WEALTH of NATIONS: Books IV-V
Adam Smith

Published by the
EAST INDIA PUBLISHING COMPANY
Ottawa, Canada

© 2022 East India Publishing Company

All rights reserved.
No part of this publication may be reproduced,
stored in a retrieval system, or transmitted, in any form, or by any
means, without the prior written
permission of the publisher.

Cover Design by EIPC © 2022
9781774265130

www.eastindiapublishing.com

CONTENTS

Book IV

Chapter I	3
Chapter II	24
Chapter III	43
Chapter IV	68
Chapter V	74
Chapter VI	110
Chapter VII	121
Chapter VIII	203
Chapter IX	222

Book V

Chapter I	249
Chapter II	363
Chapter III	451

BOOK IV

OF SYSTEMS OF POLITICAL ECONOMY

Political economy, considered as a branch of the science of a statesman or legislator, proposes two distinct objects; first, to provide a plentiful revenue or subsistence for the people, or, more properly, to enable them to provide such a revenue or subsistence for themselves; and, secondly, to supply the state or commonwealth with a revenue sufficient for the public services. It proposes to enrich both the people and the sovereign.

The different progress of opulence in different ages and nations, has given occasion to two different systems of political economy, with regard to enriching the people. The one may be called the system of commerce, the other that of agriculture. I shall endeavour to explain both as fully and distinctly as I can, and shall begin with the system of commerce. It is the modern system, and is best understood in our own country and in our own times.

CHAPTER I

OF THE PRINCIPLE OF THE COMMERCIAL OR MERCANTILE SYSTEM

That wealth consists in money, or in gold and silver, is a popular notion which naturally arises from the double function of money, as the instrument of commerce, and as the measure of value. In consequence of its being the instrument of commerce, when we have money we can more readily obtain whatever else we have occasion for, than by means of any other commodity. The great affair, we always find, is to get money. When that is obtained, there is no difficulty in making any subsequent purchase. In consequence of its being the measure of value, we estimate that of all other commodities by the quantity of money which they will exchange for. We say of a rich man, that he is worth a great deal, and of a poor man, that he is worth very little money. A frugal man, or a man eager to be rich, is said to love money; and a careless, a generous, or a profuse man, is said to be indifferent about it. To grow rich is to get money; and wealth and money, in short, are, in common language, considered as in every respect synonymous.

A rich country, in the same manner as a rich man, is supposed to be a country abounding in money; and to heap up gold and silver in any country is supposed to be the readiest way to enrich it. For some time after the discovery of America, the first inquiry of the Spaniards, when they arrived upon any unknown coast, used to be, if there was any gold or silver to be found in the neighbourhood? By the information which they received, they judged whether it was worth while to make a settlement there, or if the country was worth the conquering. Plano Carpino, a monk sent ambassador from the king of France to one of the sons of the famous Gengis Khan, says, that the Tartars used frequently to ask him, if there was plenty of sheep and oxen in the kingdom of France? Their inquiry had the same object with that of the Spaniards. They wanted to know if the country was rich enough to be worth the conquering. Among the Tartars, as among all other nations of shepherds, who are generally ignorant of the use of money, cattle are the instruments of commerce and the measures of value. Wealth, therefore, according to them, consisted in cattle, as, according to the Spaniards, it consisted in gold and silver. Of the two, the Tartar notion, perhaps, was the nearest to the truth.

Mr Locke remarks a distinction between money and other moveable goods. All other moveable goods, he says, are of so consumable a nature, that the wealth which consists in them cannot be much depended on; and a nation which abounds in them one year may, without any exportation, but merely by their own waste and extravagance, be in great want of them the next. Money, on the contrary, is a steady friend, which, though it may travel about from hand to hand, yet if it can be kept from going out of the country, is not very liable to be wasted and consumed. Gold and silver, therefore, are, according to him, the must solid and substantial part of the moveable wealth of a nation; and to multiply those metals ought, he thinks, upon that account, to be the great object of its political economy.

Others admit, that if a nation could be separated from all the world, it would be of no consequence how much or how little money circulated in it. The consumable goods, which were circulated by means of this money, would only be exchanged for a greater or a smaller number of pieces; but the real wealth or poverty of the country, they allow, would depend altogether upon the abundance or scarcity of those consumable goods. But it is otherwise, they think, with countries which have connections with foreign nations, and which are obliged to carry on foreign wars, and to maintain fleets and armies in distant countries. This, they say, cannot be done, but by sending abroad money to pay them with; and a nation cannot send much money abroad, unless it has a good deal at home. Every such nation, therefore, must endeavour, in time of peace, to accumulate gold and silver, that when occasion requires, it may have wherewithal to carry on foreign wars.

In consequence of those popular notions, all the different nations of Europe have studied, though to little purpose, every possible means of accumulating gold and silver in their respective countries. Spain and Portugal, the proprietors of the principal mines which supply Europe with those metals, have either prohibited their exportation under the severest penalties, or subjected it to a considerable duty. The like prohibition seems anciently to have made a part of the policy of most other European nations. It is even to be found, where we should least of all expect to find it, in some old Scotch acts of Parliament, which forbid, under heavy penalties, the carrying gold or silver forth of the kingdom. The like policy anciently took place both in France and England.

When those countries became commercial, the merchants found this prohibition, upon many occasions, extremely inconvenient. They could frequently buy more advantageously with gold and silver, than with any other commodity, the foreign goods which they wanted, either to import into their own, or to carry to some other foreign country. They remonstrated, therefore, against this prohibition as hurtful to trade.

They represented, first, that the exportation of gold and silver, in order to purchase foreign goods, did not always diminish the quantity of those metals in the kingdom; that, on the contrary, it might frequently increase the quantity; because, if the consumption of foreign goods was not thereby increased in the country, those goods might be re-exported to foreign countries, and being there sold for a large profit, might bring back much more treasure than was originally sent out to purchase them. Mr Mun compares this operation of foreign trade to the seed-time and harvest of agriculture. "If we only behold," says he, "the actions of the husbandman in the seed time, when he casteth away much good corn into the ground, we shall account him rather a madman than a husbandman. But when we consider his labours in the harvest, which is the end of his endeavours, we shall find the worth and plentiful increase of his actions."

They represented, secondly, that this prohibition could not hinder the exportation of gold and silver, which, on account of the smallness of their bulk in proportion to their value, could easily be smuggled abroad. That this exportation could only be prevented by a proper attention to what they called the balance of trade. That when the country exported to a greater value than it imported, a balance became due to it from foreign nations, which was necessarily paid to it in gold and silver, and thereby increased the quantity of those metals in the kingdom. But that when it imported to a greater value than it exported, a contrary balance became due to foreign nations, which was necessarily paid to them in the same manner, and thereby diminished that quantity: that in this case, to prohibit the exportation of those metals, could not prevent it, but only, by making it more dangerous, render it more expensive: that the exchange was thereby turned more against the country which owed the balance, than it otherwise might have been; the merchant who purchased a bill upon the foreign country being obliged to pay the banker who sold it, not only for the natural risk, trouble, and expense of sending the money thither, but for the extraordinary risk arising from the prohibition; but that the more the exchange was against any country, the more the balance of trade became necessarily against it; the money of that country becoming necessarily of so much less value, in comparison with that of the country to which the balance was due. That if the exchange between England and Holland, for example, was five per cent. against England, it would require 105 ounces of silver in England to purchase a bill for 100 ounces of silver in Holland: that 105 ounces of silver in England, therefore, would be worth only 100 ounces of silver in Holland, and would purchase only a proportionable quantity of Dutch goods; but that 100 ounces of silver in Holland, on the contrary, would be worth 105 ounces in England, and would purchase a proportionable quantity of English goods; that the English goods which were sold to Holland would be sold so much cheaper, and the Dutch goods which were sold to England so much dearer, by the difference of the exchange: that the one would draw so much less Dutch money to England, and the other so much more English money to Holland, as this difference amounted to: and that the balance of trade, therefore, would necessarily be so much more against England, and would require a greater balance of gold and silver to be exported to Holland.

Those arguments were partly solid and partly sophistical. They were solid, so far as they asserted that the exportation of gold and silver in trade might frequently be advantageous to the country. They were solid, too, in asserting that no prohibition could prevent their exportation, when private people found any advantage in exporting them. But they were sophistical, in supposing, that either to preserve or to augment the quantity of those metals required more the attention of government, than to preserve or to augment the quantity of any other useful commodities, which the freedom of trade, without any such attention, never fails to supply in the proper quantity. They were sophistical, too, perhaps, in asserting that the high price of exchange necessarily increased what they called the unfavourable balance of trade, or occasioned the exportation of a greater quantity of gold and silver. That high price, indeed, was extremely disadvantageous to the merchants who had any money to pay in foreign countries. They paid so much dearer for the bills which their bankers granted them upon those countries. But though the risk arising from the prohibition might occasion some extraordinary expense to the bankers, it would not necessarily carry any more money out of the country. This expense would generally be all laid out in the country, in smuggling the money out of it, and could seldom occasion the exportation of a single sixpence beyond the precise sum drawn for. The high price of exchange, too, would naturally dispose the merchants to endeavour to make their exports nearly balance their imports, in order that they might have this high exchange to pay upon as small a sum as possible. The high price of exchange, besides, must necessarily have operated as a tax, in raising the price of foreign goods, and thereby diminishing their consumption. It would tend, therefore, not to increase, but to diminish, what they called the unfavourable balance of trade, and consequently the exportation of gold and silver.

Such as they were, however, those arguments convinced the people to whom they were addressed. They were addressed by merchants to parliaments and to the councils of princes, to nobles, and to country gentlemen; by those who were supposed to understand trade, to those who were conscious to them selves that they knew nothing about the matter. That foreign trade enriched the country, experience demonstrated to the nobles and country gentlemen, as well as to the merchants; but how, or in what manner, none of them well knew. The merchants knew perfectly in what manner it enriched themselves, it was their business to know it. But to know in what manner it enriched the country, was no part of their business. The subject never came into their consideration, but when they had occasion to apply to their country for some change in the laws relating to foreign trade. It then became necessary to say something about the beneficial effects of foreign trade, and the manner in which those effects were obstructed by the laws as they then stood. To the judges who were to decide the business, it appeared a most satisfactory account of the matter, when they were told that foreign trade brought money into the country, but that the laws in question hindered it from bringing so much as it otherwise would do. Those arguments, therefore, produced the wished-for effect. The prohibition of exporting gold and silver was, in France and England, confined to the coin of those respective countries. The exportation of foreign coin and of bullion was made free. In Holland, and in some other places, this liberty was extended even to the coin of the country. The attention of government was turned away from guarding against the exportation of gold and silver, to watch over the balance of trade, as the only cause which could occasion any augmentation or diminution of those metals. From one fruitless care, it was turned away to another care much more intricate, much more embarrassing, and just equally fruitless. The title of Mun's book, England's Treasure in Foreign Trade, became a fundamental maxim in the political economy, not of England only, but of all other commercial countries. The inland or home trade, the most important of all, the trade in which an equal capital affords the greatest revenue, and creates the greatest employment to the people of the country, was considered as subsidiary only to foreign trade. It neither brought money into the country, it was said, nor carried any out of it. The country, therefore, could never become either richer or poorer by means of it, except so far as its prosperity or decay might indirectly influence the state of foreign trade.

A country that has no mines of its own, must undoubtedly draw its gold and silver from foreign countries, in the same manner as one that has no vineyards of its own must draw its wines. It does not seem necessary, however, that the attention of government should be more turned towards the one than towards the other object. A country that has wherewithal to buy wine, will always get the wine which it has occasion for; and a country that has wherewithal to buy gold and silver, will never be in want of those metals. They are to be bought for a certain price, like all other commodities; and as they are the price of all other commodities, so all other commodities are the price of those metals. We trust, with perfect security, that the freedom of trade, without any attention of government, will always supply us with the wine which we have occasion for; and we may trust, with equal security, that it will always supply us with all the gold and silver which we can afford to purchase or to employ, either in circulating our commodities or in other uses.

The quantity of every commodity which human industry can either purchase or produce, naturally regulates itself in every country according to the effectual demand, or according to the demand of those who are willing to pay the whole rent, labour, and profits, which must be paid in order to prepare and bring it to market. But no commodities regulate themselves more easily or more exactly, according to this effectual demand, than gold and silver; because, on account of the small bulk and great value of those metals, no commodities can be more easily transported from one place to another; from the places where they are cheap, to those where they are dear; from the places where they exceed, to those where they fall short of this effectual demand. If there were in England, for example, an effectual demand for an additional quantity of gold, a packet-boat could bring from Lisbon, or from wherever else it was to be had, fifty tons of gold, which could be coined into more than five millions of guineas. But if there were an effectual demand for grain to the same value, to import it would require, at five guineas a-ton, a million of tons of shipping, or a thousand ships of a thousand tons each. The navy of England would not be sufficient.

When the quantity of gold and silver imported into any country exceeds the effectual demand, no vigilance of government can prevent their exportation. All the sanguinary laws of Spain and Portugal are not able to keep their gold and silver at home. The continual importations from Peru and Brazil exceed the effectual demand of those countries, and sink the price of those metals there below that in the neighbouring countries. If, on the contrary, in any particular country, their quantity fell short of the effectual demand, so as to raise their price above that of the neighbouring countries, the government would have no occasion to take any pains to import them. If it were even to take pains to prevent their importation, it would not be able to effectuate it. Those metals, when the Spartans had got wherewithal to purchase them, broke through all the barriers which the laws of Lycurgus opposed to their entrance into Lacedaemon. All the sanguinary laws of the customs are not able to prevent the importation of the teas of the Dutch and Gottenburg East India companies; because somewhat cheaper than those of the British company. A pound of tea, however, is about a hundred times the bulk of one of the highest prices, sixteen shillings, that is commonly paid for it in silver, and more than two thousand times the bulk of the same price in gold, and, consequently, just so many times more difficult to smuggle.

It is partly owing to the easy transportation of gold and silver, from the places where they abound to those where they are wanted, that the price of those metals does not fluctuate continually, like that of the greater part of other commodities, which are hindered by their bulk from shifting their situation, when the market happens to be either over or under-stocked with them. The price of those metals, indeed, is not altogether exempted from variation; but the changes to which it is liable are generally slow, gradual, and uniform. In Europe, for example, it is supposed, without much foundation, perhaps, that during the course of the present and preceding century, they have been constantly, but gradually, sinking in their value, on account of the continual importations from the Spanish West Indies. But to make any sudden change in the price of gold and silver, so as to raise or lower at once, sensibly and remarkably, the money price of all other commodities, requires such a revolution in commerce as that occasioned by the discovery of America.

If, not withstanding all this, gold and silver should at any time fall short in a country which has wherewithal to purchase them, there are more expedients for supplying their place, than that of almost any other commodity. If the materials of manufacture are wanted, industry must stop. If provisions are wanted, the people must starve. But if money is wanted, barter will supply its place, though with a good deal of inconveniency. Buying and selling upon credit, and the different dealers compensating their credits with one another, once a-month, or once a-year, will supply it with less inconveniency. A well-regulated paper-money will supply it not only without any inconveniency, but, in some cases, with some advantages. Upon every account, therefore, the attention of government never was so unnecessarily employed, as when directed to watch over the preservation or increase of the quantity of money in any country.

No complaint, however, is more common than that of a scarcity of money. Money, like wine, must always be scarce with those who have neither wherewithal to buy it, nor credit to borrow it. Those who have either, will seldom be in want either of the money, or of the wine which they have occasion for. This complaint, however, of the scarcity of money, is not always confined to improvident spendthrifts. It is sometimes general through a whole mercantile town and the country in its neighbourhood. Over-trading is the common cause of it. Sober men, whose projects have been disproportioned to their capitals, are as likely to have neither wherewithal to buy money, nor credit to borrow it, as prodigals, whose expense has been disproportioned to their revenue. Before their projects can be brought to bear, their stock is gone, and their credit with it. They run about everywhere to borrow money, and everybody tells them that they have none to lend. Even such general complaints of the scarcity of money do not always prove that the usual number of gold and silver pieces are not circulating in the country, but that many people want those pieces who have nothing to give for them. When the profits of trade happen to be greater than ordinary over-trading becomes a general error, both among great and small dealers. They do not always send more money abroad than usual, but they buy upon credit, both at home and abroad, an unusual quantity of goods, which they send to some distant market, in hopes that the returns will come in before the demand for payment. The demand comes before the returns, and they have nothing at hand with which they can either purchase money or give solid security for borrowing. It is not any scarcity of gold and silver, but the difficulty which such people find in borrowing, and which their creditor find in getting payment, that occasions the general complaint of the scarcity of money.

It would be too ridiculous to go about seriously to prove, that wealth does not consist in money, or in gold and silver; but in what money purchases, and is valuable only for purchasing. Money, no doubt, makes always a part of the national capital; but it has already been shown that it generally makes but a small part, and always the most unprofitable part of it.

It is not because wealth consists more essentially in money than in goods, that the merchant finds it generally more easy to buy goods with money, than to buy money with goods; but because money is the known and established instrument of commerce, for which every thing is readily given in exchange, but which is not always with equal readiness to be got in exchange for every thing. The greater part of goods, besides, are more perishable than money, and he may frequently sustain a much greater loss by keeping them. When his goods are upon hand, too, he is more liable to such demands for money as he may not be able to answer, than when he has got their price in his coffers. Over and above all this, his profit arises more directly from selling than from buying; and he is, upon all these accounts, generally much more anxious to exchange his goods for money than his money for goods. But though a particular merchant, with abundance of goods in his warehouse, may sometimes be ruined by not being able to sell them in time, a nation or country is not liable to the same accident, The whole capital of a merchant frequently consists in perishable goods destined for purchasing money. But it is but a very small part of the annual produce of the land and labour of a country, which can ever be destined for purchasing gold and silver from their neighbours. The far greater part is circulated and consumed among themselves; and even of the surplus which is sent abroad, the greater part is generally destined for the purchase of other foreign goods. Though gold and silver, therefore, could not be had in exchange for the goods destined to purchase them, the nation would not be ruined. It might, indeed, suffer some loss and inconveniency, and be forced upon some of those expedients which are necessary for supplying the place of money. The annual produce of its land and labour, however, would be the same, or very nearly the same as usual; because the same, or very nearly the same consumable capital would be employed in maintaining it. And though goods do not always draw money so readily as money draws goods, in the long-run they draw it more necessarily than even it draws them. Goods can serve many other purposes besides purchasing money, but money can serve no other purpose besides purchasing goods. Money, therefore, necessarily runs after goods, but goods do not always or necessarily run after money. The man who buys, does not always mean to sell again, but frequently to use or to consume; whereas he who sells always means to buy again. The one may frequently have done the whole, but the other can never have done more than the one half of his business. It is not for its own sake that men desire money, but for the sake of what they can purchase with it.

Consumable commodities, it is said, are soon destroyed; whereas gold and silver are of a more durable nature, and were it not for this continual exportation, might be accumulated for ages together, to the incredible augmentation of the real wealth of the country. Nothing, therefore, it is pretended, can be more disadvantageous to any country, than the trade which consists in the exchange of such lasting for such perishable commodities. We do not, however, reckon that trade disadvantageous, which consists in the exchange of the hardware of England for the wines of France, and yet hardware is a very durable commodity, and were it not for this continual exportation, might too be accumulated for ages together, to the incredible augmentation of the pots and pans of the country. But it readily occurs, that the number of such utensils is in every country necessarily limited by the use which there is for them; that it would be absurd to have more pots and pans than were necessary for cooking the victuals usually consumed there; and that, if the quantity of victuals were to increase, the number of pots and pans would readily increase along with it; a part of the increased quantity of victuals being employed in purchasing them, or in maintaining an additional number of workmen whose business it was to make them. It should as readily occur, that the quantity of gold and silver is, in every country, limited by the use which there is for those metals; that their use consists in circulating commodities, as coin, and in affording a species of household furniture, as plate; that the quantity of coin in every country is regulated by the value of the commodities which are to be circulated by it; increase that value, and immediately a part of it will be sent abroad to purchase, wherever it is to be had, the additional quantity of coin requisite for circulating them: that the quantity of plate is regulated by the number and wealth of those private families who choose to indulge themselves in that sort of magnificence; increase the number and wealth of such families, and a part of this increased wealth will most probably be employed in purchasing, wherever it is to be found, an additional quantity of plate; that to attempt to increase the wealth of any country, either by introducing or by detaining in it an unnecessary quantity of gold and silver, is as absurd as it would be to attempt to increase the good cheer of private families, by obliging them to keep an unnecessary number of kitchen utensils. As the expense of purchasing those unnecessary utensils would diminish, instead of increasing, either the quantity or goodness of the family provisions; so the expense of purchasing an unnecessary quantity of gold and silver must, in every country, as necessarily diminish the wealth which feeds, clothes, and lodges, which maintains and employs the people. Gold and silver, whether in the shape of coin or of plate, are utensils, it must be remembered, as much as the furniture of the kitchen. Increase the use of them, increase the consumable commodities which are to be circulated, managed, and prepared by means of them, and you will infallibly increase the quantity; but if you attempt by extraordinary means to increase the quantity, you will as infallibly diminish the use, and even the quantity too, which in those metals can never be greater than what the use requires. Were they ever to be accumulated beyond this quantity, their transportation is so easy, and the loss which attends their lying idle and unemployed so great, that no law could prevent their being immediately sent out of the country.

It is not always necessary to accumulate gold and silver, in order to enable a country to carry on foreign wars, and to maintain fleets and armies in distant countries. Fleets and armies are maintained, not with gold and silver, but with consumable goods. The nation which, from the annual produce of its domestic industry, from the annual revenue arising out of its lands, and labour, and consumable stock, has wherewithal to purchase those consumable goods in distant countries, can maintain foreign wars there.

A nation may purchase the pay and provisions of an army in a distant country three different ways; by sending abroad either, first, some part of its accumulated gold and silver; or, secondly, some part of the annual produce of its manufactures; or, last of all, some part of its annual rude produce.

The gold and silver which can properly be considered as accumulated, or stored up in any country, may be distinguished into three parts; first, the circulating money; secondly, the plate of private families; and, last of all, the money which may have been collected by many years parsimony, and laid up in the treasury of the prince.

It can seldom happen that much can be spared from the circulating money of the country; because in that there can seldom be much redundancy. The value of goods annually bought and sold in any country requires a certain quantity of money to circulate and distribute them to their proper consumers, and can give employment to no more. The channel of circulation necessarily draws to itself a sum sufficient to fill it, and never admits any more. Something, however, is generally withdrawn from this channel in the case of foreign war. By the great number of people who are maintained abroad, fewer are maintained at home. Fewer goods are circulated there, and less money becomes necessary to circulate them. An extraordinary quantity of paper money of some sort or other, too, such as exchequer notes, navy bills, and bank bills, in England, is generally issued upon such occasions, and, by supplying the place of circulating gold and silver, gives an opportunity of sending a greater quantity of it abroad. All this, however, could afford but a poor resource for maintaining a foreign war, of great expense, and several years duration.

The melting down of the plate of private families has, upon every occasion, been found a still more insignificant one. The French, in the beginning of the last war, did not derive so much advantage from this expedient as to compensate the loss of the fashion.

The accumulated treasures of the prince have in former times afforded a much greater and more lasting resource. In the present times, if you except the king of Prussia, to accumulate treasure seems to be no part of the policy of European princes.

The funds which maintained the foreign wars of the present century, the most expensive perhaps which history records, seem to have had little dependency upon the exportation either of the circulating money, or of the plate of private families, or of the treasure of the prince. The last French war cost Great Britain upwards of £90,000,000, including not only the £75,000,000 of new debt that was contracted, but the additional 2s. in the pound land-tax, and what was annually borrowed of the sinking fund. More than two-thirds of this expense were laid out in distant countries; in Germany, Portugal, America, in the ports of the

Mediterranean, in the East and West Indies. The kings of England had no accumulated treasure. We never heard of any extraordinary quantity of plate being melted down. The circulating gold and silver of the country had not been supposed to exceed £18,000,000. Since the late recoinage of the gold, however, it is believed to have been a good deal under-rated. Let us suppose, therefore, according to the most exaggerated computation which I remember to have either seen or heard of, that, gold and silver together, it amounted to £30,000,000. Had the war been carried on by means of our money, the whole of it must, even according to this computation, have been sent out and returned again, at least twice in a period of between six and seven years. Should this be supposed, it would afford the most decisive argument, to demonstrate how unnecessary it is for government to watch over the preservation of money, since, upon this supposition, the whole money of the country must have gone from it, and returned to it again, two different times in so short a period, without any body's knowing any thing of the matter. The channel of circulation, however, never appeared more empty than usual during any part of this period. Few people wanted money who had wherewithal to pay for it. The profits of foreign trade, indeed, were greater than usual during the whole war, but especially towards the end of it. This occasioned, what it always occasions, a general over-trading in all the ports of Great Britain; and this again occasioned the usual complaint of the scarcity of money, which always follows over-trading. Many people wanted it, who had neither wherewithal to buy it, nor credit to borrow it; and because the debtors found it difficult to borrow, the creditors found it difficult to get payment. Gold and silver, however, were generally to be had for their value, by those who had that value to give for them.

The enormous expense of the late war, therefore, must have been chiefly defrayed, not by the exportation of gold and silver, but by that of British commodities of some kind or other. When the government, or those who acted under them, contracted with a merchant for a remittance to some foreign country, he would naturally endeavour to pay his foreign correspondent, upon whom he granted a bill, by sending abroad rather commodities than gold and silver. If the commodities of Great Britain were not in demand in that country, he would endeavour to send them to some other country in which he could purchase a bill upon that country. The transportation of commodities, when properly suited to the market, is always attended with a considerable profit; whereas that of gold and silver is scarce ever attended with any. When those metals are sent abroad in order to purchase foreign commodities, the merchant's profit arises, not from the purchase, but from the sale of the returns. But when they are sent abroad merely to pay a debt, he gets no returns, and consequently no profit. He naturally, therefore, exerts his invention to find out a way of paying his foreign debts, rather by the exportation of commodities, than by that of gold and silver. The great quantity of British goods, exported during the course of the late war, without bringing back any returns, is accordingly remarked by the author of the Present State of the Nation.

Besides the three sorts of gold and silver above mentioned, there is in all great commercial countries a good deal of bullion alternately imported and exported, for the purposes of foreign trade. This bullion, as it circulates among different commercial countries, in the same manner as the national coin circulates in every country, may be considered as the money of the great mercantile republic. The national coin receives its movement and direction from the commodities circulated within the precincts of each particular country; the money in the mercantile republic, from those circulated between different countries. Both are employed in facilitating exchanges, the one between different individuals of the same, the other between those of different nations. Part of this money of the great mercantile republic may have been, and probably was, employed in carrying on the late war. In time of a general war, it is natural to suppose that a movement and direction should be impressed upon it, different from what it usually follows in profound peace, that it should circulate more about the seat of the war, and be more employed in purchasing there, and in the neighbouring countries, the pay and provisions of the different armies. But whatever part of this money of the mercantile republic Great Britain may have annually employed in this manner, it must have been annually purchased, either with British commodities, or with something else that had been purchased with them; which still brings us back to commodities, to the annual produce of the land and labour of the country, as the ultimate resources which enabled us to carry on the war. It is natural, indeed, to suppose, that so great an annual expense must have been defrayed from a great annual produce. The expense of 1761, for example, amounted to more than £19,000,000. No accumulation could have supported so great an annual profusion. There is no annual produce, even of gold and silver, which could have supported it. The whole gold and silver annually imported into both Spain and Portugal, according to the best accounts, does not commonly much exceed £6,000,000 sterling, which, in some years, would scarce have paid four months expense of the late war.

The commodities most proper for being transported to distant countries, in order to purchase there either the pay and provisions of an army, or some part of the money of the mercantile republic to be employed in purchasing them, seem to be the finer and more improved manufactures; such as contain a great value in a small bulk, and can therefore be exported to a great distance at little expense. A country whose industry produces a great annual surplus of such manufactures, which are usually exported to foreign countries, may carry on for many years a very expensive foreign war, without either exporting any considerable quantity of gold and silver, or even having any such quantity to export. A considerable part of the annual surplus of its manufactures must, indeed, in this case, be exported without bringing back any returns to the country, though it does to the merchant; the government purchasing of the merchant his bills upon foreign countries, in order to purchase there the pay and provisions of an army. Some part of this surplus, however, may still continue to bring back a return. The manufacturers during; the war will have a double demand upon them, and be called upon first to work up goods to be sent abroad, for paying the bills drawn upon foreign countries for the pay and provisions of the army: and, secondly, to work up such as are necessary for purchasing the common returns that had usually been consumed in the country. In the midst of the most destructive foreign war, therefore, the greater part of manufactures may frequently flourish greatly; and, on the contrary, they may decline on the return of peace. They may flourish amidst the ruin of their country, and begin to decay upon the return of its prosperity. The different state of many different branches of the British manufactures during the late war, and for some time after the peace, may serve as an illustration of what has been just now said.

No foreign war, of great expense or duration, could conveniently be carried on by the exportation of the rude produce of the soil. The expense of sending such a quantity of it into a foreign country as might purchase the pay and provisions of an army would be too great. Few countries, too, produce much more rude produce than what is sufficient for the subsistence of their own inhabitants. To send abroad any great quantity of it, therefore, would be to send abroad a part of the necessary subsistence of the people. It is otherwise with the exportation of manufactures. The maintenance of the people employed in them is kept at home, and only the surplus part of their work is exported. Mr Hume frequently takes notice of the inability of the ancient kings of England to carry on, without interruption, any foreign war of long duration. The English in those days had nothing wherewithal to purchase the pay and provisions of their armies in foreign countries, but either the rude produce of the soil, of which no considerable part could be spared from the home consumption, or a few manufactures of the coarsest kind, of which, as well as of the rude produce, the transportation was too expensive. This inability did not arise from the want of money, but of the finer and more improved manufactures. Buying and selling was transacted by means of money in England then as well as now. The quantity of circulating money must have borne the same proportion, to the number and value of purchases and sales usually transacted at that time, which it does to those transacted at present; or, rather, it must have borne a greater proportion, because there was then no paper, which now occupies a great part of the employment of gold and silver. Among nations to whom commerce and manufactures are little known, the sovereign, upon extraordinary occasions, can seldom draw any considerable aid from his subjects, for reasons which shall be explained hereafter. It is in such countries, therefore, that he generally endeavours to accumulate a treasure, as the only resource against such emergencies. Independent of this necessity, he is, in such a situation, naturally disposed to the parsimony requisite for accumulation. In that simple state, the expense even of a sovereign is not directed by the vanity which delights in the gaudy finery of a court, but is employed in bounty to his tenants, and hospitality to his retainers. But bounty and hospitality very seldom lead to extravagance; though vanity almost always does. Every Tartar chief, accordingly, has a treasure. The treasures of Mazepa, chief of the Cossacks in the Ukraine, the famous ally of Charles XII., are said to have been very great. The French kings of the Merovingian race had all treasures. When they divided their kingdom among their different children, they divided their treasures too. The Saxon princes, and the first kings after the Conquest, seem likewise to have accumulated treasures. The first exploit of every new reign was commonly to seize the treasure of the preceding king, as the most essential measure for securing the succession. The sovereigns of improved and commercial countries are not under the same necessity of accumulating treasures, because they can generally draw from their subjects extraordinary aids upon extraordinary occasions. They are likewise less disposed to do so. They naturally, perhaps necessarily, follow the mode of the times; and their expense comes to be regulated by the same extravagant vanity which directs that of all the other great proprietors in their dominions. The insignificant pageantry of their court becomes every day more brilliant; and the expense of it not only prevents accumulation, but frequently encroaches upon the funds destined for more necessary expenses. What Dercyllidas said of the court of Persia, may be applied to that of several European princes, that he saw there much splendour, but little strength, and many servants, but few soldiers.

The importation of gold and silver is not the principal, much less the sole benefit, which a nation derives from its foreign trade. Between whatever places foreign trade is carried on, they all of them derive two distinct benefits from it. It carries out that surplus part of the produce of their land and labour for which there is no demand among them, and brings back in return for it something else for which there is a demand. It gives a value to their superfluities, by exchanging them for something else, which may satisfy a part of their wants and increase their enjoyments. By means of it, the narrowness of the home market does not hinder the division of labour in any particular branch of art or manufacture from being carried to the highest perfection. By opening a more extensive market for whatever part of the produce of their labour may exceed the home consumption, it encourages them to improve its productive power, and to augment its annual produce to the utmost, and thereby to increase the real revenue and wealth of the society. These great and important services foreign trade is continually occupied in performing to all the different countries between which it is carried on. They all derive great benefit from it, though that in which the merchant resides generally derives the greatest, as he is generally more employed in supplying the wants, and carrying out the superfluities of his own, than of any other particular country. To import the gold and silver which may be wanted into the countries which have no mines, is, no doubt a part of the business of foreign commerce. It is, however, a most insignificant part of it. A country which carried on foreign trade merely upon this account, could scarce have occasion to freight a ship in a century.

It is not by the importation of gold and silver that the discovery of America has enriched Europe. By the abundance of the American mines, those metals have become cheaper. A service of plate can now be purchased for about a third part of the corn, or a third part of the labour, which it would have cost in the fifteenth century. With the same annual expense of labour and commodities, Europe can annually purchase about three times the quantity of plate which it could have purchased at that time. But when a commodity comes to be sold for a third part of what bad been its usual price, not only those who purchased it before can purchase three times their former quantity, but it is brought down to the level of a much greater number of purchasers, perhaps to more than ten, perhaps to more than twenty times the former number. So that there may be in Europe at present, not only more than three times, but more than twenty or thirty times the quantity of plate which would have been in it, even in its present state of improvement, had the discovery of the American mines never been made. So far Europe has, no doubt, gained a real conveniency, though surely a very trifling one. The cheapness of gold and silver renders those metals rather less fit for the purposes of money than they were before. In order to make the same purchases, we must load ourselves with a greater quantity of them, and carry about a shilling in our pocket, where a groat would have done before. It is difficult to say which is most trifling, this inconveniency, or the opposite conveniency. Neither the one nor the other could have made any very essential change in the state of Europe. The discovery of America, however, certainly made a most essential one. By opening a new and inexhaustible market to all the commodities of Europe, it gave occasion to new divisions of labour and improvements of art, which in the narrow circle of the ancient commerce could never have taken place, for want of a market to take off the greater part of their produce. The productive powers of labour were improved, and its produce increased in all the different countries of Europe, and together with it the real revenue and wealth of the inhabitants. The commodities of Europe were almost all new to America, and many of those of America were new to Europe. A new set of exchanges, therefore, began to take place, which had never been thought of before, and which should naturally have proved as advantageous to the new, as it certainly did to the old continent. The savage injustice of the Europeans rendered an event, which ought to have been beneficial to all, ruinous and destructive to several of those unfortunate countries.

   The discovery of a passage to the East Indies by the Cape of Good Hope, which happened much about the same time, opened perhaps a still more extensive range to foreign commerce, than even that of America, notwithstanding the greater distance. There were but two nations in America, in any respect, superior to the savages, and these were destroyed almost as soon as discovered. The rest were mere savages. But the empires of China, Indostan, Japan, as well as several others in the East Indies, without having richer mines of gold or silver, were, in every other respect, much richer, better cultivated, and more advanced in all arts and manufactures, than either Mexico or Peru, even though we should credit, what plainly deserves no credit, the exaggerated accounts of the Spanish writers concerning the ancient state of those empires. But rich and civilized nations can always exchange to a much greater value with one another, than with savages and barbarians. Europe, however, has hitherto derived much less advantage from its commerce with the East Indies, than from that with America. The Portuguese monopolised the East India trade to themselves for about a century; and it was only indirectly, and through them, that the other nations of Europe could either send out or receive any goods from that country. When the Dutch, in the beginning of the last century, began to encroach upon them, they vested their whole East India commerce in an exclusive company. The English, French, Swedes, and Danes, have all followed their example; so that no great nation of Europe has ever yet had the benefit of a free commerce to the East Indies. No other reason need be assigned why it has never been so advantageous as the trade to America, which, between almost every nation of Europe and its own colonies, is free to all its subjects. The exclusive privileges of those East India companies, their great riches, the great favour and protection which these have procured them from their respective governments, have excited much envy against them. This envy has frequently represented their trade as altogether pernicious, on account of the great quantities of silver which it every year exports from the countries from which it is carried on. The parties concerned have replied, that their trade by this continual exportation of silver, might indeed tend to impoverish Europe in general, but not the particular country from which it was carried on; because, by the exportation of a part of the returns to other European countries, it annually brought home a much greater quantity of that metal than it carried out. Both the objection and the reply are founded in the popular notion which I have been just now examining. It is therefore unnecessary to say any thing further about either. By the annual exportation of silver to the East Indies, plate is probably somewhat dearer in Europe than it otherwise might have been; and coined silver probably purchases a larger quantity both of labour and commodities. The former of these two effects is a very small loss, the latter a very small advantage; both too insignificant to deserve any part of the public attention. The trade to the East Indies, by opening a market to the commodities of Europe, or, what comes nearly to the same thing, to the gold and silver which is purchased with those commodities, must necessarily tend to increase the annual production of European commodities, and consequently the real wealth and revenue of Europe. That it has hitherto increased them so little, is probably owing to the restraints which it everywhere labours under.

I thought it necessary, though at the hazard of being tedious, to examine at full length this popular notion, that wealth consists in money or in gold and silver. Money, in common language, as I have already observed, frequently signifies wealth; and this ambiguity of expression has rendered this popular notion so familiar to us, that even they who are convinced of its absurdity, are very apt to forget their own principles, and, in the course of their reasonings, to take it for granted as a certain and undeniable truth. Some of the best English writers upon commerce set out with observing, that the wealth of a country consists, not in its gold and silver only, but in its lands, houses, and consumable goods of all different kinds. In the course of their reasonings, however, the lands, houses, and consumable goods, seem to slip out of their memory; and the strain of their argument frequently supposes that all wealth consists in gold and silver, and that to multiply those metals is the great object of national industry and commerce.

The two principles being established, however, that wealth consisted in gold and silver, and that those metals could be brought into a country which had no mines, only by the balance of trade, or by exporting to a greater value than it imported; it necessarily became the great object of political economy to diminish as much as possible the importation of foreign goods for home consumption, and to increase as much as possible the exportation of the produce of domestic industry. Its two great engines for enriching the country, therefore, were restraints upon importation, and encouragement to exportation.

The restraints upon importation were of two kinds.

First, restraints upon the importation of such foreign goods for home consumption as could be produced at home, from whatever country they were imported.

Secondly, restraints upon the importation of goods of almost all kinds, from those particular countries with which the balance of trade was supposed to be disadvantageous.

Those different restraints consisted sometimes in high duties, and sometimes in absolute prohibitions.

Exportation was encouraged sometimes by drawbacks, sometimes by bounties, sometimes by advantageous treaties of commerce with foreign states, and sometimes by the establishment of colonies in distant countries.

Drawbacks were given upon two different occasions. When the home manufactures were subject to any duty or excise, either the whole or a part of it was frequently drawn back upon their exportation; and when foreign goods liable to a duty were imported, in order to be exported again, either the whole or a part of this duty was sometimes given back upon such exportation.

Bounties were given for the encouragement, either of some beginning manufactures, or of such sorts of industry of other kinds as were supposed to deserve particular favour.

By advantageous treaties of commerce, particular privileges were procured in some foreign state for the goods and merchants of the country, beyond what were granted to those of other countries.

By the establishment of colonies in distant countries, not only particular privileges, but a monopoly was frequently procured for the goods and merchants of the country which established them.

The two sorts of restraints upon importation above mentioned, together with these four encouragements to exportation, constitute the six principal means by which the commercial system proposes to increase the quantity of gold and silver in any country, by turning the balance of trade in its favour. I shall consider each of them in a particular chapter, and, without taking much farther notice of their supposed tendency to bring money into the country, I shall examine chiefly what are likely to be the effects of each of them upon the annual produce of its industry. According as they tend either to increase or diminish the value of this annual produce, they must evidently tend either to increase or diminish the real wealth and revenue of the country.

CHAPTER II

OF RESTRAINTS UPON IMPORTATION FROM FOREIGN COUNTRIES OF SUCH GOODS AS CAN BE PRODUCED AT HOME

By restraining, either by high duties, or by absolute prohibitions, the importation of such goods from foreign countries as can be produced at home, the monopoly of the home market is more or less secured to the domestic industry employed in producing them. Thus the prohibition of importing either live cattle or salt provisions from foreign countries, secures to the graziers of Great Britain the monopoly of the home market for butcher's meat. The high duties upon the importation of corn, which, in times of moderate plenty, amount to a prohibition, give a like advantage to the growers of that commodity. The prohibition of the importation of foreign woollen is equally favourable to the woollen manufacturers. The silk manufacture, though altogether employed upon foreign materials, has lately obtained the same advantage. The linen manufacture has not yet obtained it, but is making great strides towards it. Many other sorts of manufactures have, in the same manner obtained in Great Britain, either altogether, or very nearly, a monopoly against their countrymen. The variety of goods, of which the importation into Great Britain is prohibited, either absolutely, or under certain circumstances, greatly exceeds what can easily be suspected by those who are not well acquainted with the laws of the customs.

That this monopoly of the home market frequently gives great encouragement to that particular species of industry which enjoys it, and frequently turns towards that employment a greater share of both the labour and stock of the society than would otherwise have gone to it, cannot be doubted. But whether it tends either to increase the general industry of the society, or to give it the most advantageous direction, is not, perhaps, altogether so evident.

The general industry of the society can never exceed what the capital of the society can employ. As the number of workmen that can be kept in employment by any particular person must bear a certain proportion to his capital, so the number of those that can be continually employed by all the members of a great society must bear a certain proportion to the whole capital of the society, and never can exceed that proportion. No regulation of commerce can increase the quantity of industry in any society beyond what its capital can maintain. It can only divert a part of it into a direction into which it might not otherwise have gone; and it is by no means certain that this artificial direction is likely to be more advantageous to the society, than that into which it would have gone of its own accord.

Every individual is continually exerting himself to find out the most advantageous employment for whatever capital he can command. It is his own advantage, indeed, and not that of the society, which he has in view. But the study of his own advantage naturally, or rather necessarily, leads him to prefer that employment which is most advantageous to the society.

First, every individual endeavours to employ his capital as near home as he can, and consequently as much as he can in the support of domestic industry, provided always that he can thereby obtain the ordinary, or not a great deal less than the ordinary profits of stock.

Thus, upon equal, or nearly equal profits, every wholesale merchant naturally prefers the home trade to the foreign trade of consumption, and the foreign trade of consumption to the carrying trade. In the home trade, his capital is never so long out of his sight as it frequently is in the foreign trade of consumption. He can know better the character and situation of the persons whom he trusts; and if he should happen to be deceived, he knows better the laws of the country from which he must seek redress. In the carrying trade, the capital of the merchant is, as it were, divided between two foreign countries, and no part of it is ever necessarily brought home, or placed under his own immediate view and command. The capital which an Amsterdam merchant employs in carrying corn from Koningsberg to Lisbon, and fruit and wine from Lisbon to Koningsberg, must generally be the one half of it at Koningsberg, and the other half at Lisbon. No part of it need ever come to Amsterdam. The natural residence of such a merchant should either be at Koningsberg or Lisbon; and it can only be some very particular circumstances which can make him prefer the residence of Amsterdam. The uneasiness, however, which he feels at being separated so far from his capital, generally determines him to bring part both of the Koningsberg goods which he destines for the market of Lisbon, and of the Lisbon goods which he destines for that of Koningsberg, to Amsterdam; and though this necessarily subjects him to a double charge of loading and unloading as well as to the payment of some duties and customs, yet, for the sake of having some part of his capital always under his own view and command, he willingly submits to this extraordinary charge; and it is in this manner that every country which has any considerable share of the carrying trade, becomes always the emporium, or general market, for the goods of all the different countries whose trade it carries on. The merchant, in order to save a second loading and unloading, endeavours always to sell in the home market, as much of the goods of all those different countries as he can; and thus, so far as he can, to convert his carrying trade into a foreign trade of consumption. A merchant, in the same manner, who is engaged in the foreign trade of consumption, when he collects goods for foreign markets, will always be glad, upon equal or nearly equal profits, to sell as great a part of them at home as he can. He saves himself the risk and trouble of exportation, when, so far as he can, he thus converts his foreign trade of consumption into a home trade. Home is in this manner the centre, if I may say so, round which the capitals of the inhabitants of every country are continually circulating, and towards which they are always tending, though, by particular causes, they may sometimes be driven off and repelled from it towards more distant employments. But a capital employed in the home trade, it has already been shown, necessarily puts into motion a greater quantity of domestic industry, and gives revenue and employment to a greater number of the inhabitants of the country, than an equal capital employed in the foreign trade of consumption; and one employed in the foreign trade of consumption has the same advantage over an equal capital employed in the carrying trade. Upon equal, or only nearly equal profits, therefore, every individual naturally inclines to employ his capital in the manner in which it is likely to afford the greatest support to domestic industry, and to give revenue and employment to the greatest number of people of his own country.

Secondly, every individual who employs his capital in the support of domestic industry, necessarily endeavours so to direct that industry, that its produce may be of the greatest possible value.

The produce of industry is what it adds to the subject or materials upon which it is employed. In proportion as the value of this produce is great or small, so will likewise be the profits of the employer. But it is only for the sake of profit that any man employs a capital in the support of industry; and he will always, therefore, endeavour to employ it in the support of that industry of which the produce is likely to be of the greatest value, or to exchange for the greatest quantity either of money or of other goods.

But the annual revenue of every society is always precisely equal to the exchangeable value of the whole annual produce of its industry, or rather is precisely the same thing with that exchangeable value. As every individual, therefore, endeavours as much as he can, both to employ his capital in the support of domestic industry, and so to direct that industry that its produce maybe of the greatest value; every individual necessarily labours to render the annual revenue of the society as great as he can. He generally, indeed, neither intends to promote the public interest, nor knows how much he is promoting it. By preferring the support of domestic to that of foreign industry, he intends only his own security; and by directing that industry in such a manner as its produce may be of the greatest value, he intends only his own gain; and he is in this, as in many other cases, led by an invisible hand to promote an end which was no part of his intention. Nor is it always the worse for the society that it was no part of it. By pursuing his own interest, he frequently promotes that of the society more effectually than when he really intends to promote it. I have never known much good done by those who affected to trade for the public good. It is an affectation, indeed, not very common among merchants, and very few words need be employed in dissuading them from it.

What is the species of domestic industry which his capital can employ, and of which the produce is likely to be of the greatest value, every individual, it is evident, can in his local situation judge much better than any statesman or lawgiver can do for him. The statesman, who should attempt to direct private people in what manner they ought to employ their capitals, would not only load himself with a most unnecessary attention, but assume an authority which could safely be trusted, not only to no single person, but to no council or senate whatever, and which would nowhere be so dangerous as in the hands of a man who had folly and presumption enough to fancy himself fit to exercise it.

To give the monopoly of the home market to the produce of domestic industry, in any particular art or manufacture, is in some measure to direct private people in what manner they ought to employ their capitals, and must in almost all cases be either a useless or a hurtful regulation. If the produce of domestic can be brought there as cheap as that of foreign industry, the regulation is evidently useless. If it cannot, it must generally be hurtful. It is the maxim of every prudent master of a family, never to attempt to make at home what it will cost him more to make than to buy. The tailor does not attempt to make his own shoes, but buys them of the shoemaker. The shoemaker does not attempt to make his own clothes, but employs a tailor. The farmer attempts to make neither the one nor the other, but employs those different artificers. All of them find it for their interest to employ their whole industry in a way in which they have some advantage over their neighbours, and to purchase with a part of its produce, or, what is the same thing, with the price of a part of it, whatever else they have occasion for.

What is prudence in the conduct of every private family, can scarce be folly in that of a great kingdom. If a foreign country can supply us with a commodity cheaper than we ourselves can make it, better buy it of them with some part of the produce of our own industry, employed in a way in which we have some advantage. The general industry of the country being always in proportion to the capital which employs it, will not thereby be diminished, no more than that of the abovementioned artificers; but only left to find out the way in which it can be employed with the greatest advantage. It is certainly not employed to the greatest advantage, when it is thus directed towards an object which it can buy cheaper than it can make. The value of its annual produce is certainly more or less diminished, when it is thus turned away from producing commodities evidently of more value than the commodity which it is directed to produce. According to the supposition, that commodity could be purchased from foreign countries cheaper than it can be made at home; it could therefore have been purchased with a part only of the commodities, or, what is the same thing, with a part only of the price of the commodities, which the industry employed by an equal capital would have produced at home, had it been left to follow its natural course. The industry of the country, therefore, is thus turned away from a more to a less advantageous employment; and the exchangeable value of its annual produce, instead of being increased, according to the intention of the lawgiver, must necessarily be diminished by every such regulation.

By means of such regulations, indeed, a particular manufacture may sometimes be acquired sooner than it could have been otherwise, and after a certain time may be made at home as cheap, or cheaper, than in the foreign country. But though the industry of the society may be thus carried with advantage into a particular channel sooner than it could have been otherwise, it will by no means follow that the sum-total, either of its industry, or of its revenue, can ever be augmented by any such regulation. The industry of the society can augment only in proportion as its capital augments, and its capital can augment only in proportion to what can be gradually saved out of its revenue. But the immediate effect of every such regulation is to diminish its revenue; and what diminishes its revenue is certainly not very likely to augment its capital faster than it would have augmented of its own accord, had both capital and industry been left to find out their natural employments.

Though, for want of such regulations, the society should never acquire the proposed manufacture, it would not upon that account necessarily be the poorer in anyone period of its duration. In every period of its duration its whole capital and industry might still have been employed, though upon different objects, in the manner that was most advantageous at the time. In every period its revenue might have been the greatest which its capital could afford, and both capital and revenue might have been augmented with the greatest possible rapidity.

The natural advantages which one country has over another, in producing particular commodities, are sometimes so great, that it is acknowledged by all the world to be in vain to struggle with them. By means of glasses, hot-beds, and hot-walls, very good grapes can be raised in Scotland, and very good wine, too, can be made of them, at about thirty times the expense for which at least equally good can be brought from foreign countries. Would it be a reasonable law to prohibit the importation of all foreign wines, merely to encourage the making of claret and Burgundy in Scotland? But if there would be a manifest absurdity in turning towards any employment thirty times more of the capital and industry of the country than would be necessary to purchase from foreign countries an equal quantity of the commodities wanted, there must be an absurdity, though not altogether so glaring, yet exactly of the same kind, in turning towards any such employment a thirtieth, or even a three hundredth part more of either. Whether the advantages which one country has over another be natural or acquired, is in this respect of no consequence. As long as the one country has those advantages, and the other wants them, it will always be more advantageous for the latter rather to buy of the former than to make. It is an acquired advantage only, which one artificer has over his neighbour, who exercises another trade; and yet they both find it more advantageous to buy of one another, than to make what does not belong to their particular trades.

Merchants and manufacturers are the people who derive the greatest advantage from this monopoly of the home market. The prohibition of the importation of foreign cattle and of salt provisions, together with the high duties upon foreign corn, which in times of moderate plenty amount to a prohibition, are not near so advantageous to the graziers and farmers of Great Britain, as other regulations of the same kind are to its merchants and manufacturers. Manufactures, those of the finer kind especially, are more easily transported from one country to another than corn or cattle. It is in the fetching and carrying manufactures, accordingly, that foreign trade is chiefly employed. In manufactures, a very small advantage will enable foreigners to undersell our own workmen, even in the home market. It will require a very great one to enable them to do so in the rude produce of the soil. If the free importation of foreign manufactures were permitted, several of the home manufactures would probably suffer, and some of them perhaps go to ruin altogether, and a considerable part of the stock and industry at present employed in them, would be forced to find out some other employment. But the freest importation of the rude produce of the soil could have no such effect upon the agriculture of the country.

If the importation of foreign cattle, for example, were made ever so free, so few could be imported, that the grazing trade of Great Britain could be little affected by it. Live cattle are, perhaps, the only commodity of which the transportation is more expensive by sea than by land. By land they carry themselves to market. By sea, not only the cattle, but their food and their water too, must be carried at no small expense and inconveniency. The short sea between Ireland and Great Britain, indeed, renders the importation of Irish cattle more easy. But though the free importation of them, which was lately permitted only for a limited time, were rendered perpetual, it could have no considerable effect upon the interest of the graziers of Great Britain. Those parts of Great Britain which border upon the Irish sea are all grazing countries. Irish cattle could never be imported for their use, but must be drove through those very extensive countries, at no small expense and inconveniency, before they could arrive at their proper market. Fat cattle could not be drove so far. Lean cattle, therefore, could only be imported; and such importation could interfere not with the interest of the feeding or fattening countries, to which, by reducing the price of lean cattle it would rather be advantageous, but with that of the breeding countries only. The small number of Irish cattle imported since their importation was permitted, together with the good price at which lean cattle still continue to sell, seem to demonstrate, that even the breeding countries of Great Britain are never likely to be much affected by the free importation of Irish cattle. The common people of Ireland, indeed, are said to have sometimes opposed with violence the exportation of their cattle. But if the exporters had found any great advantage in continuing the trade, they could easily, when the law was on their side, have conquered this mobbish opposition.

Feeding and fattening countries, besides, must always be highly improved, whereas breeding countries are generally uncultivated. The high price of lean cattle, by augmenting the value of uncultivated land, is like a bounty against improvement. To any country which was highly improved throughout, it would be more advantageous to import its lean cattle than to breed them. The province of Holland, accordingly, is said to follow this maxim at present. The mountains of Scotland, Wales, and Northumberland, indeed, are countries not capable of much improvement, and seem destined by nature to be the breeding countries of Great Britain. The freest importation of foreign cattle could have no other effect than to hinder those breeding countries from taking advantage of the increasing population and improvement of the rest of the kingdom, from raising their price to an exorbitant height, and from laying a real tax upon all the more improved and cultivated parts of the country.

The freest importation of salt provisions, in the same manner, could have as little effect upon the interest of the graziers of Great Britain as that of live cattle. Salt provisions are not only a very bulky commodity, but when compared with fresh meat they are a commodity both of worse quality, and, as they cost more labour and expense, of higher price. They could never, therefore, come into competition with the fresh meat, though they might with the salt provisions of the country. They might be used for victualling ships for distant voyages, and such like uses, but could never make any considerable part of the food of the people. The small quantity of salt provisions imported from Ireland since their importation was rendered free, is an experimental proof that our graziers have nothing to apprehend from it. It does not appear that the price of butcher's meat has ever been sensibly affected by it.

Even the free importation of foreign corn could very little affect the interest of the farmers of Great Britain. Corn is a much more bulky commodity than butcher's meat. A pound of wheat at a penny is as dear as a pound of butcher's meat at fourpence. The small quantity of foreign corn imported even in times of the greatest scarcity, may satisfy our farmers that they can have nothing to fear from the freest importation. The average quantity imported, one year with another, amounts only, according to the very well informed author of the Tracts upon the Corn Trade, to 23,728 quarters of all sorts of grain, and does not exceed the five hundredth and seventy-one part of the annual consumption. But as the bounty upon corn occasions a greater exportation in years of plenty, so it must, of consequence, occasion a greater importation in years of scarcity, than in the actual state of tillage would otherwise take place. By means of it, the plenty of one year does not compensate the scarcity of another; and as the average quantity exported is necessarily augmented by it, so must likewise, in the actual state of tillage, the average quantity imported. If there were no bounty, as less corn would be exported, so it is probable that, one year with another, less would be imported than at present. The corn-merchants, the fetchers and carriers of corn between Great Britain and foreign countries, would have much less employment, and might suffer considerably; but the country gentlemen and farmers could suffer very little. It is in the corn-merchants, accordingly, rather than the country gentlemen and farmers, that I have observed the greatest anxiety for the renewal and continuation of the bounty.

Country gentlemen and farmers are, to their great honour, of all people, the least subject to the wretched spirit of monopoly. The undertaker of a great manufactory is sometimes alarmed if another work of the same kind is established within twenty miles of him; the Dutch undertaker of the woollen manufacture at Abbeville, stipulated that no work of the same kind should be established within thirty leagues of that city. Farmers and country gentlemen, on the contrary, are generally disposed rather to promote, than to obstruct, the cultivation and improvement of their neighbours farms and estates. They have no secrets, such as those of the greater part of manufacturers, but are generally rather fond of communicating to their neighbours, and of extending as far as possible any new practice which they may have found to be advantageous. "Pius quaestus", says old Cato, "stabilissimusque, minimeque invidiosus; minimeque male cogitantes sunt, qui in eo studio occupati sunt." Country gentlemen and farmers, dispersed in different parts of the country, cannot so easily combine as merchants and manufacturers, who being collected into towns, and accustomed to that exclusive corporation spirit which prevails in them, naturally endeavour to obtain, against all their countrymen, the same exclusive privilege which they generally possess against the inhabitants of their respective towns. They accordingly seem to have been the original inventors of those restraints upon the importation of foreign goods, which secure to them the monopoly of the home market. It was probably in imitation of them, and to put themselves upon a level with those who, they found, were disposed to oppress them, that the country gentlemen and farmers of Great Britain so far forgot the generosity which is natural to their station, as to demand the exclusive privilege of supplying their countrymen with corn and butcher's meat. They did not, perhaps, take time to consider how much less their interest could be affected by the freedom of trade, than that of the people whose example they followed.

To prohibit, by a perpetual law, the importation of foreign corn and cattle, is in reality to enact, that the population and industry of the country shall, at no time, exceed what the rude produce of its own soil can maintain.

There seem, however, to be two cases, in which it will generally be advantageous to lay some burden upon foreign, for the encouragement of domestic industry.

The first is, when some particular sort of industry is necessary for the defence of the country. The defence of Great Britain, for example, depends very much upon the number of its sailors and shipping. The act of navigation, therefore, very properly endeavours to give the sailors and shipping of Great Britain the monopoly of the trade of their own country, in some cases, by absolute prohibitions, and in others, by heavy burdens upon the shipping of foreign countries. The following are the principal dispositions of this act.

First, All ships, of which the owners, masters, and three-fourths of the mariners, are not British subjects, are prohibited, upon pain of forfeiting ship and cargo, from trading to the British settlements and plantations, or from being employed in the coasting trade of Great Britain.

Secondly, A great variety of the most bulky articles of importation can be brought into Great Britain only, either in such ships as are above described, or in ships of the country where those goods are produced, and of which the owners, masters, and three-fourths of the mariners, are of that particular country; and when imported even in ships of this latter kind, they are subject to double aliens duty. If imported in ships of any other country, the penalty is forfeiture of ship and goods. When this act was made, the Dutch were, what they still are, the great carriers of Europe; and by this regulation they were entirely excluded from being the carriers to Great Britain, or from importing to us the goods of any other European country.

Thirdly, A great variety of the most bulky articles of importation are prohibited from being imported, even in British ships, from any country but that in which they are produced, under pain of forfeiting ship and cargo. This regulation, too, was probably intended against the Dutch. Holland was then, as now, the great emporium for all European goods; and by this regulation, British ships were hindered from loading in Holland the goods of any other European country.

Fourthly, Salt fish of all kinds, whale fins, whalebone, oil, and blubber, not caught by and cured on board British vessels, when imported into Great Britain, are subject to double aliens duty. The Dutch, as they are still the principal, were then the only fishers in Europe that attempted to supply foreign nations with fish. By this regulation, a very heavy burden was laid upon their supplying Great Britain.

When the act of navigation was made, though England and Holland were not actually at war, the most violent animosity subsisted between the two nations. It had begun during the government of the long parliament, which first framed this act, and it broke out soon after in the Dutch wars, during that of the Protector and of Charles II. It is not impossible, therefore, that some of the regulations of this famous act may have proceeded from national animosity. They are as wise, however, as if they had all been dictated by the most deliberate wisdom. National animosity, at that particular time, aimed at the very same object which the most deliberate wisdom would have recommended, the diminution of the naval power of Holland, the only naval power which could endanger the security of England.

The act of navigation is not favourable to foreign commerce, or to the growth of that opulence which can arise from it. The interest of a nation, in its commercial relations to foreign nations, is, like that of a merchant with regard to the different people with whom he deals, to buy as cheap, and to sell as dear as possible. But it will be most likely to buy cheap, when, by the most perfect freedom of trade, it encourages all nations to bring to it the goods which it has occasion to purchase; and, for the same reason, it will be most likely to sell dear, when its markets are thus filled with the greatest number of buyers. The act of navigation, it is true, lays no burden upon foreign ships that come to export the produce of British industry. Even the ancient aliens duty, which used to be paid upon all goods, exported as well as imported, has, by several subsequent acts, been taken off from the greater part of the articles of exportation. But if foreigners, either by prohibitions or high duties, are hindered from coming to sell, they cannot always afford to come to buy; because, coming without a cargo, they must lose the freight from their own country to Great Britain. By diminishing the number of sellers, therefore, we necessarily diminish that of buyers, and are thus likely not only to buy foreign goods dearer, but to sell our own cheaper, than if there was a more perfect freedom of trade. As defence, however, is of much more importance than opulence, the act of navigation is, perhaps, the wisest of all the commercial regulations of England.

The second case, in which it will generally be advantageous to lay some burden upon foreign for the encouragement of domestic industry, is when some tax is imposed at home upon the produce of the latter. In this case, it seems reasonable that an equal tax should be imposed upon the like produce of the former. This would not give the monopoly of the borne market to domestic industry, nor turn towards a particular employment a greater share of the stock and labour of the country, than what would naturally go to it. It would only hinder any part of what would naturally go to it from being turned away by the tax into a less natural direction, and would leave the competition between foreign and domestic industry, after the tax, as nearly as possible upon the same footing as before it. In Great Britain, when any such tax is laid upon the produce of domestic industry, it is usual, at the same time, in order to stop the clamorous complaints of our merchants and manufacturers, that they will be undersold at home, to lay a much heavier duty upon the importation of all foreign goods of the same kind.

This second limitation of the freedom of trade, according to some people, should, upon most occasions, be extended much farther than to the precise foreign commodities which could come into competition with those which had been taxed at home. When the necessaries of life have been taxed in any country, it becomes proper, they pretend, to tax not only the like necessaries of life imported from other countries, but all sorts of foreign goods which can come into competition with any thing that is the produce of domestic industry. Subsistence, they say, becomes necessarily dearer in consequence of such taxes; and the price of labour must always rise with the price of the labourer's subsistence. Every commodity, therefore, which is the produce of domestic industry, though not immediately taxed itself, becomes dearer in consequence of such taxes, because the labour which produces it becomes so. Such taxes, therefore, are really equivalent, they say, to a tax upon every particular commodity produced at home. In order to put domestic upon the same footing with foreign industry, therefore, it becomes necessary, they think, to lay some duty upon every foreign commodity, equal to this enhancement of the price of the home commodities with which it can come into competition.

Whether taxes upon the necessaries of life, such as those in Great Britain upon soap, salt, leather, candles, etc. necessarily raise the price of labour, and consequently that of all other commodities, I shall consider hereafter, when I come to treat of taxes. Supposing, however, in the mean time, that they have this effect, and they have it undoubtedly, this general enhancement of the price of all commodities, in consequence of that labour, is a case which differs in the two following respects from that of a particular commodity, of which the price was enhanced by a particular tax immediately imposed upon it.

First, It might always be known with great exactness, how far the price of such a commodity could be enhanced by such a tax; but how far the general enhancement of the price of labour might affect that of every different commodity about which labour was employed, could never be known with any tolerable exactness. It would be impossible, therefore, to proportion, with any tolerable exactness, the tax of every foreign, to the enhancement of the price of every home commodity.

Secondly, Taxes upon the necessaries of life have nearly the same effect upon the circumstances of the people as a poor soil and a bad climate. Provisions are thereby rendered dearer, in the same manner as if it required extraordinary labour and expense to raise them. As, in the natural scarcity arising from soil and climate, it would be absurd to direct the people in what manner they ought to employ their capitals and industry, so is it likewise in the artificial scarcity arising from such taxes. To be left to accommodate, as well as they could, their industry to their situation, and to find out those employments in which, notwithstanding their unfavourable circumstances, they might have some advantage either in the home or in the foreign market, is what, in both cases, would evidently be most for their advantage. To lay a new-tax upon them, because they are already overburdened with taxes, and because they already pay too dear for the necessaries of life, to make them likewise pay too dear for the greater part of other commodities, is certainly a most absurd way of making amends.

Such taxes, when they have grown up to a certain height, are a curse equal to the barrenness of the earth, and the inclemency of the heavens, and yet it is in the richest and most industrious countries that they have been most generally imposed. No other countries could support so great a disorder. As the strongest bodies only can live and enjoy health under an unwholesome regimen, so the nations only, that in every sort of industry have the greatest natural and acquired advantages, can subsist and prosper under such taxes. Holland is the country in Europe in which they abound most, and which, from peculiar circumstances, continues to prosper, not by means of them, as has been most absurdly supposed, but in spite of them.

As there are two cases in which it will generally be advantageous to lay some burden upon foreign for the encouragement of domestic industry, so there are two others in which it may sometimes be a matter of deliberation, in the one, how far it is proper to continue the free importation of certain foreign goods; and, in the other, how far, or in what manner, it may be proper to restore that free importation, after it has been for some time interrupted.

The case in which it may sometimes be a matter of deliberation how far it is proper to continue the free importation of certain foreign goods, is when some foreign nation restrains, by high duties or prohibitions, the importation of some of our manufactures into their country. Revenge, in this case, naturally dictates retaliation, and that we should impose the like duties and prohibitions upon the importation of some or all of their manufactures into ours. Nations, accordingly, seldom fail to retaliate in this manner. The French have been particularly forward to favour their own manufactures, by restraining the importation of such foreign goods as could come into competition with them. In this consisted a great part of the policy of Mr Colbert, who, notwithstanding his great abilities, seems in this case to have been imposed upon by the sophistry of merchants and manufacturers, who are always demanding a monopoly against their countrymen. It is at present the opinion of the most intelligent men in France, that his operations of this kind have not been beneficial to his country. That minister, by the tariff of 1667, imposed very high duties upon a great number of foreign manufactures. Upon his refusing to moderate them in favour of the Dutch, they, in 1671, prohibited the importation of the wines, brandies, and manufactures of France. The war of 1672 seems to have been in part occasioned by this commercial dispute. The peace of Nimeguen put an end to it in 1678, by moderating some of those duties in favour of the Dutch, who in consequence took off their prohibition. It was about the same time that the French and English began mutually to oppress each other's industry, by the like duties and prohibitions, of which the French, however, seem to have set the first example, The spirit of hostility which has subsisted between the two nations ever since, has hitherto hindered them from being moderated on either side. In 1697, the Ehglish prohibited the importation of bone lace, the manufacture of Flanders. The government of that country, at that time under the dominion of Spain, prohibited, in return, the importation of English woollens. In 1700, the prohibition of importing bone lace into England was taken oft; upon condition that the importation of English woollens into Flanders should be put on the same footing as before.

There may be good policy in retaliations of this kind, when there is a probability that they will procure the repeal of the high duties or prohibitions complained of. The recovery of a great foreign market will generally more than compensate the transitory inconveniency of paying dearer during a short time for some sorts of goods. To judge whether such retaliations are likely to produce such an effect, does not, perhaps, belong so much to the science of a legislator, whose deliberations ought to be governed by general principles, which are always the same, as to the skill of that insidious and crafty animal vulgarly called a statesman or politician, whose councils are directed by the momentary fluctuations of affairs. When there is no probability that any such repeal can be procured, it seems a bad method of compensating the injury done to certain classes of our people, to do another injury ourselves, not only to those classes, but to almost all the other classes of them. When our neighbours prohibit some manufacture of ours, we generally prohibit, not only the same, for that alone would seldom affect them considerably, but some other manufacture of theirs. This may, no doubt, give encouragement to some particular class of workmen among ourselves, and, by excluding some of their rivals, may enable them to raise their price in the home market. Those workmen however, who suffered by our neighbours prohibition, will not be benefited by ours. On the contrary, they, and almost all the other classes of our citizens, will thereby be obliged to pay dearer than before for certain goods. Every such law, therefore, imposes a real tax upon the whole country, not in favour of that particular class of workmen who were injured by our neighbours prohibitions, but of some other class.

The case in which it may sometimes be a matter of deliberation, how far, or in what manner, it is proper to restore the free importation of foreign goods, after it has been for some time interrupted, is when particular manufactures, by means of high duties or prohibitions upon all foreign goods which can come into competition with them, have been so far extended as to employ a great multitude of hands. Humanity may in this case require that the freedom of trade should be restored only by slow gradations, and with a good deal of reserve and circumspection. Were those high duties and prohibitions taken away all at once, cheaper foreign goods of the same kind might be poured so fast into the home market, as to deprive all at once many thousands of our people of their ordinary employment and means of subsistence. The disorder which this would occasion might no doubt be very considerable. It would in all probability, however, be much less than is commonly imagined, for the two following reasons.

First, All those manufactures of which any part is commonly exported to other European countries without a bounty, could be very little affected by the freest importation of foreign goods. Such manufactures must be sold as cheap abroad as any other foreign goods of the same quality and kind, and consequently must be sold cheaper at home. They would still, therefore, keep possession of the home market; and though a capricious man of fashion might sometimes prefer foreign wares, merely because they were foreign, to cheaper and better goods of the same kind that were made at home, this folly could, from the nature of things, extend to so few, that it could make no sensible impression upon the general employment of the people. But a great part of all the different branches of our woollen manufacture, of our tanned leather, and of our hardware, are annually exported to other European countries without any bounty, and these are the manufactures which employ the greatest number of hands. The silk, perhaps, is the manufacture which would suffer the most by this freedom of trade, and after it the linen, though the latter much less than the former.

Secondly, Though a great number of people should, by thus restoring the freedom of trade, be thrown all at once out of their ordinary employment and common method of subsistence, it would by no means follow that they would thereby be deprived either of employment or subsistence. By the reduction of the army and navy at the end of the late war, more than 100,000 soldiers and seamen, a number equal to what is employed in the greatest manufactures, were all at once thrown out of their ordinary employment: but though they no doubt suffered some inconveniency, they were not thereby deprived of all employment and subsistence. The greater part of the seamen, it is probable, gradually betook themselves to the merchant service as they could find occasion, and in the mean time both they and the soldiers were absorbed in the great mass of the people, and employed in a great variety of occupations. Not only no great convulsion, but no sensible disorder, arose from so great a change in the situation of more than 100,000 men, all accustomed to the use of arms, and many of them to rapine and plunder. The number of vagrants was scarce anywhere sensibly increased by it; even the wages of labour were not reduced by it in any occupation, so far as I have been able to learn, except in that of seamen in the merchant service. But if we compare together the habits of a soldier and of any sort of manufacturer, we shall find that those of the latter do not tend so much to disqualify him from being employed in a new trade, as those of the former from being employed in any. The manufacturer has always been accustomed to look for his subsistence from his labour only; the soldier to expect it from his pay. Application and industry have been familiar to the one; idleness and dissipation to the other. But it is surely much easier to change the direction of industry from one sort of labour to another, than to turn idleness and dissipation to any. To the greater part of manufactures, besides, it has already been observed, there are other collateral manufactures of so similar a nature, that a workman can easily transfer his industry from one of them to another. The greater part of such workmen, too, are occasionally employed in country labour. The stock which employed them in a particular manufacture before, will still remain in the country, to employ an equal number of people in some other way. The capital of the country remaining the same, the demand for labour will likewise be the same, or very nearly the same, though it may be exerted in different places, and for different occupations. Soldiers and seamen, indeed, when discharged from the king's service, are at liberty to exercise any trade within any town or place of Great Britain or Ireland. Let the same natural liberty of exercising what species of industry they please, be restored to all his Majesty's subjects, in the same manner as to soldiers and seamen; that is, break down the exclusive privileges of corporations, and repeal the statute of apprenticeship, both which are really encroachments upon natural Liberty, and add to those the repeal of the law of settlements, so that a poor workman, when thrown out of employment, either in one trade or in one place, may seek for it in another trade or in another place, without the fear either of a prosecution or of a removal; and neither the public nor the individuals will suffer much more from the occasional disbanding some particular classes of manufacturers, than from that of the soldiers. Our manufacturers have no doubt great merit with their country, but they cannot have more than those who defend it with their blood, nor deserve to be treated with more delicacy.

To expect, indeed, that the freedom of trade should ever be entirely restored in Great Britain, is as absurd as to expect that an Oceana or Utopia should ever be established in it. Not only the prejudices of the public, but, what is much more unconquerable, the private interests of many individuals, irresistibly oppose it. Were the officers of the army to oppose, with the same zeal and unanimity, any reduction in the number of forces, with which master manufacturers set themselves against every law that is likely to increase the number of their rivals in the home market; were the former to animate their soldiers. In the same manner as the latter inflame their workmen, to attack with violence and outrage the proposers of any such regulation; to attempt to reduce the army would be as dangerous as it has now become to attempt to diminish, in any respect, the monopoly which our manufacturers have obtained against us. This monopoly has so much increased the number of some particular tribes of them, that, like an overgrown standing army, they have become formidable to the government, and, upon many occasions, intimidate the legislature. The member of parliament who supports every proposal for strengthening this monopoly, is sure to acquire not only the reputation of understanding trade, but great popularity and influence with an order of men whose numbers and wealth render them of great importance. If he opposes them, on the contrary, and still more, if he has authority enough to be able to thwart them, neither the most acknowledged probity, nor the highest rank, nor the greatest public services, can protect him from the most infamous abuse and detraction, from personal insults, nor sometimes from real danger, arising from the insolent outrage of furious and disappointed monopolists.

The undertaker of a great manufacture, who, by the home markets being suddenly laid open to the competition of foreigners, should be obliged to abandon his trade, would no doubt suffer very considerably. That part of his capital which had usually been employed in purchasing materials, and in paying his workmen, might, without much difficulty, perhaps, find another employment; but that part of it which was fixed in workhouses, and in the instruments of trade, could scarce be disposed of without considerable loss. The equitable regard, therefore, to his interest, requires that changes of this kind should never be introduced suddenly, but slowly, gradually, and after a very long warning. The legislature, were it possible that its deliberations could be always directed, not by the clamorous importunity of partial interests, but by an extensive view of the general good, ought, upon this very account, perhaps, to be particularly careful, neither to establish any new monopolies of this kind, nor to extend further those which are already established. Every such regulation introduces some degree of real disorder into the constitution of the state, which it will be difficult afterwards to cure without occasioning another disorder.

How far it may be proper to impose taxes upon the importation of foreign goods, in order not to prevent their importation, but to raise a revenue for government, I shall consider hereafter when I come to treat of taxes. Taxes imposed with a view to prevent, or even to diminish importation, are evidently as destructive of the revenue of the customs as of the freedom of trade.

CHAPTER III

OF THE EXTRAORDINARY RESTRAINTS UPON THE IMPORTATION OF GOODS OF ALMOST ALL KINDS, FROM THOSE COUNTRIES WITH WHICH THE BALANCE IS SUPPOSED TO BE DISADVANTAGEOUS

Part I—Of the Unreasonableness of those Restraints, even upon the Principles of the Commercial System

To lay extraordinary restraints upon the importation of goods of almost all kinds, from those particular countries with which the balance of trade is supposed to be disadvantageous, is the second expedient by which the commercial system proposes to increase the quantity of gold and silver. Thus, in Great Britain, Silesia lawns may be imported for home consumption, upon paying certain duties; but French cambrics and lawns are prohibited to be imported, except into the port of London, there to be warehoused for exportation. Higher duties are imposed upon the wines of France than upon those of Portugal, or indeed of any other country. By what is called the impost 1692, a duty of five-and-twenty per cent. of the rate or value, was laid upon all French goods; while the goods of other nations were, the greater part of them, subjected to much lighter duties, seldom exceeding five per cent. The wine, brandy, salt, and vinegar of France, were indeed excepted; these commodities being subjected to other heavy duties, either by other laws, or by particular clauses of the same law. In 1696, a second duty of twenty-five per cent. the first not having been thought a sufficient discouragement, was imposed upon all French goods, except brandy; together with a new duty of five-and-twenty pounds upon the ton of French wine, and another of fifteen pounds upon the ton of French vinegar. French goods have never been omitted in any of those general subsidies or duties of five per cent. which have been imposed upon all, or the greater part, of the goods enumerated in the book of rates. If we count the one-third and two-third subsidies as making a complete subsidy between them, there have been five of these general subsidies; so that, before the commencement of the present war, seventy-five per cent. may be considered as the lowest duty to which the greater part of the goods of the growth, produce, or manufacture of France, were liable. But upon the greater part of goods, those duties are equivalent to a prohibition. The French, in their turn, have, I believe, treated our goods and manufactures just as hardly; though I am not so well acquainted with the particular hardships which they have imposed upon them. Those mutual restraints have put an end to almost all fair commerce between the two nations; and smugglers are now the principal importers, either of British goods into France, or of French goods into Great Britain. The principles which I have been examining, in the foregoing chapter, took their origin from private interest and the spirit of monopoly; those which I am going te examine in this, from national prejudice and animosity. They are, accordingly, as might well be expected, still more unreasonable. They are so, even upon the principles of the commercial system.

First, Though it were certain that in the case of a free trade between France and England, for example, the balance would be in favour of France, it would by no means follow that such a trade would be disadvantageous to England, or that the general balance of its whole trade would thereby be turned more against it. If the wines of France are better and cheaper than those of Portugal, or its linens than those of Germany, it would be more advantageous for Great Britain to purchase both the wine and the foreign linen which it had occasion for of France, than of Portugal and Germany. Though the value of the annual importations from France would thereby be greatly augmented, the value of the whole annual importations would be diminished, in proportion as the French goods of the same quality were cheaper than those of the other two countries. This would be the case, even upon the supposition that the whole French goods imported were to be consumed in Great Britain.

But, Secondly, A great part of them might be re-exported to other countries, where, being sold with profit, they might bring back a return, equal in value, perhaps, to the prime cost of the whole French goods imported. What has frequently been said of the East India trade, might possibly be true of the French; that though the greater part of East India goods were bought with gold and silver, the re-exportation of a part of them to other countries brought back more gold and silver to that which carried on the trade, than the prime cost of the whole amounted to. One of the most important branches of the Dutch trade at present, consists in the carriage of French goods to other European countries. Some part even of the French wine drank in Great Britain, is clandestinely imported from Holland and Zealand. If there was either a free trade between France and England, or if French goods could be imported upon paying only the same duties as those of other European nations, to be drawn back upon exportation, England might have some share of a trade which is found so advantageous to Holland.

Thirdly, and lastly, There is no certain criterion by which we can determine on which side what is called the balance between any two countries lies, or which of them exports to the greatest value. National prejudice and animosity, prompted always by the private interest of particular traders, are the principles which generally direct our judgment upon all questions concerning it. There are two criterions, however, which have frequently been appealed to upon such occasions, the custom-house books and the course of exchange. The custom-house books, I think, it is now generally acknowledged, are a very uncertain criterion, on account of the inaccuracy of the valuation at which the greater part of goods are rated in them. The course of exchange is, perhaps, almost equally so.

When the exchange between two places, such as London and Paris, is at par, it is said to be a sign that the debts due from London to Paris are compensated by those due from Paris to London. On the contrary, when a premium is paid at London for a bill upon Paris, it is said to be a sign that the debts due from London to Paris are not compensated by those due from Paris to London, but that a balance in money must be sent out from the latter place; for the risk, trouble, and expense, of exporting which, the premium is both demanded and given. But the ordinary state of debt and credit between those two cities must necessarily be regulated, it is said, by the ordinary course of their dealings with one another. When neither of them imports from from other to a greater amount than it exports to that other, the debts and credits of each may compensate one another. But when one of them imports from the other to a greater value than it exports to that other, the former necessarily becomes indebted to the latter in a greater sum than the latter becomes indebted to it: the debts and credits of each do not compensate one another, and money must be sent out from that place of which the debts overbalance the credits. The ordinary course of exchange, therefore, being an indication of the ordinary state of debt and credit between two places, must likewise be an indication of the ordinary course of their exports and imports, as these necessarily regulate that state.

But though the ordinary course of exchange shall be allowed to be a sufficient indication of the ordinary state of debt and credit between any two places, it would not from thence follow, that the balance of trade was in favour of that place which had the ordinary state of debt and credit in its favour. The ordinary state of debt and credit between any two places is not always entirely regulated by the ordinary course of their dealings with one another, but is often influenced by that of the dealings of either with many other places. If it is usual, for example, for the merchants of England to pay for the goods which they buy of Hamburg, Dantzic, Riga, etc. by bills upon Holland, the ordinary state of debt and credit between England and Holland will not be regulated entirely by the ordinary course of the dealings of those two countries with one another, but will be influenced by that of the dealings in England with those other places. England may be obliged to send out every year money to Holland, though its annual exports to that country may exceed very much the annual value of its imports from thence, and though what is called the balance of trade may be very much in favour of England.

In the way, besides, in which the par of exchange has hitherto been computed, the ordinary course of exchange can afford no sufficient indication that the ordinary state of debt and credit is in favour of that country which seems to have, or which is supposed to have, the ordinary course of exchange in its favour; or, in other words, the real exchange may be, and in fact often is, so very different from the computed one, that, from the course of the latter, no certain conclusion can, upon many occasions, be drawn concerning that of the former.

When for a sum or money paid in England, containing, according to the standard of the English mint, a certain number of ounces of pure silver, you receive a bill for a sum of money to be paid in France, containing, according to the standard of the French mint, an equal number of ounces of pure silver, exchange is said to be at par between England and France. When you pay more, you are supposed to give a premium, and exchange is said to be against England, and in favour of France. When you pay less, you are supposed to get a premium, and exchange is said to be against France, and in favour of England.

But, first, We cannot always judge of the value of the current money of different countries by the standard of their respective mints. In some it is more, in others it is less worn, clipt, and otherwise degenerated from that standard. But the value of the current coin of every country, compared with that of any other country, is in proportion, not to the quantity of pure silver which it ought to contain, but to that which it actually does contain. Before the reformation of the silver coin in King William's time, exchange between England and Holland, computed in the usual manner, according to the standard of their respective mints, was five-and twenty per cent. against England. But the value of the current coin of England, as we learn from Mr Lowndes, was at that time rather more than five-and-twenty per cent. below its standard value. The real exchange, therefore, may even at that time have been in favour of England, notwithstanding the computed exchange was so much against it; a smaller number or ounces of pure silver, actually paid in England, may have purchased a bill for a greater number of ounces of pure silver to be paid in Holland, and the man who was supposed to give, may in reality have got the premium. The French coin was, before the late reformation of the English gold coin, much less wore than the English, and was perhaps two or three per cent. nearer its standard. If the computed exchange with France, therefore, was not more than two or three per cent. against England, the real exchange might have been in its favour. Since the reformation of the gold coin, the exchange has been constantly in favour of England, and against France.

Secondly, In some countries the expense of coinage is defrayed by the government; in others, it is defrayed by the private people, who carry their bullion to the mint, and the government even derives some revenue from the coinage. In England it is defrayed by the government; and if you carry a pound weight of standard silver to the mint, you get back sixty-two shillings, containing a pound weight of the like standard silver. In France a duty of eight per cent. is deducted for the coinage, which not only defrays the expense of it, but affords a small revenue to the government. In England, as the coinage costs nothing, the current coin can never be much more valuable than the quantity of bullion which it actually contains. In France, the workmanship, as you pay for it, adds to the value, in the same manner as to that of wrought plate. A sum of French money, therefore, containing an equal weight of pure silver, is more valuable than a sum of English money containing an equal weight of pure silver, and must require more bullion, or other commodities, to purchase it. Though the current coin of the two countries, therefore, were equally near the standards of their respective mints, a sum of English money could not well purchase a sum of French money containing an equal number of ounces of pure silver, nor, consequently, a bill upon France for such a sum. If, for such a bill, no more additional money was paid than what was sufficient to compensate the expense of the French coinage, the real exchange might be at par between the two countries; their debts and credits might mutually compensate one another, while the computed exchange was considerably in favour of France. If less than this was paid, the real exchange might be in favour of England, while the computed was in favour of France.

Thirdly, and lastly, In some places, as at Amsterdam, Hamburg, Venice, etc. foreign bills of exchange are paid in what they call bank money; while in others, as at London, Lisbon, Antwerp, Leghorn, etc. they are paid in the common currency of the country. What is called bank money, is always of more value than the same nominal sum of common currency. A thousand guilders in the bank of Amsterdam, for example, are of more value than a thousand guilders of Amsterdam currency. The difference between them is called the agio of the bank, which at Amsterdam is generally about five per cent. Supposing the current money of the two countries equally near to the standard of their respective mints, and that the one pays foreign bills in this common currency, while the other pays them in bank money, it is evident that the computed exchange may be in favour of that which pays in bank money, though the real exchange should be in favour of that which pays in current money; for the same reason that the computed exchange may be in favour of that which pays in better money, or in money nearer to its own standard, though the real exchange should be in favour of that which pays in worse. The computed exchange, before the late reformation of the gold coin, was generally against London with Amsterdam, Hamburg, Venice, and, I believe, with all other places which pay in what is called bank money. It will by no means follow, however, that the real exchange was against it. Since the reformation of the gold coin, it has been in favour of London, even with those places. The computed exchange has generally been in favour of London with Lisbon, Antwerp, Leghorn, and, if you except France, I believe with most other parts of Europe that pay in common currency; and it is not improbable that the real exchange was so too.

Digression concerning Banks of Deposit, particularly concerning that of Amsterdam

The currency of a great state, such as France or England, generally consists almost entirely of its own coin. Should this currency, therefore, be at any time worn, clipt, or otherwise degraded below its standard value, the state, by a reformation of its coin, can effectually re-establish its currency. But the currency of a small state, such as Genoa or Hamburg, can seldom consist altogether in its own coin, but must be made up, in a great measure, of the coins of all the neighbouring states with which its inhabitants have a continual intercourse. Such a state, therefore, by reforming its coin, will not always be able to reform its currency. If foreign bills of exchange are paid in this currency, the uncertain value of any sum, of what is in its own nature so uncertain, must render the exchange always very much against such a state, its currency being in all foreign states necessarily valued even below what it is worth.

In order to remedy the inconvenience to which this disadvantageous exchange must have subjected their merchants, such small states, when they began to attend to the interest of trade, have frequently enacted that foreign bills of exchange of a certain value should be paid, not in common currency, but by an order upon, or by a transfer in the books of a certain bank, established upon the credit, and under the protection of the state, this bank being always obliged to pay, in good and true money, exactly according to the standard of the state. The banks of Venice, Genoa, Amsterdam, Hamburg, and Nuremberg, seem to have been all originally established with this view, though some of them may have afterwards been made subservient to other purposes. The money of such banks, being better than the common currency of the country, necessarily bore an agio, which was greater or smaller, according as the currency was supposed to be more or less degraded below the standard of the state. The agio of the bank of Hamburg, for example, which is said to be commonly about fourteen per cent. is the supposed difference between the good standard money of the state, and the clipt, worn, and diminished currency, poured into it from all the neighbouring states.

Before 1609, the great quantity of clipt and worn foreign coin which the extensive trade of Amsterdam brought from all parts of Europe, reduced the value of its currency about nine per cent. below that of good money fresh from the mint. Such money no sooner appeared, than it was melted down or carried away, as it always is in such circumstances. The merchants, with plenty of currency, could not always find a sufficient quantity of good money to pay their bills of exchange; and the value of those bills, in spite of several regulations which were made to prevent it, became in a great measure uncertain.

In order to remedy these inconveniencies, a bank was established in 1609, under the guarantee of the city. This bank received both foreign coin, and the light and worn coin of the country, at its real intrinsic value in the good standard money of the country, deducting only so much as was necessary for defraying the expense of coinage and the other necessary expense of management. For the value which remained after this small deduction was made, it gave a credit in its books. This credit was called bank money, which, as it represented money exactly according to the standard of the mint, was always of the same real value, and intrinsically worth more than current money. It was at the same time enacted, that all bills drawn upon or negotiated at Amsterdam, of the value of 600 guilders and upwards, should be paid in bank money, which at once took away all uncertainty in the value of those bills. Every merchant, in consequence of this regulation, was obliged to keep an account with the bank, in order to pay his foreign bills of exchange, which necessarily occasioned a certain demand for bank money.

Bank money, over and above both its intrinsic superiority to currency, and the additional value which this demand necessarily gives it, has likewise some other advantages, It is secure from fire, robbery, and other accidents; the city of Amsterdam is bound for it; it can be paid away by a simple transfer, without the trouble of counting, or the risk of transporting it from one place to another. In consequence of those different advantages, it seems from the beginning to have borne an agio; and it is generally believed that all the money originally deposited in the bank, was allowed to remain there, nobody caring to demand payment of a debt which he could sell for a premium in the market. By demanding payment of the bank, the owner of a bank credit would lose this premium. As a shilling fresh from the mint will buy no more goods in the market than one of our common worn shillings, so the good and true money which might be brought from the coffers of the bank into those of a private person, being mixed and confounded with the common currency of the country, would be of no more value than that currency, from which it could no longer be readily distinguished. While it remained in the coffers of the bank, its superiority was known and ascertained. When it had come into those of a private person, its superiority could not well be ascertained without more trouble than perhaps the difference was worth. By being brought from the coffers of the bank, besides, it lost all the other advantages of bank money; its security, its easy and safe transferability, its use in paying foreign bills of exchange. Over and above all this, it could not be brought from those coffers, as will appear by and by, without previously paying for the keeping.

Those deposits of coin, or those deposits which the bank was bound to restore in coin, constituted the original capital of the bank, or the whole value of what was represented by what is called bank money. At present they are supposed to constitute but a very small part of it. In order to facilitate the trade in bullion, the bank has been for these many years in the practice of giving credit in its books, upon deposits of gold and silver bullion. This credit is generally about five per cent. below the mint price of such bullion. The bank grants at the same time what is called a recipice or receipt, entitling the person who makes the deposit, or the bearer, to take out the bullion again at any time within six months, upon transferring to the bank a quantity of bank money equal to that for which credit had been given in its books when the deposit was made, and upon paying one-fourth per cent. for the keeping, if the deposit was in silver; and one-half per cent. if it was in gold; but at the same time declaring, that in default of such payment, and upon the expiration of this term, the deposit should belong to the bank, at the price at which it had been received, or for which credit had been given in the transfer books. What is thus paid for the keeping of the deposit may be considered as a sort of warehouse rent; and why this warehouse rent should be so much dearer for gold than for silver, several different reasons have been assigned. The fineness of gold, it has been said, is more difficult to be ascertained than that of silver. Frauds are more easily practised, and occasion a greater loss in the most precious metal. Silver, besides, being the standard metal, the state, it has been said, wishes to encourage more the making of deposits of silver than those of gold.

Deposits of bullion are most commonly made when the price is somewhat lower than ordinary, and they are taken out again when it happens to rise. In Holland the market price of bullion is generally above the mint price, for the same reason that it was so in England before the late reformation of the gold coin. The difference is said to be commonly from about six to sixteen stivers upon the mark, or eight ounces of silver, of eleven parts of fine and one part alloy. The bank price, or the credit which the bank gives for the deposits of such silver (when made in foreign coin, of which the fineness is well known and ascertained, such as Mexico dollars), is twenty-two guilders the mark: the mint price is about twenty-three guilders, and the market price is from twenty-three guilders six, to twenty-three guilders sixteen stivers, or from two to three per cent. above the mint price.

The following are the prices at which the bank of Amsterdam at present {September 1775} receives bullion and coin of different kinds:

SILVER

Mexico dollars	22 Guilders / mark
French crowns	22
English silver coin	22
Mexico dollars, new coin	21 / 10
Ducatoons	3 / 0
Rix-dollars	2 / 8

Bar silver, containing 11-12ths fine silver, 21 Guilders / mark, and in this proportion down to 1-4th fine, on which 5 guilders are given. Fine bars,.................. 28 Guilders / mark.

GOLD

Portugal coin	310 Guilders / mark
Guineas	310
Louis d'ors, new	310
Ditto, old	300
New ducats	4 / 19 8 per ducat

Bar or ingot gold is received in proportion to its fineness, compared with the above foreign gold coin. Upon fine bars the bank gives 340 per mark. In general, however, something more is given upon coin of a known fineness, than upon gold and silver bars, of which the fineness cannot be ascertained but by a process of melting and assaying.

The proportions between the bank price, the mint price, and the market price of gold bullion, are nearly the same. A person can generally sell his receipt for the difference between the mint price of bullion and the market price. A receipt for bullion is almost always worth something, and it very seldom happens, therefore, that anybody suffers his receipts to expire, or allows his bullion to fall to the bank at the price at which it had been received, either by not taking it out before the end of the six months, or by neglecting to pay one fourth or one half per cent. in order to obtain a new receipt for another six months. This, however, though it happens seldom, is said to happen sometimes, and more frequently with regard to gold than with regard to silver, on account of the higher warehouse rent which is paid for the keeping of the more precious metal.

The person who, by making a deposit of bullion, obtains both a bank credit and a receipt, pays his bills of exchange as they become due, with his bank credit; and either sells or keeps his receipt, according as he judges that the price of bullion is likely to rise or to fall. The receipt and the bank credit seldom keep long together, and there is no occasion that they should. The person who has a receipt, and who wants to take out bullion, finds always plenty of bank credits, or bank money, to buy at the ordinary price, and the person who has bank money, and wants to take out bullion, finds receipts always in equal abundance.

The owners of bank credits, and the holders of receipts, constitute two different sorts of creditors against the bank. The holder of a receipt cannot draw out the bullion for which it is granted, without re-assigning to the bank a sum of bank money equal to the price at which the bullion had been received. If he has no bank money of his own, he must purchase it of those who have it. The owner of bank money cannot draw out bullion, without producing to the bank receipts for the quantity which he wants. If he has none of his own, he must buy them of those who have them. The holder of a receipt, when he purchases bank money, purchases the power of taking out a quantity of bullion, of which the mint price is five per cent. above the bank price. The agio of five per cent. therefore, which he commonly pays for it, is paid, not for an imaginary, but for a real value. The owner of bank money, when he purchases a receipt, purchases the power of taking out a quantity of bullion, of which the market price is commonly from two to three per cent. above the mint price. The price which he pays for it, therefore, is paid likewise for a real value. The price of the receipt, and the price of the bank money, compound or make up between them the full value or price of the bullion.

Upon deposits of the coin current in the country, the bank grant receipts likewise, as well as bank credits; but those receipts are frequently of no value and will bring no price in the market. Upon ducatoons, for example, which in the currency pass for three guilders three stivers each, the bank gives a credit of three guilders only, or five per cent. below their current value. It grants a receipt likewise, entitling the bearer to take out the number of ducatoons deposited at any time within six months, upon paying one fourth per cent. for the keeping. This receipt will frequently bring no price in the market. Three guilders, bank money, generally sell in the market for three guilders three stivers, the full value of the ducatoons, if they were taken out of the bank; and before they can be taken out, one-fourth per cent. must be paid for the keeping, which would be mere loss to the holder of the receipt. If the agio of the bank, however, should at any time fall to three per cent. such receipts might bring some price in the market, and might sell for one and three-fourths per cent. But the agio of the bank being now generally about five per cent. such receipts are frequently allowed to expire, or, as they express it, to fall to the bank. The receipts which are given for deposits of gold ducats fall to it yet more frequently, because a higher warehouse rent, or one half per cent. must be paid for the keeping of them, before they can be taken out again. The five per cent. which the bank gains, when deposits either of coin or bullion are allowed to fall to it, maybe considered as the warehouse rent for the perpetual keeping of such deposits.

 The sum of bank money, for which the receipts are expired, must be very considerable. It must comprehend the whole original capital of the bank, which, it is generally supposed, has been allowed to remain there from the time it was first deposited, nobody caring either to renew his receipt, or to take out his deposit, as, for the reasons already assigned, neither the one nor the other could be done without loss. But whatever may be the amount of this sum, the proportion which it bears to the whole mass of bank money is supposed to be very small. The bank of Amsterdam has, for these many years past, been the great warehouse of Europe for bullion, for which the receipts are very seldom allowed to expire, or, as they express it, to fall to the bank. The far greater part of the bank money, or of the credits upon the books of the bank, is supposed to have been created, for these many years past, by such deposits, which the dealers in bullion are continually both making and withdrawing.

 No demand can be made upon the bank, but by means of a recipice or receipt. The smaller mass of bank money, for which the receipts are expired, is mixed and confounded with the much greater mass for which they are still in force; so that, though there may be a considerable sum of bank money, for which there are no receipts, there is no specific sum or portion of it which may not at any time be demanded by one. The bank cannot be debtor to two persons for the same thing; and the owner of bank money who has no receipt, cannot demand payment of the bank till he buys one. In ordinary and quiet times, he can find no difficulty in getting one to buy at the market price, which generally corresponds with the price at which he can sell the coin or bullion it entitles him to take out of the bank.

It might be otherwise during a public calamity; an invasion, for example, such as that of the French in 1672. The owners of bank money being then all eager to draw it out of the bank, in order to have it in their own keeping, the demand for receipts might raise their price to an exorbitant height. The holders of them might form extravagant expectations, and, instead of two or three per cent. demand half the bank money for which credit had been given upon the deposits that the receipts had respectively been granted for. The enemy, informed of the constitution of the bank, might even buy them up, in order to prevent the carrying away of the treasure. In such emergencies, the bank, it is supposed, would break through its ordinary rule of making payment only to the holders of receipts. The holders of receipts, who had no bank money, must have received within two or three per cent. of the value of the deposit for which their respective receipts had been granted. The bank, therefore, it is said, would in this case make no scruple of paying, either with money or bullion, the full value of what the owners of bank money, who could get no receipts, were credited for in its books; paying, at the same time, two or three per cent. to such holders of receipts as had no bank money, that being the whole value which, in this state of things, could justly be supposed due to them.

Even in ordinary and quiet times, it is the interest of the holders of receipts to depress the agio, in order either to buy bank money (and consequently the bullion which their receipts would then enable them to take out of the bank) so much cheaper, or to sell their receipts to those who have bank money, and who want to take out bullion, so much dearer; the price of a receipt being generally equal to the difference between the market price of bank money and that of the coin or bullion for which the receipt had been granted. It is the interest of the owners of bank money, on the contrary, to raise the agio, in order either to sell their bank money so much dearer, or to buy a receipt so much cheaper. To prevent the stock-jobbing tricks which those opposite interests might sometimes occasion, the bank has of late years come to the resolution, to sell at all times bank money for currency at five per cent. agio, and to buy it in again at four per cent. agio. In consequence of this resolution, the agio can never either rise above five, or sink below four per cent.; and the proportion between the market price of bank and that of current money is kept at all times very near the proportion between their intrinsic values. Before this resolution was taken, the market price of bank money used sometimes to rise so high as nine per cent. agio, and sometimes to sink so low as par, according as opposite interests happened to influence the market.

The bank of Amsterdam professes to lend out no part of what is deposited with it, but for every guilder for which it gives credit in its books, to keep in its repositories the value of a guilder either in money or bullion. That it keeps in its repositories all the money or bullion for which there are receipts in force for which it is at all times liable to be called upon, and which in reality is continually going from it, and returning to it again, cannot well be doubted. But whether it does so likewise with regard to that part of its capital for which the receipts are long ago expired, for which, in ordinary and quiet times, it cannot be called upon, and which, in reality, is very likely to remain with it for ever, or as long as the states of the United Provinces subsist, may perhaps appear more uncertain. At Amsterdam, however, no point of faith is better established than that, for every guilder circulated as bank money, there is a correspondent guilder in gold or silver to be found in the treasures of the bank. The city is guarantee that it should be so. The bank is under the direction of the four reigning burgomasters who are changed every year. Each new set of burgomasters visits the treasure, compares it with the books, receives it upon oath, and delivers it over, with the same awful solemnity to the set which succeeds; and in that sober and religious country, oaths are not yet disregarded. A rotation of this kind seems alone a sufficient security against any practices which cannot be avowed. Amidst all the revolutions which faction has ever occasioned in the government of Amsterdam, the prevailing party has at no time accused their predecessors of infidelity in the administration of the bank. No accusation could have affected more deeply the reputation and fortune of the disgraced party; and if such an accusation could have been supported, we may be assured that it would have been brought. In 1672, when the French king was at Utrecht, the bank of Amsterdam paid so readily, as left no doubt of the fidelity with which it had observed its engagements. Some of the pieces which were then brought from its repositories, appeared to have been scorched with the fire which happened in the town-house soon after the bank was established. Those pieces, therefore, must have lain there from that time.

What may be the amount of the treasure in the bank, is a question which has long employed the speculations of the curious. Nothing but conjecture can be offered concerning it. It is generally reckoned, that there are about 2000 people who keep accounts with the bank; and allowing them to have, one with another, the value of £1500 sterling lying upon their respective accounts (a very large allowance), the whole quantity of bank money, and consequently of treasure in the bank, will amount to about £3,000,000 sterling, or, at eleven guilders the pound sterling, 33,000,000 of guilders; a great sum, and sufficient to carry on a very extensive circulation, but vastly below the extravagant ideas which some people have formed of this treasure.

The city of Amsterdam derives a considerable revenue from the bank. Besides what may be called the warehouse rent above mentioned, each person, upon first opening an account with the bank, pays a fee of ten guilders; and for every new account, three guilders three stivers; for every transfer, two stivers; and if the transfer is for less than 300 guilders, six stivers, in order to discourage the multiplicity of small transactions. The person who neglects to balance his account twice in the year, forfeits twenty-five guilders. The person who orders a transfer for more than is upon his account, is obliged to pay three per cent. for the sum overdrawn, and his order is set aside into the bargain. The bank is supposed, too, to make a considerable profit by the sale of the foreign coin or bullion which sometimes falls to it by the expiring of receipts, and which is always kept till it can be sold with advantage. It makes a profit, likewise, by selling bank money at five per cent. agio, and buying it in at four. These different emoluments amount to a good deal more than what is necessary for paying the salaries of officers, and defraying the expense of management. What is paid for the keeping of bullion upon receipts, is alone supposed to amount to a neat annual revenue of between 150,000 and 200,000 guilders. Public utility, however, and not revenue, was the original object of this institution. Its object was to relieve the merchants from the inconvenience of a disadvantageous exchange. The revenue which has arisen from it was unforeseen, and may be considered as accidental. But it is now time to return from this long digression, into which I have been insensibly led, in endeavouring to explain the reasons why the exchange between the countries which pay in what is called bank money, and those which pay in common currency, should generally appear to be in favour of the former, and against the latter. The former pay in a species of money, of which the intrinsic value is always the same, and exactly agreeable to the standard of their respective mints; the latter is a species of money, of which the intrinsic value is continually varying, and is almost always more or less below that standard.

PART II.—Of the Unreasonableness of those extraordinary Restraints, upon other Principles

In the foregoing part of this chapter, I have endeavoured to show, even upon the principles of the commercial system, how unnecessary it is to lay extraordinary restraints upon the importation of goods from those countries with which the balance of trade is supposed to be disadvantageous.

Nothing, however, can be more absurd than this whole doctrine of the balance of trade, upon which, not only these restraints, but almost all the other regulations of commerce, are founded. When two places trade with one another, this doctrine supposes that, if the balance be even, neither of them either loses or gains; but if it leans in any degree to one side, that one of them loses, and the other gains, in proportion to its declension from the exact equilibrium. Both suppositions are false. A trade, which is forced by means of bounties and monopolies, may be, and commonly is, disadvantageous to the country in whose favour it is meant to be established, as I shall endeavour to show hereafter. But that trade which, without force or constraint, is naturally and regularly carried on between any two places, is always advantageous, though not always equally so, to both.

By advantage or gain, I understand, not the increase of the quantity of gold and silver, but that of the exchangeable value of the annual produce of the land and labour of the country, or the increase of the annual revenue of its inhabitants.

If the balance be even, and if the trade between the two places consist altogether in the exchange of their native commodities, they will, upon most occasions, not only both gain, but they will gain equally, or very nearly equally; each will, in this case, afford a market for a part of the surplus produce of the other; each will replace a capital which had been employed in raising and preparing for the market this part of the surplus produce of the other, and which had been distributed among, and given revenue and maintenance to, a certain number of its inhabitants. Some part of the inhabitants of each, therefore, will directly derive their revenue and maintenance from the other. As the commodities exchanged, too, are supposed to be of equal value, so the two capitals employed in the trade will, upon most occasions, be equal, or very nearly equal; and both being employed in raising the native commodities of the two countries, the revenue and maintenance which their distribution will afford to the inhabitants of each will be equal, or very nearly equal. This revenue and maintenance, thus mutually afforded, will be greater or smaller, in proportion to the extent of their dealings. If these should annually amount to £100,000, for example, or to £1,000,000, on each side, each of them will afford an annual revenue, in the one case, of £100,000, and, in the other, of £1,000,000, to the inhabitants of the other.

If their trade should be of such a nature, that one of them exported to the other nothing but native commodities, while the returns of that other consisted altogether in foreign goods; the balance, in this case, would still be supposed even, commodities being paid for with commodities. They would, in this case too, both gain, but they would not gain equally; and the inhabitants of the country which exported nothing but native commodities, would derive the greatest revenue from the trade. If England, for example, should import from France nothing but the native commodities of that country, and not having such commodities of its own as were in demand there, should annually repay them by sending thither a large quantity of foreign goods, tobacco, we shall suppose, and East India goods; this trade, though it would give some revenue to the inhabitants of both countries, would give more to those of France than to those of England. The whole French capital annually employed in it would annually be distributed among the people of France; but that part of the English capital only, which was employed in producing the English commodities with which those foreign goods were purchased, would be annually distributed among the people of England. The greater part of it would replace the capitals which had been employed in Virginia, Indostan, and China, and which had given revenue and maintenance to the inhabitants of those distant countries. If the capitals were equal, or nearly equal, therefore, this employment of the French capital would augment much more the revenue of the people of France, than that of the English capital would the revenue of the people of England. France would, in this case, carry on a direct foreign trade of consumption with England; whereas England would carry on a round-about trade of the same kind with France. The different effects of a capital employed in the direct, and of one employed in the round-about foreign trade of consumption, have already been fully explained.

There is not, probably, between any two countries, a trade which consists altogether in the exchange, either of native commodities on both sides, or of native commodities on one side, and of foreign goods on the other. Almost all countries exchange with one another, partly native and partly foreign goods. That country, however, in whose cargoes there is the greatest proportion of native, and the least of foreign goods, will always be the principal gainer.

If it was not with tobacco and East India goods, but with gold and silver, that England paid for the commodities annually imported from France, the balance, in this case, would be supposed uneven, commodities not being paid for with commodities, but with gold and silver. The trade, however, would in this case, as in the foregoing, give some revenue to the inhabitants of both countries, but more to those of France than to those of England. It would give some revenue to those of England. The capital which had been employed in producing the English goods that purchased this gold and silver, the capital which had been distributed among, and given revenue to, certain inhabitants of England, would thereby be replaced, and enabled to continue that employment. The whole capital of England would no more be diminished by this exportation of gold and silver, than by the exportation of an equal value of any other goods. On the contrary, it would, in most cases, be augmented. No goods are sent abroad but those for which the demand is supposed to be greater abroad than at home, and of which the returns, consequently, it is expected, will be of more value at home than the commodities exported. If the tobacco which in England is worth only £100,000, when sent to France, will purchase wine which is in England worth £110,000, the exchange will augment the capital of England by £10,000. If £100,000 of English gold, in the same manner, purchase French wine, which in England is worth £110,000, this exchange will equally augment the capital of England by £10,000. As a merchant, who has £110,000 worth of wine in his cellar, is a richer man than he who has only £100,000 worth of tobacco in his warehouse, so is he likewise a richer man than he who has only £100,000 worth of gold in his coffers. He can put into motion a greater quantity of industry, and give revenue, maintenance, and employment, to a greater number of people, than either of the other two. But the capital of the country is equal to the capital of all its different inhabitants; and the quantity of industry which can be annually maintained in it is equal to what all those different capitals can maintain. Both the capital of the country, therefore, and the quantity of industry which can be annually maintained in it, must generally be augmented by this exchange. It would, indeed, be more advantageous for England that it could purchase the wines of France with its own hardware and broad cloth, than with either the tobacco of Virginia, or the gold and silver of Brazil and Peru. A direct foreign trade of consumption is always more advantageous than a round-about one. But a round-about foreign trade of consumption, which is carried on with gold and silver, does not seem to be less advantageous than any other equally round-about one. Neither is a country which has no mines, more likely to be exhausted of gold and silver by this annual exportation of those metals, than one which does not grow tobacco by the like annual exportation of that plant. As a country which has wherewithal to buy tobacco will never be long in want of it, so neither will one be long in want of gold and silver which has wherewithal to purchase those metals.

It is a losing trade, it is said, which a workman carries on with the alehouse; and the trade which a manufacturing nation would naturally carry on with a wine country, may be considered as a trade of the same nature. I answer, that the trade with the alehouse is not necessarily a losing trade. In its own nature it is just as advantageous as any other, though, perhaps, somewhat more liable to be abused. The employment of a brewer, and even that of a retailer of fermented liquors, are as necessary divisions of labour as any other. It will generally be more advantageous for a workman to buy of the brewer the quantity he has occasion for, than to brew it himself; and if he is a poor workman, it will generally be more advantageous for him to buy it by little and little of the retailer, than a large quantity of the brewer. He may no doubt buy too much of either, as he may of any other dealers in his neighbourhood; of the butcher, if he is a glutton; or of the draper, if he affects to be a beau among his companions. It is advantageous to the great body of workmen, notwithstanding, that all these trades should be free, though this freedom may be abused in all of them, and is more likely to be so, perhaps, in some than in others. Though individuals, besides, may sometimes ruin their fortunes by an excessive consumption of fermented liquors, there seems to be no risk that a nation should do so. Though in every country there are many people who spend upon such liquors more than they can afford, there are always many more who spend less. It deserves to be remarked, too, that if we consult experience, the cheapness of wine seems to be a cause, not of drunkenness, but of sobriety. The inhabitants of the wine countries are in general the soberest people of Europe; witness the Spaniards, the Italians, and the inhabitants of the southern provinces of France. People are seldom guilty of excess in what is their daily fare. Nobody affects the character of liberality and good fellowship, by being profuse of a liquor which is as cheap as small beer. On the contrary, in the countries which, either from excessive heat or cold, produce no grapes, and where wine consequently is dear and a rarity, drunkenness is a common vice, as among the northern nations, and all those who live between the tropics, the negroes, for example on the coast of Guinea. When a French regiment comes from some of the northern provinces of France, where wine is somewhat dear, to be quartered in the southern, where it is very cheap, the soldiers, I have frequently heard it observed, are at first debauched by the cheapness and novelty of good wine; but after a few months residence, the greater part of them become as sober as the rest of the inhabitants. Were the duties upon foreign wines, and the excises upon malt, beer, and ale, to be taken away all at once, it might, in the same manner, occasion in Great Britain a pretty general and temporary drunkenness among the middling and inferior ranks of people, which would probably be soon followed by a permanent and almost universal sobriety. At present, drunkenness is by no means the vice of people of fashion, or of those who can easily afford the most expensive liquors. A gentleman drunk with ale has scarce ever been seen among us. The restraints upon the wine trade in Great Britain, besides, do not so much seem calculated to hinder the people from going, if I may say so, to the alehouse, as from going where they can buy the best and cheapest liquor. They favour the wine trade of Portugal, and discourage that of France. The Portuguese, it is said, indeed, are better customers for our manufactures than the French, and should therefore be encouraged in preference to them. As they give us their custom, it is pretended we should give them ours. The sneaking arts of underling tradesmen are thus erected into political maxims for the conduct of a great empire; for it is the most underling tradesmen only who make it a rule to employ chiefly their own customers. A great trader purchases his goods always where they are cheapest and best, without regard to any little interest of this kind.

By such maxims as these, however, nations have been taught that their interest consisted in beggaring all their neighbours. Each nation has been made to look with an invidious eye upon the prosperity of all the nations with which it trades, and to consider their gain as its own loss. Commerce, which ought naturally to be, among nations as among individuals, a bond of union and friendship, has become the most fertile source of discord and animosity. The capricious ambition of kings and ministers has not, during the present and the preceding century, been more fatal to the repose of Europe, than the impertinent jealousy of merchants and manufacturers. The violence and injustice of the rulers of mankind is an ancient evil, for which, I am afraid, the nature of human affairs can scarce admit of a remedy: but the mean rapacity, the monopolizing spirit, of merchants and manufacturers, who neither are, nor ought to be, the rulers of mankind, though it cannot, perhaps, be corrected, may very easily be prevented from disturbing the tranquillity of anybody but themselves.

That it was the spirit of monopoly which originally both invented and propagated this doctrine, cannot be doubted and they who first taught it, were by no means such fools as they who believed it. In every country it always is, and must be, the interest of the great body of the people, to buy whatever they want of those who sell it cheapest. The proposition is so very manifest, that it seems ridiculous to take any pains to prove it; nor could it ever have been called in question, had not the interested sophistry of merchants and manufacturers confounded the common sense of mankind. Their interest is, in this respect, directly opposite to that of the great body of the people. As it is the interest of the freemen of a corporation to hinder the rest of the inhabitants from employing any workmen but themselves; so it is the interest of the merchants and manufacturers of every country to secure to themselves the monopoly of the home market. Hence, in Great Britain, and in most other European countries, the extraordinary duties upon almost all goods imported by alien merchants. Hence the high duties and prohibitions upon all those foreign manufactures which can come into competition with our own. Hence, too, the extraordinary restraints upon the importation of almost all sorts of goods from those countries with which the balance of trade is supposed to be disadvantageous; that is, from those against whom national animosity happens ta be most violently inflamed.

The wealth of neighbouring nations, however, though dangerous in war and politics, is certainly advantageous in trade. In a state of hostility, it may enable our enemies to maintain fleets and armies superior to our own; but in a state of peace and commerce it must likewise enable them to exchange with us to a greater value, and to afford a better market, either for the immediate produce of our own industry, or for whatever is purchased with that produce. As a rich man is likely to be a better customer to the industrious people in his neighbourhood, than a poor, so is likewise a rich nation. A rich man, indeed, who is himself a manufacturer, is a very dangerous neighbour to all those who deal in the same way. All the rest of the neighbourhood, however, by far the greatest number, profit by the good market which his expense affords them. They even profit by his underselling the poorer workmen who deal in the same way with him. The manufacturers of a rich nation, in the same manner, may no doubt be very dangerous rivals to those of their neighbours. This very competition, however, is advantageous to the great body of the people, who profit greatly, besides, by the good market which the great expense of such a nation affords them in every other way. Private people, who want to make a fortune, never think of retiring to the remote and poor provinces of the country, but resort either to the capital, or to some of the great commercial towns. They know, that where little wealth circulates, there is little to be got; but that where a great deal is in motion, some share of it may fall to them. The same maxim which would in this manner direct the common sense of one, or ten, or twenty individuals, should regulate the judgment of one, or ten, or twenty millions, and should make a whole nation regard the riches of its neighbours, as a probable cause and occasion for itself to acquire riches. A nation that would enrich itself by foreign trade, is certainly most likely to do so, when its neighbours are all rich, industrious and commercial nations. A great nation, surrounded on all sides by wandering savages and poor barbarians, might, no doubt, acquire riches by the cultivation of its own lands, and by its own interior commerce, but not by foreign trade. It seems to have been in this manner that the ancient Egyptians and the modern Chinese acquired their great wealth. The ancient Egyptians, it is said, neglected foreign commerce, and the modern Chinese, it is known, hold it in the utmost contempt, and scarce deign to afford it the decent protection of the laws. The modern maxims of foreign commerce, by aiming at the impoverishment of all our neighbours, so far as they are capable of producing their intended effect, tend to render that very commerce insignificant and contemptible.

It is in consequence of these maxims, that the commerce between France and England has, in both countries, been subjected to so many discouragements and restraints. If those two countries, however, were to consider their real interest, without either mercantile jealousy or national animosity, the commerce of France might be more advantageous to Great Britain than that of any other country, and, for the same reason, that of Great Britain to France. France is the nearest neighbour to Great Britain. In the trade between the southern coast of England and the northern and north-western coast of France, the returns might be expected, in the same manner as in the inland trade, four, five, or six times in the year. The capital, therefore, employed in this trade could, in each of the two countries, keep in motion four, five, or six times the quantity of industry, and afford employment and subsistence to four, five, or six times the number of people, which all equal capital could do in the greater part of the other branches of foreign trade. Between the parts of France and Great Britain most remote from one another, the returns might be expected, at least, once in the year; and even this trade would so far be at least equally advantageous, as the greater part of the other branches of our foreign European trade. It would be, at least, three times more advantageous than the boasted trade with our North American colonies, in which the returns were seldom made in less than three years, frequently not in less than four or five years. France, besides, is supposed to contain 24,000,000 of inhabitants. Our North American colonies were never supposed to contain more than 3,000,000; and France is a much richer country than North America; though, on account of the more unequal distribution of riches, there is much more poverty and beggary in the one country than in the other. France, therefore, could afford a market at least eight times more extensive, and, on account of the superior frequency of the returns, four-and-twenty times more advantageous than that which our North American colonies ever afforded. The trade of Great Britain would be just as advantageous to France, and, in proportion to the wealth, population, and proximity of the respective countries, would have the same superiority over that which France carries on with her own colonies.

Such is the very great difference between that trade which the wisdom of both nations has thought proper to discourage, and that which it has favoured the most.

But the very same circumstances which would have rendered an open and free commerce between the two countries so advantageous to both, have occasioned the principal obstructions to that commerce. Being neighbours, they are necessarily enemies, and the wealth and power of each becomes, upon that account, more formidable to the other; and what would increase the advantage of national friendship, serves only to inflame the violence of national animosity. They are both rich and industrious nations; and the merchants and manufacturers of each dread the competition of the skill and activity of those of the other. Mercantile jealousy is excited, and both inflames, and is itself inflamed, by the violence of national animosity, and the traders of both countries have announced, with all the passionate confidence of interested falsehood, the certain ruin of each, in consequence of that unfavourable balance of trade, which, they pretend, would be the infallible effect of an unrestrained commerce with the other.

There is no commercial country in Europe, of which the approaching ruin has not frequently been foretold by the pretended doctors of this system, from all unfavourably balance of trade. After all the anxiety, however, which they have excited about this, after all the vain attempts of almost all trading nations to turn that balance in their own favour, and against their neighbours, it does not appear that any one nation in Europe has been, in any respect, impoverished by this cause. Every town and country, on the contrary, in proportion as they have opened their ports to all nations, instead of being ruined by this free trade, as the principles of the commercial system would lead us to expect, have been enriched by it. Though there are in Europe indeed, a few towns which, in same respects, deserve the name of free ports, there is no country which does so. Holland, perhaps, approaches the nearest to this character of any, though still very remote from it; and Holland, it is acknowledged, not only derives its whole wealth, but a great part of its necessary subsistence, from foreign trade.

There is another balance, indeed, which has already been explained, very different from the balance of trade, and which, according as it happens to be either favourable or unfavourable, necessarily occasions the prosperity or decay of every nation. This is the balance of the annual produce and consumption. If the exchangeable value of the annual produce, it has already been observed, exceeds that of the annual consumption, the capital of the society must annually increase in proportion to this excess. The society in this case lives within its revenue; and what is annually saved out of its revenue, is naturally added to its capital, and employed so as to increase still further the annual produce. If the exchangeable value of the annual produce, on the contrary, fall short of the annual consumption, the capital of the society must annually decay in proportion to this deficiency. The expense of the society, in this case, exceeds its revenue, and necessarily encroaches upon its capital. Its capital, therefore, must necessarily decay, and, together with it, the exchangeable value of the annual produce of its industry.

This balance of produce and consumption is entirely different from what is called the balance of trade. It might take place in a nation which had no foreign trade, but which was entirely separated from all the world. It may take place in the whole globe of the earth, of which the wealth, population, and improvement, may be either gradually increasing or gradually decaying.

The balance of produce and consumption may be constantly in favour of a nation, though what is called the balance of trade be generally against it. A nation may import to a greater value than it exports for half a century, perhaps, together; the gold and silver which comes into it during all this time, may be all immediately sent out of it; its circulating coin may gradually decay, different sorts of paper money being substituted in its place, and even the debts, too, which it contracts in the principal nations with whom it deals, may be gradually increasing; and yet its real wealth, the exchangeable value of the annual produce of its lands and labour, may, during the same period, have been increasing in a much greater proportion. The state of our North American colonies, and of the trade which they carried on with Great Britain, before the commencement of the present disturbances, {This paragraph was written in the year 1775.} may serve as a proof that this is by no means an impossible supposition.

CHAPTER IV

OF DRAWBACKS

Merchants and manufacturers are not contented with the monopoly of the home market, but desire likewise the most extensive foreign sale for their goods. Their country has no jurisdiction in foreign nations, and therefore can seldom procure them any monopoly there. They are generally obliged, therefore, to content themselves with petitioning for certain encouragements to exportation.

Of these encouragements, what are called drawbacks seem to be the most reasonable. To allow the merchant to draw back upon exportation, either the whole, or a part of whatever excise or inland duty is imposed upon domestic industry, can never occasion the exportation of a greater quantity of goods than what would have been exported had no duty been imposed. Such encouragements do not tend to turn towards any particular employment a greater share of the capital of the country, than what would go to that employment of its own accord, but only to hinder the duty from driving away any part of that share to other employments. They tend not to overturn that balance which naturally establishes itself among all the various employments of the society, but to hinder it from being overturned by the duty. They tend not to destroy, but to preserve, what it is in most cases advantageous to preserve, the natural division and distribution of labour in the society.

The same thing may be said of the drawbacks upon the re-exportation of foreign goods imported, which, in Great Britain, generally amount to by much the largest part of the duty upon importation. By the second of the rules, annexed to the act of parliament, which imposed what is now called the old subsidy, every merchant, whether English or alien. was allowed to draw back half that duty upon exportation; the English merchant, provided the exportation took place within twelve months; the alien, provided it took place within nine months. Wines, currants, and wrought silks, were the only goods which did not fall within this rule, having other and more advantageous allowances. The duties imposed by this act of parliament were, at that time, the only duties upon the importation of foreign goods. The term within which this, and all other drawbacks could be claimed, was afterwards (by 7 Geo. I. chap. 21. sect. 10.) extended to three years.

The duties which have been imposed since the old subsidy, are, the greater part of them, wholly drawn back upon exportation. This general rule, however, is liable to a great number of exceptions; and the doctrine of drawbacks has become a much less simple matter than it was at their first institution.

Upon the exportation of some foreign goods, of which it was expected that the importation would greatly exceed what was necessary for the home consumption, the whole duties are drawn back, without retaining even half the old subsidy. Before the revolt of our North American colonies, we had the monopoly of the tobacco of Maryland and Virginia. We imported about ninety-six thousand hogsheads, and the home consumption was not supposed to exceed fourteen thousand. To facilitate the great exportation which was necessary, in order to rid us of the rest, the whole duties were drawn back, provided the exportation took place within three years.

We still have, though not altogether, yet very nearly, the monopoly of the sugars of our West Indian islands. If sugars are exported within a year, therefore, all the duties upon importation are drawn back; and if exported within three years, all the duties, except half the old subsidy, which still continues to be retained upon the exportation of the greater part of goods. Though the importation of sugar exceeds a good deal what is necessary for the home consumption, the excess is inconsiderable, in comparison of what it used to be in tobacco.

Some goods, the particular objects of the jealousy of our own manufacturers, are prohibited to be imported for home consumption. They may, however, upon paying certain duties, be imported and warehoused for exportation. But upon such exportation no part of these duties is drawn back. Our manufacturers are unwilling, it seems, that even this restricted importation should be encouraged, and are afraid lest some part of these goods should be stolen out of the warehouse, and thus come into competition with their own. It is under these regulations only that we can import wrought silks, French cambrics and lawns, calicoes, painted, printed, stained, or dyed, etc.

We are unwilling even to be the carriers of French goods, and choose rather to forego a profit to ourselves than to suffer those whom we consider as our enemies to make any profit by our means. Not only half the old subsidy, but the second twenty-five per cent. is retained upon the exportation of all French goods.

By the fourth of the rules annexed to the old subsidy, the drawback allowed upon the exportation of all wines amounted to a great deal more than half the duties which were at that time paid upon their importation; and it seems at that time to have been the object of the legislature to give somewhat more than ordinary encouragement to the carrying trade in wine. Several of the other duties, too which were imposed either at the same time or subsequent to the old subsidy, what is called the additional duty, the new subsidy, the one-third and two-thirds subsidies, the impost 1692, the tonnage on wine, were allowed to be wholly drawn back upon exportation. All those duties, however, except the additional duty and impost 1692, being paid down in ready money upon importation, the interest of so large a sum occasioned an expense, which made it unreasonable to expect any profitable carrying trade in this article. Only a part, therefore of the duty called the impost on wine, and no part of the twenty-five pounds the ton upon French wines, or of the duties imposed in 1745, in 1763, and in 1778, were allowed to be drawn back upon exportation. The two imposts of five per cent. imposed in 1779 and 1781, upon all the former duties of customs, being allowed to be wholly drawn back upon the exportation of all other goods, were likewise allowed to be drawn back upon that of wine. The last duty that has been particularly imposed upon wine, that of 1780, is allowed to be wholly drawn back; an indulgence which, when so many heavy duties are retained, most probably could never occasion the exportation of a single ton of wine. These rules took place with regard to all places of lawful exportation, except the British colonies in America.

The 15th Charles II, chap. 7, called an act for the encouragement of trade, had given Great Britain the monopoly of supplying the colonies with all the commodities of the growth or manufacture of Europe, and consequently with wines. In a country of so extensive a coast as our North American and West Indian colonies, where our authority was always so very slender, and where the inhabitants were allowed to carry out in their own ships their non-enumerated commodities, at first to all parts of Europe, and afterwards to all parts of Europe south of Cape Finisterre, it is not very probable that this monopoly could ever be much respected; and they probably at all times found means of bringing back some cargo from the countries to which they were allowed to carry out one. They seem, however, to have found some difficulty in importing European wines from the places of their growth; and they could not well import them from Great Britain, where they were loaded with many heavy duties, of which a considerable part was not drawn back upon exportation. Madeira wine, not being an European commodity, could be imported directly into America and the West Indies, countries which, in all their non-enumerated commodities, enjoyed a free trade to the island of Madeira. These circumstances had probably introduced that general taste for Madeira wine, which our officers found established in all our colonies at the commencement of the war which began in 1755, and which they brought back with them to the mother country, where that wine had not been much in fashion before. Upon the conclusion of that war, in 1763 (by the 4th Geo. III, chap. 15, sect. 12), all the duties except £3, 10s. were allowed to be drawn back upon the exportation to the colonies of all wines, except French wines, to the commerce and consumption of which national prejudice would allow no sort of encouragement. The period between the granting of this indulgence and the revolt of our North American colonies, was probably too short to admit of any considerable change in the customs of those countries.

The same act which, in the drawbacks upon all wines, except French wines, thus favoured the colonies so much more than other countries, in those upon the greater part of other commodities, favoured them much less. Upon the exportation of the greater part of commodities to other countries, half the old subsidy was drawn back. But this law enacted, that no part of that duty should be drawn back upon the exportation to the colonies of any commodities of the growth or manufacture either of Europe or the East Indies, except wines, white calicoes, and muslins.

Drawbacks were, perhaps, originally granted for the encouragement of the carrying trade, which, as the freight of the ship is frequently paid by foreigners in money, was supposed to be peculiarly fitted for bringing gold and silver into the country. But though the carrying trade certainly deserves no peculiar encouragement, though the motive of the institution was, perhaps, abundantly foolish, the institution itself seems reasonable enough. Such drawbacks cannot force into this trade a greater share of the capital of the country than what would have gone to it of its own accord, had there been no duties upon importation; they only prevent its being excluded altogether by those duties. The carrying trade, though it deserves no preference, ought not to be precluded, but to be left free, like all other trades. It is a necessary resource to those capitals which cannot find employment, either in the agriculture or in the manufactures of the country, either in its home trade, or in its foreign trade of consumption.

The revenue of the customs, instead of suffering, profits from such drawbacks, by that part of the duty which is retained. If the whole duties had been retained, the foreign goods upon which they are paid could seldom have been exported, nor consequently imported, for want of a market. The duties, therefore, of which a part is retained, would never have been paid.

These reasons seem sufficiently to justify drawbacks, and would justify them, though the whole duties, whether upon the produce of domestic industry or upon foreign goods, were always drawn back upon exportation. The revenue of excise would, in this case indeed, suffer a little, and that of the customs a good deal more; but the natural balance of industry, the natural division and distribution of labour, which is always more or less disturbed by such duties, would be more nearly re-established by such a regulation.

These reasons, however, will justify drawbacks only upon exporting goods to those countries which are altogether foreign and independent, not to those in which our merchants and manufacturers enjoy a monopoly. A drawback, for example, upon the exportation of European goods to our American colonies, will not always occasion a greater exportation than what would have taken place without it. By means of the monopoly which our merchants and manufacturers enjoy there, the same quantity might frequently, perhaps, be sent thither, though the whole duties were retained. The drawback, therefore, may frequently be pure loss to the revenue of excise and customs, without altering the state of the trade, or rendering it in any respect more extensive. How far such drawbacks can be justified as a proper encouragement to the industry of our colonies, or how far it is advantageous to the mother country that they should be exempted from taxes which are paid by all the rest of their fellow-subjects, will appear hereafter, when I come to treat of colonies.

Drawbacks, however, it must always be understood, are useful only in those cases in which the goods, for the exportation of which they are given, are really exported to some foreign country, and not clandestinely re-imported into our own. That some drawbacks, particularly those upon tobacco, have frequently been abused in this manner, and have given occasion to many frauds, equally hurtful both to the revenue and to the fair trader, is well known.

CHAPTER V

OF BOUNTIES

Bounties upon exportation are, in Great Britain, frequently petitioned for, and sometimes granted, to the produce of particular branches of domestic industry. By means of them, our merchants and manufacturers, it is pretended, will be enabled to sell their goods as cheap or cheaper than their rivals in the foreign market. A greater quantity, it is said, will thus be exported, and the balance of trade consequently turned more in favour of our own country. We cannot give our workmen a monopoly in the foreign, as we have done in the home market. We cannot force foreigners to buy their goods, as we have done our own countrymen. The next best expedient, it has been thought, therefore, is to pay them for buying. It is in this manner that the mercantile system proposes to enrich the whole country, and to put money into all our pockets, by means of the balance of trade.

Bounties, it is allowed, ought to be given to those branches of trade only which cannot be carried on without them. But every branch of trade in which the merchant can sell his goods for a price which replaces to him, with the ordinary profits of stock, the whole capital employed in preparing and sending them to market, can be carried on without a bounty. Every such branch is evidently upon a level with all the other branches of trade which are carried on without bounties, and cannot, therefore, require one more than they. Those trades only require bounties, in which the merchant is obliged to sell his goods for a price which does not replace to him his capital, together with the ordinary profit, or in which he is obliged to sell them for less than it really cost him to send them to market. The bounty is given in order to make up this loss, and to encourage him to continue, or, perhaps, to begin a trade, of which the expense is supposed to be greater than the returns, of which every operation eats up a part of the capital employed in it, and which is of such a nature, that if all other trades resembled it, there would soon be no capital left in the country.

The trades, it is to be observed, which are carried on by means of bounties, are the only ones which can be carried on between two nations for any considerable time together, in such a manner as that one of them shall always and regularly lose, or sell its goods for less than it really cost to send them to market. But if the bounty did not repay to the merchant what he would otherwise lose upon the price of his goods, his own interest would soon oblige him to employ his stock in another way, or to find out a trade in which the price of the goods would replace to him, with the ordinary profit, the capital employed in sending them to market. The effect of bounties, like that of all the other expedients of the mercantile system, can only be to force the trade of a country into a channel much less advantageous than that in which it would naturally run of its own accord.

The ingenious and well-informed author of the Tracts upon the Corn Trade has shown very clearly, that since the bounty upon the exportation of corn was first established, the price of the corn exported, valued moderately enough, has exceeded that of the corn imported, valued very high, by a much greater sum than the amount of the whole bounties which have been paid during that period. This, he imagines, upon the true principles of the mercantile system, is a clear proof that this forced corn trade is beneficial to the nation, the value of the exportation exceeding that of the importation by a much greater sum than the whole extraordinary expense which the public has been at in order to get it exported. He does not consider that this extraordinary expense, or the bounty, is the smallest part of the expense which the exportation of corn really costs the society. The capital which the farmer employed in raising it must likewise be taken into the account. Unless the price of the corn, when sold in the foreign markets, replaces not only the bounty, but this capital, together with the ordinary profits of stock, the society is a loser by the difference, or the national stock is so much diminished. But the very reason for which it has been thought necessary to grant a bounty, is the supposed insufficiency of the price to do this.

The average price of corn, it has been said, has fallen considerably since the establishment of the bounty. That the average price of corn began to fall somewhat towards the end of the last century, and has continued to do so during the course of the sixty-four first years of the present, I have already endeavoured to show. But this event, supposing it to be real, as I believe it to be, must have happened in spite of the bounty, and cannot possibly have happened in consequence of it. It has happened in France, as well as in England, though in France there was not only no bounty, but, till 1764, the exportation of corn was subjected to a general prohibition. This gradual fall in the average price of grain, it is probable, therefore, is ultimately owing neither to the one regulation nor to the other, but to that gradual and insensible rise in the real value of silver, which, in the first book of this discourse, I have endeavoured to show, has taken place in the general market of Europe during the course of the present century. It seems to be altogether impossible that the bounty could ever contribute to lower the price of grain.

In years of plenty, it has already been observed, the bounty, by occasioning an extraordinary exportation, necessarily keeps up the price of corn in the home market above what it would naturally fall to. To do so was the avowed purpose of the institution. In years of scarcity, though the bounty is frequently suspended, yet the great exportation which it occasions in years of plenty, must frequently hinder, more or less, the plenty of one year from relieving the scarcity of another. Both in years of plenty and in years of scarcity, therefore, the bounty necessarily tends to raise the money price of corn somewhat higher than it otherwise would be in the home market.

That in the actual state of tillage the bounty must necessarily have this tendency, will not, I apprehend, be disputed by any reasonable person. But it has been thought by many people, that it tends to encourage tillage, and that in two different ways; first, by opening a more extensive foreign market to the corn of the farmer, it tends, they imagine, to increase the demand for, and consequently the production of, that commodity; and, secondly by securing to him a better price than he could otherwise expect in the actual state of tillage, it tends, they suppose, to encourage tillage. This double encouragement must they imagine, in a long period of years, occasion such an increase in the production of corn, as may lower its price in the home market, much more than the bounty can raise it in the actual state which tillage may, at the end of that period, happen to be in.

I answer, that whatever extension of the foreign market can be occasioned by the bounty must, in every particular year, be altogether at the expense of the home market; as every bushel of corn, which is exported by means of the bounty, and which would not have been exported without the bounty, would have remained in the home market to increase the consumption, and to lower the price of that commodity.

The corn bounty, it is to be observed, as well as every other bounty upon exportation, imposes two different taxes upon the people; first, the tax which they are obliged to contribute, in order to pay the bounty; and, secondly, the tax which arises from the advanced price of the commodity in the home market, and which, as the whole body of the people are purchasers of corn, must, in this particular commodity, be paid by the whole body of the people. In this particular commodity, therefore, this second tax is by much the heaviest of the two. Let us suppose that, taking one year with another, the bounty of 5s. upon the exportation of the quarter of wheat raises the price of that commodity in the home market only 6d. the bushel, or 4s. the quarter higher than it otherwise would have been in the actual state of the crop. Even upon this very moderate supposition, the great body of the people, over and above contributing the tax which pays the bounty of 5s. upon every quarter of wheat exported, must pay another of 4s. upon every quarter which they themselves consume. But according to the very well informed author of the Tracts upon the Corn Trade, the average proportion of the corn exported to that consumed at home, is not more than that of one to thirty-one. For every 5s. therefore, which they contribute to the payment of the first tax, they must contribute £6:4s. to the payment of the second. So very heavy a tax upon the first necessary of life-must either reduce the subsistence of the labouring poor, or it must occasion some augmentation in their pecuniary wages, proportionable to that in the pecuniary price of their subsistence. So far as it operates in the one way, it must reduce the ability of the labouring poor to educate and bring up their children, and must, so far, tend to restrain the population of the country. So far as it operates in the other, it must reduce the ability of the employers of the poor, to employ so great a number as they otherwise might do, and must so far tend to restrain the industry of the country. The extraordinary exportation of corn, therefore occasioned by the bounty, not only in every particular year diminishes the home, just as much as it extends the foreign market and consumption, but, by restraining the population and industry of the country, its final tendency is to stint and restrain the gradual extension of the home market; and thereby, in the long-run, rather to diminish than to augment the whole market and consumption of corn.

This enhancement of the money price of corn, however, it has been thought, by rendering that commodity more profitable to the farmer, must necessarily encourage its production.

I answer, that this might be the case, if the effect of the bounty was to raise the real price of corn, or to enable the farmer, with an equal quantity of it, to maintain a greater number of labourers in the same manner, whether liberal, moderate, or scanty, than other labourers are commonly maintained in his neighbourhood. But neither the bounty, it is evident, nor any other human institution, can have any such effect. It is not the real, but the nominal price of corn, which can in any considerable degree be affected by the bounty. And though the tax, which that institution imposes upon the whole body of the people, may be very burdensome to those who pay it, it is of very little advantage to those who receive it.

The real effect of the bounty is not so much to raise the real value of corn, as to degrade the real value of silver; or to make an equal quantity of it exchange for a smaller quantity, not only of corn, but of all other home made commodities; for the money price of corn regulates that of all other home made commodities.

It regulates the money price of labour, which must always be such as to enable the labourer to purchase a quantity of corn sufficient to maintain him and his family, either in the liberal, moderate, or scanty manner, in which the advancing, stationary, or declining, circumstances of the society, oblige his employers to maintain him.

It regulates the money price of all the other parts of the rude produce of land, which, in every period of improvement, must bear a certain proportion to that of corn, though this proportion is different in different periods. It regulates, for example, the money price of grass and hay, of butcher's meat, of horses, and the maintenance of horses, of land carriage consequently, or of the greater part of the inland commerce of the country.

By regulating the money price of all the other parts of the rude produce of land, it regulates that of the materials of almost all manufactures; by regulating the money price of labour, it regulates that of manufacturing art and industry; and by regulating both, it regulates that of the complete manufacture. The money price of labour, and of every thing that is the produce, either of land or labour, must necessarily either rise or fall in proportion to the money price of corn.

Though in consequence of the bounty, therefore, the farmer should be enabled to sell his corn for 4s. the bushel, instead of 3s:6d. and to pay his landlord a money rent proportionable to this rise in the money price of his produce; yet if, in consequence of this rise in the price of corn, 4s. will purchase no more home made goods of any other kind than 3s. 6d. would have done before, neither the circumstances of the farmer, nor those of the landlord, will be much mended by this change. The farmer will not be able to cultivate much better; the landlord will not be able to live much better. In the purchase of foreign commodities, this enhancement in the price of corn may give them some little advantage. In that of home made commodities, it can give them none at all. And almost the whole expense of the farmer, and the far greater part even of that of the landlord, is in home made commodities.

That degradation in the value of silver, which is the effect of the fertility of the mines, and which operates equally, or very nearly equally, through the greater part of the commercial world, is a matter of very little consequence to any particular country. The consequent rise of all money prices, though it does not make those who receive them really richer, does not make them really poorer. A service of plate becomes really cheaper, and every thing else remains precisely of the same real value as before.

But that degradation in the value of silver, which, being the effect either of the peculiar situation or of the political institutions of a particular country, takes place only in that country, is a matter of very great consequence, which, far from tending to make anybody really richer, tends to make every body really poorer. The rise in the money price of all commodities, which is in this case peculiar to that country, tends to discourage more or less every sort of industry which is carried on within it, and to enable foreign nations, by furnishing almost all sorts of goods for a smaller quantity of silver than its own workmen can afford to do, to undersell them, not only in the foreign, but even in the home market.

It is the peculiar situation of Spain and Portugal, as proprietors of the mines, to be the distributers of gold and silver to all the other countries of Europe. Those metals ought naturally, therefore, to be somewhat cheaper in Spain and Portugal than in any other part of Europe. The difference, however, should be no more than the amount of the freight and insurance; and, on account of the great value and small bulk of those metals, their freight is no great matter, and their insurance is the same as that of any other goods of equal value. Spain and Portugal, therefore, could suffer very little from their peculiar situation, if they did not aggravate its disadvantages by their political institutions.

Spain by taxing, and Portugal by prohibiting, the exportation of gold and silver, load that exportation with the expense of smuggling, and raise the value of those metals in other countries so much more above what it is in their own, by the whole amount of this expense. When you dam up a stream of water, as soon as the dam is full, as much water must run over the dam-head as if there was no dam at all. The prohibition of exportation cannot detain a greater quantity of gold and silver in Spain and Portugal, than what they can afford to employ, than what the annual produce of their land and labour will allow them to employ, in coin, plate, gilding, and other ornaments of gold and silver. When they have got this quantity, the dam is full, and the whole stream which flows in afterwards must run over. The annual exportation of gold and silver from Spain and Portugal, accordingly, is, by all accounts, notwithstanding these restraints, very near equal to the whole annual importation. As the water, however, must always be deeper behind the dam-head than before it, so the quantity of gold and silver which these restraints detain in Spain and Portugal, must, in proportion to the annual produce of their land and labour, be greater than what is to be found in other countries. The higher and stronger the dam-head, the greater must be the difference in the depth of water behind and before it. The higher the tax, the higher the penalties with which the prohibition is guarded, the more vigilant and severe the police which looks after the execution of the law, the greater must be the difference in the proportion of gold and silver to the annual produce of the land and labour of Spain and Portugal, and to that of other countries. It is said, accordingly, to be very considerable, and that you frequently find there a profusion of plate in houses, where there is nothing else which would in other countries be thought suitable or correspondent to this sort of magnificence. The cheapness of gold and silver, or, what is the same thing, the dearness of all commodities, which is the necessary effect of this redundancy of the precious metals, discourages both the agriculture and manufactures of Spain and Portugal, and enables foreign nations to supply them with many sorts of rude, and with almost all sorts of manufactured produce, for a smaller quantity of gold and silver than what they themselves can either raise or make them for at home. The tax and prohibition operate in two different ways. They not only lower very much the value of the precious metals in Spain and Portugal, but by detaining there a certain quantity of those metals which would otherwise flow over other countries, they keep up their value in those other countries somewhat above what it otherwise would be, and thereby give those countries a double advantage in their commerce with Spain and Portugal. Open the flood-gates, and there will presently be less water above, and more below the dam-head, and it will soon come to a level in both places. Remove the tax and the prohibition, and as the quantity of gold and silver will diminish considerably in Spain and Portugal, so it will increase somewhat in other countries; and the value of those metals, their proportion to the annual produce of land and labour, will soon come to a level, or very near to a level, in all. The loss which Spain and Portugal could sustain by this exportation of their gold and silver, would be altogether nominal and imaginary. The nominal value of their goods, and of the annual produce of their land and labour, would fall, and would be expressed or represented by a smaller quantity of silver than before; but their real value would be the same as before, and would be sufficient to maintain, command, and employ the same quantity of labour. As the nominal value of their goods would fall, the real value of what remained of their gold and silver would rise, and a smaller quantity of those metals would answer all the same purposes of commerce and circulation which had employed a greater quantity before. The gold and silver which would go abroad would not go abroad for nothing, but would bring back an equal value of goods of some kind or other. Those goods, too, would not be all matters of mere luxury and expense, to be consumed by idle people, who produce nothing in return for their consumption. As the real wealth and revenue of idle people would not be augmented by this extraordinary exportation of gold and silver, so neither would their consumption be much augmented by it. Those goods would probably, the greater part of them, and certainly some part of them, consist in materials, tools, and provisions, for the employment and maintenance of industrious people, who would reproduce, with a profit, the full value of their consumption. A part of the dead stock of the society would thus be turned into active stock, and would put into motion a greater quantity of industry than had been employed before. The annual produce of their land and labour would immediately be augmented a little, and in a few years would probably be augmented a great deal; their industry being thus relieved from one of the most oppressive burdens which it at present labours under.

    The bounty upon the exportation of corn necessarily operates exactly in the same way as this absurd policy of Spain and Portugal. Whatever be the actual state of tillage, it renders our corn somewhat dearer in the home market than it otherwise would be in that state, and somewhat cheaper in the foreign; and as the average money price of corn regulates, more or less, that of all other commodities, it lowers the value of silver considerably in the one, and tends to raise it a little in the other. It enables foreigners, the Dutch in particular, not only to eat our corn cheaper than they otherwise could do, but sometimes to eat it cheaper than even our own people can do upon the same occasions; as we are assured by an excellent authority, that of Sir Matthew Decker. It hinders our own workmen from furnishing their goods for so small a quantity of silver as they otherwise might do, and enables the Dutch to furnish theirs for a smaller. It tends to render our manufactures somewhat dearer in every market, and theirs somewhat cheaper, than they otherwise would be, and consequently to give their industry a double advantage over our own.

The bounty, as it raises in the home market, not so much the real, as the nominal price of our corn; as it augments, not the quantity of labour which a certain quantity of corn can maintain and employ, but only the quantity of silver which it will exchange for; it discourages our manufactures, without rendering any considerable service, either to our farmers or country gentlemen. It puts, indeed, a little more money into the pockets of both, and it will perhaps be somewhat difficult to persuade the greater part of them that this is not rendering them a very considerable service. But if this money sinks in its value, in the quantity of labour, provisions, and home-made commodities of all different kinds which it is capable of purchasing, as much as it rises in its quantity, the service will be little more than nominal and imaginary.

There is, perhaps, but one set of men in the whole commonwealth to whom the bounty either was or could be essentially serviceable. These were the corn merchants, the exporters and importers of corn. In years of plenty, the bounty necessarily occasioned a greater exportation than would otherwise have taken place; and by hindering the plenty of the one year from relieving the scarcity of another, it occasioned in years of scarcity a greater importation than would otherwise have been necessary. It increased the business of the corn merchant in both; and in the years of scarcity, it not only enabled him to import a greater quantity, but to sell it for a better price, and consequently with a greater profit, than he could otherwise have made, if the plenty of one year had not been more or less hindered from relieving the scarcity of another. It is in this set of men, accordingly, that I have observed the greatest zeal for the continuance or renewal of the bounty.

Our country gentlemen, when they imposed the high duties upon the exportation of foreign corn, which in times of moderate plenty amount to a prohibition, and when they established the bounty, seem to have imitated the conduct of our manufacturers. By the one institution, they secured to themselves the monopoly of the home market, and by the other they endeavoured to prevent that market from ever being overstocked with their commodity. By both they endeavoured to raise its real value, in the same manner as our manufacturers had, by the like institutions, raised the real value of many different sorts of manufactured goods. They did not, perhaps, attend to the great and essential difference which nature has established between corn and almost every other sort of goods. When, either by the monopoly of the home market, or by a bounty upon exportation, you enable our woollen or linen manufacturers to sell their goods for somewhat a better price than they otherwise could get for them, you raise, not only the nominal, but the real price of those goods; you render them equivalent to a greater quantity of labour and subsistence; you increase not only the nominal, but the real profit, the real wealth and revenue of those manufacturers; and you enable them, either to live better themselves, or to employ a greater quantity of labour in those particular manufactures. You really encourage those manufactures, and direct towards them a greater quantity of the industry of the country than what would properly go to them of its own accord. But when, by the like institutions, you raise the nominal or money price of corn, you do not raise its real value; you do not increase the real wealth, the real revenue, either of our farmers or country gentlemen; you do not encourage the growth of corn, because you do not enable them to maintain and employ more labourers in raising it. The nature of things has stamped upon corn a real value, which cannot be altered by merely altering its money price. No bounty upon exportation, no monopoly of the home market, can raise that value. The freest competition cannot lower it, Through the world in general, that value is equal to the quantity of labour which it can maintain, and in every particular place it is equal to the quantity of labour which it can maintain in the way, whether liberal, moderate, or scanty, in which labour is commonly maintained in that place. Woollen or linen cloth are not the regulating commodities by which the real value of all other commodities must be finally measured and determined; corn is. The real value of every other commodity is finally measured and determined by the proportion which its average money price bears to the average money price of corn. The real value of corn does not vary with those variations in its average money price, which sometimes occur from one century to another; it is the real value of silver which varies with them.

Bounties upon the exportation of any homemade commodity are liable, first, to that general objection which may be made to all the different expedients of the mercantile system; the objection of forcing some part of the industry of the country into a channel less advantageous than that in which it would run of its own accord; and, secondly, to the particular objection of forcing it not only into a channel that is less advantageous, but into one that is actually disadvantageous; the trade which cannot be carried on but by means of a bounty being necessarily a losing trade. The bounty upon the exportation of corn is liable to this further objection, that it can in no respect promote the raising of that particular commodity of which it was meant to encourage the production. When our country gentlemen, therefore, demanded the establishment of the bounty, though they acted in imitation of our merchants and manufacturers, they did not act with that complete comprehension of their own interest, which commonly directs the conduct of those two other orders of people. They loaded the public revenue with a very considerable expense: they imposed a very heavy tax upon the whole body of the people; but they did not, in any sensible degree, increase the real value of their own commodity; and by lowering somewhat the real value of silver, they discouraged, in some degree, the general industry of the country, and, instead of advancing, retarded more or less the improvement of their own lands, which necessarily depend upon the general industry of the country.

To encourage the production of any commodity, a bounty upon production, one should imagine, would have a more direct operation than one upon exportation. It would, besides, impose only one tax upon the people, that which they must contribute in order to pay the bounty. Instead of raising, it would tend to lower the price of the commodity in the home market; and thereby, instead of imposing a second tax upon the people, it might, at least in part, repay them for what they had contributed to the first. Bounties upon production, however, have been very rarely granted. The prejudices established by the commercial system have taught us to believe, that national wealth arises more immediately from exportation than from production. It has been more favoured, accordingly, as the more immediate means of bringing money into the country. Bounties upon production, it has been said too, have been found by experience more liable to frauds than those upon exportation. How far this is true, I know not. That bounties upon exportation have been abused, to many fraudulent purposes, is very well known. But it is not the interest of merchants and manufacturers, the great inventors of all these expedients, that the home market should be overstocked with their goods; an event which a bounty upon production might sometimes occasion. A bounty upon exportation, by enabling them to send abroad their surplus part, and to keep up the price of what remains in the home market, effectually prevents this. Of all the expedients of the mercantile system, accordingly, it is the one of which they are the fondest. I have known the different undertakers of some particular works agree privately among themselves to give a bounty out of their own pockets upon the exportation of a certain proportion of the goods which they dealt in. This expedient succeeded so well, that it more than doubled the price of their goods in the home market, notwithstanding a very considerable increase in the produce. The operation of the bounty upon corn must have been wonderfully different, if it has lowered the money price of that commodity.

Something like a bounty upon production, however, has been granted upon some particular occasions. The tonnage bounties given to the white herring and whale fisheries may, perhaps, be considered as somewhat of this nature. They tend directly, it may be supposed, to render the goods cheaper in the home market than they otherwise would be. In other respects, their effects, it must be acknowledged, are the same as those of bounties upon exportation. By means of them, a part of the capital of the country is employed in bringing goods to market, of which the price does not repay the cost, together with the ordinary profits of stock.

But though the tonnage bounties to those fisheries do not contribute to the opulence of the nation, it may, perhaps, be thought that they contribute to its defence, by augmenting the number of its sailors and shipping. This, it may be alleged, may sometimes be done by means of such bounties, at a much smaller expense than by keeping up a great standing navy, if I may use such an expression, in the same way as a standing army.

Notwithstanding these favourable allegations, however, the following considerations dispose me to believe, that in granting at least one of these bounties, the legislature has been very grossly imposed upon:

First, The herring-buss bounty seems too large.

From the commencement of the winter fishing 1771, to the end of the winter fishing 1781, the tonnage bounty upon the herring-buss fishery has been at thirty shillings the ton. During these eleven years, the whole number of barrels caught by the herring-buss fishery of Scotland amounted to 378,347. The herrings caught and cured at sea are called sea-sticks. In order to render them what are called merchantable herrings, it is necessary to repack them with an additional quantity of salt; and in this case, it is reckoned, that three barrels of sea-sticks are usually repacked into two barrels of merchantable herrings. The number of barrels of merchantable herrings, therefore, caught during these eleven years, will amount only, according to this account, to 252,231¼. During these eleven years, the tonnage bounties paid amounted to £155,463:11s. or 8s:2¼d. upon every barrel of sea-sticks, and to 12s:3¾d. upon every barrel of merchantable herrings.

The salt with which these herrings are cured is sometimes Scotch, and sometimes foreign salt; both which are delivered, free of all excise duty, to the fish-curers. The excise duty upon Scotch salt is at present 1s:6d., that upon foreign salt 10s. the bushel. A barrel of herrings is supposed to require about one bushel and one-fourth of a bushel foreign salt. Two bushels are the supposed average of Scotch salt. If the herrings are entered for exportation, no part of this duty is paid up; if entered for home consumption, whether the herrings were cured with foreign or with Scotch salt, only one shilling the barrel is paid up. It was the old Scotch duty upon a bushel of salt, the quantity which, at a low estimation, had been supposed necessary for curing a barrel of herrings. In Scotland, foreign salt is very little used for any other purpose but the curing of fish. But from the 5th April 1771 to the 5th April 1782, the quantity of foreign salt imported amounted to 936,974 bushels, at eighty-four pounds the bushel; the quantity of Scotch salt delivered from the works to the fish-curers, to no more than 168,226, at fifty-six pounds the bushel only. It would appear, therefore, that it is principally foreign salt that is used in the fisheries. Upon every barrel of herrings exported, there is, besides, a bounty of 2s:8d. and more than two-thirds of the buss-caught herrings are exported. Put all these things together, and you will find that, during these eleven years, every barrel of buss-caught herrings, cured with Scotch salt, when exported, has cost government 17s:11¾d.; and, when entered for home consumption, 14s:3¾d.; and that every barrel cured with foreign salt, when exported, has cost government £1:7:5¾d.; and, when entered for home consumption, £1:3:9¾d. The price of a barrel of good merchantable herrings runs from seventeen and eighteen to four and five-

and-twenty shillings; about a guinea at an average. {See the accounts at the end of this Book.}

Secondly, The bounty to the white-herring fishery is a tonnage bounty, and is proportioned to the burden of the ship, not to her diligence or success in the fishery; and it has, I am afraid, been too common for the vessels to fit out for the sole purpose of catching, not the fish but the bounty. In the year 1759, when the bounty was at fifty shillings the ton, the whole buss fishery of Scotland brought in only four barrels of sea-sticks. In that year, each barrel of sea-sticks cost government, in bounties alone, £113:15s.; each barrel of merchantable herrings £159:7:6.

Thirdly, The mode of fishing, for which this tonnage bounty in the white herring fishery has been given (by busses or decked vessels from twenty to eighty tons burden), seems not so well adapted to the situation of Scotland, as to that of Holland, from the practice of which country it appears to have been borrowed. Holland lies at a great distance from the seas to which herrings are known principally to resort, and can, therefore, carry on that fishery only in decked vessels, which can carry water and provisions sufficient for a voyage to a distant sea; but the Hebrides, or Western Islands, the islands of Shetland, and the northern and north-western coasts of Scotland, the countries in whose neighbourhood the herring fishery is principally carried on, are everywhere intersected by arms of the sea, which run up a considerable way into the land, and which, in the language of the country, are called sea-lochs. It is to these sea-lochs that the herrings principally resort during the seasons in which they visit these seas; for the visits of this, and, I am assured, of many other sorts of fish, are not quite regular and constant. A boat-fishery, therefore, seems to be the mode of fishing best adapted to the peculiar situation of Scotland, the fishers carrying the herrings on shore as fast as they are taken, to be either cured or consumed fresh. But the great encouragement which a bounty of 30s. the ton gives to the buss-fishery, is necessarily a discouragement to the boat-fishery, which, having no such bounty, cannot bring its cured fish to market upon the same terms as the buss-fishery. The boat-fishery; accordingly, which, before the establishment of the buss-bounty, was very considerable, and is said to have employed a number of seamen, not inferior to what the buss-fishery employs at present, is now gone almost entirely to decay. Of the former extent, however, of this now ruined and abandoned fishery, I must acknowledge that I cannot pretend to speak with much precision. As no bounty was-paid upon the outfit of the boat-fishery, no account was taken of it by the officers of the customs or salt duties.

Fourthly, In many parts of Scotland, during certain seasons of the year, herrings make no inconsiderable part of the food of the common people. A bounty which tended to lower their price in the home market, might contribute a good deal to the relief of a great number of our fellow-subjects, whose circumstances are by no means affluent. But the herring-bus bounty contributes to no such good purpose. It has ruined the boat fishery, which is by far the best adapted for the supply of the home market; and the additional bounty of 2s:8d. the barrel upon exportation, carries the greater part, more than two-thirds, of the produce of the buss-fishery abroad. Between thirty and forty years ago, before the establishment of the buss-bounty, 16s. the barrel, I have been assured, was the common price of white herrings. Between ten and fifteen years ago, before the boat-fishery was entirely ruined, the price was said to have run from seventeen to twenty shillings the barrel. For these last five years, it has, at an average, been at twenty-five shillings the barrel. This high price, however, may have been owing to the real scarcity of the herrings upon the coast of Scotland. I must observe, too, that the cask or barrel, which is usually sold with the herrings, and of which the price is included in all the foregoing prices, has, since the commencement of the American war, risen to about double its former price, or from about 3s. to about 6s. I must likewise observe, that the accounts I have received of the prices of former times, have been by no means quite uniform and consistent, and an old man of great accuracy and experience has assured me, that, more than fifty years ago, a guinea was the usual price of a barrel of good merchantable herrings; and this, I imagine, may still be looked upon as the average price. All accounts, however, I think, agree that the price has not been lowered in the home market in consequence of the buss-bounty.

When the undertakers of fisheries, after such liberal bounties have been bestowed upon them, continue to sell their commodity at the same, or even at a higher price than they were accustomed to do before, it might be expected that their profits should be very great; and it is not improbable that those of some individuals may have been so. In general, however, I have every reason to believe they have been quite otherwise. The usual effect of such bounties is, to encourage rash undertakers to adventure in a business which they do not understand; and what they lose by their own negligence and ignorance, more than compensates all that they can gain by the utmost liberality of government. In 1750, by the same act which first gave the bounty of 30s. the ton for the encouragement of the white herring fishery (the 23d Geo. II. chap. 24), a joint stock company was erected, with a capital of £500,000, to which the subscribers (over and above all other encouragements, the tonnage bounty just now mentioned, the exportation bounty of 2s:8d. the barrel, the delivery of both British and foreign salt duty free) were, during the space of fourteen years, for every hundred pounds which they subscribed and paid into the stock of the society, entitled to three pounds a-year, to be paid by the receiver-general of the customs in equal half-yearly payments. Besides this great company, the residence of whose governor and directors was to be in London, it was declared lawful to erect different fishing chambers in all the different out-ports of the kingdom, provided a sum not less than £10,000 was subscribed into the capital of each, to be managed at its own risk, and for its own profit and loss. The same annuity, and the same encouragements of all kinds, were given to the trade of those inferior chambers as to that of the great company. The subscription of the great company was soon filled up, and several different fishing chambers were erected in the different out-ports of the kingdom. In spite of all these encouragements, almost all those different companies, both great and small, lost either the whole or the greater part of their capitals; scarce a vestige now remains of any of them, and the white-herring fishery is now entirely, or almost entirely, carried on by private adventurers.

If any particular manufacture was necessary, indeed, for the defence of the society, it might not always be prudent to depend upon our neighbours for the supply; and if such manufacture could not otherwise be supported at home, it might not be unreasonable that all the other branches of industry should be taxed in order to support it. The bounties upon the exportation of British made sail-cloth, and British made gunpowder, may, perhaps, both be vindicated upon this principle.

But though it can very seldom be reasonable to tax the industry of the great body of the people, in order to support that of some particular class of manufacturers; yet, in the wantonness of great prosperity, when the public enjoys a greater revenue than it knows well what to do with, to give such bounties to favourite manufactures, may, perhaps, be as natural as to incur any other idle expense. In public, as well as in private expenses, great wealth, may, perhaps, frequently be admitted as an apology for great folly. But there must surely be something more than ordinary absurdity in continuing such profusion in times of general difficulty and distress.

What is called a bounty, is sometimes no more than a drawback, and, consequently, is not liable to the same objections as what is properly a bounty. The bounty, for example, upon refined sugar exported, may be considered as a drawback of the duties upon the brown and Muscovado sugars, from which it is made; the bounty upon wrought silk exported, a drawback of the duties upon raw and thrown silk imported; the bounty upon gunpowder exported, a drawback of the duties upon brimstone and saltpetre imported. In the language of the customs, those allowances only are called drawbacks which are given upon goods exported in the same form in which they are imported. When that form has been so altered by manufacture of any kind as to come under a new denomination, they are called bounties.

Premiums given by the public to artists and manufacturers, who excel in their particular occupations, are not liable to the same objections as bounties. By encouraging extraordinary dexterity and ingenuity, they serve to keep up the emulation of the workmen actually employed in those respective occupations, and are not considerable enough to turn towards any one of them a greater share of the capital of the country than what would go to it of its own accord. Their tendency is not to overturn the natural balance of employments, but to render the work which is done in each as perfect and complete as possible. The expense of premiums, besides, is very trifling, that of bounties very great. The bounty upon corn alone has sometimes cost the public, in one year, more than £300,000.

Bounties are sometimes called premiums, as drawbacks are sometimes called bounties. But we must, in all cases, attend to the nature of the thing, without paying any regard to the word.

Digression concerning the Corn Trade and Corn Laws

I cannot conclude this chapter concerning bounties, without observing, that the praises which have been bestowed upon the law which establishes the bounty upon the exportation of corn, and upon that system of regulations which is connected with it, are altogether unmerited. A particular examination of the nature of the corn trade, and of the principal British laws which relate to it, will sufficiently demonstrate the truth of this assertion. The great importance of this subject must justify the length of the digression.

The trade of the corn merchant is composed of four different branches, which, though they may sometimes be all carried on by the same person, are, in their own nature, four separate and distinct trades. These are, first, the trade of the inland dealer; secondly, that of the merchant-importer for home consumption; thirdly, that of the merchant-exporter of home produce for foreign consumption; and, fourthly, that of the merchant-carrier, or of the importer of corn, in order to export it again.

I. The interest of the inland dealer, and that of the great body of the people, how opposite soever they may at first appear, are, even in years of the greatest scarcity, exactly the same. It is his interest to raise the price of his corn as high as the real scarcity of the season requires, and it can never be his interest to raise it higher. By raising the price, he discourages the consumption, and puts every body more or less, but particularly the inferior ranks of people, upon thrift and good management. If, by raising it too high, he discourages the consumption so much that the supply of the season is likely to go beyond the consumption of the season, and to last for some time after the next crop begins to come in, he runs the hazard, not only of losing a considerable part of his corn by natural causes, but of being obliged to sell what remains of it for much less than what he might have had for it several months before. If, by not raising the price high enough, he discourages the consumption so little, that the supply of the season is likely to fall short of the consumption of the season, he not only loses a part of the profit which he might otherwise have made, but he exposes the people to suffer before the end of the season, instead of the hardships of a dearth, the dreadful horrors of a famine. It is the interest of the people that their daily, weekly, and monthly consumption should be proportioned as exactly as possible to the supply of the season. The interest of the inland corn dealer is the same. By supplying them, as nearly as he can judge, in this proportion, he is likely to sell all his corn for the highest price, and with the greatest profit; and his knowledge of the state of the crop, and of his daily, weekly, and monthly sales, enables him to judge, with more or less accuracy, how far they really are supplied in this manner. Without intending the interest of the people, he is necessarily led, by a regard to his own interest, to treat them, even in years of scarcity, pretty much in the same manner as the prudent master of a vessel is sometimes obliged to treat his crew. When he foresees that provisions are likely to run short, he puts them upon short allowance. Though from excess of caution he should sometimes do this without any real necessity, yet all the inconveniencies which his crew can thereby suffer are inconsiderable, in comparison of the danger, misery, and ruin, to which they might sometimes be exposed by a less provident conduct. Though, from excess of avarice, in the same manner, the inland corn merchant should sometimes raise the price of his corn somewhat higher than the scarcity of the season requires, yet all the inconveniencies which the people can suffer from this conduct, which effectually secures them from a famine in the end of the season, are inconsiderable, in comparison of what they might have been exposed to by a more liberal way of dealing in the beginning of it the corn merchant himself is likely to suffer the most by this excess of avarice; not only from the indignation which it generally excites against him, but, though he should escape the effects of this indignation, from the quantity of corn which it necessarily leaves upon his hands in the end of the season, and which, if the next season happens to prove favourable, he must always sell for a much lower price than he might otherwise have had.

 Were it possible, indeed, for one great company of merchants to possess themselves of the whole crop of an extensive country, it might perhaps be their interest to deal with it, as the Dutch are said to do with the spiceries of the Moluccas, to destroy or throw away a considerable part of it, in order to keep up the price of the rest. But it is scarce possible, even by the violence of law, to establish such an extensive monopoly with regard to corn; and wherever the law leaves the trade free, it is of all commodities the least liable to be engrossed or monopolised by the force a few large capitals, which buy up the greater part of it. Not only its value far exceeds what the capitals of a few private men are capable of purchasing; but, supposing they were capable of purchasing it, the manner in which it is produced renders this purchase altogether impracticable. As, in every civilized country, it is the commodity of which the annual consumption is the greatest; so a greater quantity of industry is annually employed in producing corn than in producing any other commodity. When it first comes from the ground, too, it is necessarily divided among a greater number of owners than any other commodity; and these owners can never be collected into one place, like a number of independent manufacturers, but are necessarily scattered through all the different corners of the country. These first owners either immediately supply the consumers in their own neighbourhood, or they supply other inland dealers, who supply those consumers. The inland dealers in corn, therefore, including both the farmer and the baker, are necessarily more numerous than the dealers in any other commodity; and their dispersed situation renders it altogether impossible for them to enter into any general combination. If, in a year of scarcity, therefore, any of them should find that he had a good deal more corn upon hand than, at the current price, he could hope to dispose of before the end of the season, he would never think of keeping up this price to his own loss, and to the sole benefit of his rivals and competitors, but would immediately lower it, in order to get rid of his corn before the new crop began to come in. The same motives, the same interests, which would thus regulate the conduct of any one dealer, would regulate that of every other, and oblige them all in general to sell their corn at the price which, according to the best of their judgment, was most suitable to the scarcity or plenty of the season.

Whoever examines, with attention, the history of the dearths and famines which have afflicted any part of Europe during either the course of the present or that of the two preceding centuries, of several of which we have pretty exact accounts, will find, I believe, that a dearth never has arisen from any combination among the inland dealers in corn, nor from any other cause but a real scarcity, occasioned sometimes, perhaps, and in some particular places, by the waste of war, but in by far the greatest number of cases by the fault of the seasons; and that a famine has never arisen from any other cause but the violence of government attempting, by improper means, to remedy the inconveniencies of a dearth.

In an extensive corn country, between all the different parts of which there is a free commerce and communication, the scarcity occasioned by the most unfavourable seasons can never be so great as to produce a famine; and the scantiest crop, if managed with frugality and economy, will maintain, through the year, the same number of people that are commonly fed in a more affluent manner by one of moderate plenty. The seasons most unfavourable to the crop are those of excessive drought or excessive rain. But as corn grows equally upon high and low lands, upon grounds that are disposed to be too wet, and upon those that are disposed to be too dry, either the drought or the rain, which is hurtful to one part of the country, is favourable to another; and though, both in the wet and in the dry season, the crop is a good deal less than in one more properly tempered; yet, in both, what is lost in one part of the country is in some measure compensated by what is gained in the other. In rice countries, where the crop not only requires a very moist soil, but where, in a certain period of its growing, it must be laid under water, the effects of a drought are much more dismal. Even in such countries, however, the drought is, perhaps, scarce ever so universal as necessarily to occasion a famine, if the government would allow a free trade. The drought in Bengal, a few years ago, might probably have occasioned a very great dearth. Some improper regulations, some injudicious restraints, imposed by the servants of the East India Company upon the rice trade, contributed, perhaps, to turn that dearth into a famine.

When the government, in order to remedy the inconveniencies of a dearth, orders all the dealers to sell their corn at what it supposes a reasonable price, it either hinders them from bringing it to market, which may sometimes produce a famine even in the beginning of the season; or, if they bring it thither, it enables the people, and thereby encourages them to consume it so fast as must necessarily produce a famine before the end of the season. The unlimited, unrestrained freedom of the corn trade, as it is the only effectual preventive of the miseries of a famine, so it is the best palliative of the inconveniencies of a dearth; for the inconveniencies of a real scarcity cannot be remedied; they can only be palliated. No trade deserves more the full protection of the law, and no trade requires it so much; because no trade is so much exposed to popular odium.

In years of scarcity, the inferior ranks of people impute their distress to the avarice of the corn merchant, who becomes the object of their hatred and indignation. Instead of making profit upon such occasions, therefore, he is often in danger of being utterly ruined, and of having his magazines plundered and destroyed by their violence. It is in years of scarcity, however, when prices are high, that the corn merchant expects to make his principal profit. He is generally in contract with some farmers to furnish him, for a certain number of years, with a certain quantity of corn, at a certain price. This contract price is settled according to what is supposed to be the moderate and reasonable, that is, the ordinary or average price, which, before the late years of scarcity, was commonly about 28s. for the quarter of wheat, and for that of other grain in proportion. In years of scarcity, therefore, the corn merchant buys a great part of his corn for the ordinary price, and sells it for a much higher. That this extraordinary profit, however, is no more than sufficient to put his trade upon a fair level with other trades, and to compensate the many losses which he sustains upon other occasions, both from the perishable nature of the commodity itself, and from the frequent and unforeseen fluctuations of its price, seems evident enough, from this single circumstance, that great fortunes are as seldom made in this as in any other trade. The popular odium, however, which attends it in years of scarcity, the only years in which it can be very profitable, renders people of character and fortune averse to enter into it. It is abandoned to an inferior set of dealers; and millers, bakers, meal-men, and meal-factors, together with a number of wretched hucksters, are almost the only middle people that, in the home market, come between the grower and the consumer.

The ancient policy of Europe, instead of discountenancing this popular odium against a trade so beneficial to the public, seems, on the contrary, to have authorised and encouraged it.

By the 5th and 6th of Edward VI cap. 14, it was enacted, that whoever should buy any corn or grain, with intent to sell it again, should be reputed an unlawful engrosser, and should, for the first fault, suffer two months imprisonment, and forfeit the value of the corn; for the second, suffer six months imprisonment, and forfeit double the value; and, for the third, be set in the pillory, suffer imprisonment during the king's pleasure, and forfeit all his goods and chattels. The ancient policy of most other parts of Europe was no better than that of England.

Our ancestors seem to have imagined, that the people would buy their corn cheaper of the farmer than of the corn merchant, who, they were afraid, would require, over and above the price which he paid to the farmer, an exorbitant profit to himself. They endeavoured, therefore, to annihilate his trade altogether. They even endeavoured to hinder, as much as possible, any middle man of any kind from coming in between the grower and the consumer; and this was the meaning of the many restraints which they imposed upon the trade of those whom they called kidders, or carriers of corn; a trade which nobody was allowed to exercise without a licence, ascertaining his qualifications as a man of probity and fair dealing. The authority of three justices of the peace was, by the statute of Edward VI. necessary in order to grant this licence. But even this restraint was afterwards thought insufficient, and, by a statute of Elizabeth, the privilege of granting it was confined to the quarter-sessions.

The ancient policy of Europe endeavoured, in this manner, to regulate agriculture, the great trade of the country, by maxims quite different from those which it established with regard to manufactures, the great trade of the towns. By leaving a farmer no other customers but either the consumers or their immediate factors, the kidders and carriers of corn, it endeavoured to force him to exercise the trade, not only of a farmer, but of a corn merchant, or corn retailer. On the contrary, it, in many cases, prohibited the manufacturer from exercising the trade of a shopkeeper, or from selling his own goods by retail. It meant, by the one law, to promote the general interest of the country, or to render corn cheap, without, perhaps, its being well understood how this was to be done. By the other, it meant to promote that of a particular order of men, the shopkeepers, who would be so much undersold by the manufacturer, it was supposed, that their trade would be ruined, if he was allowed to retail at all.

The manufacturer, however, though he had been allowed to keep a shop, and to sell his own goods by retail, could not have undersold the common shopkeeper. Whatever part of his capital he might have placed in his shop, he must have withdrawn it from his manufacture. In order to carry on his business on a level with that of other people, as he must have had the profit of a manufacturer on the one part, so he must have had that of a shopkeeper upon the other. Let us suppose, for example, that in the particular town where he lived, ten per cent. was the ordinary profit both of manufacturing and shopkeeping stock; he must in this case have charged upon every piece of his own goods, which he sold in his shop, a profit of twenty per cent. When he carried them from his workhouse to his shop, he must have valued them at the price for which he could have sold them to a dealer or shopkeeper, who would have bought them by wholesale. If he valued them lower, he lost a part of the profit of his manufacturing capital. When, again, he sold them from his shop, unless he got the same price at which a shopkeeper would have sold them, he lost a part of the profit of his shop-keeping capital. Though he might appear, therefore, to make a double profit upon the same piece of goods, yet, as these goods made successively a part of two distinct capitals, he made but a single profit upon the whole capital employed about them; and if he made less than his profit, he was a loser, and did not employ his whole capital with the same advantage as the greater part of his neighbours.

What the manufacturer was prohibited to do, the farmer was in some measure enjoined to do; to divide his capital between two different employments; to keep one part of it in his granaries and stack-yard, for supplying the occasional demands of the market, and to employ the other in the cultivation of his land. But as he could not afford to employ the latter for less than the ordinary profits of farming stock, so he could as little afford to employ the former for less than the ordinary profits of mercantile stock. Whether the stock which really carried on the business of a corn merchant belonged to the person who was called a farmer, or to the person who was called a corn merchant, an equal profit was in both cases requisite, in order to indemnify its owner for employing it in this manner, in order to put his business on a level with other trades, and in order to hinder him from having an interest to change it as soon as possible for some other. The farmer, therefore, who was thus forced to exercise the trade of a corn merchant, could not afford to sell his corn cheaper than any other corn merchant would have been obliged to do in the case of a free competition.

The dealer who can employ his whole stock in one single branch of business, has an advantage of the same kind with the workman who can employ his whole labour in one single operation. As the latter acquires a dexterity which enables him, with the same two hands, to perform a much greater quantity of work, so the former acquires so easy and ready a method of transacting his business, of buying and disposing of his goods, that with the same capital he can transact a much greater quantity of business. As the one can commonly afford his work a good deal cheaper, so the other can commonly afford his goods somewhat cheaper, than if his stock and attention were both employed about a greater variety of objects. The greater part of manufacturers could not afford to retail their own goods so cheap as a vigilant and active shopkeeper, whose sole business it was to buy them by wholesale and to retail them again. The greater part of farmers could still less afford to retail their own corn, to supply the inhabitants of a town, at perhaps four or five miles distance from the greater part of them, so cheap as a vigilant and active corn merchant, whose sole business it was to purchase corn by wholesale, to collect it into a great magazine, and to retail it again.

The law which prohibited the manufacturer from exercising the trade of a shopkeeper, endeavoured to force this division in the employment of stock to go on faster than it might otherwise have done. The law which obliged the farmer to exercise the trade of a corn merchant, endeavoured to hinder it from going on so fast. Both laws were evident violations of natural liberty, and therefore unjust; and they were both, too, as impolitic as they were unjust. It is the interest of every society, that things of this kind should never either he forced or obstructed. The man who employs either his labour or his stock in a greater variety of ways than his situation renders necessary, can never hurt his neighbour by underselling him. He may hurt himself, and he generally does so. Jack-of-all-trades will never be rich, says the proverb. But the law ought always to trust people with the care of their own interest, as in their local situations they must generally be able to judge better of it than the legislature can do. The law, however, which obliged the farmer to exercise the trade of a corn merchant was by far the most pernicious of the two.

It obstructed not only that division in the employment of stock which is so advantageous to every society, but it obstructed likewise the improvement and cultivation of the land. By obliging the farmer to carry on two trades instead of one, it forced him to divide his capital into two parts, of which one only could be employed in cultivation. But if he had been at liberty to sell his whole crop to a corn merchant as fast as he could thresh it out, his whole capital might have returned immediately to the land, and have been employed in buying more cattle, and hiring more servants, in order to improve and cultivate it better. But by being obliged to sell his corn by retail, he was obliged to keep a great part of his capital in his granaries and stack-yard through the year, and could not therefore cultivate so well as with the same capital he might otherwise have done. This law, therefore, necessarily obstructed the improvement of the land, and, instead of tending to render corn cheaper, must have tended to render it scarcer, and therefore dearer, than it would otherwise have been.

After the business of the farmer, that of the corn merchant is in reality the trade which, if properly protected and encouraged, would contribute the most to the raising of corn. It would support the trade of the farmer, in the same manner as the trade of the wholesale dealer supports that of the manufacturer.

The wholesale dealer, by affording a ready market to the manufacturer, by taking his goods off his hand as fast as he can make them, and by sometimes even advancing their price to him before he has made them, enables him to keep his whole capital, and sometimes even more than his whole capital, constantly employed in manufacturing, and consequently to manufacture a much greater quantity of goods than if he was obliged to dispose of them himself to the immediate consumers, or even to the retailers. As the capital of the wholesale merchant, too, is generally sufficient to replace that of many manufacturers, this intercourse between him and them interests the owner of a large capital to support the owners of a great number of small ones, and to assist them in those losses and misfortunes which might otherwise prove ruinous to them.

An intercourse of the same kind universally established between the farmers and the corn merchants, would be attended with effects equally beneficial to the farmers. They would be enabled to keep their whole capitals, and even more than their whole capitals constantly employed in cultivation. In case of any of those accidents to which no trade is more liable than theirs, they would find in their ordinary customer, the wealthy corn merchant, a person who had both an interest to support them, and the ability to do it; and they would not, as at present, be entirely dependent upon the forbearance of their landlord, or the mercy of his steward. Were it possible, as perhaps it is not, to establish this intercourse universally, and all at once; were it possible to turn all at once the whole farming stock of the kingdom to its proper business, the cultivation of land, withdrawing it from every other employment into which any part of it may be at present diverted; and were it possible, in order to support and assist, upon occasion, the operations of this great stock, to provide all at once another stock almost equally great; it is not, perhaps, very easy to imagine how great, how extensive, and how sudden, would be the improvement which this change of circumstances would alone produce upon the whole face of the country.

The statute of Edward VI. therefore, by prohibiting as much as possible any middle man from coming in between the grower and the consumer, endeavoured to annihilate a trade, of which the free exercise is not only the best palliative of the inconveniencies of a dearth, but the best preventive of that calamity; after the trade of the farmer, no trade contributing so much to the growing of corn as that of the corn merchant.

The rigour of this law was afterwards softened by several subsequent statutes, which successively permitted the engrossing of corn when the price of wheat should not exceed 20s. and 24s. 32s. and 40s. the quarter. At last, by the 15th of Charles II. c.7, the engrossing or buying of corn, in order to sell it again, as long as the price of wheat did not exceed 48s. the quarter, and that of other grain in proportion, was declared lawful to all persons not being forestallers, that is, not selling again in the same market within three months. All the freedom which the trade of the inland corn dealer has ever yet enjoyed was bestowed upon it by this statute. The statute of the twelfth of the present king, which repeals almost all the other ancient laws against engrossers and forestallers, does not repeal the restrictions of this particular statute, which therefore still continue in force.

This statute, however, authorises in some measure two very absurd popular prejudices.

First, It supposes, that when the price of wheat has risen so high as 48s. the quarter, and that of other grain in proportion, corn is likely to be so engrossed as to hurt the people. But, from what has been already said, it seems evident enough, that corn can at no price be so engrossed by the inland dealers as to hurt the people; and 48s. the quarter, besides, though it may be considered as a very high price, yet, in years of scarcity, it is a price which frequently takes place immediately after harvest, when scarce any part of the new crop can be sold off, and when it is impossible even for ignorance to suppose that any part of it can be so engrossed as to hurt the people.

Secondly, It supposes that there is a certain price at which corn is likely to be forestalled, that is, bought up in order to be sold again soon after in the same market, so as to hurt the people. But if a merchant ever buys up corn, either going to a particular market, or in a particular market, in order to sell it again soon after in the same market, it must be because he judges that the market cannot be so liberally supplied through the whole season as upon that particular occasion, and that the price, therefore, must soon rise. If he judges wrong in this, and if the price does not rise, he not only loses the whole profit of the stock which he employs in this manner, but a part of the stock itself, by the expense and loss which necessarily attend the storing and keeping of corn. He hurts himself, therefore, much more essentially than he can hurt even the particular people whom he may hinder from supplying themselves upon that particular market day, because they may afterwards supply themselves just as cheap upon any other market day. If he judges right, instead of hurting the great body of the people, he renders them a most important service. By making them feel the inconveniencies of a dearth somewhat earlier than they otherwise might do, he prevents their feeling them afterwards so severely as they certainly would do, if the cheapness of price encouraged them to consume faster than suited the real scarcity of the season. When the scarcity is real, the best thing that can be done for the people is, to divide the inconvenience of it as equally as possible, through all the different months and weeks and days of the year. The interest of the corn merchant makes him study to do this as exactly as he can; and as no other person can have either the same interest, or the same knowledge, or the same abilities, to do it so exactly as he, this most important operation of commerce ought to be trusted entirely to him; or, in other words, the corn trade, so far at least as concerns the supply of the home market, ought to be left perfectly free.

The popular fear of engrossing and forestalling may be compared to the popular terrors and suspicions of witchcraft. The unfortunate wretches accused of this latter crime were not more innocent of the misfortunes imputed to them, than those who have been accused of the former. The law which put an end to all prosecutions against witchcraft, which put it out of any man's power to gratify his own malice by accusing his neighbour of that imaginary crime, seems effectually to have put an end to those fears and suspicions, by taking away the great cause which encouraged and supported them. The law which would restore entire freedom to the inland trade of corn, would probably prove as effectual to put an end to the popular fears of engrossing and forestalling.

The 15th of Charles II. c. 7, however, with all its imperfections, has, perhaps, contributed more, both to the plentiful supply of the home market, and to the increase of tillage, than any other law in the statute book. It is from this law that the inland corn trade has derived all the liberty and protection which it has ever yet enjoyed; and both the supply of the home market and the interest of tillage are much more effectually promoted by the inland, than either by the importation or exportation trade.

The proportion of the average quantity of all sorts of grain imported into Great Britain to that of all sorts of grain consumed, it has been computed by the author of the Tracts upon the Corn Trade, does not exceed that of one to five hundred and seventy. For supplying the home market, therefore, the importance of the inland trade must be to that of the importation trade as five hundred and seventy to one.

The average quantity of all sorts of grain exported from Great Britain does not, according to the same author, exceed the one-and-thirtieth part of the annual produce. For the encouragement of tillage, therefore, by providing a market for the home produce, the importance of the inland trade must be to that of the exportation trade as thirty to one.

I have no great faith in political arithmetic, and I mean not to warrant the exactness of either of these computations. I mention them only in order to show of how much less consequence, in the opinion of the most judicious and experienced persons, the foreign trade of corn is than the home trade. The great cheapness of corn in the years immediately preceding the establishment of the bounty may, perhaps with reason, be ascribed in some measure to the operation of this statute of Charles II. which had been enacted about five-and-twenty years before, and which had, therefore, full time to produce its effect.

A very few words will sufficiently explain all that I have to say concerning the other three branches of the corn trade.

II. The trade of the merchant-importer of foreign corn for home consumption, evidently contributes to the immediate supply of the home market, and must so far be immediately beneficial to the great body of the people. It tends, indeed, to lower somewhat the average money price of corn, but not to diminish its real value, or the quantity of labour which it is capable of maintaining. If importation was at all times free, our farmers and country gentlemen would probably, one year with another, get less money for their corn than they do at present, when importation is at most times in effect prohibited; but the money which they got would be of more value, would buy more goods of all other kinds, and would employ more labour. Their real wealth, their real revenue, therefore, would be the same as at present, though it might be expressed by a smaller quantity of silver, and they would neither be disabled nor discouraged from cultivating corn as much as they do at present. On the contrary, as the rise in the real value of silver, in consequence of lowering the money price of corn, lowers somewhat the money price of all other commodities, it gives the industry of the country where it takes place some advantage in all foreign markets and thereby tends to encourage and increase that industry. But the extent of the home market for corn must be in proportion to the general industry of the country where it grows, or to the number of those who produce something else, and therefore, have something else, or, what comes to the same thing, the price of something else, to give in exchange for corn. But in every country, the home market, as it is the nearest and most convenient, so is it likewise the greatest and most important market for corn. That rise in the real value of silver, therefore, which is the effect of lowering the average money price of corn, tends to enlarge the greatest and most important market for corn, and thereby to encourage, instead of discouraging its growth.

By the 22d of Charles II. c. 13, the importation of wheat, whenever the price in the home market did not exceed 53s:4d. the quarter, was subjected to a duty of 16s. the quarter; and to a duty of 8s. whenever the price did not exceed £4. The former of these two prices has, for more than a century past, taken place only in times of very great scarcity; and the latter has, so far as I know, not taken place at all. Yet, till wheat has risen above this latter price, it was, by this statute, subjected to a very high duty; and, till it had risen above the former, to a duty which amounted to a prohibition. The importation of other sorts of grain was restrained at rates and by duties, in proportion to the value of the grain, almost equally high. Before the 13th of the present king, the following were the duties payable upon the importation of the different sorts of grain:

Grain.	Duties.		Duties	Duties.
Beans to 28s. per qr.	19s:10d. after till 40s.		16s:8d.	then 12d.
Barley to 28s. -	19s:10d.	- 32s.	16s.	- 12d.
Malt is prohibited by the annual malt-tax bill.				
Oats to 16s. -	5s:10d. after		-	9½d.
Pease to 40s. -	16s:0d. after		-	9¾d.
Rye to 36s. -	19s:10d. till 40s.		16s:8d	- 12d.
Wheat to 44s. -	21s:9d. till 53s:4d.		17s.	- 8s.
	till £4, and after that about			1s:4d.
Buck-wheat to 32s. per qr.	to pay 16s.			

These different duties were imposed, partly by the 22d of Charles II. in place of the old subsidy, partly by the new subsidy, by the one-third and two-thirds subsidy, and by the subsidy 1747. Subsequent laws still further increased those duties.

The distress which, in years of scarcity, the strict execution of those laws might have brought upon the people, would probably have been very great; but, upon such occasions, its execution was generally suspended by temporary statutes, which permitted, for a limited time, the importation of foreign corn. The necessity of these temporary statutes sufficiently demonstrates the impropriety of this general one.

These restraints upon importation, though prior to the establishment of the bounty, were dictated by the same spirit, by the same principles, which afterwards enacted that regulation. How hurtful soever in themselves, these, or some other restraints upon importation, became necessary in consequence of that regulation. If, when wheat was either below 48s. the quarter, or not much above it, foreign corn could have been imported, either duty free, or upon paying only a small duty, it might have been exported again, with the benefit of the bounty, to the great loss of the public revenue, and to the entire perversion of the institution, of which the object was to extend the market for the home growth, not that for the growth of foreign countries.

III. The trade of the merchant-exporter of corn for foreign consumption, certainly does not contribute directly to the plentiful supply of the home market. It does so, however, indirectly. From whatever source this supply maybe usually drawn, whether from home growth, or from foreign importation, unless more corn is either usually grown, or usually imported into the country, than what is usually consumed in it, the supply of the home market can never be very plentiful. But unless the surplus can, in all ordinary cases, be exported, the growers will be careful never to grow more, and the importers never to import more, than what the bare consumption of the home market requires. That market will very seldom be overstocked; but it will generally be understocked; the people, whose business it is to supply it, being generally afraid lest their goods should be left upon their hands. The prohibition of exportation limits the improvement and cultivation of the country to what the supply of its own inhabitants require. The freedom of exportation enables it to extend cultivation for the supply of foreign nations.

By the 12th of Charles II. c.4, the exportation of corn was permitted whenever the price of wheat did not exceed 40s. the quarter, and that of other grain in proportion. By the 15th of the same prince, this liberty was extended till the price of wheat exceeded 48s. the quarter; and by the 22d, to all higher prices. A poundage, indeed, was to be paid to the king upon such exportation; but all grain was rated so low in the book of rates, that this poundage amounted only, upon wheat to 1s., upon oats to 4d., and upon all other grain to 6d. the quarter. By the 1st of William and Mary, the act which established this bounty, this small duty was virtually taken off whenever the price of wheat did not exceed 48s. the quarter; and by the 11th and 12th of William III. c. 20, it was expressly taken off at all higher prices.

The trade of the merchant-exporter was, in this manner, not only encouraged by a bounty, but rendered much more free than that of the inland dealer. By the last of these statutes, corn could be engrossed at any price for exportation; but it could not be engrossed for inland sale, except when the price did not exceed 48s. the quarter. The interest of the inland dealer, however, it has already been shown, can never be opposite to that of the great body of the people. That of the merchant-exporter may, and in fact sometimes is. If, while his own country labours under a dearth, a neighbouring country should be afflicted with a famine, it might be his interest to carry corn to the latter country, in such quantities as might very much aggravate the calamities of the dearth. The plentiful supply of the home market was not the direct object of those statutes; but, under the pretence of encouraging agriculture, to raise the money price of corn as high as possible, and thereby to occasion, as much as possible, a constant dearth in the home market. By the discouragement of importation, the supply of that market; even in times of great scarcity, was confined to the home growth; and by the encouragement of exportation, when the price was so high as 48s. the quarter, that market was not, even in times of considerable scarcity, allowed to enjoy the whole of that growth. The temporary laws, prohibiting, for a limited time, the exportation of corn, and taking off, for a limited time, the duties upon its importation, expedients to which Great Britain has been obliged so frequently to have recourse, sufficiently demonstrate the impropriety of her general system. Had that system been good, she would not so frequently have been reduced to the necessity of departing from it.

Were all nations to follow the liberal system of free exportation and free importation, the different states into which a great continent was divided, would so far resemble the different provinces of a great empire. As among the different provinces of a great empire, the freedom of the inland trade appears, both from reason and experience, not only the best palliative of a dearth, but the most effectual preventive of a famine; so would the freedom of the exportation and importation trade be among the different states into which a great continent was divided. The larger the continent, the easier the communication through all the different parts of it, both by land and by water, the less would any one particular part of it ever be exposed to either of these calamities, the scarcity of any one country being more likely to be relieved by the plenty of some other. But very few countries have entirely adopted this liberal system. The freedom of the corn trade is almost everywhere more or less restrained, and in many countries is confined by such absurd regulations, as frequently aggravate the unavoidable misfortune of a dearth into the dreadful calamity of a famine. The demand of such countries for corn may frequently become so great and so urgent, that a small state in their neighbourhood, which happened at the same time to be labouring under some degree of dearth, could not venture to supply them without exposing itself to the like dreadful calamity. The very bad policy of one country may thus render it, in some measure, dangerous and imprudent to establish what would otherwise be the best policy in another. The unlimited freedom of exportation, however, would be much less dangerous in great states, in which the growth being much greater, the supply could seldom be much affected by any quantity or corn that was likely to be exported. In a Swiss canton, or in some of the little states in Italy, it may, perhaps, sometimes be necessary to restrain the exportation of corn. In such great countries as France or England, it scarce ever can. To hinder, besides, the farmer from sending his goods at all times to the best market, is evidently to sacrifice the ordinary laws of justice to an idea of public utility, to a sort of reasons of state; an act or legislative authority which ought to be exercised only, which can be pardoned only, in cases of the most urgent necessity. The price at which exportation of corn is prohibited, if it is ever to be prohibited, ought always to be a very high price.

The laws concerning corn may everywhere be compared to the laws concerning religion. The people feel themselves so much interested in what relates either to their subsistence in this life, or to their happiness in a life to come, that government must yield to their prejudices, and, in order to preserve the public tranquillity, establish that system which they approve of. It is upon this account, perhaps, that we so seldom find a reasonable system established with regard to either of those two capital objects.

IV. The trade of the merchant-carrier, or of the importer of foreign corn, in order to export it again, contributes to the plentiful supply of the home market. It is not, indeed, the direct purpose of his trade to sell his corn there; but he will generally be willing to do so, and even for a good deal less money than he might expect in a foreign market; because he saves in this manner the expense of loading and unloading, of freight and insurance. The inhabitants of the country which, by means of the carrying trade, becomes the magazine and storehouse for the supply of other countries, can very seldom be in want themselves. Though the carrying trade must thus contribute to reduce the average money price of corn in the home market, it would not thereby lower its real value; it would only raise somewhat the real value of silver.

The carrying trade was in effect prohibited in Great Britain, upon all ordinary occasions, by the high duties upon the importation of foreign corn, of the greater part of which there was no drawback; and upon extraordinary occasions, when a scarcity made it necessary to suspend those duties by temporary statutes, exportation was always prohibited. By this system of laws, therefore, the carrying trade was in effect prohibited.

That system of laws, therefore, which is connected with the establishment of the bounty, seems to deserve no part of the praise which has been bestowed upon it. The improvement and prosperity of Great Britain, which has been so often ascribed to those laws, may very easily be accounted for by other causes. That security which the laws in Great Britain give to every man, that he shall enjoy the fruits of his own labour, is alone sufficient to make any country flourish, notwithstanding these and twenty other absurd regulations of commerce; and this security was perfected by the Revolution, much about the same time that the bounty was established. The natural effort of every individual to better his own condition, when suffered to exert itself with freedom and security, is so powerful a principle, that it is alone, and without any assistance, not only capable of carrying on the society to wealth and prosperity, but of surmounting a hundred impertinent obstructions, with which the folly of human laws too often encumbers its operations: though the effect of those obstructions is always, more or less, either to encroach upon its freedom, or to diminish its security. In Great Britain industry is perfectly secure; and though it is far from being perfectly free, it is as free or freer than in any other part of Europe.

Though the period of the greatest prosperity and improvement of Great Britain has been posterior to that system of laws which is connected with the bounty, we must not upon that account, impute it to those laws. It has been posterior likewise to the national debt; but the national debt has most assuredly not been the cause of it.

Though the system of laws which is connected with the bounty, has exactly the same tendency with the practice of Spain and Portugal, to lower somewhat the value of the precious metals in the country where it takes place; yet Great Britain is certainly one of the richest countries in Europe, while Spain and Portugal are perhaps amongst the most beggarly. This difference of situation, however, may easily be accounted for from two different causes. First, the tax in Spain, the prohibition in Portugal of exporting gold and silver, and the vigilant police which watches over the execution of those laws, must, in two very poor countries, which between them import annually upwards of six millions sterling, operate not only more directly, but much more forcibly, in reducing the value of those metals there, than the corn laws can do in Great Britain. And, secondly, this bad policy is not in those countries counterbalanced by the general liberty and security of the people. Industry is there neither free nor secure; and the civil and ecclesiastical governments of both Spain and Portugal are such as would alone be sufficient to perpetuate their present state of poverty, even though their regulations of commerce were as wise as the greatest part of them are absurd and foolish.

The 13th of the present king, c. 43, seems to have established a new system with regard to the corn laws, in many respects better than the ancient one, but in one or two respects perhaps not quite so good.

By this statute, the high duties upon importation for home consumption are taken off, so soon as the price of middling wheat rises to 48s. the quarter; that of middling rye, pease, or beans, to 32s.; that of barley to 24s.; and that of oats to 16s.; and instead of them, a small duty is imposed of only 6d upon the quarter of wheat, and upon that or other grain in proportion. With regard to all those different sorts of grain, but particularly with regard to wheat, the home market is thus opened to foreign supplies, at prices considerably lower than before.

By the same statute, the old bounty of 5s. upon the exportation of wheat, ceases so soon as the price rises to 44s. the quarter, instead of 48s. the price at which it ceased before; that of 2s:6d. upon the exportation of barley, ceases so soon as the price rises to 22s. instead of 24s. the price at which it ceased before; that of 2s:6d. upon the exportation of oatmeal, ceases so soon as the price rises to 14s. instead of 15s. the price at which it ceased before. The bounty upon rye is reduced from 3s:6d. to 3s. and it ceases so soon as the price rises to 28s. instead of 32s. the price at which it ceased before. If bounties are as improper as I have endeavoured to prove them to be, the sooner they cease, and the lower they are, so much the better.

The same statute permits, at the lowest prices, the importation of corn in order to be exported again, duty free, provided it is in the mean time lodged in a warehouse under the joint locks of the king and the importer. This liberty, indeed, extends to no more than twenty-five of the different ports of Great Britain. They are, however, the principal ones; and there may not, perhaps, be warehouses proper for this purpose in the greater part of the others.

So far this law seems evidently an improvement upon the ancient system.

But by the same law, a bounty of 2s. the quarter is given for the exportation of oats, whenever the price does not exceed fourteen shillings. No bounty had ever been given before for the exportation of this grain, no more than for that of pease or beans.

By the same law, too, the exportation of wheat is prohibited so soon as the price rises to forty-four shillings the quarter; that of rye so soon as it rises to twenty-eight shillings; that of barley so soon as it rises to twenty-two shillings; and that of oats so soon as they rise to fourteen shillings. Those several prices seem all of them a good deal too low; and there seems to be an impropriety, besides, in prohibiting exportation altogether at those precise prices at which that bounty, which was given in order to force it, is withdrawn. The bounty ought certainly either to have been withdrawn at a much lower price, or exportation ought to have been allowed at a much higher.

So far, therefore, this law seems to be inferior to the ancient system. With all its imperfections, however, we may perhaps say of it what was said of the laws of Solon, that though not the best in itself, it is the best which the interest, prejudices, and temper of the times, would admit of. It may perhaps in due time prepare the way for a better.

CHAPTER VI

OF TREATIES OF COMMERCE

When a nation binds itself by treaty, either to permit the entry of certain goods from one foreign country which it prohibits from all others, or to exempt the goods of one country from duties to which it subjects those of all others, the country, or at least the merchants and manufacturers of the country, whose commerce is so favoured, must necessarily derive great advantage from the treaty. Those merchants and manufacturers enjoy a sort of monopoly in the country which is so indulgent to them. That country becomes a market, both more extensive and more advantageous for their goods: more extensive, because the goods of other nations being either excluded or subjected to heavier duties, it takes off a greater quantity of theirs; more advantageous, because the merchants of the favoured country, enjoying a sort of monopoly there, will often sell their goods for a better price than if exposed to the free competition of all other nations.

Such treaties, however, though they may be advantageous to the merchants and manufacturers of the favoured, are necessarily disadvantageous to those of the favouring country. A monopoly is thus granted against them to a foreign nation; and they must frequently buy the foreign goods they have occasion for, dearer than if the free competition of other nations was admitted. That part of its own produce with which such a nation purchases foreign goods, must consequently be sold cheaper; because, when two things are exchanged for one another, the cheapness of the one is a necessary consequence, or rather is the same thing, with the dearness of the other. The exchangeable value of its annual produce, therefore, is likely to be diminished by every such treaty. This diminution, however, can scarce amount to any positive loss, but only to a lessening of the gain which it might otherwise make. Though it sells its goods cheaper than it otherwise might do, it will not probably sell them for less than they cost; nor, as in the case of bounties, for a price which will not replace the capital employed in bringing them to market, together with the ordinary profits of stock. The trade could not go on long if it did. Even the favouring country, therefore, may still gain by the trade, though less than if there was a free competition.

Some treaties of commerce, however, have been supposed advantageous, upon principles very different from these; and a commercial country has sometimes granted a monopoly of this kind, against itself, to certain goods of a foreign nation, because it expected, that in the whole commerce between them, it would annually sell more than it would buy, and that a balance in gold and silver would be annually returned to it. It is upon this principle that the treaty of commerce between England and Portugal, concluded in 1703 by Mr Methuen, has been so much commended. The following is a literal translation of that treaty, which consists of three articles only.

ART. I. His sacred royal majesty of Portugal promises, both in his own name and that of his successors, to admit for ever hereafter, into Portugal, the woollen cloths, and the rest of the woollen manufactures of the British, as was accustomed, till they were prohibited by the law; nevertheless upon this condition:

ART. II. That is to say, that her sacred royal majesty of Great Britain shall, in her own name, and that of her successors, be obliged, for ever hereafter, to admit the wines of the growth of Portugal into Britain; so that at no time, whether there shall be peace or war between the kingdoms of Britain and France, any thing more shall be demanded for these wines by the name of custom or duty, or by whatsoever other title, directly or indirectly, whether they shall be imported into Great Britain in pipes or hogsheads, or other casks, than what shall be demanded for the like quantity or measure of French wine, deducting or abating a third part of the custom or duty. But if, at any time, this deduction or abatement of customs, which is to be made as aforesaid, shall in any manner be attempted and prejudiced, it shall be just and lawful for his sacred royal majesty of Portugal, again to prohibit the woollen cloths, and the rest of the British woollen manufactures.

ART. III. The most excellent lords the plenipotentiaries promise and take upon themselves, that their above named masters shall ratify this treaty; and within the space of two months the ratification shall be exchanged.

By this treaty, the crown of Portugal becomes bound to admit the English woollens upon the same footing as before the prohibition; that is, not to raise the duties which had been paid before that time. But it does not become bound to admit them upon any better terms than those of any other nation, of France or Holland, for example. The crown of Great Britain, on the contrary, becomes bound to admit the wines of Portugal, upon paying only two-thirds of the duty which is paid for those of France, the wines most likely to come into competition with them. So far this treaty, therefore, is evidently advantageous to Portugal, and disadvantageous to Great Britain.

It has been celebrated, however, as a masterpiece of the commercial policy of England. Portugal receives annually from the Brazils a greater quantity of gold than can be employed in its domestic commerce, whether in the shape of coin or of plate. The surplus is too valuable to be allowed to lie idle and locked up in coffers; and as it can find no advantageous market at home, it must, notwithstanding; any prohibition, be sent abroad, and exchanged for something for which there is a more advantageous market at home. A large share of it comes annually to England, in return either for English goods, or for those of other European nations that receive their returns through England. Mr Barretti was informed, that the weekly packet-boat from Lisbon brings, one week with another, more than £50,000 in gold to England. The sum had probably been exaggerated. It would amount to more than £2,600,000 a year, which is more than the Brazils are supposed to afford.

Our merchants were, some years ago, out of humour with the crown of Portugal. Some privileges which had been granted them, not by treaty, but by the free grace of that crown, at the solicitation, indeed, it is probable, and in return for much greater favours, defence and protection from the crown of Great Britain, had been either infringed or revoked. The people, therefore, usually most interested in celebrating the Portugal trade, were then rather disposed to represent it as less advantageous than it had commonly been imagined. The far greater part, almost the whole, they pretended, of this annual importation of gold, was not on account of Great Britain, but of other European nations; the fruits and wines of Portugal annually imported into Great Britain nearly compensating the value of the British goods sent thither.

Let us suppose, however, that the whole was on account of Great Britain, and that it amounted to a still greater sum than Mr Barretti seems to imagine; this trade would not, upon that account, be more advantageous than any other, in which, for the same value sent out, we received an equal value of consumable goods in return.

It is but a very small part of this importation which, it can be supposed, is employed as an annual addition, either to the plate or to the coin of the kingdom. The rest must all be sent abroad, and exchanged for consumable goods of some kind or other. But if those consumable goods were purchased directly with the produce of English industry, it would be more for the advantage of England, than first to purchase with that produce the gold of Portugal, and afterwards to purchase with that gold those consumable goods. A direct foreign trade of consumption is always more advantageous than a round-about one; and to bring the same value of foreign goods to the home market requires a much smaller capital in the one way than in the ether. If a smaller share of its industry, therefore, had been employed in producing goods fit for the Portugal market, and a greater in producing those lit for the other markets, where those consumable goods for which there is a demand in Great Britain are to be had, it would have been more for the advantage of England. To procure both the gold which it wants for its own use, and the consumable goods, would, in this way, employ a much smaller capital than at present. There would be a spare capital, therefore, to be employed for other purposes, in exciting an additional quantity of industry, and in raising a greater annual produce.

Though Britain were entirely excluded from the Portugal trade, it could find very little difficulty in procuring all the annual supplies of gold which it wants, either for the purposes of plate, or of coin, or of foreign trade. Gold, like every other commodity, is always somewhere or another to be got for its value by those who have that value to give for it. The annual surplus of gold in Portugal, besides, would still be sent abroad, and though not carried away by Great Britain, would be carried away by some other nation, which would be glad to sell it again for its price, in the same manner as Great Britain does at present. In buying gold of Portugal, indeed, we buy it at the first hand; whereas, in buying it of any other nation, except Spain, we should buy it at the second, and might pay somewhat dearer. This difference, however, would surely be too insignificant to deserve the public attention.

Almost all our gold, it is said, comes from Portugal. With other nations, the balance of trade is either against as, or not much in our favour. But we should remember, that the more gold we import from one country, the less we must necessarily import from all others. The effectual demand for gold, like that for every other commodity, is in every country limited to a certain quantity. If nine-tenths of this quantity are imported from one country, there remains a tenth only to be imported from all others. The more gold, besides, that is annually imported from some particular countries, over and above what is requisite for plate and for coin, the more must necessarily be exported to some others: and the more that most insignificant object of modern policy, the balance of trade, appears to be in our favour with some particular countries, the more it must necessarily appear to be against us with many others.

It was upon this silly notion, however, that England could not subsist without the Portugal trade, that, towards the end of the late war, France and Spain, without pretending either offence or provocation, required the king of Portugal to exclude all British ships from his ports, and, for the security of this exclusion, to receive into them French or Spanish garrisons. Had the king of Portugal submitted to those ignominious terms which his brother-in-law the king of Spain proposed to him, Britain would have been freed from a much greater inconveniency than the loss of the Portugal trade, the burden of supporting a very weak ally, so unprovided of every thing for his own defence, that the whole power of England, had it been directed to that single purpose, could scarce, perhaps, have defended him for another campaign. The loss of the Portugal trade would, no doubt, have occasioned a considerable embarrassment to the merchants at that time engaged in it, who might not, perhaps, have found out, for a year or two, any other equally advantageous method of employing their capitals; and in this would probably have consisted all the inconveniency which England could have suffered from this notable piece of commercial policy.

The great annual importation of gold and silver is neither for the purpose of plate nor of coin, but of foreign trade. A round-about foreign trade of consumption can be carried on more advantageously by means of these metals than of almost any other goods. As they are the universal instruments of commerce, they are more readily received in return for all commodities than any other goods; and, on account of their small bulk and great value, it costs less to transport them backward and forward from one place to another than almost any other sort of merchandize, and they lose less of their value by being so transported. Of all the commodities, therefore, which are bought in one foreign country, for no other purpose but to be sold or exchanged again for some other goods in another, there are none so convenient as gold and silver. In facilitating all the different round-about foreign trades of consumption which are carried on in Great Britain, consists the principal advantage of the Portugal trade; and though it is not a capital advantage, it is, no doubt, a considerable one.

That any annual addition which, it can reasonably be supposed, is made either to the plate or to the coin of the kingdom, could require but a very small annual importation of gold and silver, seems evident enough; and though we had no direct trade with Portugal, this small quantity could always, somewhere or another, be very easily got.

Though the goldsmiths trade be very considerable in Great Britain, the far greater part of the new plate which they annually sell, is made from other old plate melted down; so that the addition annually made to the whole plate of the kingdom cannot be very great, and could require but a very small annual importation.

It is the same case with the coin. Nobody imagines, I believe, that even the greater part of the annual coinage, amounting, for ten years together, before the late reformation of the gold coin, to upwards of £800,000 a-year in gold, was an annual addition to the money before current in the kingdom. In a country where the expense of the coinage is defrayed by the government, the value of the coin, even when it contains its full standard weight of gold and silver, can never be much greater than that of an equal quantity of those metals uncoined, because it requires only the trouble of going to the mint, and the delay, perhaps, of a few weeks, to procure for any quantity of uncoined gold and silver an equal quantity of those metals in coin; but in every country the greater part of the current coin is almost always more or less worn, or otherwise degenerated from its standard. In Great Britain it was, before the late reformation, a good deal so, the gold being more than two per cent., and the silver more than eight per cent. below its standard weight. But if forty-four guineas and a-half, containing their full standard weight, a pound weight of gold, could purchase very little more than a pound weight of uncoined gold; forty-four guineas and a-half, wanting a part of their weight, could not purchase a pound weight, and something was to be added, in order to make up the deficiency. The current price of gold bullion at market, therefore, instead of being the same with the mint price, or £46:14:6, was then about £47:14s., and sometimes about £48. When the greater part of the coin, however, was in this degenerate condition, forty four guineas and a-half, fresh from the mint, would purchase no more goods in the market than any other ordinary guineas; because, when they came into the coffers of the merchant, being confounded with other money, they could not afterwards be distinguished without more trouble than the difference was worth. Like other guineas, they were worth no more than £46:14:6. If thrown into the melting pot, however, they produced, without any sensible loss, a pound weight of standard gold, which could be sold at any time for between £47:14s. and £48, either in gold or silver, as fit for all the purposes of coin as that which had been melted down. There was an evident profit, therefore, in melting down new-coined money; and it was done so instantaneously, that no precaution of government could prevent it. The operations of the mint were, upon this account, somewhat like the web of Penelope; the work that was done in the day was undone in the night. The mint was employed, not so much in making daily additions to the coin, as in replacing the very best part of it, which was daily melted down.

Were the private people who carry their gold and silver to the mint to pay themselves for the coinage, it would add to the value of those metals, in the same manner as the fashion does to that of plate. Coined gold and silver would be more valuable than uncoined. The seignorage, if it was not exorbitant, would add to the bullion the whole value of the duty; because, the government having everywhere the exclusive privilege of coining, no coin can come to market cheaper than they think proper to afford it. If the duty was exorbitant, indeed, that is, if it was very much above the real value of the labour and expense requisite for coinage, false coiners, both at home and abroad, might be encouraged, by the great difference between the value of bullion and that of coin, to pour in so great a quantity of counterfeit money as might reduce the value of the government money. In France, however, though the seignorage is eight per cent., no sensible inconveniency of this kind is found to arise from it. The dangers to which a false coiner is everywhere exposed, if he lives in the country of which he counterfeits the coin, and to which his agents or correspondents are exposed, if he lives in a foreign country, are by far too great to be incurred for the sake of a profit of six or seven per cent.

The seignorage in France raises the value of the coin higher than in proportion to the quantity of pure gold which it contains. Thus, by the edict of January 1726, the mint price of fine gold of twenty-four carats was fixed at seven hundred and forty livres nine sous and one denier one-eleventh the mark of eight Paris ounces. {See Dictionnaire des Monnoies, tom. ii. article Seigncurage, p. 439, par 81. Abbot de

Bazinghen, Conseiller-Commissaire en la Cour des Monnoies à Paris.} The gold coin of France, making an allowance for the remedy of the mint, contains twenty-one carats and three-fourths of fine gold, and two carats one-fourth of alloy. The mark of standard gold, therefore, is worth no more than about six hundred and seventy-one livres ten deniers. But in France this mark of standard gold is coined into thirty louis d'ors of twenty-four livres each, or into seven hundred and twenty livres. The coinage, therefore, increases the value of a mark of standard gold bullion, by the difference between six hundred and seventy-one livres ten deniers and seven hundred and twenty livres, or by forty-eight livres nineteen sous and two deniers.

A seignorage will, in many cases, take away altogether, and will in all cases diminish, the profit of melting down the new coin. This profit always arises from the difference between the quantity of bullion which the common currency ought to contain and that which it actually does contain. If this difference is less than the seignorage, there will be loss instead of profit. If it is equal to the seignorage, there will be neither profit nor loss. If it is greater than the seignorage, there will, indeed, be some profit, but less than if there was no seignorage. If, before the late reformation of the gold coin, for example, there had been a seignorage of five per cent. upon the coinage, there would have been a loss of three per cent. upon the melting down of the gold coin. If the seignorage had been two per cent., there would have been neither profit nor loss. If the seignorage had been one per cent., there would have been a profit but of one per cent. only, instead of two per cent. Wherever money is received by tale, therefore, and not by weight, a seignorage is the most effectual preventive of the melting down of the coin, and, for the same reason, of its exportation. It is the best and heaviest pieces that are commonly either melted down or exported, because it is upon such that the largest profits are made.

The law for the encouragement of the coinage, by rendering it duty-free, was first enacted during the reign of Charles II. for a limited time, and afterwards continued, by different prolongations, till 1769, when it was rendered perpetual. The bank of England, in order to replenish their coffers with money, are frequently obliged to carry bullion to the mint; and it was more for their interest, they probably imagined, that the coinage should be at the expense of the government than at their own. It was probably out of complaisance to this great company, that the government agreed to render this law perpetual. Should the custom of weighing gold, however, come to be disused, as it is very likely to be on account of its inconveniency; should the gold coin of England come to be received by tale, as it was before the late recoinage this great company may, perhaps, find that they have, upon this, as upon some other occasions, mistaken their own interest not a little.

Before the late recoinage, when the gold currency of England was two per cent. below its standard weight, as there was no seignorage, it was two per cent. below the value of that quantity of standard gold bullion which it ought to have contained. When this great company, therefore, bought gold bullion in order to have it coined, they were obliged to pay for it two per cent. more than it was worth after the coinage. But if there had been a seignorage of two per cent. upon the coinage, the common gold currency, though two per cent. below its standard weight, would, notwithstanding, have been equal in value to the quantity of standard gold which it ought to have contained; the value of the fashion compensating in this case the diminution of the weight. They would, indeed, have had the seignorage to pay, which being two per cent., their loss upon the whole transaction would have been two per cent., exactly the same, but no greater than it actually was.

If the seignorage had been five per cent. and the gold currency only two per cent. below its standard weight, the bank would, in this case, have gained three per cent. upon the price of the bullion; but as they would have had a seignorage of five per cent. to pay upon the coinage, their loss upon the whole transaction would, in the same manner, have been exactly two per cent.

If the seignorage had been only one per cent., and the gold currency two per cent. below its standard weight, the bank would, in this case, have lost only one per cent. upon the price of the bullion; but as they would likewise have had a seignorage of one per cent. to pay, their loss upon the whole transaction would have been exactly two per cent., in the same manner as in all other cases.

If there was a reasonable seignorage, while at the same time the coin contained its full standard weight, as it has done very nearly since the late recoinage, whatever the bank might lose by the seignorage, they would gain upon the price of the bullion; and whatever they might gain upon the price of the bullion, they would lose by the seignorage. They would neither lose nor gain, therefore, upon the whole transaction, and they would in this, as in all the foregoing cases, be exactly in the same situation as if there was no seignorage.

When the tax upon a commodity is so moderate as not to encourage smuggling, the merchant who deals in it, though he advances, does not properly pay the tax, as he gets it back in the price of the commodity. The tax is finally paid by the last purchaser or consumer. But money is a commodity, with regard to which every man is a merchant. Nobody buys it but in order to sell it again; and with regard to it there is, in ordinary cases, no last purchaser or consumer. When the tax upon coinage, therefore, is so moderate as not to encourage false coining, though every body advances the tax, nobody finally pays it; because every body gets it back in the advanced value of the coin.

A moderate seignorage, therefore, would not, in any case, augment the expense of the bank, or of any other private persons who carry their bullion to the mint in order to be coined; and the want of a moderate seignorage does not in any case diminish it. Whether there is or is not a seignorage, if the currency contains its full standard weight, the coinage costs nothing to anybody; and if it is short of that weight, the coinage must always cost the difference between the quantity of bullion which ought to be contained in it, and that which actually is contained in it.

The government, therefore, when it defrays the expense of coinage, not only incurs some small expense, but loses some small revenue which it might get by a proper duty; and neither the bank, nor any other private persons, are in the smallest degree benefited by this useless piece of public generosity.

The directors of the bank, however, would probably be unwilling to agree to the imposition of a seignorage upon the authority of a speculation which promises them no gain, but only pretends to insure them from any loss. In the present state of the gold coin, and as long as it continues to be received by weight, they certainly would gain nothing by such a change. But if the custom of weighing the gold coin should ever go into disuse, as it is very likely to do, and if the gold coin should ever fall into the same state of degradation in which it was before the late recoinage, the gain, or more properly the savings, of the bank, in consequence of the imposition of a seignorage, would probably be very considerable. The bank of England is the only company which sends any considerable quantity of bullion to the mint, and the burden of the annual coinage falls entirely, or almost entirely, upon it. If this annual coinage had nothing to do but to repair the unavoidable losses and necessary wear and tear of the coin, it could seldom exceed fifty thousand, or at most a hundred thousand pounds. But when the coin is degraded below its standard weight, the annual coinage must, besides this, fill up the large vacuities which exportation and the melting pot are continually making in the current coin. It was upon this account, that during the ten or twelve years immediately preceding the late reformation of the gold coin, the annual coinage amounted, at an average, to more than £850,000. But if there had been a seignorage of four or five per cent. upon the gold coin, it would probably, even in the state in which things then were, have put an effectual stop to the business both of exportation and of the melting pot. The bank, instead of losing every year about two and a half per cent. upon the bullion which was to be coined into more than eight hundred and fifty thousand pounds, or incurring an annual loss of more than £21,250 pounds, would not probably have incurred the tenth part of that loss.

The revenue allotted by parliament for defraying the expense of the coinage is but fourteen thousand pounds a-year; and the real expense which it costs the government, or the fees of the officers of the mint, do not, upon ordinary occasions, I am assured, exceed the half of that sum. The saving of so very small a sum, or even the gaining of another, which could not well be much larger, are objects too inconsiderable, it may be thought, to deserve the serious attention of government. But the saving of eighteen or twenty thousand pounds a-year, in case of an event which is not improbable, which has frequently happened before, and which is very likely to happen again, is surely an object which well deserves the serious attention, even of so great a company as the bank of England.

Some of the foregoing reasonings and observations might, perhaps, have been more properly placed in those chapters of the first book which treat of the origin and use of money, and of the difference between the real and the nominal price of commodities. But as the law for the encouragement of coinage derives its origin from those vulgar prejudices which have been introduced by the mercantile system, I judged it more proper to reserve them for this chapter. Nothing could be more agreeable to the spirit of that system than a sort of bounty upon the production of money, the very thing which, it supposes, constitutes the wealth of every nation. It is one of its many admirable expedients for enriching the country.

CHAPTER VII

OF COLONIES

PART I. Of the Motives for Establishing New Colonies

The interest which occasioned the first settlement of the different European colonies in America and the West Indies, was not altogether so plain and distinct as that which directed the establishment of those of ancient Greece and Rome.

All the different states of ancient Greece possessed, each of them, but a very small territory; and when the people in anyone of them multiplied beyond what that territory could easily maintain, a part of them were sent in quest of a new habitation, in some remote and distant part of the world; the warlike neighbours who surrounded them on all sides, rendering it difficult for any of them to enlarge very much its territory at home. The colonies of the Dorians resorted chiefly to Italy and Sicily, which, in the times preceding the foundation of Rome, were inhabited by barbarous and uncivilized nations; those of the Ionians and Aeolians, the two other great tribes of the Greeks, to Asia Minor and the islands of the Aegean sea, of which the inhabitants sewn at that time to have been pretty much in the same state as those of Sicily and Italy. The mother city, though she considered the colony as a child, at all times entitled to great favour and assistance, and owing in return much gratitude and respect, yet considered it as an emancipated child, over whom she pretended to claim no direct authority or jurisdiction. The colony settled its own form of government, enacted its own laws, elected its own magistrates, and made peace or war with its neighbours, as an independent state, which had no occasion to wait for the approbation or consent of the mother city. Nothing can be more plain and distinct than the interest which directed every such establishment.

Rome, like most of the other ancient republics, was originally founded upon an agrarian law, which divided the public territory, in a certain proportion, among the different citizens who composed the state. The course of human affairs, by marriage, by succession, and by alienation, necessarily deranged this original division, and frequently threw the lands which had been allotted for the maintenance of many different families, into the possession of a single person. To remedy this disorder, for such it was supposed to be, a law was made, restricting the quantity of land which any citizen could possess to five hundred jugera; about 350 English acres. This law, however, though we read of its having been executed upon one or two occasions, was either neglected or evaded, and the inequality of fortunes went on continually increasing. The greater part of the citizens had no land; and without it the manners and customs of those times rendered it difficult for a freeman to maintain his independency. In the present times, though a poor man has no land of his own, if he has a little stock, he may either farm the lands of another, or he may carry on some little retail trade; and if he has no stock, he may find employment either as a country labourer, or as an artificer. But among the ancient Romans, the lands of the rich were all cultivated by slaves, who wrought under an overseer, who was likewise a slave; so that a poor freeman had little chance of being employed either as a farmer or as a labourer. All trades and manufactures, too, even the retail trade, were carried on by the slaves of the rich for the benefit of their masters, whose wealth, authority, and protection, made it difficult for a poor freeman to maintain the competition against them. The citizens, therefore, who had no land, had scarce any other means of subsistence but the bounties of the candidates at the annual elections. The tribunes, when they had a mind to animate the people against the rich and the great, put them in mind of the ancient divisions of lands, and represented that law which restricted this sort of private property as the fundamental law of the republic. The people became clamorous to get land, and the rich and the great, we may believe, were perfectly determined not to give them any part of theirs. To satisfy them in some measure, therefore, they frequently proposed to send out a new colony. But conquering Rome was, even upon such occasions, under no necessity of turning out her citizens to seek their fortune, if one may so, through the wide world, without knowing where they were to settle. She assigned them lands generally in the conquered provinces of Italy, where, being within the dominions of the republic, they could never form any independent state, but were at best but a sort of corporation, which, though it had the power of enacting bye-laws for its own government, was at all times subject to the correction, jurisdiction, and legislative authority of the mother city. The sending out a colony of this kind not only gave some satisfaction to the people, but often established a sort of garrison, too, in a newly conquered province, of which the obedience might otherwise have been doubtful. A Roman colony, therefore, whether we consider the nature of the establishment itself, or the motives for making it, was altogether different from a Greek one. The words, accordingly, which in the original languages denote those different establishments, have very different meanings. The Latin word (colonia) signifies simply a plantation. The Greek word (apoixia), on the contrary, signifies a separation of dwelling, a departure from home, a going out of the house. But though the Roman colonies were, in many respects, different from the Greek ones, the interest which prompted to establish them was equally plain and distinct. Both institutions derived their origin, either from irresistible necessity, or from clear and evident utility.

The establishment of the European colonies in America and the West Indies arose from no necessity; and though the utility which has resulted from them has been very great, it is not altogether so clear and evident. It was not understood at their first establishment, and was not the motive, either of that establishment, or of the discoveries which gave occasion to it; and the nature, extent, and limits of that utility, are not, perhaps, well understood at this day.

The Venetians, during the fourteenth and fifteenth centuries, carried on a very advantageous commerce in spiceries and other East India goods, which they distributed among the other nations of Europe. They purchased them chiefly in Egypt, at that time under the dominion of the Mamelukes, the enemies of the Turks, of whom the Venetians were the enemies; and this union of interest, assisted by the money of Venice, formed such a connexion as gave the Venetians almost a monopoly of the trade.

The great profits of the Venetians tempted the avidity of the Portuguese. They had been endeavouring, during the course of the fifteenth century, to find out by sea a way to the countries from which the Moors brought them ivory and gold dust across the desert. They discovered the Madeiras, the Canaries, the Azores, the Cape de Verd islands, the coast of Guinea, that of Loango, Congo, Angola, and Benguela, and, finally, the Cape of Good Hope. They had long wished to share in the profitable traffic of the Venetians, and this last discovery opened to them a probable prospect of doing so. In 1497, Vasco de Gamo sailed from the port of Lisbon with a fleet of four ships, and, after a navigation of eleven months, arrived upon the coast of Indostan; and thus completed a course of discoveries which had been pursued with great steadiness, and with very little interruption, for near a century together.

Some years before this, while the expectations of Europe were in suspense about the projects of the Portuguese, of which the success appeared yet to be doubtful, a Genoese pilot formed the yet more daring project of sailing to the East Indies by the west. The situation of those countries was at that time very imperfectly known in Europe. The few European travellers who had been there, had magnified the distance, perhaps through simplicity and ignorance; what was really very great, appearing almost infinite to those who could not measure it; or, perhaps, in order to increase somewhat more the marvellous of their own adventures in visiting regions so immensely remote from Europe. The longer the way was by the east, Columbus very justly concluded, the shorter it would be by the west. He proposed, therefore, to take that way, as both the shortest and the surest, and he had the good fortune to convince Isabella of Castile of the probability of his project. He sailed from the port of Palos in August 1492, near five years before the expedition of Vasco de Gamo set out from Portugal; and, after a voyage of between two and three months, discovered first some of the small Bahama or Lucyan islands, and afterwards the great island of St. Domingo.

But the countries which Columbus discovered, either in this or in any of his subsequent voyages, had no resemblance to those which he had gone in quest of. Instead of the wealth, cultivation, and populousness of China and Indostan, he found, in St. Domingo, and in all the other parts of the new world which he ever visited, nothing but a country quite covered with wood, uncultivated, and inhabited only by some tribes of naked and miserable savages. He was not very willing, however, to believe that they were not the same with some of the countries described by Marco Polo, the first European who had visited, or at least had left behind him any description of China or the East Indies; and a very slight resemblance, such as that which he found between the name of Cibao, a mountain in St. Domingo, and that of Cipange, mentioned by Marco Polo, was frequently sufficient to make him return to this favourite prepossession, though contrary to the clearest evidence. In his letters to Ferdinand and Isabella, he called the countries which he had discovered the Indies. He entertained no doubt but that they were the extremity of those which had been described by Marco Polo, and that they were not very distant from the Ganges, or from the countries which had been conquered by Alexander. Even when at last convinced that they were different, he still flattered himself that those rich countries were at no great distance; and in a subsequent voyage, accordingly, went in quest of them along the coast of Terra Firma, and towards the Isthmus of Darien.

In consequence of this mistake of Columbus, the name of the Indies has stuck to those unfortunate countries ever since; and when it was at last clearly discovered that the new were altogether different from the old Indies, the former were called the West, in contradistinction to the latter, which were called the East Indies.

It was of importance to Columbus, however, that the countries which he had discovered, whatever they were, should be represented to the court of Spain as of very great consequence; and, in what constitutes the real riches of every country, the animal and vegetable productions of the soil, there was at that time nothing which could well justify such a representation of them.

The cori, something between a rat and a rabbit, and supposed by Mr Buffon to be the same with the aperea of Brazil, was the largest viviparous quadruped in St. Domingo. This species seems never to have been very numerous; and the dogs and cats of the Spaniards are said to have long ago almost entirely extirpated it, as well as some other tribes of a still smaller size. These, however, together with a pretty large lizard, called the ivana or iguana, constituted the principal part of the animal food which the land afforded.

The vegetable food of the inhabitants, though, from their want of industry, not very abundant, was not altogether so scanty. It consisted in Indian corn, yams, potatoes, bananas, etc., plants which were then altogether unknown in Europe, and which have never since been very much esteemed in it, or supposed to yield a sustenance equal to what is drawn from the common sorts of grain and pulse, which have been cultivated in this part of the world time out of mind.

The cotton plant, indeed, afforded the material of a very important manufacture, and was at that time, to Europeans, undoubtedly the most valuable of all the vegetable productions of those islands. But though, in the end of the fifteenth century, the muslins and other cotton goods of the East Indies were much esteemed in every part of Europe, the cotton manufacture itself was not cultivated in any part of it. Even this production, therefore, could not at that time appear in the eyes of Europeans to be of very great consequence.

Finding nothing, either in the animals or vegetables of the newly discovered countries which could justify a very advantageous representation of them, Columbus turned his view towards their minerals; and in the richness of their productions of this third kingdom, he flattered himself he had found a full compensation for the insignificancy of those of the other two. The little bits of gold with which the inhabitants ornamented their dress, and which, he was informed, they frequently found in the rivulets and torrents which fell from the mountains, were sufficient to satisfy him that those mountains abounded with the richest gold mines. St. Domingo, therefore, was represented as a country abounding with gold, and upon that account (according to the prejudices not only of the present times, but of those times), an inexhaustible source of real wealth to the crown and kingdom of Spain. When Columbus, upon his return from his first voyage, was introduced with a sort of triumphal honours to the sovereigns of Castile and Arragon, the principal productions of the countries which he had discovered were carried in solemn procession before him. The only valuable part of them consisted in some little fillets, bracelets, and other ornaments of gold, and in some bales of cotton. The rest were mere objects of vulgar wonder and curiosity; some reeds of an extraordinary size, some birds of a very beautiful plumage, and some stuffed skins of the huge alligator and manati; all of which were preceded by six or seven of the wretched natives, whose singular colour and appearance added greatly to the novelty of the show.

In consequence of the representations of Columbus, the council of Castile determined to take possession of the countries of which the inhabitants were plainly incapable of defending themselves. The pious purpose of converting them to Christianity sanctified the injustice of the project. But the hope of finding treasures of gold there was the sole motive which prompted to undertake it; and to give this motive the greater weight, it was proposed by Columbus, that the half of all the gold and silver that should be found there, should belong to the crown. This proposal was approved of by the council.

As long as the whole, or the greater part of the gold which the first adventurers imported into Europe was got by so very easy a method as the plundering of the defenceless natives, it was not perhaps very difficult to pay even this heavy tax; but when the natives were once fairly stript of all that they had, which, in St. Domingo, and in all the other countries discovered by Columbus, was done completely in six or eight years, and when, in order to find more, it had become necessary to dig for it in the mines, there was no longer any possibility of paying this tax. The rigorous exaction of it, accordingly, first occasioned, it is said, the total abandoning of the mines of St. Domingo, which have never been wrought since. It was soon reduced, therefore, to a third; then to a fifth; afterwards to a tenth; and at last to a twentieth part of the gross produce of the gold mines. The tax upon silver continued for a long time to be a fifth of the gross produce. It was reduced to a tenth only in the course of the present century. But the first adventurers do not appear to have been much interested about silver. Nothing less precious than gold seemed worthy of their attention.

All the other enterprizes of the Spaniards in the New World, subsequent to those of Columbus, seem to have been prompted by the same motive. It was the sacred thirst of gold that carried Ovieda, Nicuessa, and Vasco Nugnes de Balboa, to the Isthmus of Darien; that carried Cortes to Mexico, Almagro and Pizarro to Chili and Peru. When those adventurers arrived upon any unknown coast, their first inquiry was always if there was any gold to be found there; and according to the information which they received concerning this particular, they determined either to quit the country or to settle in it.

Of all those expensive and uncertain projects, however, which bring bankruptcy upon the greater part of the people who engage in them, there is none, perhaps, more perfectly ruinous than the search after new silver and gold mines. It is, perhaps, the most disadvantageous lottery in the world, or the one in which the gain of those who draw the prizes bears the least proportion to the loss of those who draw the blanks; for though the prizes are few, and the blanks many, the common price of a ticket is the whole fortune of a very rich man. Projects of mining, instead of replacing the capital employed in them, together with the ordinary profits of stock, commonly absorb both capital and profit. They are the projects, therefore, to which, of all others, a prudent lawgiver, who desired to increase the capital of his nation, would least choose to give any extraordinary encouragement, or to turn towards them a greater share of that capital than what would go to them of its own accord. Such, in reality, is the absurd confidence which almost all men have in their own good fortune, that wherever there is the least probability of success, too great a share of it is apt to go to them of its own accord.

But though the judgment of sober reason and experience concerning such projects has always been extremely unfavourable, that of human avidity has commonly been quite otherwise. The same passion which has suggested to so many people the absurd idea of the philosopher's stone, has suggested to others the equally absurd one of immense rich mines of gold and silver. They did not consider that the value of those metals has, in all ages and nations, arisen chiefly from their scarcity, and that their scarcity has arisen from the very small quantities of them which nature has anywhere deposited in one place, from the hard and intractable substances with which she has almost everywhere surrounded those small quantities, and consequently from the labour and expense which are everywhere necessary in order to penetrate, and get at them. They flattered themselves that veins of those metals might in many places be found, as large and as abundant as those which are commonly found of lead, or copper, or tin, or iron. The dream of Sir Waiter Raleigh, concerning the golden city and country of El Dorado, may satisfy us, that even wise men are not always exempt from such strange delusions. More than a hundred years after the death of that great man, the Jesuit Gumila was still convinced of the reality of that wonderful country, and expressed, with great warmth, and, I dare say, with great sincerity, how happy he should be to carry the light of the gospel to a people who could so well reward the pious labours of their missionary.

In the countries first discovered by the Spaniards, no gold and silver mines are at present known which are supposed to be worth the working. The quantities of those metals which the first adventurers are said to have found there, had probably been very much magnified, as well as the fertility of the mines which were wrought immediately after the first discovery. What those adventurers were reported to have found, however, was sufficient to inflame the avidity of all their countrymen. Every Spaniard who sailed to America expected to find an El Dorado. Fortune, too, did upon this what she has done upon very few other occasions. She realized in some measure the extravagant hopes of her votaries; and in the discovery and conquest of Mexico and Peru (of which the one happened about thirty, and the other about forty, years after the first expedition of Columbus), she presented them with something not very unlike that profusion of the precious metals which they sought for.

A project of commerce to the East Indies, therefore, gave occasion to the first discovery of the West. A project of conquest gave occasion to all the establishments of the Spaniards in those newly discovered countries. The motive which excited them to this conquest was a project of gold and silver mines; and a course of accidents which no human wisdom could foresee, rendered this project much more successful than the undertakers had any reasonable grounds for expecting.

The first adventurers of all the other nations of Europe who attempted to make settlements in America, were animated by the like chimerical views; but they were not equally successful. It was more than a hundred years after the first settlement of the Brazils, before any silver, gold, or diamond mines, were discovered there. In the English, French, Dutch, and Danish colonies, none have ever yet been discovered, at least none that are at present supposed to be worth the working. The first English settlers in North America, however, offered a fifth of all the gold and silver which should be found there to the king, as a motive for granting them their patents. In the patents of Sir Waiter Raleigh, to the London and Plymouth companies, to the council of Plymouth, etc. this fifth was accordingly reserved to the crown. To the expectation of finding gold and silver mines, those first settlers, too, joined that of discovering a north-west passage to the East Indies. They have hitherto been disappointed in both.

PART II. Causes of the Prosperity of New Colonies

The colony of a civilized nation which takes possession either of a waste country, or of one so thinly inhabited that the natives easily give place to the new settlers, advances more rapidly to wealth and greatness than any other human society.

The colonies carry out with them a knowledge of agriculture and of other useful arts, superior to what can grow up of its own accord, in the course of many centuries, among savage and barbarous nations. They carry out with them, too, the habit of subordination, some notion of the regular government which takes place in their own country, of the system of laws which support it, and of a regular administration of justice; and they naturally establish something of the same kind in the new settlement. But among savage and barbarous nations, the natural progress of law and government is still slower than the natural progress of arts, after law and government have been so far established as is necessary for their protection. Every colonist gets more land than he can possibly cultivate. He has no rent, and scarce any taxes, to pay. No landlord shares with him in its produce, and, the share of the sovereign is commonly but a trifle. He has every motive to render as great as possible a produce which is thus to be almost entirely his own. But his land is commonly so extensive, that, with all his own industry, and with all the industry of other people whom he can get to employ, he can seldom make it produce the tenth part of what it is capable of producing. He is eager, therefore, to collect labourers from all quarters, and to reward them with the most liberal wages. But those liberal wages, joined to the plenty and cheapness of land, soon make those labourers leave him, in order to become landlords themselves, and to reward with equal liberality other labourers, who soon leave them for the same reason that they left their first master. The liberal reward of labour encourages marriage. The children, during the tender years of infancy, are well fed and properly taken care of; and when they are grown up, the value of their labour greatly overpays their maintenance. When arrived at maturity, the high price of labour, and the low price of land, enable them to establish themselves in the same manner as their fathers did before them.

In other countries, rent and profit eat up wages, and the two superior orders of people oppress the inferior one; but in new colonies, the interest of the two superior orders obliges them to treat the inferior one with more generosity and humanity, at least where that inferior one is not in a state of slavery. Waste lands, of the greatest natural fertility, are to be had for a trifle. The increase of revenue which the proprietor, who is always the undertaker, expects from their improvement, constitutes his profit, which, in these circumstances, is commonly very great; but this great profit cannot be made, without employing the labour of other people in clearing and cultivating the land; and the disproportion between the great extent of the land and the small number of the people, which commonly takes place in new colonies, makes it difficult for him to get this labour. He does not, therefore, dispute about wages, but is willing to employ labour at any price. The high wages of labour encourage population. The cheapness and plenty of good land encourage improvement, and enable the proprietor to pay those high wages. In those wages consists almost the whole price of the land; and though they are high, considered as the wages of labour, they are low, considered as the price of what is so very valuable. What encourages the progress of population and improvement, encourages that of real wealth and greatness.

The progress of many of the ancient Greek colonies towards wealth and greatness seems accordingly to have been very rapid. In the course of a century or two, several of them appear to have rivalled, and even to have surpassed, their mother cities. Syracuse and Agrigentum in Sicily, Tarentum and Locri in Italy, Ephesus and Miletus in Lesser Asia, appear, by all accounts, to have been at least equal to any of the cities of ancient Greece. Though posterior in their establishment, yet all the arts of refinement, philosophy, poetry, and eloquence, seem to have been cultivated as early, and to have been improved as highly in them as in any part of the mother country. The schools of the two oldest Greek philosophers, those of Thales and Pythagoras, were established, it is remarkable, not in ancient Greece, but the one in an Asiatic, the other in an Italian colony. All those colonies had established themselves in countries inhabited by savage and barbarous nations, who easily gave place to the new settlers. They had plenty of good land; and as they were altogether independent of the mother city, they were at liberty to manage their own affairs in the way that they judged was most suitable to their own interest.

The history of the Roman colonies is by no means so brilliant. Some of them, indeed, such as Florence, have, in the course of many ages, and after the fall of the mother city, grown up to be considerable states. But the progress of no one of them seems ever to have been very rapid. They were all established in conquered provinces, which in most cases had been fully inhabited before. The quantity of land assigned to each colonist was seldom very considerable, and, as the colony was not independent, they were not always at liberty to manage their own affairs in the way that they judged was most suitable to their own interest.

In the plenty of good land, the European colonies established in America and the West Indies resemble, and even greatly surpass, those of ancient Greece. In their dependency upon the mother state, they resemble those of ancient Rome; but their great distance from Europe has in all of them alleviated more or less the effects of this dependency. Their situation has placed them less in the view, and less in the power of their mother country. In pursuing their interest their own way, their conduct has upon many occasions been overlooked, either because not known or not understood in Europe; and upon some occasions it has been fairly suffered and submitted to, because their distance rendered it difficult to restrain it. Even the violent and arbitrary government of Spain has, upon many occasions, been obliged to recall or soften the orders which had been given for the government of her colonies, for fear of a general insurrection. The progress of all the European colonies in wealth, population, and improvement, has accordingly been very great.

The crown of Spain, by its share of the gold and silver, derived some revenue from its colonies from the moment of their first establishment. It was a revenue, too, of a nature to excite in human avidity the most extravagant expectation of still greater riches. The Spanish colonies, therefore, from the moment of their first establishment, attracted very much the attention of their mother country; while those of the other European nations were for a long time in a great measure neglected. The former did not, perhaps, thrive the better in consequence of this attention, nor the latter the worse in consequence of this neglect. In proportion to the extent of the country which they in some measure possess, the Spanish colonies are considered as less populous and thriving than those of almost any other European nation. The progress even of the Spanish colonies, however, in population and improvement, has certainly been very rapid and very great. The city of Lima, founded since the conquest, is represented by Ulloa as containing fifty thousand inhabitants near thirty years ago. Quito, which had been but a miserable hamlet of Indians, is represented by the same author as in his time equally populous. Gemel i Carreri, a pretended traveller, it is said, indeed, but who seems everywhere to have written upon extreme good information, represents the city of Mexico as containing a hundred thousand inhabitants; a number which, in spite of all the exaggerations of the Spanish writers, is probably more than five times greater than what it contained in the time of Montezuma. These numbers exceed greatly those of Boston, New York, and Philadelphia, the three greatest cities of the English colonies. Before the conquest of the Spaniards, there were no cattle fit for draught, either in Mexico or Peru. The lama was their only beast of burden, and its strength seems to have been a good deal inferior to that of a common ass. The plough was unknown among them. They were ignorant of the use of iron. They had no coined money, nor any established instrument of commerce of any kind. Their commerce was carried on by barter. A sort of wooden spade was their principal instrument of agriculture. Sharp stones served them for knives and hatchets to cut with; fish bones, and the hard sinews of certain animals, served them with needles to sew with; and these seem to have been their principal instruments of trade. In this state of things, it seems impossible that either of those empires could have been so much improved or so well cultivated as at present, when they are plentifully furnished with all sorts of European cattle, and when the use of iron, of the plough, and of many of the arts of Europe, have been introduced among them. But the populousness of every country must be in proportion to the degree of its improvement and cultivation. In spite of the cruel destruction of the natives which followed the conquest, these two great empires are probably more populous now than they ever were before; and the people are surely very different; for we must acknowledge, I apprehend, that the Spanish creoles are in many respects superior to the ancient Indians.

After the settlements of the Spaniards, that of the Portuguese in Brazil is the oldest of any European nation in America. But as for a long time after the first discovery neither gold nor silver mines were found in it, and as it afforded upon that account little or no revenue to the crown, it was for a long time in a great measure neglected; and during this state of neglect, it grew up to be a great and powerful colony. While Portugal was under the dominion of Spain, Brazil was attacked by the Dutch, who got possession of seven of the fourteen provinces into which it is divided. They expected soon to conquer the other seven, when Portugal recovered its independency by the elevation of the family of Braganza to the throne. The Dutch, then, as enemies to the Spaniards, became friends to the Portuguese, who were likewise the enemies of the Spaniards. They agreed, therefore, to leave that part of Brazil which they had not conquered to the king of Portugal, who agreed to leave that part which they had conquered to them, as a matter not worth disputing about, with such good allies. But the Dutch government soon began to oppress the Portuguese colonists, who, instead of amusing themselves with complaints, took arms against their new masters, and by their own valour and resolution, with the connivance, indeed, but without any avowed assistance from the mother country, drove them out of Brazil. The Dutch, therefore, finding it impossible to keep any part of the country to themselves, were contented that it should be entirely restored to the crown of Portugal. In this colony there are said to be more than six hundred thousand people, either Portuguese or descended from Portuguese, creoles, mulattoes, and a mixed race between Portuguese and Brazilians. No one colony in

America is supposed to contain so great a number of people of European extraction.

Towards the end of the fifteenth, and during the greater part of the sixteenth century, Spain and Portugal were the two great naval powers upon the ocean; for though the commerce of Venice extended to every part of Europe, its fleet had scarce ever sailed beyond the Mediterranean. The Spaniards, in virtue of the first discovery, claimed all America as their own; and though they could not hinder so great a naval power as that of Portugal from settling in Brazil, such was at that time the terror of their name, that the greater part of the other nations of Europe were afraid to establish themselves in any other part of that great continent. The French, who attempted to settle in Florida, were all murdered by the Spaniards. But the declension of the naval power of this latter nation, in consequence of the defeat or miscarriage of what they called their invincible armada, which happened towards the end of the sixteenth century, put it out of their power to obstruct any longer the settlements of the other European nations. In the course of the seventeenth century, therefore, the English, French, Dutch, Danes, and Swedes, all the great nations who had any ports upon the ocean, attempted to make some settlements in the new world.

The Swedes established themselves in New Jersey; and the number of Swedish families still to be found there sufficiently demonstrates, that this colony was very likely to prosper, had it been protected by the mother country. But being neglected by Sweden, it was soon swallowed up by the Dutch colony of New York, which again, in 1674, fell under the dominion of the English.

The small islands of St. Thomas and Santa Cruz, are the only countries in the new world that have ever been possessed by the Danes. These little settlements, too, were under the government of an exclusive company, which had the sole right, both of purchasing the surplus produce of the colonies, and of supplying them with such goods of other countries as they wanted, and which, therefore, both in its purchases and sales, had not only the power of oppressing them, but the greatest temptation to do so. The government of an exclusive company of merchants is, perhaps, the worst of all governments for any country whatever. It was not, however, able to stop altogether the progress of these colonies, though it rendered it more slow and languid. The late king of Denmark dissolved this company, and since that time the prosperity of these colonies has been very great.

The Dutch settlements in the West, as well as those in the East Indies, were originally put under the government of an exclusive company. The progress of some of them, therefore, though it has been considerable in comparison with that of almost any country that has been long peopled and established, has been languid and slow in comparison with that of the greater part of new colonies. The colony of Surinam, though very considerable, is still inferior to the greater part of the sugar colonies of the other European nations. The colony of Nova Belgia, now divided into the two provinces of New York and New Jersey, would probably have soon become considerable too, even though it had remained under the government of the Dutch. The plenty and cheapness of good land are such powerful causes of prosperity, that the very worst government is scarce capable of checking altogether the efficacy of their operation. The great distance, too, from the mother country, would enable the colonists to evade more or less, by smuggling, the monopoly which the company enjoyed against them. At present, the company allows all Dutch ships to trade to Surinam, upon paying two and a-half per cent. upon the value of their cargo for a license; and only reserves to itself exclusively, the direct trade from Africa to America, which consists almost entirely in the slave trade. This relaxation in the exclusive privileges of the company, is probably the principal cause of that degree of prosperity which that colony at present enjoys. Curacoa and Eustatia, the two principal islands belonging to the Dutch, are free ports, open to the ships of all nations; and this freedom, in the midst of better colonies, whose ports are open to those of one nation only, has been the great cause of the prosperity of those two barren islands.

The French colony of Canada was, during the greater part of the last century, and some part of the present, under the government of an exclusive company. Under so unfavourable an administration, its progress was necessarily very slow, in comparison with that of other new colonies; but it became much more rapid when this company was dissolved, after the fall of what is called the Mississippi scheme. When the English got possession of this country, they found in it near double the number of inhabitants which father Charlevoix had assigned to it between twenty and thirty years before. That jesuit had travelled over the whole country, and had no inclination to represent it as less inconsiderable than it really was.

The French colony of St. Domingo was established by pirates and freebooters, who, for a long time, neither required the protection, nor acknowledged the authority of France; and when that race of banditti became so far citizens as to acknowledge this authority, it was for a long time necessary to exercise it with very great gentleness. During this period, the population and improvement of this colony increased very fast. Even the oppression of the exclusive company, to which it was for some time subjected with all the other colonies of France, though it no doubt retarded, had not been able to stop its progress altogether. The course of its prosperity returned as soon as it was relieved from that oppression. It is now the most important of the sugar colonies of the West Indies, and its produce is said to be greater than that of all the English sugar colonies put together. The other sugar colonies of France are in general all very thriving.

But there are no colonies of which the progress has been more rapid than that of the English in North America.

Plenty of good land, and liberty to manage their own affairs their own way, seem to be the two great causes of the prosperity of all new colonies.

In the plenty of good land, the English colonies of North America, though no doubt very abundantly provided, are, however, inferior to those of the Spaniards and Portuguese, and not superior to some of those possessed by the French before the late war. But the political institutions of the English colonies have been more favourable to the improvement and cultivation of this land, than those of the other three nations.

First, The engrossing of uncultivated land, though it has by no means been prevented altogether, has been more restrained in the English colonies than in any other. The colony law, which imposes upon every proprietor the obligation of improving and cultivating, within a limited time, a certain proportion of his lands, and which, in case of failure, declares those neglected lands grantable to any other person; though it has not perhaps been very strictly executed, has, however, had some effect.

Secondly, In Pennsylvania there is no right of primogeniture, and lands, like moveables, are divided equally among all the children of the family. In three of the provinces of New England, the oldest has only a double share, as in the Mosaical law. Though in those provinces, therefore, too great a quantity of land should sometimes be engrossed by a particular individual, it is likely, in the course of a generation or two, to be sufficiently divided again. In the other English colonies, indeed, the right of primogeniture takes place, as in the law of England: But in all the English colonies, the tenure of the lands, which are all held by free soccage, facilitates alienation; and the grantee of an extensive tract of land generally finds it for his interest to alienate, as fast as he can, the greater part of it, reserving only a small quit-rent. In the Spanish and Portuguese colonies, what is called the right of majorazzo takes place in the succession of all those great estates to which any title of honour is annexed. Such estates go all to one person, and are in effect entailed and unalienable. The French colonies, indeed, are subject to the custom of Paris, which, in the inheritance of land, is much more favourable to the younger children than the law of England. But, in the French colonies, if any part of an estate, held by the noble tenure of chivalry and homage, is alienated, it is, for a limited time, subject to the right of redemption, either by the heir of the superior, or by the heir of the family; and all the largest estates of the country are held by such noble tenures, which necessarily embarrass alienation. But, in a new colony, a great uncultivated estate is likely to be much more speedily divided by alienation than by succession. The plenty and cheapness of good land, it has already been observed, are the principal causes of the rapid prosperity of new colonies. The engrossing of land, in effect, destroys this plenty and cheapness. The engrossing of uncultivated land, besides, is the greatest obstruction to its improvement; but the labour that is employed in the improvement and cultivation of land affords the greatest and most valuable produce to the society. The produce of labour, in this case, pays not only its own wages and the profit of the stock which employs it, but the rent of the land too upon which it is employed. The labour of the English colonies, therefore, being more employed in the improvement and cultivation of land, is likely to afford a greater and more valuable produce than that of any of the other three nations, which, by the engrossing of land, is more or less diverted towards other employments.

Thirdly, The labour of the English colonists is not only likely to afford a greater and more valuable produce, but, in consequence of the moderation of their taxes, a greater proportion of this produce belongs to themselves, which they may store up and employ in putting into motion a still greater quantity of labour. The English colonists have never yet contributed any thing towards the defence of the mother country, or towards the support of its civil government. They themselves, on the contrary, have hitherto been defended almost entirely at the expense of the mother country; but the expense of fleets and armies is out of all proportion greater than the necessary expense of civil government. The expense of their own civil government has always been very moderate. It has generally been confined to what was necessary for paying competent salaries to the governor, to the judges, and to some other officers of police, and for maintaining a few of the most useful public works. The expense of the civil establishment of Massachusetts Bay, before the commencement of the present disturbances, used to be but about £18;000 a-year; that of New Hampshire and Rhode Island, £3500 each; that of Connecticut, £4000; that of New York and Pennsylvania, £4500 each; that of New Jersey, £1200; that of Virginia and South Carolina, £8000 each. The civil establishments of Nova Scotia and Georgia are partly supported by an annual grant of parliament; but Nova Scotia pays, besides, about £7000 a-year towards the public expenses of the colony, and Georgia about £2500 a-year. All the different civil establishments in North America, in short, exclusive of those of Maryland and North Carolina, of which no exact account has been got, did not, before the commencement of the present disturbances, cost the inhabitants above £64,700 a-year; an ever memorable example, at how small an expense three millions of people may not only be governed but well governed. The most important part of the expense of government, indeed, that of defence and protection, has constantly fallen upon the mother country. The ceremonial, too, of the civil government in the colonies, upon the reception of a new governor, upon the opening of a new assembly, etc. though sufficiently decent, is not accompanied with any expensive pomp or parade. Their ecclesiastical government is conducted upon a plan equally frugal. Tithes are unknown among them; and their clergy, who are far from being numerous, are maintained either by moderate stipends, or by the voluntary contributions of the people. The power of Spain and Portugal, on the contrary, derives some support from the taxes levied upon their colonies. France, indeed, has never drawn any considerable revenue from its colonies, the taxes which it levies upon them being generally spent among them. But the colony government of all these three nations is conducted upon a much more extensive plan, and is accompanied with a much more expensive ceremonial. The sums spent upon the reception of a new viceroy of Peru, for example, have frequently been enormous. Such ceremonials are not only real taxes paid by the rich colonists upon those particular occasions, but they serve to introduce among them the habit of vanity and expense upon all other occasions. They are not only very grievous occasional taxes, but they contribute to establish perpetual taxes, of the same kind, still more grievous; the ruinous taxes of private luxury and extravagance. In the colonies of all those three nations, too, the ecclesiastical government is extremely oppressive. Tithes take place in all of them, and are levied with the utmost rigour in those of Spain and Portugal. All of them, besides, are oppressed with a numerous race of mendicant friars, whose beggary being not only licensed but consecrated by religion, is a most grievous tax upon the poor people, who are most carefully taught that it is a duty to give, and a very great sin to refuse them their charity. Over and above all this, the clergy are, in all of them, the greatest engrossers of land.

Fourthly, In the disposal of their surplus produce, or of what is over and above their own consumption, the English colonies have been more favoured, and have been allowed a more extensive market, than those of any other European nation. Every European nation has endeavoured, more or less, to monopolize to itself the commerce of its colonies, and, upon that account, has prohibited the ships of foreign nations from trading to them, and has prohibited them from importing European goods from any foreign nation. But the manner in which this monopoly has been exercised in different nations, has been very different.

Some nations have given up the whole commerce of their colonies to an exclusive company, of whom the colonists were obliged to buy all such European goods as they wanted, and to whom they were obliged to sell the whole of their surplus produce. It was the interest of the company, therefore, not only to sell the former as dear, and to buy the latter as cheap as possible, but to buy no more of the latter, even at this low price, than what they could dispose of for a very high price in Europe. It was their interest not only to degrade in all cases the value of the surplus produce of the colony, but in many cases to discourage and keep down the natural increase of its quantity. Of all the expedients that can well be contrived to stunt the natural growth of a new colony, that of an exclusive company is undoubtedly the most effectual. This, however, has been the policy of Holland, though their company, in the course of the present century, has given up in many respects the exertion of their exclusive privilege. This, too, was the policy of Denmark, till the reign of the late king. It has occasionally been the policy of France; and of late, since 1755, after it had been abandoned by all other nations on account of its absurdity, it has become the policy of Portugal, with regard at least to two of the principal provinces of Brazil, Pernambucco, and Marannon.

Other nations, without establishing an exclusive company, have confined the whole commerce of their colonies to a particular port of the mother country, from whence no ship was allowed to sail, but either in a fleet and at a particular season, or, if single, in consequence of a particular license, which in most cases was very well paid for. This policy opened, indeed, the trade of the colonies to all the natives of the mother country, provided they traded from the proper port, at the proper season, and in the proper vessels. But as all the different merchants, who joined their stocks in order to fit out those licensed vessels, would find it for their interest to act in concert, the trade which was carried on in this manner would necessarily be conducted very nearly upon the same principles as that of an exclusive company. The profit of those merchants would be almost equally exorbitant and oppressive. The colonies would be ill supplied, and would be obliged both to buy very dear, and to sell very cheap. This, however, till within these few years, had always been the policy of Spain; and the price of all European goods, accordingly, is said to have been enormous in the Spanish West Indies. At Quito, we are told by Ulloa, a pound of iron sold for about 4s:6d., and a pound of steel for about 6s:9d. sterling. But it is chiefly in order to purchase European goods that the colonies part with their own produce. The more, therefore, they pay for the one, the less they really get for the other, and the dearness of the one is the same thing with the cheapness of the other. The policy of Portugal is, in this respect, the same as the ancient policy of Spain, with regard to all its colonies, except Pernambucco and Marannon; and with regard to these it has lately adopted a still worse.

Other nations leave the trade of their colonies free to all their subjects, who may carry it on from all the different ports of the mother country, and who have occasion for no other license than the common despatches of the custom-house. In this case the number and dispersed situation of the different traders renders it impossible for them to enter into any general combination, and their competition is sufficient to hinder them from making very exorbitant profits. Under so liberal a policy, the colonies are enabled both to sell their own produce, and to buy the goods of Europe at a reasonable price; but since the dissolution of the Plymouth company, when our colonies were but in their infancy, this has always been the policy of England. It has generally, too, been that of France, and has been uniformly so since the dissolution of what in England is commonly called their Mississippi company. The profits of the trade, therefore, which France and England carry on with their colonies, though no doubt somewhat higher than if the competition were free to all other nations, are, however, by no means exorbitant; and the price of European goods, accordingly, is not extravagantly high in the greater past of the colonies of either of those nations.

In the exportation of their own surplus produce, too, it is only with regard to certain commodities that the colonies of Great Britain are confined to the market of the mother country. These commodities having been enumerated in the act of navigation, and in some other subsequent acts, have upon that account been called enumerated commodities. The rest are called non-enumerated, and may be exported directly to other countries, provided it is in British or plantation ships, of which the owners and three fourths of the mariners are British subjects.

Among the non-enumerated commodities are some of the most important productions of America and the West Indies, grain of all sorts, lumber, salt provisions, fish, sugar, and rum.

Grain is naturally the first and principal object of the culture of all new colonies. By allowing them a very extensive market for it, the law encourages them to extend this culture much beyond the consumption of a thinly inhabited country, and thus to provide beforehand an ample subsistence for a continually increasing population.

In a country quite covered with wood, where timber consequently is of little or no value, the expense of clearing the ground is the principal obstacle to improvement. By allowing the colonies a very extensive market for their lumber, the law endeavours to facilitate improvement by raising the price of a commodity which would otherwise be of little value, and thereby enabling them to make some profit of what would otherwise be mere expense.

In a country neither half peopled nor half cultivated, cattle naturally multiply beyond the consumption of the inhabitants, and are often, upon that account, of little or no value. But it is necessary, it has already been shown, that the price of cattle should bear a certain proportion to that of corn, before the greater part of the lands of any country can be improved. By allowing to American cattle, in all shapes, dead and alive, a very extensive market, the law endeavours to raise the value of a commodity, of which the high price is so very essential to improvement. The good effects of this liberty, however, must be somewhat diminished by the 4th of Geo. III. c. 15, which puts hides and skins among the enumerated commodities, and thereby tends to reduce the value of American cattle.

To increase the shipping and naval power of Great Britain by the extension of the fisheries of our colonies, is an object which the legislature seems to have had almost constantly in view. Those fisheries, upon this account, have had all the encouragement which freedom can give them, and they have flourished accordingly. The New England fishery, in particular, was, before the late disturbances, one of the most important, perhaps, in the world. The whale fishery which, notwithstanding an extravagant bounty, is in Great Britain carried on to so little purpose, that in the opinion of many people (which I do not, however, pretend to warrant), the whole produce does not much exceed the value of the bounties which are annually paid for it, is in New England carried on, without any bounty, to a very great extent. Fish is one of the principal articles with which the North Americans trade to Spain, Portugal, and the Mediterranean.

Sugar was originally an enumerated commodity, which could only be exported to Great Britain; but in 1751, upon a representation of the sugar-planters, its exportation was permitted to all parts of the world. The restrictions, however, with which this liberty was granted, joined to the high price of sugar in Great Britain, have rendered it in a great measure ineffectual. Great Britain and her colonies still continue to be almost the sole market for all sugar produced in the British plantations. Their consumption increases so fast, that, though in consequence of the increasing improvement of Jamaica, as well as of the ceded islands, the importation of sugar has increased very greatly within these twenty years, the exportation to foreign countries is said to be not much greater than before.

Rum is a very important article in the trade which the Americans carry on to the coast of Africa, from which they bring back negro slaves in return.

If the whole surplus produce of America, in grain of all sorts, in salt provisions, and in fish, had been put into the enumeration, and thereby forced into the market of Great Britain, it would have interfered too much with the produce of the industry of our own people. It was probably not so much from any regard to the interest of America, as from a jealousy of this interference, that those important commodities have not only been kept out of the enumeration, but that the importation into Great Britain of all grain, except rice, and of all salt provisions, has, in the ordinary state of the law, been prohibited.

The non-enumerated commodities could originally be exported to all parts of the world. Lumber and rice having been once put into the enumeration, when they were afterwards taken out of it, were confined, as to the European market, to the countries that lie south of Cape Finisterre. By the 6th of George III. c. 52, all non-enumerated commodities were subjected to the like restriction. The parts of Europe which lie south of Cape Finisterre are not manufacturing countries, and we are less jealous of the colony ships carrying home from them any manufactures which could interfere with our own.

The enumerated commodities are of two sorts; first, such as are either the peculiar produce of America, or as cannot be produced, or at least are not produced in the mother country. Of this kind are molasses, coffee, cocoa-nuts, tobacco, pimento, ginger, whalefins, raw silk, cotton, wool, beaver, and other peltry of America, indigo, fustick, and other dyeing woods; secondly, such as are not the peculiar produce of America, but which are, and may be produced in the mother country, though not in such quantities as to supply the greater part of her demand, which is principally supplied from foreign countries. Of this kind are all naval stores, masts, yards, and bowsprits, tar, pitch, and turpentine, pig and bar iron, copper ore, hides and skins, pot and pearl ashes. The largest importation of commodities of the first kind could not discourage the growth, or interfere with the sale, of any part of the produce of the mother country. By confining them to the home market, our merchants, it was expected, would not only be enabled to buy them cheaper in the plantations, and consequently to sell them with a better profit at home, but to establish between the plantations and foreign countries an advantageous carrying trade, of which Great Britain was necessarily to be the centre or emporium, as the European country into which those commodities were first to be imported. The importation of commodities of the second kind might be so managed too, it was supposed, as to interfere, not with the sale of those of the same kind which were produced at home, but with that of those which were imported from foreign countries; because, by means of proper duties, they might be rendered always somewhat dearer than the former, and yet a good deal cheaper than the latter. By confining such commodities to the home market, therefore, it was proposed to discourage the produce, not of

Great Britain, but of some foreign countries with which the balance of trade was believed to be unfavourable to Great Britain.

The prohibition of exporting from the colonies to any other country but Great Britain, masts, yards, and bowsprits, tar, pitch, and turpentine, naturally tended to lower the price of timber in the colonies, and consequently to increase the expense of clearing their lands, the principal obstacle to their improvement. But about the beginning of the present century, in 1703, the pitch and tar company of Sweden endeavoured to raise the price of their commodities to Great Britain, by prohibiting their exportation, except in their own ships, at their own price, and in such quantities as they thought proper. In order to counteract this notable piece of mercantile policy, and to render herself as much as possible independent, not only of Sweden, but of all the other northern powers, Great Britain gave a bounty upon the importation of naval stores from America; and the effect of this bounty was to raise the price of timber in America much more than the confinement to the home market could lower it; and as both regulations were enacted at the same time, their joint effect was rather to encourage than to discourage the clearing of land in America.

Though pig and bar iron, too, have been put among the enumerated commodities, yet as, when imported from America, they are exempted from considerable duties to which they are subject when imported front any other country, the one part of the regulation contributes more to encourage the erection of furnaces in America than the other to discourage it. There is no manufacture which occasions so great a consumption of wood as a furnace, or which can contribute so much to the clearing of a country overgrown with it.

The tendency of some of these regulations to raise the value of timber in America, and thereby to facilitate the clearing of the land, was neither, perhaps, intended nor understood by the legislature. Though their beneficial effects, however, have been in this respect accidental, they have not upon that account been less real.

The most perfect freedom of trade is permitted between the British colonies of America and the West Indies, both in the enumerated and in the non-enumerated commodities Those colonies are now become so populous and thriving, that each of them finds in some of the others a great and extensive market for every part of its produce. All of them taken together, they make a great internal market for the produce of one another.

The liberality of England, however, towards the trade of her colonies, has been confined chiefly to what concerns the market for their produce, either in its rude state, or in what may be called the very first stage of manufacture. The more advanced or more refined manufactures, even of the colony produce, the merchants and manufacturers of Great Britain chuse to reserve to themselves, and have prevailed upon the legislature to prevent their establishment in the colonies, sometimes by high duties, and sometimes by absolute prohibitions.

While, for example, Muscovado sugars from the British plantations pay, upon importation, only 6s:4d. the hundred weight, white sugars pay £1:1:1; and refined, either double or single, in loaves, £4:2:5 8/20ths. When those high duties were imposed, Great Britain was the sole, and she still continues to be, the principal market, to which the sugars of the British colonies could be exported. They amounted, therefore, to a prohibition, at first of claying or refining sugar for any foreign market, and at present of claying or refining it for the market which takes off, perhaps, more than nine-tenths of the whole produce. The manufacture of claying or refining sugar, accordingly, though it has flourished in all the sugar colonies of France, has been little cultivated in any of those of England, except for the market of the colonies themselves. While Grenada was in the hands of the French, there was a refinery of sugar, by claying, at least upon almost every plantation. Since it fell into those of the English, almost all works of this kind have been given up; and there are at present (October 1773), I am assured, not above two or three remaining in the island. At present, however, by an indulgence of the custom-house, clayed or refined sugar, if reduced from loaves into powder, is commonly imported as Muscovado.

While Great Britain encourages in America the manufacturing of pig and bar iron, by exempting them from duties to which the like commodities are subject when imported from any other country, she imposes an absolute prohibition upon the erection of steel furnaces and slit-mills in any of her American plantations. She will not suffer her colonies to work in those more refined manufactures, even for their own consumption; but insists upon their purchasing of her merchants and manufacturers all goods of this kind which they have occasion for.

She prohibits the exportation from one province to another by water, and even the carriage by land upon horseback, or in a cart, of hats, of wools, and woollen goods, of the produce of America; a regulation which effectually prevents the establishment of any manufacture of such commodities for distant sale, and confines the industry of her colonists in this way to such coarse and household manufactures as a private family commonly makes for its own use, or for that of some of its neighbours in the same province.

To prohibit a great people, however, from making all that they can of every part of their own produce, or from employing their stock and industry in the way that they judge most advantageous to themselves, is a manifest violation of the most sacred rights of mankind. Unjust, however, as such prohibitions may be, they have not hitherto been very hurtful to the colonies. Land is still so cheap, and, consequently, labour so dear among them, that they can import from the mother country almost all the more refined or more advanced manufactures cheaper than they could make them for themselves. Though they had not, therefore, been prohibited from establishing such manufactures, yet, in their present state of improvement, a regard to their own interest would probably have prevented them from doing so. In their present state of improvement, those prohibitions, perhaps, without cramping their industry, or restraining it from any employment to which it would have gone of its own accord, are only impertinent badges of slavery imposed upon them, without any sufficient reason, by the groundless jealousy of the merchants and manufacturers of the mother country. In a more advanced state, they might be really oppressive and insupportable.

Great Britain, too, as she confines to her own market some of the most important productions of the colonies, so, in compensation, she gives to some of them an advantage in that market, sometimes by imposing higher duties upon the like productions when imported from other countries, and sometimes by giving bounties upon their importation from the colonies. In the first way, she gives an advantage in the home market to the sugar, tobacco, and iron of her own colonies; and, in the second, to their raw silk, to their hemp and flax, to their indigo, to their naval stores, and to their building timber. This second way of encouraging the colony produce, by bounties upon importation, is, so far as I have been able to learn, peculiar to Great Britain: the first is not. Portugal does not content herself with imposing higher duties upon the importation of tobacco from any other country, but prohibits it under the severest penalties.

With regard to the importation of goods from Europe, England has likewise dealt more liberally with her colonies than any other nation.

Great Britain allows a part, almost always the half, generally a larger portion, and sometimes the whole, of the duty which is paid upon the importation of foreign goods, to be drawn back upon their exportation to any foreign country. No independent foreign country, it was easy to foresee, would receive them, if they came to it loaded with the heavy duties to which almost all foreign goods are subjected on their importation into Great Britain. Unless, therefore, some part of those duties was drawn back upon exportation, there was an end of the carrying trade; a trade so much favoured by the mercantile system.

Our colonies, however, are by no means independent foreign countries; and Great Britain having assumed to herself the exclusive right of supplying them with all goods from Europe, might have forced them (in the same manner as other countries have done their colonies) to receive such goods loaded with all the same duties which they paid in the mother country. But, on the contrary, till 1763, the same drawbacks were paid upon the exportation of the greater part of foreign goods to our colonies, as to any independent foreign country. In 1763, indeed, by the 4th of Geo. III. c. 15, this indulgence was a good deal abated, and it was enacted, "That no part of the duty called the old subsidy should be drawn back for any goods of the growth, production, or manufacture of Europe or the East Indies, which should be exported from this kingdom to any British colony or plantation in America; wines, white calicoes, and muslins, excepted." Before this law, many different sorts of foreign goods might have been bought cheaper in the plantations than in the mother country, and some may still.

Of the greater part of the regulations concerning the colony trade, the merchants who carry it on, it must be observed, have been the principal advisers. We must not wonder, therefore, if, in a great part of them, their interest has been more considered than either that of the colonies or that of the mother country. In their exclusive privilege of supplying the colonies with all the goods which they wanted from Europe, and of purchasing all such parts of their surplus produce as could not interfere with any of the trades which they themselves carried on at home, the interest of the colonies was sacrificed to the interest of those merchants. In allowing the same drawbacks upon the re-exportation of the greater part of European and East India goods to the colonies, as upon their re-exportation to any independent country, the interest of the mother country was sacrificed to it, even according to the mercantile ideas of that interest. It was for the interest of the merchants to pay as little as possible for the foreign goods which they sent to the colonies, and, consequently, to get back as much as possible of the duties which they advanced upon their importation into Great Britain. They might thereby be enabled to sell in the colonies, either the same quantity of goods with a greater profit, or a greater quantity with the same profit, and, consequently, to gain something either in the one way or the other. It was likewise for the interest of the colonies to get all such goods as cheap, and in as great abundance as possible. But this might not always be for the interest of the mother country. She might frequently suffer, both in her revenue, by giving back a great part of the duties which had been paid upon the importation of such goods; and in her manufactures, by being undersold in the colony market, in consequence of the easy terms upon which foreign manufactures could be carried thither by means of those drawbacks. The progress of the linen manufacture of Great Britain, it is commonly said, has been a good deal retarded by the drawbacks upon the re-exportation of German linen to the American colonies.

But though the policy of Great Britain, with regard to the trade of her colonies, has been dictated by the same mercantile spirit as that of other nations, it has, however, upon the whole, been less illiberal and oppressive than that of any of them.

In every thing except their foreign trade, the liberty of the English colonists to manage their own affairs their own way, is complete. It is in every respect equal to that of their fellow-citizens at home, and is secured in the same manner, by an assembly of the representatives of the people, who claim the sole right of imposing taxes for the support of the colony government. The authority of this assembly overawes the executive power; and neither the meanest nor the most obnoxious colonist, as long as he obeys the law, has any thing to fear from the resentment, either of the governor, or of any other civil or military officer in the province. The colony assemblies, though, like the house of commons in England, they are not always a very equal representation of the people, yet they approach more nearly to that character; and as the executive power either has not the means to corrupt them, or, on account of the support which it receives from the mother country, is not under the necessity of doing so, they are, perhaps, in general more influenced by the inclinations of their constituents. The councils, which, in the colony legislatures, correspond to the house of lords in Great Britain, are not composed of a hereditary nobility. In some of the colonies, as in three of the governments of New England, those councils are not appointed by the king, but chosen by the representatives of the people. In none of the English colonies is there any hereditary nobility. In all of them, indeed, as in all other free countries, the descendant of an old colony family is more respected than an upstart of equal merit and fortune; but he is only more respected, and he has no privileges by which he can be troublesome to his neighbours. Before the commencement of the present disturbances, the colony assemblies had not only the legislative, but a part of the executive power. In Connecticut and Rhode Island, they elected the governor. In the other colonies, they appointed the revenue officers, who collected the taxes imposed by those respective assemblies, to whom those officers were immediately responsible. There is more equality, therefore, among the English colonists than among the inhabitants of the mother country. Their manners are more re publican; and their governments, those of three of the provinces of New England in particular, have hitherto been more republican too.

The absolute governments of Spain, Portugal, and France, on the contrary, take place in their colonies; and the discretionary powers which such governments commonly delegate to all their inferior officers are, on account of the great distance, naturally exercised there with more than ordinary violence. Under all absolute governments, there is more liberty in the capital than in any other part of the country. The sovereign himself can never have either interest or inclination to pervert the order of justice, or to oppress the great body of the people. In the capital, his presence overawes, more or less, all his inferior officers, who, in the remoter provinces, from whence the complaints of the people are less likely to reach him, can exercise their tyranny with much more safety. But the European colonies in America are more remote than the most distant provinces of the greatest empires which had ever been known before. The government of the English colonies is, perhaps, the only one which, since the world began, could give perfect security to the inhabitants of so very distant a province. The administration of the French colonies, however, has always been conducted with much more gentleness and moderation than that of the Spanish and Portuguese. This superiority of conduct is suitable both to the character of the French nation, and to what forms the character of every nation, the nature of their government, which, though arbitrary and violent in comparison with that of Great Britain, is legal and free in comparison with those of Spain and Portugal.

It is in the progress of the North American colonies, however, that the superiority of the English policy chiefly appears. The progress of the sugar colonies of France has been at least equal, perhaps superior, to that of the greater part of those of England; and yet the sugar colonies of England enjoy a free government, nearly of the same kind with that which takes place in her colonies of North America. But the sugar colonies of France are not discouraged, like those of England, from refining their own sugar; and what is still of greater importance, the genius of their government naturally introduces a better management of their negro slaves.

In all European colonies, the culture of the sugar-cane is carried on by negro slaves. The constitution of those who have been born in the temperate climate of Europe could not, it is supposed, support the labour of digging the ground under the burning sun of the West Indies; and the culture of the sugar-cane, as it is managed at present, is all hand labour; though, in the opinion of many, the drill plough might be introduced into it with great advantage. But, as the profit and success of the cultivation which is carried on by means of cattle, depend very much upon the good management of those cattle; so the profit and success of that which is carried on by slaves must depend equally upon the good management of those slaves; and in the good management of their slaves the French planters, I think it is generally allowed, are superior to the English. The law, so far as it gives some weak protection to the slave against the violence of his master, is likely to be better executed in a colony where the government is in a great measure arbitrary, than in one where it is altogether free. In every country where the unfortunate law of slavery is established, the magistrate, when he protects the slave, intermeddles in some measure in the management of the private property of the master; and, in a free country, where the master is, perhaps, either a member of the colony assembly, or an elector of such a member, he dares not do this but with the greatest caution and circumspection. The respect which he is obliged to pay to the master, renders it more difficult for him to protect the slave. But in a country where the government is in a great measure arbitrary, where it is usual for the magistrate to intermeddle even in the management of the private property of individuals, and to send them, perhaps, a lettre de cachet, if they do not manage it according to his liking, it is much easier for him to give some protection to the slave; and common humanity naturally disposes him to do so. The protection of the magistrate renders the slave less contemptible in the eyes of his master, who is thereby induced to consider him with more regard, and to treat him with more gentleness. Gentle usage renders the slave not only more faithful, but more intelligent, and, therefore, upon a double account, more useful. He approaches more to the condition of a free servant, and may possess some degree of integrity and attachment to his master's interest; virtues which frequently belong to free servants, but which never can belong to a slave, who is treated as slaves commonly are in countries where the master is perfectly free and secure.

That the condition of a slave is better under an arbitrary than under a free government, is, I believe, supported by the history of all ages and nations. In the Roman history, the first time we read of the magistrate interposing to protect the slave from the violence of his master, is under the emperors. When Vidius Pollio, in the presence of Augustus, ordered one of his slaves, who had committed a slight fault, to be cut into pieces and thrown into his fish-pond, in order to feed his fishes, the emperor commanded him, with indignation, to emancipate immediately, not only that slave, but all the others that belonged to him. Under the republic no magistrate could have had authority enough to protect the slave, much less to punish the master.

The stock, it is to be observed, which has improved the sugar colonies of France, particularly the great colony of St Domingo, has been raised almost entirely from the gradual improvement and cultivation of those colonies. It has been almost altogether the produce of the soil and of the industry of the colonists, or, what comes to the same thing, the price of that produce, gradually accumulated by good management, and employed in raising a still greater produce. But the stock which has improved and cultivated the sugar colonies of England, has, a great part of it, been sent out from England, and has by no means been altogether the produce of the soil and industry of the colonists. The prosperity of the English sugar colonies has been in a great measure owing to the great riches of England, of which a part has overflowed, if one may say so, upon these colonies. But the prosperity of the sugar colonies of France has been entirely owing to the good conduct of the colonists, which must therefore have had some superiority over that of the English; and this superiority has been remarked in nothing so much as in the good management of their slaves.

Such have been the general outlines of the policy of the different European nations with regard to their colonies.

The policy of Europe, therefore, has very little to boast of, either in the original establishment, or, so far as concerns their internal government, in the subsequent prosperity of the colonies of America.

Folly and injustice seem to have been the principles which presided over and directed the first project of establishing those colonies; the folly of hunting after gold and silver mines, and the injustice of coveting the possession of a country whose harmless natives, far from having ever injured the people of Europe, had received the first adventurers with every mark of kindness and hospitality.

The adventurers, indeed, who formed some of the latter establishments, joined to the chimerical project of finding gold and silver mines, other motives more reasonable and more laudable; but even these motives do very little honour to the policy of Europe.

The English puritans, restrained at home, fled for freedom to America, and established there the four governments of New England. The English catholics, treated with much greater injustice, established that of Maryland; the quakers, that of Pennsylvania. The Portuguese Jews, persecuted by the inquisition, stript of their fortunes, and banished to Brazil, introduced, by their example, some sort of order and industry among the transported felons and strumpets by whom that colony was originally peopled, and taught them the culture of the sugar-cane. Upon all these different occasions, it was not the wisdom and policy, but the disorder and injustice of the European governments, which peopled and cultivated America.

In effectuation some of the most important of these establishments, the different governments of Europe had as little merit as in projecting them. The conquest of Mexico was the project, not of the council of Spain, but of a governor of Cuba; and it was effectuated by the spirit of the bold adventurer to whom it was entrusted, in spite of every thing which that governor, who soon repented of having trusted such a person, could do to thwart it. The conquerors of Chili and Peru, and of almost all the other Spanish settlements upon the continent of America, carried out with them no other public encouragement, but a general permission to make settlements and conquests in the name of the king of Spain. Those adventures were all at the private risk and expense of the adventurers. The government of Spain contributed scarce any thing to any of them. That of England contributed as little towards effectuating the establishment of some of its most important colonies in North America.

When those establishments were effectuated, and had become so considerable as to attract the attention of the mother country, the first regulations which she made with regard to them, had always in view to secure to herself the monopoly of their commerce; to confine their market, and to enlarge her own at their expense, and, consequently, rather to damp and discourage, than to quicken and forward the course of their prosperity. In the different ways in which this monopoly has been exercised, consists one of the most essential differences in the policy of the different European nations with regard to their colonies. The best of them all, that of England, is only somewhat less illiberal and oppressive than that of any of the rest.

In what way, therefore, has the policy of Europe contributed either to the first establishment, or to the present grandeur of the colonies of America? In one way, and in one way only, it has contributed a good deal. Magna virum mater! It bred and formed the men who were capable of achieving such great actions, and of laying the foundation of so great an empire; and there is no other quarter of the world; of which the policy is capable of forming, or has ever actually, and in fact, formed such men. The colonies owe to the policy of Europe the education and great views of their active and enterprizing founders; and some of the greatest and most important of them, so far as concerns their internal government, owe to it scarce anything else.

PART III. Of the Advantages which Europe has derived From the Discovery of America, and from that of a Passage to the East Indies by the Cape of Good Hope

Such are the advantages which the colonies of America have derived from the policy of Europe.

What are those which Europe has derived from the discovery and colonization of America?

Those advantages may be divided, first, into the general advantages which Europe, considered as one great country, has derived from those great events; and, secondly, into the particular advantages which each colonizing country has derived from the colonies which particularly belong to it, in consequence of the authority or dominion which it exercises over them.

The general advantages which Europe, considered as one great country, has derived from the discovery and colonization of America, consist, first, in the increase of its enjoyments; and, secondly, in the augmentation of its industry.

The surplus produce of America imported into Europe, furnishes the inhabitants of this great continent with a variety of commodities which they could not otherwise have possessed; some for conveniency and use, some for pleasure, and some for ornament; and thereby contributes to increase their enjoyments.

The discovery and colonization of America, it will readily be allowed, have contributed to augment the industry, first, of all the countries which trade to it directly, such as Spain, Portugal, France, and England; and, secondly, of all those which, without trading to it directly, send, through the medium of other countries, goods to it of their own produce, such as Austrian Flanders, and some provinces of Germany, which, through the medium of the countries before mentioned, send to it a considerable quantity of linen and other goods. All such countries have evidently gained a more extensive market for their surplus produce, and must consequently have been encouraged to increase its quantity.

But that those great events should likewise have contributed to encourage the industry of countries such as Hungary and Poland, which may never, perhaps, have sent a single commodity of their own produce to America, is not, perhaps, altogether so evident. That those events have done so, however, cannot be doubted. Some part of the produce of America is consumed in Hungary and Poland, and there is some demand there for the sugar, chocolate, and tobacco, of that new quarter of the world. But those commodities must be purchased with something which is either the produce of the industry of Hungary and Poland, or with something which had been purchased with some part of that produce. Those commodities of America are new values, new equivalents, introduced into Hungary and Poland, to be exchanged there for the surplus produce of these countries. By being carried thither, they create a new and more extensive market for that surplus produce. They raise its value, and thereby contribute to encourage its increase. Though no part of it may ever be carried to America, it may be carried to other countries, which purchase it with a part of their share of the surplus produce of America, and it may find a market by means of the circulation of that trade which was originally put into motion by the surplus produce of America.

Those great events may even have contributed to increase the enjoyments, and to augment the industry, of countries which not only never sent any commodities to America, but never received any from it. Even such countries may have received a greater abundance of other commodities from countries, of which the surplus produce had been augmented by means of the American trade. This greater abundance, as it must necessarily have increased their enjoyments, so it must likewise have augmented their industry. A greater number of new equivalents, of some kind or other, must have been presented to them to be exchanged for the surplus produce of that industry. A more extensive market must have been created for that surplus produce, so as to raise its value, and thereby encourage its increase. The mass of commodities annually thrown into the great circle of European commerce, and by its various revolutions annually distributed among all the different nations comprehended within it, must have been augmented by the whole surplus produce of America. A greater share of this greater mass, therefore, is likely to have fallen to each of those nations, to have increased their enjoyments, and augmented their industry.

The exclusive trade of the mother countries tends to diminish, or at least to keep down below what they would otherwise rise to, both the enjoyments and industry of all those nations in general, and of the American colonies in particular. It is a dead weight upon the action of one of the great springs which puts into motion a great part of the business of mankind. By rendering the colony produce dearer in all other countries, it lessens its consumption, and thereby cramps the industry of the colonies, and both the enjoyments and the industry of all other countries, which both enjoy less when they pay more for what they enjoy, and produce less when they get less for what they produce. By rendering the produce of all other countries dearer in the colonies, it cramps in the same manner the industry of all other colonies, and both the enjoyments and the industry of the colonies. It is a clog which, for the supposed benefit of some particular countries, embarrasses the pleasures and encumbers the industry of all other countries, but of the colonies more than of any other. It not only excludes as much as possible all other countries from one particular market, but it confines as much as possible the colonies to one particular market; and the difference is very great between being excluded from one particular market when all others are open, and being confined to one particular market when all others are shut up. The surplus produce of the colonies, however, is the original source of all that increase of enjoyments and industry which Europe derives from the discovery and colonization of America, and the exclusive trade of the mother countries tends to render this source much less abundant than it otherwise would be.

The particular advantages which each colonizing country derives from the colonies which particularly belong to it, are of two different kinds; first, those common advantages which every empire derives from the provinces subject to its dominion; and, secondly, those peculiar advantages which are supposed to result from provinces of so very peculiar a nature as the European colonies of America.

The common advantages which every empire derives from the provinces subject to its dominion consist, first, in the military force which they furnish for its defence; and, secondly, in the revenue which they furnish for the support of its civil government. The Roman colonies furnished occasionally both the one and the other. The Greek colonies sometimes furnished a military force, but seldom any revenue. They seldom acknowledged themselves subject to the dominion of the mother city. They were generally her allies in war, but very seldom her subjects in peace.

The European colonies of America have never yet furnished any military force for the defence of the mother country. The military force has never yet been sufficient for their own defence; and in the different wars in which the mother countries have been engaged, the defence of their colonies has generally occasioned a very considerable distraction of the military force of those countries. In this respect, therefore, all the European colonies have, without exception, been a cause rather of weakness than of strength to their respective mother countries.

The colonies of Spain and Portugal only have contributed any revenue towards the defence of the mother country, or the support of her civil government. The taxes which have been levied upon those of other European nations, upon those of England in particular, have seldom been equal to the expense laid out upon them in time of peace, and never sufficient to defray that which they occasioned in time of war. Such colonies, therefore, have been a source of expense, and not of revenue, to their respective mother countries.

The advantages of such colonies to their respective mother countries, consist altogether in those peculiar advantages which are supposed to result from provinces of so very peculiar a nature as the European colonies of America; and the exclusive trade, it is acknowledged, is the sole source of all those peculiar advantages.

In consequence of this exclusive trade, all that part of the surplus produce of the English colonies, for example, which consists in what are called enumerated commodities, can be sent to no other country but England. Other countries must afterwards buy it of her. It must be cheaper, therefore, in England than it can be in any other country, and must contribute more to increase the enjoyments of England than those of any other country. It must likewise contribute more to encourage her industry. For all those parts of her own surplus produce which England exchanges for those enumerated commodities, she must get a better price than any other countries can get for the like parts of theirs, when they exchange them for the same commodities. The manufactures of England, for example, will purchase a greater quantity of the sugar and tobacco of her own colonies than the like manufactures of other countries can purchase of that sugar and tobacco. So far, therefore, as the manufactures of England and those of other countries are both to be exchanged for the sugar and tobacco of the English colonies, this superiority of price gives an encouragement to the former beyond what the latter can, in these circumstances, enjoy. The exclusive trade of the colonies, therefore, as it diminishes, or at least keeps down below what they would otherwise rise to, both the enjoyments and the industry of the countries which do not possess it, so it gives an evident advantage to the countries which do possess it over those other countries.

This advantage, however, will, perhaps, be found to be rather what may be called a relative than an absolute advantage, and to give a superiority to the country which enjoys it, rather by depressing the industry and produce of other countries, than by raising those of that particular country above what they would naturally rise to in the case of a free trade.

The tobacco of Maryland and Virginia, for example, by means of the monopoly which England enjoys of it, certainly comes cheaper to England than it can do to France to whom England commonly sells a considerable part of it. But had France and all other European countries been at all times allowed a free trade to Maryland and Virginia, the tobacco of those colonies might by this time have come cheaper than it actually does, not only to all those other countries, but likewise to England. The produce of tobacco, in consequence of a market so much more extensive than any which it has hitherto enjoyed, might, and probably would, by this time have been so much increased as to reduce the profits of a tobacco plantation to their natural level with those of a corn plantation, which it is supposed they are still somewhat above. The price of tobacco might, and probably would, by this time have fallen somewhat lower than it is at present. An equal quantity of the commodities, either of England or of those other countries, might have purchased in Maryland and Virginia a greater quantity of tobacco than it can do at present, and consequently have been sold there for so much a better price. So far as that weed, therefore, can, by its cheapness and abundance, increase the enjoyments, or augment the industry, either of England or of any other country, it would probably, in the case of a free trade, have produced both these effects in somewhat a greater degree than it can do at present. England, indeed, would not, in this case, have had any advantage over other countries. She might have bought the tobacco of her colonies somewhat cheaper, and consequently have sold some of her own commodities somewhat dearer, than she actually does; but she could neither have bought the one cheaper, nor sold the other dearer, than any other country might have done. She might, perhaps, have gained an absolute, but she would certainly have lost a relative advantage.

In order, however, to obtain this relative advantage in the colony trade, in order to execute the invidious and malignant project of excluding, as much as possible, other nations from any share in it, England, there are very probable reasons for believing, has not only sacrificed a part of the absolute advantage which she, as well as every other nation, might have derived from that trade, but has subjected herself both to an absolute and to a relative disadvantage in almost every other branch of trade.

When, by the act of navigation, England assumed to herself the monopoly of the colony trade, the foreign capitals which had before been employed in it, were necessarily withdrawn from it. The English capital, which had before carried on but a part of it, was now to carry on the whole. The capital which had before supplied the colonies with but a part of the goods which they wanted from Europe, was now all that was employed to supply them with the whole. But it could not supply them with the whole; and the goods with which it did supply them were necessarily sold very dear. The capital which had before bought but a part of the surplus produce of the colonies, was now all that was employed to buy the whole. But it could not buy the whole at any thing near the old price; and therefore, whatever it did buy, it necessarily bought very cheap. But in an employment of capital, in which the merchant sold very dear, and bought very cheap, the profit must have been very great, and much above the ordinary level of profit in other branches of trade. This superiority of profit in the colony trade could not fail to draw from other branches of trade a part of the capital which had before been employed in them. But this revulsion of capital, as it must have gradually increased the competition of capitals in the colony trade, so it must have gradually diminished that competition in all those other branches of trade; as it must have gradually lowered the profits of the one, so it must have gradually raised those of the other, till the profits of all came to a new level, different from, and somewhat higher, than that at which they had been before.

This double effect of drawing capital from all other trades, and of raising the rate of profit somewhat higher than it otherwise would have been in all trades, was not only produced by this monopoly upon its first establishment, but has continued to be produced by it ever since.

First, This monopoly has been continually drawing capital from all other trades, to be employed in that of the colonies.

Though the wealth of Great Britain has increased very much since the establishment of the act of navigation, it certainly has not increased in the same proportion as that or the colonies. But the foreign trade of every country naturally increases in proportion to its wealth, its surplus produce in proportion to its whole produce; and Great Britain having engrossed to herself almost the whole of what may be called the foreign trade of the colonies, and her capital not having increased in the same proportion as the extent of that trade, she could not carry it on without continually withdrawing from other branches of trade some part of the capital which had before been employed in them, as well as withholding from them a great deal more which would otherwise have gone to them. Since the establishment of the act of navigation, accordingly, the colony trade has been continually increasing, while many other branches of foreign trade, particularly of that to other parts of Europe, have been continually decaying. Our manufactures for foreign sale, instead of being suited, as before the act of navigation, to the neighbouring market of Europe, or to the more distant one of the countries which lie round the

Mediterranean sea, have the greater part of them, been accommodated to the still more distant one of the colonies; to the market in which they have the monopoly, rather than to that in which they have many competitors. The causes of decay in other branches of foreign trade, which, by Sir Matthew Decker and other writers, have been sought for in the excess and improper mode of taxation, in the high price of labour, in the increase of luxury, etc. may all be found in the overgrowth of the colony trade. The mercantile capital of Great Britain, though very great, yet not being infinite, and though greatly increased since the act of navigation, yet not being increased in the same proportion as the colony trade, that trade could not possibly be carried on without withdrawing some part of that capital from other branches of trade, nor consequently without some decay of those other branches.

England, it must be observed, was a great trading country, her mercantile capital was very great, and likely to become still greater and greater every day, not only before the act of navigation had established the monopoly of the corn trade, but before that trade was very considerable. In the Dutch war, during the government of Cromwell, her navy was superior to that of Holland; and in that which broke out in the beginning of the reign of Charles II., it was at least equal, perhaps superior to the united navies of France and Holland. Its superiority, perhaps, would scarce appear greater in the present times, at least if the Dutch navy were to bear the same proportion to the Dutch commerce now which it did then. But this great naval power could not, in either of those wars, be owing to the act of navigation. During the first of them, the plan of that act had been but just formed; and though, before the breaking out of the second, it had been fully enacted by legal authority, yet no part of it could have had time to produce any considerable effect, and least of all that part which established the exclusive trade to the colonies. Both the colonies and their trade were inconsiderable then, in comparison of what they are how. The island of Jamaica was an unwholesome desert, little inhabited, and less cultivated. New York and New Jersey were in the possession of the Dutch, the half of St. Christopher's in that of the French. The island of Antigua, the two Carolinas, Pennsylvania, Georgia, and Nova Scotia, were not planted. Virginia, Maryland, and New England were planted; and though they were very thriving colonies, yet there was not perhaps at that time, either in Europe or America, a single person who foresaw, or even suspected, the rapid progress which they have since made in wealth, population, and improvement. The island of Barbadoes, in short, was the only British colony of any consequence, of which the condition at that time bore any resemblance to what it is at present. The trade of the colonies, of which England, even for some time after the act of navigation, enjoyed but a part (for the act of navigation was not very strictly executed till several years after it was enacted), could not at that time be the cause of the great trade of England, nor of the great naval power which was supported by that trade. The trade which at that time supported that great naval power was the trade of Europe, and of the countries which lie round the Mediterranean sea. But the share which Great Britain at present enjoys of that trade could not support any such great naval power. Had the growing trade of the colonies been left free to all nations, whatever share of it might have fallen to Great Britain, and a very considerable share would probably have fallen to her, must have been all an addition to this great trade of which she was before in possession. In consequence of the monopoly, the increase of the colony trade has not so much occasioned an addition to the trade which Great Britain had before, as a total change in its direction.

Secondly, This monopoly has necessarily contributed to keep up the rate of profit, in all the different branches of British trade, higher than it naturally would have been, had all nations been allowed a free trade to the British colonies.

The monopoly of the colony trade, as it necessarily drew towards that trade a greater proportion of the capital of Great Britain than what would have gone to it of its own accord, so, by the expulsion of all foreign capitals, it necessarily reduced the whole quantity of capital employed in that trade below what it naturally would have been in the case of a free trade. But, by lessening the competition of capitals in that branch of trade, it necessarily raised the rate of profit in that branch. By lessening, too, the competition of British capitals in all other branches of trade, it necessarily raised the rate of British profit in all those other branches. Whatever may have been, at any particular period since the establishment of the act of navigation, the state or extent of the mercantile capital of Great Britain, the monopoly of the colony trade must, during the continuance of that state, have raised the ordinary rate of British profit higher than it otherwise would have been, both in that and in all the other branches of British trade. If, since the establishment of the act of navigation, the ordinary rate of British profit has fallen considerably, as it certainly has, it must have fallen still lower, had not the monopoly established by that act contributed to keep it up.

But whatever raises, in any country, the ordinary rate of profit higher than it otherwise would be, necessarily subjects that country both to an absolute, and to a relative disadvantage in every branch of trade of which she has not the monopoly.

It subjects her to an absolute disadvantage; because, in such branches of trade, her merchants cannot get this greater profit without selling dearer than they otherwise would do, both the goods of foreign countries which they import into their own, and the goods of their own country which they export to foreign countries. Their own country must both buy dearer and sell dearer; must both buy less, and sell less; must both enjoy less and produce less, than she otherwise would do.

It subjects her to a relative disadvantage; because, in such branches of trade, it sets other countries, which are not subject to the same absolute disadvantage, either more above her or less below her, than they otherwise would be. It enables them both to enjoy more and to produce more, in proportion to what she enjoys and produces. It renders their superiority greater, or their inferiority less, than it otherwise would be. By raising the price of her produce above what it otherwise would be, it enables the merchants of other countries to undersell her in foreign markets, and thereby to justle her out of almost all those branches of trade, of which she has not the monopoly.

Our merchants frequently complain of the high wages of British labour, as the cause of their manufactures being undersold in foreign markets; but they are silent about the high profits of stock. They complain of the extravagant gain of other people; but they say nothing of their own. The high profits of British stock, however, may contribute towards raising the price of British manufactures, in many cases, as much, and in some perhaps more, than the high wages of British labour.

It is in this manner that the capital of Great Britain, one may justly say, has partly been drawn and partly been driven from the greater part of the different branches of trade of which she has not the monopoly; from the trade of Europe, in particular, and from that of the countries which lie round the Mediterranean sea.

It has partly been drawn from those branches of trade, by the attraction of superior profit in the colony trade, in consequence of the continual increase of that trade, and of the continual insufficiency of the capital which had carried it on one year to carry it on the next.

It has partly been driven from them, by the advantage which the high rate of profit established in Great Britain gives to other countries, in all the different branches of trade of which Great Britain has not the monopoly.

As the monopoly of the colony trade has drawn from those other branches a part of the British capital, which would otherwise have been employed in them, so it has forced into them many foreign capitals which would never have gone to them, had they not been expelled from the colony trade. In those other branches of trade, it has diminished the competition of British capitals, and thereby raised the rate of British profit higher than it otherwise would have been. On the contrary, it has increased the competition of foreign capitals, and thereby sunk the rate of foreign profit lower than it otherwise would have been. Both in the one way and in the other, it must evidently have subjected Great Britain to a relative disadvantage in all those other branches of trade.

The colony trade, however, it may perhaps be said, is more advantageous to Great Britain than any other; and the monopoly, by forcing into that trade a greater proportion of the capital of Great Britain than what would otherwise have gone to it, has turned that capital into an employment, more advantageous to the country than any other which it could have found.

The most advantageous employment of any capital to the country to which it belongs, is that which maintains there the greatest quantity of productive labour, and increases the most the annual produce of the land and labour of that country. But the quantity of productive labour which any capital employed in the foreign trade of consumption can maintain, is exactly in proportion, it has been shown in the second book, to the frequency of its returns. A capital of a thousand pounds, for example, employed in a foreign trade of consumption, of which the returns are made regularly once in the year, can keep in constant employment, in the country to which it belongs, a quantity of productive labour, equal to what a thousand pounds can maintain there for a year. If the returns are made twice or thrice in the year, it can keep in constant employment a quantity of productive labour, equal to what two or three thousand pounds can maintain there for a year. A foreign trade of consumption carried on with a neighbouring, is, upon that account, in general, more advantageous than one carried on with a distant country; and, for the same reason, a direct foreign trade of consumption, as it has likewise been shown in the second book, is in general more advantageous than a round-about one.

But the monopoly of the colony trade, so far as it has operated upon the employment of the capital of Great Britain, has, in all cases, forced some part of it from a foreign trade of consumption carried on with a neighbouring, to one carried on with a more distant country, and in many cases from a direct foreign trade of consumption to a round-about one.

First, The monopoly of the colony trade has, in all cases, forced some part of the capital of Great Britain from a foreign trade of consumption carried on with a neighbouring, to one carried on with a more distant country.

It has, in all cases, forced some part of that capital from the trade with Europe, and with the countries which lie round the Mediterranean sea, to that with the more distant regions of America and the West Indies; from which the returns are necessarily less frequent, not only on account of the greater distance, but on account of the peculiar circumstances of those countries. New colonies, it has already been observed, are always understocked. Their capital is always much less than what they could employ with great profit and advantage in the improvement and cultivation of their land. They have a constant demand, therefore, for more capital than they have of their own; and, in order to supply the deficiency of their own, they endeavour to borrow as much as they can of the mother country, to whom they are, therefore, always in debt. The most common way in which the colonies contract this debt, is not by borrowing upon bond of the rich people of the mother country, though they sometimes do this too, but by running as much in arrear to their correspondents, who supply them with goods from Europe, as those correspondents will allow them. Their annual returns frequently do not amount to more than a third, and sometimes not to so great a proportion of what they owe. The whole capital, therefore, which their correspondents advance to them, is seldom returned to Britain in less than three, and sometimes not in less than four or five years. But a British capital of a thousand pounds, for example, which is returned to Great Britain only once in five years, can keep in constant employment only one-fifth part of the British industry which it could maintain, if the whole was returned once in the year; and, instead of the quantity of industry which a thousand pounds could maintain for a year, can keep in constant employment the quantity only which two hundred pounds can maintain for a year. The planter, no doubt, by the high price which he pays for the goods from Europe, by the interest upon the bills which he grants at distant dates, and by the commission upon the renewal of those which he grants at near dates, makes up, and probably more than makes up, all the loss which his correspondent can sustain by this delay. But, though he make up the loss of his correspondent, he cannot make up that of Great Britain. In a trade of which the returns are very distant, the profit of the merchant may be as great or greater than in one in which they are very frequent and near; but the advantage of the country in which he resides, the quantity of productive labour constantly maintained there, the annual produce of the land and labour, must always be much less. That the returns of the trade to America, and still more those of that to the West Indies, are, in general, not only more distant, but more irregular and more uncertain, too, than those of the trade to any part of Europe, or even of the countries which lie round the Mediterranean sea, will readily be allowed, I imagine, by everybody who has any experience of those different branches of trade.

Secondly, The monopoly of the colony trade, has, in many cases, forced some part of the capital of Great Britain from a direct foreign trade of consumption, into a round-about one.

Among the enumerated commodities which can be sent to no other market but Great Britain, there are several of which the quantity exceeds very much the consumption of Great Britain, and of which, a part, therefore, must be exported to other countries. But this cannot be done without forcing some part of the capital of Great Britain into a round-about foreign trade of consumption. Maryland, and Virginia, for example, send annually to Great Britain upwards of ninety-six thousand hogsheads of tobacco, and the consumption of Great Britain is said not to exceed fourteen thousand. Upwards of eighty-two thousand hogsheads, therefore, must be exported to other countries, to France, to Holland, and, to the countries which lie round the Baltic and Mediterranean seas. But that part of the capital of Great Britain which brings those eighty-two thousand hogsheads to Great Britain, which re-exports them from thence to those other countries, and which brings back from those other countries to Great Britain either goods or money in return, is employed in a round-about foreign trade of consumption; and is necessarily forced into this employment, in order to dispose of this great surplus. If we would compute in how many years the whole of this capital is likely to come back to Great Britain, we must add to the distance of the American returns that of the returns from those other countries. If, in the direct foreign trade of consumption which we carry on with America, the whole capital employed frequently does not come back in less than three or four years, the whole capital employed in this round-about one is not likely to come back in less than four or five. If the one can keep in constant employment but a third or a fourth part of the domestic industry which could be maintained by a capital returned once in the year, the other can keep in constant employment but a fourth or a fifth part of that industry. At some of the outports a credit is commonly given to those foreign correspondents to whom they export them tobacco. At the port of London, indeed, it is commonly sold for ready money: the rule is Weigh and pay. At the port of London, therefore, the final returns of the whole round-about trade are more distant than the returns from America, by the time only which the goods may lie unsold in the warehouse; where, however, they may sometimes lie long enough. But, had not the colonies been confined to the market of Great Britain for the sale of their tobacco, very little more of it would probably have come to us than what was necessary for the home consumption. The goods which Great Britain purchases at present for her own consumption with the great surplus of tobacco which she exports to other countries, she would, in this case, probably have purchased with the immediate produce of her own industry, or with some part of her own manufactures. That produce, those manufactures, instead of being almost entirely suited to one great market, as at present, would probably have been fitted to a great number of smaller markets. Instead of one great round-about foreign trade of consumption, Great Britain would probably have carried on a great number of small direct foreign trades of the same kind. On account of the frequency of the returns, a part, and probably but a small part, perhaps not above a third or a fourth of the capital which at present carries on this great round-about trade, might have been sufficient to carry on all those small direct ones; might have kept in constant employment an equal quantity of British industry; and have equally supported the annual produce of the land and labour of Great Britain. All the purposes of this trade being, in this manner, answered by a much smaller capital, there would have been a large spare capital to apply to other purposes; to improve the lands, to increase the manufactures, and to extend the commerce of Great Britain; to come into competition at least with the other British capitals employed in all those different ways, to reduce the rate of profit in them all, and thereby to give to Great Britain, in all of them, a superiority over other countries, still greater than what she at present enjoys.

The monopoly of the colony trade, too, has forced some part of the capital of Great Britain from all foreign trade of consumption to a carrying trade; and, consequently from supporting more or less the industry of Great Britain, to be employed altogether in supporting partly that of the colonies, and partly that of some other countries.

The goods, for example, which are annually purchased with the great surplus of eighty-two thousand hogsheads of tobacco annually re-exported from Great Britain, are not all consumed in Great Britain. Part of them, linen from Germany and Holland, for example, is returned to the colonies for their particular consumption. But that part of the capital of Great Britain which buys the tobacco with which this linen is afterwards bought, is necessarily withdrawn from supporting the industry of Great Britain, to be employed altogether in supporting, partly that of the colonies, and partly that of the particular countries who pay for this tobacco with the produce of their own industry.

The monopoly of the colony trade, besides, by forcing towards it a much greater proportion of the capital of Great Britain than what would naturally have gone to it, seems to have broken altogether that natural balance which would otherwise have taken place among all the different branches of British industry. The industry of Great Britain, instead of being accommodated to a great number of small markets, has been principally suited to one great market. Her commerce, instead of running in a great number of small channels, has been taught to run principally in one great channel. But the whole system of her industry and commerce has thereby been rendered less secure; the whole state of her body politic less healthful than it otherwise would have been. In her present condition, Great Britain resembles one of those unwholesome bodies in which some of the vital parts are overgrown, and which, upon that account, are liable to many dangerous disorders, scarce incident to those in which all the parts are more properly proportioned. A small stop in that great blood-vessel, which has been artificially swelled beyond its natural dimensions, and through which an unnatural proportion of the industry and commerce of the country has been forced to circulate, is very likely to bring on the most dangerous disorders upon the whole body politic. The expectation of a rupture with the colonies, accordingly, has struck the people of Great Britain with more terror than they ever felt for a Spanish armada, or a

French invasion. It was this terror, whether well or ill grounded, which rendered the repeal of the stamp act, among the merchants at least, a popular measure. In the total exclusion from the colony market, was it to last only for a few years, the greater part of our merchants used to fancy that they foresaw an entire stop to their trade; the greater part of our master manufacturers, the entire ruin of their business; and the greater part of our workmen, an end of their employment. A rupture with any of our neighbours upon the continent, though likely, too, to occasion some stop or interruption in the employments of some of all these different orders of people, is foreseen, however, without any such general emotion. The blood, of which the circulation is stopt in some of the smaller vessels, easily disgorges itself into the greater, without occasioning any dangerous disorder; but, when it is stopt in any of the greater vessels, convulsions, apoplexy, or death, are the immediate and unavoidable consequences. If but one of those overgrown manufactures, which, by means either of bounties or of the monopoly of the home and colony markets, have been artificially raised up to any unnatural height, finds some small stop or interruption in its employment, it frequently occasions a mutiny and disorder alarming to government, and embarrassing even to the deliberations of the legislature. How great, therefore, would be the disorder and confusion, it was thought, which must necessarily be occasioned by a sudden and entire stop in the employment of so great a proportion of our principal manufacturers?

Some moderate and gradual relaxation of the laws which give to Great Britain the exclusive trade to the colonies, till it is rendered in a great measure free, seems to be the only expedient which can, in all future times, deliver her from this danger; which can enable her, or even force her, to withdraw some part of her capital from this overgrown employment, and to turn it, though with less profit, towards other employments; and which, by gradually diminishing one branch of her industry, and gradually increasing all the rest, can, by degrees, restore all the different branches of it to that natural, healthful, and proper proportion, which perfect liberty necessarily establishes, and which perfect liberty can alone preserve. To open the colony trade all at once to all nations, might not only occasion some transitory inconveniency, but a great permanent loss, to the greater part of those whose industry or capital is at present engaged in it. The sudden loss of the employment, even of the ships which import the eighty-two thousand hogsheads of tobacco, which are over and above the consumption of Great Britain, might alone be felt very sensibly. Such are the unfortunate effects of all the regulations of the mercantile system. They not only introduce very dangerous disorders into the state of the body politic, but disorders which it is often difficult to remedy, without occasioning, for a time at least, still greater disorders. In what manner, therefore, the colony trade ought gradually to be opened; what are the restraints which ought first, and what are those which ought last, to be taken away; or in what manner the natural system of perfect liberty and justice ought gradually to be restored, we must leave to the wisdom of future statesmen and legislators to determine.

Five different events, unforeseen and unthought of, have very fortunately concurred to hinder Great Britain from feeling, so sensibly as it was generally expected she would, the total exclusion which has now taken place for more than a year (from the first of December 1774) from a very important branch of the colony trade, that of the twelve associated provinces of North America. First, those colonies, in preparing themselves for their non-importation agreement, drained Great Britain completely of all the commodities which were fit for their market; secondly, the extra ordinary demand of the Spanish flota has, this year, drained Germany and the north of many commodities, linen in particular, which used to come into competition, even in the British market, with the manufactures of Great Britain; thirdly, the peace between Russia and Turkey has occasioned an extraordinary demand from the Turkey market, which, during the distress of the country, and while a Russian fleet was cruizing in the Archipelago, had been very poorly supplied; fourthly, the demand of the north of Europe for the manufactures of Great Britain has been increasing from year to year, for some time past; and, fifthly, the late partition, and consequential pacification of Poland, by opening the market of that great country, have, this year, added an extraordinary demand from thence to the increasing demand of the north. These events are all, except the fourth, in their nature transitory and accidental; and the exclusion from so important a branch of the colony trade, if unfortunately it should continue much longer, may still occasion some degree of distress. This distress, however, as it will come on gradually, will be felt much less severely than if it had come on all at once; and, in the mean time, the industry and capital of the country may find a new employment and direction, so as to prevent this distress from ever rising to any considerable height.

The monopoly of the colony trade, therefore, so far as it has turned towards that trade a greater proportion of the capital of Great Britain than what would otherwise have gone to it, has in all cases turned it, from a foreign trade of consumption with a neighbouring, into one with a more distant country; in many cases from a direct foreign trade of consumption into a round-about one; and, in some cases, from all foreign trade of consumption into a carrying trade. It has, in all cases, therefore, turned it from a direction in which it would have maintained a greater quantity of productive labour, into one in which it can maintain a much smaller quantity. By suiting, besides, to one particular market only, so great a part of the industry and commerce of Great Britain, it has rendered the whole state of that industry and commerce more precarious and less secure, than if their produce had been accommodated to a greater variety of markets.

We must carefully distinguish between the effects of the colony trade and those of the monopoly of that trade. The former are always and necessarily beneficial; the latter always and necessarily hurtful. But the former are so beneficial, that the colony trade, though subject to a monopoly, and, notwithstanding the hurtful effects of that monopoly, is still, upon the whole, beneficial, and greatly beneficial, though a good deal less so than it otherwise would be.

The effect of the colony trade, in its natural and free state, is to open a great though distant market, for such parts of the produce of British industry as may exceed the demand of the markets nearer home, of those of Europe, and of the countries which lie round the Mediterranean sea. In its natural and free state, the colony trade, without drawing from those markets any part of the produce which had ever been sent to them, encourages Great Britain to increase the surplus continually, by continually presenting new equivalents to be exchanged for it. In its natural and free state, the colony trade tends to increase the quantity of productive labour in Great Britain, but without altering in any respect the direction of that which had been employed there before. In the natural and free state of the colony trade, the competition of all other nations would hinder the rate of profit from rising above the common level, either in the new market, or in the new employment. The new market, without drawing any thing from the old one, would create, if one may say so, a new produce for its own supply; and that new produce would constitute a new capital for carrying on the new employment, which, in the same manner, would draw nothing from the old one.

The monopoly of the colony trade, on the contrary, by excluding the competition of other nations, and thereby raising the rate of profit, both in the new market and in the new employment, draws produce from the old market, and capital from the old employment. To augment our share of the colony trade beyond what it otherwise would be, is the avowed purpose of the monopoly. If our share of that trade were to be no greater with, than it would have been without the monopoly, there could have been no reason for establishing the monopoly. But whatever forces into a branch of trade, of which the returns are slower and more distant than those of the greater part of other trades, a greater proportion of the capital of any country, than what of its own accord would go to that branch, necessarily renders the whole quantity of productive labour annually maintained there, the whole annual produce of the land and labour of that country, less than they otherwise would be. It keeps down the revenue of the inhabitants of that country below what it would naturally rise to, and thereby diminishes their power of accumulation. It not only hinders, at all times, their capital from maintaining so great a quantity of productive labour as it would otherwise maintain, but it hinders it from increasing so fast as it would otherwise increase, and, consequently, from maintaining a still greater quantity of productive labour.

The natural good effects of the colony trade, however, more than counterbalance to Great Britain the bad effects of the monopoly; so that, monopoly and altogether, that trade, even as it is carried on at present, is not only advantageous, but greatly advantageous. The new market and the new employment which are opened by the colony trade, are of much greater extent than that portion of the old market and of the old employment which is lost by the monopoly. The new produce and the new capital which has been created, if one may say so, by the colony trade, maintain in Great Britain a greater quantity of productive labour than what can have been thrown out of employment by the revulsion of capital from other trades of which the returns are more frequent. If the colony trade, however, even as it is carried on at present, is advantageous to Great Britain, it is not by means of the monopoly, but in spite of the monopoly.

It is rather for the manufactured than for the rude produce of Europe, that the colony trade opens a new market. Agriculture is the proper business of all new colonies; a business which the cheapness of land renders more advantageous than any other. They abound, therefore, in the rude produce of land; and instead of importing it from other countries, they have generally a large surplus to export. In new colonies, agriculture either draws hands from all other employments, or keeps them from going to any other employment. There are few hands to spare for the necessary, and none for the ornamental manufactures. The greater part of the manufactures of both kinds they find it cheaper to purchase of other countries than to make for themselves. It is chiefly by encouraging the manufactures of Europe, that the colony trade indirectly encourages its agriculture. The manufacturers of Europe, to whom that trade gives employment, constitute a new market for the produce of the land, and the most advantageous of all markets; the home market for the corn and cattle, for the bread and butcher's meat of Europe, is thus greatly extended by means of the trade to America.

But that the monopoly of the trade of populous and thriving colonies is not alone sufficient to establish, or even to maintain, manufactures in any country, the examples of Spain and Portugal sufficiently demonstrate. Spain and Portugal were manufacturing countries before they had any considerable colonies. Since they had the richest and most fertile in the world, they have both ceased to be so.

In Spain and Portugal, the bad effects of the monopoly, aggravated by other causes, have, perhaps, nearly overbalanced the natural good effects of the colony trade. These causes seem to be other monopolies of different kinds: the degradation of the value of gold and silver below what it is in most other countries; the exclusion from foreign markets by improper taxes upon exportation, and the narrowing of the home market, by still more improper taxes upon the transportation of goods from one part of the country to another; but above all, that irregular and partial administration of justice which often protects the rich and powerful debtor from the pursuit of his injured creditor, and which makes the industrious part of the nation afraid to prepare goods for the consumption of those haughty and great men, to whom they dare not refuse to sell upon credit, and from whom they are altogether uncertain of repayment.

In England, on the contrary, the natural good effects of the colony trade, assisted by other causes, have in a great measure conquered the bad effects of the monopoly. These causes seem to be, the general liberty of trade, which, notwithstanding some restraints, is at least equal, perhaps superior, to what it is in any other country; the liberty of exporting, duty free, almost all sorts of goods which are the produce of domestic industry, to almost any foreign country; and what, perhaps, is of still greater importance, the unbounded liberty of transporting them from one part of our own country to any other, without being obliged to give any account to any public office, without being liable to question or examination of any kind; but, above all, that equal and impartial administration of justice, which renders the rights of the meanest British subject respectable to the greatest, and which, by securing to every man the fruits of his own industry, gives the greatest and most effectual encouragement to every sort of industry.

If the manufactures of Great Britain, however, have been advanced, as they certainly have, by the colony trade, it has not been by means of the monopoly of that trade, but in spite of the monopoly. The effect of the monopoly has been, not to augment the quantity, but to alter the quality and shape of a part of the manufactures of Great Britain, and to accommodate to a market, from which the returns are slow and distant, what would otherwise have been accommodated to one from which the returns are frequent and near. Its effect has consequently been, to turn a part of the capital of Great Britain from an employment in which it would have maintained a greater quantity of manufacturing industry, to one in which it maintains a much smaller, and thereby to diminish, instead of increasing, the whole quantity of manufacturing industry maintained in Great Britain.

The monopoly of the colony trade, therefore, like all the other mean and malignant expedients of the mercantile system, depresses the industry of all other countries, but chiefly that of the colonies, without in the least increasing, but on the contrary diminishing, that of the country in whose favour it is established.

The monopoly hinders the capital of that country, whatever may, at any particular time, be the extent of that capital, from maintaining so great a quantity of productive labour as it would otherwise maintain, and from affording so great a revenue to the industrious inhabitants as it would otherwise afford. But as capital can be increased only by savings from revenue, the monopoly, by hindering it from affording so great a revenue as it would otherwise afford, necessarily hinders it from increasing so fast as it would otherwise increase, and consequently from maintaining a still greater quantity of productive labour, and affording a still greater revenue to the industrious inhabitants of that country. One great original source of revenue, therefore, the wages of labour, the monopoly must necessarily have rendered, at all times, less abundant than it otherwise would have been.

By raising the rate of mercantile profit, the monopoly discourages the improvement of land. The profit of improvement depends upon the difference between what the land actually produces, and what, by the application of a certain capital, it can be made to produce. If this difference affords a greater profit than what can be drawn from an equal capital in any mercantile employment, the improvement of land will draw capital from all mercantile employments. If the profit is less, mercantile employments will draw capital from the improvement of land. Whatever, therefore, raises the rate of mercantile profit, either lessens the superiority, or increases the inferiority of the profit of improvement: and, in the one case, hinders capital from going to improvement, and in the other draws capital from it; but by discouraging improvement, the monopoly necessarily retards the natural increase of another great original source of revenue, the rent of land. By raising the rate of profit, too, the monopoly necessarily keeps up the market rate of interest higher than it otherwise would be. But the price of land, in proportion to the rent which it affords, the number of years purchase which is commonly paid for it, necessarily falls as the rate of interest rises, and rises as the rate of interest falls. The monopoly, therefore, hurts the interest of the landlord two different ways, by retarding the natural increase, first, of his rent, and, secondly, of the price which he would get for his land, in proportion to the rent which it affords.

The monopoly, indeed, raises the rate of mercantile profit and thereby augments somewhat the gain of our merchants. But as it obstructs the natural increase of capital, it tends rather to diminish than to increase the sum total of the revenue which the inhabitants of the country derive from the profits of stock; a small profit upon a great capital generally affording a greater revenue than a great profit upon a small one. The monopoly raises the rate of profit, but it hinders the sum of profit from rising so high as it otherwise would do.

All the original sources of revenue, the wages of labour, the rent of land, and the profits of stock, the monopoly renders much less abundant than they otherwise would be. To promote the little interest of one little order of men in one country, it hurts the interest of all other orders of men in that country, and of all the men in all other countries.

It is solely by raising the ordinary rate of profit, that the monopoly either has proved, or could prove, advantageous to any one particular order of men. But besides all the bad effects to the country in general, which have already been mentioned as necessarily resulting from a higher rate of profit, there is one more fatal, perhaps, than all these put together, but which, if we may judge from experience, is inseparably connected with it. The high rate of profit seems everywhere to destroy that parsimony which, in other circumstances, is natural to the character of the merchant. When profits are high, that sober virtue seems to be superfluous, and expensive luxury to suit better the affluence of his situation. But the owners of the great mercantile capitals are necessarily the leaders and conductors of the whole industry of every nation; and their example has a much greater influence upon the manners of the whole industrious part of it than that of any other order of men. If his employer is attentive and parsimonious, the workman is very likely to be so too; but if the master is dissolute and disorderly, the servant, who shapes his work according to the pattern which his master prescribes to him, will shape his life, too, according to the example which he sets him. Accumulation is thus prevented in the hands of all those who are naturally the most disposed to accumulate; and the funds destined for the maintenance of productive labour, receive no augmentation from the revenue of those who ought naturally to augment them the most. The capital of the country, instead of increasing, gradually dwindles away, and the quantity of productive labour maintained in it grows every day less and less. Have the exorbitant profits of the merchants of Cadiz and Lisbon augmented the capital of Spain and Portugal? Have they alleviated the poverty, have they promoted the industry, of those two beggarly countries? Such has been the tone of mercantile expense in those two trading cities, that those exorbitant profits, far from augmenting the general capital of the country, seem scarce to have been sufficient to keep up the capitals upon which they were made. Foreign capitals are every day intruding themselves, if I may say so, more and more into the trade of Cadiz and Lisbon. It is to expel those foreign capitals from a trade which their own grows every day more and more insufficient for carrying on, that the Spaniards and Portuguese endeavour every day to straiten more and more the galling bands of their absurd monopoly. Compare the mercantile manners of Cadiz and Lisbon with those of Amsterdam, and you will be sensible how differently the conduct and character of merchants are affected by the high and by the low profits of stock. The merchants of London, indeed, have not yet generally become such magnificent lords as those of Cadiz and Lisbon; but neither are they in general such attetitive and parsimonious burghers as those of Amsterdam. They are supposed, however, many of them, to be a good deal richer than the greater part of the former, and not quire so rich as many of the latter: but the rate of their profit is commonly much lower than that of the former, and a good deal higher than that of the latter. Light come, light go, says the proverb; and the ordinary tone of expense seems everywhere to be regulated, not so much according to the real ability of spending, as to the supposed facility of getting money to spend.

It is thus that the single advantage which the monopoly procures to a single order of men, is in many different ways hurtful to the general interest of the country.

To found a great empire for the sole purpose of raising up a people of customers, may at first sight, appear a project fit only for a nation of shopkeepers. It is, however, a project altogether unfit for a nation of shopkeepers, but extremely fit for a nation whose government is influenced by shopkeepers. Such statesmen, and such statesmen only, are capable of fancying that they will find some advantage in employing the blood and treasure of their fellow-citizens, to found and maintain such an empire. Say to a shopkeeper, Buy me a good estate, and I shall always buy my clothes at your shop, even though I should pay somewhat dearer than what I can have them for at other shops; and you will not find him very forward to embrace your proposal. But should any other person buy you such an estate, the shopkeeper will be much obliged to your benefactor if he would enjoin you to buy all your clothes at his shop. England purchased for some of her subjects, who found themselves uneasy at home, a great estate in a distant country. The price, indeed, was very small, and instead of thirty years purchase, the ordinary price of land in the present times, it amounted to little more than the expense of the different equipments which made the first discovery, reconnoitered the coast, and took a fictitious possession of the country. The land was good, and of great extent; and the cultivators having plenty of good ground to work upon, and being for some time at liberty to sell their produce where they pleased, became, in the course of little more than thirty or forty years (between 1620 and 1660), so numerous and thriving a people, that the shopkeepers and other traders of England wished to secure to themselves the monopoly of their custom. Without pretending, therefore, that they had paid any part, either of the original purchase money, or of the subsequent expense of improvement, they petitioned the parliament, that the cultivators of America might for the future be confined to their shop; first, for buying all the goods which they wanted from Europe; and, secondly, for selling all such parts of their own produce as those traders might find it convenient to buy. For they did not find it convenient to buy every part of it. Some parts of it imported into England, might have interfered with some of the trades which they themselves carried on at home. Those particular parts of it, therefore, they were willing that the colonists should sell where they could; the farther off the better; and upon that account proposed that their market should be confined to the countries south of Cape Finisterre. A clause in the famous act of navigation established this truly shopkeeper proposal into a law.

The maintenance of this monopoly has hitherto been the principal, or more properly, perhaps, the sole end and purpose of the dominion which Great Britain assumes over her colonies. In the exclusive trade, it is supposed, consists the great advantage of provinces, which have never yet afforded either revenue or military force for the support of the civil government, or the defence of the mother country. The monopoly is the principal badge of their dependency, and it is the sole fruit which has hitherto been gathered from that dependency. Whatever expense Great Britain has hitherto laid out in maintaining this dependency, has really been laid out in order to support this monopoly. The expense of the ordinary peace establishment of the colonies amounted, before the commencement of the present disturbances to the pay of twenty regiments of foot; to the expense of the artillery, stores, and extraordinary provisions, with which it was necessary to supply them; and to the expense of a very considerable naval force, which was constantly kept up, in order to guard from the smuggling vessels of other nations, the immense coast of North America, and that of our West Indian islands. The whole expense of this peace establishment was a charge upon the revenue of Great Britain, and was, at the same time, the smallest part of what the dominion of the colonies has cost the mother country. If we would know the amount of the whole, we must add to the annual expense of this peace establishment, the interest of the sums which, in consequence of their considering her colonies as provinces subject to her dominion, Great Britain has, upon different occasions, laid out upon their defence. We must add to it, in particular, the whole expense of the late war, and a great part of that of the war which preceded it. The late war was altogether a colony quarrel;

and the whole expense of it, in whatever part of the world it might have been laid out, whether in Germany or the East Indies, ought justly to be stated to the account of the colonies. It amounted to more than ninety millions sterling, including not only the new debt which was contracted, but the two shillings in the pound additional land tax, and the sums which were every year borrowed from the sinking fund. The Spanish war which began in 1739 was principally a colony quarrel. Its principal object was to prevent the search of the colony ships, which carried on a contraband trade with the Spanish Main. This whole expense is, in reality, a bounty which has been given in order to support a monopoly. The pretended purpose of it was to encourage the manufactures, and to increase the commerce of Great Britain. But its real effect has been to raise the rate of mercantile profit, and to enable our merchants to turn into a branch of trade, of which the returns are more slow and distant than those of the greater part of other trades, a greater proportion of their capital than they otherwise would have done; two events which, if a bounty could have prevented, it might perhaps have been very well worth while to give such a bounty.

Under the present system of management, therefore, Great Britain derives nothing but loss from the dominion which she assumes over her colonies.

To propose that Great Britain should voluntarily give up all authority over her colonies, and leave them to elect their own magistrates, to enact their own laws, and to make peace and war, as they might think proper, would be to propose such a measure as never was, and never will be, adopted by any nation in the world. No nation ever voluntarily gave up the dominion of any province, how troublesome soever it might be to govern it, and how small soever the revenue which it afforded might be in proportion to the expense which it occasioned. Such sacrifices, though they might frequently be agreeable to the interest, are always mortifying to the pride of every nation; and, what is perhaps of still greater consequence, they are always contrary to the private interest of the governing part of it, who would thereby be deprived of the disposal of many places of trust and profit, of many opportunities of acquiring wealth and distinction, which the possession of the most turbulent, and, to the great body of the people, the most unprofitable province, seldom fails to afford. The most visionary enthusiasts would scarce be capable of proposing such a measure, with any serious hopes at least of its ever being adopted. If it was adopted, however, Great Britain would not only be immediately freed from the whole annual expense of the peace establishment of the colonies, but might settle with them such a treaty of commerce as would effectually secure to her a free trade, more advantageous to the great body of the people, though less so to the merchants, than the monopoly which she at present enjoys. By thus parting good friends, the natural affection of the colonies to the mother country, which, perhaps, our late dissensions have well nigh extinguished, would quickly revive. It might dispose them not only to respect, for whole centuries together, that treaty of commerce which they had concluded with us at parting, but to favour us in war as well as in trade, and instead of turbulent and factious subjects, to become our most faithful, affectionate, and generous allies; and the same sort of parental affection on the one side, and filial respect on the other, might revive between Great Britain and her colonies, which used to subsist between those of ancient Greece and the mother city from which they descended.

In order to render any province advantageous to the empire to which it belongs, it ought to afford, in time of peace, a revenue to the public, sufficient not only for defraying the whole expense of its own peace establishment, but for contributing its proportion to the support of the general government of the empire. Every province necessarily contributes, more or less, to increase the expense of that general government. If any particular province, therefore, does not contribute its share towards defraying this expense, an unequal burden must be thrown upon some other part of the empire. The extraordinary revenue, too, which every province affords to the public in time of war, ought, from parity of reason, to bear the same proportion to the extraordinary revenue of the whole empire, which its ordinary revenue does in time of peace. That neither the ordinary nor extraordinary revenue which Great Britain derives from her colonies, bears this proportion to the whole revenue of the British empire, will readily be allowed. The monopoly, it has been supposed, indeed, by increasing the private revenue of the people of Great Britain, and thereby enabling them to pay greater taxes, compensates the deficiency of the public revenue of the colonies. But this monopoly, I have endeavoured to show, though a very grievous tax upon the colonies, and though it may increase the revenue of a particular order of men in Great Britain, diminishes, instead of increasing, that of the great body of the people, and consequently diminishes, instead of increasing, the ability of the great body of the people to pay taxes. The men, too, whose revenue the monopoly increases, constitute a particular order, which it is both absolutely impossible to tax beyond the proportion of other orders, and extremely impolitic even to attempt to tax beyond that proportion, as I shall endeavour to show in the following book. No particular resource, therefore, can be drawn from this particular order.

The colonies may be taxed either by their own assemblies, or by the parliament of Great Britain.

That the colony assemblies can never be so managed as to levy upon their constituents a public revenue, sufficient, not only to maintain at all times their own civil and military establishment, but to pay their proper proportion of the expense of the general government of the British empire, seems not very probable. It was a long time before even the parliament of England, though placed immediately under the eye of the sovereign, could be brought under such a system of management, or could be rendered sufficiently liberal in their grants for supporting the civil and military establishments even of their own country. It was only by distributing among the particular members of parliament a great part either of the offices, or of the disposal of the offices arising from this civil and military establishment, that such a system of management could be established, even with regard to the parliament of England. But the distance of the colony assemblies from the eye of the sovereign, their number, their dispersed situation, and their various constitutions, would render it very difficult to manage them in the same manner, even though the sovereign had the same means of doing it; and those means are wanting. It would be absolutely impossible to distribute among all the leading members of all the colony assemblies such a share, either of the offices, or of the disposal of the offices, arising from the general government of the British empire, as to dispose them to give up their popularity at home, and to tax their constituents for the support of that general government, of which almost the whole emoluments were to be divided among people who were strangers to them. The unavoidable ignorance of administration, besides, concerning the relative importance of the different members of those different assemblies, the offences which must frequently be given, the blunders which must constantly be committed, in attempting to manage them in this manner, seems to render such a system of management altogether impracticable with regard to them.

The colony assemblies, besides, cannot be supposed the proper judges of what is necessary for the defence and support of the whole empire. The care of that defence and support is not entrusted to them. It is not their business, and they have no regular means of information concerning it. The assembly of a province, like the vestry of a parish, may judge very properly concerning the affairs of its own particular district, but can have no proper means of judging concerning those of the whole empire. It cannot even judge properly concerning the proportion which its own province bears to the whole empire, or concerning the relative degree of its wealth and importance, compared with the other provinces; because those other provinces are not under the inspection and superintendency of the assembly of a particular province. What is necessary for the defence and support of the whole empire, and in what proportion each part ought to contribute, can be judged of only by that assembly which inspects and super-intends the affairs of the whole empire.

It has been proposed, accordingly, that the colonies should be taxed by requisition, the parliament of Great Britain determining the sum which each colony ought to pay, and the provincial assembly assessing and levying it in the way that suited best the circumstances of the province. What concerned the whole empire would in this way be determined by the assembly which inspects and superintends the affairs of the whole empire; and the provincial affairs of each colony might still be regulated by its own assembly. Though the colonies should, in this case, have no representatives in the British parliament, yet, if we may judge by experience, there is no probability that the parliamentary requisition would be unreasonable. The parliament of England has not, upon any occasion, shewn the smallest disposition to overburden those parts of the empire which are not represented in parliament. The islands of Guernsey and Jersey, without any means of resisting the authority of parliament, are more lightly taxed than any part of Great Britain. Parliament, in attempting to exercise its supposed right, whether well or ill grounded, of taxing the colonies, has never hitherto demanded of them anything which even approached to a just proportion to what was paid by their fellow subjects at home. If the contribution of the colonies, besides, was to rise or fall in proportion to the rise or fall of the land-tax, parliament could not tax them without taxing, at the same time, its own constituents, and the colonies might, in this case, be considered as virtually represented in parliament.

Examples are not wanting of empires in which all the different provinces are not taxed, if I may be allowed the expression, in one mass; but in which the sovereign regulates the sum which each province ought to pay, and in some provinces assesses and levies it as he thinks proper; while in others he leaves it to be assessed and levied as the respective states of each province shall determine. In some provinces of France, the king not only imposes what taxes he thinks proper, but assesses and levies them in the way he thinks proper. From others he demands a certain sum, but leaves it to the states of each province to assess and levy that sum as they think proper. According to the scheme of taxing by requisition, the parliament of Great Britain would stand nearly in the same situation towards the colony assemblies, as the king of France does towards the states of those provinces which still enjoy the privilege of having states of their own, the provinces of France which are supposed to be the best governed.

But though, according to this scheme, the colonies could have no just reason to fear that their share of the public burdens should ever exceed the proper proportion to that of their fellow-citizens at home, Great Britain might have just reason to fear that it never would amount to that proper proportion. The parliament of Great Britain has not, for some time past, had the same established authority in the colonies, which the French king has in those provinces of France which still enjoy the privilege of having states of their own. The colony assemblies, if they were not very favourably disposed (and unless more skilfully managed than they ever have been hitherto, they are not very likely to be so), might still find many pretences for evading or rejecting the most reasonable requisitions of parliament. A French war breaks out, we shall suppose; ten millions must immediately be raised, in order to defend the seat of the empire. This sum must be borrowed upon the credit of some parliamentary fund mortgaged for paying the interest. Part of this fund parliament proposes to raise by a tax to be levied in Great Britain; and part of it by a requisition to all the different colony assemblies of America and the West Indies. Would people readily advance their money upon the credit of a fund which partly depended upon the good humour of all those assemblies, far distant from the seat of the war, and sometimes, perhaps, thinking themselves not much concerned in the event of it? Upon such a fund, no more money would probably be advanced than what the tax to be levied in Great Britain might be supposed to answer for. The whole burden of the debt contracted on account of the war would in this manner fall, as it always has done hitherto, upon Great Britain; upon a part of the empire, and not upon the whole empire. Great Britain is, perhaps, since the world began, the only state which, as it has extended its empire, has only increased its expense, without once augmenting its resources. Other states have generally disburdened themselves, upon their subject and subordinate provinces, of the most considerable part of the expense of defending the empire. Great Britain has hitherto suffered her subject and subordinate provinces to disburden themselves upon her of almost this whole expense. In order to put Great Britain upon a footing of equality with her own colonies, which the law has hitherto supposed to be subject and subordinate, it seems necessary, upon the scheme of taxing them by parliamentary requisition, that parliament should have some means of rendering its requisitions immediately effectual, in case the colony assemblies should attempt to evade or reject them; and what those means are, it is not very easy to conceive, and it has not yet been explained.

Should the parliament of Great Britain, at the same time, be ever fully established in the right of taxing the colonies, even independent of the consent of their own assemblies, the importance of those assemblies would, from that moment, be at an end, and with it, that of all the leading men of British America. Men desire to have some share in the management of public affairs, chiefly on account of the importance which it gives them. Upon the power which the greater part of the leading men, the natural aristocracy of every country, have of preserving or defending their respective importance, depends the stability and duration of every system of free government. In the attacks which those leading men are continually making upon the importance of one another, and in the defence of their own, consists the whole play of domestic faction and ambition. The leading men of America, like those of all other countries, desire to preserve their own importance. They feel, or imagine, that if their assemblies, which they are fond of calling parliaments, and of considering as equal in authority to the parliament of Great Britain, should be so far degraded as to become the humble ministers and executive officers of that parliament, the greater part of their own importance would be at an end. They have rejected, therefore, the proposal of being taxed by parliamentary requisition, and, like other ambitious and high-spirited men, have rather chosen to draw the sword in defence of their own importance.

Towards the declension of the Roman republic, the allies of Rome, who had borne the principal burden of defending the state and extending the empire, demanded to be admitted to all the privileges of Roman citizens. Upon being refused, the social war broke out. During the course of that war, Rome granted those privileges to the greater part of them, one by one, and in proportion as they detached themselves from the general confederacy. The parliament of Great Britain insists upon taxing the colonies; and they refuse to be taxed by a parliament in which they are not represented. If to each colony which should detach itself from the general confederacy, Great Britain should allow such a number of representatives as suited the proportion of what it contributed to the public revenue of the empire, in consequence of its being subjected to the same taxes, and in compensation admitted to the same freedom of trade with its fellow-subjects at home; the number of its representatives to be augmented as the proportion of its contribution might afterwards augment; a new method of acquiring importance, a new and more dazzling object of ambition, would be presented to the leading men of each colony. Instead of piddling for the little prizes which are to be found in what may be called the paltry raffle of colony faction, they might then hope, from the presumption which men naturally have in their own ability and good fortune, to draw some of the great prizes which sometimes come from the wheel of the great state lottery of British politics. Unless this or some other method is fallen upon, and there seems to be none more obvious than this, of preserving the importance and of gratifying the ambition of the leading men of America, it is not very probable that they will ever voluntarily submit to us; and we ought to consider, that the blood which must be shed in forcing them to do so, is, every drop of it, the blood either of those who are, or of those whom we wish to have for our fellow citizens. They are very weak who flatter themselves that, in the state to which things have come, our colonies will be easily conquered by force alone. The persons who now govern the resolutions of what they call their continental congress, feel in themselves at this moment a degree of importance which, perhaps, the greatest subjects in Europe scarce feel. From shopkeepers, tradesmen, and attorneys, they are become statesmen and legislators, and are employed in contriving a new form of government for an extensive empire, which, they flatter themselves, will become, and which, indeed, seems very likely to become, one of the greatest and most formidable that ever was in the world. Five hundred different people, perhaps, who, in different ways, act immediately under the continental congress, and five hundred thousand, perhaps, who act under those five hundred, all feel, in the same manner, a proportionable rise in their own importance. Almost every individual of the governing party in America fills, at present, in his own fancy, a station superior, not only to what he had ever filled before, but to what he had ever expected to fill; and unless some new object of ambition is presented either to him or to his leaders, if he has the ordinary spirit of a man, he will die in defence of that station.

It is a remark of the President Heynaut, that we now read with pleasure the account of many little transactions of the Ligue, which, when they happened, were not, perhaps, considered as very important pieces of news. But everyman then, says he, fancied himself of some importance; and the innumerable memoirs which have come down to us from those times, were the greater part of them written by people who took pleasure in recording and magnifying events, in which they flattered themselves they had been considerable actors. How obstinately the city of Paris, upon that occasion, defended itself, what a dreadful famine it supported, rather than submit to the best, and afterwards the most beloved of all the French kings, is well known. The greater part of the citizens, or those who governed the greater part of them, fought in defence of their own importance, which, they foresaw, was to be at an end whenever the ancient government should be re-established. Our colonies, unless they can be induced to consent to a union, are very likely to defend themselves, against the best of all mother countries, as obstinately as the city of Paris did against one of the best of kings.

The idea of representation was unknown in ancient times. When the people of one state were admitted to the right of citizenship in another, they had no other means of exercising that right, but by coming in a body to vote and deliberate with the people of that other state. The admission of the greater part of the inhabitants of Italy to the privileges of Roman citizens, completely ruined the Roman republic. It was no longer possible to distinguish between who was, and who was not, a Roman citizen. No tribe could know its own members. A rabble of any kind could be introduced into the assemblies of the people, could drive out the real citizens, and decide upon the affairs of the republic, as if they themselves had been such. But though America were to send fifty or sixty new representatives to parliament, the door-keeper of the house of commons could not find any great difficulty in distinguishing between who was and who was not a member. Though the Roman constitution, therefore, was necessarily ruined by the union of Rome with the allied states of Italy, there is not the least probability that the British constitution would be hurt by the union of Great Britain with her colonies. That constitution, on the contrary, would be completed by it, and seems to be imperfect without it. The assembly which deliberates and decides concerning the affairs of every part of the empire, in order to be properly informed, ought certainly to have representatives from every part of it. That this union, however, could be easily effectuated, or that difficulties, and great difficulties, might not occur in the execution, I do not pretend. I have yet heard of none, however, which appear insurmountable. The principal, perhaps, arise, not from the nature of things, but from the prejudices and opinions of the people, both on this and on the other side of the Atlantic.

We on this side the water are afraid lest the multitude of American representatives should overturn the balance of the constitution, and increase too much either the influence of the crown on the one hand, or the force of the democracy on the other. But if the number of American representatives were to be in proportion to the produce of American taxation, the number of people to be managed would increase exactly in proportion to the means of managing them, and the means of managing to the number of people to be managed. The monarchical and democratical parts of the constitution would, after the union, stand exactly in the same degree of relative force with regard to one another as they had done before.

The people on the other side of the water are afraid lest their distance from the seat of government might expose them to many oppressions; but their representatives in parliament, of which the number ought from the first to be considerable, would easily be able to protect them from all oppression. The distance could not much weaken the dependency of the representative upon the constituent, and the former would still feel that he owed his seat in parliament, and all the consequence which he derived from it, to the good-will of the latter. It would be the interest of the former, therefore, to cultivate that good-will, by complaining, with all the authority of a member of the legislature, of every outrage which any civil or military officer might be guilty of in those remote parts of the empire. The distance of America from the seat of government, besides, the natives of that country might flatter themselves, with some appearance of reason too, would not be of very long continuance. Such has hitherto been the rapid progress of that country in wealth, population, and improvement, that in the course of little more than a century, perhaps, the produce of the American might exceed that of the British taxation. The seat of the empire would then naturally remove itself to that part of the empire which contributed most to the general defence and support of the whole.

The discovery of America, and that of a passage to the East Indies by the Cape of Good Hope, are the two greatest and most important events recorded in the history of mankind. Their consequences have already been great; but, in the short period of between two and three centuries which has elapsed since these discoveries were made, it is impossible that the whole extent of their consequences can have been seen. What benefits or what misfortunes to mankind may hereafter result from those great events, no human wisdom can foresee. By uniting in some measure the most distant parts of the world, by enabling them to relieve one another's wants, to increase one another's enjoyments, and to encourage one another's industry, their general tendency would seem to be beneficial. To the natives, however, both of the East and West Indies, all the commercial benefits which can have resulted from those events have been sunk and lost in the dreadful misfortunes which they have occasioned. These misfortunes, however, seem to have arisen rather from accident than from any thing in the nature of those events themselves. At the particular time when these discoveries were made, the superiority of force happened to be so great on the side of the Europeans, that they were enabled to commit with impunity every sort of injustice in those remote countries. Hereafter, perhaps, the natives of those countries may grow stronger, or those of Europe may grow weaker; and the inhabitants of all the different quarters of the world may arrive at that equality of courage and force which, by inspiring mutual fear, can alone overawe the injustice of independent nations into some sort of respect for the rights of one another. But nothing seems more likely to establish this equality of force, than that mutual communication of knowledge, and of all sorts of improvements, which an extensive commerce from all countries to all countries naturally, or rather necessarily, carries along with it.

In the mean time, one of the principal effects of those discoveries has been, to raise the mercantile system to a degree of splendour and glory which it could never otherwise have attained to. It is the object of that system to enrich a great nation, rather by trade and manufactures than by the improvement and cultivation of land, rather by the industry of the towns than by that of the country. But in consequence of those discoveries, the commercial towns of Europe, instead of being the manufacturers and carriers for but a very small part of the world (that part of Europe which is washed by the Atlantic ocean, and the countries which lie round the Baltic and Mediterranean seas), have now become the manufacturers for the numerous and thriving cultivators of America, and the carriers, and in some respects the manufacturers too, for almost all the different nations of Asia, Africa, and America. Two new worlds have been opened to their industry, each of them much greater and more extensive than the old one, and the market of one of them growing still greater and greater every day.

The countries which possess the colonies of America, and which trade directly to the East Indies, enjoy indeed the whole show and splendour of this great commerce. Other countries, however, notwithstanding all the invidious restraints by which it is meant to exclude them, frequently enjoy a greater share of the real benefit of it. The colonies of Spain and Portugal, for example, give more real encouragement to the industry of other countries than to that of Spain and Portugal. In the single article of linen alone, the consumption of those colonies amounts, it is said (but I do not pretend to warrant the quantity), to more than three millions sterling a-year. But this great consumption is almost entirely supplied by France, Flanders, Holland, and Germany. Spain and Portugal furnish but a small part of it. The capital which supplies the colonies with this great quantity of linen, is annually distributed among, and furnishes a revenue to, the inhabitants of those other countries. The profits of it only are spent in Spain and Portugal, where they help to support the sumptuous profusion of the merchants of Cadiz and Lisbon.

Even the regulations by which each nation endeavours to secure to itself the exclusive trade of its own colonies, are frequently more hurtful to the countries in favour of which they are established, than to those against which they are established. The unjust oppression of the industry of other countries falls back, if I may say so, upon the heads of the oppressors, and crushes their industry more than it does that of those other countries. By those regulations, for example, the merchant of Hamburg must send the linen which he destines for the American market to London, and he must bring back from thence the tobacco which he destines for the German market; because he can neither send the one directly to America, nor bring the other directly from thence. By this restraint he is probably obliged to sell the one somewhat cheaper, and to buy the other somewhat dearer, than he otherwise might have done; and his profits are probably somewhat abridged by means of it. In this trade, however, between Hamburg and London, he certainly receives the returns of his capital much more quickly than he could possibly have done in the direct trade to America, even though we should suppose, what is by no means the case, that the payments of America were as punctual as those of London. In the trade, therefore, to which those regulations confine the merchant of Hamburg, his capital can keep in constant employment a much greater quantity of German industry than he possibly could have done in the trade from which he is excluded. Though the one employment, therefore, may to him perhaps be less profitable than the other, it cannot be less advantageous to his country. It is quite otherwise with the employment into which the monopoly naturally attracts, if I may say so, the capital of the London merchant. That employment may, perhaps, be more profitable to him than the greater part of other employments; but on account of the slowness of the returns, it cannot be more advantageous to his country.

After all the unjust attempts, therefore, of every country in Europe to engross to itself the whole advantage of the trade of its own colonies, no country has yet been able to engross to itself any thing but the expense of supporting in time of peace, and of defending in time of war, the oppressive authority which it assumes over them. The inconveniencies resulting from the possession of its colonies, every country has engrossed to itself completely. The advantages resulting from their trade, it has been obliged to share with many other countries.

At first sight, no doubt, the monopoly of the great commerce of America naturally seems to be an acquisition of the highest value. To the undiscerning eye of giddy ambition it naturally presents itself, amidst the confused scramble of politics and war, as a very dazzling object to fight for. The dazzling splendour of the object, however, the immense greatness of the commerce, is the very quality which renders the monopoly of it hurtful, or which makes one employment, in its own nature necessarily less advantageous to the country than the greater part of other employments, absorb a much greater proportion of the capital of the country than what would otherwise have gone to it.

The mercantile stock of every country, it has been shown in the second book, naturally seeks, if one may say so, the employment most advantageous to that country. If it is employed in the carrying trade, the country to which it belongs becomes the emporium of the goods of all the countries whose trade that stock carries on. But the owner of that stock necessarily wishes to dispose of as great a part of those goods as he can at home. He thereby saves himself the trouble, risk, and expense of exportation; and he will upon that account be glad to sell them at home, not only for a much smaller price, but with somewhat a smaller profit, than he might expect to make by sending them abroad. He naturally, therefore, endeavours as much as he can to turn his carrying trade into a foreign trade of consumption, If his stock, again, is employed in a foreign trade of consumption, he will, for the same reason, be glad to dispose of, at home, as great a part as he can of the home goods which he collects in order to export to some foreign market, and he will thus endeavour, as much as he can, to turn his foreign trade of consumption into a home trade. The mercantile stock of every country naturally courts in this manner the near, and shuns the distant employment: naturally courts the employment in which the returns are frequent, and shuns that in which they are distant and slow; naturally courts the employment in which it can maintain the greatest quantity of productive labour in the country to which it belongs, or in which its owner resides, and shuns that in which it can maintain there the smallest quantity. It naturally courts the employment which in ordinary cases is most advantageous, and shuns that which in ordinary cases is least advantageous to that country.

But if, in any one of those distant employments, which in ordinary cases are less advantageous to the country, the profit should happen to rise somewhat higher than what is sufficient to balance the natural preference which is given to nearer employments, this superiority of profit will draw stock from those nearer employments, till the profits of all return to their proper level. This superiority of profit, however, is a proof that, in the actual circumstances of the society, those distant employments are somewhat understocked in proportion to other employments, and that the stock of the society is not distributed in the properest manner among all the different employments carried on in it. It is a proof that something is either bought cheaper or sold dearer than it ought to be, and that some particular class of citizens is more or less oppressed, either by paying more, or by getting less than what is suitable to that equality which ought to take place, and which naturally does take place, among all the different classes of them. Though the same capital never will maintain the same quantity of productive labour in a distant as in a near employment, yet a distant employment maybe as necessary for the welfare of the society as a near one; the goods which the distant employment deals in being necessary, perhaps, for carrying on many of the nearer employments. But if the profits of those who deal in such goods are above their proper level, those goods will be sold dearer than they ought to be, or somewhat above their natural price, and all those engaged in the nearer employments will be more or less oppressed by this high price. Their interest, therefore, in this case, requires, that some stock should be withdrawn from those nearer employments, and turned towards that distant one, in order to reduce its profits to their proper level, and the price of the goods which it deals in to their natural price. In this extraordinary case, the public interest requires that some stock should be withdrawn from those employments which, in ordinary cases, are more advantageous, and turned towards one which, in ordinary cases, is less advantageous to the public; and, in this extraordinary case, the natural interests and inclinations of men coincide as exactly with the public interests as in all other ordinary cases, and lead them to withdraw stock from the near, and to turn it towards the distant employments.

It is thus that the private interests and passions of individuals naturally dispose them to turn their stock towards the employments which in ordinary cases, are most advantageous to the society. But if from this natural preference they should turn too much of it towards those employments, the fall of profit in them, and the rise of it in all others, immediately dispose them to alter this faulty distribution. Without any intervention of law, therefore, the private interests and passions of men naturally lead them to divide and distribute the stock of every society among all the different employments carried on in it; as nearly as possible in the proportion which is most agreeable to the interest of the whole society.

All the different regulations of the mercantile system necessarily derange more or less this natural and most advantageous distribution of stock. But those which concern the trade to America and the East Indies derange it, perhaps, more than any other; because the trade to those two great continents absorbs a greater quantity of stock than any two other branches of trade. The regulations, however, by which this derangement is effected in those two different branches of trade, are not altogether the same. Monopoly is the great engine of both; but it is a different sort of monopoly. Monopoly of one kind or another, indeed, seems to be the sole engine of the mercantile system.

In the trade to America, every nation endeavours to engross as much as possible the whole market of its own colonies, by fairly excluding all other nations from any direct trade to them. During the greater part of the sixteenth century, the Portuguese endeavoured to manage the trade to the East Indies in the same manner, by claiming the sole right of sailing in the Indian seas, on account of the merit of having first found out the road to them. The Dutch still continue to exclude all other European nations from any direct trade to their spice islands. Monopolies of this kind are evidently established against all other European nations, who are thereby not only excluded from a trade to which it might be convenient for them to turn some part of their stock, but are obliged to buy the goods which that trade deals in, somewhat dearer than if they could import them themselves directly from the countries which produced them.

But since the fall of the power of Portugal, no European nation has claimed the exclusive right of sailing in the Indian seas, of which the principal ports are now open to the ships of all European nations. Except in Portugal, however, and within these few years in France, the trade to the East Indies has, in every European country, been subjected to an exclusive company. Monopolies of this kind are properly established against the very nation which erects them. The greater part of that nation are thereby not only excluded from a trade to which it might be convenient for them to turn some part of their stock, but are obliged to buy the goods which that trade deals in somewhat dearer than if it was open and free to all their countrymen. Since the establishment of the English East India company, for example, the other inhabitants of England, over and above being excluded from the trade, must have paid, in the price of the East India goods which they have consumed, not only for all the extraordinary profits which the company may have made upon those goods in consequence of their monopoly, but for all the extraordinary waste which the fraud and abuse inseparable from the management of the affairs of so great a company must necessarily have occasioned. The absurdity of this second kind of monopoly, therefore, is much more manifest than that of the first.

Both these kinds of monopolies derange more or less the natural distribution of the stock of the society; but they do not always derange it in the same way.

Monopolies of the first kind always attract to the particular trade in which they are established a greater proportion of the stock of the society than what would go to that trade of its own accord.

Monopolies of the second kind may sometimes attract stock towards the particular trade in which they are established, and sometimes repel it from that trade, according to different circumstances. In poor countries, they naturally attract towards that trade more stock than would otherwise go to it. In rich countries, they naturally repel from it a good deal of stock which would otherwise go to it.

Such poor countries as Sweden and Denmark, for example, would probably have never sent a single ship to the East Indies, had not the trade been subjected to an exclusive company. The establishment of such a company necessarily encourages adventurers. Their monopoly secures them against all competitors in the home market, and they have the same chance for foreign markets with the traders of other nations. Their monopoly shows them the certainty of a great profit upon a considerable quantity of goods, and the chance of a considerable profit upon a great quantity. Without such extraordinary encouragement, the poor traders of such poor countries would probably never have thought of hazarding their small capitals in so very distant and uncertain an adventure as the trade to the East Indies must naturally have appeared to them.

Such a rich country as Holland, on the contrary, would probably, in the case of a free trade, send many more ships to the East Indies than it actually does. The limited stock of the Dutch East India company probably repels from that trade many great mercantile capitals which would otherwise go to it. The mercantile capital of Holland is so great, that it is, as it were, continually overflowing, sometimes into the public funds of foreign countries, sometimes into loans to private traders and adventurers of foreign countries, sometimes into the most round-about foreign trades of consumption, and sometimes into the carrying trade. All near employments being completely filled up, all the capital which can be placed in them with any tolerable profit being already placed in them, the capital of Holland necessarily flows towards the most distant employments. The trade to the East Indies, if it were altogether free, would probably absorb the greater part of this redundant capital. The East Indies offer a market both for the manufactures of Europe, and for the gold and silver, as well as for the several other productions of America, greater and more extensive than both Europe and America put together.

Every derangement of the natural distribution of stock is necessarily hurtful to the society in which it takes place; whether it be by repelling from a particular trade the stock which would otherwise go to it, or by attracting towards a particular trade that which would not otherwise come to it. If, without any exclusive company, the trade of Holland to the East Indies would be greater than it actually is, that country must suffer a considerable loss, by part of its capital being excluded from the employment most convenient for that port. And, in the same manner, if, without an exclusive company, the trade of Sweden and Denmark to the East Indies would be less than it actually is, or, what perhaps is more probable, would not exist at all, those two countries must likewise suffer a considerable loss, by part of their capital being drawn into an employment which must be more or less unsuitable to their present circumstances. Better for them, perhaps, in the present circumstances, to buy East India goods of other nations, even though they should pay somewhat dearer, than to turn so great a part of their small capital to so very distant a trade, in which the returns are so very slow, in which that capital can maintain so small a quantity of productive labour at home, where productive labour is so much wanted, where so little is done, and where so much is to do.

Though without an exclusive company, therefore, a particular country should not be able to carry on any direct trade to the East Indies, it will not from thence follow, that such a company ought to be established there, but only that such a country ought not, in these circumstances, to trade directly to the East Indies. That such companies are not in general necessary for carrying on the East India trade, is sufficiently demonstrated by the experience of the Portuguese, who enjoyed almost the whole of it for more than a century together, without any exclusive company.

No private merchant, it has been said, could well have capital sufficient to maintain factors and agents in the different ports of the East Indies, in order to provide goods for the ships which he might occasionally send thither; and yet, unless he was able to do this, the difficulty of finding a cargo might frequently make his ships lose the season for returning; and the expense of so long a delay would not only eat up the whole profit of the adventure, but frequently occasion a very considerable loss. This argument, however, if it proved any thing at all, would prove that no one great branch of trade could be carried on without an exclusive company, which is contrary to the experience of all nations. There is no great branch of trade, in which the capital of any one private merchant is sufficient for carrying on all the subordinate branches which must be carried on, in order to carry on the principal one. But when a nation is ripe for any great branch of trade, some merchants naturally turn their capitals towards the principal, and some towards the subordinate branches of it; and though all the different branches of it are in this manner carried on, yet it very seldom happens that they are all carried on by the capital of one private merchant. If a nation, therefore, is ripe for the East India trade, a certain portion of its capital will naturally divide itself among all the different branches of that trade. Some of its merchants will find it for their interest to reside in the East Indies, and to employ their capitals there in providing goods for the ships which are to be sent out by other merchants who reside in Europe. The settlements which different European nations have obtained in the East Indies, if they were taken from the exclusive companies to which they at present belong, and put under the immediate protection of the sovereign, would render this residence both safe and easy, at least to the merchants of the particular nations to whom those settlements belong. If, at any particular time, that part of the capital of any country which of its own accord tended and inclined, if I may say so, towards the East India trade, was not sufficient for carrying on all those different branches of it, it would be a proof that, at that particular time, that country was not ripe for that trade, and that it would do better to buy for some time, even at a higher price, from other European nations, the East India goods it had occasion for, than to import them itself directly from the East Indies. What it might lose by the high price of those goods, could seldom be equal to the loss which it would sustain by the distraction of a large portion of its capital from other employments more necessary, or more useful, or more suitable to its circumstances and situation, than a direct trade to the East Indies.

Though the Europeans possess many considerable settlements both upon the coast of Africa and in the East Indies, they have not yet established, in either of those countries, such numerous and thriving colonies as those in the islands and continent of America. Africa, however, as well as several of the countries comprehended under the general name of the East Indies, is inhabited by barbarous nations. But those nations were by no means so weak and defenceless as the miserable and helpless Americans; and in proportion to the natural fertility of the countries which they inhabited, they were, besides, much more populous. The most barbarous nations either of Africa or of the East Indies, were shepherds; even the Hottentots were so. But the natives of every part of America, except Mexico and Peru, were only hunters and the difference is very great between the number of shepherds and that of hunters whom the same extent of equally fertile territory can maintain. In Africa and the East Indies, therefore, it was more difficult to displace the natives, and to extend the European plantations over the greater part of the lands of the original inhabitants. The genius of exclusive companies, besides, is unfavourable, it has already been observed, to the growth of new colonies, and has probably been the principal cause of the little progress which they have made in the East Indies. The Portuguese carried on the trade both to Africa and the East Indies, without any exclusive companies; and their settlements at Congo, Angola, and Benguela, on the coast of Africa, and at Goa in the East Indies though much depressed by superstition and every sort of bad government, yet bear some resemblance to the colonies of America, and are partly inhabited by Portuguese who have been established there for several generations. The Dutch settlements at the Cape of Good Hope and at Batavia, are at present the most considerable colonies which the Europeans have established, either in Africa or in the East Indies; and both those settlements are peculiarly fortunate in their situation. The Cape of Good Hope was inhabited by a race of people almost as barbarous, and quite as incapable of defending themselves, as the natives of America. It is, besides, the half-way house, if one may say so, between Europe and the East Indies, at which almost every European ship makes some stay, both in going and returning. The supplying of those ships with every sort of fresh provisions, with fruit, and sometimes with wine, affords alone a very extensive market for the surplus produce of the colonies. What the Cape of Good Hope is between Europe and every part of the East Indies, Batavia is between the principal countries of the East Indies. It lies upon the most frequented road from Indostan to China and Japan, and is nearly about mid-way upon that road. Almost all the ships too, that sail between Europe and China, touch at Batavia; and it is, over and above all this, the centre and principal mart of what is called the country trade of the East Indies; not only of that part of it which is carried on by Europeans, but of that which is carried on by the native Indians; and vessels navigated by the inhabitants of China and Japan, of Tonquin, Malacca, Cochin-China, and the island of Celebes, are frequently to be seen in its port. Such advantageous situations have enabled those two colonies to surmount all the obstacles which the oppressive genius of an exclusive company may have occasionally opposed to their growth. They have enabled Batavia to surmount the additional disadvantage of perhaps the most unwholesome climate in the world.

The English and Dutch companies, though they have established no considerable colonies, except the two above mentioned, have both made considerable conquests in the East Indies. But in the manner in which they both govern their new subjects, the natural genius of an exclusive company has shewn itself most distinctly. In the spice islands, the Dutch are said to burn all the spiceries which a fertile season produces, beyond what they expect to dispose of in Europe with such a profit as they think sufficient. In the islands where they have no settlements, they give a premium to those who collect the young blossoms and green leaves of the clove and nutmeg trees, which naturally grow there, but which this savage policy has now, it is said, almost completely extirpated. Even in the islands where they have settlements, they have very much reduced, it is said, the number of those trees. If the produce even of their own islands was much greater than what suited their market, the natives, they suspect, might find means to convey some part of it to other nations; and the best way, they imagine, to secure their own monopoly, is to take care that no more shall grow than what they themselves carry to market. By different arts of oppression, they have reduced the population of several of the Moluccas nearly to the number which is sufficient to supply with fresh provisions, and other necessaries of life, their own insignificant garrisons, and such of their ships as occasionally come there for a cargo of spices. Under the government even of the Portuguese, however, those islands are said to have been tolerably well inhabited. The English company have not yet had time to establish in Bengal so perfectly destructive a system. The plan of their government, however, has had exactly the same tendency. It has not been uncommon, I am well assured, for the chief, that is, the first clerk or a factory, to order a peasant to plough up a rich field of poppies, and sow it with rice, or some other grain. The pretence was, to prevent a scarcity of provisions; but the real reason, to give the chief an opportunity of selling at a better price a large quantity of opium which he happened then to have upon hand. Upon other occasions, the order has been reversed; and a rich field of rice or other grain has been ploughed up, in order to make room for a plantation of poppies, when the chief foresaw that extraordinary profit was likely to be made by opium.

The servants of the company have, upon several occasions, attempted to establish in their own favour the monopoly of some of the most important branches, not only of the foreign, but of the inland trade of the country. Had they been allowed to go on, it is impossible that they should not, at some time or another, have attempted to restrain the production of the particular articles of which they had thus usurped the monopoly, not only to the quantity which they themselves could purchase, but to that which they could expect to sell with such a profit as they might think sufficient. In the course of a century or two, the policy of the English company would, in this manner, have probably proved as completely destructive as that of the Dutch.

Nothing, however, can be more directly contrary to the real interest of those companies, considered as the sovereigns of the countries which they have conquered, than this destructive plan. In almost all countries, the revenue of the sovereign is drawn from that of the people. The greater the revenue of the people, therefore, the greater the annual produce of their land and labour, the more they can afford to the sovereign. It is his interest, therefore, to increase as much as possible that annual produce. But if this is the interest of every sovereign, it is peculiarly so of one whose revenue, like that of the sovereign of Bengal, arises chiefly from a land-rent. That rent must necessarily be in proportion to the quantity and value of the produce; and both the one and the other must depend upon the extent of the market. The quantity will always be suited, with more or less exactness, to the consumption of those who can afford to pay for it; and the price which they will pay will always be in proportion to the eagerness of their competition. It is the interest of such a sovereign, therefore, to open the most extensive market for the produce of his country, to allow the most perfect freedom of commerce, in order to increase as much as possible the number and competition of buyers; and upon this account to abolish, not only all monopolies, but all restraints upon the transportation of the home produce from one part of the country to another, upon its exportation to foreign countries, or upon the importation of goods of any kind for which it can be exchanged. He is in this manner most likely to increase both the quantity and value of that produce, and consequently of his own share of it, or of his own revenue.

But a company of merchants, are, it seems, incapable of considering themselves as sovereigns, even after they have become such. Trade, or buying in order to sell again, they still consider as their principal business, and by a strange absurdity, regard the character of the sovereign as but an appendix to that of the merchant; as something which ought to be made subservient to it, or by means of which they may be enabled to buy cheaper in India, and thereby to sell with a better profit in Europe. They endeavour, for this purpose, to keep out as much as possible all competitors from the market of the countries which are subject to their government, and consequently to reduce, at least, some part of the surplus produce of those countries to what is barely sufficient for supplying their own demand, or to what they can expect to sell in Europe, with such a profit as they may think reasonable. Their mercantile habits draw them in this manner, almost necessarily, though perhaps insensibly, to prefer, upon all ordinary occasions, the little and transitory profit of the monopolist to the great and permanent revenue of the sovereign; and would gradually lead them to treat the countries subject to their government nearly as the Dutch treat the Moluccas. It is the interest of the East India company, considered as sovereigns, that the European goods which are carried to their Indian dominions should be sold there as cheap as possible; and that the Indian goods which are brought from thence should bring there as good a price, or should be sold there as dear as possible. But the reverse of this is their interest as merchants. As sovereigns, their interest is exactly the same with that of the country which they govern. As merchants, their interest is directly opposite to that interest.

But if the genius of such a government, even as to what concerns its direction in Europe, is in this manner essentially, and perhaps incurably faulty, that of its administration in India is still more so. That administration is necessarily composed of a council of merchants, a profession no doubt extremely respectable, but which in no country in the world carries along with it that sort of authority which naturally overawes the people, and without force commands their willing obedience. Such a council can command obedience only by the military force with which they are accompanied; and their government is, therefore, necessarily military and despotical. Their proper business, however, is that of merchants. It is to sell, upon their master's account, the European goods consigned to them, and to buy, in return, Indian goods for the European market. It is to sell the one as dear, and to buy the other as cheap as possible, and consequently to exclude, as much as possible, all rivals from the particular market where they keep their shop. The genius of the administration, therefore, so far as concerns the trade of the company, is the same as that of the direction. It tends to make government subservient to the interest of monopoly, and consequently to stunt the natural growth of some parts, at least, of the surplus produce of the country, to what is barely sufficient for answering the demand of the company.

All the members of the administration besides, trade more or less upon their own account; and it is in vain to prohibit them from doing so. Nothing can be more completely foolish than to expect that the clerk of a great counting-house, at ten thousand miles distance, and consequently almost quite out of sight, should, upon a simple order from their master, give up at once doing any sort of business upon their own account abandon for ever all hopes of making a fortune, of which they have the means in their hands; and content themselves with the moderate salaries which those masters allow them, and which, moderate as they are, can seldom be augmented, being commonly as large as the real profits of the company trade can afford. In such circumstances, to prohibit the servants of the company from trading upon their own account, can have scarce any other effect than to enable its superior servants, under pretence of executing their master's order, to oppress such of the inferior ones as have had the misfortune to fall under their displeasure. The servants naturally endeavour to establish the same monopoly in favour of their own private trade as of the public trade of the company. If they are suffered to act as they could wish, they will establish this monopoly openly and directly, by fairly prohibiting all other people from trading in the articles in which they choose to deal; and this, perhaps, is the best and least oppressive way of establishing it. But if, by an order from Europe, they are prohibited from doing this, they will, notwithstanding, endeavour to establish a monopoly of the same kind secretly and indirectly, in a way that is much more destructive to the country. They will employ the whole authority of government, and pervert the administration of Justice, in order to harass and ruin those who interfere with them in any branch of commerce, which by means of agents, either concealed, or at least not publicly avowed, they may choose to carry on. But the private trade of the servants will naturally extend to a much greater variety of articles than the public trade of the company. The public trade of the company extends no further than the trade with Europe, and comprehends a part only of the foreign trade of the country. But the private trade of the servants may extend to all the different branches both of its inland and foreign trade. The monopoly of the company can tend only to stunt the natural growth of that part of the surplus produce which, in the case of a free trade, would be exported to Europe. That of the servants tends to stunt the natural growth of every part of the produce in which they choose to deal; of what is destined for home consumption, as well as of what is destined for exportation; and consequently to degrade the cultivation of the whole country, and to reduce the number of its inhabitants. It tends to reduce the quantity of every sort of produce, even that of the necessaries of life, whenever the servants of the country choose to deal in them, to what those servants can both afford to buy and expect to sell with such a profit as pleases them.

From the nature of their situation, too, the servants must be more disposed to support with rigourous severity their own interest, against that of the country which they govern, than their masters can be to support theirs. The country belongs to their masters, who cannot avoid having some regard for the interest of what belongs to them; but it does not belong to the servants. The real interest of their masters, if they were capable of understanding it, is the same with that of the country; {The interest of every proprietor of India stock, however, is by no means the same with that of the country in the government of which his vote gives him some influence.—See book v, chap. 1, part ii.} and it is from ignorance chiefly, and the meanness of mercantile prejudice, that they ever oppress it. But the real interest of the servants is by no means the same with that of the country, and the most perfect information would not necessarily put an end to their oppressions. The regulations, accordingly, which have been sent out from Europe, though they have been frequently weak, have upon most occasions been well meaning. More intelligence, and perhaps less good meaning, has sometimes appeared in those established by the servants in India. It is a very singular government in which every member of the administration wishes to get out of the country, and consequently to have done with the government, as soon as he can, and to whose interest, the day after he has left it, and carried his whole fortune with him, it is perfectly indifferent though the whole country was swallowed up by an earthquake.

I mean not, however, by any thing which I have here said, to throw any odious imputation upon the general character of the servants of the East India company, and touch less upon that of any particular persons. It is the system of government, the situation in which they are placed, that I mean to censure, not the character of those who have acted in it. They acted as their situation naturally directed, and they who have clamoured the loudest against them would probably not have acted better themselves. In war and negotiation, the councils of Madras and Calcutta, have upon several occasions, conducted themselves with a resolution and decisive wisdom, which would have done honour to the senate of Rome in the best days of that republic. The members of those councils, however, had been bred to professions very different from war and politics. But their situation alone, without education, experience, or even example, seems to have formed in them all at once the great qualities which it required, and to have inspired them both with abilities and virtues which they themselves could not well know that they possessed. If upon some occasions, therefore, it has animated them to actions of magnanimity which could not well have been expected from them, we should not wonder if, upon others, it has prompted them to exploits of somewhat a different nature.

Such exclusive companies, therefore, are nuisances in every respect; always more or less inconvenient to the countries in which they are established, and destructive to those which have the misfortune to fall under their government.

CHAPTER VIII

CONCLUSION OF THE MERCANTILE SYSTEM

Though the encouragement of exportation, and the discouragement of importation, are the two great engines by which the mercantile system proposes to enrich every country, yet, with regard to some particular commodities, it seems to follow an opposite plan: to discourage exportation, and to encourage importation. Its ultimate object, however, it pretends, is always the same, to enrich the country by an advantageous balance of trade. It discourages the exportation of the materials of manufacture, and of the instruments of trade, in order to give our own workmen an advantage, and to enable them to undersell those of other nations in all foreign markets; and by restraining, in this manner, the exportation of a few commodities, of no great price, it proposes to occasion a much greater and more valuable exportation of others. It encourages the importation of the materials of manufacture, in order that our own people may be enabled to work them up more cheaply, and thereby prevent a greater and more valuable importation of the manufactured commodities. I do not observe, at least in our statute book, any encouragement given to the importation of the instruments of trade. When manufactures have advanced to a certain pitch of greatness, the fabrication of the instruments of trade becomes itself the object of a great number of very important manufactures. To give any particular encouragement to the importation of such instruments, would interfere too much with the interest of those manufactures. Such importation, therefore, instead of being encouraged, has frequently been prohibited. Thus the importation of wool cards, except from Ireland, or when brought in as wreck or prize goods, was prohibited by the 3rd of Edward IV.; which prohibition was renewed by the 39th of Elizabeth, and has been continued and rendered perpetual by subsequent laws.

The importation of the materials of manufacture has sometimes been encouraged by an exemption from the duties to which other goods are subject, and sometimes by bounties.

The importation of sheep's wool from several different countries, of cotton wool from all countries, of undressed flax, of the greater part of dyeing drugs, of the greater part of undressed hides from Ireland, or the British colonies, of seal skins from the British Greenland fishery, of pig and bar iron from the British colonies, as well as of several other materials of manufacture, has been encouraged by an exemption from all duties, if properly entered at the custom-house. The private interest of our merchants and manufacturers may, perhaps, have extorted from the legislature these exemptions, as well as the greater part of our other commercial regulations. They are, however, perfectly just and reasonable; and if, consistently with the necessities of the state, they could be extended to all the other materials of manufacture, the public would certainly be a gainer.

The avidity of our great manufacturers, however, has in some cases extended these exemptions a good deal beyond what can justly be considered as the rude materials of their work. By the 24th Geo. II. chap. 46, a small duty of only 1d. the pound was imposed upon the importation of foreign brown linen yarn, instead of much higher duties, to which it had been subjected before, viz. of 6d. the pound upon sail yarn, of 1s. the pound upon all French and Dutch yarn, and of £2:13:4 upon the hundred weight of all spruce or Muscovia yarn. But our manufacturers were not long satisfied with this reduction: by the 29th of the same king, chap. 15, the same law which gave a bounty upon the exportation of British and Irish linen, of which the price did not exceed 18d. the yard, even this small duty upon the importation of brown linen yarn was taken away. In the different operations, however, which are necessary for the preparation of linen yarn, a good deal more industry is employed, than in the subsequent operation of preparing linen cloth from linen yarn. To say nothing of the industry of the flax-growers and flaxdressers, three or four spinners at least are necessary in order to keep one weaver in constant employment; and more than four-fifths of the whole quantity of labour necessary for the preparation of linen cloth, is employed in that of linen yarn; but our spinners are poor people; women commonly scattered about in all different parts of the country, without support or protection. It is not by the sale of their work, but by that of the complete work of the weavers, that our great master manufacturers make their profits. As it is their interest to sell the complete manufacture as dear, so it is to buy the materials as cheap as possible. By extorting from the legislature bounties upon the exportation of their own linen, high duties upon the importation of all foreign linen, and a total prohibition of the home consumption of some sorts of French linen, they endeavour to sell their own goods as dear as possible. By encouraging the importation of foreign linen yarn, and thereby bringing it into competition with that which is made by our own people, they endeavour to buy the work of the poor spinners as cheap as possible. They are as intent to keep down the wages of their own weavers, as the earnings of the poor spinners; and it is by no means for the benefit of the workmen that they endeavour either to raise the price of the complete work, or to lower that of the rude materials. It is the industry which is carried on for the benefit of the rich and the powerful, that is principally encouraged by our mercantile system. That which is carried on for the benefit of the poor and the indigent is too often either neglected or oppressed.

Both the bounty upon the exportation of linen, and the exemption from the duty upon the importation of foreign yarn, which were granted only for fifteen years, but continued by two different prolongations, expire with the end of the session of parliament which shall immediately follow the 24th of June 1786.

The encouragement given to the importation of the materials of manufacture by bounties, has been principally confined to such as were imported from our American plantations.

The first bounties of this kind were those granted about the beginning of the present century, upon the importation of naval stores from America. Under this denomination were comprehended timber fit for masts, yards, and bowsprits; hemp, tar, pitch, and turpentine. The bounty, however, of £1 the ton upon masting-timber, and that of £6 the ton upon hemp, were extended to such as should be imported into England from Scotland. Both these bounties continued, without any variation, at the same rate, till they were severally allowed to expire; that upon hemp on the 1st of January 1741, and that upon masting-timber at the end of the session of parliament immediately following the 24th June 1781.

The bounties upon the importation of tar, pitch, and turpentine, underwent, during their continuance, several alterations. Originally, that upon tar was £4 the ton; that upon pitch the same; and that upon turpentine £3 the ton. The bounty of £4 the ton upon tar was afterwards confined to such as had been prepared in a particular manner; that upon other good, clean, and merchantable tar was reduced to £2:4s. the ton. The bounty upon pitch was likewise reduced to £1, and that upon turpentine to £1:10s. the ton.

The second bounty upon the importation of any of the materials of manufacture, according to the order of time, was that granted by the 21st Geo. II. chap.30, upon the importation of indigo from the British plantations. When the plantation indigo was worth three-fourths of the price of the best French indigo, it was, by this act, entitled to a bounty of 6d. the pound. This bounty, which, like most others, was granted only for a limited time, was continued by several prolongations, but was reduced to 4d. the pound. It was allowed to expire with the end of the session of parliament which followed the 25th March 1781.

The third bounty of this kind was that granted (much about the time that we were beginning sometimes to court, and sometimes to quarrel with our American colonies), by the 4th. Geo. III. chap. 26, upon the importation of hemp, or undressed flax, from the British plantations. This bounty was granted for twenty-one years, from the 24th June 1764 to the 24th June 1785. For the first seven years, it was to be at the rate of £8 the ton; for the second at £6; and for the third at £4. It was not extended to Scotland, of which the climate (although hemp is sometimes raised there in small quantities, and of an inferior quality) is not very fit for that produce. Such a bounty upon the importation of Scotch flax in England would have been too great a discouragement to the native produce of the southern part of the united kingdom.

The fourth bounty of this kind was that granted by the 5th Geo. III. chap. 45, upon the importation of wood from America. It was granted for nine years from the 1st January 1766 to the 1st January 1775. During the first three years, it was to be for every hundred-and-twenty good deals, at the rate of £1, and for every load containing fifty cubic feet of other square timber, at the rate of 12s. For the second three years, it was for deals, to be at the rate of 15s., and for other squared timber at the rate of 8s.; and for the third three years, it was for deals, to be at the rate of 10s.; and for every other squared timber at the rate of 5s.

The fifth bounty of this kind was that granted by the 9th Geo. III. chap. 38, upon the importation of raw silk from the British plantations. It was granted for twenty-one years, from the 1st January 1770, to the 1st January 1791. For the first seven years, it was to be at the rate of £25 for every hundred pounds value; for the second, at £20; and for the third, at £15. The management of the silk-worm, and the preparation of silk, requires so much hand-labour, and labour is so very dear in America, that even this great bounty, I have been informed, was not likely to produce any considerable effect.

The sixth Bounty of this kind was that granted by 11th Geo. III. chap. 50, for the importation of pipe, hogshead, and barrelstaves and leading from the British plantations. It was granted for nine years, from 1st January 1772 to the 1st January 1781. For the first three years, it was, for a certain quantity of each, to be at the rate of £6; for the second three years at £4; and for the third three years at £2.

The seventh and last bounty of this kind was that granted by the 19th Geo. III chap. 37, upon the importation of hemp from Ireland. It was granted in the same manner as that for the importation of hemp and undressed flax from America, for twenty-one years, from the 24th June 1779 to the 24th June 1800. The term is divided likewise into three periods, of seven years each; and in each of those periods, the rate of the Irish bounty is the same with that of the American. It does not, however, like the American bounty, extend to the importation of undressed flax. It would have been too great a discouragement to the cultivation of that plant in Great Britain. When this last bounty was granted, the British and Irish legislatures were not in much better humour with one another, than the British and American had been before. But this boon to Ireland, it is to be hoped, has been granted under more fortunate auspices than all those to America. The same commodities, upon which we thus gave bounties, when imported from America, were subjected to considerable duties when imported from any other country. The interest of our American colonies was regarded as the same with that of the mother country. Their wealth was considered as our wealth. Whatever money was sent out to them, it was said, came all back to us by the balance of trade, and we could never become a farthing the poorer by any expense which we could lay out upon them. They were our own in every respect, and it was an expense laid out upon the improvement of our own property, and for the profitable employment of our own people. It is unnecessary, I apprehend, at present to say anything further, in order to expose the folly of a system which fatal experience has now sufficiently exposed. Had our American colonies really been a part of Great Britain, those bounties might have been considered as bounties upon production, and would still have been liable to all the objections to which such bounties are liable, but to no other.

The exportation of the materials of manufacture is sometimes discouraged by absolute prohibitions, and sometimes by high duties.

Our woollen manufacturers have been more successful than any other class of workmen, in persuading the legislature that the prosperity of the nation depended upon the success and extension of their particular business. They have not only obtained a monopoly against the consumers, by an absolute prohibition of importing woollen cloths from any foreign country; but they have likewise obtained another monopoly against the sheep farmers and growers of wool, by a similar prohibition of the exportation of live sheep and wool. The severity of many of the laws which have been enacted for the security of the revenue is very justly complained of, as imposing heavy penalties upon actions which, antecedent to the statutes that declared them to be crimes, had always been understood to be innocent. But the cruellest of our revenue laws, I will venture to affirm, are mild and gentle, in comparison to some of those which the clamour of our merchants and manufacturers has extorted from the legislature, for the support of their own absurd and oppressive monopolies. Like the laws of Draco, these laws may be said to be all written in blood.

By the 8th of Elizabeth, chap. 3, the exporter of sheep, lambs, or rams, was for the first offence, to forfeit all his goods for ever, to suffer a year's imprisonment, and then to have his left hand cut off in a market town, upon a market day, to be there nailed up; and for the second offence, to be adjudged a felon, and to suffer death accordingly. To prevent the breed of our sheep from being propagated in foreign countries, seems to have been the object of this law. By the 13th and 14th of Charles II. chap. 18, the exportation of wool was made felony, and the exporter subjected to the same penalties and forfeitures as a felon.

For the honour of the national humanity, it is to be hoped that neither of these statutes was ever executed. The first of them, however, so far as I know, has never been directly repealed, and serjeant Hawkins seems to consider it as still in force. It may, however, perhaps be considered as virtually repealed by the 12th of Charles II. chap. 32, sect. 3, which, without expressly taking away the penalties imposed by former statutes, imposes a new penalty, viz. that of 20s. for every sheep exported, or attempted to be exported, together with the forfeiture of the sheep, and of the owner's share of the sheep. The second of them was expressly repealed by the 7th and 8th of William III. chap. 28, sect. 4, by which it is declared that "Whereas the statute of the 13th and 14th of king Charles II. made against the exportation of wool, among other things in the said act mentioned, doth enact the same to be deemed felony, by the severity of which penalty the prosecution of offenders hath not been so effectually put in execution; be it therefore enacted, by the authority aforesaid, that so much of the said act, which relates to the making the said offence felony, be repealed and made void."

The penalties, however, which are either imposed by this milder statute, or which, though imposed by former statutes, are not repealed by this one, are still sufficiently severe. Besides the forfeiture of the goods, the exporter incurs the penalty of 3s. for every pound weight of wool, either exported or attempted to be exported, that is, about four or five times the value. Any merchant, or other person convicted of this offence, is disabled from requiring any debt or account belonging to him from any factor or other person. Let his fortune be what it will, whether he is or is not able to pay those heavy penalties, the law means to ruin him completely. But, as the morals of the great body of the people are not yet so corrupt as those of the contrivers of this statute, I have not heard that any advantage has ever been taken of this clause. If the person convicted of this offence is not able to pay the penalties within three months after judgment, he is to be transported for seven years; and if he returns before the expiration of that term, he is liable to the pains of felony, without benefit of clergy. The owner of the ship, knowing this offence, forfeits all his interest in the ship and furniture. The master and mariners, knowing this offence, forfeit all their goods and chattels, and suffer three months imprisonment. By a subsequent statute, the master suffers six months imprisonment.

In order to prevent exportation, the whole inland commerce of wool is laid under very burdensome and oppressive restrictions. It cannot be packed in any box, barrel, cask, case, chest, or any other package, but only in packs of leather or pack-cloth, on which must be marked on the outside the words WOOL or YARN, in large letters, not less than three inches long, on pain of forfeiting the same and the package, and 8s. for every pound weight, to be paid by the owner or packer. It cannot be loaden on any horse or cart, or carried by land within five miles of the coast, but between sun-rising, and sun-setting, on pain of forfeiting the same, the horses and carriages. The hundred next adjoining to the sea coast, out of, or through which the wool is carried or exported, forfeits £20, if the wool is under the value of £10; and if of greater value, then treble that value, together with treble costs, to be sued for within the year. The execution to be against any two of the inhabitants, whom the sessions must reimburse, by an assessment on the other inhabitants, as in the cases of robbery. And if any person compounds with the hundred for less than this penalty, he is to be imprisoned for five years; and any other person may prosecute. These regulations take place through the whole kingdom.

But in the particular counties of Kent and Sussex, the restrictions are still more troublesome. Every owner of wool within ten miles of the sea coast must give an account in writing, three days after shearing, to the next officer of the customs, of the number of his fleeces, and of the places where they are lodged. And before he removes any part of them, he must give the like notice of the number and weight of the fleeces, and of the name and abode of the person to whom they are sold, and of the place to which it is intended they should be carried. No person within fifteen miles of the sea, in the said counties, can buy any wool, before he enters into bond to the king, that no part of the wool which he shall so buy shall be sold by him to any other person within fifteen miles of the sea. If any wool is found carrying towards the sea side in the said counties, unless it has been entered and security given as aforesaid, it is forfeited, and the offender also forfeits 3s. for every pound weight, if any person lay any wool, not entered as aforesaid, within fifteen miles of the sea, it must be seized and forfeited; and if, after such seizure, any person shall claim the same, he must give security to the exchequer, that if he is cast upon trial he shall pay treble costs, besides all other penalties.

When such restrictions are imposed upon the inland trade, the coasting trade, we may believe, cannot be left very free. Every owner of wool, who carrieth, or causeth to be carried, any wool to any port or place on the sea coast, in order to be from thence transported by sea to any other place or port on the coast, must first cause an entry thereof to be made at the port from whence it is intended to be conveyed, containing the weight, marks, and number, of the packages, before he brings the same within five miles of that port, on pain of forfeiting the same, and also the horses, carts, and other carriages; and also of suffering and forfeiting, as by the other laws in force against the exportation of wool. This law, however (1st of William III. chap. 32), is so very indulgent as to declare, that this shall not hinder any person from carrying his wool home from the place of shearing, though it be within five miles of the sea, provided that in ten days after shearing, and before he remove the wool, he do under his hand certify to the next officer of the customs the true number of fleeces, and where it is housed; and do not remove the same, without certifying to such officer, under his hand, his intention so to do, three days before. Bond must be given that the wool to be carried coast-ways is to be landed at the particular port for which it is entered outwards; and if my part of it is landed without the presence of an officer, not only the forfeiture of the wool is incurred, as in other goods, but the usual additional penalty of 3s. for every pound weight is likewise incurred.

Our woollen manufacturers, in order to justify their demand of such extraordinary restrictions and regulations, confidently asserted, that English wool was of a peculiar quality, superior to that of any other country; that the wool of other countries could not, without some mixture of it, be wrought up into any tolerable manufacture; that fine cloth could not be made without it; that England, therefore, if the exportation of it could be totally prevented, could monopolize to herself almost the whole woollen trade of the world; and thus, having no rivals, could sell at what price she pleased, and in a short time acquire the most incredible degree of wealth by the most advantageous balance of trade. This doctrine, like most other doctrines which are confidently asserted by any considerable number of people, was, and still continues to be, most implicitly believed by a much greater number: by almost all those who are either unacquainted with the woollen trade, or who have not made particular inquiries. It is, however, so perfectly false, that English wool is in any respect necessary for the making of fine cloth, that it is altogether unfit for it. Fine cloth is made altogether of Spanish wool. English wool, cannot be even so mixed with Spanish wool, as to enter into the composition without spoiling and degrading, in some degree, the fabric of the cloth.

It has been shown in the foregoing part of this work, that the effect of these regulations has been to depress the price of English wool, not only below what it naturally would be in the present times, but very much below what it actually was in the time of Edward III. The price of Scotch wool, when, in consequence of the Union, it became subject to the same regulations, is said to have fallen about one half. It is observed by the very accurate and intelligent author of the Memoirs of Wool, the Reverend Mr. John Smith, that the price of the best English wool in England, is generally below what wool of a very inferior quality commonly sells for in the market of Amsterdam. To depress the price of this commodity below what may be called its natural and proper price, was the avowed purpose of those regulations; and there seems to be no doubt of their having produced the effect that was expected from them.

This reduction of price, it may perhaps be thought, by discouraging the growing of wool, must have reduced very much the annual produce of that commodity, though not below what it formerly was, yet below what, in the present state of things, it would probably have been, had it, in consequence of an open and free market, been allowed to rise to the natural and proper price. I am, however, disposed to believe, that the quantity of the annual produce cannot have been much, though it may, perhaps, have been a little affected by these regulations. The growing of wool is not the chief purpose for which the sheep farmer employs his industry and stock. He expects his profit, not so much from the price of the fleece, as from that of the carcase; and the average or ordinary price of the latter must even, in many cases, make up to him whatever deficiency there may be in the average or ordinary price of the former. It has been observed, in the foregoing part of this work, that 'whatever regulations tend to sink the price, either of wool or of raw hides, below what it naturally would be, must, in an improved and cultivated country, have some tendency to raise the price of butcher's meat. The price, both of the great and small cattle which are fed on improved and cultivated land, must be sufficient to pay the rent which the landlord, and the profit which the farmer, has reason to expect from improved and cultivated land. If it is not, they will soon cease to feed them. Whatever part of this price, therefore, is not paid by the wool and the hide, must be paid by the carcase. The less there is paid for the one, the more must be paid for the other. In what manner this price is to be divided upon the different parts of the beast, is indifferent to the landlords and farmers, provided it is all paid to them. In an improved and cultivated country, therefore, their interest as landlords and farmers cannot be much affected by such regulations, though their interest as consumers may, by the rise in the price of provisions.' According to this reasoning, therefore, this degradation in the price of wool is not likely, in an improved and cultivated country, to occasion any diminution in the annual produce of that commodity; except so far as, by raising the price of mutton, it may somewhat diminish the demand for, and consequently the production of, that particular species of butcher's meat, Its effect, however, even in this way, it is probable, is not very considerable.

But though its effect upon the quantity of the annual produce may not have been very considerable, its effect upon the quality, it may perhaps be thought, must necessarily have been very great. The degradation in the quality of English wool, if not below what it was in former times, yet below what it naturally would have been in the present state of improvement and cultivation, must have been, it may perhaps be supposed, very nearly in proportion to the degradation of price. As the quality depends upon the breed, upon the pasture, and upon the management and cleanliness of the sheep, during the whole progress of the growth of the fleece, the attention to these circumstances, it may naturally enough be imagined, can never be greater than in proportion to the recompence which the price of the fleece is likely to make for the labour and expense which that attention requires. It happens, however, that the goodness of the fleece depends, in a great measure, upon the health, growth, and bulk of the animal: the same attention which is necessary for the improvement of the carcase is, in some respect, sufficient for that of the fleece. Notwithstanding the degradation of price, English wool is said to have been improved considerably during the course even of the present century. The improvement, might, perhaps, have been greater if the price had been better; but the lowness of price, though it may have obstructed, yet certainly it has not altogether prevented that improvement.

The violence of these regulations, therefore, seems to have affected neither the quantity nor the quality of the annual produce of wool, so much as it might have been expected to do (though I think it probable that it may have affected the latter a good deal more than the former); and the interest of the growers of wool, though it must have been hurt in some degree, seems upon the whole, to have been much less hurt than could well have been imagined.

These considerations, however, will not justify the absolute prohibition of the exportation of wool; but they will fully justify the imposition of a considerable tax upon that exportation.

To hurt, in any degree, the interest of any one order of citizens, for no other purpose but to promote that of some other, is evidently contrary to that justice and equality of treatment which the sovereign owes to all the different orders of his subjects. But the prohibition certainly hurts, in some degree, the interest of the growers of wool, for no other purpose but to promote that of the manufacturers.

Every different order of citizens is bound to contribute to the support of the sovereign or commonwealth. A tax of five, or even of ten shillings, upon the exportation of every tod of wool, would produce a very considerable revenue to the sovereign. It would hurt the interest of the growers somewhat less than the prohibition, because it would not probably lower the price of wool quite so much. It would afford a sufficient advantage to the manufacturer, because, though he might not buy his wool altogether so cheap as under the prohibition, he would still buy it at least five or ten shillings cheaper than any foreign manufacturer could buy it, besides saving the freight and insurance which the other would be obliged to pay. It is scarce possible to devise a tax which could produce any considerable revenue to the sovereign, and at the same time occasion so little inconveniency to anybody.

The prohibition, notwithstanding all the penalties which guard it, does not prevent the exportation of wool. It is exported, it is well known, in great quantities. The great difference between the price in the home and that in the foreign market, presents such a temptation to smuggling, that all the rigour of the law cannot prevent it. This illegal exportation is advantageous to nobody but the smuggler. A legal exportation, subject to a tax, by affording a revenue to the sovereign, and thereby saving the imposition of some other, perhaps more burdensome and inconvenient taxes, might prove advantageous to all the different subjects of the state.

The exportation of fuller's earth, or fuller's clay, supposed to be necessary for preparing and cleansing the woollen manufactures, has been subjected to nearly the same penalties as the exportation of wool. Even tobacco-pipe clay, though acknowledged to be different from fuller's clay, yet, on account of their resemblance, and because fuller's clay might sometimes be exported as tobacco-pipe clay, has been laid under the same prohibitions and penalties.

By the 13th and 14th of Charles II. chap, 7, the exportation, not only of raw hides, but of tanned leather, except in the shape of boots, shoes, or slippers, was prohibited; and the law gave a monopoly to our boot-makers and shoe-makers, not only against our graziers, but against our tanners. By subsequent statutes, our tanners have got themselves exempted from this monopoly, upon paying a small tax of only one shilling on the hundred weight of tanned leather, weighing one hundred and twelve pounds. They have obtained likewise the drawback of two-thirds of the excise duties imposed upon their commodity, even when exported without further manufacture. All manufactures of leather may be exported duty free; and the exporter is besides entitled to the drawback of the whole duties of excise. Our graziers still continue subject to the old monopoly. Graziers, separated from one another, and dispersed through all the different corners of the country, cannot, without great difficulty, combine together for the purpose either of imposing monopolies upon their fellow-citizens, or of exempting themselves from such as may have been imposed upon them by other people. Manufacturers of all kinds, collected together in numerous bodies in all great cities, easily can. Even the horns of cattle are prohibited to be exported; and the two insignificant trades of the horner and comb-maker enjoy, in this respect, a monopoly against the graziers.

Restraints, either by prohibitions, or by taxes, upon the exportation of goods which are partially, but not completely manufactured, are not peculiar to the manufacture of leather. As long as anything remains to be done, in order to fit any commodity for immediate use and consumption, our manufacturers think that they themselves ought to have the doing of it. Woollen yarn and worsted are prohibited to be exported, under the same penalties as wool even white cloths we subject to a duty upon exportation; and our dyers have so far obtained a monopoly against our clothiers. Our clothiers would probably have been able to defend themselves against it; but it happens that the greater part of our principal clothiers are themselves likewise dyers. Watch-cases, clock-cases, and dial-plates for clocks and watches, have been prohibited to be exported. Our clock-makers and watch-makers are, it seems, unwilling that the price of this sort of workmanship should be raised upon them by the competition of foreigners.

By some old statutes of Edward III, Henry VIII. and Edward VI. the exportation of all metals was prohibited. Lead and tin were alone excepted, probably on account of the great abundance of those metals; in the exportation of which a considerable part of the trade of the kingdom in those days consisted. For the encouragement of the mining trade, the 5th of William and Mary, chap.17, exempted from this prohibition iron, copper, and mundic metal made from British ore. The exportation of all sorts of copper bars, foreign as well as British, was afterwards permitted by the 9th and 10th of William III. chap 26. The exportation of unmanufactured brass, of what is called gun-metal, bell-metal, and shroff metal, still continues to be prohibited. Brass manufactures of all sorts may be exported duty free.

The exportation of the materials of manufacture, where it is not altogether prohibited, is, in many cases, subjected to considerable duties.

By the 8th Geo. I. chap.15, the exportation of all goods, the produce of manufacture of Great Britain, upon which any duties had been imposed by former statutes, was rendered duty free. The following goods, however, were excepted: alum, lead, lead-ore, tin, tanned leather, copperas, coals, wool, cards, white woollen cloths, lapis calaminaris, skins of all sorts, glue, coney hair or wool, hares wool, hair of all sorts, horses, and litharge of lead. If you except horses, all these are either materials of manufacture, or incomplete manufactures (which may be considered as materials for still further manufacture), or instruments of trade. This statute leaves them subject to all the old duties which had ever been imposed upon them, the old subsidy, and one per cent. outwards.

By the same statute, a great number of foreign drugs for dyers use are exempted from all duties upon importation. Each of them, however, is afterwards subjected to a certain duty, not indeed a very heavy one, upon exportation. Our dyers, it seems, while they thought it for their interest to encourage the importation of those drugs, by an exemption from all duties, thought it likewise for their own interest to throw some small discouragement upon their exportation. The avidity, however, which suggested this notable piece of mercantile ingenuity, most probably disappointed itself of its object. It necessarily taught the importers to be more careful than they might otherwise have been, that their importation should not exceed what was necessary for the supply of the home market. The home market was at all times likely to be more scantily supplied; the commodities were at all times likely to be somewhat dearer there than they would have been, had the exportation been rendered as free as the importation.

By the above-mentioned statute, gum senega, or gum arabic, being among the enumerated dyeing drugs, might be imported duty free. They were subjected, indeed, to a small poundage duty, amounting only to threepence in the hundred weight, upon their re-exportation. France enjoyed, at that time, an exclusive trade to the country most productive of those drugs, that which lies in the neighbourhood of the Senegal; and the British market could not be easily supplied by the immediate importation of them from the place of growth. By the 25th Geo. II. therefore, gum senega was allowed to be imported (contrary to the general dispositions of the act of navigation) from any part of Europe. As the law, however, did not mean to encourage this species of trade, so contrary to the general principles of the mercantile policy of England, it imposed a duty of ten shillings the hundred weight upon such importation, and no part of this duty was to be afterwards drawn back upon its exportation. The successful war which began in 1755 gave Great Britain the same exclusive trade to those countries which France had enjoyed before. Our manufactures, as soon as the peace was made, endeavoured to avail themselves of this advantage, and to establish a monopoly in their own favour both against the growers and against the importers of this commodity. By the 5th of Geo. III. therefore, chap. 37, the exportation of gum senega, from his majesty's dominions in Africa, was confined to Great Britain, and was subjected to all the same restrictions, regulations, forfeitures, and penalties, as that of the enumerated commodities of the British colonies in America and the West Indies. Its importation, indeed, was subjected to a small duty of sixpence the hundred weight; but its re-exportation was subjected to the enormous duty of one pound ten shillings the hundred weight. It was the intention of our manufacturers, that the whole produce of those countries should be imported into Great Britain; and in order that they themselves might be enabled to buy it at their own price, that no part of it should be exported again, but at such an expense as would sufficiently discourage that exportation. Their avidity, however, upon this, as well as upon many other occasions, disappointed itself of its object. This enormous duty presented such a temptation to smuggling, that great quantities of this commodity were clandestinely exported, probably to all the manufacturing countries of Europe, but particularly to Holland, not only from Great Britain, but from Africa. Upon this account, by the 14th Geo. III. chap.10, this duty upon exportation was reduced to five shillings the hundred weight.

In the book of rates, according to which the old subsidy was levied, beaver skins were estimated at six shillings and eight pence a piece; and the different subsidies and imposts which, before the year 1722, had been laid upon their importation, amounted to one-fifth part of the rate, or to sixteen pence upon each skin; all of which, except half the old subsidy, amounting only to twopence, was drawn back upon exportation. This duty, upon the importation of so important a material of manufacture, had been thought too high; and, in the year 1722, the rate was reduced to two shillings and sixpence, which reduced the duty upon importation to sixpence, and of this only one-half was to be drawn back upon exportation. The same successful war put the country most productive of beaver under the dominion of Great Britain; and beaver skins being among the enumerated commodities, the exportation from America was consequently confined to the market of Great Britain. Our manufacturers soon bethought themselves of the advantage which they might make of this circumstance; and in the year 1764, the duty upon the importation of beaver skin was reduced to one penny, but the duty upon exportation was raised to sevenpence each skin, without any drawback of the duty upon importation. By the same law, a duty of eighteen pence the pound was imposed upon the exportation of beaver wool or woumbs, without making any alteration in the duty upon the importation of that commodity, which, when imported by British, and in British shipping, amounted at that time to between fourpence and fivepence the piece.

Coals may be considered both as a material of manufacture, and as an instrument of trade. Heavy duties, accordingly, have been imposed upon their exportation, amounting at present (1783) to more than five shillings the ton, or more than fifteen shillings the chaldron, Newcastle measure; which is, in most cases, more than the original value of the commodity at the coal-pit, or even at the shipping port for exportation.

The exportation, however, of the instruments of trade, properly so called, is commonly restrained, not by high duties, but by absolute prohibitions. Thus, by the 7th and 8th of William III chap.20, sect.8, the exportation of frames or engines for knitting gloves or stockings, is prohibited, under the penalty, not only of the forfeiture of such frames or engines, so exported, or attempted to be exported, but of forty pounds, one half to the king, the other to the person who shall inform or sue for the same. In the same manner, by the 14th Geo. III. chap. 71, the exportation to foreign parts, of any utensils made use of in the cotton, linen, woollen, and silk manufactures, is prohibited under the penalty, not only of the forfeiture of such utensils, but of two hundred pounds, to be paid by the person who shall offend in this manner; and likewise of two hundred pounds, to be paid by the master of the ship, who shall knowingly suffer such utensils to be loaded on board his ship.

When such heavy penalties were imposed upon the exportation of the dead instruments of trade, it could not well be expected that the living instrument, the artificer, should be allowed to go free. Accordingly, by the 5th Geo. I. chap. 27, the person who shall be convicted of enticing any artificer, of or in any of the manufactures of Great Britain, to go into any foreign parts, in order to practise or teach his trade, is liable, for the first offence, to be fined in any sum not exceeding one hundred pounds, and to three months imprisonment, and until the fine shall be paid; and for the second offence, to be fined in any sum, at the discretion of the court, and to imprisonment for twelve months, and until the fine shall be paid. By the 23d Geo. II. chap. 13, this penalty is increased, for the first offence, to five hundred pounds for every artificer so enticed, and to twelve months imprisonment, and until the fine shall be paid; and for the second offence, to one thousand pounds, and to two years imprisonment, and until the fine shall be paid.

By the former of these two statutes, upon proof that any person has been enticing any artificer, or that any artificer has promised or contracted to go into foreign parts, for the purposes aforesaid, such artificer may be obliged to give security, at the discretion of the court, that he shall not go beyond the seas, and may be committed to prison until he give such security.

If any artificer has gone beyond the seas, and is exercising or teaching his trade in any foreign country, upon warning being given to him by any of his majesty's ministers or consuls abroad, or by one of his majesty's secretaries of state, for the time being, if he does not, within six months after such warning, return into this realm, and from henceforth abide and inhabit continually within the same, he is from thenceforth declared incapable of taking any legacy devised to him within this kingdom, or of being executor or administrator to any person, or of taking any lands within this kingdom, by descent, devise, or purchase. He likewise forfeits to the king all his lands, goods, and chattels; is declared an alien in every respect; and is put out of the king's protection.

It is unnecessary, I imagine, to observe how contrary such regulations are to the boasted liberty of the subject, of which we affect to be so very jealous; but which, in this case, is so plainly sacrificed to the futile interests of our merchants and manufacturers.

The laudable motive of all these regulations, is to extend our own manufactures, not by their own improvement, but by the depression of those of all our neighbours, and by putting an end, as much as possible, to the troublesome competition of such odious and disagreeable rivals. Our master manufacturers think it reasonable that they themselves should have the monopoly of the ingenuity of all their countrymen. Though by restraining, in some trades, the number of apprentices which can be employed at one time, and by imposing the necessity of a long apprenticeship in all trades, they endeavour, all of them, to confine the knowledge of their respective employments to as small a number as possible; they are unwilling, however, that any part of this small number should go abroad to instruct foreigners.

Consumption is the sole end and purpose of all production; and the interest of the producer ought to be attended to, only so far as it may be necessary for promoting that of the consumer.

The maxim is so perfectly self-evident, that it would be absurd to attempt to prove it. But in the mercantile system, the interest of the consumer is almost constantly sacrificed to that of the producer; and it seems to consider production, and not consumption, as the ultimate end and object of all industry and commerce.

In the restraints upon the importation of all foreign commodities which can come into competition with those of our own growth or manufacture, the interest of the home consumer is evidently sacrificed to that of the producer. It is altogether for the benefit of the latter, that the former is obliged to pay that enhancement of price which this monopoly almost always occasions.

It is altogether for the benefit of the producer, that bounties are granted upon the exportation of some of his productions. The home consumer is obliged to pay, first the tax which is necessary for paying the bounty; and, secondly, the still greater tax which necessarily arises from the enhancement of the price of the commodity in the home market.

By the famous treaty of commerce with Portugal, the consumer is prevented by duties from purchasing of a neighbouring country, a commodity which our own climate does not produce; but is obliged to purchase it of a distant country, though it is acknowledged, that the commodity of the distant country is of a worse quality than that of the near one. The home consumer is obliged to submit to this inconvenience, in order that the producer may import into the distant country some of his productions, upon more advantageous terms than he otherwise would have been allowed to do. The consumer, too, is obliged to pay whatever enhancement in the price of those very productions this forced exportation may occasion in the home market.

But in the system of laws which has been established for the management of our American and West Indian colonies, the interest of the home consumer has been sacrificed to that of the producer, with a more extravagant profusion than in all our other commercial regulations. A great empire has been established for the sole purpose of raising up a nation of customers, who should be obliged to buy, from the shops of our different producers, all the goods with which these could supply them. For the sake of that little enhancement of price which this monopoly might afford our producers, the home consumers have been burdened with the whole expense of maintaining and defending that empire. For this purpose, and for this purpose only, in the two last wars, more than two hundred millions have been spent, and a new debt of more than a hundred and seventy millions has been contracted, over and above all that had been expended for the same purpose in former wars. The interest of this debt alone is not only greater than the whole extraordinary profit which, it never could be pretended, was made by the monopoly of the colony trade, but than the whole value of that trade, or than the whole value of the goods which, at an average, have been annually exported to the colonies.

It cannot be very difficult to determine who have been the contrivers of this whole mercantile system; not the consumers, we may believe, whose interest has been entirely neglected; but the producers, whose interest has been so carefully attended to; and among this latter class, our merchants and manufacturers have been by far the principal architects. In the mercantile regulations which have been taken notice of in this chapter, the interest of our manufacturers has been most peculiarly attended to; and the interest, not so much of the consumers, as that of some other sets of producers, has been sacrificed to it.

CHAPTER IX

OF THE AGRICULTURAL SYSTEMS, OR OF THOSE SYSTEMS OF POLITICAL ECONOMY WHICH REPRESENT THE PRODUCE OF LAND, AS EITHER THE SOLE OR THE PRINCIPAL SOURCE OF THE REVENUE AND WEALTH OF EVERY COUNTRY

The agricultural systems of political economy will not require so long an explanation as that which I have thought it necessary to bestow upon the mercantile or commercial system.

That system which represents the produce of land as the sole source of the revenue and wealth of every country, has so far as I know, never been adopted by any nation, and it at present exists only in the speculations of a few men of great learning and ingenuity in France. It would not, surely, be worth while to examine at great length the errors of a system which never has done, and probably never will do, any harm in any part of the world. I shall endeavour to explain, however, as distinctly as I can, the great outlines of this very ingenious system.

Mr. Colbert, the famous minister of Lewis XIV. was a man of probity, of great industry, and knowledge of detail; of great experience and acuteness in the examination of public accounts; and of abilities, in short, every way fitted for introducing method and good order into the collection and expenditure of the public revenue. That minister had unfortunately embraced all the prejudices of the mercantile system, in its nature and essence a system of restraint and regulation, and such as could scarce fail to be agreeable to a laborious and plodding man of business, who had been accustomed to regulate the different departments of public offices, and to establish the necessary checks and controls for confining each to its proper sphere. The industry and commerce of a great country, he endeavoured to regulate upon the same model as the departments of a public office; and instead of allowing every man to pursue his own interest his own way, upon the liberal plan of equality, liberty, and justice, he bestowed upon certain branches of industry extraordinary privileges, while he laid others under as extraordinary restraints. He was not only disposed, like other European ministers, to encourage more the industry of the towns than that of the country; but, in order to support the industry of the towns, he was willing even to depress and keep down that of the country. In order to render provisions cheap to the inhabitants of the towns, and thereby to encourage manufactures and foreign commerce, he prohibited altogether the exportation of corn, and thus excluded the inhabitants of the country from every foreign market, for by far the most important part of the produce of their industry. This prohibition, joined to the restraints imposed by the ancient provincial laws of France upon the transportation of corn from one province to another, and to the arbitrary and degrading taxes which are levied upon the cultivators in almost all the provinces, discouraged and kept down the agriculture of that country very much below the state to which it would naturally have risen in so very fertile a soil, and so very happy a climate. This state of discouragement and depression was felt more or less in every different part of the country, and many different inquiries were set on foot concerning the causes of it. One of those causes appeared to be the preference given, by the institutions of Mr. Colbert, to the industry of the towns above that of the country.

If the rod be bent too much one way, says the proverb, in order to make it straight, you must bend it as much the other. The French philosophers, who have proposed the system which represents agriculture as the sole source of the revenue and wealth of every country, seem to have adopted this proverbial maxim; and, as in the plan of Mr. Colbert, the industry of the towns was certainly overvalued in comparison with that of the country, so in their system it seems to be as certainly under-valued.

The different orders of people, who have ever been supposed to contribute in any respect towards the annual produce of the land and labour of the country, they divide into three classes. The first is the class of the proprietors of land. The second is the class of the cultivators, of farmers and country labourers, whom they honour with the peculiar appellation of the productive class. The third is the class of artificers, manufacturers, and merchants, whom they endeavour to degrade by the humiliating appellation of the barren or unproductive class.

The class of proprietors contributes to the annual produce, by the expense which they may occasionally lay out upon the improvement of the land, upon the buildings, drains, inclosures, and other ameliorations, which they may either make or maintain upon it, and by means of which the cultivators are enabled, with the same capital, to raise a greater produce, and consequently to pay a greater rent. This advanced rent may be considered as the interest or profit due to the proprietor, upon the expense or capital which he thus employs in the improvement of his land. Such expenses are in this system called ground expenses (depenses foncieres).

The cultivators or farmers contribute to the annual produce, by what are in this system called the original and annual expenses (depenses primitives, et depenses annuelles), which they lay out upon the cultivation of the land. The original expenses consist in the instruments of husbandry, in the stock of cattle, in the seed, and in the maintenance of the farmer's family, servants, and cattle, during at least a great part of the first year of his occupancy, or till he can receive some return from the land. The annual expenses consist in the seed, in the wear and tear of instruments of husbandry, and in the annual maintenance of the farmer's servants and cattle, and of his family too, so far as any part of them can be considered as servants employed in cultivation. That part of the produce of the land which remains to him after paying the rent, ought to be sufficient, first, to replace to him, within a reasonable time, at least during the term of his occupancy, the whole of his original expenses, together with the ordinary profits of stock; and, secondly, to replace to him annually the whole of his annual expenses, together likewise with the ordinary profits of stock. Those two sorts of expenses are two capitals which the farmer employs in cultivation; and unless they are regularly restored to him, together with a reasonable profit, he cannot carry on his employment upon a level with other employments; but, from a regard to his own interest, must desert it as soon as possible, and seek some other. That part of the produce of the land which is thus necessary for enabling the farmer to continue his business, ought to be considered as a fund sacred to cultivation, which, if the landlord violates, he necessarily reduces the produce of his own land, and, in a few years, not only disables the farmer from paying this racked rent, but from paying the reasonable rent which he might otherwise have got for his land. The rent which properly belongs to the landlord, is no more than the neat produce which remains after paying, in the completest manner, all the necessary expenses which must be previously laid out, in order to raise the gross or the whole produce. It is because the labour of the cultivators, over and above paying completely all those necessary expenses, affords a neat produce of this kind, that this class of people are in this system peculiarly distinguished by the honourable appellation of the productive class. Their original and annual expenses are for the same reason called, In this system, productive expenses, because, over and above replacing their own value, they occasion the annual reproduction of this neat produce.

The ground expenses, as they are called, or what the landlord lays out upon the improvement of his land, are, in this system, too, honoured with the appellation of productive expenses. Till the whole of those expenses, together with the ordinary profits of stock, have been completely repaid to him by the advanced rent which he gets from his land, that advanced rent ought to be regarded as sacred and inviolable, both by the church and by the king; ought to be subject neither to tithe nor to taxation. If it is otherwise, by discouraging the improvement of land, the church discourages the future increase of her own tithes, and the king the future increase of his own taxes. As in a well ordered state of things, therefore, those ground expenses, over and above reproducing in the completest manner their own value, occasion likewise, after a certain time, a reproduction of a neat produce, they are in this system considered as productive expenses.

The ground expenses of the landlord, however, together with the original and the annual expenses of the farmer, are the only three sorts of expenses which in this system are considered as productive. All other expenses, and all other orders of people, even those who, in the common apprehensions of men, are regarded as the most productive, are, in this account of things, represented as altogether barren and unproductive.

Artificers and manufacturers, in particular, whose industry, in the common apprehensions of men, increases so much the value of the rude produce of land, are in this system represented as a class of people altogether barren and unproductive. Their labour, it is said, replaces only the stock which employs them, together with its ordinary profits. That stock consists in the materials, tools, and wages, advanced to them by their employer; and is the fund destined for their employment and maintenance. Its profits are the fund destined for the maintenance of their employer. Their employer, as he advances to them the stock of materials, tools, and wages, necessary for their employment, so he advances to himself what is necessary for his own maintenance; and this maintenance he generally proportions to the profit which he expects to make by the price of their work. Unless its price repays to him the maintenance which he advances to himself, as well as the materials, tools, and wages, which he advances to his workmen, it evidently does not repay to him the whole expense which he lays out upon it. The profits of manufacturing stock, therefore, are not, like the rent of land, a neat produce which remains after completely repaying the whole expense which must be laid out in order to obtain them. The stock of the farmer yields him a profit, as well as that of the master manufacturer; and it yields a rent likewise to another person, which that of the master manufacturer does not. The expense, therefore, laid out in employing and maintaining artificers and manufacturers, does no more than continue, if one may say so, the existence of its own value, and does not produce any new value. It is, therefore, altogether a barren and unproductive expense. The expense, on the contrary, laid out in employing farmers and country labourers, over and above continuing the existence of its own value, produces a new value the rent of the landlord. It is, therefore, a productive expense.

Mercantile stock is equally barren and unproductive with manufacturing stock. It only continues the existence of its own value, without producing any new value. Its profits are only the repayment of the maintenance which its employer advances to himself during the time that he employs it, or till he receives the returns of it. They are only the repayment of a part of the expense which must be laid out in employing it.

The labour of artificers and manufacturers never adds any thing to the value of the whole annual amount of the rude produce of the land. It adds, indeed, greatly to the value of some particular parts of it. But the consumption which, in the mean time, it occasions of other parts, is precisely equal to the value which it adds to those parts; so that the value of the whole amount is not, at any one moment of time, in the least augmented by it. The person who works the lace of a pair of fine ruffles for example, will sometimes raise the value of, perhaps, a pennyworth of flax to £30 sterling. But though, at first sight, he appears thereby to multiply the value of a part of the rude produce about seven thousand and two hundred times, he in reality adds nothing to the value of the whole annual amount of the rude produce. The working of that lace costs him, perhaps, two years labour. The £30 which he gets for it when it is finished, is no more than the repayment of the subsistence which he advances to himself during the two years that he is employed about it. The value which, by every day's, month's, or year's labour, he adds to the flax, does no more than replace the value of his own consumption during that day, month, or year. At no moment of time, therefore, does he add any thing to the value of the whole annual amount of the rude produce of the land: the portion of that produce which he is continually consuming, being always equal to the value which he is continually producing. The extreme poverty of the greater part of the persons employed in this expensive, though trifling manufacture, may satisfy us that the price of their work does not, in ordinary cases, exceed the value of their subsistence. It is otherwise with the work of farmers and country labourers. The rent of the landlord is a value which, in ordinary cases, it is continually producing over and above replacing, in the most complete manner, the whole consumption, the whole expense laid out upon the employment and maintenance both of the workmen and of their employer.

Artificers, manufacturers, and merchants, can augment the revenue and wealth of their society by parsimony only; or, as it is expressed in this system, by privation, that is, by depriving themselves of a part of the funds destined for their own subsistence. They annually reproduce nothing but those funds. Unless, therefore, they annually save some part of them, unless they annually deprive themselves of the enjoyment of some part of them, the revenue and wealth of their society can never be, in the smallest degree, augmented by means of their industry. Farmers and country labourers, on the contrary, may enjoy completely the whole funds destined for their own subsistence, and yet augment, at the same time, the revenue and wealth of their society. Over and above what is destined for their own subsistence, their industry annually affords a neat produce, of which the augmentation necessarily augments the revenue and wealth of their society. Nations, therefore, which, like France or England, consist in a great measure, of proprietors and cultivators, can be enriched by industry and enjoyment. Nations, on the contrary, which, like Holland and Hamburgh, are composed chiefly of merchants, artificers, and manufacturers, can grow rich only through parsimony and privation. As the interest of nations so differently circumstanced is very different, so is likewise the common character of the people. In those of the former kind, liberality, frankness, and good fellowship, naturally make a part of their common character; in the latter, narrowness, meanness, and a selfish disposition, averse to all social pleasure and enjoyment.

The unproductive class, that of merchants, artificers, and manufacturers, is maintained and employed altogether at the expense of the two other classes, of that of proprietors, and of that of cultivators. They furnish it both with the materials of its work, and with the fund of its subsistence, with the corn and cattle which it consumes while it is employed about that work. The proprietors and cultivators finally pay both the wages of all the workmen of the unproductive class, and the profits of all their employers. Those workmen and their employers are properly the servants of the proprietors and cultivators. They are only servants who work without doors, as menial servants work within. Both the one and the other, however, are equally maintained at the expense of the same masters. The labour of both is equally unproductive. It adds nothing to the value of the sum total of the rude produce of the land. Instead of increasing the value of that sum total, it is a charge and expense which must be paid out of it.

The unproductive class, however, is not only useful, but greatly useful, to the other two classes. By means of the industry of merchants, artificers, and manufacturers, the proprietors and cultivators can purchase both the foreign goods and the manufactured produce of their own country, which they have occasion for, with the produce of a much smaller quantity of their own labour, than what they would be obliged to employ, if they were to attempt, in an awkward and unskilful manner, either to import the one, or to make the other, for their own use. By means of the unproductive class, the cultivators are delivered from many cares, which would otherwise distract their attention from the cultivation of land. The superiority of produce, which in consequence of this undivided attention, they are enabled to raise, is fully sufficient to pay the whole expense which the maintenance and employment of the unproductive class costs either the proprietors or themselves. The industry of merchants, artificers, and manufacturers, though in its own nature altogether unproductive, yet contributes in this manner indirectly to increase the produce of the land. It increases the productive powers of productive labour, by leaving it at liberty to confine itself to its proper employment, the cultivation of land; and the plough goes frequently the easier and the better, by means of the labour of the man whose business is most remote from the plough.

It can never be the interest of the proprietors and cultivators, to restrain or to discourage, in any respect, the industry of merchants, artificers, and manufacturers. The greater the liberty which this unproductive class enjoys, the greater will be the competition in all the different trades which compose it, and the cheaper will the other two classes be supplied, both with foreign goods and with the manufactured produce of their own country.

It can never be the interest of the unproductive class to oppress the other two classes. It is the surplus produce of the land, or what remains after deducting the maintenance, first of the cultivators, and afterwards of the proprietors, that maintains and employs the unproductive class. The greater this surplus, the greater must likewise be the maintenance and employment of that class. The establishment of perfect justice, of perfect liberty, and of perfect equality, is the very simple secret which most effectually secures the highest degree of prosperity to all the three classes.

The merchants, artificers, and manufacturers of those mercantile states, which, like Holland and Hamburgh, consist chiefly of this unproductive class, are in the same manner maintained and employed altogether at the expense of the proprietors and cultivators of land. The only difference is, that those proprietors and cultivators are, the greater part of them, placed at a most inconvenient distance from the merchants, artificers, and manufacturers, whom they supply with the materials of their work and the fund of their subsistence; are the inhabitants of other countries, and the subjects of other governments.

Such mercantile states, however, are not only useful, but greatly useful, to the inhabitants of those other countries. They fill up, in some measure, a very important void; and supply the place of the merchants, artificers, and manufacturers, whom the inhabitants of those countries ought to find at home, but whom, from some defect in their policy, they do not find at home.

It can never be the interest of those landed nations, if I may call them so, to discourage or distress the industry of such mercantile states, by imposing high duties upon their trade, or upon the commodities which they furnish. Such duties, by rendering those commodities dearer, could serve only to sink the real value of the surplus produce of their own land, with which, or, what comes to the same thing, with the price of which those commodities are purchased. Such duties could only serve to discourage the increase of that surplus produce, and consequently the improvement and cultivation of their own land. The most effectual expedient, on the contrary, for raising the value of that surplus produce, for encouraging its increase, and consequently the improvement and cultivation of their own land, would be to allow the most perfect freedom to the trade of all such mercantile nations.

This perfect freedom of trade would even be the most effectual expedient for supplying them, in due time, with all the artificers, manufacturers, and merchants, whom they wanted at home; and for filling up, in the properest and most advantageous manner, that very important void which they felt there.

The continual increase of the surplus produce of their land would, in due time, create a greater capital than what would be employed with the ordinary rate of profit in the improvement and cultivation of land; and the surplus part of it would naturally turn itself to the employment of artificers and manufacturers, at home. But these artificers and manufacturers, finding at home both the materials of their work and the fund of their subsistence, might immediately, even with much less art and skill be able to work as cheap as the little artificers and manufacturers of such mercantile states, who had both to bring from a greater distance. Even though, from want of art and skill, they might not for some time be able to work as cheap, yet, finding a market at home, they might be able to sell their work there as cheap as that of the artificers and manufacturers of such mercantile states, which could not be brought to that market but from so great a distance; and as their art and skill improved, they would soon be able to sell it cheaper. The artificers and manufacturers of such mercantile states, therefore, would immediately be rivalled in the market of those landed nations, and soon after undersold and justled out of it altogether. The cheapness of the manufactures of those landed nations, in consequence of the gradual improvements of art and skill, would, in due time, extend their sale beyond the home market, and carry them to many foreign markets, from which they would, in the same manner, gradually justle out many of the manufacturers of such mercantile nations.

This continual increase, both of the rude and manufactured produce of those landed nations, would, in due time, create a greater capital than could, with the ordinary rate of profit, be employed either in agriculture or in manufactures. The surplus of this capital would naturally turn itself to foreign trade and be employed in exporting, to foreign countries, such parts of the rude and manufactured produce of its own country, as exceeded the demand of the home market. In the exportation of the produce of their own country, the merchants of a landed nation would have an advantage of the same kind over those of mercantile nations, which its artificers and manufacturers had over the artificers and manufacturers of such nations; the advantage of finding at home that cargo, and those stores and provisions, which the others were obliged to seek for at a distance.

With inferior art and skill in navigation, therefore, they would be able to sell that cargo as cheap in foreign markets as the merchants of such mercantile nations; and with equal art and skill they would be able to sell it cheaper. They would soon, therefore, rival those mercantile nations in this branch of foreign trade, and, in due time, would justle them out of it altogether.

According to this liberal and generous system, therefore, the most advantageous method in which a landed nation can raise up artificers, manufacturers, and merchants of its own, is to grant the most perfect freedom of trade to the artificers, manufacturers, and merchants of all other nations. It thereby raises the value of the surplus produce of its own land, of which the continual increase gradually establishes a fund, which, in due time, necessarily raises up all the artificers, manufacturers, and merchants, whom it has occasion for.

When a landed nation on the contrary, oppresses, either by high duties or by prohibitions, the trade of foreign nations, it necessarily hurts its own interest in two different ways. First, by raising the price of all foreign goods, and of all sorts of manufactures, it necessarily sinks the real value of the surplus produce of its own land, with which, or, what comes to the same thing, with the price of which, it purchases those foreign goods and manufactures. Secondly, by giving a sort of monopoly of the home market to its own merchants, artificers, and manufacturers, it raises the rate of mercantile and manufacturing profit, in proportion to that of agricultural profit; and, consequently, either draws from agriculture a part of the capital which had before been employed in it, or hinders from going to it a part of what would otherwise have gone to it. This policy, therefore, discourages agriculture in two different ways; first, by sinking the real value of its produce, and thereby lowering the rate of its profits; and, secondly, by raising the rate of profit in all other employments. Agriculture is rendered less advantageous, and trade and manufactures more advantageous, than they otherwise would be; and every man is tempted by his own interest to turn, as much as he can, both his capital and his industry from the former to the latter employments.

Though, by this oppressive policy, a landed nation should be able to raise up artificers, manufacturers, and merchants of its own, somewhat sooner than it could do by the freedom of trade; a matter, however, which is not a little doubtful; yet it would raise them up, if one may say so, prematurely, and before it was perfectly ripe for them. By raising up too hastily one species of industry, it would depress another more valuable species of industry. By raising up too hastily a species of industry which duly replaces the stock which employs it, together with the ordinary profit, it would depress a species of industry which, over and above replacing that stock, with its profit, affords likewise a neat produce, a free rent to the landlord. It would depress productive labour, by encouraging too hastily that labour which is altogether barren and unproductive.

In what manner, according to this system, the sum total of the annual produce of the land is distributed among the three classes above mentioned, and in what manner the labour of the unproductive class does no more than replace the value of its own consumption, without increasing in any respect the value of that sum total, is represented by Mr Quesnai, the very ingenious and profound author of this system, in some arithmetical formularies. The first of these formularies, which, by way of eminence, he peculiarly distinguishes by the name of the Economical Table, represents the manner in which he supposes this distribution takes place, in a state of the most perfect liberty, and, therefore, of the highest prosperity; in a state where the annual produce is such as to afford the greatest possible neat produce, and where each class enjoys its proper share of the whole annual produce. Some subsequent formularies represent the manner in which he supposes this distribution is made in different states of restraint and regulation; in which, either the class of proprietors, or the barren and unproductive class, is more favoured than the class of cultivators; and in which either the one or the other encroaches, more or less, upon the share which ought properly to belong to this productive class. Every such encroachment, every violation of that natural distribution, which the most perfect liberty would establish, must, according to this system, necessarily degrade, more or less, from one year to another, the value and sum total of the annual produce, and must necessarily occasion a gradual declension in the real wealth and revenue of the society; a declension, of which the progress must be quicker or slower, according to the degree of this encroachment, according as that natural distribution, which the most perfect liberty would establish, is more or less violated. Those subsequent formularies represent the different degrees of declension which, according to this system, correspond to the different degrees in which this natural distribution of things is violated.

Some speculative physicians seem to have imagined that the health of the human body could be preserved only by a certain precise regimen of diet and exercise, of which every, the smallest violation, necessarily occasioned some degree of disease or disorder proportionate to the degree of the violation. Experience, however, would seem to shew, that the human body frequently preserves, to all appearance at least, the most perfect state of health under a vast variety of different regimens; even under some which are generally believed to be very far from being perfectly wholesome. But the healthful state of the human body, it would seem, contains in itself some unknown principle of preservation, capable either of preventing or of correcting, in many respects, the bad effects even of a very faulty regimen. Mr Quesnai, who was himself a physician, and a very speculative physician, seems to have entertained a notion of the same kind concerning the political body, and to have imagined that it would thrive and prosper only under a certain precise regimen, the exact regimen of perfect liberty and perfect justice. He seems not to have considered, that in the political body, the natural effort which every man is continually making to better his own condition, is a principle of preservation capable of preventing and correcting, in many respects, the bad effects of a political economy, in some degree both partial and oppressive. Such a political economy, though it no doubt retards more or less, is not always capable of stopping altogether, the natural progress of a nation towards wealth and prosperity, and still less of making it go backwards. If a nation could not prosper without the enjoyment of perfect liberty and perfect justice, there is not in the world a nation which could ever have prospered. In the political body, however, the wisdom of nature has fortunately made ample provision for remedying many of the bad effects of the folly and injustice of man; it the same manner as it has done in the natural body, for remedying those of his sloth and intemperance.

The capital error of this system, however, seems to lie in its representing the class of artificers, manufacturers, and merchants, as altogether barren and unproductive. The following observations may serve to shew the impropriety of this representation:—

First, this class, it is acknowledged, reproduces annually the value of its own annual consumption, and continues, at least, the existence of the stock or capital which maintains and employs it. But, upon this account alone, the denomination of barren or unproductive should seem to be very improperly applied to it. We should not call a marriage barren or unproductive, though it produced only a son and a daughter, to replace the father and mother, and though it did not increase the number of the human species, but only continued it as it was before. Farmers and country labourers, indeed, over and above the stock which maintains and employs them, reproduce annually a neat produce, a free rent to the landlord. As a marriage which affords three children is certainly more productive than one which affords only two, so the labour of farmers and country labourers is certainly more productive than that of merchants, artificers, and manufacturers. The superior produce of the one class, however, does not, render the other barren or unproductive.

Secondly, it seems, on this account, altogether improper to consider artificers, manufacturers, and merchants, in the same light as menial servants. The labour of menial servants does not continue the existence of the fund which maintains and employs them. Their maintenance and employment is altogether at the expense of their masters, and the work which they perform is not of a nature to repay that expense. That work consists in services which perish generally in the very instant of their performance, and does not fix or realize itself in any vendible commodity, which can replace the value of their wages and maintenance. The labour, on the contrary, of artificers, manufacturers, and merchants, naturally does fix and realize itself in some such vendible commodity. It is upon this account that, in the chapter in which I treat of productive and unproductive labour, I have classed artificers, manufacturers, and merchants among the productive labourers, and menial servants among the barren or unproductive.

Thirdly, it seems, upon every supposition, improper to say, that the labour of artificers, manufacturers, and merchants, does not increase the real revenue of the society. Though we should suppose, for example, as it seems to be supposed in this system, that the value of the daily, monthly, and yearly consumption of this class was exactly equal to that of its daily, monthly, and yearly production; yet it would not from thence follow, that its labour added nothing to the real revenue, to the real value of the annual produce of the land and labour of the society. An artificer, for example, who, in the first six months after harvest, executes ten pounds worth of work, though he should, in the same time, consume ten pounds worth of corn and other necessaries, yet really adds the value of ten pounds to the annual produce of the land and labour of the society. While he has been consuming a half-yearly revenue of ten pounds worth of corn and other necessaries, he has produced an equal value of work, capable of purchasing, either to himself, or to some other person, an equal half-yearly revenue. The value, therefore, of what has been consumed and produced during these six months, is equal, not to ten, but to twenty pounds. It is possible, indeed, that no more than ten pounds worth of this value may ever have existed at any one moment of time. But if the ten pounds worth of corn and other necessaries which were consumed by the artificer, had been consumed by a soldier, or by a menial servant, the value of that part of the annual produce which existed at the end of the six months, would have been ten pounds less than it actually is in consequence of the labour of the artificer. Though the value of what the artificer produces, therefore, should not, at any one moment of time, be supposed greater than the value he consumes, yet, at every moment of time, the actually existing value of goods in the market is, in consequence of what he produces, greater than it otherwise would be.

When the patrons of this system assert, that the consumption of artificers, manufacturers, and merchants, is equal to the value of what they produce, they probably mean no more than that their revenue, or the fund destined for their consumption, is equal to it. But if they had expressed themselves more accurately, and only asserted, that the revenue of this class was equal to the value of what they produced, it might readily have occurred to the reader, that what would naturally be saved out of this revenue, must necessarily increase more or less the real wealth of the society. In order, therefore, to make out something like an argument, it was necessary that they should express themselves as they have done; and this argument, even supposing things actually were as it seems to presume them to be, turns out to be a very inconclusive one.

Fourthly, farmers and country labourers can no more augment, without parsimony, the real revenue, the annual produce of the land and labour of their society, than artificers, manufacturers, and merchants. The annual produce of the land and labour of any society can be augmented only in two ways; either, first, by some improvement in the productive powers of the useful labour actually maintained within it; or, secondly, by some increase in the quantity of that labour.

The improvement in the productive powers of useful labour depends, first, upon the improvement in the ability of the workman; and, secondly, upon that of the machinery with which he works. But the labour of artificers and manufacturers, as it is capable of being more subdivided, and the labour of each workman reduced to a greater simplicity of operation, than that of farmers and country labourers; so it is likewise capable of both these sorts of improvement in a much higher degree {See book i chap. 1.} In this respect, therefore, the class of cultivators can have no sort of advantage over that of artificers and manufacturers.

The increase in the quantity of useful labour actually employed within any society must depend altogether upon the increase of the capital which employs it; and the increase of that capital, again, must be exactly equal to the amount of the savings from the revenue, either of the particular persons who manage and direct the employment of that capital, or of some other persons, who lend it to them. If merchants, artificers, and manufacturers are, as this system seems to suppose, naturally more inclined to parsimony and saving than proprietors and cultivators, they are, so far, more likely to augment the quantity of useful labour employed within their society, and consequently to increase its real revenue, the annual produce of its land and labour.

Fifthly and lastly, though the revenue of the inhabitants of every country was supposed to consist altogether, as this system seems to suppose, in the quantity of subsistence which their industry could procure to them; yet, even upon this supposition, the revenue of a trading and manufacturing country must, other things being equal, always be much greater than that of one without trade or manufactures. By means of trade and manufactures, a greater quantity of subsistence can be annually imported into a particular country, than what its own lands, in the actual state of their cultivation, could afford. The inhabitants of a town, though they frequently possess no lands of their own, yet draw to themselves, by their industry, such a quantity of the rude produce of the lands of other people, as supplies them, not only with the materials of their work, but with the fund of their subsistence. What a town always is with regard to the country in its neighbourhood, one independent state or country may frequently be with regard to other independent states or countries. It is thus that Holland draws a great part of its subsistence from other countries; live cattle from Holstein and Jutland, and corn from almost all the different countries of Europe. A small quantity of manufactured produce, purchases a great quantity of rude produce. A trading and manufacturing country, therefore, naturally purchases, with a small part of its manufactured produce, a great part of the rude produce of other countries; while, on the contrary, a country without trade and manufactures is generally obliged to purchase, at the expense of a great part of its rude produce, a very small part of the manufactured produce of other countries. The one exports what can subsist and accommodate but a very few, and imports the subsistence and accommodation of a great number. The other exports the accommodation and subsistence of a great number, and imports that of a very few only. The inhabitants of the one must always enjoy a much greater quantity of subsistence than what their own lands, in the actual state of their cultivation, could afford. The inhabitants of the other must always enjoy a much smaller quantity.

This system, however, with all its imperfections, is perhaps the nearest approximation to the truth that has yet been published upon the subject of political economy; and is upon that account, well worth the consideration of every man who wishes to examine with attention the principles of that very important science. Though in representing the labour which is employed upon land as the only productive labour, the notions which it inculcates are, perhaps, too narrow and confined; yet in representing the wealth of nations as consisting, not in the unconsumable riches of money, but in the consumable goods annually reproduced by the labour of the society, and in representing perfect liberty as the only effectual expedient for rendering this annual reproduction the greatest possible, its doctrine seems to be in every respect as just as it is generous and liberal. Its followers are very numerous; and as men are fond of paradoxes, and of appearing to understand what surpasses the comprehensions of ordinary people, the paradox which it maintains, concerning the unproductive nature of manufacturing labour, has not, perhaps, contributed a little to increase the number of its admirers. They have for some years past made a pretty considerable sect, distinguished in the French republic of letters by the name of the Economists. Their works have certainly been of some service to their country; not only by bringing into general discussion, many subjects which had never been well examined before, but by influencing, in some measure, the public administration in favour of agriculture. It has been in consequence of their representations, accordingly, that the agriculture of France has been delivered from several of the oppressions which it before laboured under. The term, during which such a lease can be granted, as will be valid against every future purchaser or proprietor of the land, has been prolonged from nine to twenty-seven years. The ancient provincial restraints upon the transportation of corn from one province of the kingdom to another, have been entirely taken away; and the liberty of exporting it to all foreign countries, has been established as the common law of the kingdom in all ordinary cases. This sect, in their works, which are very numerous, and which treat not only of what is properly called Political Economy, or of the nature and causes or the wealth of nations, but of every other branch of the system of civil government, all follow implicitly, and without any sensible variation, the doctrine of Mr. Qttesnai. There is, upon this account, little variety in the greater part of their works. The most distinct and best connected account of this doctrine is to be found in a little book written by Mr. Mercier de la Riviere, some time intendant of Martinico, entitled, The natural and essential Order of Political Societies. The admiration of this whole sect for their master, who was himself a man of the greatest modesty and simplicity, is not inferior to that of any of the ancient philosophers for the founders of their respective systems. 'There have been since the world began,' says a very diligent and respectable author, the Marquis de Mirabeau, 'three great inventions which have principally given stability to political societies, independent of many other inventions which have enriched and adorned them. The first is the invention of writing, which alone gives human nature the power of transmitting, without alteration, its laws, its contracts, its annals, and its discoveries. The second is the invention of money, which binds together all the relations between civilized societies. The third is the economical table, the result of the other two, which completes them both by perfecting their object; the great discovery of our age, but of which our posterity will reap the benefit.'

As the political economy of the nations of modern Europe has been more favourable to manufactures and foreign trade, the industry of the towns, than to agriculture, the industry of the country; so that of other nations has followed a different plan, and has been more favourable to agriculture than to manufactures and foreign trade.

The policy of China favours agriculture more than all other employments. In China, the condition of a labourer is said to be as much superior to that of an artificer, as in most parts of Europe that of an artificer is to that of a labourer. In China, the great ambition of every man is to get possession of a little bit of land, either in property or in lease; and leases are there said to be granted upon very moderate terms, and to be sufficiently secured to the lessees. The Chinese have little respect for foreign trade. Your beggarly commerce! was the language in which the mandarins of Pekin used to talk to Mr. De Lange, the Russian envoy, concerning it {See the Journal of Mr. De Lange, in Bell's Travels, vol. ii. p. 258, 276, 293.}. Except with Japan, the Chinese carry on, themselves, and in their own bottoms, little or no foreign trade; and it is only into one or two ports of their kingdom that they even admit the ships of foreign nations. Foreign trade, therefore, is, in China, every way confined within a much narrower circle than that to which it would naturally extend itself, if more freedom was allowed to it, either in their own ships, or in those of foreign nations.

Manufactures, as in a small bulk they frequently contain a great value, and can upon that account be transported at less expense from one country to another than most parts of rude produce, are, in almost all countries, the principal support of foreign trade. In countries, besides, less extensive, and less favourably circumstanced for inferior commerce than China, they generally require the support of foreign trade. Without an extensive foreign market, they could not well flourish, either in countries so moderately extensive as to afford but a narrow home market, or in countries where the communication between one province and another was so difficult, as to render it impossible for the goods of any particular place to enjoy the whole of that home market which the country could afford. The perfection of manufacturing industry, it must be remembered, depends altogether upon the division of labour; and the degree to which the division of labour can be introduced into any manufacture, is necessarily regulated, it has already been shewn, by the extent of the market. But the great extent of the empire of China, the vast multitude of its inhabitants, the variety of climate, and consequently of productions in its different provinces, and the easy communication by means of water-carriage between the greater part of them, render the home market of that country of so great extent, as to be alone sufficient to support very great manufactures, and to admit of very considerable subdivisions of labour. The home market of China is, perhaps, in extent, not much inferior to the market of all the different countries of Europe put together. A more extensive foreign trade, however, which to this great home market added the foreign market of all the rest of the world, especially if any considerable part of this trade was carried on in Chinese ships, could scarce fail to increase very much the manufactures of China, and to improve very much the productive powers of its manufacturing industry. By a more extensive navigation, the Chinese would naturally learn the art of using and constructing, themselves, all the different machines made use of in other countries, as well as the other improvements of art and industry which are practised in all the different parts of the world. Upon their present plan, they have little opportunity of improving themselves by the example of any other nation, except that of the Japanese.

The policy of ancient Egypt, too, and that of the Gentoo government of Indostan, seem to have favoured agriculture more than all other employments.

Both in ancient Egypt and Indostan, the whole body of the people was divided into different casts or tribes each of which was confined, from father to son, to a particular employment, or class of employments. The son of a priest was necessarily a priest; the son of a soldier, a soldier; the son of a labourer, a labourer; the son of a weaver, a weaver; the son of a tailor, a tailor, etc. In both countries, the cast of the priests holds the highest rank, and that of the soldiers the next; and in both countries the cast of the farmers and labourers was superior to the casts of merchants and manufacturers.

The government of both countries was particularly attentive to the interest of agriculture. The works constructed by the ancient sovereigns of Egypt, for the proper distribution of the waters of the Nile, were famous in antiquity, and the ruined remains of some of them are still the admiration of travellers. Those of the same kind which were constructed by the ancient sovereigns of Indostan, for the proper distribution of the waters of the Ganges, as well as of many other rivers, though they have been less celebrated, seem to have been equally great. Both countries, accordingly, though subject occasionally to dearths, have been famous for their great fertility. Though both were extremely populous, yet, in years of moderate plenty, they were both able to export great quantities of grain to their neighbours.

The ancient Egyptians had a superstitious aversion to the sea; and as the Gentoo religion does not permit its followers to light a fire, nor consequently to dress any victuals, upon the water, it, in effect, prohibits them from all distant sea voyages. Both the Egyptians and Indians must have depended almost altogether upon the navigation of other nations for the exportation of their surplus produce; and this dependency, as it must have confined the market, so it must have discouraged the increase of this surplus produce. It must have discouraged, too, the increase of the manufactured produce, more than that of the rude produce. Manufactures require a much more extensive market than the most important parts of the rude produce of the land. A single shoemaker will make more than 300 pairs of shoes in the year; and his own family will not, perhaps, wear out six pairs. Unless, therefore, he has the custom of, at least, 50 such families as his own, he cannot dispose of the whole product of his own labour. The most numerous class of artificers will seldom, in a large country, make more than one in 50, or one in a 100, of the whole number of families contained in it. But in such large countries, as France and England, the number of people employed in agriculture has, by some authors been computed at a half, by others at a third and by no author that I know of, at less that a fifth of the whole inhabitants of the country. But as the produce of the agriculture of both France and England is, the far greater part of it, consumed at home, each person employed in it must, according to these computations, require little more than the custom of one, two, or, at most, of four such families as his own, in order to dispose of the whole produce of his own labour. Agriculture, therefore, can support itself under the discouragement of a confined market much better than manufactures. In both ancient Egypt and Indostan, indeed, the confinement of the foreign market was in some measure compensated by the conveniency of many inland navigations, which opened, in the most advantageous manner, the whole extent of the home market to every part of the produce of every different district of those countries. The great extent of Indostan, too, rendered the home market of that country very great, and sufficient to support a great variety of manufactures. But the small extent of ancient Egypt, which was never equal to England, must at all times, have rendered the home market of that country too narrow for supporting any great variety of manufactures. Bengal accordingly, the province of Indostan which commonly exports the greatest quantity of rice, has always been more remarkable for the exportation of a great variety of manufactures, than for that of its grain. Ancient Egypt, on the contrary, though it exported some manufactures, fine linen in particular, as well as some other goods, was always most distinguished for its great exportation of grain. It was long the granary of the Roman empire.

The sovereigns of China, of ancient Egypt, and of the different kingdoms into which Indostan has, at different times, been divided, have always derived the whole, or by far the most considerable part, of their revenue, from some sort of land tax or land rent. This land tax, or land rent, like the tithe in Europe, consisted in a certain proportion, a fifth, it is said, of the produce of the land, which was either delivered in kind, or paid in money, according to a certain valuation, and which, therefore, varied from year to year, according to all the variations of the produce.

It was natural, therefore, that the sovereigns of those countries should be particularly attentive to the interests of agriculture, upon the prosperity or declension of which immediately depended the yearly increase or diminution of their own revenue.

The policy of the ancient republics of Greece, and that of Rome, though it honoured agriculture more than manufactures or foreign trade, yet seems rather to have discouraged the latter employments, than to have given any direct or intentional encouragement to the former. In several of the ancient states of Greece, foreign trade was prohibited altogether; and in several others, the employments of artificers and manufacturers were considered as hurtful to the strength and agility of the human body, as rendering it incapable of those habits which their military and gymnastic exercises endeavoured to form in it, and as thereby disqualifying it, more or less, for undergoing the fatigues and encountering the dangers of war. Such occupations were considered as fit only for slaves, and the free citizens of the states were prohibited from exercising them. Even in those states where no such prohibition took place, as in Rome and Athens, the great body of the people were in effect excluded from all the trades which are now commonly exercised by the lower sort of the inhabitants of towns. Such trades were, at Athens and Rome, all occupied by the slaves of the rich, who exercised them for the benefit of their masters, whose wealth, power, and protection, made it almost impossible for a poor freeman to find a market for his work, when it came into competition with that of the slaves of the rich. Slaves, however, are very seldom inventive; and all the most important improvements, either in machinery, or in the arrangement and distribution of work, which facilitate and abridge labour have been the discoveries of freemen. Should a slave propose any improvement of this kind, his master would be very apt to consider the proposal as the suggestion of laziness, and of a desire to save his own labour at the master's expense. The poor slave, instead of reward would probably meet with much abuse, perhaps with some punishment. In the manufactures carried on by slaves, therefore, more labour must generally have been employed to execute the same quantity of work, than in those carried on by freemen. The work of the farmer must, upon that account, generally have been dearer than that of the latter. The Hungarian mines, it is remarked by Mr. Montesquieu, though not richer, have always been wrought with less expense, and therefore with more profit, than the Turkish mines in their neighbourhood. The Turkish mines are wrought by slaves; and the arms of those slaves are the only machines which the Turks have ever thought of employing. The Hungarian mines are wrought by freemen, who employ a great deal of machinery, by which they facilitate and abridge their own labour. From the very little that is known about the price of manufactures in the times of the Greeks and Romans, it would appear that those of the finer sort were excessively dear. Silk sold for its weight in gold. It was not, indeed, in those times an European manufacture; and as it was all brought from the East Indies, the distance of the carriage may in some measure account for the greatness of the price. The price, however, which a lady, it is said, would sometimes pay for a piece of very fine linen, seems to have been equally extravagant; and as linen was always either an European, or at farthest, an Egyptian manufacture, this high price can be accounted for only by the great expense of the labour which must have been employed about It, and the expense of this labour again could arise from nothing but the awkwardness of the machinery which is made use of. The price of fine woollens, too, though not quite so extravagant, seems, however, to have been much above that of the present times. Some cloths, we are told by Pliny {Plin. 1. ix.c.39.}, dyed in a particular manner, cost a hundred denarii, or £3:6s:8d. the pound weight. Others, dyed in another manner, cost a thousand denarii the pound weight, or £33:6s:8d. The Roman pound, it must be remembered, contained only twelve of our avoirdupois ounces. This high price, indeed, seems to have been principally owing to the dye. But had not the cloths themselves been much dearer than any which are made in the present times, so very expensive a dye would not probably have been bestowed upon them. The disproportion would have been too great between the value of the accessory and that of the principal. The price mentioned by the same author {Plin. 1. viii.c.48.}, of some triclinaria, a sort of woollen pillows or cushions made use of to lean upon as they reclined upon their couches at table, passes all credibility; some of them being said to have cost more than £30,000, others more than £300,000. This high price, too, is not said to have arisen from the dye. In the dress of the people of fashion of both sexes, there seems to have been much less variety, it is observed by Dr. Arbuthnot, in ancient than in modern times; and the very little variety which we find in that of the ancient statues, confirms his observation. He infers from this, that their dress must, upon the whole, have been cheaper than ours; but the conclusion does not seem to follow. When the expense of fashionable dress is very great, the variety must be very small. But when, by the improvements in the productive powers of manufacturing art and industry, the expense of any one dress comes to be very moderate, the variety will naturally be very great. The rich, not being able to distinguish themselves by the expense of any one dress, will naturally endeavour to do so by the multitude and variety of their dresses.

The greatest and most important branch of the commerce of every nation, it has already been observed, is that which is carried on between the inhabitants of the town and those of the country. The inhabitants of the town draw from the country the rude produce, which constitutes both the materials of their work and the fund of their subsistence; and they pay for this rude produce, by sending back to the country a certain portion of it manufactured and prepared for immediate use. The trade which is carried on between these two different sets of people, consists ultimately in a certain quantity of rude produce exchanged for a certain quantity of manufactured produce. The dearer the latter, therefore, the cheaper the former; and whatever tends in any country to raise the price of manufactured produce, tends to lower that of the rude produce of the land, and thereby to discourage agriculture. The smaller the quantity of manufactured produce, which any given quantity of rude produce, or, what comes to the same thing, which the price of any given quantity of rude produce, is capable of purchasing, the smaller the exchangeable value of that given quantity of rude produce; the smaller the encouragement which either the landlord has to increase its quantity by improving, or the farmer by cultivating the land. Whatever, besides, tends to diminish in any country the number of artificers and manufacturers, tends to diminish the home market, the most important of all markets, for the rude produce of the land, and thereby still further to discourage agriculture.

Those systems, therefore, which preferring agriculture to all other employments, in order to promote it, impose restraints upon manufactures and foreign trade, act contrary to the very end which they propose, and indirectly discourage that very species of industry which they mean to promote. They are so far, perhaps, more inconsistent than even the mercantile system. That system, by encouraging manufactures and foreign trade more than agriculture, turns a certain portion of the capital of the society, from supporting a more advantageous, to support a less advantageous species of industry. But still it really, and in the end, encourages that species of industry which it means to promote. Those agricultural systems, on the contrary, really, and in the end, discourage their own favourite species of industry.

It is thus that every system which endeavours, either, by extraordinary encouragements to draw towards a particular species of industry a greater share of the capital of the society than what would naturally go to it, or, by extraordinary restraints, to force from a particular species of industry some share of the capital which would otherwise be employed in it, is, in reality, subversive of the great purpose which it means to promote. It retards, instead of accelerating the progress of the society towards real wealth and greatness; and diminishes, instead of increasing, the real value of the annual produce of its land and labour.

All systems, either of preference or of restraint, therefore, being thus completely taken away, the obvious and simple system of natural liberty establishes itself of its own accord. Every man, as long as he does not violate the laws of justice, is left perfectly free to pursue his own interest his own way, and to bring both his industry and capital into competition with those of any other man, or order of men. The sovereign is completely discharged from a duty, in the attempting to perform which he must always be exposed to innumerable delusions, and for the proper performance of which, no human wisdom or knowledge could ever be sufficient; the duty of superintending the industry of private people, and of directing it towards the employments most suitable to the interests of the society. According to the system of natural liberty, the sovereign has only three duties to attend to; three duties of great importance, indeed, but plain and intelligible to common understandings: first, the duty of protecting the society from the violence and invasion of other independent societies; secondly, the duty of protecting, as far as possible, every member of the society from the injustice or oppression of every other member of it, or the duty of establishing an exact administration of justice; and, thirdly, the duty of erecting and maintaining certain public works, and certain public institutions, which it can never be for the interest of any individual, or small number of individuals to erect and maintain; because the profit could never repay the expense to any individual, or small number of individuals, though it may frequently do much more than repay it to a great society.

The proper performance of those several duties of the sovereign necessarily supposes a certain expense; and this expense again necessarily requires a certain revenue to support it. In the following book, therefore,

I shall endeavour to explain, first, what are the necessary expenses of the sovereign or commonwealth; and which of those expenses ought to be defrayed by the general contribution of the whole society; and which of them, by that of some particular part only, or of some particular members of the society: secondly, what are the different methods in which the whole society may be made to contribute towards defraying the expenses incumbent on the whole society; and what are the principal advantages and inconveniencies of each of those methods: and thirdly, what are the reasons and causes which have induced almost all modern governments to mortgage some part of this revenue, or to contract debts; and what have been the effects of those debts upon the real wealth, the annual produce of the land and labour of the society. The following book, therefore, will naturally be divided into three chapters.

BOOK V

OF THE REVENUE OF THE SOVEREIGN OR COMMONWEALTH

CHAPTER I

OF THE EXPENSES OF THE SOVEREIGN OR COMMONWEALTH

PART I. Of the Expense of Defence

The first duty of the sovereign, that of protecting the society from the violence and invasion of other independent societies, can be performed only by means of a military force. But the expense both of preparing this military force in time of peace, and of employing it in time of war, is very different in the different states of society, in the different periods of improvement.

Among nations of hunters, the lowest and rudest state of society, such as we find it among the native tribes of North America, every man is a warrior, as well as a hunter. When he goes to war, either to defend his society, or to revenge the injuries which have been done to it by other societies, he maintains himself by his own labour, in the same manner as when he lives at home. His society (for in this state of things there is properly neither sovereign nor commonwealth) is at no sort of expense, either to prepare him for the field, or to maintain him while he is in it.

Among nations of shepherds, a more advanced state of society, such as we find it among the Tartars and Arabs, every man is, in the same manner, a warrior. Such nations have commonly no fixed habitation, but live either in tents, or in a sort of covered waggons, which are easily transported from place to place. The whole tribe, or nation, changes its situation according to the different seasons of the year, as well as according to other accidents. When its herds and flocks have consumed the forage of one part of the country, it removes to another, and from that to a third. In the dry season, it comes down to the banks of the rivers; in the wet season, it retires to the upper country. When such a nation goes to war, the warriors will not trust their herds and flocks to the feeble defence of their old men, their women and children; and their old men, their women and children, will not be left behind without defence, and without subsistence. The whole nation, besides, being accustomed to a wandering life, even in time of peace, easily takes the field in time of war. Whether it marches as an army, or moves about as a company of herdsmen, the way of life is nearly the same, though the object proposed by it be very different. They all go to war together, therefore, and everyone does as well as he can. Among the Tartars, even the women have been frequently known to engage in battle. If they conquer, whatever belongs to the hostile tribe is the recompence of the victory; but if they are vanquished, all is lost; and not only their herds and flocks, but their women and children become the booty of the conqueror. Even the greater part of those who survive the action are obliged to submit to him for the sake of immediate subsistence. The rest are commonly dissipated and dispersed in the desert.

The ordinary life, the ordinary exercise of a Tartar or Arab, prepares him sufficiently for war. Running, wrestling, cudgel-playing, throwing the javelin, drawing the bow, etc. are the common pastimes of those who live in the open air, and are all of them the images of war. When a Tartar or Arab actually goes to war, he is maintained by his own herds and flocks, which he carries with him, in the same manner as in peace. His chief or sovereign (for those nations have all chiefs or sovereigns) is at no sort of expense in preparing him for the field; and when he is in it, the chance of plunder is the only pay which he either expects or requires.

An army of hunters can seldom exceed two or three hundred men. The precarious subsistence which the chace affords, could seldom allow a greater number to keep together for any considerable time. An army of shepherds, on the contrary, may sometimes amount to two or three hundred thousand. As long as nothing stops their progress, as long as they can go on from one district, of which they have consumed the forage, to another, which is yet entire; there seems to be scarce any limit to the number who can march on together. A nation of hunters can never be formidable to the civilized nations in their neighbourhood; a nation of shepherds may. Nothing can be more contemptible than an Indian war in North America; nothing, on the contrary, can be more dreadful than a Tartar invasion has frequently been in Asia. The judgment of Thucydides, that both Europe and Asia could not resist the Scythians united, has been verified by the experience of all ages. The inhabitants of the extensive, but defenceless plains of Scythia or Tartary, have been frequently united under the dominion of the chief of some conquering horde or clan; and the havock and devastation of Asia have always signalized their union. The inhabitants of the inhospitable deserts of Arabia, the other great nation of shepherds, have never been united but once, under Mahomet and his immediate successors. Their union, which was more the effect of religious enthusiasm than of conquest, was signalized in the same manner. If the hunting nations of America should ever become shepherds, their neighbourhood would be much more dangerous to the European colonies than it is at present.

In a yet more advanced state of society, among those nations of husbandmen who have little foreign commerce, and no other manufactures but those coarse and household ones, which almost every private family prepares for its own use, every man, in the same manner, either is a warrior, or easily becomes such. Those who live by agriculture generally pass the whole day in the open air, exposed to all the inclemencies of the seasons. The hardiness of their ordinary life prepares them for the fatigues of war, to some of which their necessary occupations bear a great analogy. The necessary occupation of a ditcher prepares him to work in the trenches, and to fortify a camp, as well as to inclose a field. The ordinary pastimes of such husbandmen are the same as those of shepherds, and are in the same manner the images of war. But as husbandmen have less leisure than shepherds, they are not so frequently employed in those pastimes. They are soldiers but soldiers not quite so much masters of their exercise. Such as they are, however, it seldom costs the sovereign or commonwealth any expense to prepare them for the field.

Agriculture, even in its rudest and lowest state, supposes a settlement, some sort of fixed habitation, which cannot be abandoned without great loss. When a nation of mere husbandmen, therefore, goes to war, the whole people cannot take the field together. The old men, the women and children, at least, must remain at home, to take care of the habitation. All the men of the military age, however, may take the field, and in small nations of this kind, have frequently done so. In every nation, the men of the military age are supposed to amount to about a fourth or a fifth part of the whole body of the people. If the campaign, too, should begin after seedtime, and end before harvest, both the husbandman and his principal labourers can be spared from the farm without much loss. He trusts that the work which must be done in the mean time, can be well enough executed by the old men, the women, and the children. He is not unwilling, therefore, to serve without pay during a short campaign; and it frequently costs the sovereign or commonwealth as little to maintain him in the field as to prepare him for it. The citizens of all the different states of ancient Greece seem to have served in this manner till after the second Persian war; and the people of Peloponnesus till after the Peloponnesian war. The Peloponnesians, Thucydides observes, generally left the field in the summer, and returned home to reap the harvest. The Roman people, under their kings, and during the first ages of the republic, served in the same manner. It was not till the seige of Veii, that they who staid at home began to contribute something towards maintaining those who went to war. In the European monarchies, which were founded upon the ruins of the Roman empire, both before, and for some time after, the establishment of what is properly called the feudal law, the great lords, with all their immediate dependents, used to serve the crown at their own expense. In the field, in the same manner as at home, they maintained themselves by their own revenue, and not by any stipend or pay which they received from the king upon that particular occasion.

In a more advanced state of society, two different causes contribute to render it altogether impossible that they who take the field should maintain themselves at their own expense. Those two causes are, the progress of manufactures, and the improvement in the art of war.

Though a husbandman should be employed in an expedition, provided it begins after seedtime, and ends before harvest, the interruption of his business will not always occasion any considerable diminution of his revenue. Without the intervention of his labour, Nature does herself the greater part of the work which remains to be done. But the moment that an artificer, a smith, a carpenter, or a weaver, for example, quits his workhouse, the sole source of his revenue is completely dried up. Nature does nothing for him; he does all for himself. When he takes the field, therefore, in defence of the public, as he has no revenue to maintain himself, he must necessarily be maintained by the public. But in a country, of which a great part of the inhabitants are artificers and manufacturers, a great part of the people who go to war must be drawn from those classes, and must, therefore, be maintained by the public as long as they are employed in its service.

When the art of war, too, has gradually grown up to be a very intricate and complicated science; when the event of war ceases to be determined, as in the first ages of society, by a single irregular skirmish or battle; but when the contest is generally spun out through several different campaigns, each of which lasts during the greater part of the year; it becomes universally necessary that the public should maintain those who serve the public in war, at least while they are employed in that service. Whatever, in time of peace, might be the ordinary occupation of those who go to war, so very tedious and expensive a service would otherwise be by far too heavy a burden upon them. After the second Persian war, accordingly, the armies of Athens seem to have been generally composed of mercenary troops, consisting, indeed, partly of citizens, but partly, too, of foreigners; and all of them equally hired and paid at the expense of the state. From the time of the siege of Veii, the armies of Rome received pay for their service during the time which they remained in the field. Under the feudal governments, the military service, both of the great lords, and of their immediate dependents, was, after a certain period, universally exchanged for a payment in money, which was employed to maintain those who served in their stead.

The number of those who can go to war, in proportion to the whole number of the people, is necessarily much smaller in a civilized than in a rude state of society. In a civilized society, as the soldiers are maintained altogether by the labour of those who are not soldiers, the number of the former can never exceed what the latter can maintain, over and above maintaining, in a manner suitable to their respective stations, both themselves and the other officers of government and law, whom they are obliged to maintain. In the little agrarian states of ancient Greece, a fourth or a fifth part of the whole body of the people considered the themselves as soldiers, and would sometimes, it is said, take the field. Among the civilized nations of modern Europe, it is commonly computed, that not more than the one hundredth part of the inhabitants of any country can be employed as soldiers, without ruin to the country which pays the expense of their service.

The expense of preparing the army for the field seems not to have become considerable in any nation, till long after that of maintaining it in the field had devolved entirely upon the sovereign or commonwealth. In all the different republics of ancient Greece, to learn his military exercises, was a necessary part of education imposed by the state upon every free citizen. In every city there seems to have been a public field, in which, under the protection of the public magistrate, the young people were taught their different exercises by different masters. In this very simple institution consisted the whole expense which any Grecian state seems ever to have been at, in preparing its citizens for war. In ancient Rome, the exercises of the Campus Martius answered the same purpose with those of the Gymnasium in ancient Greece. Under the feudal governments, the many public ordinances, that the citizens of every district should practise archery, as well as several other military exercises, were intended for promoting the same purpose, but do not seem to have promoted it so well. Either from want of interest in the officers entrusted with the execution of those ordinances, or from some other cause, they appear to have been universally neglected; and in the progress of all those governments, military exercises seem to have gone gradually into disuse among the great body of the people.

In the republics of ancient Greece and Rome, during the whole period of their existence, and under the feudal governments, for a considerable time after their first establishment, the trade of a soldier was not a separate, distinct trade, which constituted the sole or principal occupation of a particular class of citizens; every subject of the state, whatever might be the ordinary trade or occupation by which he gained his livelihood, considered himself, upon all ordinary occasions, as fit likewise to exercise the trade of a soldier, and, upon many extraordinary occasions, as bound to exercise it.

The art of war, however, as it is certainly the noblest of all arts, so, in the progress of improvement, it necessarily becomes one of the most complicated among them. The state of the mechanical, as well as some other arts, with which it is necessarily connected, determines the degree of perfection to which it is capable of being carried at any particular time. But in order to carry it to this degree of perfection, it is necessary that it should become the sole or principal occupation of a particular class of citizens; and the division of labour is as necessary for the improvement of this, as of every other art. Into other arts, the division of labour is naturally introduced by the prudence of individuals, who find that they promote their private interest better by confining themselves to a particular trade, than by exercising a great number. But it is the wisdom of the state only, which can render the trade of a soldier a particular trade, separate and distinct from all others. A private citizen, who, in time of profound peace, and without any particular encouragement from the public, should spend the greater part of his time in military exercises, might, no doubt, both improve himself very much in them, and amuse himself very well; but he certainly would not promote his own interest. It is the wisdom of the state only, which can render it for his interest to give up the greater part of his time to this peculiar occupation; and states have not always had this wisdom, even when their circumstances had become such, that the preservation of their existence required that they should have it.

A shepherd has a great deal of leisure; a husbandman, in the rude state of husbandry, has some; an artificer or manufacturer has none at all. The first may, without any loss, employ a great deal of his time in martial exercises; the second may employ some part of it; but the last cannot employ a single hour in them without some loss, and his attention to his own interest naturally leads him to neglect them altogether. Those improvements in husbandry, too, which the progress of arts and manufactures necessarily introduces, leave the husbandman as little leisure as the artificer. Military exercises come to be as much neglected by the inhabitants of the country as by those of the town, and the great body of the people becomes altogether unwarlike. That wealth, at the same time, which always follows the improvements of agriculture and manufactures, and which, in reality, is no more than the accumulated produce of those improvements, provokes the invasion of all their neighbours. An industrious, and, upon that account, a wealthy nation, is of all nations the most likely to be attacked; and unless the state takes some new measure for the public defence, the natural habits of the people render them altogether incapable of defending themselves.

In these circumstances, there seem to be but two methods by which the state can make any tolerable provision for the public defence.

It may either, first, by means of a very rigorous police, and in spite of the whole bent of the interest, genius, and inclinations of the people, enforce the practice of military exercises, and oblige either all the citizens of the military age, or a certain number of them, to join in some measure the trade of a soldier to whatever other trade or profession they may happen to carry on.

Or, secondly, by maintaining and employing a certain number of citizens in the constant practice of military exercises, it may render the trade of a soldier a particular trade, separate and distinct from all others.

If the state has recourse to the first of those two expedients, its military force is said to consist in a militia; if to the second, it is said to consist in a standing army. The practice of military exercises is the sole or principal occupation of the soldiers of a standing army, and the maintenance or pay which the state affords them is the principal and ordinary fund of their subsistence. The practice of military exercises is only the occasional occupation of the soldiers of a militia, and they derive the principal and ordinary fund of their subsistence from some other occupation. In a militia, the character of the labourer, artificer, or tradesman, predominates over that of the soldier; in a standing army, that of the soldier predominates over every other character; and in this distinction seems to consist the essential difference between those two different species of military force.

Militias have been of several different kinds. In some countries, the citizens destined for defending the state seem to have been exercised only, without being, if I may say so, regimented; that is, without being divided into separate and distinct bodies of troops, each of which performed its exercises under its own proper and permanent officers. In the republics of ancient Greece and Rome, each citizen, as long as he remained at home, seems to have practised his exercises, either separately and independently, or with such of his equals as he liked best; and not to have been attached to any particular body of troops, till he was actually called upon to take the field. In other countries, the militia has not only been exercised, but regimented. In England, in Switzerland, and, I believe, in every other country of modern Europe, where any imperfect military force of this kind has been established, every militiaman is, even in time of peace, attached to a particular body of troops, which performs its exercises under its own proper and permanent officers.

Before the invention of fire-arms, that army was superior in which the soldiers had, each individually, the greatest skill and dexterity in the use of their arms. Strength and agility of body were of the highest consequence, and commonly determined the fate of battles. But this skill and dexterity in the use of their arms could be acquired only, in the same manner as fencing is at present, by practising, not in great bodies, but each man separately, in a particular school, under a particular master, or with his own particular equals and companions. Since the invention of fire-arms, strength and agility of body, or even extraordinary dexterity and skill in the use of arms, though they are far from being of no consequence, are, however, of less consequence. The nature of the weapon, though it by no means puts the awkward upon a level with the skilful, puts him more nearly so than he ever was before. All the dexterity and skill, it is supposed, which are necessary for using it, can be well enough acquired by practising in great bodies.

Regularity, order, and prompt obedience to command, are qualities which, in modern armies, are of more importance towards determining the fate of battles, than the dexterity and skill of the soldiers in the use of their arms. But the noise of fire-arms, the smoke, and the invisible death to which every man feels himself every moment exposed, as soon as he comes within cannon-shot, and frequently a long time before the battle can be well said to be engaged, must render it very difficult to maintain any considerable degree of this regularity, order, and prompt obedience, even in the beginning of a modern battle. In an ancient battle, there was no noise but what arose from the human voice; there was no smoke, there was no invisible cause of wounds or death. Every man, till some mortal weapon actually did approach him, saw clearly that no such weapon was near him. In these circumstances, and among troops who had some confidence in their own skill and dexterity in the use of their arms, it must have been a good deal less difficult to preserve some degree of regularity and order, not only in the beginning, but through the whole progress of an ancient battle, and till one of the two armies was fairly defeated. But the habits of regularity, order, and prompt obedience to command, can be acquired only by troops which are exercised in great bodies.

A militia, however, in whatever manner it may be either disciplined or exercised, must always be much inferior to a well disciplined and well exercised standing army.

The soldiers who are exercised only once a week, or once a-month, can never be so expert in the use of their arms, as those who are exercised every day, or every other day; and though this circumstance may not be of so much consequence in modern, as it was in ancient times, yet the acknowledged superiority of the Prussian troops, owing, it is said, very much to their superior expertness in their exercise, may satisfy us that it is, even at this day, of very considerable consequence.

The soldiers, who are bound to obey their officer only once a-week, or once a-month, and who are at all other times at liberty to manage their own affairs their own way, without being, in any respect, accountable to him, can never be under the same awe in his presence, can never have the same disposition to ready obedience, with those whose whole life and conduct are every day directed by him, and who every day even rise and go to bed, or at least retire to their quarters, according to his orders. In what is called discipline, or in the habit of ready obedience, a militia must always be still more inferior to a standing army, than it may sometimes be in what is called the manual exercise, or in the management and use of its arms. But, in modern war, the habit of ready and instant obedience is of much greater consequence than a considerable superiority in the management of arms.

Those militias which, like the Tartar or Arab militia, go to war under the same chieftains whom they are accustomed to obey in peace, are by far the best. In respect for their officers, in the habit of ready obedience, they approach nearest to standing armies. The Highland militia, when it served under its own chieftains, had some advantage of the same kind. As the Highlanders, however, were not wandering, but stationary shepherds, as they had all a fixed habitation, and were not, in peaceable times, accustomed to follow their chieftain from place to place; so, in time of war, they were less willing to follow him to any considerable distance, or to continue for any long time in the field. When they had acquired any booty, they were eager to return home, and his authority was seldom sufficient to detain them. In point of obedience, they were always much inferior to what is reported of the Tartars and Arabs. As the Highlanders, too, from their stationary life, spend less of their time in the open air, they were always less accustomed to military exercises, and were less expert in the use of their arms than the Tartars and Arabs are said to be.

A militia of any kind, it must be observed, however, which has served for several successive campaigns in the field, becomes in every respect a standing army. The soldiers are every day exercised in the use of their arms, and, being constantly under the command of their officers, are habituated to the same prompt obedience which takes place in standing armies. What they were before they took the field, is of little importance. They necessarily become in every respect a standing army, after they have passed a few campaigns in it. Should the war in America drag out through another campaign, the American militia may become, in every respect, a match for that standing army, of which the valour appeared, in the last war at least, not inferior to that of the hardiest veterans of France and Spain.

This distinction being well understood, the history of all ages, it will be found, hears testimony to the irresistible superiority which a well regulated standing army has over a militia.

One of the first standing armies, of which we have any distinct account in any well authenticated history, is that of Philip of Macedon. His frequent wars with the Thracians, Illyrians, Thessalians, and some of the Greek cities in the neighbourhood of Macedon, gradually formed his troops, which in the beginning were probably militia, to the exact discipline of a standing army. When he was at peace, which he was very seldom, and never for any long time together, he was careful not to disband that army. It vanquished and subdued, after a long and violent struggle, indeed, the gallant and well exercised militias of the principal republics of ancient Greece; and afterwards, with very little struggle, the effeminate and ill exercised militia of the great Persian empire. The fall of the Greek republics, and of the Persian empire was the effect of the irresistible superiority which a standing arm has over every other sort of militia. It is the first great revolution in the affairs of mankind of which history has preserved any distinct and circumstantial account.

The fall of Carthage, and the consequent elevation of Rome, is the second. All the varieties in the fortune of those two famous republics may very well be accounted for from the same cause.

From the end of the first to the beginning of the second Carthaginian war, the armies of Carthage were continually in the field, and employed under three great generals, who succeeded one another in the command; Amilcar, his son-in-law Asdrubal, and his son Annibal: first in chastising their own rebellious slaves, afterwards in subduing the revolted nations of Africa; and lastly, in conquering the great kingdom of Spain. The army which Annibal led from Spain into Italy must necessarily, in those different wars, have been gradually formed to the exact discipline of a standing army. The Romans, in the meantime, though they had not been altogether at peace, yet they had not, during this period, been engaged in any war of very great consequence; and their military discipline, it is generally said, was a good deal relaxed. The Roman armies which Annibal encountered at Trebi, Thrasymenus, and Cannae, were militia opposed to a standing army. This circumstance, it is probable, contributed more than any other to determine the fate of those battles.

The standing army which Annibal left behind him in Spain had the like superiority over the militia which the Romans sent to oppose it; and, in a few years, under the command of his brother, the younger Asdrubal, expelled them almost entirely from that country.

Annibal was ill supplied from home. The Roman militia, being continually in the field, became, in the progress of the war, a well disciplined and well exercised standing army; and the superiority of Annibal grew every day less and less. Asdrubal judged it necessary to lead the whole, or almost the whole, of the standing army which he commanded in Spain, to the assistance of his brother in Italy. In this march, he is said to have been misled by his guides; and in a country which he did not know, was surprised and attacked, by another standing army, in every respect equal or superior to his own, and was entirely defeated.

When Asdrubal had left Spain, the great Scipio found nothing to oppose him but a militia inferior to his own. He conquered and subdued that militia, and, in the course of the war, his own militia necessarily became a well disciplined and well exercised standing army. That standing army was afterwards carried to Africa, where it found nothing but a militia to oppose it. In order to defend Carthage, it became necessary to recal the standing army of Annibal. The disheartened and frequently defeated African militia joined it, and, at the battle of Zama, composed the greater part of the troops of Annibal. The event of that day determined the fate of the two rival republics.

From the end of the second Carthaginian war till the fall of the Roman republic, the armies of Rome were in every respect standing armies. The standing army of Macedon made some resistance to their arms. In the height of their grandeur, it cost them two great wars, and three great battles, to subdue that little kingdom, of which the conquest would probably have been still more difficult, had it not been for the cowardice of its last king. The militias of all the civilized nations of the ancient world, of Greece, of Syria, and of Egypt, made but a feeble resistance to the standing armies of Rome. The militias of some barbarous nations defended themselves much better. The Scythian or Tartar militia, which Mithridates drew from the countries north of the Euxine and Caspian seas, were the most formidable enemies whom the Romans had to encounter after the second Carthaginian war. The Parthian and German militias, too, were always respectable, and upon several occasions, gained very considerable advantages over the Roman armies. In general, however, and when the Roman armies were well commanded, they appear to have been very much superior; and if the Romans did not pursue the final conquest either of Parthia or Germany, it was probably because they judged that it was not worth while to add those two barbarous countries to an empire which was already too large. The ancient Parthians appear to have been a nation of Scythian or Tartar extraction, and to have always retained a good deal of the manners of their ancestors. The ancient Germans were, like the Scythians or Tartars, a nation of wandering shepherds, who went to war under the same chiefs whom they were accustomed to follow in peace. 'Their militia was exactly of the same kind with that of the Scythians or Tartars, from whom, too, they were probably descended.

Many different causes contributed to relax the discipline of the Roman armies. Its extreme severity was, perhaps, one of those causes. In the days of their grandeur, when no enemy appeared capable of opposing them, their heavy armour was laid aside as unnecessarily burdensome, their laborious exercises were neglected, as unnecessarily toilsome. Under the Roman emperors, besides, the standing armies of Rome, those particularly which guarded the German and Pannonian frontiers, became dangerous to their masters, against whom they used frequently to set up their own generals. In order to render them less formidable, according to some authors, Dioclesian, according to others, Constantine, first withdrew them from the frontier, where they had always before been encamped in great bodies, generally of two or three legions each, and dispersed them in small bodies through the different provincial towns, from whence they were scarce ever removed, but when it became necessary to repel an invasion. Small bodies of soldiers, quartered in trading and manufacturing towns, and seldom removed from those quarters, became themselves trades men, artificers, and manufacturers. The civil came to predominate over the military character; and the standing armies of Rome gradually degenerated into a corrupt, neglected, and undisciplined militia, incapable of resisting the attack of the German and Scythian militias, which soon afterwards invaded the western empire. It was only by hiring the militia of some of those nations to oppose to that of others, that the emperors were for some time able to defend themselves. The fall of the western empire is the third great revolution in the affairs of mankind, of which ancient history has preserved any distinct or circumstantial account. It was brought about by the irresistible superiority which the militia of a barbarous has over that of a civilized nation; which the militia of a nation of shepherds has over that of a nation of husbandmen, artificers, and manufacturers. The victories which have been gained by militias have generally been, not over standing armies, but over other militias, in exercise and discipline inferior to themselves. Such were the victories which the Greek militia gained over that of the Persian empire; and such, too, were those which, in later times, the Swiss militia gained over that of the Austrians and Burgundians.

The military force of the German and Scythian nations, who established themselves upon ruins of the western empire, continued for some time to be of the same kind in their new settlements, as it had been in their original country. It was a militia of shepherds and husbandmen, which, in time of war, took the field under the command of the same chieftains whom it was accustomed to obey in peace. It was, therefore, tolerably well exercised, and tolerably well disciplined. As arts and industry advanced, however, the authority of the chieftains gradually decayed, and the great body of the people had less time to spare for military exercises. Both the discipline and the exercise of the feudal militia, therefore, went gradually to ruin, and standing armies were gradually introduced to supply the place of it. When the expedient of a standing army, besides, had once been adopted by one civilized nation, it became necessary that all its neighbours should follow the example. They soon found that their safety depended upon their doing so, and that their own militia was altogether incapable of resisting the attack of such an army.

The soldiers of a standing army, though they may never have seen an enemy, yet have frequently appeared to possess all the courage of veteran troops, and, the very moment that they took the field, to have been fit to face the hardiest and most experienced veterans. In 1756, when the Russian army marched into Poland, the valour of the Russian soldiers did not appear inferior to that of the Prussians, at that time supposed to be the hardiest and most experienced veterans in Europe. The Russian empire, however, had enjoyed a profound peace for near twenty years before, and could at that time have very few soldiers who had ever seen an enemy. When the Spanish war broke out in 1739, England had enjoyed a profound peace for about eight-and-twenty years. The valour of her soldiers, however, far from being corrupted by that long peace, was never more distinguished than in the attempt upon Carthagena, the first unfortunate exploit of that unfortunate war. In a long peace, the generals, perhaps, may sometimes forget their skill; but where a well regulated standing army has been kept up, the soldiers seem never to forget their valour.

When a civilized nation depends for its defence upon a militia, it is at all times exposed to be conquered by any barbarous nation which happens to be in its neighbourhood. The frequent conquests of all the civilized countries in Asia by the Tartars, sufficiently demonstrates the natural superiority which the militia of a barbarous has over that of a civilized nation. A well regulated standing army is superior to every militia. Such an army, as it can best be maintained by an opulent and civilized nation, so it can alone defend such a nation against the invasion of a poor and barbarous neighbour. It is only by means of a standing army, therefore, that the civilization of any country can be perpetuated, or even preserved, for any considerable time.

As it is only by means of a well regulated standing army, that a civilized country can be defended, so it is only by means of it that a barbarous country can be suddenly and tolerably civilized. A standing army establishes, with an irresistible force, the law of the sovereign through the remotest provinces of the empire, and maintains some degree of regular government in countries which could not otherwise admit of any. Whoever examines with attention, the improvements which Peter the Great introduced into the Russian empire, will find that they almost all resolve themselves into the establishment of a well regulated standing army. It is the instrument which executes and maintains all his other regulations. That degree of order and internal peace, which that empire has ever since enjoyed, is altogether owing to the influence of that army.

Men of republican principles have been jealous of a standing army, as dangerous to liberty. It certainly is so, wherever the interest of the general, and that of the principal officers, are not necessarily connected with the support of the constitution of the state. The standing army of Caesar destroyed the Roman republic. The standing army of Cromwell turned the long parliament out of doors. But where the sovereign is himself the general, and the principal nobility and gentry of the country the chief officers of the army; where the military force is placed under the command of those who have the greatest interest in the support of the civil authority, because they have themselves the greatest share of that authority, a standing army can never be dangerous to liberty. On the contrary, it may, in some cases, be favourable to liberty. The security which it gives to the sovereign renders unnecessary that troublesome jealousy, which, in some modern republics, seems to watch over the minutest actions, and to be at all times ready to disturb the peace of every citizen. Where the security of the magistrate, though supported by the principal people of the country, is endangered by every popular discontent; where a small tumult is capable of bringing about in a few hours a great revolution, the whole authority of government must be employed to suppress and punish every murmur and complaint against it. To a sovereign, on the contrary, who feels himself supported, not only by the natural aristocracy of the country, but by a well regulated standing army, the rudest, the most groundless, and the most licentious remonstrances, can give little disturbance. He can safely pardon or neglect them, and his consciousness of his own superiority naturally disposes him to do so. That degree of liberty which approaches to licentiousness, can be tolerated only in countries where the sovereign is secured by a well regulated standing army. It is in such countries only, that the public safety does not require that the sovereign should be trusted with any discretionary power, for suppressing even the impertinent wantonness of this licentious liberty.

The first duty of the sovereign, therefore, that of defending the society from the violence and injustice of other independent societies, grows gradually more and more expensive, as the society advances in civilization. The military force of the society, which originally cost the sovereign no expense, either in time of peace, or in time of war, must, in the progress of improvement, first be maintained by him in time of war, and afterwards even in time of peace.

The great change introduced into the art of war by the invention of fire-arms, has enhanced still further both the expense of exercising and disciplining any particular number of soldiers in time of peace, and that of employing them in time of war. Both their arms and their ammunition are become more expensive. A musket is a more expensive machine than a javelin or a bow and arrows; a cannon or a mortar, than a balista or a catapulta. The powder which is spent in a modern review is lost irrecoverably, and occasions a very considerable expense. The javelins and arrows which were thrown or shot in an ancient one, could easily be picked up again, and were, besides, of very little value. The cannon and the mortar are not only much dearer, but much heavier machines than the balista or catapulta; and require a greater expense, not only to prepare them for the field, but to carry them to it. As the superiority of the modern artillery, too, over that of the ancients, is very great; it has become much more difficult, and consequently much more expensive, to fortify a town, so as to resist, even for a few weeks, the attack of that superior artillery. In modern times, many different causes contribute to render the defence of the society more expensive. The unavoidable effects of the natural progress of improvement have, in this respect, been a good deal enhanced by a great revolution in the art of war, to which a mere accident, the invention of gunpowder, seems to have given occasion.

In modern war, the great expense of firearms gives an evident advantage to the nation which can best afford that expense; and, consequently, to an opulent and civilized, over a poor and barbarous nation. In ancient times, the opulent and civilized found it difficult to defend themselves against the poor and barbarous nations. In modern times, the poor and barbarous find it difficult to defend themselves against the opulent and civilized. The invention of fire-arms, an invention which at first sight appears to be so pernicious, is certainly favourable, both to the permanency and to the extension of civilization.

PART II. Of the Expense of Justice

The second duty of the sovereign, that of protecting, as far as possible, every member of the society from the injustice or oppression of every other member of it, or the duty of establishing an exact administration of justice, requires two very different degrees of expense in the different periods of society.

Among nations of hunters, as there is scarce any property, or at least none that exceeds the value of two or three days labour; so there is seldom any established magistrate, or any regular administration of justice. Men who have no property, can injure one another only in their persons or reputations. But when one man kills, wounds, beats, or defames another, though he to whom the injury is done suffers, he who does it receives no benefit. It is otherwise with the injuries to property. The benefit of the person who does the injury is often equal to the loss of him who suffers it. Envy, malice, or resentment, are the only passions which can prompt one man to injure another in his person or reputation. But the greater part of men are not very frequently under the influence of those passions; and the very worst men are so only occasionally. As their gratification, too, how agreeable soever it may be to certain characters, is not attended with any real or permanent advantage, it is, in the greater part of men, commonly restrained by prudential considerations. Men may live together in society with some tolerable degree of security, though there is no civil magistrate to protect them from the injustice of those passions. But avarice and ambition in the rich, in the poor the hatred of labour and the love of present ease and enjoyment, are the passions which prompt to invade property; passions much more steady in their operation, and much more universal in their influence. Wherever there is a great property, there is great inequality. For one very rich man, there must be at least five hundred poor, and the affluence of the few supposes the indigence of the many. The affluence of the rich excites the indignation of the poor, who are often both driven by want, and prompted by envy to invade his possessions. It is only under the shelter of the civil magistrate, that the owner of that valuable property, which is acquired by the labour of many years, or perhaps of many successive generations, can sleep a single night in security. He is at all times surrounded by unknown enemies, whom, though he never provoked, he can never appease, and from whose injustice he can be protected only by the powerful arm of the civil magistrate, continually held up to chastise it. The acquisition of valuable and extensive property, therefore, necessarily requires the establishment of civil government. Where there is no property, or at least none that exceeds the value of two or three days labour, civil government is not so necessary.

Civil government supposes a certain subordination. But as the necessity of civil government gradually grows up with the acquisition of valuable property; so the principal causes, which naturally introduce subordination, gradually grow up with the growth of that valuable property.

The causes or circumstances which naturally introduce subordination, or which naturally and antecedent to any civil institution, give some men some superiority over the greater part of their brethren, seem to be four in number.

The first of those causes or circumstances, is the superiority of personal qualifications, of strength, beauty, and agility of body; of wisdom and virtue; of prudence, justice, fortitude, and moderation of mind. The qualifications of the body, unless supported by those of the mind, can give little authority in any period of society. He is a very strong man, who, by mere strength of body, can force two weak ones to obey him. The qualifications of the mind can alone give very great authority. They are however, invisible qualities; always disputable, and generally disputed. No society, whether barbarous or civilized, has ever found it convenient to settle the rules of precedency of rank and subordination, according to those invisible qualities; but according to something that is more plain and palpable.

The second of those causes or circumstances, is the superiority of age. An old man, provided his age is not so far advanced as to give suspicion of dotage, is everywhere more respected than a young man of equal rank, fortune, and abilities. Among nations of hunters, such as the native tribes of North America, age is the sole foundation of rank and precedency. Among them, father is the appellation of a superior; brother, of an equal; and son, of an inferior. In the most opulent and civilized nations, age regulates rank among those who are in every other respect equal; and among whom, therefore, there is nothing else to regulate it. Among brothers and among sisters, the eldest always takes place; and in the succession of the paternal estate, every thing which cannot be divided, but must go entire to one person, such as a title of honour, is in most cases given to the eldest. Age is a plain and palpable quality, which admits of no dispute.

The third of those causes or circumstances, is the superiority of fortune. The authority of riches, however, though great in every age of society, is, perhaps, greatest in the rudest ages of society, which admits of any considerable inequality of fortune. A Tartar chief, the increase of whose flocks and herds is sufficient to maintain a thousand men, cannot well employ that increase in any other way than in maintaining a thousand men. The rude state of his society does not afford him any manufactured produce any trinkets or baubles of any kind, for which he can exchange that part of his rude produce which is over and above his own consumption. The thousand men whom he thus maintains, depending entirely upon him for their subsistence, must both obey his orders in war, and submit to his jurisdiction in peace. He is necessarily both their general and their judge, and his chieftainship is the necessary effect of the superiority of his fortune. In an opulent and civilized society, a man may possess a much greater fortune, and yet not be able to command a dozen of people. Though the produce of his estate may be sufficient to maintain, and may, perhaps, actually maintain, more than a thousand people, yet, as those people pay for every thing which they get from him, as he gives scarce any thing to any body but in exchange for an equivalent, there is scarce anybody who considers himself as entirely dependent upon him, and his authority extends only over a few menial servants. The authority of fortune, however, is very great, even in an opulent and civilized society. That it is much greater than that either of age or of personal qualities, has been the constant complaint of every period of society which admitted of any considerable inequality of fortune. The first period of society, that of hunters, admits of no such inequality. Universal poverty establishes their universal equality; and the superiority, either of age or of personal qualities, are the feeble, but the sole foundations of authority and subordination. There is, therefore, little or no authority or subordination in this period of society. The second period of society, that of shepherds, admits of very great inequalities of fortune, and there is no period in which the superiority of fortune gives so great authority to those who possess it. There is no period, accordingly, in which authority and subordination are more perfectly established. The authority of an Arabian scherif is very great; that of a Tartar khan altogether despotical.

The fourth of those causes or circumstances, is the superiority of birth. Superiority of birth supposes an ancient superiority of fortune in the family of the person who claims it. All families are equally ancient; and the ancestors of the prince, though they may be better known, cannot well be more numerous than those of the beggar. Antiquity of family means everywhere the antiquity either of wealth, or of that greatness which is commonly either founded upon wealth, or accompanied with it. Upstart greatness is everywhere less respected than ancient greatness. The hatred of usurpers, the love of the family of an ancient monarch, are in a great measure founded upon the contempt which men naturally have for the former, and upon their veneration for the latter. As a military officer submits, without reluctance, to the authority of a superior by whom he has always been commanded, but cannot bear that his inferior should be set over his head; so men easily submit to a family to whom they and their ancestors have always submitted; but are fired with indignation when another family, in whom they had never acknowledged any such superiority, assumes a dominion over them.

The distinction of birth, being subsequent to the inequality of fortune, can have no place in nations of hunters, among whom all men, being equal in fortune, must likewise be very nearly equal in birth. The son of a wise and brave man may, indeed, even among them, be somewhat more respected than a man of equal merit, who has the misfortune to be the son of a fool or a coward. The difference, however will not be very great; and there never was, I believe, a great family in the world, whose illustration was entirely derived from the inheritance of wisdom and virtue.

The distinction of birth not only may, but always does, take place among nations of shepherds. Such nations are always strangers to every sort of luxury, and great wealth can scarce ever be dissipated among them by improvident profusion. There are no nations, accordingly, who abound more in families revered and honoured on account of their descent from a long race of great and illustrious ancestors; because there are no nations among whom wealth is likely to continue longer in the same families.

Birth and fortune are evidently the two circumstances which principally set one man above another. They are the two great sources of personal distinction, and are, therefore, the principal causes which naturally establish authority and subordination among men. Among nations of shepherds, both those causes operate with their full force. The great shepherd or herdsman, respected on account of his great wealth, and of the great number of those who depend upon him for subsistence, and revered on account of the nobleness of his birth, and of the immemorial antiquity or his illustrious family, has a natural authority over all the inferior shepherds or herdsmen of his horde or clan. He can command the united force of a greater number of people than any of them. His military power is greater than that of any of them. In time of war, they are all of them naturally disposed to muster themselves under his banner, rather than under that of any other person; and his birth and fortune thus naturally procure to him some sort of executive power. By commanding, too, the united force of a greater number of people than any of them, he is best able to compel any one of them, who may have injured another, to compensate the wrong. He is the person, therefore, to whom all those who are too weak to defend themselves naturally look up for protection. It is to him that they naturally complain of the injuries which they imagine have been done to them; and his interposition, in such cases, is more easily submitted to, even by the person complained of, than that of any other person would be. His birth and fortune thus naturally procure him some sort of judicial authority.

It is in the age of shepherds, in the second period of society, that the inequality of fortune first begins to take place, and introduces among men a degree of authority and subordination, which could not possibly exist before. It thereby introduces some degree of that civil government which is indispensably necessary for its own preservation; and it seems to do this naturally, and even independent of the consideration of that necessity. The consideration of that necessity comes, no doubt, afterwards, to contribute very much to maintain and secure that authority and subordination. The rich, in particular, are necessarily interested to support that order of things, which can alone secure them in the possession of their own advantages. Men of inferior wealth combine to defend those of superior wealth in the possession of their property, in order that men of superior wealth may combine to defend them in the possession of theirs. All the inferior shepherds and herdsmen feel, that the security of their own herds and flocks depends upon the security of those of the great shepherd or herdsman; that the maintenance of their lesser authority depends upon that of his greater authority; and that upon their subordination to him depends his power of keeping their inferiors in subordination to them. They constitute a sort of little nobility, who feel themselves interested to defend the property, and to support the authority, of their own little sovereign, in order that he may be able to defend their property, and to support their authority. Civil government, so far as it is instituted for the security of property, is, in reality, instituted for the defence of the rich against the poor, or of those who have some property against those who have none at all.

The judicial authority of such a sovereign, however, far from being a cause of expense, was, for a long time, a source of revenue to him. The persons who applied to him for justice were always willing to pay for it, and a present never failed to accompany a petition. After the authority of the sovereign, too, was thoroughly established, the person found guilty, over and above the satisfaction which he was obliged to make to the party, was like-wise forced to pay an amercement to the sovereign. He had given trouble, he had disturbed, he had broke the peace of his lord the king, and for those offences an amercement was thought due. In the Tartar governments of Asia, in the governments of Europe which were founded by the German and Scythian nations who overturned the Roman empire, the administration of justice was a considerable source of revenue, both to the sovereign, and to all the lesser chiefs or lords who exercised under him any particular jurisdiction, either over some particular tribe or clan, or over some particular territory or district. Originally, both the sovereign and the inferior chiefs used to exercise this jurisdiction in their own persons. Afterwards, they universally found it convenient to delegate it to some substitute, bailiff, or judge. This substitute, however, was still obliged to account to his principal or constituent for the profits of the jurisdiction. Whoever reads the instructions (They are to be found in Tyrol's History of England) which were given to the judges of the circuit in the time of Henry II will see clearly that those judges were a sort of itinerant factors, sent round the country for the purpose of levying certain branches of the king's revenue. In those days, the administration of justice not only afforded a certain revenue to the sovereign, but, to procure this revenue, seems to have been one of the principal advantages which he proposed to obtain by the administration of justice.

This scheme of making the administration of justice subservient to the purposes of revenue, could scarce fail to be productive of several very gross abuses. The person who applied for justice with a large present in his hand, was likely to get something more than justice; while he who applied for it with a small one was likely to get something less. Justice, too, might frequently be delayed, in order that this present might be repeated. The amercement, besides, of the person complained of, might frequently suggest a very strong reason for finding him in the wrong, even when he had not really been so. That such abuses were far from being uncommon, the ancient history of every country in Europe bears witness.

When the sovereign or chief exercises his judicial authority in his own person, how much soever he might abuse it, it must have been scarce possible to get any redress; because there could seldom be any body powerful enough to call him to account. When he exercised it by a bailiff, indeed, redress might sometimes be had. If it was for his own benefit only, that the bailiff had been guilty of an act of injustice, the sovereign himself might not always be unwilling to punish him, or to oblige him to repair the wrong. But if it was for the benefit of his sovereign; if it was in order to make court to the person who appointed him, and who might prefer him, that he had committed any act of oppression; redress would, upon most occasions, be as impossible as if the sovereign had committed it himself. In all barbarous governments, accordingly, in all those ancient governments of Europe in particular, which were founded upon the ruins of the Roman empire, the administration of justice appears for a long time to have been extremely corrupt; far from being quite equal and impartial, even under the best monarchs, and altogether profligate under the worst.

Among nations of shepherds, where the sovereign or chief is only the greatest shepherd or herdsman of the horde or clan, he is maintained in the same manner as any of his vassals or subjects, by the increase of his own herds or flocks. Among those nations of husbandmen, who are but just come out of the shepherd state, and who are not much advanced beyond that state, such as the Greek tribes appear to have been about the time of the Trojan war, and our German and Scythian ancestors, when they first settled upon the ruins of the western empire; the sovereign or chief is, in the same manner, only the greatest landlord of the country, and is maintained in the same manner as any other landlord, by a revenue derived from his own private estate, or from what, in modern Europe, was called the demesne of the crown. His subjects, upon ordinary occasions, contribute nothing to his support, except when, in order to protect them from the oppression of some of their fellow-subjects, they stand in need of his authority. The presents which they make him upon such occasions constitute the whole ordinary revenue, the whole of the emoluments which, except, perhaps, upon some very extraordinary emergencies, he derives from his dominion over them. When Agamemnon, in Homer, offers to Achilles, for his friendship, the sovereignty of seven Greek cities, the sole advantage which he mentions as likely to be derived from it was, that the people would honour him with presents. As long as such presents, as long as the emoluments of justice, or what may be called the fees of court, constituted, in this manner, the whole ordinary revenue which the sovereign derived from his sovereignty, it could not well be expected, it could not even decently be proposed, that he should give them up altogether. It might, and it frequently was proposed, that he should regulate and ascertain them. But after they had been so regulated and ascertained, how to hinder a person who was all-powerful from extending them beyond those regulations, was still very difficult, not to say impossible. During the continuance of this state of things, therefore, the corruption of justice, naturally resulting from the arbitrary and uncertain nature of those presents, scarce admitted of any effectual remedy.

But when, from different causes, chiefly from the continually increasing expense of defending the nation against the invasion of other nations, the private estate of the sovereign had become altogether insufficient for defraying the expense of the sovereignty; and when it had become necessary that the people should, for their own security, contribute towards this expense by taxes of different kinds; it seems to have been very commonly stipulated, that no present for the administration of justice should, under any pretence, be accepted either by the sovereign, or by his bailiffs and substitutes, the judges. Those presents, it seems to have been supposed, could more easily be abolished altogether, than effectually regulated and ascertained. Fixed salaries were appointed to the judges, which were supposed to compensate to them the loss of whatever might have been their share of the ancient emoluments of justice; as the taxes more than compensated to the sovereign the loss of his. Justice was then said to be administered gratis.

Justice, however, never was in reality administered gratis in any country. Lawyers and attorneys, at least, must always be paid by the parties; and if they were not, they would perform their duty still worse than they actually perform it. The fees annually paid to lawyers and attorneys, amount, in every court, to a much greater sum than the salaries of the judges. The circumstance of those salaries being paid by the crown, can nowhere much diminish the necessary expense of a law-suit. But it was not so much to diminish the expense, as to prevent the corruption of justice, that the judges were prohibited from receiving my present or fee from the parties.

The office of judge is in itself so very honourable, that men are willing to accept of it, though accompanied with very small emoluments. The inferior office of justice of peace, though attended with a good deal of trouble, and in most cases with no emoluments at all, is an object of ambition to the greater part of our country gentlemen. The salaries of all the different judges, high and low, together with the whole expense of the administration and execution of justice, even where it is not managed with very good economy, makes, in any civilized country, but a very inconsiderable part of the whole expense of government.

The whole expense of justice, too, might easily be defrayed by the fees of court; and, without exposing the administration of justice to any real hazard of corruption, the public revenue might thus be entirely discharged from a certain, though perhaps but a small incumbrance. It is difficult to regulate the fees of court effectually, where a person so powerful as the sovereign is to share in them and to derive any considerable part of his revenue from them. It is very easy, where the judge is the principal person who can reap any benefit from them. The law can very easily oblige the judge to respect the regulation though it might not always be able to make the sovereign respect it. Where the fees of court are precisely regulated and ascertained where they are paid all at once, at a certain period of every process, into the hands of a cashier or receiver, to be by him distributed in certain known proportions among the different judges after the process is decided and not till it is decided; there seems to be no more danger of corruption than when such fees are prohibited altogether. Those fees, without occasioning any considerable increase in the expense of a law-suit, might be rendered fully sufficient for defraying the whole expense of justice. But not being paid to the judges till the process was determined, they might be some incitement to the diligence of the court in examining and deciding it. In courts which consisted of a considerable number of judges, by proportioning the share of each judge to the number of hours and days which he had employed in examining the process, either in the court, or in a committee, by order of the court, those fees might give some encouragement to the diligence of each particular judge. Public services are never better performed, than when their reward comes only in consequence of their being performed, and is proportioned to the diligence employed in performing them. In the different parliaments of France, the fees of court (called epices and vacations) constitute the far greater part of the emoluments of the judges. After all deductions are made, the neat salary paid by the crown to a counsellor or judge in the parliament of Thoulouse, in rank and dignity the second parliament of the kingdom, amounts only to 150 livres, about £6:11s. sterling a-year. About seven years ago, that sum was in the same place the ordinary yearly wages of a common footman. The distribution of these epices, too, is according to the diligence of the judges. A diligent judge gains a comfortable, though moderate revenue, by his office; an idle one gets little more than his salary. Those parliaments are, perhaps, in many respects, not very convenient courts of justice; but they have never been accused; they seem never even to have been suspected of corruption.

    The fees of court seem originally to have been the principal support of the different courts of justice in England. Each court endeavoured to draw to itself as much business as it could, and was, upon that account, willing to take cognizance of many suits which were not originally intended to fall under its jurisdiction. The court of king's bench, instituted for the trial of criminal causes only, took cognizance of civil suits; the plaintiff pretending that the defendant, in not doing him justice, had been guilty of some trespass or misdemeanour. The court of exchequer, instituted for the levying of the king's revenue, and for enforcing the payment of such debts only as were due to the king, took cognizance of all other contract debts; the planitiff alleging that he could not pay the king, because the defendant would not pay him. In consequence of such fictions, it came, in many cases, to depend altogether upon the parties, before what court they would choose to have their cause tried, and each court endeavoured, by superior dispatch and impartiality, to draw to itself as many causes as it could. The present admirable constitution of the courts of justice in England was, perhaps, originally, in a great measure, formed by this emulation, which anciently took place between their respective judges: each judge endeavouring to give, in his own court, the speediest and most effectual remedy which the law would admit, for every sort of injustice. Originally, the courts of law gave damages only for breach of contract. The court of chancery, as a court of conscience, first took upon it to enforce the specific performance of agreements. When the breach of contract consisted in the non-payment of money, the damage sustained could be compensated in no other way than by ordering payment, which was equivalent to a specific performance of the agreement. In such cases, therefore, the remedy of the courts of law was sufficient. It was not so in others. When the tenant sued his lord for having unjustly outed him of his lease, the damages which he recovered were by no means equivalent to the possession of the land. Such causes, therefore, for some time, went all to the court of chancery, to the no small loss of the courts of law. It was to draw back such causes to themselves, that the courts of law are said to have invented the artificial and fictitious writ of ejectment, the most effectual remedy for an unjust outer or dispossession of land.

A stamp-duty upon the law proceedings of each particular court, to be levied by that court, and applied towards the maintenance of the judges, and other officers belonging to it, might in the same manner, afford a revenue sufficient for defraying the expense of the administration of justice, without bringing any burden upon the general revenue of the society. The judges, indeed, might in this case, be under the temptation of multiplying unnecessarily the proceedings upon every cause, in order to increase, as much as possible, the produce of such a stamp-duty. It has been the custom in modern Europe to regulate, upon most occasions, the payment of the attorneys and clerks of court according to the number of pages which they had occasion to write; the court, however, requiring that each page should contain so many lines, and each line so many words. In order to increase their payment, the attorneys and clerks have contrived to multiply words beyond all necessity, to the corruption of the law language of, I believe, every court of justice in Europe. A like temptation might, perhaps, occasion a like corruption in the form of law proceedings.

But whether the administration of justice be so contrived as to defray its own expense, or whether the judges be maintained by fixed salaries paid to them from some other fund, it does not seen necessary that the person or persons entrusted with the executive power should be charged with the management of that fund, or with the payment of those salaries. That fund might arise from the rent of landed estates, the management of each estate being entrusted to the particular court which was to be maintained by it. That fund might arise even from the interest of a sum of money, the lending out of which might, in the same manner, be entrusted to the court which was to be maintained by it. A part, though indeed but a small part of the salary of the judges of the court of session in Scotland, arises from the interest of a sum of money. The necessary instability of such a fund seems, however, to render it an improper one for the maintenance of an institution which ought to last for ever.

The separation of the judicial from the executive power, seems originally to have arisen from the increasing business of the society, in consequence of its increasing improvement. The administration of justice became so laborious and so complicated a duty, as to require the undivided attention of the person to whom it was entrusted. The person entrusted with the executive power, not having leisure to attend to the decision of private causes himself, a deputy was appointed to decide them in his stead. In the progress of the Roman greatness, the consul was too much occupied with the political affairs of the state, to attend to the administration of justice. A praetor, therefore, was appointed to administer it in his stead. In the progress of the European monarchies, which were founded upon the ruins of the Roman empire, the sovereigns and the great lords came universally to consider the administration of justice as an office both too laborious and too ignoble for them to execute in their own persons. They universally, therefore, discharged themselves of it, by appointing a deputy, bailiff or judge.

When the judicial is united to the executive power, it is scarce possible that justice should not frequently be sacrificed to what is vulgarly called politics. The persons entrusted with the great interests of the state may even without any corrupt views, sometimes imagine it necessary to sacrifice to those interests the rights of a private man. But upon the impartial administration of justice depends the liberty of every individual, the sense which he has of his own security. In order to make every individual feel himself perfectly secure in the possession of every right which belongs to him, it is not only necessary that the judicial should be separated from the executive power, but that it should be rendered as much as possible independent of that power. The judge should not be liable to be removed from his office according to the caprice of that power. The regular payment of his salary should not depend upon the good will, or even upon the good economy of that power.

PART III. Of the Expense of public Works and public Institutions

The third and last duty of the sovereign or commonwealth, is that of erecting and maintaining those public institutions and those public works, which though they may be in the highest degree advantageous to a great society, are, however, of such a nature, that the profit could never repay the expense to any individual, or small number of individuals; and which it, therefore, cannot be expected that any individual, or small number of individuals, should erect or maintain. The performance of this duty requires, too, very different degrees of expense in the different periods of society.

After the public institutions and public works necessary for the defence of the society, and for the administration of justice, both of which have already been mentioned, the other works and institutions of this kind are chiefly for facilitating the commerce of the society, and those for promoting the instruction of the people. The institutions for instruction are of two kinds: those for the education of the youth, and those for the instruction of people of all ages. The consideration of the manner in which the expense of those different sorts of public works and institutions may be most properly defrayed will divide this third part of the present chapter into three different articles.

ARTICLE I.—Of the public Works and Institutions for facilitating the Commerce of the Society

And, first, of those which are necessary for facilitating Commerce in general.

That the erection and maintenance of the public works which facilitate the commerce of any country, such as good roads, bridges, navigable canals, harbours, etc. must require very different degrees of expense in the different periods of society, is evident without any proof. The expense of making and maintaining the public roads of any country must evidently increase with the annual produce of the land and labour of that country, or with the quantity and weight of the goods which it becomes necessary to fetch and carry upon those roads. The strength of a bridge must be suited to the number and weight of the carriages which are likely to pass over it. The depth and the supply of water for a navigable canal must be proportioned to the number and tonnage of the lighters which are likely to carry goods upon it; the extent of a harbour, to the number of the shipping which are likely to take shelter in it.

It does not seem necessary that the expense of those public works should be defrayed from that public revenue, as it is commonly called, of which the collection and application are in most countries, assigned to the executive power. The greater part of such public works may easily be so managed, as to afford a particular revenue, sufficient for defraying their own expense without bringing any burden upon the general revenue of the society.

A highway, a bridge, a navigable canal, for example, may, in most cases, be both made add maintained by a small toll upon the carriages which make use of them; a harbour, by a moderate port-duty upon the tonnage of the shipping which load or unload in it. The coinage, another institution for facilitating commerce, in many countries, not only defrays its own expense, but affords a small revenue or a seignorage to the sovereign. The post-office, another institution for the same purpose, over and above defraying its own expense, affords, in almost all countries, a very considerable revenue to the sovereign.

When the carriages which pass over a highway or a bridge, and the lighters which sail upon a navigable canal, pay toll in proportion to their weight or their tonnage, they pay for the maintenance of those public works exactly in proportion to the wear and tear which they occasion of them. It seems scarce possible to invent a more equitable way of maintaining such works. This tax or toll, too, though it is advanced by the carrier, is finally paid by the consumer, to whom it must always be charged in the price of the goods. As the expense of carriage, however, is very much reduced by means of such public works, the goods, notwithstanding the toll, come cheaper to the consumer than they could otherwise have done, their price not being so much raised by the toll, as it is lowered by the cheapness of the carriage. The person who finally pays this tax, therefore, gains by the application more than he loses by the payment of it. His payment is exactly in proportion to his gain. It is, in reality, no more than a part of that gain which he is obliged to give up, in order to get the rest. It seems impossible to imagine a more equitable method of raising a tax. When the toll upon carriages of luxury, upon coaches, post-chaises, etc. is made somewhat higher in proportion to their weight, than upon carriages of necessary use, such as carts, waggons, etc. the indolence and vanity of the rich is made to contribute, in a very easy manner, to the relief of the poor, by rendering cheaper the transportation of heavy goods to all the different parts of the country.

When high-roads, bridges, canals, etc. are in this manner made and supported by the commerce which is carried on by means of them, they can be made only where that commerce requires them, and, consequently, where it is proper to make them. Their expense, too, their grandeur and magnificence, must be suited to what that commerce can afford to pay. They must be made, consequently, as it is proper to make them. A magnificent high-road cannot be made through a desert country, where there is little or no commerce, or merely because it happens to lead to the country villa of the intendant of the province, or to that of some great lord, to whom the intendant finds it convenient to make his court. A great bridge cannot be thrown over a river at a place where nobody passes, or merely to embellish the view from the windows of a neighbouring palace; things which sometimes happen in countries, where works of this kind are carried on by any other revenue than that which they themselves are capable of affording.

In several different parts of Europe, the toll or lock-duty upon a canal is the property of private persons, whose private interest obliges them to keep up the canal. If it is not kept in tolerable order, the navigation necessarily ceases altogether, and, along with it, the whole profit which they can make by the tolls. If those tolls were put under the management of commissioners, who had themselves no interest in them, they might be less attentive to the maintenance of the works which produced them. The canal of Languedoc cost the king of France and the province upwards of thirteen millions of livres, which (at twenty-eight livres the mark of silver, the value of French money in the end of the last century) amounted to upwards of nine hundred thousand pounds sterling. When that great work was finished, the most likely method, it was found, of keeping it in constant repair, was to make a present of the tolls to Riquet, the engineer who planned and conducted the work. Those tolls constitute, at present, a very large estate to the different branches of the family of that gentleman, who have, therefore, a great interest to keep the work in constant repair. But had those tolls been put under the management of commissioners, who had no such interest, they might perhaps, have been dissipated in ornamental and unnecessary expenses, while the most essential parts of the works were allowed to go to ruin.

The tolls for the maintenance of a highroad cannot, with any safety, be made the property of private persons. A high-road, though entirely neglected, does not become altogether impassable, though a canal does. The proprietors of the tolls upon a high-road, therefore, might neglect altogether the repair of the road, and yet continue to levy very nearly the same tolls. It is proper, therefore, that the tolls for the maintenance of such a work should be put under the management of commissioners or trustees.

In Great Britain, the abuses which the trustees have committed in the management of those tolls, have, in many cases, been very justly complained of. At many turnpikes, it has been said, the money levied is more than double of what is necessary for executing, in the completest manner, the work, which is often executed in a very slovenly manner, and sometimes not executed at all. The system of repairing the high-roads by tolls of this kind, it must be observed, is not of very long standing. We should not wonder, therefore, if it has not yet been brought to that degree of perfection of which it seems capable. If mean and improper persons are frequently appointed trustees; and if proper courts of inspection and account have not yet been established for controlling their conduct, and for reducing the tolls to what is barely sufficient for executing the work to be done by them; the recency of the institution both accounts and apologizes for those defects, of which, by the wisdom of parliament, the greater part may, in due time, be gradually remedied.

The money levied at the different turnpikes in Great Britain, is supposed to exceed so much what is necessary for repairing the roads, that the savings which, with proper economy, might be made from it, have been considered, even by some ministers, as a very great resource, which might, at some time or another, be applied to the exigencies of the state. Government, it has been said, by taking the management of the turnpikes into its own hands, and by employing the soldiers, who would work for a very small addition to their pay, could keep the roads in good order, at a much less expense than it can be done by trustees, who have no other workmen to employ, but such as derive their whole subsistence from their wages. A great revenue, half a million, perhaps {Since publishing the two first editions of this book, I have got good reasons to believe that all the turnpike tolls levied in Great Britain do not produce a neat revenue that amounts to half a million; a sum which, under the management of government, would not be sufficient to keep in repair five of the principal roads in the kingdom}, it has been pretended, might in this manner be gained, without laying any new burden upon the people; and the turnpike roads might be made to contribute to the general expense of the state, in the same manner as the post-office does at present.

That a considerable revenue might be gained in this manner, I have no doubt, though probably not near so much as the projectors of this plan have supposed. The plan itself, however, seems liable to several very important objections.

First, If the tolls which are levied at the turnpikes should ever be considered as one of the resources for supplying the exigencies of the state, they would certainly be augmented as those exigencies were supposed to require. According to the policy of Great Britain, therefore, they would probably he augmented very fast. The facility with which a great revenue could be drawn from them, would probably encourage administration to recur very frequently te this resource. Though it may, perhaps, be more than doubtful whether half a million could by any economy be saved out of the present tolls, it can scarcely be doubted, but that a million might be saved out of them, if they were doubled; and perhaps two millions, if they were tripled {I have now good reason to believe that all these conjectural sums are by much too large.}. This great revenue, too, might be levied without the appointment of a single new officer to collect and receive it. But the turnpike tolls, being continually augmented in this manner, instead of facilitating the inland commerce of the country, as at present, would soon become a very great incumbrance upon it. The expense of transporting all heavy goods from one part of the country to another, would soon be so much increased, the market for all such goods, consequently, would soon be so much narrowed, that their production would be in a great measure discouraged, and the most important branches of the domestic industry of the country annihilated altogether.

Secondly, A tax upon carriages, in proportion to their weight, though a very equal tax when applied to the sole purpose of repairing the roads, is a very unequal one when applied to any other purpose, or to supply the common exigencies of the state. When it is applied to the sole purpose above mentioned, each carriage is supposed to pay exactly for the wear and tear which that carriage occasions of the roads. But when it is applied to any other purpose, each carriage is supposed to pay for more than that wear and tear, and contributes to the supply of some other exigency of the state. But as the turnpike toll raises the price of goods in proportion to their weight and not to their value, it is chiefly paid by the consumers of coarse and bulky, not by those of precious and light commodities. Whatever exigency of the state, therefore, this tax might be intended to supply, that exigency would be chiefly supplied at the expense of the poor, not of the rich; at the expense of those who are least able to supply it, not of those who are most able.

Thirdly, If government should at any time neglect the reparation of the high-roads, it would be still more difficult, than it is at present, to compel the proper application of any part of the turnpike tolls. A large revenue might thus be levied upon the people, without any part of it being applied to the only purpose to which a revenue levied in this manner ought ever to be applied. If the meanness and poverty of the trustees of turnpike roads render it sometimes difficult, at present, to oblige them to repair their wrong; their wealth and greatness would render it ten times more so in the case which is here supposed.

In France, the funds destined for the reparation of the high-roads are under the immediate direction of the executive power. Those funds consist, partly in a certain number of days labour, which the country people are in most parts of Europe obliged to give to the reparation of the highways; and partly in such a portion of the general revenue of the state as the king chooses to spare from his other expenses.

By the ancient law of France, as well as by that of most other parts of Europe, the labour of the country people was under the direction of a local or provincial magistracy, which had no immediate dependency upon the king's council. But, by the present practice, both the labour of the country people, and whatever other fund the king may choose to assign for the reparation of the high-roads in any particular province or generality, are entirely under the management of the intendant; an officer who is appointed and removed by the king's council who receives his orders from it, and is in constant correspondence with it. In the progress of despotism, the authority of the executive power gradually absorbs that of every other power in the state, and assumes to itself the management of every branch of revenue which is destined for any public purpose. In France, however, the great post-roads, the roads which make the communication between the principal towns of the kingdom, are in general kept in good order; and, in some provinces, are even a good deal superior to the greater part of the turnpike roads of England. But what we call the cross roads, that is, the far greater part of the roads in the country, are entirely neglected, and are in many places absolutely impassable for any heavy carriage. In some places it is even dangerous to travel on horseback, and mules are the only conveyance which can safely be trusted. The proud minister of an ostentatious court, may frequently take pleasure in executing a work of splendour and magnificence, such as a great highway, which is frequently seen by the principal nobility, whose applauses not only flatter his vanity, but even contribute to support his interest at court. But to execute a great number of little works, in which nothing that can be done can make any great appearance, or excite the smallest degree of admiration in any traveller, and which, in short, have nothing to recommend them but their extreme utility, is a business which appears, in every respect, too mean and paltry to merit the attention of so great a magistrate. Under such an administration therefore, such works are almost always entirely neglected.

In China, and in several other governments of Asia, the executive power charges itself both with the reparation of the high-roads, and with the maintenance of the navigable canals. In the instructions which are given to the governor of each province, those objects, it is said, are constantly recommended to him, and the judgment which the court forms of his conduct is very much regulated by the attention which he appears to have paid to this part of his instructions. This branch of public police, accordingly, is said to be very much attended to in all those countries, but particularly in China, where the high-roads, and still more the navigable canals, it is pretended, exceed very much every thing of the same kind which is known in Europe. The accounts of those works, however, which have been transmitted to Europe, have generally been drawn up by weak and wondering travellers; frequently by stupid and lying missionaries. If they had been examined by more intelligent eyes, and if the accounts of them had been reported by more faithful witnesses, they would not, perhaps, appear to be so wonderful. The account which Bernier gives of some works of this kind in Indostan, falls very short of what had been reported of them by other travellers, more disposed to the marvellous than he was. It may too, perhaps, be in those countries, as it is in France, where the great roads, the great communications, which are likely to be the subjects of conversation at the court and in the capital, are attended to, and all the rest neglected. In China, besides, in Indostan, and in several other governments of Asia, the revenue of the sovereign arises almost altogether from a land tax or land rent, which rises or falls with the rise and fall of the annual produce of the land. The great interest of the sovereign, therefore, his revenue, is in such countries necessarily and immediately connected with the cultivation of the land, with the greatness of its produce, and with the value of its produce. But in order to render that produce both as great and as valuable as possible, it is necessary to procure to it as extensive a market as possible, and consequently to establish the freest, the easiest, and the least expensive communication between all the different parts of the country; which can be done only by means of the best roads and the best navigable canals. But the revenue of the sovereign does not, in any part of Europe, arise chiefly from a land tax or land rent. In all the great kingdoms of Europe, perhaps, the greater part of it may ultimately depend upon the produce of the land: but that dependency is neither so immediate nor so evident. In Europe, therefore, the sovereign does not feel himself so directly called upon to promote the increase, both in quantity and value of the produce of the land, or, by maintaining good roads and canals, to provide the most extensive market for that produce. Though it should be true, therefore, what I apprehend is not a little doubtful, that in some parts of Asia this department of the public police is very properly managed by the executive power, there is not the least probability that, during the present state of things, it could be tolerably managed by that power in any part of Europe.

Even those public works, which are of such a nature that they cannot afford any revenue for maintaining themselves, but of which the conveniency is nearly confined to some particular place or district, are always better maintained by a local or provincial revenue, under the management of a local and provincial administration, than by the general revenue of the state, of which the executive power must always have the management. Were the streets of London to be lighted and paved at the expense of the treasury, is there any probability that they would be so well lighted and paved as they are at present, or even at so small an expense? The expense, besides, instead of being raised by a local tax upon the inhabitants of each particular street, parish, or district in London, would, in this case, be defrayed out of the general revenue of the state, and would consequently be raised by a tax upon all the inhabitants of the kingdom, of whom the greater part derive no sort of benefit from the lighting and paving of the streets of London.

The abuses which sometimes creep into the local and provincial administration of a local and provincial revenue, how enormous soever they may appear, are in reality, however, almost always very trifling in comparison of those which commonly take place in the administration and expenditure of the revenue of a great empire. They are, besides, much more easily corrected. Under the local or provincial administration of the justices of the peace in Great Britain, the six days labour which the country people are obliged to give to the reparation of the highways, is not always, perhaps, very judiciously applied, but it is scarce ever exacted with any circumstance of cruelty or oppression. In France, under the administration of the intendants, the application is not always more judicious, and the exaction is frequently the most cruel and oppressive. Such corvees, as they are called, make one of the principal instruments of tyranny by which those officers chastise any parish or communeaute, which has had the misfortune to fall under their displeasure.

Of the public Works and Institution which are necessary for facilitating particular Branches of Commerce

The object of the public works and institutions above mentioned, is to facilitate commerce in general. But in order to facilitate some particular branches of it, particular institutions are necessary, which again require a particular and extraordinary expense.

Some particular branches of commerce which are carried on with barbarous and uncivilized nations, require extraordinary protection. An ordinary store or counting-house could give little security to the goods of the merchants who trade to the western coast of Africa. To defend them from the barbarous natives, it is necessary that the place where they are deposited should be in some measure fortified. The disorders in the government of Indostan have been supposed to render a like precaution necessary, even among that mild and gentle people; and it was under pretence of securing their persons and property from violence, that both the English and French East India companies were allowed to erect the first forts which they possessed in that country. Among other nations, whose vigorous government will suffer no strangers to possess any fortified place within their territory, it may be necessary to maintain some ambassador, minister, or consul, who may both decide, according to their own customs, the differences arising among his own countrymen, and, in their disputes with the natives, may by means of his public character, interfere with more authority and afford them a more powerful protection than they could expect from any private man. The interests of commerce have frequently made it necessary to maintain ministers in foreign countries, where the purposes either of war or alliance would not have required any. The commerce of the Turkey company first occasioned the establishment of an ordinary ambassador at Constantinople. The first English embassies to Russia arose altogether from commercial interests. The constant interference with those interests, necessarily occasioned between the subjects of the different states of Europe, has probably introduced the custom of keeping, in all neighbouring countries, ambassadors or ministers constantly resident, even in the time of peace. This custom, unknown to ancient times, seems not to be older than the end of the fifteenth, or beginning of the sixteenth century; that is, than the time when commerce first began to extend itself to the greater part of the nations of Europe, and when they first began to attend to its interests.

It seems not unreasonable, that the extraordinary expense which the protection of any particular branch of commerce may occasion, should be defrayed by a moderate tax upon that particular branch; by a moderate fine, for example, to be paid by the traders when they first enter into it; or, what is more equal, by a particular duty of so much per cent. upon the goods which they either import into, or export out of, the particular countries with which it is carried on. The protection of trade, in general, from pirates and freebooters, is said to have given occasion to the first institution of the duties of customs. But, if it was thought reasonable to lay a general tax upon trade, in order to defray the expense of protecting trade in general, it should seem equally reasonable to lay a particular tax upon a particular branch of trade, in order to defray the extraordinary expense of protecting that branch.

The protection of trade, in general, has always been considered as essential to the defence of the commonwealth, and, upon that account, a necessary part of the duty of the executive power. The collection and application of the general duties of customs, therefore, have always been left to that power. But the protection of any particular branch of trade is a part of the general protection of trade; a part, therefore, of the duty of that power; and if nations always acted consistently, the particular duties levied for the purposes of such particular protection, should always have been left equally to its disposal. But in this respect, as well as in many others, nations have not always acted consistently; and in the greater part of the commercial states of Europe, particular companies of merchants have had the address to persuade the legislature to entrust to them the performance of this part of the duty of the sovereign, together with all the powers which are necessarily connected with it.

These companies, though they may, perhaps, have been useful for the first introduction of some branches of commerce, by making, at their own expense, an experiment which the state might not think it prudent to make, have in the long-run proved, universally, either burdensome or useless, and have either mismanaged or confined the trade.

When those companies do not trade upon a joint stock, but are obliged to admit any person, properly qualified, upon paying a certain fine, and agreeing to submit to the regulations of the company, each member trading upon his own stock, and at his own risk, they are called regulated companies. When they trade upon a joint stock, each member sharing in the common profit or loss, in proportion to his share in this stock, they are called joint-stock companies. Such companies, whether regulated or joint-stock, sometimes have, and sometimes have not, exclusive privileges.

Regulated companies resemble, in every respect, the corporation of trades, so common in the cities and towns of all the different countries of Europe; and are a sort of enlarged monopolies of the same kind. As no inhabitant of a town can exercise an incorporated trade, without first obtaining his freedom in the incorporation, so, in most cases, no subject of the state can lawfully carry on any branch of foreign trade, for which a regulated company is established, without first becoming a member of that company. The monopoly is more or less strict, according as the terms of admission are more or less difficult, and according as the directors of the company have more or less authority, or have it more or less in their power to manage in such a manner as to confine the greater part of the trade to themselves and their particular friends. In the most ancient regulated companies, the privileges of apprenticeship were the same as in other corporations, and entitled the person who had served his time to a member of the company, to become himself a member, either without paying any fine, or upon paying a much smaller one than what was exacted of other people. The usual corporation spirit, wherever the law does not restrain it, prevails in all regulated companies. When they have been allowed to act according to their natural genius, they have always, in order to confine the competition to as small a number of persons as possible, endeavoured to subject the trade to many burdensome regulations. When the law has restrained them from doing this, they have become altogether useless and insignificant.

The regulated companies for foreign commerce which at present subsist in Great Britain, are the ancient merchant-adventurers company, now commonly called the Hamburgh company, the Russia company, the Eastland company, the Turkey company, and the African company.

The terms of admission into the Hamburgh company are now said to be quite easy; and the directors either have it not in their power to subject the trade to any troublesome restraint or regulations, or, at least, have not of late exercised that power. It has not always been so. About the middle of the last century, the fine for admission was fifty, and at one time one hundred pounds, and the conduct of the company was said to be extremely oppressive. In 1643, in 1645, and in 1661, the clothiers and free traders of the west of England complained of them to parliament, as of monopolists, who confined the trade, and oppressed the manufactures of the country. Though those complaints produced no act of parliament, they had probably intimidated the company so far, as to oblige them to reform their conduct. Since that time, at least, there have been no complaints against them. By the 10th and 11th of William III. c.6, the fine for admission into the Russia company was reduced to five pounds; and by the 25th of Charles II. c.7, that for admission into the Eastland company to forty shillings; while, at the same time, Sweden, Denmark, and Norway, all the countries on the north side of the Baltic, were exempted from their exclusive charter. The conduct of those companies had probably given occasion to those two acts of parliament. Before that time, Sir Josiah Child had represented both these and the Hamburgh company as extremely oppressive, and imputed to their bad management the low state of the trade, which we at that time carried on to the countries comprehended within their respective charters. But though such companies may not, in the present times, be very oppressive, they are certainly altogether useless. To be merely useless, indeed, is perhaps, the highest eulogy which can ever justly be bestowed upon a regulated company; and all the three companies above mentioned seem, in their present state, to deserve this eulogy.

The fine for admission into the Turkey company was formerly twenty-five pounds for all persons under twenty-six years of age, and fifty pounds for all persons above that age. Nobody but mere merchants could be admitted; a restriction which excluded all shop-keepers and retailers. By a bye-law, no British manufactures could be exported to Turkey but in the general ships of the company; and as those ships sailed always from the port of London, this restriction confined the trade to that expensive port, and the traders to those who lived in London and in its neighbourhood. By another bye-law, no person living within twenty miles of London, and not free of the city, could be admitted a member; another restriction which, joined to the foregoing, necessarily excluded all but the freemen of London. As the time for the loading and sailing of those general ships depended altogether upon the directors, they could easily fill them with their own goods, and those of their particular friends, to the exclusion of others, who, they might pretend, had made their proposals too late. In this state of things, therefore, this company was, in every respect, a strict and oppressive monopoly. Those abuses gave occasion to the act of the 26th of George II. c. 18, reducing the fine for admission to twenty pounds for all persons, without any distinction of ages, or any restriction, either to mere merchants, or to the freemen of London; and granting to all such persons the liberty of exporting, from all the ports of Great Britain, to any port in Turkey, all British goods, of which the exportation was not prohibited, upon paying both the general duties of customs, and the particular duties assessed for defraying the necessary expenses of the company; and submitting, at the same time, to the lawful authority of the British ambassador and consuls resident in Turkey, and to the bye-laws of the company duly enacted. To prevent any oppression by those bye-laws, it was by the same act ordained, that if any seven members of the company conceived themselves aggrieved by any bye-law which should be enacted after the passing of this act, they might appeal to the board of trade and plantations (to the authority of which a committee of the privy council has now succeeded), provided such appeal was brought within twelve months after the bye-law was enacted; and that, if any seven members conceived themselves aggrieved by any bye-law which had been enacted before the passing of this act, they might bring a like appeal, provided it was within twelve months after the day on which this act was to take place. The experience of one year, however, may not always be sufficient to discover to all the members of a great company the pernicious tendency of a particular bye-law; and if several of them should afterwards discover it, neither the board of trade, nor the committee of council, can afford them any redress. The object, besides, of the greater part of the bye-laws of all regulated companies, as well as of all other corporations, is not so much to oppress those who are already members, as to discourage others from becoming so; which may be done, not only by a high fine, but by many other contrivances. The constant view of such companies is always to raise the rate of their own profit as high as they can; to keep the market, both for the goods which they export, and for those which they import, as much understocked as they can; which can be done only by restraining the competition, or by discouraging new adventurers from entering into the trade. A fine, even of twenty pounds, besides, though it may not, perhaps, be sufficient to discourage any man from entering into the Turkey trade, with an intention to continue in it, may be enough to discourage a speculative merchant from hazarding a single adventure in it. In all trades, the regular established traders, even though not incorporated, naturally combine to raise profits, which are noway so likely to be kept, at all times, down to their proper level, as by the occasional competition of speculative adventurers. The Turkey trade, though in some measure laid open by this act of parliament, is still considered by many people as very far from being altogether free. The Turkey company contribute to maintain an ambassador and two or three consuls, who, like other public ministers, ought to be maintained altogether by the state, and the trade laid open to all his majesty's subjects. The different taxes levied by the company, for this and other corporation purposes, might afford a revenue much more than sufficient to enable a state to maintain such ministers.

Regulated companies, it was observed by Sir Josiah Child, though they had frequently supported public ministers, had never maintained any forts or garrisons in the countries to which they traded; whereas joint-stock companies frequently had. And, in reality, the former seem to be much more unfit for this sort of service than the latter. First, the directors of a regulated company have no particular interest in the prosperity of the general trade of the company, for the sake of which such forts and garrisons are maintained. The decay of that general trade may even frequently contribute to the advantage of their own private trade; as, by diminishing the number of their competitors, it may enable them both to buy cheaper, and to sell dearer. The directors of a joint-stock company, on the contrary, having only their share in the profits which are made upon the common stock committed to their management, have no private trade of their own, of which the interest can be separated from that of the general trade of the company. Their private interest is connected with the prosperity of the general trade of the company, and with the maintenance of the forts and garrisons which are necessary for its defence. They are more likely, therefore, to have that continual and careful attention which that maintenance necessarily requires. Secondly, The directors of a joint-stock company have always the management of a large capital, the joint stock of the company, a part of which they may frequently employ, with propriety, in building, repairing, and maintaining such necessary forts and garrisons. But the directors of a regulated company, having the management of no common capital, have no other fund to employ in this way, but the casual revenue arising from the admission fines, and from the corporation duties imposed upon the trade of the company. Though they had the same interest, therefore, to attend to the maintenance of such forts and garrisons, they can seldom have the same ability to render that attention effectual. The maintenance of a public minister, requiring scarce any attention, and but a moderate and limited expense, is a business much more suitable both to the temper and abilities of a regulated company.

Long after the time of Sir Josiah Child, however, in 1750, a regulated company was established, the present company of merchants trading to Africa; which was expressly charged at first with the maintenance of all the British forts and garrisons that lie between Cape Blanc and the Cape of Good Hope, and afterwards with that of those only which lie between Cape Rouge and the Cape of Good Hope. The act which establishes this company (the 23rd of George II. c.51), seems to have had two distinct objects in view; first, to restrain effectually the oppressive and monopolizing spirit which is natural to the directors of a regulated company; and, secondly, to force them, as much as possible, to give an attention, which is not natural to them, towards the maintenance of forts and garrisons.

For the first of these purposes, the fine for admission is limited to forty shillings. The company is prohibited from trading in their corporate capacity, or upon a joint stock; from borrowing money upon common seal, or from laying any restraints upon the trade, which may be carried on freely from all places, and by all persons being British subjects, and paying the fine. The government is in a committee of nine persons, who meet at London, but who are chosen annually by the freemen of the company at London, Bristol, and Liverpool; three from each place. No committeeman can be continued in office for more than three years together. Any committee-man might be removed by the board of trade and plantations, now by a committee of council, after being heard in his own defence. The committee are forbid to export negroes from Africa, or to import any African goods into Great Britain. But as they are charged with the maintenance of forts and garrisons, they may, for that purpose export from Great Britain to Africa goods and stores of different kinds. Out of the moneys which they shall receive from the company, they are allowed a sum, not exceeding eight hundred pounds, for the salaries of their clerks and agents at London, Bristol, and Liverpool, the house-rent of their offices at London, and all other expenses of management, commission, and agency, in England. What remains of this sum, after defraying these different expenses, they may divide among themselves, as compensation for their trouble, in what manner they think proper. By this constitution, it might have been expected, that the spirit of monopoly would have been effectually restrained, and the first of these purposes sufficiently answered. It would seem, however, that it had not. Though by the 4th of George III. c.20, the fort of Senegal, with all its dependencies, had been invested in the company of merchants trading to Africa, yet, in the year following (by the 5th of George III. c.44), not only Senegal and its dependencies, but the whole coast, from the port of Sallee, in South Barbary, to Cape Rouge, was exempted from the jurisdiction of that company, was vested in the crown, and the trade to it declared free to all his majesty's subjects. The company had been suspected of restraining the trade and of establishing some sort of improper monopoly. It is not, however, very easy to conceive how, under the regulations of the 23d George II. they could do so. In the printed debates of the house of commons, not always the most authentic records of truth, I observe, however, that they have been accused of this. The members of the committee of nine being all merchants, and the governors and factors in their different forts and settlements being all dependent upon them, it is not unlikely that the latter might have given peculiar attention to the consignments and commissions of the former, which would establish a real monopoly.

For the second of these purposes, the maintenance of the forts and garrisons, an annual sum has been allotted to them by parliament, generally about £13,000. For the proper application of this sum, the committee is obliged to account annually to the cursitor baron of exchequer; which account is afterwards to be laid before parliament. But parliament, which gives so little attention to the application of millions, is not likely to give much to that of £13,000 a-year; and the cursitor baron of exchequer, from his profession and education, is not likely to be profoundly skilled in the proper expense of forts and garrisons. The captains of his majesty's navy, indeed, or any other commissioned officers, appointed by the board of admiralty, may inquire into the condition of the forts and garrisons, and report their observations to that board. But that board seems to have no direct jurisdiction over the committee, nor any authority to correct those whose conduct it may thus inquire into; and the captains of his majesty's navy, besides, are not supposed to be always deeply learned in the science of fortification. Removal from an office, which can be enjoyed only for the term of three years, and of which the lawful emoluments, even during that term, are so very small, seems to be the utmost punishment to which any committee-man is liable, for any fault, except direct malversation, or embezzlement, either of the public money, or of that of the company; and the fear of the punishment can never be a motive of sufficient weight to force a continual and careful attention to a business to which he has no other interest to attend. The committee are accused of having sent out bricks and stones from England for the reparation of Cape Coast Castle, on the coast of Guinea; a business for which parliament had several times granted an extraordinary sum of money. These bricks and stones, too, which had thus been sent upon so long a voyage, were said to have been of so bad a quality, that it was necessary to rebuild, from the foundation, the walls which had been repaired with them. The forts and garrisons which lie north of Cape Rouge, are not only maintained at the expense of the state, but are under the immediate government of the executive power; and why those which lie south of that cape, and which, too, are, in part at least, maintained at the expense of the state, should be under a different government, it seems not very easy even to imagine a good reason. The protection of the Mediterranean trade was the original purpose or pretence of the garrisons of Gibraltar and Minorca; and the maintenance and government of those garrisons have always been, very properly, committed, not to the Turkey company, but to the executive power. In the extent of its dominion consists, in a great measure, the pride and dignity of that power; and it is not very likely to fail in attention to what is necessary for the defence of that dominion. The garrisons at Gibraltar and Minorca, accordingly, have never been neglected. Though Minorca has been twice taken, and is now probably lost for ever, that disaster has never been imputed to any neglect in the executive power. I would not, however, be understood to insinuate, that either of those expensive garrisons was ever, even in the smallest degree, necessary for the purpose for which they were originally dismembered from the Spanish monarchy. That dismemberment, perhaps, never served any other real purpose than to alienate from England her natural ally the king of Spain, and to unite the two principal branches of the house of

Bourbon in a much stricter and more permanent alliance than the ties of blood could ever have united them.

Joint-stock companies, established either by royal charter, or by act of parliament, are different in several respects, not only from regulated companies, but from private copartneries.

First, In a private copartnery, no partner without the consent of the company, can transfer his share to another person, or introduce a new member into the company. Each member, however, may, upon proper warning, withdraw from the copartnery, and demand payment from them of his share of the common stock. In a joint-stock company, on the contrary, no member can demand payment of his share from the company; but each member can, without their consent, transfer his share to another person, and thereby introduce a new member. The value of a share in a joint stock is always the price which it will bring in the market; and this may be either greater or less in any proportion, than the sum which its owner stands credited for in the stock of the company.

Secondly, In a private copartnery, each partner is bound for the debts contracted by the company, to the whole extent of his fortune. In a joint-stock company, on the contrary, each partner is bound only to the extent of his share.

The trade of a joint-stock company is always managed by a court of directors. This court, indeed, is frequently subject, in many respects, to the control of a general court of proprietors. But the greater part of these proprietors seldom pretend to understand any thing of the business of the company; and when the spirit of faction happens not to prevail among them, give themselves no trouble about it, but receive contentedly such halfyearly or yearly dividend as the directors think proper to make to them. This total exemption front trouble and front risk, beyond a limited sum, encourages many people to become adventurers in joint-stock companies, who would, upon no account, hazard their fortunes in any private copartnery. Such companies, therefore, commonly draw to themselves much greater stocks, than any private copartnery can boast of. The trading stock of the South Sea company at one time amounted to upwards of thirty-three millions eight hundred thousand pounds. The divided capital of the Bank of England amounts, at present, to ten millions seven hundred and eighty thousand pounds. The directors of such companies, however, being the managers rather of other people's money than of their own, it cannot well be expected that they should watch over it with the same anxious vigilance with which the partners in a private copartnery frequently watch over their own. Like the stewards of a rich man, they are apt to consider attention to small matters as not for their master's honour, and very easily give themselves a dispensation from having it. Negligence and profusion, therefore, must always prevail, more or less, in the management of the affairs of such a company. It is upon this account, that joint-stock companies for foreign trade have seldom been able to maintain the competition against private adventurers. They have, accordingly, very seldom succeeded without an exclusive privilege; and frequently have not succeeded with one. Without an exclusive privilege, they have commonly mismanaged the trade. With an exclusive privilege, they have both mismanaged and confined it.

The Royal African company, the predecessors of the present African company, had an exclusive privilege by charter; but as that charter had not been confirmed by act of parliament, the trade, in consequence of the declaration of rights, was, soon after the Revolution, laid open to all his majesty's subjects. The Hudson's Bay company are, as to their legal rights, in the same situation as the Royal African company. Their exclusive charter has not been confirmed by act of parliament. The South Sea company, as long as they continued to be a trading company, had an exclusive privilege confirmed by act of parliament; as have likewise the present united company of merchants trading to the East Indies.

The Royal African company soon found that they could not maintain the competition against private adventurers, whom, notwithstanding the declaration of rights, they continued for some time to call interlopers, and to persecute as such. In 1698, however, the private adventurers were subjected to a duty of ten per cent. upon almost all the different branches of their trade, to be employed by the company in the maintenance of their forts and garrisons. But, notwithstanding this heavy tax, the company were still unable to maintain the competition. Their stock and credit gradually declined. In 1712, their debts had become so great, that a particular act of parliament was thought necessary, both for their security and for that of their creditors. It was enacted, that the resolution of two-thirds of these creditors in number and value should bind the rust, both with regard to the time which should be allowed to the company for the payment of their debts, and with regard to any other agreement which it might be thought proper to make with them concerning those debts. In 1730, their affairs were in so great disorder, that they were altogether incapable of maintaining their forts and garrisons, the sole purpose and pretext of their institution. From that year till their final dissolution, the parliament judged it necessary to allow the annual sum of £10,000 for that purpose. In 1732, after having been for many years losers by the trade of carrying negroes to the West Indies, they at last resolved to give it up altogether; to sell to the private traders to America the negroes which they purchased upon the coast; and to employ their servants in a trade to the inland parts of Africa for gold dust, elephants teeth, dyeing drugs, etc. But their success in this more confined trade was not greater than in their former extensive one. Their affairs continued to go gradually to decline, till at last, being in every respect a bankrupt company, they were dissolved by act of parliament, and their forts and garrisons vested in the present regulated company of merchants trading to Africa. Before the erection of the Royal African company, there had been three other joint-stock companies successively established, one after another, for the African trade. They were all equally unsuccessful. They all, however, had exclusive charters, which, though not confirmed by act of parliament, were in those days supposed to convey a real exclusive privilege.

The Hudson's Bay company, before their misfortunes in the late war, had been much more fortunate than the Royal African company. Their necessary expense is much smaller. The whole number of people whom they maintain in their different settlements and habitations, which they have honoured with the name of forts, is said not to exceed a hundred and twenty persons. This number, however, is sufficient to prepare beforehand the cargo of furs and other goods necessary for loading their ships, which, on account of the ice, can seldom remain above six or eight weeks in those seas. This advantage of having a cargo ready prepared, could not, for several years, be acquired by private adventurers; and without it there seems to be no possibility of trading to Hudson's Bay. The moderate capital of the company, which, it is said, does not exceed one hundred and ten thousand pounds, may, besides, be sufficient to enable them to engross the whole, or almost the whole trade and surplus produce, of the miserable though extensive country comprehended within their charter. No private adventurers, accordingly, have ever attempted to trade to that country in competition with them. This company, therefore, have always enjoyed an exclusive trade, in fact, though they may have no right to it in law. Over and above all this, the moderate capital of this company is said to be divided among a very small number of proprietors. But a joint-stock company, consisting of a small number of proprietors, with a moderate capital, approaches very nearly to the nature of a private copartnery, and may be capable of nearly the same degree of vigilance and attention. It is not to be wondered at, therefore, if, in consequence of these different advantages, the Hudson's Bay company had, before the late war, been able to carry on their trade with a considerable degree of success. It does not seem probable, however, that their profits ever approached to what the late Mr Dobbs imagined them. A much more sober and judicious writer, Mr Anderson, author of the Historical and Chronological Deduction of Commerce, very justly observes, that upon examining the accounts which Mr Dobbs himself has given for several years together, of their exports and imports, and upon making proper allowances for their extraordinary risk and expense, it does not appear that their profits deserve to be envied, or that they can much, if at all, exceed the ordinary profits of trade.

The South Sea company never had any forts or garrisons to maintain, and therefore were entirely exempted from one great expense, to which other joint-stock companies for foreign trade are subject; but they had an immense capital divided among an immense number of proprietors. It was naturally to be expected, therefore, that folly, negligence, and profusion, should prevail in the whole management of their affairs. The knavery and extravagance of their stock-jobbing projects are sufficiently known, and the explication of them would be foreign to the present subject. Their mercantile projects were not much better conducted. The first trade which they engaged in, was that of supplying the Spanish West Indies with negroes, of which (in consequence of what was called the Assiento Contract granted them by the treaty of Utrecht) they had the exclusive privilege. But as it was not expected that much profit could be made by this trade, both the Portuguese and French companies, who had enjoyed it upon the same terms before them, having been ruined by it, they were allowed, as compensation, to send annually a ship of a certain burden, to trade directly to the Spanish West Indies. Of the ten voyages which this annual ship was allowed to make, they are said to have gained considerably by one, that of the Royal Caroline, in 1731; and to have been losers, more or less, by almost all the rest. Their ill success was imputed, by their factors and agents, to the extortion and oppression of the Spanish government; but was, perhaps, principally owing to the profusion and depredations of those very factors and agents; some of whom are said to have acquired great fortunes, even in one year. In 1734, the company petitioned the king, that they might be allowed to dispose of the trade and tonnage of their annual ship, on account of the little profit which they made by it, and to accept of such equivalent as they could obtain from the king of Spain.

In 1724, this company had undertaken the whale fishery. Of this, indeed, they had no monopoly; but as long as they carried it on, no other British subjects appear to have engaged in it. Of the eight voyages which their ships made to Greenland, they were gainers by one, and losers by all the rest. After their eighth and last voyage, when they had sold their ships, stores, and utensils, they found that their whole loss upon this branch, capital and interest included, amounted to upwards of £237,000.

In 1722, this company petitioned the parliament to be allowed to divide their immense capital of more than thirty-three millions eight hundred thousand pounds, the whole of which had been lent to government, into two equal parts; the one half, or upwards of £16,900,000, to be put upon the same footing with other government annuities, and not to be subject to the debts contracted, or losses incurred, by the directors of the company, in the prosecution of their mercantile projects; the other half to remain as before, a trading stock, and to be subject to those debts and losses. The petition was too reasonable not to be granted. In 1733, they again petitioned the parliament, that three-fourths of their trading stock might be turned into annuity stock, and only one-fourth remain as trading stock, or exposed to the hazards arising from the bad management of their directors. Both their annuity and trading stocks had, by this time, been reduced more than two millions each, by several different payments from government; so that this fourth amounted only to £3,662,784:8:6. In 1748, all the demands of the company upon the king of Spain, in consequence of the assiento contract, were, by the treaty of Aix-la-Chapelle, given up for what was supposed an equivalent. An end was put to their trade with the Spanish West Indies; the remainder of their trading stock was turned into an annuity stock; and the company ceased, in every respect, to be a trading company.

It ought to be observed, that in the trade which the South Sea company carried on by means of their annual ship, the only trade by which it ever was expected that they could make any considerable profit, they were not without competitors, either in the foreign or in the home market. At Carthagena, Porto Bello, and La Vera Cruz, they had to encounter the competition of the Spanish merchants, who brought from Cadiz to those markets European goods, of the same kind with the outward cargo of their ship; and in England they had to encounter that of the English merchants, who imported from Cadiz goods of the Spanish West Indies, of the same kind with the inward cargo. The goods, both of the Spanish and English merchants, indeed, were, perhaps, subject to higher duties. But the loss occasioned by the negligence, profusion, and malversation of the servants of the company, had probably been a tax much heavier than all those duties. That a joint-stock company should be able to carry on successfully any branch of foreign trade, when private adventurers can come into any sort of open and fair competition with them, seems contrary to all experience.

The old English East India company was established in 1600, by a charter from Queen Elizabeth. In the first twelve voyages which they fitted out for India, they appear to have traded as a regulated company, with separate stocks, though only in the general ships of the company. In 1612, they united into a joint stock. Their charter was exclusive, and, though not confirmed by act of parliament, was in those days supposed to convey a real exclusive privilege. For many years, therefore, they were not much disturbed by interlopers. Their capital, which never exceeded £744,000, and of which £50 was a share, was not so exorbitant, nor their dealings so extensive, as to afford either a pretext for gross negligence and profusion, or a cover to gross malversation. Notwithstanding some extraordinary losses, occasioned partly by the malice of the Dutch East India company, and partly by other accidents, they carried on for many years a successful trade. But in process of time, when the principles of liberty were better understood, it became every day more and more doubtful, how far a royal charter, not confirmed by act of parliament, could convey an exclusive privilege. Upon this question the decisions of the courts of justice were not uniform, but varied with the authority of government, and the humours of the times. Interlopers multiplied upon them; and towards the end of the reign of Charles II., through the whole of that of James II., and during a part of that of William III., reduced them to great distress. In 1698, a proposal was made to parliament, of advancing two millions to government, at eight per cent. provided the subscribers were erected into a new East India company, with exclusive privileges. The old East India company offered seven hundred thousand pounds, nearly the amount of their capital, at four per cent. upon the same conditions. But such was at that time the state of public credit, that it was more convenient for government to borrow two millions at eight per cent. than seven hundred thousand pounds at four. The proposal of the new subscribers was accepted, and a new East India company established in consequence. The old East India company, however, had a right to continue their trade till 1701. They had, at the same time, in the name of their treasurer, subscribed very artfully three hundred and fifteen thousand pounds into the stock of the new. By a negligence in the expression of the act of parliament, which vested the East India trade in the subscribers to this loan of two millions, it did not appear evident that they were all obliged to unite into a joint stock. A few private traders, whose subscriptions amounted only to seven thousand two hundred pounds, insisted upon the privilege of trading separately upon their own stocks, and at their own risks. The old East India company had a right to a separate trade upon their own stock till 1701; and they had likewise, both before and after that period, a right, like that or other private traders, to a separate trade upon the £315,000, which they had subscribed into the stock of the new company. The competition of the two companies with the private traders, and with one another, is said to have well nigh ruined both. Upon a subsequent occasion, in 1750, when a proposal was made to parliament for putting the trade under the management of a regulated company, and thereby laying it in some measure open, the East India company, in opposition to this proposal, represented, in very strong terms, what had been, at this time, the miserable effects, as they thought them, of this competition. In India, they said, it raised the price of goods so high, that they were not worth the buying; and in England, by overstocking the market, it sunk their price so low, that no profit could be made by them. That by a more plentiful supply, to the great advantage and conveniency of the public, it must have reduced very much the price of India goods in the English market, cannot well be doubted; but that it should have raised very much their price in the Indian market, seems not very probable, as all the extraordinary demand which that competition could occasion must have been but as a drop of water in the immense ocean of Indian commerce. The increase of demand, besides, though in the beginning it may sometimes raise the price of goods, never fails to lower it in the long-run. It encourages production, and thereby increases the competition of the producers, who, in order to undersell one another, have recourse to new divisions or labour and new improvements of art, which might never otherwise have been thought of. The miserable effects of which the company complained, were the cheapness of consumption, and the encouragement given to production; precisely the two effects which it is the great business of political economy to promote. The competition, however, of which they gave this doleful account, had not been allowed to be of long continuance. In 1702, the two companies were, in some measure, united by an indenture tripartite, to which the queen was the third party; and in 1708, they were by act of parliament, perfectly consolidated into one company, by their present name of the United Company of Merchants trading to the East Indies. Into this act it was thought worth while to insert a clause, allowing the separate traders to continue their trade till Michaelmas 1711; but at the same time empowering the directors, upon three years notice, to redeem their little capital of seven thousand two hundred pounds, and thereby to convert the whole stock of the company into a joint stock. By the same act, the capital of the company, in consequence of a new loan to government, was augmented from two millions to three millions two hundred thousand pounds. In 1743, the company advanced another million to government. But this million being raised, not by a call upon the proprietors, but by selling annuities and contracting bond-debts, it did not augment the stock upon which the proprietors could claim a dividend. It augmented, however, their trading stock, it being equally liable with the other three millions two hundred thousand pounds, to the losses sustained, and debts contracted by the company in prosecution of their mercantile projects. From 1708, or at least from 1711, this company, being delivered from all competitors, and fully established in the monopoly of the English commerce to the East Indies, carried on a successful trade, and from their profits, made annually a moderate dividend to their proprietors. During the French war, which began in 1741, the ambition of Mr. Dupleix, the French governor of Pondicherry, involved them in the wars of the Carnatic, and in the politics of the Indian princes. After many signal successes, and equally signal losses, they at last lost Madras, at that time their principal settlement in India. It was restored to them by the treaty of Aix-la-Chapelle; and, about this time the spirit of war and conquest seems to have taken possession of their servants in India, and never since to have left them. During the French war, which began in 1755, their arms partook of the general good fortune of those of Great Britain. They defended Madras, took Pondicherry, recovered Calcutta, and acquired the revenues of a rich and extensive territory, amounting, it was then said, to upwards of three millions a-year. They remained for several years in quiet possession of this revenue; but in 1767, administration laid claim to their territorial acquisitions, and the revenue arising from them, as of right belonging to the crown; and the company, in compensation for this claim, agreed to pay to government £400,000 a-year. They had, before this, gradually augmented their dividend from about six to ten per cent.; that is, upon their capital of three millions two hundred thousand pounds, they had increased it by £128,000, or had raised it from one hundred and ninety-two thousand to three hundred and twenty thousand pounds a-year. They were attempting about this time to raise it still further, to twelve and a-half per cent., which would have made their annual payments to their proprietors equal to what they had agreed to pay annually to government, or to £400,000 a-year. But during the two years in which their agreement with government was to take place, they were restrained from any further increase of dividend by two successive acts of parliament, of which the object was to enable them to make a speedier progress in the payment of their debts, which were at this time estimated at upwards of six or seven millions sterling. In 1769, they renewed their agreement with government for five years more, and stipulated, that during the course of that period, they should be allowed gradually to increase their dividend to twelve and a-half per cent; never increasing it, however, more than one per cent. in one year. This increase of dividend, therefore, when it had risen to its utmost height, could augment their annual payments, to their proprietors and government together, but by £680,000, beyond what they had been before their late territorial acquisitions. What the gross revenue of those territorial acquisitions was supposed to amount to, has already been mentioned; and by an account brought by the Cruttenden East Indiaman in 1769, the neat revenue, clear of all deductions and military charges, was stated at two millions forty-eight thousand seven hundred and forty-seven pounds. They were said, at the same time, to possess another revenue, arising partly from lands, but chiefly from the customs established at their different settlements, amounting to £439,000. The profits of their trade, too, according to the evidence of their chairman before the house of commons, amounted, at this time, to at least £400,000 a-year; according to that of their accountant, to at least £500,000; according to the lowest account, at least equal to the highest dividend that was to be paid to their proprietors. So great a revenue might certainly have afforded an augmentation of £680,000 in their annual payments;

and, at the same time, have left a large sinking fund, sufficient for the speedy reduction of their debt. In 1773, however, their debts, instead of being reduced, were augmented by an arrear to the treasury in the payment of the four hundred thousand pounds; by another to the custom-house for duties unpaid; by a large debt to the bank, for money borrowed; and by a fourth, for bills drawn upon them from India, and wantonly accepted, to the amount of upwards of twelve hundred thousand pounds. The distress which these accumulated claims brought upon them, obliged them not only to reduce all at once their dividend to six per cent. but to throw themselves upon the mercy of govermnent, and to supplicate, first, a release from the further payment of the stipulated £400,000 a-year; and, secondly, a loan of fourteen hundred thousand, to save them from immediate bankruptcy. The great increase of their fortune had, it seems, only served to furnish their servants with a pretext for greater profusion, and a cover for greater malversation, than in proportion even to that increase of fortune. The conduct of their servants in India, and the general state of their affairs both in India and in Europe, became the subject of a parliamentary inquiry: in consequence of which, several very important alterations were made in the constitution of their government, both at home and abroad. In India, their principal settlements or Madras, Bombay, and Calcutta, which had before been altogether independent of one another, were subjected to a governor-general, assisted by a council of four assessors, parliament assuming to itself the first nomination of this governor and council, who were to reside at Calcutta; that city having now become, what Madras was before, the most important of the English settlements in India. The court of the Mayor of Calcutta, originally instituted for the trial of mercantile causes, which arose in the city and neighbourhood, had gradually extended its jurisdiction with the extension of the empire. It was now reduced and confined to the original purpose of its institution. Instead of it, a new supreme court of judicature was established, consisting of a chief justice and three judges, to be appointed by the crown. In Europe, the qualification necessary to entitle a proprietor to vote at their general courts was raised, from five hundred pounds, the original price of a share in the stock of the company, to a thousand pounds. In order to vote upon this qualification, too, it was declared necessary, that he should have possessed it, if acquired by his own purchase, and not by inheritance, for at least one year, instead of six months, the term requisite before. The court of twenty-four directors had before been chosen annually; but it was now enacted, that each director should, for the future, be chosen for four years; six of them, however, to go out of office by rotation every year, and not be capable of being rechosen at the election of the six new directors for the ensuing year. In consequence of these alterations, the courts, both of the proprietors and directors, it was expected, would be likely to act with more dignity and steadiness than they had usually done before. But it seems impossible, by any alterations, to render those courts, in any respect, fit to govern, or even to share in the government of a great empire; because the greater part of their members must always have too little interest in the prosperity of that empire, to give any serious attention to what may promote it. Frequently a man of great, sometimes even a man of small fortune, is willing to purchase a thousand pounds share in India stock, merely for the influence which he expects to aquire by a vote in the court of proprietors. It gives him a share, though not in the plunder, yet in the appointment of the plunderers of India; the court of directors, though they make that appointment, being necessarily more or less under the influence of the proprietors, who not only elect those directors, but sometimes over-rule the appointments of their servants in India. Provided he can enjoy this influence for a few years, and thereby provide for a certain number of his friends, he frequently cares little about the dividend, or even about the value of the stock upon which his vote is founded. About the prosperity of the great empire, in the government of which that vote gives him a share, he seldom cares at all. No other sovereigns ever were, or, from the nature of things, ever could be, so perfectly indifferent about the happiness or misery of their subjects, the improvement or waste of their dominions, the glory or disgrace of their administration, as, from irresistible moral causes, the greater part of the proprietors of such a mercantile company are, and necessarily must be. This indifference, too, was more likely to be increased than diminished by some of the new regulations which were made in consequence of the parliamentary inquiry. By a resolution of the house of commons, for example, it was declared, that when the £1,400,000 lent to the company by government, should be paid, and their bond-debts be reduced to £1,500,000, they might then, and not till then, divide eight per cent. upon their capital; and that whatever remained of their revenues and neat profits at home should be divided into four parts; three of them to be paid into the exchequer for the use of the public, and the fourth to be reserved as a fund, either for the further reduction of their bond-debts, or for the discharge of other contingent exigencies which the company might labour under. But if the company were bad stewards and bad sovereigns, when the whole of their neat revenue and profits belonged to themselves, and were at their own disposal, they were surely not likely to be better when three-fourths of them were to belong to other people, and the other fourth, though to be laid out for the benefit of the company, yet to be so under the inspection and with the approbation of other people.

It might be more agreeable to the company, that their own servants and dependants should have either the pleasure of wasting, or the profit of embezzling, whatever surplus might remain, after paying the proposed dividend of eight per cent. than that it should come into the hands of a set of people with whom those resolutions could scarce fail to set them in some measure at variance. The interest of those servants and dependants might so far predominate in the court of proprietors, as sometimes to dispose it to support the authors of depredations which had been committed in direct violation of its own authority. With the majority of proprietors, the support even of the authority of their own court might sometimes be a matter of less consequence than the support of those who had set that authority at defiance.

The regulations of 1773, accordingly, did not put an end to the disorder of the company's government in India. Notwithstanding that, during a momentary fit of good conduct, they had at one time collected into the treasury of Calcutta more than £3,000,000 sterling; notwithstanding that they had afterwards extended either their dominion or their depredations over a vast accession of some of the richest and most fertile countries in India, all was wasted and destroyed. They found themselves altogether unprepared to stop or resist the incursion of Hyder Ali; and in consequence of those disorders, the company is now (1784) in greater distress than ever; and, in order to prevent immediate bankruptcy, is once more reduced to supplicate the assistance of government. Different plans have been proposed by the different parties in parliament for the better management of its affairs; and all those plans seem to agree in supposing, what was indeed always abundantly evident, that it is altogether unfit to govern its territorial possessions. Even the company itself seems to be convinced of its own incapacity so far, and seems, upon that account willing to give them up to government.

With the right of possessing forts and garrisons in distant and barbarous countries is necessarily connected the right of making peace and war in those countries. The joint-stock companies, which have had the one right, have constantly exercised the other, and have frequently had it expressly conferred upon them. How unjustly, how capriciously, how cruelly, they have commonly exercised it, is too well known from recent experience.

When a company of merchants undertake, at their own risk and expense, to establish a new trade with some remote and barbarous nation, it may not be unreasonable to incorporate them into a joint-stock company, and to grant them, in case of their success, a monopoly of the trade for a certain number of years. It is the easiest and most natural way in which the state can recompense them for hazarding a dangerous and expensive experiment, of which the public is afterwards to reap the benefit. A temporary monopoly of this kind may be vindicated, upon the same principles upon which a like monopoly of a new machine is granted to its inventor, and that of a new book to its author. But upon the expiration of the term, the monopoly ought certainly to determine; the forts and garrisons, if it was found necessary to establish any, to be taken into the hands of government, their value to be paid to the company, and the trade to be laid open to all the subjects of the state. By a perpetual monopoly, all the other subjects of the state are taxed very absurdly in two different ways: first, by the high price of goods, which, in the case of a free trade, they could buy much cheaper; and, secondly, by their total exclusion from a branch of business which it might be both convenient and profitable for many of them to carry on. It is for the most worthless of all purposes, too, that they are taxed in this manner. It is merely to enable the company to support the negligence, profusion, and malversation of their own servants, whose disorderly conduct seldom allows the dividend of the company to exceed the ordinary rate of profit in trades which are altogether free, and very frequently makes a fall even a good deal short of that rate. Without a monopoly, however, a joint-stock company, it would appear from experience, cannot long carry on any branch of foreign trade. To buy in one market, in order to sell with profit in another, when there are many competitors in both; to watch over, not only the occasional variations in the demand, but the much greater and more frequent variations in the competition, or in the supply which that demand is likely to get from other people; and to suit with dexterity and judgment both the quantity and quality of each assortment of goods to all these circumstances, is a species of warfare, of which the operations are continually changing, and which can scarce ever be conducted successfully, without such an unremitting exertion of vigilance and attention as cannot long be expected from the directors of a joint-stock company. The East India company, upon the redemption of their funds, and the expiration of their exclusive privilege, have a right, by act of parliament, to continue a corporation with a joint stock, and to trade in their corporate capacity to the East Indies, in common with the rest of their fellow subjects. But in this situation, the superior vigilance and attention of a private adventurer would, in all probability, soon make them weary of the trade.

An eminent French author, of great knowledge in matters of political economy, the Abbe Morellet, gives a list of fifty-five joint-stock companies for foreign trade, which have been established in different parts of Europe since the year 1600, and which, according to him, have all failed from mismanagement, notwithstanding they had exclusive privileges. He has been misinformed with regard to the history of two or three of them, which were not joint-stock companies and have not failed. But, in compensation, there have been several joint-stock companies which have failed, and which he has omitted.

The only trades which it seems possible for a joint-stock company to carry on successfully, without an exclusive privilege, are those, of which all the operations are capable of being reduced to what is called a routine, or to such a uniformity of method as admits of little or no variation. Of this kind is, first, the banking trade; secondly, the trade of insurance from fire and from sea risk, and capture in time of war; thirdly, the trade of making and maintaining a navigable cut or canal; and, fourthly, the similar trade of bringing water for the supply of a great city.

Though the principles of the banking trade may appear somewhat abstruse, the practice is capable of being reduced to strict rules. To depart upon any occasion from those rules, in consequence of some flattering speculation of extraordinary gain, is almost always extremely dangerous and frequently fatal to the banking company which attempts it. But the constitution of joint-stock companies renders them in general, more tenacious of established rules than any private copartnery. Such companies, therefore, seem extremely well fitted for this trade. The principal banking companies in Europe, accordingly, are joint-stock companies, many of which manage their trade very successfully without any exclusive privilege. The bank of England has no other exclusive privilege, except that no other banking company in England shall consist of more than six persons. The two banks of Edinburgh are joint-stock companies, without any exclusive privilege.

The value of the risk, either from fire, or from loss by sea, or by capture, though it cannot, perhaps, be calculated very exactly, admits, however, of such a gross estimation, as renders it, in some degree, reducible to strict rule and method. The trade of insurance, therefore, may be carried on successfully by a joint-stock company, without any exclusive privilege. Neither the London Assurance, nor the Royal Exchange Assurance companies have any such privilege.

When a navigable cut or canal has been once made, the management of it becomes quite simple and easy, and it is reducible to strict rule and method. Even the making of it is so, as it may be contracted for with undertakers, at so much a mile, and so much a lock. The same thing may be said of a canal, an aqueduct, or a great pipe for bringing water to supply a great city. Such under-takings, therefore, may be, and accordingly frequently are, very successfully managed by joint-stock companies, without any exclusive privilege.

To establish a joint-stock company, however, for any undertaking, merely because such a company might be capable of managing it successfully; or, to exempt a particular set of dealers from some of the general laws which take place with regard to all their neighbours, merely because they might be capable of thriving, if they had such an exemption, would certainly not be reasonable. To render such an establishment perfectly reasonable, with the circumstance of being reducible to strict rule and method, two other circumstances ought to concur. First, it ought to appear with the clearest evidence, that the undertaking is of greater and more general utility than the greater part of common trades; and, secondly, that it requires a greater capital than can easily be collected into a private copartnery. If a moderate capital were sufficient, the great utility of the undertaking would not be a sufficient reason for establishing a joint-stock company; because, in this case, the demand for what it was to produce, would readily and easily be supplied by private adventurers. In the four trades above mentioned, both those circumstances concur.

The great and general utility of the banking trade, when prudently managed, has been fully explained in the second book of this Inquiry. But a public bank, which is to support public credit, and, upon particular emergencies, to advance to government the whole produce of a tax, to the amount, perhaps, of several millions, a year or two before it comes in, requires a greater capital than can easily be collected into any private copartnery.

The trade of insurance gives great security to the fortunes of private people, and, by dividing among a great many that loss which would ruin an individual, makes it fall light and easy upon the whole society. In order to give this security, however, it is necessary that the insurers should have a very large capital. Before the establishment of the two joint-stock companies for insurance in London, a list, it is said, was laid before the attorney-general, of one hundred and fifty private usurers, who had failed in the course of a few years.

That navigable cuts and canals, and the works which are sometimes necessary for supplying a great city with water, are of great and general utility, while, at the same time, they frequently require a greater expense than suits the fortunes of private people, is sufficiently obvious.

Except the four trades above mentioned, I have not been able to recollect any other, in which all the three circumstances requisite for rendering reasonable the establishment of a joint-stock company concur. The English copper company of London, the lead-smelting company, the glass-grinding company, have not even the pretext of any great or singular utility in the object which they pursue; nor does the pursuit of that object seem to require any expense unsuitable to the fortunes of many private men. Whether the trade which those companies carry on, is reducible to such strict rule and method as to render it fit for the management of a joint-stock company, or whether they have any reason to boast of their extraordinary profits, I do not pretend to know. The mine-adventurers company has been long ago bankrupt. A share in the stock of the British Linen company of Edinburgh sells, at present, very much below par, though less so than it did some years ago. The joint-stock companies, which are established for the public-spirited purpose of promoting some particular manufacture, over and above managing their own affairs ill, to the diminution of the general stock of the society, can, in other respects, scarce ever fail to do more harm than good. Notwithstanding the most upright intentions, the unavoidable partiality of their directors to particular branches of the manufacture, of which the undertakers mislead and impose upon them, is a real discouragement to the rest, and necessarily breaks, more or less, that natural proportion which would otherwise establish itself between judicious industry and profit, and which, to the general industry of the country, is of all encouragements the greatest and the most effectual.

ART. II.—Of the Expense of the Institution for the Education of Youth

The institutions for the education of the youth may, in the same manner, furnish a revenue sufficient for defraying their own expense. The fee or honorary, which the scholar pays to the master, naturally constitutes a revenue of this kind.

Even where the reward of the master does not arise altogether from this natural revenue, it still is not necessary that it should be derived from that general revenue of the society, of which the collection and application are, in most countries, assigned to the executive power. Through the greater part of Europe, accordingly, the endowment of schools and colleges makes either no charge upon that general revenue, or but a very small one. It everywhere arises chiefly from some local or provincial revenue, from the rent of some landed estate, or from the interest of some sum of money, allotted and put under the management of trustees for this particular purpose, sometimes by the sovereign himself, and sometimes by some private donor.

Have those public endowments contributed in general, to promote the end of their institution? Have they contributed to encourage the diligence, and to improve the abilities, of the teachers? Have they directed the course of education towards objects more useful, both to the individual and to the public, than those to which it would naturally have gone of its own accord? It should not seem very difficult to give at least a probable answer to each of those questions.

In every profession, the exertion of the greater part of those who exercise it, is always in proportion to the necessity they are under of making that exertion. This necessity is greatest with those to whom the emoluments of their profession are the only source from which they expect their fortune, or even their ordinary revenue and subsistence. In order to acquire this fortune, or even to get this subsistence, they must, in the course of a year, execute a certain quantity of work of a known value; and, where the competition is free, the rivalship of competitors, who are all endeavouring to justle one another out of employment, obliges every man to endeavour to execute his work with a certain degree of exactness. The greatness of the objects which are to be acquired by success in some particular professions may, no doubt, sometimes animate the exertions of a few men of extraordinary spirit and ambition. Great objects, however, are evidently not necessary, in order to occasion the greatest exertions. Rivalship and emulation render excellency, even in mean professions, an object of ambition, and frequently occasion the very greatest exertions. Great objects, on the contrary, alone and unsupported by the necessity of application, have seldom been sufficient to occasion any considerable exertion. In England, success in the profession of the law leads to some very great objects of ambition; and yet how few men, born to easy fortunes, have ever in this country been eminent in that profession?

The endowments of schools and colleges have necessarily diminished, more or less, the necessity of application in the teachers. Their subsistence, so far as it arises from their salaries, is evidently derived from a fund, altogether independent of their success and reputation in their particular professions.

In some universities, the salary makes but a part, and frequently but a small part, of the emoluments of the teacher, of which the greater part arises from the honoraries or fees of his pupils. The necessity of application, though always more or less diminished, is not, in this case, entirely taken away. Reputation in his profession is still of some importance to him, and he still has some dependency upon the affection, gratitude, and favourable report of those who have attended upon his instructions; and these favourable sentiments he is likely to gain in no way so well as by deserving them, that is, by the abilities and diligence with which he discharges every part of his duty.

In other universities, the teacher is prohibited from receiving any honorary or fee from his pupils, and his salary constitutes the whole of the revenue which he derives from his office. His interest is, in this case, set as directly in opposition to his duty as it is possible to set it. It is the interest of every man to live as much at his ease as he can; and if his emoluments are to be precisely the same, whether he does or does not perform some very laborious duty, it is certainly his interest, at least as interest is vulgarly understood, either to neglect it altogether, or, if he is subject to some authority which will not suffer him to do this, to perform it in as careless and slovenly a manner as that authority will permit. If he is naturally active and a lover of labour, it is his interest to employ that activity in any way from which he can derive some advantage, rather than in the performance of his duty, from which he can derive none.

If the authority to which he is subject resides in the body corporate, the college, or university, of which he himself is a member, and in which the greater part of the other members are, like himself, persons who either are, or ought to be teachers, they are likely to make a common cause, to be all very indulgent to one another, and every man to consent that his neighbour may neglect his duty, provided he himself is allowed to neglect his own. In the university of Oxford, the greater part of the public professors have, for these many years, given up altogether even the pretence of teaching.

If the authority to which he is subject resides, not so much in the body corporate, of which he is a member, as in some other extraneous persons, in the bishop of the diocese, for example, in the governor of the province, or, perhaps, in some minister of state, it is not, indeed, in this case, very likely that he will be suffered to neglect his duty altogether. All that such superiors, however, can force him to do, is to attend upon his pupils a certain number of hours, that is, to give a certain number of lectures in the week, or in the year. What those lectures shall be, must still depend upon the diligence of the teacher; and that diligence is likely to be proportioned to the motives which he has for exerting it. An extraneous jurisdiction of this kind, besides, is liable to be exercised both ignorantly and capriciously. In its nature, it is arbitrary and discretionary; and the persons who exercise it, neither attending upon the lectures of the teacher themselves, nor perhaps understanding the sciences which it is his business to teach, are seldom capable of exercising it with judgment. From the insolence of office, too, they are frequently indifferent how they exercise it, and are very apt to censure or deprive him of his office wantonly and without any just cause. The person subject to such jurisdiction is necessarily degraded by it, and, instead of being one of the most respectable, is rendered one of the meanest and most contemptible persons in the society. It is by powerful protection only, that he can effectually guard himself against the bad usage to which he is at all times exposed; and this protection he is most likely to gain, not by ability or diligence in his profession, but by obsequiousness to the will of his superiors, and by being ready, at all times, to sacrifice to that will the rights, the interest, and the honour of the body corporate, of which he is a member. Whoever has attended for any considerable time to the administration of a French university, must have had occasion to remark the effects which naturally result from an arbitrary and extraneous jurisdiction of this kind.

Whatever forces a certain number of students to any college or university, independent of the merit or reputation of the teachers, tends more or less to diminish the necessity of that merit or reputation.

The privileges of graduates in arts, in law, physic, and divinity, when they can be obtained only by residing a certain number of years in certain universities, necessarily force a certain number of students to such universities, independent of the merit or reputation of the teachers. The privileges of graduates are a sort of statutes of apprenticeship, which have contributed to the improvement of education just as the other statutes of apprenticeship have to that of arts and manufactures.

The charitable foundations of scholarships, exhibitions, bursaries, etc. necessarily attach a certain number of students to certain colleges, independent altogether of the merit of those particular colleges. Were the students upon such charitable foundations left free to choose what college they liked best, such liberty might perhaps contribute to excite some emulation among different colleges. A regulation, on the contrary, which prohibited even the independent members of every particular college from leaving it, and going to any other, without leave first asked and obtained of that which they meant to abandon, would tend very much to extinguish that emulation.

If in each college, the tutor or teacher, who was to instruct each student in all arts and sciences, should not be voluntarily chosen by the student, but appointed by the head of the college; and if, in case of neglect, inability, or bad usage, the student should not be allowed to change him for another, without leave first asked and obtained; such a regulation would not only tend very much to extinguish all emulation among the different tutors of the same college, but to diminish very much, in all of them, the necessity of diligence and of attention to their respective pupils. Such teachers, though very well paid by their students, might be as much disposed to neglect them, as those who are not paid by them at all or who have no other recompense but their salary.

If the teacher happens to be a man of sense, it must be an unpleasant thing to him to be conscious, while he is lecturing to his students, that he is either speaking or reading nonsense, or what is very little better than nonsense. It must, too, be unpleasant to him to observe, that the greater part of his students desert his lectures; or perhaps, attend upon them with plain enough marks of neglect, contempt, and derision. If he is obliged, therefore, to give a certain number of lectures, these motives alone, without any other interest, might dispose him to take some pains to give tolerably good ones. Several different expedients, however, may be fallen upon, which will effectually blunt the edge of all those incitements to diligence. The teacher, instead of explaining to his pupils himself the science in which he proposes to instruct them, may read some book upon it; and if this book is written in a foreign and dead language, by interpreting it to them into their own, or, what would give him still less trouble, by making them interpret it to him, and by now and then making an occasional remark upon it, he may flatter himself that he is giving a lecture. The slightest degree of knowledge and application will enable him to do this, without exposing himself to contempt or derision, by saying any thing that is really foolish, absurd, or ridiculous. The discipline of the college, at the same time, may enable him to force all his pupils to the most regular attendance upon his sham lecture, and to maintain the most decent and respectful behaviour during the whole time of the performance.

The discipline of colleges and universities is in general contrived, not for the benefit of the students, but for the interest, or, more properly speaking, for the ease of the masters. Its object is, in all cases, to maintain the authority of the master, and, whether he neglects or performs his duty, to oblige the students in all cases to behave to him as if he performed it with the greatest diligence and ability. It seems to presume perfect wisdom and virtue in the one order, and the greatest weakness and folly in the other. Where the masters, however, really perform their duty, there are no examples, I believe, that the greater part of the students ever neglect theirs. No discipline is ever requisite to force attendance upon lectures which are really worth the attending, as is well known wherever any such lectures are given. Force and restraint may, no doubt, be in some degree requisite, in order to oblige children, or very young boys, to attend to those parts of education, which it is thought necessary for them to acquire during that early period of life; but after twelve or thirteen years of age, provided the master does his duty, force or restraint can scarce ever be necessary to carry on any part of education. Such is the generosity of the greater part of young men, that so far from being disposed to neglect or despise the instructions of their master, provided he shews some serious intention of being of use to them, they are generally inclined to pardon a great deal of incorrectness in the performance of his duty, and sometimes even to conceal from the public a good deal of gross negligence.

Those parts of education, it is to be observed, for the teaching of which there are no public institutions, are generally the best taught. When a young man goes to a fencing or a dancing school, he does not, indeed, always learn to fence or to dance very well; but he seldom fails of learning to fence or to dance. The good effects of the riding school are not commonly so evident. The expense of a riding school is so great, that in most places it is a public institution. The three most essential parts of literary education, to read, write, and account, it still continues to be more common to acquire in private than in public schools; and it very seldom happens, that anybody fails of acquiring them to the degree in which it is necessary to acquire them.

In England, the public schools are much less corrupted than the universities. In the schools, the youth are taught, or at least may be taught, Greek and Latin; that is, everything which the masters pretend to teach, or which it is expected they should teach. In the universities, the youth neither are taught, nor always can find any proper means of being taught the sciences, which it is the business of those incorporated bodies to teach. The reward of the schoolmaster, in most cases, depends principally, in some cases almost entirely, upon the fees or honoraries of his scholars. Schools have no exclusive privileges. In order to obtain the honours of graduation, it is not necessary that a person should bring a certificate of his having studied a certain number of years at a public school. If, upon examination, he appears to understand what is taught there, no questions are asked about the place where he learnt it.

The parts of education which are commonly taught in universities, it may perhaps be said, are not very well taught. But had it not been for those institutions, they would not have been commonly taught at all; and both the individual and the public would have suffered a good deal from the want of those important parts of education.

The present universities of Europe were originally, the greater part of them, ecclesiastical corporations, instituted for the education of churchmen. They were founded by the authority of the pope; and were so entirely under his immediate protection, that their members, whether masters or students, had all of them what was then called the benefit of clergy, that is, were exempted from the civil jurisdiction of the countries in which their respective universities were situated, and were amenable only to the ecclesiastical tribunals. What was taught in the greater part of those universities was suitable to the end of their institution, either theology, or something that was merely preparatory to theology.

When Christianity was first established by law, a corrupted Latin had become the common language of all the western parts of Europe. The service of the church, accordingly, and the translation of the Bible which were read in churches, were both in that corrupted Latin; that is, in the common language of the country, After the irruption of the barbarous nations who overturned the Roman empire, Latin gradually ceased to be the language of any part of Europe. But the reverence of the people naturally preserves the established forms and ceremonies of religion long after the circumstances which first introduced and rendered them reasonable, are no more. Though Latin, therefore, was no longer understood anywhere by the great body of the people, the whole service of the church still continued to be performed in that language. Two different languages were thus established in Europe, in the same manner as in ancient Egypt: a language of the priests, and a language of the people; a sacred and a profane, a learned and an unlearned language. But it was necessary that the priests should understand something of that sacred and learned language in which they were to officiate; and the study of the Latin language therefore made, from the beginning, an essential part of university education.

It was not so with that either of the Greek or of the Hebrew language. The infallible decrees of the church had pronounced the Latin translation of the Bible, commonly called the Latin Vulgate, to have been equally dictated by divine inspiration, and therefore of equal authority with the Greek and Hebrew originals. The knowledge of those two languages, therefore, not being indispensably requisite to a churchman, the study of them did not for along time make a necessary part of the common course of university education. There are some Spanish universities, I am assured, in which the study of the Greek language has never yet made any part of that course. The first reformers found the Greek text of the New Testament, and even the Hebrew text of the Old, more favourable to their opinions than the vulgate translation, which, as might naturally be supposed, had been gradually accommodated to support the doctrines of the Catholic Church. They set themselves, therefore, to expose the many errors of that translation, which the Roman catholic clergy were thus put under the necessity of defending or explaining. But this could not well be done without some knowledge of the original languages, of which the study was therefore gradually introduced into the greater part of universities; both of those which embraced, and of those which rejected, the doctrines of the reformation. The Greek language was connected with every part of that classical learning, which, though at first principally cultivated by catholics and Italians, happened to come into fashion much about the same time that the doctrines of the reformation were set on foot. In the greater part of universities, therefore, that language was taught previous to the study of philosophy, and as soon as the student had made some progress in the Latin. The Hebrew language having no connection with classical learning, and, except the Holy Scriptures, being the language of not a single book in any esteem the study of it did not commonly commence till after that of philosophy, and when the student had entered upon the study of theology.

Originally, the first rudiments, both of the Greek and Latin languages, were taught in universities; and in some universities they still continue to be so. In others, it is expected that the student should have previously acquired, at least, the rudiments of one or both of those languages, of which the study continues to make everywhere a very considerable part of university education.

The ancient Greek philosophy was divided into three great branches; physics, or natural philosophy; ethics, or moral philosophy; and logic. This general division seems perfectly agreeable to the nature of things.

The great phenomena of nature, the revolutions of the heavenly bodies, eclipses, comets; thunder and lightning, and other extraordinary meteors; the generation, the life, growth, and dissolution of plants and animals; are objects which, as they necessarily excite the wonder, so they naturally call forth the curiosity of mankind to inquire into their causes. Superstition first attempted to satisfy this curiosity, by referring all those wonderful appearances to the immediate agency of the gods. Philosophy afterwards endeavoured to account for them from more familiar causes, or from such as mankind were better acquainted with, than the agency of the gods. As those great phenomena are the first objects of human curiosity, so the science which pretends to explain them must naturally have been the first branch of philosophy that was cultivated. The first philosophers, accordingly, of whom history has preserved any account, appear to have been natural philosophers.

In every age and country of the world, men must have attended to the characters, designs, and actions of one another; and many reputable rules and maxims for the conduct of human life must have been laid down and approved of by common consent. As soon as writing came into fashion, wise men, or those who fancied themselves such, would naturally endeavour to increase the number of those established and respected maxims, and to express their own sense of what was either proper or improper conduct, sometimes in the more artificial form of apologues, like what are called the fables of Aesop; and sometimes in the more simple one of apophthegms or wise sayings, like the proverbs of Solomon, the verses of Theognis and Phocyllides, and some part of the works of Hesiod. They might continue in this manner, for a long time, merely to multiply the number of those maxims of prudence and morality, without even attempting to arrange them in any very distinct or methodical order, much less to connect them together by one or more general principles, from which they were all deducible, like effects from their natural causes. The beauty of a systematical arrangement of different observations, connected by a few common principles, was first seen in the rude essays of those ancient times towards a system of natural philosophy. Something of the same kind was afterwards attempted in morals. The maxims of common life were arranged in some methodical order, and connected together by a few common principles, in the same manner as they had attempted to arrange and connect the phenomena of nature. The science which pretends to investigate and explain those connecting principles, is what is properly called Moral Philosophy.

Different authors gave different systems, both of natural and moral philosophy. But the arguments by which they supported those different systems, far from being always demonstrations, were frequently at best but very slender probabilities, and sometimes mere sophisms, which had no other foundation but the inaccuracy and ambiguity of common language. Speculative systems, have, in all ages of the world, been adopted for reasons too frivolous to have determined the judgment of any man of common sense, in a matter of the smallest pecuniary interest. Gross sophistry has scarce ever had any influence upon the opinions of mankind, except in matters of philosophy and speculation; and in these it has frequently had the greatest. The patrons of each system of natural and moral philosophy, naturally endeavoured to expose the weakness of the arguments adduced to support the systems which were opposite to their own. In examining those arguments, they were necessarily led to consider the difference between a probable and a demonstrative argument, between a fallacious and a conclusive one; and logic, or the science of the general principles of good and bad reasoning, necessarily arose out of the observations which a scrutiny of this kind gave occasion to; though, in its origin, posterior both to physics and to ethics, it was commonly taught, not indeed in all, but in the greater part of the ancient schools of philosophy, previously to either of those sciences. The student, it seems to have been thought, ought to understand well the difference between good and bad reasoning, before he was led to reason upon subjects of so great importance.

This ancient division of philosophy into three parts was, in the greater part of the universities of Europe, changed for another into five.

In the ancient philosophy, whatever was taught concerning the nature either of the human mind or of the Deity, made a part of the system of physics. Those beings, in whatever their essence might be supposed to consist, were parts of the great system of the universe, and parts, too, productive of the most important effects. Whatever human reason could either conclude or conjecture concerning them, made, as it were, two chapters, though no doubt two very important ones, of the science which pretended to give an account of the origin and revolutions of the great system of the universe. But in the universities of Europe, where philosophy was taught only as subservient to theology, it was natural to dwell longer upon these two chapters than upon any other of the science. They were gradually more and more extended, and were divided into many inferior chapters; till at last the doctrine of spirits, of which so little can be known, came to take up as much room in the system of philosophy as the doctrine of bodies, of which so much can be known. The doctrines concerning those two subjects were considered as making two distinct sciences. What are called metaphysics, or pneumatics, were set in opposition to physics, and were cultivated not only as the more sublime, but, for the purposes of a particular profession, as the more useful science of the two. The proper subject of experiment and observation, a subject in which a careful attention is capable of making so many useful discoveries, was almost entirely neglected. The subject in which, after a very few simple and almost obvious truths, the most careful attention can discover nothing but obscurity and uncertainty, and can consequently produce nothing but subtleties and sophisms, was greatly cultivated.

When those two sciences had thus been set in opposition to one another, the comparison between them naturally gave birth to a third, to what was called ontology, or the science which treated of the qualities and attributes which were common to both the subjects of the other two sciences. But if subtleties and sophisms composed the greater part of the metaphysics or pneumatics of the schools, they composed the whole of this cobweb science of ontology, which was likewise sometimes called metaphysics.

Wherein consisted the happiness and perfection of a man, considered not only as an individual, but as the member of a family, of a state, and of the great society of mankind, was the object which the ancient moral philosophy proposed to investigate. In that philosophy, the duties of human life were treated of as subservient to the happiness and perfection of human life, But when moral, as well as natural philosophy, came to be taught only as subservient to theology, the duties of human life were treated of as chiefly subservient to the happiness of a life to come. In the ancient philosophy, the perfection of virtue was represented as necessarily productive, to the person who possessed it, of the most perfect happiness in this life. In the modern philosophy, it was frequently represented as generally, or rather as almost always, inconsistent with any degree of happiness in this life; and heaven was to be earned only by penance and mortification, by the austerities and abasement of a monk, not by the liberal, generous, and spirited conduct of a man. Casuistry, and an ascetic morality, made up, in most cases, the greater part of the moral philosophy of the schools. By far the most important of all the different branches of philosophy became in this manner by far the most corrupted.

Such, therefore, was the common course of philosophical education in the greater part of the universities in Europe. Logic was taught first; ontology came in the second place; pneumatology, comprehending the doctrine concerning the nature of the human soul and of the Deity, in the third; in the fourth followed a debased system of moral philosophy, which was considered as immediately connected with the doctrines of pneumatology, with the immortality of the human soul, and with the rewards and punishments which, from the justice of the Deity, were to be expected in a life to come: a short and superficial system of physics usually concluded the course.

The alterations which the universities of Europe thus introduced into the ancient course of philosophy were all meant for the education of ecclesiastics, and to render it a more proper introduction to the study of theology. But the additional quantity of subtlety and sophistry, the casuistry and ascetic morality which those alterations introduced into it, certainly did not render it more for the education of gentlemen or men of the world, or more likely either to improve the understanding or to mend the heart.

This course of philosophy is what still continues to be taught in the greater part of the universities of Europe, with more or less diligence, according as the constitution of each particular university happens to render diligence more or less necessary to the teachers. In some of the richest and best endowed universities, the tutors content themselves with teaching a few unconnected shreds and parcels of this corrupted course; and even these they commonly teach very negligently and superficially.

The improvements which, in modern times have been made in several different branches of philosophy, have not, the greater part of them, been made in universities, though some, no doubt, have. The greater part of universities have not even been very forward to adopt those improvements after they were made; and several of those learned societies have chosen to remain, for a long time, the sanctuaries in which exploded systems and obsolete prejudices found shelter and protection, after they had been hunted out of every other corner of the world. In general, the richest and best endowed universities have been slowest in adopting those improvements, and the most averse to permit any considerable change in the established plan of education. Those improvements were more easily introduced into some of the poorer universities, in which the teachers, depending upon their reputation for the greater part of their subsistence, were obliged to pay more attention to the current opinions of the world.

But though the public schools and universities of Europe were originally intended only for the education of a particular profession, that of churchmen; and though they were not always very diligent in instructing their pupils, even in the sciences which were supposed necessary for that profession; yet they gradually drew to themselves the education of almost all other people, particularly of almost all gentlemen and men of fortune. No better method, it seems, could be fallen upon, of spending, with any advantage, the long interval between infancy and that period of life at which men begin to apply in good earnest to the real business of the world, the business which is to employ them during the remainder of their days. The greater part of what is taught in schools and universities, however, does not seem to be the most proper preparation for that business.

In England, it becomes every day more and more the custom to send young people to travel in foreign countries immediately upon their leaving school, and without sending them to any university. Our young people, it is said, generally return home much improved by their travels.

A young man, who goes abroad at seventeen or eighteen, and returns home at one-and-twenty, returns three or four years older than he was when he went abroad; and at that age it is very difficult not to improve a good deal in three or four years. In the course of his travels, he generally acquires some knowledge of one or two foreign languages; a knowledge, however, which is seldom sufficient to enable him either to speak or write them with propriety. In other respects, he commonly returns home more conceited, more unprincipled, more dissipated, and more incapable of my serious application, either to study or to business, than he could well have become in so short a time had he lived at home. By travelling so very young, by spending in the most frivolous dissipation the most precious years of his life, at a distance from the inspection and control of his parents and relations, every useful habit, which the earlier parts of his education might have had some tendency to form in him, instead of being riveted and confirmed, is almost necessarily either weakened or effaced. Nothing but the discredit into which the universities are allowing themselves to fall, could ever have brought into repute so very absurd a practice as that of travelling at this early period of life. By sending his son abroad, a father delivers himself, at least for some time, from so disagreeable an object as that of a son unemployed, neglected, and going to ruin before his eyes.

Such have been the effects of some of the modern institutions for education.

Different plans and different institutions for education seem to have taken place in other ages and nations

In the republics of ancient Greece, every free citizen was instructed, under the direction of the public magistrate, in gymnastic exercises and in music. By gymnastic exercises, it was intended to harden his body, to sharpen his courage, and to prepare him for the fatigues and dangers of war; and as the Greek militia was, by all accounts, one of the best that ever was in the world, this part of their public education must have answered completely the purpose for which it was intended. By the other part, music, it was proposed, at least by the philosophers and historians, who have given us an account of those institutions, to humanize the mind, to soften the temper, and to dispose it for performing all the social and moral duties of public and private life.

In ancient Rome, the exercises of the Campus Martius answered the same purpose as those of the Gymnasium in ancient Greece, and they seem to have answered it equally well. But among the Romans there was nothing which corresponded to the musical education of the Greeks. The morals of the Romans, however, both in private and public life, seem to have been, not only equal, but, upon the whole, a good deal superior to those of the Greeks. That they were superior in private life, we have the express testimony of Polybius, and of Dionysius of Halicarnassus, two authors well acquainted with both nations; and the whole tenor of the Greek and Roman history bears witness to the superiority of the public morals of the Romans. The good temper and moderation of contending factions seem to be the most essential circumstances in the public morals of a free people. But the factions of the Greeks were almost always violent and sanguinary; whereas, till the time of the Gracchi, no blood had ever been shed in any Roman faction; and from the time of the Gracchi, the Roman republic may be considered as in reality dissolved. Notwithstanding, therefore, the very respectable authority of Plato, Aristotle, and Polybius, and notwithstanding the very ingenious reasons by which Mr. Montesquieu endeavours to support that authority, it seems probable that the musical education of the Greeks had no great effect in mending their morals, since, without any such education, those of the Romans were, upon the whole, superior. The respect of those ancient sages for the institutions of their ancestors had probably disposed them to find much political wisdom in what was, perhaps, merely an ancient custom, continued, without interruption, from the earliest period of those societies, to the times in which they had arrived at a considerable degree of refinement. Music and dancing are the great amusements of almost all barbarous nations, and the great accomplishments which are supposed to fit any man for entertaining his society. It is so at this day among the negroes on the coast of Africa. It was so among the ancient Celtes, among the ancient Scandinavians, and, as we may learn from Homer, among the ancient Greeks, in the times preceding the Trojan war. When the Greek tribes had formed themselves into little republics, it was natural that the study of those accomplishments should for a long time make a part of the public and common education of the people.

The masters who instructed the young people, either in music or in military exercises, do not seem to have been paid, or even appointed by the state, either in Rome or even at Athens, the Greek republic of whose laws and customs we are the best informed. The state required that every free citizen should fit himself for defending it in war, and should upon that account, learn his military exercises. But it left him to learn them of such masters as he could find; and it seems to have advanced nothing for this purpose, but a public field or place of exercise, in which he should practise and perform them.

In the early ages, both of the Greek and Roman republics, the other parts of education seem to have consisted in learning to read, write, and account, according to the arithmetic of the times. These accomplishments the richer citizens seem frequently to have acquired at home, by the assistance of some domestic pedagogue, who was, generally, either a slave or a freedman; and the poorer citizens in the schools of such masters as made a trade of teaching for hire. Such parts of education, however, were abandoned altogether to the care of the parents or guardians of each individual. It does not appear that the state ever assumed any inspection or direction of them. By a law of Solon, indeed, the children were acquitted from maintaining those parents who had neglected to instruct them in some profitable trade or business.

In the progress of refinement, when philosophy and rhetoric came into fashion, the better sort of people used to send their children to the schools of philosophers and rhetoricians, in order to be instructed in these fashionable sciences. But those schools were not supported by the public. They were, for a long time, barely tolerated by it. The demand for philosophy and rhetoric was, for a long time, so small, that the first professed teachers of either could not find constant employment in any one city, but were obliged to travel about from place to place. In this manner lived Zeno of Elea, Protagoras, Gorgias, Hippias, and many others. As the demand increased, the school, both of philosophy and rhetoric, became stationary, first in Athens, and afterwards in several other cities. The state, however, seems never to have encouraged them further, than by assigning to some of them a particular place to teach in, which was sometimes done, too, by private donors. The state seems to have assigned the Academy to Plato, the Lyceum to Aristotle, and the Portico to Zeno of Citta, the founder of the Stoics. But Epicurus bequeathed his gardens to his own school. Till about the time of Marcus Antoninus, however, no teacher appears to have had any salary from the public, or to have had any other emoluments, but what arose from the honorarius or fees of his scholars. The bounty which that philosophical emperor, as we learn from Lucian, bestowed upon one of the teachers of philosophy, probably lasted no longer than his own life. There was nothing equivalent to the privileges of graduation; and to have attended any of those schools was not necessary, in order to be permitted to practise any particular trade or profession. If the opinion of their own utility could not draw scholars to them, the law neither forced anybody to go to them, nor rewarded anybody for having gone to them. The teachers had no jurisdiction over their pupils, nor any other authority besides that natural authority which superior virtue and abilities never fail to procure from young people towards those who are entrusted with any part of their education.

At Rome, the study of the civil law made a part of the education, not of the greater part of the citizens, but of some particular families. The young people, however, who wished to acquire knowledge in the law, had no public school to go to, and had no other method of studying it, than by frequenting the company of such of their relations and friends as were supposed to understand it. It is, perhaps, worth while to remark, that though the laws of the twelve tables were many of them copied from those of some ancient Greek republics, yet law never seems to have grown up to be a science in any republic of ancient Greece. In Rome it became a science very early, and gave a considerable degree of illustration to those citizens who had the reputation of understanding it. In the republics of ancient Greece, particularly in Athens, the ordinary courts of justice consisted of numerous, and therefore disorderly, bodies of people, who frequently decided almost at random, or as clamour, faction, and party-spirit, happened to determine. The ignominy of an unjust decision, when it was to be divided among five hundred, a thousand, or fifteen hundred people (for some of their courts were so very numerous), could not fall very heavy upon any individual. At Rome, on the contrary, the principal courts of justice consisted either of a single judge, or of a small number of judges, whose characters, especially as they deliberated always in public, could not fail to be very much affected by any rash or unjust decision. In doubtful cases such courts, from their anxiety to avoid blame, would naturally endeavour to shelter themselves under the example or precedent of the judges who had sat before them, either in the same or in some other court. This attention to practice and precedent, necessarily formed the Roman law into that regular and orderly system in which it has been delivered down to us; and the like attention has had the like effects upon the laws of every other country where such attention has taken place. The superiority of character in the Romans over that of the Greeks, so much remarked by Polybius and Dionysius of Halicarnassus, was probably more owing to the better constitution of their courts of justice, than to any of the circumstances to which those authors ascribe it. The Romans are said to have been particularly distinguished for their superior respect to an oath. But the people who were accustomed to make oath only before some diligent and well informed court of justice, would naturally be much more attentive to what they swore, than they who were accustomed to do the same thing before mobbish and disorderly assemblies.

The abilities, both civil and military, of the Greeks and Romans, will readily be allowed to have been at least equal to those of any modern nation. Our prejudice is perhaps rather to overrate them. But except in what related to military exercises, the state seems to have been at no pains to form those great abilities; for I cannot be induced to believe that the musical education of the Greeks could be of much consequence in forming them. Masters, however, had been found, it seems, for instructing the better sort of people among those nations, in every art and science in which the circumstances of their society rendered it necessary or convenient for them to be instructed. The demand for such instruction produced, what it always produces, the talent for giving it; and the emulation which an unrestrained competition never fails to excite, appears to have brought that talent to a very high degree of perfection. In the attention which the ancient philosophers excited, in the empire which they acquired over the opinions and principles of their auditors, in the faculty which they possessed of giving a certain tone and character to the conduct and conversation of those auditors, they appear to have been much superior to any modern teachers. In modern times, the diligence of public teachers is more or less corrupted by the circumstances which render them more or less independent of their success and reputation in their particular professions. Their salaries, too, put the private teacher, who would pretend to come into competition with them, in the same state with a merchant who attempts to trade without a bounty, in competition with those who trade with a considerable one. If he sells his goods at nearly the same price, he cannot have the same profit; and poverty and beggary at least, if not bankruptcy and ruin, will infallibly be his lot. If he attempts to sell them much dearer, he is likely to have so few customers, that his circumstances will not be much mended. The privileges of graduation, besides, are in many countries necessary, or at least extremely convenient, to most men of learned professions, that is, to the far greater part of those who have occasion for a learned education. But those privileges can be obtained only by attending the lectures of the public teachers. The most careful attendance upon the ablest instructions of any private teacher cannot always give any title to demand them. It is from these different causes that the private teacher of any of the sciences, which are commonly taught in universities, is, in modern times, generally considered as in the very lowest order of men of letters. A man of real abilities can scarce find out a more humiliating or a more unprofitable employment to turn them to. The endowments of schools and colleges have in this manner not only corrupted the diligence of public teachers, but have rendered it almost impossible to have any good private ones.

Were there no public institutions for education, no system, no science, would be taught, for which there was not some demand, or which the circumstances of the times did not render it either necessary or convenient, or at least fashionable to learn. A private teacher could never find his account in teaching either an exploded and antiquated system of a science acknowledged to be useful, or a science universally believed to be a mere useless and pedantic heap of sophistry and nonsense. Such systems, such sciences, can subsist nowhere but in those incorporated societies for education, whose prosperity and revenue are in a great measure independent of their industry. Were there no public institutions for education, a gentleman, after going through, with application and abilities, the most complete course of education which the circumstances of the times were supposed to afford, could not come into the world completely ignorant of everything which is the common subject of conversation among gentlemen and men of the world.

There are no public institutions for the education of women, and there is accordingly nothing useless, absurd, or fantastical, in the common course of their education. They are taught what their parents or guardians judge it necessary or useful for them to learn, and they are taught nothing else. Every part of their education tends evidently to some useful purpose; either to improve the natural attractions of their person, or to form their mind to reserve, to modesty, to chastity, and to economy; to render them both likely to became the mistresses of a family, and to behave properly when they have become such. In every part of her life, a woman feels some conveniency or advantage from every part of her education. It seldom happens that a man, in any part of his life, derives any conveniency or advantage from some of the most laborious and troublesome parts of his education.

Ought the public, therefore, to give no attention, it may be asked, to the education of the people? Or, if it ought to give any, what are the different parts of education which it ought to attend to in the different orders of the people? and in what manner ought it to attend to them?

In some cases, the state of society necessarily places the greater part of individuals in such situations as naturally form in them, without any attention of government, almost all the abilities and virtues which that state requires, or perhaps can admit of. In other cases, the state of the society does not place the greater part of individuals in such situations; and some attention of government is necessary, in order to prevent the almost entire corruption and degeneracy of the great body of the people.

In the progress of the division of labour, the employment of the far greater part of those who live by labour, that is, of the great body of the people, comes to be confined to a few very simple operations; frequently to one or two. But the understandings of the greater part of men are necessarily formed by their ordinary employments. The man whose whole life is spent in performing a few simple operations, of which the effects, too, are perhaps always the same, or very nearly the same, has no occasion to exert his understanding, or to exercise his invention, in finding out expedients for removing difficulties which never occur. He naturally loses, therefore, the habit of such exertion, and generally becomes as stupid and ignorant as it is possible for a human creature to become. The torpor of his mind renders him not only incapable of relishing or bearing a part in any rational conversation, but of conceiving any generous, noble, or tender sentiment, and consequently of forming any just judgment concerning many even of the ordinary duties of private life. Of the great and extensive interests of his country he is altogether incapable of judging; and unless very particular pains have been taken to render him otherwise, he is equally incapable of defending his country in war. The uniformity of his stationary life naturally corrupts the courage of his mind, and makes him regard, with abhorrence, the irregular, uncertain, and adventurous life of a soldier. It corrupts even the activity of his body, and renders him incapable of exerting his strength with vigour and perseverance in any other employment, than that to which he has been bred. His dexterity at his own particular trade seems, in this manner, to be acquired at the expense of his intellectual, social, and martial virtues.

But in every improved and civilized society, this is the state into which the labouring poor, that is, the great body of the people, must necessarily fall, unless government takes some pains to prevent it.

It is otherwise in the barbarous societies, as they are commonly called, of hunters, of shepherds, and even of husbandmen in that rude state of husbandry which precedes the improvement of manufactures, and the extension of foreign commerce. In such societies, the varied occupations of every man oblige every man to exert his capacity, and to invent expedients for removing difficulties which are continually occurring. Invention is kept alive, and the mind is not suffered to fall into that drowsy stupidity, which, in a civilized society, seems to benumb the understanding of almost all the inferior ranks of people. In those barbarous societies, as they are called, every man, it has already been observed, is a warrior. Every man, too, is in some measure a statesman, and can form a tolerable judgment concerning the interest of the society, and the conduct of those who govern it. How far their chiefs are good judges in peace, or good leaders in war, is obvious to the observation of almost every single man among them. In such a society, indeed, no man can well acquire that improved and refined understanding which a few men sometimes possess in a more civilized state. Though in a rude society there is a good deal of variety in the occupations of every individual, there is not a great deal in those of the whole society. Every man does, or is capable of doing, almost every thing which any other man does, or is capable of being. Every man has a considerable degree of knowledge, ingenuity, and invention but scarce any man has a great degree. The degree, however, which is commonly possessed, is generally sufficient for conducting the whole simple business of the society. In a civilized state, on the contrary, though there is little variety in the occupations of the greater part of individuals, there is an almost infinite variety in those of the whole society. These varied occupations present an almost infinite variety of objects to the contemplation of those few, who, being attached to no particular occupation themselves, have leisure and inclination to examine the occupations of other people. The contemplation of so great a variety of objects necessarily exercises their minds in endless comparisons and combinations, and renders their understandings, in an extraordinary degree, both acute and comprehensive. Unless those few, however, happen to be placed in some very particular situations, their great abilities, though honourable to themselves, may contribute very little to the good government or happiness of their society. Notwithstanding the great abilities of those few, all the nobler parts of the human character may be, in a great measure, obliterated and extinguished in the great body of the people.

The education of the common people requires, perhaps, in a civilized and commercial society, the attention of the public, more than that of people of some rank and fortune. People of some rank and fortune are generally eighteen or nineteen years of age before they enter upon that particular business, profession, or trade, by which they propose to distinguish themselves in the world. They have, before that, full time to acquire, or at least to fit themselves for afterwards acquiring, every accomplishment which can recommend them to the public esteem, or render them worthy of it. Their parents or guardians are generally sufficiently anxious that they should be so accomplished, and are in most cases, willing enough to lay out the expense which is necessary for that purpose. If they are not always properly educated, it is seldom from the want of expense laid out upon their education, but from the improper application of that expense. It is seldom from the want of masters, but from the negligence and incapacity of the masters who are to be had, and from the difficulty, or rather from the impossibility, which there is, in the present state of things, of finding any better. The employments, too, in which people of some rank or fortune spend the greater part of their lives, are not, like those of the common people, simple and uniform. They are almost all of them extremely complicated, and such as exercise the head more than the hands. The understandings of those who are engaged in such employments, can seldom grow torpid for want of exercise. The employments of people of some rank and fortune, besides, are seldom such as harass them from morning to night. They generally have a good deal of leisure, during which they may perfect themselves in every branch, either of useful or ornamental knowledge, of which they may have laid the foundation, or for which they may have acquired some taste in the earlier part of life.

It is otherwise with the common people. They have little time to spare for education. Their parents can scarce afford to maintain them, even in infancy. As soon as they are able to work, they must apply to some trade, by which they can earn their subsistence. That trade, too, is generally so simple and uniform, as to give little exercise to the understanding; while, at the same time, their labour is both so constant and so severe, that it leaves them little leisure and less inclination to apply to, or even to think of any thing else.

But though the common people cannot, in any civilized society, be so well instructed as people of some rank and fortune; the most essential parts of education, however, to read, write, and account, can be acquired at so early a period of life, that the greater part, even of those who are to be bred to the lowest occupations, have time to acquire them before they can be employed in those occupations. For a very small expense, the public can facilitate, can encourage and can even impose upon almost the whole body of the people, the necessity of acquiring those most essential parts of education.

The public can facilitate this acquisition, by establishing in every parish or district a little school, where children maybe taught for a reward so moderate, that even a common labourer may afford it; the master being partly, but not wholly, paid by the public; because, if he was wholly, or even principally, paid by it, he would soon learn to neglect his business. In Scotland, the establishment of such parish schools has taught almost the whole common people to read, and a very great proportion of them to write and account. In England, the establishment of charity schools has had an effect of the same kind, though not so universally, because the establishment is not so universal. If, in those little schools, the books by which the children are taught to read, were a little more instructive than they commonly are; and if, instead of a little smattering in Latin, which the children of the common people are sometimes taught there, and which can scarce ever be of any use to them, they were instructed in the elementary parts of geometry and mechanics; the literary education of this rank of people would, perhaps, be as complete as can be. There is scarce a common trade, which does not afford some opportunities of applying to it the principles of geometry and mechanics, and which would not, therefore, gradually exercise and improve the common people in those principles, the necessary introduction to the most sublime, as well as to the most useful sciences.

The public can encourage the acquisition of those most essential parts of education, by giving small premiums, and little badges of distinction, to the children of the common people who excel in them.

The public can impose upon almost the whole body of the people the necessity of acquiring the most essential parts of education, by obliging every man to undergo an examination or probation in them, before he can obtain the freedom in any corporation, or be allowed to set up any trade, either in a village or town corporate.

It was in this manner, by facilitating the acquisition of their military and gymnastic exercises, by encouraging it, and even by imposing upon the whole body of the people the necessity of learning those exercises, that the Greek and Roman republics maintained the martial spirit of their respective citizens. They facilitated the acquisition of those exercises, by appointing a certain place for learning and practising them, and by granting to certain masters the privilege of teaching in that place. Those masters do not appear to have had either salaries or exclusive privileges of any kind. Their reward consisted altogether in what they got from their scholars; and a citizen, who had learnt his exercises in the public gymnasia, had no sort of legal advantage over one who had learnt them privately, provided the latter had learned them equally well. Those republics encouraged the acquisition of those exercises, by bestowing little premiums and badges of distinction upon those who excelled in them. To have gained a prize in the Olympic, Isthmian, or Nemaean games, gave illustration, not only to the person who gained it, but to his whole family and kindred. The obligation which every citizen was under, to serve a certain number of years, if called upon, in the armies of the republic, sufficiently imposed the necessity of learning those exercises, without which he could not be fit for that service.

That in the progress of improvement, the practice of military exercises, unless government takes proper pains to support it, goes gradually to decay, and, together with it, the martial spirit of the great body of the people, the example of modern Europe sufficiently demonstrates. But the security of every society must always depend, more or less, upon the martial spirit of the great body of the people. In the present times, indeed, that martial spirit alone, and unsupported by a well-disciplined standing army, would not, perhaps, be sufficient for the defence and security of any society. But where every citizen had the spirit of a soldier, a smaller standing army would surely be requisite. That spirit, besides, would necessarily diminish very much the dangers to liberty, whether real or imaginary, which are commonly apprehended from a standing army. As it would very much facilitate the operations of that army against a foreign invader; so it would obstruct them as much, if unfortunately they should ever be directed against the constitution of the state.

The ancient institutions of Greece and Rome seem to have been much more effectual for maintaining the martial spirit of the great body of the people, than the establishment of what are called the militias of modern times. They were much more simple. When they were once established, they executed themselves, and it required little or no attention from government to maintain them in the most perfect vigour. Whereas to maintain, even in tolerable execution, the complex regulations of any modern militia, requires the continual and painful attention of government, without which they are constantly falling into total neglect and disuse. The influence, besides, of the ancient institutions, was much more universal. By means of them, the whole body of the people was completely instructed in the use of arms; whereas it is but a very small part of them who can ever be so instructed by the regulations of any modern militia, except, perhaps, that of Switzerland. But a coward, a man incapable either of defending or of revenging himself, evidently wants one of the most essential parts of the character of a man. He is as much mutilated and deformed in his mind as another is in his body, who is either deprived of some of its most essential members, or has lost the use of them. He is evidently the more wretched and miserable of the two; because happiness and misery, which reside altogether in the mind, must necessarily depend more upon the healthful or unhealthful, the mutilated or entire state of the mind, than upon that of the body. Even though the martial spirit of the people were of no use towards the defence of the society, yet, to prevent that sort of mental mutilation, deformity, and wretchedness, which cowardice necessarily involves in it, from spreading themselves through the great body of the people, would still deserve the most serious attention of government; in the same manner as it would deserve its most serious attention to prevent a leprosy, or any other loathsome and offensive disease, though neither mortal nor dangerous, from spreading itself among them; though, perhaps, no other public good might result from such attention, besides the prevention of so great a public evil.

    The same thing may be said of the gross ignorance and stupidity which, in a civilized society, seem so frequently to benumb the understandings of all the inferior ranks of people. A man without the proper use of the intellectual faculties of a man, is, if possible, more contemptible than even a coward, and seems to be mutilated and deformed in a still more essential part of the character of human nature. Though the state was to derive no advantage from the instruction of the inferior ranks of people, it would still deserve its attention that they should not be altogether uninstructed. The state, however, derives no inconsiderable advantage from their instruction. The more they are instructed, the less liable they are to the delusions of enthusiasm and superstition, which, among ignorant nations frequently occasion the most dreadful disorders. An instructed and intelligent people, besides, are always more decent and orderly than an ignorant and stupid one. They feel themselves, each individually, more respectable, and more likely to obtain the respect of their lawful superiors, and they are, therefore, more disposed to respect those superiors. They are more disposed to examine, and more capable of seeing through, the interested complaints of faction and sedition; and they are, upon that account, less apt to be misled into any wanton or unnecessary opposition to the measures of government. In free countries, where the safety of government depends very much upon the favourable judgment which the people may form of its conduct, it must surely be of the highest importance, that they should not be disposed to judge rashly or capriciously concerning it.

Art. III.—Of the Expense of the Institutions for the Instruction of People of all Ages

The institutions for the instruction of people of all ages, are chiefly those for religious instruction. This is a species of instruction, of which the object is not so much to render the people good citizens in this world, as to prepare them for another and a better world in the life to come. The teachers of the doctrine which contains this instruction, in the same manner as other teachers, may either depend altogether for their subsistence upon the voluntary contributions of their hearers; or they may derive it from some other fund, to which the law of their country may entitle them; such as a landed estate, a tythe or land tax, an established salary or stipend. Their exertion, their zeal and industry, are likely to be much greater in the former situation than in the latter. In this respect, the teachers of a new religion have always had a considerable advantage in attacking those ancient and established systems, of which the clergy, reposing themselves upon their benefices, had neglected to keep up the fervour of faith and devotion in the great body of the people; and having given themselves up to indolence, were become altogether incapable of making any vigorous exertion in defence even of their own establishment. The clergy of an established and well endowed religion frequently become men of learning and elegance, who possess all the virtues of gentlemen, or which can recommend them to the esteem of gentlemen; but they are apt gradually to lose the qualities, both good and bad, which gave them authority and influence with the inferior ranks of people, and which had perhaps been the original causes of the success and establishment of their religion. Such a clergy, when attacked by a set of popular and bold, though perhaps stupid and ignorant enthusiasts, feel themselves as perfectly defenceless as the indolent, effeminate, and full fed nations of the southern parts of Asia, when they were invaded by the active, hardy, and hungry Tartars of the north. Such a clergy, upon such an emergency, have commonly no other resource than to call upon the civil magistrate to persecute, destroy, or drive out their adversaries, as disturbers of the public peace. It was thus that the Roman catholic clergy called upon the civil magistrate to persecute the protestants, and the church of England to persecute the dissenters; and that in general every religious sect, when it has once enjoyed, for a century or two, the security of a legal establishment, has found itself incapable of making any vigorous defence against any new sect which chose to attack its doctrine or discipline. Upon such occasions, the advantage, in point of learning and good writing, may sometimes be on the side of the established church. But the arts of popularity, all the arts of gaining proselytes, are constantly on the side of its adversaries. In England, those arts have been long neglected by the well endowed clergy of the established church, and are at present chiefly cultivated by the dissenters and by the methodists. The independent provisions, however, which in many places have been made for dissenting teachers, by means of voluntary subscriptions, of trust rights, and other evasions of the law, seem very much to have abated the zeal and activity of those teachers. They have many of them become very learned, ingenious, and respectable men; but they have in general ceased to be very popular preachers. The methodists, without half the learning of the dissenters, are much more in vogue.

In the church of Rome the industry and zeal of the inferior clergy are kept more alive by the powerful motive of self-interest, than perhaps in any established protestant church. The parochial clergy derive many of them, a very considerable part of their subsistence from the voluntary oblations of the people; a source of revenue, which confession gives them many opportunities of improving. The mendicant orders derive their whole subsistence from such oblations. It is with them as with the hussars and light infantry of some armies; no plunder, no pay. The parochial clergy are like those teachers whose reward depends partly upon their salary, and partly upon the fees or honoraries which they get from their pupils; and these must always depend, more or less, upon their industry and reputation. The mendicant orders are like those teachers whose subsistence depends altogether upon their industry. They are obliged, therefore, to use every art which can animate the devotion of the common people. The establishment of the two great mendicant orders of St Dominic and St. Francis, it is observed by Machiavel, revived, in the thirteenth and fourteenth centuries, the languishing faith and devotion of the catholic church. In Roman catholic countries, the spirit of devotion is supported altogether by the monks, and by the poorer parochial clergy. The great dignitaries of the church, with all the accomplishments of gentlemen and men of the world, and sometimes with those of men of learning, are careful to maintain the necessary discipline over their inferiors, but seldom give themselves any trouble about the instruction of the people.

"Most of the arts and professions in a state," says by far the most illustrious philosopher and historian of the present age, "are of such a nature, that, while they promote the interests of the society, they are also useful or agreeable to some individuals; and, in that case, the constant rule of the magistrate, except, perhaps, on the first introduction of any art, is, to leave the profession to itself, and trust its encouragement to the individuals who reap the benefit of it. The artizans, finding their profits to rise by the favour of their customers, increase, as much as possible, their skill and industry; and as matters are not disturbed by any injudicious tampering, the commodity is always sure to be at all times nearly proportioned to the demand.

"But there are also some callings which, though useful and even necessary in a state, bring no advantage or pleasure to any individual; and the supreme power is obliged to alter its conduct with regard to the retainers of those professions. It must give them public encouragement in order to their subsistence; and it must provide against that negligence to which they will naturally be subject, either by annexing particular honours to profession, by establishing a long subordination of ranks, and a strict dependence, or by some other expedient. The persons employed in the finances, fleets, and magistracy, are instances of this order of men.

"It may naturally be thought, at first sight, that the ecclesiastics belong to the first class, and that their encouragement, as well as that of lawyers and physicians, may safely be entrusted to the liberality of individuals, who are attached to their doctrines, and who find benefit or consolation from their spiritual ministry and assistance. Their industry and vigilance will, no doubt, be whetted by such an additional motive; and their skill in the profession, as well as their address in governing the minds of the people, must receive daily increase, from their increasing practice, study, and attention.

"But if we consider the matter more closely, we shall find that this interested diligence of the clergy is what every wise legislator will study to prevent; because, in every religion except the true, it is highly pernicious, and it has even a natural tendency to pervert the truth, by infusing into it a strong mixture of superstition, folly, and delusion. Each ghostly practitioner, in order to render himself more precious and sacred in the eyes of his retainers, will inspire them with the most violent abhorrence of all other sects, and continually endeavour, by some novelty, to excite the languid devotion of his audience. No regard will be paid to truth, morals, or decency, in the doctrines inculcated. Every tenet will be adopted that best suits the disorderly affections of the human frame. Customers will be drawn to each conventicle by new industry and address, in practising on the passions and credulity of the populace. And, in the end, the civil magistrate will find that he has dearly paid for his intended frugality, in saving a fixed establishment for the priests; and that, in reality, the most decent and advantageous composition, which he can make with the spiritual guides, is to bribe their indolence, by assigning stated salaries to their profession, and rendering it superfluous for them to be farther active, than merely to prevent their flock from straying in quest of new pastors. And in this manner ecclesiastical establishments, though commonly they arose at first from religious views, prove in the end advantageous to the political interests of society."

But whatever may have been the good or bad effects of the independent provision of the clergy, it has, perhaps, been very seldom bestowed upon them from any view to those effects. Times of violent religious controversy have generally been times of equally violent political faction. Upon such occasions, each political party has either found it, or imagined it, for his interest, to league itself with some one or other of the contending religious sects. But this could be done only by adopting, or, at least, by favouring the tenets of that particular sect. The sect which had the good fortune to be leagued with the conquering party necessarily shared in the victory of its ally, by whose favour and protection it was soon enabled, in some degree, to silence and subdue all its adversaries. Those adversaries had generally leagued themselves with the enemies of the conquering party, and were, therefore the enemies of that party. The clergy of this particular sect having thus become complete masters of the field, and their influence and authority with the great body of the people being in its highest vigour, they were powerful enough to overawe the chiefs and leaders of their own party, and to oblige the civil magistrate to respect their opinions and inclinations. Their first demand was generally that he should silence and subdue all their adversaries; and their second, that he should bestow an independent provision on themselves. As they had generally contributed a good deal to the victory, it seemed not unreasonable that they should have some share in the spoil. They were weary, besides, of humouring the people, and of depending upon their caprice for a subsistence. In making this demand, therefore, they consulted their own ease and comfort, without troubling themselves about the effect which it might have, in future times, upon the influence and authority of their order. The civil magistrate, who could comply with their demand only by giving them something which he would have chosen much rather to take, or to keep to himself, was seldom very forward to grant it. Necessity, however, always forced him to submit at last, though frequently not till after many delays, evasions, and affected excuses.

But if politics had never called in the aid of religion, had the conquering party never adopted the tenets of one sect more than those of another, when it had gained the victory, it would probably have dealt equally and impartially with all the different sects, and have allowed every man to choose his own priest, and his own religion, as he thought proper. There would, and, in this case, no doubt, have been, a great multitude of religious sects. Almost every different congregation might probably have had a little sect by itself, or have entertained some peculiar tenets of its own. Each teacher, would, no doubt, have felt himself under the necessity of making the utmost exertion, and of using every art, both to preserve and to increase the number of his disciples. But as every other teacher would have felt himself under the same necessity, the success of no one teacher, or sect of teachers, could have been very great. The interested and active zeal of religious teachers can be dangerous and troublesome only where there is either but one sect tolerated in the society, or where the whole of a large society is divided into two or three great sects; the teachers of each acting by concert, and under a regular discipline and subordination. But that zeal must be altogether innocent, where the society is divided into two or three hundred, or, perhaps, into as many thousand small sects, of which no one could be considerable enough to disturb the public tranquillity. The teachers of each sect, seeing themselves surrounded on all sides with more adversaries than friends, would be obliged to learn that candour and moderation which are so seldom to be found among the teachers of those great sects, whose tenets, being supported by the civil magistrate, are held in veneration by almost all the inhabitants of extensive kingdoms and empires, and who, therefore, see nothing round them but followers, disciples, and humble admirers. The teachers of each little sect, finding themselves almost alone, would be obliged to respect those of almost every other sect; and the concessions which they would mutually find in both convenient and agreeable to make one to another, might in time, probably reduce the doctrine of the greater part of them to that pure and rational religion, free from every mixture of absurdity, imposture, or fanaticism, such as wise men have, in all ages of the world, wished to see established; but such as positive law has, perhaps, never yet established, and probably never will establish in any country; because, with regard to religion, positive law always has been, and probably always will be, more or less influenced by popular superstition and enthusiasm. This plan of ecclesiastical government, or, more properly, of no ecclesiastical government, was what the sect called Independents (a sect, no doubt, of very wild enthusiasts), proposed to establish in England towards the end of the civil war. If it had been established, though of a very unphilosophical origin, it would probably, by this time, have been productive of the most philosophical good temper and moderation with regard to every sort of religious principle. It has been established in Pennsylvania, where, though the quakers happen to be the most numerous, the law, in reality, favours no one sect more than another; and it is there said to have been productive of this philosophical good temper and moderation.

But though this equality of treatment should not be productive of this good temper and moderation in all, or even in the greater part of the religious sects of a particular country; yet, provided those sects were sufficiently numerous, and each of them consequently too small to disturb the public tranquillity, the excessive zeal of each for its particular tenets could not well be productive of any very hurtful effects, but, on the contrary, of several good ones; and if the government was perfectly decided, both to let them all alone, and to oblige them all to let alone one another, there is little danger that they would not of their own accord, subdivide themselves fast enough, so as soon to become sufficiently numerous.

In every civilized society, in every society where the distinction of ranks has once been completely established, there have been always two different schemes or systems of morality current at the same time; of which the one may be called the strict or austere; the other the liberal, or, if you will, the loose system. The former is generally admired and revered by the common people; the latter is commonly more esteemed and adopted by what are called the people of fashion. The degree of disapprobation with which we ought to mark the vices of levity, the vices which are apt to arise from great prosperity, and from the excess of gaiety and good humour, seems to constitute the principal distinction between those two opposite schemes or systems. In the liberal or loose system, luxury, wanton, and even disorderly mirth, the pursuit of pleasure to some degree of intemperance, the breach of chastity, at least in one of the two sexes, etc. provided they are not accompanied with gross indecency, and do not lead to falsehood and injustice, are generally treated with a good deal of indulgence, and are easily either excused or pardoned altogether. In the austere system, on the contrary, those excesses are regarded with the utmost abhorrence and detestation. The vices of levity are always ruinous to the common people, and a single week's thoughtlessness and dissipation is often sufficient to undo a poor workman for ever, and to drive him, through despair, upon committing the most enormous crimes. The wiser and better sort of the common people, therefore, have always the utmost abhorrence and detestation of such excesses, which their experience tells them are so immediately fatal to people of their condition. The disorder and extravagance of several years, on the contrary, will not always ruin a man of fashion; and people of that rank are very apt to consider the power of indulging in some degree of excess, as one of the advantages of their fortune; and the liberty of doing so without censure or reproach, as one of the privileges which belong to their station. In people of their own station, therefore, they regard such excesses with but a small degree of disapprobation, and censure them either very slightly or not at all.

Almost all religious sects have begun among the common people, from whom they have generally drawn their earliest, as well as their most numerous proselytes. The austere system of morality has, accordingly, been adopted by those sects almost constantly, or with very few exceptions; for there have been some. It was the system by which they could best recommend themselves to that order of people, to whom they first proposed their plan of reformation upon what had been before established. Many of them, perhaps the greater part of them, have even endeavoured to gain credit by refining upon this austere system, and by carrying it to some degree of folly and extravagance; and this excessive rigour has frequently recommended them, more than any thing else, to the respect and veneration of the common people.

A man of rank and fortune is, by his station, the distinguished member of a great society, who attend to every part of his conduct, and who thereby oblige him to attend to every part of it himself. His authority and consideration depend very much upon the respect which this society bears to him. He dares not do anything which would disgrace or discredit him in it; and he is obliged to a very strict observation of that species of morals, whether liberal or austere, which the general consent of this society prescribes to persons of his rank and fortune. A man of low condition, on the contrary, is far from being a distinguished member of any great society. While he remains in a country village, his conduct may be attended to, and he may be obliged to attend to it himself. In this situation, and in this situation only, he may have what is called a character to lose. But as soon as he comes into a great city, he is sunk in obscurity and darkness. His conduct is observed and attended to by nobody; and he is, therefore, very likely to neglect it himself, and to abandon himself to every sort of low profligacy and vice. He never emerges so effectually from this obscurity, his conduct never excites so much the attention of any respectable society, as by his becoming the member of a small religious sect. He from that moment acquires a degree of consideration which he never had before. All his brother sectaries are, for the credit of the sect, interested to observe his conduct; and, if he gives occasion to any scandal, if he deviates very much from those austere morals which they almost always require of one another, to punish him by what is always a very severe punishment, even where no evil effects attend it, expulsion or excommunication from the sect. In little religious sects, accordingly, the morals of the common people have been almost always remarkably regular and orderly; generally much more so than in the established church. The morals of those little sects, indeed, have frequently been rather disagreeably rigorous and unsocial.

There are two very easy and effectual remedies, however, by whose joint operation the state might, without violence, correct whatever was unsocial or disagreeably rigorous in the morals of all the little sects into which the country was divided.

The first of those remedies is the study of science and philosophy, which the state might render almost universal among all people of middling or more than middling rank and fortune; not by giving salaries to teachers in order to make them negligent and idle, but by instituting some sort of probation, even in the higher and more difficult sciences, to be undergone by every person before he was permitted to exercise any liberal profession, or before he could be received as a candidate for any honourable office, of trust or profit. If the state imposed upon this order of men the necessity of learning, it would have no occasion to give itself any trouble about providing them with proper teachers. They would soon find better teachers for themselves, than any whom the state could provide for them. Science is the great antidote to the poison of enthusiasm and superstition; and where all the superior ranks of people were secured from it, the inferior ranks could not be much exposed to it.

The second of those remedies is the frequency and gaiety of public diversions. The state, by encouraging, that is, by giving entire liberty to all those who, from their own interest, would attempt, without scandal or indecency, to amuse and divert the people by painting, poetry, music, dancing; by all sorts of dramatic representations and exhibitions; would easily dissipate, in the greater part of them, that melancholy and gloomy humour which is almost always the nurse of popular superstition and enthusiasm. Public diversions have always been the objects of dread and hatred to all the fanatical promoters of those popular frenzies. The gaiety and good humour which those diversions inspire, were altogether inconsistent with that temper of mind which was fittest for their purpose, or which they could best work upon. Dramatic representations, besides, frequently exposing their artifices to public ridicule, and sometimes even to public execration, were, upon that account, more than all other diversions, the objects of their peculiar abhorrence.

In a country where the law favoured the teachers of no one religion more than those of another, it would not be necessary that any of them should have any particular or immediate dependency upon the sovereign or executive power; or that he should have anything to do either in appointing or in dismissing them from their offices. In such a situation, he would have no occasion to give himself any concern about them, further than to keep the peace among them, in the same manner as among the rest of his subjects, that is, to hinder them from persecuting, abusing, or oppressing one another. But it is quite otherwise in countries where there is an established or governing religion. The sovereign can in this case never be secure, unless he has the means of influencing in a considerable degree the greater part of the teachers of that religion.

    The clergy of every established church constitute a great incorporation. They can act in concert, and pursue their interest upon one plan, and with one spirit as much as if they were under the direction of one man; and they are frequently, too, under such direction. Their interest as an incorporated body is never the same with that of the sovereign, and is sometimes directly opposite to it. Their great interest is to maintain their authority with the people, and this authority depends upon the supposed certainty and importance of the whole doctrine which they inculcate, and upon the supposed necessity of adopting every part of it with the most implicit faith, in order to avoid eternal misery. Should the sovereign have the imprudence to appear either to deride, or doubt himself of the most trifling part of their doctrine, or from humanity, attempt to protect those who did either the one or the other, the punctilious honour of a clergy, who have no sort of dependency upon him, is immediately provoked to proscribe him as a profane person, and to employ all the terrors of religion, in order to oblige the people to transfer their allegiance to some more orthodox and obedient prince. Should he oppose any of their pretensions or usurpations, the danger is equally great. The princes who have dared in this manner to rebel against the church, over and above this crime of rebellion, have generally been charged, too, with the additional crime of heresy, notwithstanding their solemn protestations of their faith, and humble submission to every tenet which she thought proper to prescribe to them. But the authority of religion is superior to every other authority. The fears which it suggests conquer all other fears. When the authorized teachers of religion propagate through the great body of the people, doctrines subversive of the authority of the sovereign, it is by violence only, or by the force of a standing army, that he can maintain his authority. Even a standing army cannot in this case give him any lasting security; because if the soldiers are not foreigners, which can seldom be the case, but drawn from the great body of the people, which must almost always be the case, they are likely to be soon corrupted by those very doctrines. The revolutions which the turbulence of the Greek clergy was continually occasioning at Constantinople, as long as the eastern empire subsisted; the convulsions which, during the course of several centuries, the turbulence of the Roman clergy was continually occasioning in every part of Europe, sufficiently demonstrate how precarious and insecure must always be the situation of the sovereign, who has no proper means of influencing the clergy of the established and governing religion of his country.

Articles of faith, as well as all other spiritual matters, it is evident enough, are not within the proper department of a temporal sovereign, who, though he may be very well qualified for protecting, is seldom supposed to be so for instructing the people. With regard to such matters, therefore, his authority can seldom be sufficient to counterbalance the united authority of the clergy of the established church. The public tranquillity, however, and his own security, may frequently depend upon the doctrines which they may think proper to propagate concerning such matters. As he can seldom directly oppose their decision, therefore, with proper weight and authority, it is necessary that he should be able to influence it; and he can influence it only by the fears and expectations which he may excite in the greater part of the individuals of the order. Those fears and expectations may consist in the fear of deprivation or other punishment, and in the expectation of further preferment.

In all Christian churches, the benefices of the clergy are a sort of freeholds, which they enjoy, not during pleasure, but during life or good behaviour. If they held them by a more precarious tenure, and were liable to be turned out upon every slight disobligation either of the sovereign or of his ministers, it would perhaps be impossible for them to maintain their authority with the people, who would then consider them as mercenary dependents upon the court, in the sincerity of whose instructions they could no longer have any confidence. But should the sovereign attempt irregularly, and by violence, to deprive any number of clergymen of their freeholds, on account, perhaps, of their having propagated, with more than ordinary zeal, some factious or seditious doctrine, he would only render, by such persecution, both them and their doctrine ten times more popular, and therefore ten times more troublesome and dangerous, than they had been before. Fear is in almost all cases a wretched instrument of govermnent, and ought in particular never to be employed against any order of men who have the smallest pretensions to independency. To attempt to terrify them, serves only to irritate their bad humour, and to confirm them in an opposition, which more gentle usage, perhaps, might easily induce them either to soften, or to lay aside altogether. The violence which the French government usually employed in order to oblige all their parliaments, or sovereign courts of justice, to enregister any unpopular edict, very seldom succeeded. The means commonly employed, however, the imprisonment of all the refractory members, one would think, were forcible enough. The princes of the house of Stuart sometimes employed the like means in order to influence some of the members of the parliament of England, and they generally found them equally intractable. The parliament of England is now managed in another manner; and a very small experiment, which the duke of Choiseul made, about twelve years ago, upon the parliament of Paris, demonstrated sufficiently that all the parliaments of France might have been managed still more easily in the same manner. That experiment was not pursued. For though management and persuasion are always the easiest and safest instruments of government as force and violence are the worst and the most dangerous; yet such, it seems, is the natural insolence of man, that he almost always disdains to use the good instrument, except when he cannot or dare not use the bad one. The French government could and durst use force, and therefore disdained to use management and persuasion. But there is no order of men, it appears I believe, from the experience of all ages, upon whom it is so dangerous or rather so perfectly ruinous, to employ force and violence, as upon the respected clergy of an established church. The rights, the privileges, the personal liberty of every individual ecclesiastic, who is upon good terms with his own order, are, even in the most despotic governments, more respected than those of any other person of nearly equal rank and fortune. It is so in every gradation of despotism, from that of the gentle and mild government of Paris, to that of the violent and furious government of Constantinople. But though this order of men can scarce ever be forced, they may be managed as easily as any other; and the security of the sovereign, as well as the public tranquillity, seems to depend very much upon the means which he has of managing them; and those means seem to consist altogether in the preferment which he has to bestow upon them.

In the ancient constitution of the Christian church, the bishop of each diocese was elected by the joint votes of the clergy and of the people of the episcopal city. The people did not long retain their right of election; and while they did retain it, they almost always acted under the influence of the clergy, who, in such spiritual matters, appeared to be their natural guides. The clergy, however, soon grew weary of the trouble of managing them, and found it easier to elect their own bishops themselves. The abbot, in the same manner, was elected by the monks of the monastery, at least in the greater part of abbacies. All the inferior ecclesiastical benefices comprehended within the diocese were collated by the bishop, who bestowed them upon such ecclesiastics as he thought proper. All church preferments were in this manner in the disposal of the church. The sovereign, though he might have some indirect influence in those elections, and though it was sometimes usual to ask both his consent to elect, and his approbation of the election, yet had no direct or sufficient means of managing the clergy. The ambition of every clergyman naturally led him to pay court, not so much to his sovereign as to his own order, from which only he could expect preferment.

Through the greater part of Europe, the pope gradually drew to himself, first the collation of almost all bishoprics and abbacies, or of what were called consistorial benefices, and afterwards, by various machinations and pretences, of the greater part of inferior benefices comprehended within each diocese, little more being left to the bishop than what was barely necessary to give him a decent authority with his own clergy. By this arrangement the condition of the sovereign was still worse than it had been before. The clergy of all the different countries of Europe were thus formed into a sort of spiritual army, dispersed in different quarters indeed, but of which all the movements and operations could now be directed by one head, and conducted upon one uniform plan. The clergy of each particular country might be considered as a particular detachment of that army, of which the operations could easily be supported and seconded by all the other detachments quartered in the different countries round about. Each detachment was not only independent of the sovereign of the country in which it was quartered, and by which it was maintained, but dependent upon a foreign sovereign, who could at any time turn its arms against the sovereign of that particular country, and support them by the arms of all the other detachments.

Those arms were the most formidable that can well be imagined.

In the ancient state of Europe, before the establishment of arts and manufactures, the wealth of the clergy gave them the same sort of influence over the common people which that of the great barons gave them over their respective vassals, tenants, and retainers. In the great landed estates, which the mistaken piety both of princes and private persons had bestowed upon the church, jurisdictions were established, of the same kind with those of the great barons, and for the same reason. In those great landed estates, the clergy, or their bailiffs, could easily keep the peace, without the support or assistance either of the king or of any other person; and neither the king nor any other person could keep the peace there without the support and assistance of the clergy. The jurisdictions of the clergy, therefore, in their particular baronies or manors, were equally independent, and equally exclusive of the authority of the king's courts, as those of the great temporal lords. The tenants of the clergy were, like those of the great barons, almost all tenants at will, entirely dependent upon their immediate lords, and, therefore, liable to be called out at pleasure, in order to fight in any quarrel in which the clergy might think proper to engage them. Over and above the rents of those estates, the clergy possessed in the tithes a very large portion of the rents of all the other estates in every kingdom of Europe. The revenues arising from both those species of rents were, the greater part of them, paid in kind, in corn, wine, cattle, poultry, etc. The quantity exceeded greatly what the clergy could themselves consume; and there were neither arts nor manufactures, for the produce of which they could exchange the surplus. The clergy could derive advantage from this immense surplus in no other way than by employing it, as the great barons employed the like surplus of their revenues, in the most profuse hospitality, and in the most extensive charity. Both the hospitality and the charity of the ancient clergy, accordingly, are said to have been very great. They not only maintained almost the whole poor of every kingdom, but many knights and gentlemen had frequently no other means of subsistence than by travelling about from monastery to monastery, under pretence of devotion, but in reality to enjoy the hospitality of the clergy. The retainers of some particular prelates were often as numerous as those of the greatest lay-lords; and the retainers of all the clergy taken together were, perhaps, more numerous than those of all the lay-lords. There was always much more union among the clergy than among the lay-lords. The former were under a regular discipline and subordination to the papal authority. The latter were under no regular discipline or subordination, but almost always equally jealous of one another, and of the king. Though the tenants and retainers of the clergy, therefore, had both together been less numerous than those of the great lay-lords, and their tenants were probably much less numerous, yet their union would have rendered them more formidable. The hospitality and charity of the clergy, too, not only gave them the command of a great temporal force, but increased very much the weight of their spiritual weapons. Those virtues procured them the highest respect and veneration among all the inferior ranks of people, of whom many were constantly, and almost all occasionally, fed by them. Everything belonging or related to so popular an order, its possessions, its privileges, its doctrines, necessarily appeared sacred in the eyes of the common people; and every violation of them, whether real or pretended, the highest act of sacrilegious wickedness and profaneness. In this state of things, if the sovereign frequently found it difficult to resist the confederacy of a few of the great nobility, we cannot wonder that he should find it still more so to resist the united force of the clergy of his own dominions, supported by that of the clergy of all the neighbouring dominions. In such circumstances, the wonder is, not that he was sometimes obliged to yield, but that he ever was able to resist.

The privileges of the clergy in those ancient times (which to us, who live in the present times, appear the most absurd), their total exemption from the secular jurisdiction, for example, or what in England was called the benefit of clergy, were the natural, or rather the necessary, consequences of this state of things. How dangerous must it have been for the sovereign to attempt to punish a clergyman for any crime whatever, if his order were disposed to protect him, and to represent either the proof as insufficient for convicting so holy a man, or the punishment as too severe to be inflicted upon one whose person had been rendered sacred by religion? The sovereign could, in such circumstances, do no better than leave him to be tried by the ecclesiastical courts, who, for the honour of their own order, were interested to restrain, as much as possible, every member of it from committing enormous crimes, or even from giving occasion to such gross scandal as might disgust the minds of the people.

In the state in which things were, through the greater part of Europe, during the tenth, eleventh, twelfth, and thirteenth centuries, and for some time both before and after that period, the constitution of the church of Rome may be considered as the most formidable combination that ever was formed against the authority and security of civil government, as well as against the liberty, reason, and happiness of mankind, which can flourish only where civil government is able to protect them. In that constitution, the grossest delusions of superstition were supported in such a manner by the private interests of so great a number of people, as put them out of all danger from any assault of human reason; because, though human reason might, perhaps, have been able to unveil, even to the eyes of the common people, some of the delusions of superstition, it could never have dissolved the ties of private interest. Had this constitution been attacked by no other enemies but the feeble efforts of human reason, it must have endured for ever. But that immense and well-built fabric, which all the wisdom and virtue of man could never have shaken, much less have overturned, was, by the natural course of things, first weakened, and afterwards in part destroyed; and is now likely, in the course of a few centuries more, perhaps, to crumble into ruins altogether.

The gradual improvements of arts, manufactures, and commerce, the same causes which destroyed the power of the great barons, destroyed, in the same manner, through the greater part of Europe, the whole temporal manufactures, and commerce, the clergy, like the great barons, found something for which they could exchange their rude produce, and thereby discovered the means of spending their whole revenues upon their own persons, without giving any considerable share of them to other people. Their charity became gradually less extensive, their hospitality less liberal, or less profuse. Their retainers became consequently less numerous, and, by degrees, dwindled away altogether. The clergy, too, like the great barons, wished to get a better rent from their landed estates, in order to spend it, in the same manner, upon the gratification of their own private vanity and folly. But this increase of rent could be got only by granting leases to their tenants, who thereby became, in a great measure, independent of them. The ties of interest, which bound the inferior ranks of people to the clergy, were in this manner gradually broken and dissolved. They were even broken and dissolved sooner than those which bound the same ranks of people to the great barons; because the benefices of the church being, the greater part of them, much smaller than the estates of the great barons, the possessor of each benefice was much sooner able to spend the whole of its revenue upon his own person. During the greater part of the fourteenth and fifteenth centuries, the power of the great barons was, through the greater part of

Europe, in full vigour. But the temporal power of the clergy, the absolute command which they had once had over the great body of the people was very much decayed. The power of the church was, by that time, very nearly reduced, through the greater part of Europe, to what arose from their spiritual authority; and even that spiritual authority was much weakened, when it ceased to be supported by the charity and hospitality of the clergy. The inferior ranks of people no longer looked upon that order as they had done before; as the comforters of their distress, and the relievers of their indigence. On the contrary, they were provoked and disgusted by the vanity, luxury, and expense of the richer clergy, who appeared to spend upon their own pleasures what had always before been regarded as the patrimony of the poor.

In this situation of things, the sovereigns in the different states of Europe endeavoured to recover the influence which they had once had in the disposal of the great benefices of the church; by procuring to the deans and chapters of each diocese the restoration of their ancient right of electing the bishop; and to the monks of each abbacy that of electing the abbot. The re-establishing this ancient order was the object of several statutes enacted in England during the course of the fourteenth century, particularly of what is called the statute of provisors; and of the pragmatic sanction, established in France in the fifteenth century. In order to render the election valid, it was necessary that the sovereign should both consent to it before hand, and afterwards approve of the person elected; and though the election was still supposed to be free, he had, however all the indirect means which his situation necessarily afforded him, of influencing the clergy in his own dominions. Other regulations, of a similar tendency, were established in other parts of Europe. But the power of the pope, in the collation of the great benefices of the church, seems, before the reformation, to have been nowhere so effectually and so universally restrained as in France and England. The concordat afterwards, in the sixteenth century, gave to the kings of France the absolute right of presenting to all the great, or what are called the consistorial, benefices of the Gallican church.

Since the establishment of the pragmatic sanction and of the concordat, the clergy of France have in general shewn less respect to the decrees of the papal court, than the clergy of any other catholic country. In all the disputes which their sovereign has had with the pope, they have almost constantly taken part with the former. This independency of the clergy of France upon the court of Rome seems to be principally founded upon the pragmatic sanction and the concordat. In the earlier periods of the monarchy, the clergy of France appear to have been as much devoted to the pope as those of any other country. When Robert, the second prince of the Capetian race, was most unjustly excommunicated by the court of Rome, his own servants, it is said, threw the victuals which came from his table to the dogs, and refused to taste any thing themselves which had been polluted by the contact of a person in his situation. They were taught to do so, it may very safely be presumed, by the clergy of his own dominions.

The claim of collating to the great benefices of the church, a claim in defence of which the court of Rome had frequently shaken, and sometimes overturned, the thrones of some of the greatest sovereigns in Christendom, was in this manner either restrained or modified, or given up altogether, in many different parts of Europe, even before the time of the reformation. As the clergy had now less influence over the people, so the state had more influence over the clergy. The clergy, therefore, had both less power, and less inclination, to disturb the state.

The authority of the church of Rome was in this state of declension, when the disputes which gave birth to the reformation began in Germany, and soon spread themselves through every part of Europe. The new doctrines were everywhere received with a high degree of popular favour. They were propagated with all that enthusiastic zeal which commonly animates the spirit of party, when it attacks established authority. The teachers of those doctrines, though perhaps, in other respects, not more learned than many of the divines who defended the established church, seem in general to have been better acquainted with ecclesiastical history, and with the origin and progress of that system of opinions upon which the authority of the church was established; and they had thereby the advantage in almost every dispute. The austerity of their manners gave them authority with the common people, who contrasted the strict regularity of their conduct with the disorderly lives of the greater part of their own clergy. They possessed, too, in a much higher degree than their adversaries, all the arts of popularity and of gaining proselytes; arts which the lofty and dignified sons of the church had long neglected, as being to them in a great measure useless. The reason of the new doctrines recommended them to some, their novelty to many; the hatred and contempt of the established clergy to a still greater number: but the zealous, passionate, and fanatical, though frequently coarse and rustic eloquence, with which they were almost everywhere inculcated, recommended them to by far the greatest number.

The success of the new doctrines was almost everywhere so great, that the princes, who at that time happened to be on bad terms with the court of Rome, were, by means of them, easily enabled, in their own dominions, to overturn the church, which having lost the respect and veneration of the inferior ranks of people, could make scarce any resistance. The court of Rome had disobliged some of the smaller princes in the northern parts of Germany, whom it had probably considered as too insignificant to be worth the managing. They universally, therefore, established the reformation in their own dominions. The tyranny of Christiern II., and of Troll archbishop of Upsal, enabled Gustavus Vasa to expel them both from Sweden. The pope favoured the tyrant and the archbishop, and Gustavus Vasa found no difficulty in establishing the reformation in Sweden. Christiern II. was afterwards deposed from the throne of Denmark, where his conduct had rendered him as odious as in Sweden. The pope, however, was still disposed to favour him; and Frederic of Holstein, who had mounted the throne in his stead, revenged himself, by following the example of Gustavus Vasa. The magistrates of Berne and Zurich, who had no particular quarrel with the pope, established with great ease the reformation in their respective cantons, where just before some of the clergy had, by an imposture somewhat grosser than ordinary, rendered the whole order both odious and contemptible.

In this critical situation of its affairs the papal court was at sufficient pains to cultivate the friendship of the powerful sovereigns of France and Spain, of whom the latter was at that time emperor of Germany. With their assistance, it was enabled, though not without great difficulty, and much bloodshed, either to suppress altogether, or to obstruct very much, the progress of the reformation in their dominions. It was well enough inclined, too, to be complaisant to the king of England. But from the circumstances of the times, it could not be so without giving offence to a still greater sovereign, Charles V., king of Spain and emperor of Germany. Henry VIII., accordingly, though he did not embrace himself the greater part of the doctrines of the reformation, was yet enabled, by their general prevalence, to suppress all the monasteries, and to abolish the authority of the church of Rome in his dominions. That he should go so far, though he went no further, gave some satisfaction to the patrons of the reformation, who, having got possession of the government in the reign of his son and successor completed, without any difficulty, the work which Henry VIII. had begun.

In some countries, as in Scotland, where the government was weak, unpopular, and not very firmly established, the reformation was strong enough to overturn, not only the church, but the state likewise, for attempting to support the church.

Among the followers of the reformation, dispersed in all the different countries of Europe, there was no general tribunal, which, like that of the court of Rome, or an oecumenical council, could settle all disputes among them, and, with irresistible authority, prescribe to all of them the precise limits of orthodoxy. When the followers of the reformation in one country, therefore, happened to differ from their brethren in another, as they had no common judge to appeal to, the dispute could never be decided; and many such disputes arose among them. Those concerning the government of the church, and the right of conferring ecclesiastical benefices, were perhaps the most interesting to the peace and welfare of civil society. They gave birth, accordingly, to the two principal parties or sects among the followers of the reformation, the Lutheran and Calvinistic sects, the only sects among them, of which the doctrine and discipline have ever yet been established by law in any part of Europe.

The followers of Luther, together with what is called the church of England, preserved more or less of the episcopal government, established subordination among the clergy, gave the sovereign the disposal of all the bishoprics, and other consistorial benefices within his dominions, and thereby rendered him the real head of the church; and without depriving the bishop of the right of collating to the smaller benefices within his diocese, they, even to those benefices, not only admitted, but favoured the right of presentation, both in the sovereign and in all other lay patrons. This system of church government was, from the beginning, favourable to peace and good order, and to submission to the civil sovereign. It has never, accordingly, been the occasion of any tumult or civil commotion in any country in which it has once been established. The church of England, in particular, has always valued herself, with great reason, upon the unexceptionable loyalty of her principles. Under such a government, the clergy naturally endeavour to recommend themselves to the sovereign, to the court, and to the nobility and gentry of the country, by whose influence they chiefly expect to obtain preferment. They pay court to those patrons, sometimes, no doubt, by the vilest flattery and assentation; but frequently, too, by cultivating all those arts which best deserve, and which are therefore most likely to gain them, the esteem of people of rank and fortune; by their knowledge in all the different branches of useful and ornamental learning, by the decent liberality of their manners, by the social good humour of their conversation, and by their avowed contempt of those absurd and hypocritical austerities which fanatics inculcate and pretend to practise, in order to draw upon themselves the veneration, and upon the greater part of men of rank and fortune, who avow that they do not practise them, the abhorrence of the common people. Such a clergy, however, while they pay their court in this manner to the higher ranks of life, are very apt to neglect altogether the means of maintaining their influence and authority with the lower. They are listened to, esteemed, and respected by their superiors; but before their inferiors they are frequently incapable of defending, effectually, and to the conviction of such hearers, their own sober and moderate doctrines, against the most ignorant enthusiast who chooses to attack them.

The followers of Zuinglius, or more properly those of Calvin, on the contrary, bestowed upon the people of each parish, whenever the church became vacant, the right of electing their own pastor; and established, at the same time, the most perfect equality among the clergy. The former part of this institution, as long as it remained in vigour, seems to have been productive of nothing but disorder and confusion, and to have tended equally to corrupt the morals both of the clergy and of the people. The latter part seems never to have had any effects but what were perfectly agreeable.

As long as the people of each parish preserved the right of electing their own pastors, they acted almost always under the influence of the clergy, and generally of the most factious and fanatical of the order. The clergy, in order to preserve their influence in those popular elections, became, or affected to become, many of them, fanatics themselves, encouraged fanaticism among the people, and gave the preference almost always to the most fanatical candidate. So small a matter as the appointment of a parish priest, occasioned almost always a violent contest, not only in one parish, but in all the neighbouring parishes who seldom failed to take part in the quarrel. When the parish happened to be situated in a great city, it divided all the inhabitants into two parties; and when that city happened, either to constitute itself a little republic, or to be the head and capital of a little republic, as in the case with many of the considerable cities in Switzerland and Holland, every paltry dispute of this kind, over and above exasperating the animosity of all their other factions, threatened to leave behind it, both a new schism in the church, and a new faction in the state. In those small republics, therefore, the magistrate very soon found it necessary, for the sake of preserving the public peace, to assume to himself the right of presenting to all vacant benefices. In Scotland, the most extensive country in which this presbyterian form of church government has ever been established, the rights of patronage were in effect abolished by the act which established presbytery in the beginning of the reign of William III. That act, at least, put in the power of certain classes of people in each parish to purchase, for a very small price, the right of electing their own pastor. The constitution which this act established, was allowed to subsist for about two-and-twenty years, but was abolished by the 10th of queen Anne, ch.12, on account of the confusions and disorders which this more popular mode of election had almost everywhere occasioned. In so extensive a country as Scotland, however, a tumult in a remote parish was not so likely to give disturbance to government as in a smaller state. The 10th of queen Anne restored the rights of patronage. But though, in Scotland, the law gives the benefice, without any exception to the person presented by the patron; yet the church requires sometimes (for she has not in this respect been very uniform in her decisions) a certain concurrence of the people, before she will confer upon the presentee what is called the cure of souls, or the ecclesiastical jurisdiction in the parish. She sometimes, at least, from an affected concern for the peace of the parish, delays the settlement till this concurrence can be procured. The private tampering of some of the neighbouring clergy, sometimes to procure, but more frequently to prevent this concurrence, and the popular arts which they cultivate, in order to enable them upon such occasions to tamper more effectually, are perhaps the causes which principally keep up whatever remains of the old fanatical spirit, either in the clergy or in the people of Scotland.

The equality which the presbyterian form of church government establishes among the clergy, consists, first, in the equality of authority or ecclesiastical jurisdiction; and, secondly, in the equality of benefice. In all presbyterian churches, the equality of authority is perfect; that of benefice is not so. The difference, however, between one benefice and another, is seldom so considerable, as commonly to tempt the possessor even of the small one to pay court to his patron, by the vile arts of flattery and assentation, in order to get a better. In all the presbyterian churches, where the rights of patronage are thoroughly established, it is by nobler and better arts, that the established clergy in general endeavour to gain the favour of their superiors; by their learning, by the irreproachable regularity of their life, and by the faithful and diligent discharge of their duty. Their patrons even frequently complain of the independency of their spirit, which they are apt to construe into ingratitude for past favours, but which, at worse, perhaps, is seldom anymore than that indifference which naturally arises from the consciousness that no further favours of the kind are ever to be expected. There is scarce, perhaps, to be found anywhere in Europe, a more learned, decent, independent, and respectable set of men, than the greater part of the presbyterian clergy of Holland, Geneva, Switzerland, and Scotland.

Where the church benefices are all nearly equal, none of them can be very great; and this mediocrity of benefice, though it may be, no doubt, carried too far, has, however, some very agreeable effects. Nothing but exemplary morals can give dignity to a man of small fortune. The vices of levity and vanity necessarily render him ridiculous, and are, besides, almost as ruinous to him as they are to the common people. In his own conduct, therefore, he is obliged to follow that system of morals which the common people respect the most. He gains their esteem and affection, by that plan of life which his own interest and situation would lead him to follow. The common people look upon him with that kindness with which we naturally regard one who approaches somewhat to our own condition, but who, we think, ought to be in a higher. Their kindness naturally provokes his kindness. He becomes careful to instruct them, and attentive to assist and relieve them. He does not even despise the prejudices of people who are disposed to be so favourable to him, and never treats them with those contemptuous and arrogant airs, which we so often meet with in the proud dignitaries of opulent and well endowed churches. The presbyterian clergy, accordingly, have more influence over the minds of the common people, than perhaps the clergy of any other established church. It is, accordingly, in presbyterian countries only, that we ever find the common people converted, without persecution completely, and almost to a man, to the established church.

In countries where church benefices are, the greater part of them, very moderate, a chair in a university is generally a better establishment than a church benefice. The universities have, in this case, the picking and chusing of their members from all the churchmen of the country, who, in every country, constitute by far the most numerous class of men of letters. Where church benefices, on the contrary, are many of them very considerable, the church naturally draws from the universities the greater part of their eminent men of letters; who generally find some patron, who does himself honour by procuring them church preferment. In the former situation, we are likely to find the universities filled with the most eminent men of letters that are to be found in the country. In the latter, we are likely to find few eminent men among them, and those few among the youngest members of the society, who are likely, too, to be drained away from it, before they can have acquired experience and knowledge enough to be of much use to it. It is observed by Mr. de Voltaire, that father Porée, a jesuit of no great eminence in the republic of letters, was the only professor they had ever had in France, whose works were worth the reading. In a country which has produced so many eminent men of letters, it must appear somewhat singular, that scarce one of them should have been a professor in a university. The famous Cassendi was, in the beginning of his life, a professor in the university of Aix. Upon the first dawning of his genius, it was represented to him, that by going into the church he could easily find a much more quiet and comfortable subsistence, as well as a better situation for pursuing his studies; and he immediately followed the advice. The observation of Mr. de Voltaire may be applied, I believe, not only to France, but to all other Roman Catholic countries. We very rarely find in any of them an eminent man of letters, who is a professor in a university, except, perhaps, in the professions of law and physic; professions from which the church is not so likely to draw them. After the church of Rome, that of England is by far the richest and best endowed church in Christendom. In England, accordingly, the church is continually draining the universities of all their best and ablest members; and an old college tutor who is known and distinguished in Europe as an eminent man of letters, is as rarely to be found there as in any Roman catholic country, In Geneva, on the contrary, in the protestant cantons of Switzerland, in the protestant countries of Germany, in Holland, in Scotland, in Sweden, and Denmark, the most eminent men of letters whom those countries have produced, have, not all indeed, but the far greater part of them, been professors in universities. In those countries, the universities are continually draining the church of all its most eminent men of letters.

It may, perhaps, be worth while to remark, that, if we except the poets, a few orators, and a few historians, the far greater part of the other eminent men of letters, both of Greece and Rome, appear to have been either public or private teachers; generally either of philosophy or of rhetoric. This remark will be found to hold true, from the days of Lysias and Isocrates, of Plato and Aristotle, down to those of Plutarch and Epictetus, Suetonius, and Quintilian. To impose upon any man the necessity of teaching, year after year, in any particular branch of science seems in reality to be the most effectual method for rendering him completely master of it himself. By being obliged to go every year over the same ground, if he is good for any thing, he necessarily becomes, in a few years, well acquainted with every part of it, and if, upon any particular point, he should form too hasty an opinion one year, when he comes, in the course of his lectures to reconsider the same subject the year thereafter, he is very likely to correct it. As to be a teacher of science is certainly the natural employment of a mere man of letters; so is it likewise, perhaps, the education which is most likely to render him a man of solid learning and knowledge. The mediocrity of church benefices naturally tends to draw the greater part of men of letters in the country where it takes place, to the employment in which they can be the most useful to the public, and at the same time to give them the best education, perhaps, they are capable of receiving. It tends to render their learning both as solid as possible, and as useful as possible.

The revenue of every established church, such parts of it excepted as may arise from particular lands or manors, is a branch, it ought to be observed, of the general revenue of the state, which is thus diverted to a purpose very different from the defence of the state. The tithe, for example, is a real land tax, which puts it out of the power of the proprietors of land to contribute so largely towards the defence of the state as they otherwise might be able to do. The rent of land, however, is, according to some, the sole fund; and, according to others, the principal fund, from which, in all great monarchies, the exigencies of the state must be ultimately supplied. The more of this fund that is given to the church, the less, it is evident, can be spared to the state. It may be laid down as a certain maxim, that all other things being supposed equal, the richer the church, the poorer must necessarily be, either the sovereign on the one hand, or the people on the other; and, in all cases, the less able must the state be to defend itself. In several protestant countries, particularly in all the protestant cantons of Switzerland, the revenue which anciently belonged to the Roman catholic church, the tithes and church lands, has been found a fund sufficient, not only to afford competent salaries to the established clergy, but to defray, with little or no addition, all the other expenses of the state. The magistrates of the powerful canton of Berne, in particular, have accumulated, out of the savings from this fund, a very large sum, supposed to amount to several millions; part of which is deposited in a public treasure, and part is placed at interest in what are called the public funds of the different indebted nations of Europe; chiefly in those of France and Great Britain. What may be the amount of the whole expense which the church, either of Berne, or of any other protestant canton, costs the state, I do not pretend to know. By a very exact account it appears, that, in 1755, the whole revenue of the clergy of the church of Scotland, including their glebe or church lands, and the rent of their manses or dwelling-houses, estimated according to a reasonable valuation, amounted only to £68,514:1:5 1/12d. This very moderate revenue affords a decent subsistence to nine hundred and forty-four ministers. The whole expense of the church, including what is occasionally laid out for the building and reparation of churches, and of the manses of ministers, cannot well be supposed to exceed eighty or eighty-five thousand pounds a-year. The most opulent church in Christendom does not maintain better the uniformity of faith, the fervour of devotion, the spirit of order, regularity, and austere morals, in the great body of the people, than this very poorly endowed church of Scotland. All the good effects, both civil and religious, which an established church can be supposed to produce, are produced by it as completely as by any other. The greater part of the protestant churches of Switzerland, which, in general, are not better endowed than the church of Scotland, produce those effects in a still higher degree. In the greater part of the protestant cantons, there is not a single person to be found, who does not profess himself to be of the established church. If he professes himself to be of any other, indeed, the law obliges him to leave the canton. But so severe, or, rather, indeed, so oppressive a law, could never have been executed in such free countries, had not the diligence of the clergy beforehand converted to the established church the whole body of the people, with the exception of, perhaps, a few individuals only. In some parts of Switzerland, accordingly, where, from the accidental union of a protestant and Roman catholic country, the conversion has not been so complete, both religions are not only tolerated, but established by law.

The proper performance of every service seems to require, that its pay or recompence should be, as exactly as possible, proportioned to the nature of the service. If any service is very much underpaid, it is very apt to suffer by the meanness and incapacity of the greater part of those who are employed in it. If it is very much overpaid, it is apt to suffer, perhaps still more, by their negligence and idleness. A man of a large revenue, whatever may be his profession, thinks he ought to live like other men of large revenues; and to spend a great part of his time in festivity, in vanity, and in dissipation. But in a clergyman, this train of life not only consumes the time which ought to be employed in the duties of his function, but in the eyes of the common people, destroys almost entirely that sanctity of character, which can alone enable him to perform those duties with proper weight and authority.

PART IV. Of the Expense of supporting the Dignity of the Sovereign

Over and above the expenses necessary for enabling the sovereign to perform his several duties, a certain expense is requisite for the support of his dignity. This expense varies, both with the different periods of improvement, and with the different forms of government.

In an opulent and improved society, where all the different orders of people are growing every day more expensive in their houses, in their furniture, in their tables, in their dress, and in their equipage; it cannot well be expected that the sovereign should alone hold out against the fashion. He naturally, therefore, or rather necessarily, becomes more expensive in all those different articles too. His dignity even seems to require that he should become so.

As, in point of dignity, a monarch is more raised above his subjects than the chief magistrate of any republic is ever supposed to be above his fellow-citizens; so a greater expense is necessary for supporting that higher dignity. We naturally expect more splendour in the court of a king, than in the mansion-house of a doge or burgo-master.

CONCLUSION

The expense of defending the society, and that of supporting the dignity of the chief magistrate, are both laid out for the general benefit of the whole society. It is reasonable, therefore, that they should be defrayed by the general contribution of the whole society; all the different members contributing, as nearly as possible, in proportion to their respective abilities.

The expense of the administration of justice, too, may no doubt be considered as laid out for the benefit of the whole society. There is no impropriety, therefore, in its being defrayed by the general contribution of the whole society. The persons, however, who give occasion to this expense, are those who, by their injustice in one way or another, make it necessary to seek redress or protection from the courts of justice. The persons, again, most immediately benefited by this expense, are those whom the courts of justice either restore to their rights, or maintain in their rights. The expense of the administration of justice, therefore, may very properly be defrayed by the particular contribution of one or other, or both, of those two different sets of persons, according as different occasions may require, that is, by the fees of court. It cannot be necessary to have recourse to the general contribution of the whole society, except for the conviction of those criminals who have not themselves any estate or fund sufficient for paying those fees.

Those local or provincial expenses, of which the benefit is local or provincial (what is laid out, for example, upon the police of a particular town or district), ought to be defrayed by a local or provincial revenue, and ought to be no burden upon the general revenue of the society. It is unjust that the whole society should contribute towards an expense, of which the benefit is confined to a part of the society.

The expense of maintaining good roads and communications is, no doubt, beneficial to the whole society, and may, therefore, without any injustice, be defrayed by the general contributions of the whole society. This expense, however, is most immediately and directly beneficial to those who travel or carry goods from one place to another, and to those who consume such goods. The turnpike tolls in England, and the duties called peages in other countries, lay it altogether upon those two different sets of people, and thereby discharge the general revenue of the society from a very considerable burden.

The expense of the institutions for education and religious instruction, is likewise, no doubt, beneficial to the whole society, and may, therefore, without injustice, be defrayed by the general contribution of the whole society. This expense, however, might, perhaps, with equal propriety, and even with some advantage, be defrayed altogether by those who receive the immediate benefit of such education and instruction, or by the voluntary contribution of those who think they have occasion for either the one or the other.

When the institutions, or public works, which are beneficial to the whole society, either cannot be maintained altogether, or are not maintained altogether, by the contribution of such particular members of the society as are most immediately benefited by them; the deficiency must, in most cases, be made up by the general contribution of the whole society. The general revenue of the society, over and above defraying the expense of defending the society, and of supporting the dignity of the chief magistrate, must make up for the deficiency of many particular branches of revenue. The sources of this general or public revenue, I shall endeavour to explain in the following chapter.

CHAPTER II

OF THE SOURCES OF THE GENERAL OR PUBLIC REVENUE OF THE SOCIETY

The revenue which must defray, not only the expense of defending the society and of supporting the dignity of the chief magistrate, but all the other necessary expenses of government, for which the constitution of the state has not provided any particular revenue may be drawn, either, first, from some fund which peculiarly belongs to the sovereign or commonwealth, and which is independent of the revenue of the people; or, secondly, from the revenue of the people.

PART I. Of the Funds, or Sources, of Revenue, which may peculiarly belong to the Sovereign or Commonwealth

The funds, or sources, of revenue, which may peculiarly belong to the sovereign or commonwealth, must consist, either in stock, or in land.

The sovereign, like, any other owner of stock, may derive a revenue from it, either by employing it himself, or by lending it. His revenue is, in the one case, profit, in the other interest.

The revenue of a Tartar or Arabian chief consists in profit. It arises principally from the milk and increase of his own herds and flocks, of which he himself superintends the management, and is the principal shepherd or herdsman of his own horde or tribe. It is, however, in this earliest and rudest state of civil government only, that profit has ever made the principal part of the public revenue of a monarchical state.

Small republics have sometimes derived a considerable revenue from the profit of mercantile projects. The republic of Hamburgh is said to do so from the profits of a public wine-cellar and apothecary's shop. {See Memoires concernant les Droits et Impositions en Europe, tome i. page 73. This work was compiled by the order of the court, for the use of a commission employed for some years past in considering the proper means for reforming the finances of France. The account of the

French taxes, which takes up three volumes in quarto, may be regarded as perfectly authentic. That of those of other European nations was compiled from such information as the French ministers at the different courts could procure. It is much shorter, and probably not quite so exact as that of the French taxes.} That state cannot be very great, of which the sovereign has leisure to carry on the trade of a wine-merchant or an apothecary. The profit of a public bank has been a source of revenue to more considerable states. It has been so, not only to Hamburgh, but to Venice and Amsterdam. A revenue of this kind has even by some people been thought not below the attention of so great an empire as that of Great Britain. Reckoning the ordinary dividend of the bank of England at five and a-half per cent., and its capital at ten millions seven hundred and eighty thousand pounds, the neat annual profit, after paying the expense of management, must amount, it is said, to five hundred and ninety-two thousand nine hundred pounds. Government, it is pretended, could borrow this capital at three per cent. interest, and, by taking the management of the bank into its own hands, might make a clear profit of two hundred and sixty-nine thousand five hundred pounds a-year. The orderly, vigilant, and parsimonious administration of such aristocracies as those of Venice and Amsterdam, is extremely proper, it appears from experience, for the management of a mercantile project of this kind. But whether such a government as that of England, which, whatever may be its virtues, has never been famous for good economy; which, in time of peace, has generally conducted itself with the slothful and negligent profusion that is, perhaps, natural to monarchies; and, in time of war, has constantly acted with all the thoughtless extravagance that democracies are apt to fall into, could be safely trusted with the management of such a project, must at least be a good deal more doubtful.

The post-office is properly a mercantile project. The government advances the expense of establishing the different offices, and of buying or hiring the necessary horses or carriages, and is repaid, with a large profit, by the duties upon what is carried. It is, perhaps, the only mercantile project which has been successfully managed by, I believe, every sort of government. The capital to be advanced is not very considerable. There is no mystery in the business. The returns are not only certain but immediate.

Princes, however, have frequently engaged in many other mercantile projects, and have been willing, like private persons, to mend their fortunes, by becoming adventurers in the common branches of trade. They have scarce ever succeeded. The profusion with which the affairs of princes are always managed, renders it almost impossible that they should. The agents of a prince regard the wealth of their master as inexhaustible; are careless at what price they buy, are careless at what price they sell, are careless at what expense they transport his goods from one place to another. Those agents frequently live with the profusion of princes; and sometimes, too, in spite of that profusion, and by a proper method of making up their accounts, acquire the fortunes of princes. It was thus, as we are told by Machiavel, that the agents of Lorenzo of Medicis, not a prince of mean abilities, carried on his trade. The republic of Florence was several times obliged to pay the debt into which their extravagance had involved him. He found it convenient, accordingly to give up the business of merchant, the business to which his family had originally owed their fortune, and, in the latter part of his life, to employ both what remained of that fortune, and the revenue of the state, of which he had the disposal, in projects and expenses more suitable to his station.

No two characters seem more inconsistent than those of trader and sovereign. If the trading spirit of the English East India company renders them very bad sovereigns, the spirit of sovereignty seems to have rendered them equally bad traders. While they were traders only, they managed their trade successfully, and were able to pay from their profits a moderate dividend to the proprietors of their stock. Since they became sovereigns, with a revenue which, it is said, was originally more than three millions sterling, they have been obliged to beg the ordinary assistance of government, in order to avoid immediate bankruptcy. In their former situation, their servants in India considered themselves as the clerks of merchants; in their present situation, those servants consider themselves as the ministers of sovereigns.

A state may sometimes derive some part of its public revenue from the interest of money, as well as from the profits of stock. If it has amassed a treasure, it may lend a part of that treasure, either to foreign states, or to its own subjects.

The canton of Berne derives a considerable revenue by lending a part of its treasure to foreign states, that is, by placing it in the public funds of the different indebted nations of Europe, chiefly in those of France and England. The security of this revenue must depend, first, upon the security of the funds in which it is placed, or upon the good faith of the government which has the management of them; and, secondly, upon the certainty or probability of the continuance of peace with the debtor nation. In the case of a war, the very first act of hostility on the part of the debtor nation might be the forfeiture of the funds of its credit. This policy of lending money to foreign states is, so far as I know peculiar to the canton of Berne.

The city of Hamburgh {See Memoire concernant les Droites et Impositions en Europe tome i p. 73.} has established a sort of public pawn-shop, which lends money to the subjects of the state, upon pledges, at six per cent. interest. This pawn-shop, or lombard, as it is called, affords a revenue, it is pretended, to the state, of a hundred and fifty thousand crowns, which, at four and sixpence the crown, amounts to £33,750 sterling.

The government of Pennsylvania, without amassing any treasure, invented a method of lending, not money, indeed, but what is equivalent to money, to its subjects. By advancing to private people, at interest, and upon land security to double the value, paper bills of credit, to be redeemed fifteen years after their date; and, in the mean time, made transferable from hand to hand, like banknotes, and declared by act of assembly to be a legal tender in all payments from one inhabitant of the province to another, it raised a moderate revenue, which went a considerable way towards defraying an annual expense of about £4,500, the whole ordinary expense of that frugal and orderly government. The success of an expedient of this kind must have depended upon three different circumstances: first, upon the demand for some other instrument of commerce, besides gold and silver money, or upon the demand for such a quantity of consumable stock as could not be had without sending abroad the greater part of their gold and silver money, in order to purchase it; secondly, upon the good credit of the government which made use of this expedient; and, thirdly, upon the moderation with which it was used, the whole value of the paper bills of credit never exceeding that of the gold and silver money which would have been necessary for carrying on their circulation, had there been no paper bills of credit. The same expedient was, upon different occasions, adopted by several other American colonies; but, from want of this moderation, it produced, in the greater part of them, much more disorder than conveniency.

The unstable and perishable nature of stock and credit, however, renders them unfit to be trusted to as the principal funds of that sure, steady, and permanent revenue, which can alone give security and dignity to government. The government of no great nation, that was advanced beyond the shepherd state, seems ever to have derived the greater part of its public revenue from such sources.

Land is a fund of more stable and permanent nature; and the rent of public lands, accordingly, has been the principal source of the public revenue of many a great nation that was much advanced beyond the shepherd state. From the produce or rent of the public lands, the ancient republics of Greece and Italy derived for a long time the greater part of that revenue which defrayed the necessary expenses of the commonwealth. The rent of the crown lands constituted for a long time the greater part of the revenue of the ancient sovereigns of Europe.

War, and the preparation for war, are the two circumstances which, in modern times, occasion the greater part of the necessary expense or all great states. But in the ancient republics of Greece and Italy, every citizen was a soldier, and both served, and prepared himself for service, at his own expense. Neither of those two circumstances, therefore, could occasion any very considerable expense to the state. The rent of a very moderate landed estate might be fully sufficient for defraying all the other necessary expenses of government.

In the ancient monarchies of Europe, the manners and customs of the time sufficiently prepared the great body of the people for war; and when they took the field, they were, by the condition of their feudal tenures, to be maintained either at their own expense, or at that of their immediate lords, without bringing any new charge upon the sovereign. The other expenses of government were, the greater part of them, very moderate. The administration of justice, it has been shewn, instead of being a cause of expense was a source of revenue. The labour of the country people, for three days before, and for three days after, harvest, was thought a fund sufficient for making and maintaining all the bridges, highways, and other public works, which the commerce of the country was supposed to require. In those days the principal expense of the sovereign seems to have consisted in the maintenance of his own family and household. The officers of his household, accordingly, were then the great officers of state. The lord treasurer received his rents. The lord steward and lord chamberlain looked after the expense of his family. The care of his stables was committed to the lord constable and the lord marshal. His houses were all built in the form of castles, and seem to have been the principal fortresses which he possessed. The keepers of those houses or castles might be considered as a sort of military governors. They seem to have been the only military officers whom it was necessary to maintain in time of peace. In these circumstances, the rent of a great landed estate might, upon ordinary occasions, very well defray all the necessary expenses of government.

In the present state of the greater part of the civilized monarchies of Europe, the rent of all the lands in the country, managed as they probably would be, if they all belonged to one proprietor, would scarce, perhaps, amount to the ordinary revenue which they levy upon the people even in peaceable times. The ordinary revenue of Great Britain, for example, including not only what is necessary for defraying the current expense of the year, but for paying the interest of the public debts, and for sinking a part of the capital of those debts, amounts to upwards of ten millions a-year. But the land tax, at four shillings in the pound, falls short of two millions a-year. This land tax, as it is called however, is supposed to be one-fifth, not only of the rent of all the land, but of that of all the houses, and of the interest of all the capital stock of Great Britain, that part of it only excepted which is either lent to the public, or employed as farming stock in the cultivation of land. A very considerable part of the produce of this tax arises from the rent of houses and the interest of capital stock. The land tax of the city of London, for example, at four shillings in the pound, amounts to £123,399: 6: 7; that of the city of Westminster to £63,092: 1: 5; that of the palaces of Whitehall and St. James's, to £30,754: 6: 3. A certain proportion of the land tax is, in the same manner, assessed upon all the other cities and towns corporate in the kingdom; and arises almost altogether, either from the rent of houses, or from what is supposed to be the interest of trading and capital stock. According to the estimation, therefore, by which Great Britain is rated to the land tax, the whole mass of revenue arising from the rent of all the lands, from that of all the houses, and from the interest of all the capital stock, that part of it only excepted which is either lent to the public, or employed in the cultivation of land, does not exceed ten millions sterling a-year, the ordinary revenue which government levies upon the people, even in peaceable times. The estimation by which Great Britain is rated to the land tax is, no doubt, taking the whole kingdom at an average, very much below the real value; though in several particular counties and districts it is said to be nearly equal to that value. The rent of the lands alone, exclusive of that of houses and of the interest of stock, has by many people been estimated at twenty millions; an estimation made in a great measure at random, and which, I apprehend, is as likely to be above as below the truth. But if the lands of Great Britain, in the present state of their cultivation, do not afford a rent of more than twenty millions a-year, they could not well afford the half, most probably not the fourth part of that rent, if they all belonged to a single proprietor, and were put under the negligent, expensive, and oppressive management of his factors and agents. The crown lands of Great Britain do not at present afford the fourth part of the rent which could probably be drawn from them if they were the property of private persons. If the crown lands were more extensive, it is probable, they would be still worse managed.

The revenue which the great body of the people derives from land is, in proportion, not to the rent, but to the produce of the land. The whole annual produce of the land of every country, if we except what is reserved for seed, is either annually consumed by the great body of the people, or exchanged for something else that is consumed by them. Whatever keeps down the produce of the land below what it would otherwise rise to, keeps down the revenue of the great body of the people, still more than it does that of the proprietors of land. The rent of land, that portion of the produce which belongs to the proprietors, is scarce anywhere in Great Britain supposed to be more than a third part of the whole produce. If the land which, in one state of cultivation, affords a revenue of ten millions sterling a-year, would in another afford a rent of twenty millions; the rent being, in both cases, supposed a third part of the produce, the revenue of the proprietors would be less than it otherwise might be, by ten millions a-year only; but the revenue of the great body of the people would be less than it otherwise might be, by thirty millions a-year, deducting only what would be necessary for seed. The population of the country would be less by the number of people which thirty millions a-year, deducting always the seed, could maintain, according to the particular mode of living, and expense which might take place in the different ranks of men, among whom the remainder was distributed.

Though there is not at present in Europe, any civilized state of any kind which derives the greater part of its public revenue from the rent of lands which are the property of the state; yet, in all the great monarchies of Europe, there are still many large tracts of land which belong to the crown. They are generally forest, and sometimes forests where, after travelling several miles, you will scarce find a single tree; a mere waste and loss of country, in respect both of produce and population. In every great monarchy of Europe, the sale of the crown lands would produce a very large sum of money, which, if applied to the payment of the public debts, would deliver from mortgage a much greater revenue than any which those lands have ever afforded to the crown. In countries where lands, improved and cultivated very highly, and yielding, at the time of sale, as great a rent as can easily be got from them, commonly sell at thirty years purchase; the unimproved, uncultivated, and low-rented crown lands, might well be expected to sell at forty, fifty, or sixty years purchase. The crown might immediately enjoy the revenue which this great price would redeem from mortgage. In the course of a few years, it would probably enjoy another revenue. When the crown lands had become private property, they would, in the course of a few years, become well improved and well cultivated. The increase of their produce would increase the population of the country, by augmenting the revenue and consumption of the people. But the revenue which the crown derives from the duties or custom and excise, would necessarily increase with the revenue and consumption of the people.

The revenue which, in any civilized monarchy, the crown derives from the crown lands, though it appears to cost nothing to individuals, in reality costs more to the society than perhaps any other equal revenue which the crown enjoys. It would, in all cases, be for the interest of the society, to replace this revenue to the crown by some other equal revenue, and to divide the lands among the people, which could not well be done better, perhaps, than by exposing them to public sale.

Lands, for the purposes of pleasure and magnificence, parks, gardens, public walks, etc. possessions which are everywhere considered as causes of expense, not as sources of revenue, seem to be the only lands which, in a great and civilized monarchy, ought to belong to the crown.

Public stock and public lands, therefore, the two sources of revenue which may peculiarly belong to the sovereign or commonwealth, being both improper and insufficient funds for defraying the necessary expense of any great and civilized state; it remains that this expense must, the greater part of it, be defrayed by taxes of one kind or another; the people contributing a part of their own private revenue, in order to make up a public revenue to the sovereign or commonwealth.

PART II. Of Taxes

The private revenue of individuals, it has been shown in the first book of this Inquiry, arises, ultimately from three different sources; rent, profit, and wages. Every tax must finally be paid from some one or other of those three different sources of revenue, or from all of them indifferently. I shall endeavour to give the best account I can, first, of those taxes which, it is intended should fall upon rent; secondly, of those which, it is intended should fall upon profit; thirdly, of those which, it is intended should fall upon wages; and fourthly, of those which, it is intended should fall indifferently upon all those three different sources of private revenue. The particular consideration of each of these four different sorts of taxes will divide the second part of the present chapter into four articles, three of which will require several other subdivisions. Many of these taxes, it will appear from the following review, are not finally paid from the fund, or source of revenue, upon which it is intended they should fall.

Before I enter upon the examination of particular taxes, it is necessary to premise the four following maxims with regard to taxes in general.

1. The subjects of every state ought to contribute towards the support of the government, as nearly as possible, in proportion to their respective abilities; that is, in proportion to the revenue which they respectively enjoy under the protection of the state. The expense of government to the individuals of a great nation, is like the expense of management to the joint tenants of a great estate, who are all obliged to contribute in proportion to their respective interests in the estate. In the observation or neglect of this maxim, consists what is called the equality or inequality of taxation. Every tax, it must be observed once for all, which falls finally upon one only of the three sorts of revenue above mentioned, is necessarily unequal, in so far as it does not affect the other two. In the following examination of different taxes, I shall seldom take much farther notice of this sort of inequality; but shall, in most cases, confine my observations to that inequality which is occasioned by a particular tax falling unequally upon that particular sort of private revenue which is affected by it.

2. The tax which each individual is bound to pay, ought to be certain and not arbitrary. The time of payment, the manner of payment, the quantity to be paid, ought all to be clear and plain to the contributor, and to every other person. Where it is otherwise, every person subject to the tax is put

more or less in the power of the tax-gatherer, who can either aggravate the tax upon any obnoxious contributor, or extort, by the terror of such aggravation, some present or perquisite to himself. The uncertainty of taxation encourages the insolence, and favours the corruption, of an order of men who are naturally unpopular, even where they are neither insolent nor corrupt. The certainty of what each individual ought to pay is, in taxation, a matter of so great importance, that a very considerable degree of inequality, it appears, I believe, from the experience of all nations, is not near so great an evil as a very small degree of uncertainty.

3. Every tax ought to be levied at the time, or in the manner, in which it is most likely to be convenient for the contributor to pay it. A tax upon the rent of land or of houses, payable at the same term at which such rents are usually paid, is levied at the time when it is most likely to be convenient for the contributor to pay; or when he is most likely to have wherewithall to pay. Taxes upon such consumable goods as are articles of luxury, are all finally paid by the consumer, and generally in a manner that is very convenient for him. He pays them by little and little, as he has occasion to buy the goods. As he is at liberty too, either to buy or not to buy, as he pleases, it must be his own fault if he ever suffers any considerable inconveniency from such taxes.

4. Every tax ought to be so contrived, as both to take out and to keep out of the pockets of the people as little as possible, over and above what it brings into the public treasury of the state. A tax may either take out or keep out of the pockets of the people a great deal more than it brings into the public treasury, in the four following ways. First, the levying of it may require a great number of officers, whose salaries may eat up the greater part of the produce of the tax, and whose perquisites may impose another additional tax upon the people. Secondly, it may obstruct the industry of the people, and discourage them from applying to certain branches of business which might give maintenance and employment to great multitudes. While it obliges the people to pay, it may thus diminish, or perhaps destroy, some of the funds which might enable them more easily to do so. Thirdly, by the forfeitures and other penalties which those unfortunate individuals incur, who attempt unsuccessfully to evade the tax, it may frequently ruin them, and thereby put an end to the benefit which the community might have received from the employment of their capitals. An injudicious tax offers a great temptation to smuggling. But the penalties of smuggling must arise in proportion to the temptation.

The law, contrary to all the ordinary principles of justice, first creates the temptation, and then punishes those who yield to it; and it commonly enhances the punishment, too, in proportion to the very circumstance which ought certainly to alleviate it, the temptation to commit the crime. {See Sketches of the History of Man page 474, and Seq.} Fourthly, by subjecting the people to the frequent visits and the odious examination of the tax-gatherers, it may expose them to much unnecessary trouble, vexation, and oppression; and though vexation is not, strictly speaking, expense, it is certainly equivalent to the expense at which every man would be willing to redeem himself from it. It is in some one or other of these four different ways, that taxes are frequently so much more burdensome to the people than they are beneficial to the sovereign.

The evident justice and utility of the foregoing maxims have recommended them, more or less, to the attention of all nations. All nations have endeavoured, to the best of their judgment, to render their taxes as equal as they could contrive; as certain, as convenient to the contributor, both the time and the mode of payment, and in proportion to the revenue which they brought to the prince, as little burdensome to the people. The following short review of some of the principal taxes which have taken place in different ages and countries, will show, that the endeavours of all nations have not in this respect been equally successful.

ARTICLE I.—Taxes upon Rent—Taxes upon the Rent of Land

A tax upon the rent of land may either be imposed according to a certain canon, every district being valued at a curtain rent, which valuation is not afterwards to be altered; or it may be imposed in such a manner, as to vary with every variation in the real rent of the land, and to rise or fall with the improvement or declension of its cultivation.

A land tax which, like that of Great Britain, is assessed upon each district according to a certain invariable canon, though it should be equal at the time of its first establishment, necessarily becomes unequal in process of time, according to the unequal degrees of improvement or neglect in the cultivation of the different parts of the country. In England, the valuation, according to which the different counties and parishes were assessed to the land tax by the 4th of William and Mary, was very unequal even at its first establishment. This tax, therefore, so far offends against the first of the four maxims above mentioned. It is perfectly agreeable to the other three. It is perfectly certain. The time of payment for the tax, being the same as that for the rent, is as convenient as it can be to the contributor. Though the landlord is, in all cases, the real contributor, the tax is commonly advanced by the tenant, to whom the landlord is obliged to allow it in the payment of the rent. This tax is levied by a much smaller number of officers than any other which affords nearly the same revenue. As the tax upon each district does not rise with the rise of the rent, the sovereign does not share in the profits of the landlord's improvements. Those improvements sometimes contribute, indeed, to the discharge of the other landlords of the district. But the aggravation of the tax, which this may sometimes occasion upon a particular estate, is always so very small, that it never can discourage those improvements, nor keep down the produce of the land below what it would otherwise rise to. As it has no tendency to diminish the quantity, it can have none to raise the price of that produce. It does not obstruct the industry of the people; it subjects the landlord to no other inconveniency besides the unavoidable one of paying the tax. The advantage, however, which the land-lord has derived from the invariable constancy of the valuation, by which all the lands of Great Britain are rated to the land-tax, has been principally owing to some circumstances altogether extraneous to the nature of the tax.

It has been owing in part, to the great prosperity of almost every part of the country, the rents of almost all the estates of Great Britain having, since the time when this valuation was first established, been continually rising, and scarce any of them having fallen. The landlords, therefore, have almost all gained the difference between the tax which they would have paid, according to the present rent of their estates, and that which they actually pay according to the ancient valuation. Had the state of the country been different, had rents been gradually falling in consequence of the declension of cultivation, the landlords would almost all have lost this difference. In the state of things which has happened to take place since the revolution, the constancy of the valuation has been advantageous to the landlord and hurtful to the sovereign. In a different state of things it might have been advantageous to the sovereign and hurtful to the landlord.

As the tax is made payable in money, so the valuation of the land is expressed in money. Since the establishment of this valuation, the value of silver has been pretty uniform, and there has been no alteration in the standard of the coin, either as to weight or fineness. Had silver risen considerably in its value, as it seems to have done in the course of the two centuries which preceded the discovery of the mines of America, the constancy of the valuation might have proved very oppressive to the landlord. Had silver fallen considerably in its value, as it certainly did for about a century at least after the discovery of those mines, the same constancy of valuation would have reduced very much this branch of the revenue of the sovereign. Had any considerable alteration been made in the standard of the money, either by sinking the same quantity of silver to a lower denomination, or by raising it to a higher; had an ounce of silver, for example, instead of being coined into five shillings and two pence, been coined either into pieces which bore so low a denomination as two shillings and seven pence, or into pieces which bore so high a one as ten shillings and four pence, it would, in the one case, have hurt the revenue of the proprietor, in the other that of the sovereign.

In circumstances, therefore, somewhat different from those which have actually taken place, this constancy of valuation might have been a very great inconveniency, either to the contributors or to the commonwealth. In the course of ages, such circumstances, however, must at some time or other happen. But though empires, like all the other works of men, have all hitherto proved mortal, yet every empire aims at immortality. Every constitution, therefore, which it is meant should be as permanent as the empire itself, ought to be convenient, not in certain circumstances only, but in all circumstances; or ought to be suited, not to those circumstances which are transitory, occasional, or accidental, but to those which are necessary, and therefore always the same.

A tax upon the rent of land, which varies with every variation of the rent, or which rises and falls according to the improvement or neglect of cultivation, is recommended by that sect of men of letters in France, who call themselves the economists, as the most equitable of all taxes. All taxes, they pretend, fall ultimately upon the rent of land, and ought, therefore, to be imposed equally upon the fund which must finally pay them. That all taxes ought to fall as equally as possible upon the fund which must finally pay them, is certainly true. But without entering into the disagreeable discussion of the metaphysical arguments by which they support their very ingenious theory, it will sufficiently appear, from the following review, what are the taxes which fall finally upon the rent of the land, and what are those which fall finally upon some other fund.

In the Venetian territory, all the arable lands which are given in lease to farmers are taxed at a tenth of the rent. {Memoires concernant les Droits, p. 240, 241.} The leases are recorded in a public register, which is kept by the officers of revenue in each province or district. When the proprietor cultivates his own lands, they are valued according to an equitable estimation, and he is allowed a deduction of one-fifth of the tax; so that for such land he pays only eight instead of ten per cent. of the supposed rent.

A land-tax of this kind is certainly more equal than the land-tax of England. It might not, perhaps, be altogether so certain, and the assessment of the tax might frequently occasion a good deal more trouble to the landlord. It might, too, be a good deal more expensive in the levying.

Such a system of administration, however, might, perhaps, be contrived, as would in a great measure both prevent this uncertainty, and moderate this expense.

The landlord and tenant, for example, might jointly be obliged to record their lease in a public register. Proper penalties might be enacted against concealing or misrepresenting any of the conditions; and if part of those penalties were to be paid to either of the two parties who informed against and convicted the other of such concealment or misrepresentation, it would effectually deter them from combining together in order to defraud the public revenue. All the conditions of the lease might be sufficiently known from such a record.

Some landlords, instead of raising the rent, take a fine for the renewal of the lease. This practice is, in most cases, the expedient of a spendthrift, who, for a sum of ready money sells a future revenue of much greater value. It is, in most cases, therefore, hurtful to the landlord; it is frequently hurtful to the tenant; and it is always hurtful to the community. It frequently takes from the tenant so great a part of his capital, and thereby diminishes so much his ability to cultivate the land, that he finds it more difficult to pay a small rent than it would otherwise have been to pay a great one. Whatever diminishes his ability to cultivate, necessarily keeps down, below what it would otherwise have been, the most important part of the revenue of the community. By rendering the tax upon such fines a good deal heavier than upon the ordinary rent, this hurtful practice might be discouraged, to the no small advantage of all the different parties concerned, of the landlord, of the tenant, of the sovereign, and of the whole community.

Some leases prescribe to the tenant a certain mode of cultivation, and a certain succession of crops, during the whole continuance of the lease. This condition, which is generally the effect of the landlord's conceit of his own superior knowledge (a conceit in most cases very ill-founded), ought always to be considered as an additional rent, as a rent in service, instead of a rent in money. In order to discourage the practice, which is generally a foolish one, this species of rent might be valued rather high, and consequently taxed somewhat higher than common money-rents.

Some landlords, instead of a rent in money, require a rent in kind, in corn, cattle, poultry, wine, oil, etc.; others, again, require a rent in service. Such rents are always more hurtful to the tenant than beneficial to the landlord. They either take more, or keep more out of the pocket of the former, than they put into that of the latter. In every country where they take place, the tenants are poor and beggarly, pretty much according to the degree in which they take place. By valuing, in the same manner, such rents rather high, and consequently taxing them somewhat higher than common money-rents, a practice which is hurtful to the whole community, might, perhaps, be sufficiently discouraged.

When the landlord chose to occupy himself a part of his own lands, the rent might be valued according to an equitable arbitration of the farmers and landlords in the neighbourhood, and a moderate abatement of the tax might be granted to him, in the same manner as in the Venetian territory, provided the rent of the lands which he occupied did not exceed a certain sum. It is of importance that the landlord should be encouraged to cultivate a part of his own land. His capital is generally greater than that of the tenant, and, with less skill, he can frequently raise a greater produce. The landlord can afford to try experiments, and is generally disposed to do so. His unsuccessful experiments occasion only a moderate loss to himself. His successful ones contribute to the improvement and better cultivation of the whole country. It might be of importance, however, that the abatement of the tax should encourage him to cultivate to a certain extent only. If the landlords should, the greater part of them, be tempted to farm the whole of their own lands, the country (instead of sober and industrious tenants, who are bound by their own interest to cultivate as well as their capital and skill will allow them) would be filled with idle and profligate bailiffs, whose abusive management would soon degrade the cultivation, and reduce the annual produce of the land, to the diminution, not only of the revenue of their masters, but of the most important part of that of the whole society.

Such a system of administration might, perhaps, free a tax of this kind from any degree of uncertainty, which could occasion either oppression or inconveniency to the contributor; and might, at the same time, serve to introduce into the common management of land such a plan of policy as might contribute a good deal to the general improvement and good cultivation of the country.

The expense of levying a land-tax, which varied with every variation of the rent, would, no doubt, be somewhat greater than that of levying one which was always rated according to a fixed valuation. Some additional expense would necessarily be incurred, both by the different register-offices which it would be proper to establish in the different districts of the country, and by the different valuations which might occasionally be made of the lands which the proprietor chose to occupy himself. The expense of all this, however, might be very moderate, and much below what is incurred in the levying of many other taxes, which afford a very inconsiderable revenue in comparison of what might easily be drawn from a tax of this kind.

The discouragement which a variable land-tax of this kind might give to the improvement of land, seems to be the most important objection which can be made to it. The landlord would certainly be less disposed to improve, when the sovereign, who contributed nothing to the expense, was to share in the profit of the improvement. Even this objection might, perhaps, be obviated, by allowing the landlord, before he began his improvement, to ascertain, in conjunction with the officers of revenue, the actual value of his lands, according to the equitable arbitration of a certain number of landlords and farmers in the neighbourhood, equally chosen by both parties: and by rating him, according to this valuation, for such a number of years as might be fully sufficient for his complete indemnification. To draw the attention of the sovereign towards the improvement of the land, from a regard to the increase of his own revenue, is one or the principal advantages proposed by this species of land-tax. The term, therefore, allowed, for the indemnification of the landlord, ought not to be a great deal longer than what was necessary for that purpose, lest the remoteness of the interest should discourage too much this attention. It had better, however, be somewhat too long, than in any respect too short. No incitement to the attention of the sovereign can ever counterbalance the smallest discouragement to that of the landlord. The attention of the sovereign can be, at best, but a very general and vague consideration of what is likely to contribute to the better cultivation of the greater part of his dominions. The attention of the landlord is a particular and minute consideration of what is likely to be the most advantageous application of every inch of ground upon his estate. The principal attention of the sovereign ought to be, to encourage, by every means in his power, the attention both of the landlord and of the farmer, by allowing both to pursue their own interest in their own way, and according to their own judgment; by giving to both the most perfect security that they shall enjoy the full recompence of their own industry; and by procuring to both the most extensive market for every part of their produce, in consequence of establishing the easiest and safest communications, both by land and by water, through every part of his own dominions, as well as the most unbounded freedom of exportation to the dominions of all other princes.

If, by such a system of administration, a tax of this kind could be so managed as to give, not only no discouragement, but, on the contrary, some encouragement to the improvement or land, it does not appear likely to occasion any other inconveniency to the landlord, except always the unavoidable one of being obliged to pay the tax. In all the variations of the state of the society, in the improvement and in the declension of agriculture; in all the variations in the value of silver, and in all those in the standard of the coin, a tax of this kind would, of its own accord, and without any attention of government, readily suit itself to the actual situation of things, and would be equally just and equitable in all those different changes. It would, therefore, be much more proper to be established as a perpetual and unalterable regulation, or as what is called a fundamental law of the commonwealth, than any tax which was always to be levied according to a certain valuation.

Some states, instead of the simple and obvious expedient of a register of leases, have had recourse to the laborious and expensive one of an actual survey and valuation of all the lands in the country. They have suspected, probably, that the lessor and lessee, in order to defraud the public revenue, might combine to conceal the real terms of the lease. Doomsday-book seems to have been the result of a very accurate survey of this kind.

In the ancient dominions of the king of Prussia, the land-tax is assessed according to an actual survey and valuation, which is reviewed and altered from time to time. {Memoires concernant les Droits, etc. tom, i. p. 114, 115, 116, etc.} According to that valuation, the lay proprietors pay from twenty to twenty-five per cent. of their revenue; ecclesiastics from forty to forty-five per cent. The survey and valuation of Silesia was made by order of the present king, it is said, with great accuracy. According to that valuation, the lands belonging to the bishop of Breslaw are taxed at twenty-five per cent. of their rent. The other revenues of the ecclesiastics of both religions at fifty per cent. The commanderies of the Teutonic order, and of that of Malta, at forty per cent. Lands held by a noble tenure, at thirty-eight and one-third per cent. Lands held by a base tenure, at thirty-five and one-third per cent.

The survey and valuation of Bohemia is said to have been the work of more than a hundred years. It was not perfected till after the peace of 1748, by the orders of the present empress queen. {Id. tom i. p.85, 84.} The survey of the duchy of Milan, which was begun in the time of Charles VI., was not perfected till after 1760. It is esteemed one of the most accurate that has ever been made. The survey of Savoy and Piedmont was executed under the orders of the late king of Sardinia. {Id. p. 280, etc.; also p, 287. etc. to 316.}

In the dominions of the king of Prussia, the revenue of the church is taxed much higher than that of lay proprietors. The revenue of the church is, the greater part of it, a burden upon the rent of land. It seldom happens that any part of it is applied towards the improvement of land; or is so employed as to contribute, in any respect, towards increasing the revenue of the great body of the people. His Prussian majesty had probably, upon that account, thought it reasonable that it should contribute a good deal more towards relieving the exigencies of the state. In some countries, the lands of the church are exempted from all taxes. In others, they are taxed more lightly than other lands. In the duchy of Milan, the lands which the church possessed before 1575, are rated to the tax at a third only or their value.

In Silesia, lands held by a noble tenure are taxed three per cent. higher than those held by a base tenure. The honours and privileges of different kinds annexed to the former, his Prussian majesty had probably imagined, would sufficiently compensate to the proprietor a small aggravation of the tax; while, at the same time, the humiliating inferiority of the latter would be in some measure alleviated, by being taxed somewhat more lightly. In other countries, the system of taxation, instead of alleviating, aggravates this inequality. In the dominions of the king of Sardinia, and in those provinces of France which are subject to what is called the real or predial taille, the tax falls altogether upon the lands held by a base tenure. Those held by a noble one are exempted.

A land tax assessed according to a general survey and valuation, how equal soever it may be at first, must, in the course of a very moderate period of time, become unequal. To prevent its becoming so would require the continual and painful attention of government to all the variations in the state and produce of every different farm in the country. The governments of Prussia, of Bohemia, of Sardinia, and of the duchy of Milan, actually exert an attention of this kind; an attention so unsuitable to the nature of government, that it is not likely to be of long continuance, and which, if it is continued, will probably, in the long-run, occasion much more trouble and vexation than it can possibly bring relief to the contributors.

In 1666, the generality of Montauban was assessed to the real or predial taille, according, it is said, to a very exact survey and valuation. {Memoires concernant les Droits, etc. tom. ii p. 139, etc.} By 1727, this assessment had become altogether unequal. In order to remedy this inconveniency, government has found no better expedient, than to impose upon the whole generality an additional tax of a hundred and twenty thousand livres. This additional tax is rated upon all the different districts subject to the taille according to the old assessment. But it is levied only upon those which, in the actual state of things, are by that assessment under-taxed; and it is applied to the relief of those which, by the same assessment, are over-taxed. Two districts, for example, one of which ought, in the actual state of things, to be taxed at nine hundred, the other at eleven hundred livres, are, by the old assessment, both taxed at a thousand livres. Both these districts are, by the additional tax, rated at eleven hundred livres each. But this additional tax is levied only upon the district under-charged, and it is applied altogether to the relief of that overcharged, which consequently pays only nine hundred livres. The government neither gains nor loses by the additional tax, which is applied altogether to remedy the inequalities arising from the old assessment. The application is pretty much regulated according to the discretion of the intendant of the generality, and must, therefore, be in a great measure arbitrary.

Taxes which are proportioned, not in the Rent,
but to the Produce of Land

Taxes upon the produce of land are, In reality, taxes upon the rent; and though they may be originally advanced by the farmer, are finally paid by the landlord. When a certain portion of the produce is to be paid away for a tax, the farmer computes as well as he can, what the value of this portion is, one year with another, likely to amount to, and he makes a proportionable abatement in the rent which he agrees to pay to the landlord. There is no farmer who does not compute beforehand what the church tythe, which is a land tax of this kind, is, one year with another, likely to amount to.

The tythe, and every other land tax of this kind, under the appearance of perfect equality, are very unequal taxes; a certain portion of the produce being in different situations, equivalent to a very different portion of the rent. In some very rich lands, the produce is so great, that the one half of it is fully sufficient to replace to the farmer his capital employed in cultivation, together with the ordinary profits of farming stock in the neighbourhood. The other half, or, what comes to the same thing, the value of the other half, he could afford to pay as rent to the landlord, if there was no tythe. But if a tenth of the produce is taken from him in the way of tythe, he must require an abatement of the fifth part of his rent, otherwise he cannot get back his capital with the ordinary profit. In this case, the rent of the landlord, instead of amounting to a half, or five-tenths of the whole produce, will amount only to four-tenths of it. In poorer lands, on the contrary, the produce is sometimes so small, and the expense of cultivation so great, that it requires four-fifths of the whole produce, to replace to the farmer his capital with the ordinary profit. In this case, though there was no tythe, the rent of the landlord could amount to no more than one-fifth or two-tenths of the whole produce. But if the farmer pays one-tenth of the produce in the way of tythe, he must require an equal abatement of the rent of the landlord, which will thus be reduced to one-tenth only of the whole produce. Upon the rent of rich lands the tythe may sometimes be a tax of no more than one-fifth part, or four shillings in the pound; whereas upon that of poorer lands, it may sometimes be a tax of one half, or of ten shillings in the pound.

The tythe, as it is frequently a very unequal tax upon the rent, so it is always a great discouragement, both to the improvements of the landlord, and to the cultivation of the farmer. The one cannot venture to make the most important, which are generally the most expensive improvements; nor the other to raise the most valuable, which are generally, too, the most expensive crops; when the church, which lays out no part of the expense, is to share so very largely in the profit. The cultivation of madder was, for a long time, confined by the tythe to the United Provinces, which, being presbyterian countries, and upon that account exempted from this destructive tax, enjoyed a sort of monopoly of that useful dyeing drug against the rest of Europe. The late attempts to introduce the culture of this plant into England, have been made only in consequence of the statute, which enacted that five shillings an acre should be received in lieu of all manner of tythe upon madder.

As through the greater part of Europe, the church, so in many different countries of Asia, the state, is principally supported by a land tax, proportioned not to the rent, but to the produce of the land. In China, the principal revenue of the sovereign consists in a tenth part of the produce of all the lands of the empire. This tenth part, however, is estimated so very moderately, that, in many provinces, it is said not to exceed a thirtieth part of the ordinary produce. The land tax or land rent which used to be paid to the Mahometan government of Bengal, before that country fell into the hands of the English East India company, is said to have amounted to about a fifth part of the produce. The land tax of ancient Egypt is said likewise to have amounted to a fifth part.

In Asia, this sort of land tax is said to interest the sovereign in the improvement and cultivation of land. The sovereigns of China, those of Bengal while under the Mahometan govermnent, and those of ancient Egypt, are said, accordingly, to have been extremely attentive to the making and maintaining of good roads and navigable canals, in order to increase, as much as possible, both the quantity and value of every part of the produce of the land, by procuring to every part of it the most extensive market which their own dominions could afford. The tythe of the church is divided into such small portions that no one of its proprietors can have any interest of this kind. The parson of a parish could never find his account, in making a road or canal to a distant part of the country, in order to extend the market for the produce of his own particular parish. Such taxes, when destined for the maintenance of the state, have some advantages, which may serve in some measure to balance their inconveniency. When destined for the maintenance of the church, they are attended with nothing but inconveniency.

Taxes upon the produce of land may be levied, either in kind, or, according to a certain valuation in money.

The parson of a parish, or a gentleman of small fortune who lives upon his estate, may sometimes, perhaps find some advantage in receiving, the one his tythe, and the other his rent, in kind. The quantity to be collected, and the district within which it is to be collected, are so small, that they both can oversee, with their own eyes, the collection and disposal of every part of what is due to them. A gentleman of great fortune, who lived in the capital, would be in danger of suffering much by the neglect, and more by the fraud, of his factors and agents, if the rents of an estate in a distant province were to be paid to him in this manner. The loss of the sovereign, from the abuse and depredation of his tax-gatherers, would necessarily be much greater. The servants of the most careless private person are, perhaps, more under the eye of their master than those of the most careful prince; and a public revenue, which was paid in kind, would suffer so much from the mismanagement of the collectors, that a very small part of what was levied upon the people would ever arrive at the treasury of the prince. Some part of the public revenue of China, however, is said to be paid in this manner. The mandarins and other tax-gatherers will, no doubt, find their advantage in continuing the practice of a payment, which is so much more liable to abuse than any payment in money.

A tax upon the produce of land, which is levied in money, may be levied, either according to a valuation, which varies with all the variations of the market price; or according to a fixed valuation, a bushel of wheat, for example, being always valued at one and the same money price, whatever may be the state of the market. The produce of a tax levied in the former way will vary only according to the variations in the real produce of the land, according to the improvement or neglect of cultivation. The produce of a tax levied in the latter way will vary, not only according to the variations in the produce of the land, but according both to those in the value of the precious metals, and those in the quantity of those metals which is at different times contained in coin of the same denomination. The produce of the former will always bear the same proportion to the value of the real produce of the land. The produce of the latter may, at different times, bear very different proportions to that value.

When, instead either of a certain portion of the produce of land, or of the price of a certain portion, a certain sum of money is to be paid in full compensation for all tax or tythe; the tax becomes, in this case, exactly of the same nature with the land tax of England. It neither rises nor falls with the rent of the land. It neither encourages nor discourages improvement. The tythe in the greater part of those parishes which pay what is called a modus, in lieu of all other tythe is a tax of this kind. During the Mahometan government of Bengal, instead of the payment in kind of the fifth part of the produce, a modus, and, it is said, a very moderate one, was established in the greater part of the districts or zemindaries of the country. Some of the servants of the East India company, under pretence of restoring the public revenue to its proper value, have, in some provinces, exchanged this modus for a payment in kind. Under their management, this change is likely both to discourage cultivation, and to give new opportunities for abuse in the collection of the public revenue, which has fallen very much below what it was said to have been when it first fell under the management of the company. The servants of the company may, perhaps, have profited by the change, but at the expense, it is probable, both of their masters and of the country.

Taxes upon the Rent of Houses

The rent of a house may be distinguished into two parts, of which the one may very properly be called the building-rent; the other is commonly called the ground-rent.

The building-rent is the interest or profit of the capital expended in building the house. In order to put the trade of a builder upon a level with other trades, it is necessary that this rent should be sufficient, first, to pay him the same interest which he would have got for his capital, if he had lent it upon good security; and, secondly, to keep the house in constant repair, or, what comes to the same thing, to replace, within a certain term of years, the capital which had been employed in building it. The building-rent, or the ordinary profit of building, is, therefore, everywhere regulated by the ordinary interest of money. Where the market rate of interest is four per cent. the rent of a house, which, over and above paying the ground-rent, affords six or six and a-half per cent. upon the whole expense of building, may, perhaps, afford a sufficient profit to the builder. Where the market rate of interest is five per cent. it may perhaps require seven or seven and a half per cent. If, in proportion to the interest of money, the trade of the builders affords at any time much greater profit than this, it will soon draw so much capital from other trades as will reduce the profit to its proper level. If it affords at any time much less than this, other trades will soon draw so much capital from it as will again raise that profit.

Whatever part of the whole rent of a house is over and above what is sufficient for affording this reasonable profit, naturally goes to the ground-rent; and, where the owner of the ground and the owner of the building are two different persons, is, in most cases, completely paid to the former. This surplus rent is the price which the inhabitant of the house pays for some real or supposed advantage of the situation. In country houses, at a distance from any great town, where there is plenty of ground to chuse upon, the ground-rent is scarce anything, or no more than what the ground which the house stands upon would pay, if employed in agriculture. In country villas, in the neighbourhood of some great town, it is sometimes a good deal higher; and the peculiar conveniency or beauty of situation is there frequently very well paid for. Ground-rents are generally highest in the capital, and in those particular parts of it where there happens to be the greatest demand for houses, whatever be the reason of that demand, whether for trade and business, for pleasure and society, or for mere vanity and fashion.

A tax upon house-rent, payable by the tenant, and proportioned to the whole rent of each house, could not, for any considerable time at least, affect the building-rent. If the builder did not get his reasonable profit, he would be obliged to quit the trade; which, by raising the demand for building, would, in a short time, bring back his profit to its proper level with that of other trades. Neither would such a tax fall altogether upon the ground-rent; but it would divide itself in such a manner, as to fall partly upon the inhabitant of the house, and partly upon the owner of the ground.

Let us suppose, for example, that a particular person judges that he can afford for house-rent all expense of sixty pounds a-year; and let us suppose, too, that a tax of four shillings in the pound, or of one-fifth, payable by the inhabitant, is laid upon house-rent. A house of sixty pounds rent will, in that case, cost him seventy-two pounds a-year, which is twelve pounds more than he thinks he can afford. He will, therefore, content himself with a worse house, or a house of fifty pounds rent, which, with the additional ten pounds that he must pay for the tax, will make up the sum of sixty pounds a-year, the expense which he judges he can afford, and, in order to pay the tax, he will give up a part of the additional conveniency which he might have had from a house of ten pounds a-year more rent. He will give up, I say, a part of this additional conveniency; for he will seldom be obliged to give up the whole, but will, in consequence of the tax, get a better house for fifty pounds a-year, than he could have got if there had been no tax for as a tax of this kind, by taking away this particular competitor, must diminish the competition for houses of sixty pounds rent, so it must likewise diminish it for those of fifty pounds rent, and in the same manner for those of all other rents, except the lowest rent, for which it would for some time increase the competition. But the rents of every class of houses for which the competition was diminished, would necessarily be more or less reduced. As no part of this reduction, however, could for any considerable time at least, affect the building-rent, the whole of it must, in the long-run, necessarily fall upon the ground-rent. The final payment of this tax, therefore, would fall partly upon the inhabitant of the house, who, in order to pay his share, would be obliged to give up a part of his conveniency; and partly upon the owner of the ground, who, in order to pay his share, would be obliged to give up a part of his revenue. In what proportion this final payment would be divided between them, it is not, perhaps, very easy to ascertain. The division would probably be very different in different circumstances, and a tax of this kind might, according to those different circumstances, affect very unequally, both the inhabitant of the house and the owner of the ground.

The inequality with which a tax of this kind might fall upon the owners of different ground-rents, would arise altogether from the accidental inequality of this division. But the inequality with which it might fall upon the inhabitants of different houses, would arise, not only from this, but from another cause. The proportion of the expense of house-rent to the whole expense of living, is different in the different degrees of fortune. It is, perhaps, highest in the highest degree, and it diminishes gradually through the inferior degrees, so as in general to be lowest in the lowest degree. The necessaries of life occasion the great expense of the poor. They find it difficult to get food, and the greater part of their little revenue is spent in getting it. The luxuries and vanities of life occasion the principal expense of the rich; and a magnificent house embellishes and sets off to the best advantage all the other luxuries and vanities which they possess. A tax upon house-rents, therefore, would in general fall heaviest upon the rich; and in this sort of inequality there would not, perhaps, be any thing very unreasonable. It is not very unreasonable that the rich should contribute to the public expense, not only in proportion to their revenue, but something more than in that proportion.

The rent of houses, though it in some respects resembles the rent of land, is in one respect essentially different from it. The rent of land is paid for the use of a productive subject. The land which pays it produces it. The rent of houses is paid for the use of an unproductive subject. Neither the house, nor the ground which it stands upon, produce anything. The person who pays the rent, therefore, must draw it from some other source of revenue, distinct from and independent of this subject. A tax upon the rent of houses, so far as it falls upon the inhabitants, must be drawn from the same source as the rent itself, and must be paid from their revenue, whether derived from the wages of labour, the profits of stock, or the rent of land. So far as it falls upon the inhabitants, it is one of those taxes which fall, not upon one only, but indifferently upon all the three different sources of revenue; and is, in every respect, of the same nature as a tax upon any other sort of consumable commodities. In general, there is not perhaps, any one article of expense or consumption by which the liberality or narrowness of a man's whole expense can be better judged of than by his house-rent. A proportional tax upon this particular article of expense might, perhaps, produce a more considerable revenue than any which has hitherto been drawn from it in any part of Europe. If the tax, indeed, was very high, the greater part of people would endeavour to evade it as much as they could, by contenting themselves with smaller houses, and by turning the greater part of their expense into some other channel.

 The rent of houses might easily be ascertained with sufficient accuracy, by a policy of the same kind with that which would be necessary for ascertaining the ordinary rent of land. Houses not inhabited ought to pay no tax. A tax upon them would fall altogether upon the proprietor, who would thus be taxed for a subject which afforded him neither conveniency nor revenue. Houses inhabited by the proprietor ought to be rated, not according to the expense which they might have cost in building, but according to the rent which an equitable arbitration might judge them likely to bring if leased to a tenant. If rated according to the expense which they might have cost in building, a tax of three or four shillings in the pound, joined with other taxes, would ruin almost all the rich and great families of this, and, I believe, of every other civilized country. Whoever will examine with attention the different town and country houses of some of the richest and greatest families in this country, will find that, at the rate of only six and a-half, or seven per cent. upon the original expense of building, their house-rent is nearly equal to the whole neat rent of their estates. It is the accumulated expense of several successive generations, laid out upon objects of great beauty and magnificence, indeed, but, in proportion to what they cost, of very small exchangeable value. {Since the first publication of this book, a tax nearly upon the above-mentioned principles has been imposed.}

Ground-rents are a still more proper subject of taxation than the rent of houses. A tax upon ground-rents would not raise the rent of houses; it would fall altogether upon the owner of the ground-rent, who acts always as a monopolist, and exacts the greatest rent which can be got for the use of his ground. More or less can be got for it, according as the competitors happen to be richer or poorer, or can afford to gratify their fancy for a particular spot of ground at a greater or smaller expense. In every country, the greatest number of rich competitors is in the capital, and it is there accordingly that the highest ground-rents are always to be found. As the wealth of those competitors would in no respect be increased by a tax upon ground-rents, they would not probably be disposed to pay more for the use of the ground. Whether the tax was to be advanced by the inhabitant or by the owner of the ground, would be of little importance. The more the inhabitant was obliged to pay for the tax, the less he would incline to pay for the ground; so that the final payment of the tax would fall altogether upon the owner of the ground-rent. The ground-rents of uninhabited houses ought to pay no tax. Both ground-rents, and the ordinary rent of land, are a species of revenue which the owner, in many cases, enjoys without any care or attention of his own. Though a part of this revenue should be taken from him in order to defray the expenses of the state, no discouragement will thereby be given to any sort of industry. The annual produce of the land and labour of the society, the real wealth and revenue of the great body of the people, might be the same after such a tax as before. Ground-rents, and the ordinary rent of land, are therefore, perhaps, the species of revenue which can best bear to have a peculiar tax imposed upon them.

Ground-rents seem, in this respect, a more proper subject of peculiar taxation, than even the ordinary rent of land. The ordinary rent of land is, in many cases, owing partly, at least, to the attention and good management of the landlord. A very heavy tax might discourage, too much, this attention and good management. Ground-rents, so far as they exceed the ordinary rent of land, are altogether owing to the good government of the sovereign, which, by protecting the industry either of the whole people or of the inhabitants of some particular place, enables them to pay so much more than its real value for the ground which they build their houses upon; or to make to its owner so much more than compensation for the loss which he might sustain by this use of it. Nothing can be more reasonable, than that a fund, which owes its existence to the good government of the state, should be taxed peculiarly, or should contribute something more than the greater part of other funds, towards the support of that government.

Though, in many different countries of Europe, taxes have been imposed upon the rent of houses, I do not know of any in which ground-rents have been considered as a separate subject of taxation. The contrivers of taxes have, probably, found some difficulty in ascertaining what part of the rent ought to be considered as ground-rent, and what part ought to be considered as building-rent. It should not, however, seem very difficult to distinguish those two parts of the rent from one another.

In Great Britain the rent of houses is supposed to be taxed in the same proportion as the rent of land, by what is called the annual land tax. The valuation, according to which each different parish and district is assessed to this tax, is always the same. It was originally extremely unequal, and it still continues to be so. Through the greater part of the kingdom this tax falls still more lightly upon the rent of houses than upon that of land. In some few districts only, which were originally rated high, and in which the rents of houses have fallen considerably, the land tax of three or four shillings in the pound is said to amount to an equal proportion of the real rent of houses. Untenanted houses, though by law subject to the tax, are, in most districts, exempted from it by the favour of the assessors; and this exemption sometimes occasions some little variation in the rate of particular houses, though that of the district is always the same. Improvements of rent, by new buildings, repairs, etc. go to the discharge of the district, which occasions still further variations in the rate of particular houses.

In the province of Holland, {Memoires concernant les Droits, etc. p. 223.} every house is taxed at two and a-half per cent. of its value, without any regard, either to the rent which it actually pays, or to the circumstance of its being tenanted or untenanted. There seems to be a hardship in obliging the proprietor to pay a tax for an untenanted house, from which he can derive no revenue, especially so very heavy a tax. In Holland, where the market rate of interest does not exceed three per cent., two and a-half per cent. upon the whole value of the house must, in most cases, amount to more than a third of the building-rent, perhaps of the whole rent. The valuation, indeed, according to which the houses are rated, though very unequal, is said to be always below the real value. When a house is rebuilt, improved, or enlarged, there is a new valuation, and the tax is rated accordingly.

The contrivers of the several taxes which in England have, at different times, been imposed upon houses, seem to have imagined that there was some great difficulty in ascertaining, with tolerable exactness, what was the real rent of every house. They have regulated their taxes, therefore, according to some more obvious circumstance, such as they had probably imagined would, in most cases, bear some proportion to the rent.

The first tax of this kind was hearth-money; or a tax of two shillings upon every hearth. In order to ascertain how many hearths were in the house, it was necessary that the tax-gatherer should enter every room in it. This odious visit rendered the tax odious. Soon after the Revolution, therefore, it was abolished as a badge of slavery.

The next tax of this kind was a tax of two shillings upon every dwelling-house inhabited. A house with ten windows to pay four shillings more. A house with twenty windows and upwards to pay eight shillings. This tax was afterwards so far altered, that houses with twenty windows, and with less than thirty, were ordered to pay ten shillings, and those with thirty windows and upwards to pay twenty shillings. The number of windows can, in most cases, be counted from the outside, and, in all cases, without entering every room in the house. The visit of the tax-gatherer, therefore, was less offensive in this tax than in the hearth-money.

This tax was afterwards repealed, and in the room of it was established the window-tax, which has undergone two several alterations and augmentations. The window tax, as it stands at present (January 1775), over and above the duty of three shillings upon every house in England, and of one shilling upon every house in Scotland, lays a duty upon every window, which in England augments gradually from twopence, the lowest rate upon houses with not more than seven windows, to two shillings, the highest rate upon houses with twenty-five windows and upwards.

The principal objection to all such taxes is their inequality; an inequality of the worst kind, as they must frequently fall much heavier upon the poor than upon the rich. A house of ten pounds rent in a country town, may sometimes have more windows than a house of five hundred pounds rent in London; and though the inhabitant of the former is likely to be a much poorer man than that of the latter, yet, so far as his contribution is regulated by the window tax, he must contribute more to the support of the state. Such taxes are, therefore, directly contrary to the first of the four maxims above mentioned. They do not seem to offend much against any of the other three.

The natural tendency of the window tax, and of all other taxes upon houses, is to lower rents. The more a man pays for the tax, the less, it is evident, he can afford to pay for the rent. Since the imposition of the window tax, however, the rents of houses have, upon the whole, risen more or less, in almost every town and village of Great Britain, with which I am acquainted. Such has been, almost everywhere, the increase of the demand for houses, that it has raised the rents more than the window tax could sink them; one of the many proofs of the great prosperity of the country, and of the increasing revenue of its inhabitants. Had it not been for the tax, rents would probably have risen still higher.

ARTICLE II.—Taxes upon Profit, or upon the Revenue arising from Stock

The revenue or profit arising from stock naturally divides itself into two parts; that which pays the interest, and which belongs to the owner of the stock; and that surplus part which is over and above what is necessary for paying the interest.

This latter part of profit is evidently a subject not taxable directly. It is the compensation, and, in most cases, it is no more than a very moderate compensation for the risk and trouble of employing the stock. The employer must have this compensation, otherwise he cannot, consistently with his own interest, continue the employment. If he was taxed directly, therefore, in proportion to the whole profit, he would be obliged either to raise the rate of his profit, or to charge the tax upon the interest of money; that is, to pay less interest. If he raised the rate of his profit in proportion to the tax, the whole tax, though it might be advanced by him, would be finally paid by one or other of two different sets of people, according to the different ways in which he might employ the stock of which he had the management. If he employed it as a farming stock, in the cultivation of land, he could raise the rate of his profit only by retaining a greater portion, or, what comes to the same thing, the price of a greater portion, of the produce of the land; and as this could be done only by a reduction of rent, the final payment of the tax would fall upon the landlord. If he employed it as a mercantile or manufacturing stock, he could raise the rate of his profit only by raising the price of his goods; in which case, the final payment of the tax would fall altogether upon the consumers of those goods. If he did not raise the rate of his profit, he would be obliged to charge the whole tax upon that part of it which was allotted for the interest of money. He could afford less interest for whatever stock he borrowed, and the whole weight of the tax would, in this case, fall ultimately upon the interest of money. So far as he could not relieve himself from the tax in the one way, he would be obliged to relieve himself in the other.

The interest of money seems, at first sight, a subject equally capable of being taxed directly as the rent of land. Like the rent of land, it is a neat produce, which remains, after completely compensating the whole risk and trouble of employing the stock. As a tax upon the rent of land cannot raise rents, because the neat produce which remains, after replacing the stock of the farmer, together with his reasonable profit, cannot be greater after the tax than before it, so, for the same reason, a tax upon the interest of money could not raise the rate of interest; the quantity of stock or money in the country, like the quantity of land, being supposed to remain the same after the tax as before it. The ordinary rate of profit, it has been shewn, in the first book, is everywhere regulated by the quantity of stock to be employed, in proportion to the quantity of the employment, or of the business which must be done by it. But the quantity of the employment, or of the business to be done by stock, could neither be increased nor diminished by any tax upon the interest of money. If the quantity of the stock to be employed, therefore, was neither increased nor diminished by it, the ordinary rate of profit would necessarily remain the same. But the portion of this profit, necessary for compensating the risk and trouble of the employer, would likewise remain the same; that risk and trouble being in no respect altered. The residue, therefore, that portion which belongs to the owner of the stock, and which pays the interest of money, would necessarily remain the same too. At first sight, therefore, the interest of money seems to be a subject as fit to be taxed directly as the rent of land.

There are, however, two different circumstances, which render the interest of money a much less proper subject of direct taxation than the rent of land.

First, the quantity and value of the land which any man possesses, can never be a secret, and can always be ascertained with great exactness. But the whole amount of the capital stock which he possesses is almost always a secret, and can scarce ever be ascertained with tolerable exactness. It is liable, besides, to almost continual variations. A year seldom passes away, frequently not a month, sometimes scarce a single day, in which it does not rise or fall more or less. An inquisition into every man's private circumstances, and an inquisition which, in order to accommodate the tax to them, watched over all the fluctuations of his fortune, would be a source of such continual and endless vexation as no person could support.

Secondly, land is a subject which cannot be removed; whereas stock easily may. The proprietor of land is necessarily a citizen of the particular country in which his estate lies. The proprietor of stock is properly a citizen of the world, and is not necessarily attached to any particular country. He would be apt to abandon the country in which he was exposed to a vexatious inquisition, in order to be assessed to a burdensome tax; and would remove his stock to some other country, where he could either carry on his business, or enjoy his fortune more at his ease. By removing his stock, he would put an end to all the industry which it had maintained in the country which he left. Stock cultivates land; stock employs labour. A tax which tended to drive away stock from any particular country, would so far tend to dry up every source of revenue, both to the sovereign and to the society. Not only the profits of stock, but the rent of land, and the wages of labour, would necessarily be more or less diminished by its removal.

The nations, accordingly, who have attempted to tax the revenue arising from stock, instead of any severe inquisition of this kind, have been obliged to content themselves with some very loose, and, therefore, more or less arbitrary estimation. The extreme inequality and uncertainty of a tax assessed in this manner, can be compensated only by its extreme moderation; in consequence of which, every man finds himself rated so very much below his real revenue, that he gives himself little disturbance though his neighbour should be rated somewhat lower.

By what is called the land tax in England, it was intended that the stock should be taxed in the same proportion as land. When the tax upon land was at four shillings in the pound, or at one-fifth of the supposed rent, it was intended that stock should be taxed at one-fifth of the supposed interest. When the present annual land tax was first imposed, the legal rate of interest was six per cent. Every hundred pounds stock, accordingly, was supposed to be taxed at twenty-four shillings, the fifth part of six pounds. Since the legal rate of interest has been reduced to five per cent. every hundred pounds stock is supposed to be taxed at twenty shillings only. The sum to be raised, by what is called the land tax, was divided between the country and the principal towns. The greater part of it was laid upon the country; and of what was laid upon the towns, the greater part was assessed upon the houses. What remained to be assessed upon the stock or trade of the towns (for the stock upon the land was not meant to be taxed) was very much below the real value of that stock or trade. Whatever inequalities, therefore, there might be in the original assessment, gave little disturbance. Every parish and district still continues to be rated for its land, its houses, and its stock, according to the original assessment; and the almost universal prosperity of the country, which, in most places, has raised very much the value of all these, has rendered those inequalities of still less importance now. The rate, too, upon each district, continuing always the same, the uncertainty of this tax, so far as it might he assessed upon the stock of any individual, has been very much diminished, as well as rendered of much less consequence. If the greater part of the lands of England are not rated to the land tax at half their actual value, the greater part of the stock of England is, perhaps, scarce rated at the fiftieth part of its actual value. In some towns, the whole land tax is assessed upon houses; as in Westminster, where stock and trade are free. It is otherwise in London.

In all countries, a severe inquisition into the circumstances of private persons has been carefully avoided.

At Hamburg, {Memoires concernant les Droits, tom. i, p.74} every inhabitant is obliged to pay to the state one fourth per cent. of all that he possesses; and as the wealth of the people of Hamburg consists principally in stock, this tax maybe considered as a tax upon stock. Every man assesses himself, and, in the presence of the magistrate, puts annually into the public coffer a certain sum of money, which he declares upon oath, to be one fourth per cent. of all that he possesses, but without declaring what it amounts to, or being liable to any examination upon that subject. This tax is generally supposed to be paid with great fidelity. In a small republic, where the people have entire confidence in their magistrates, are convinced of the necessity of the tax for the support of the state, and believe that it will be faithfully applied to that purpose, such conscientious and voluntary payment may sometimes be expected. It is not peculiar to the people of Hamburg.

The canton of Underwald, in Switzerland, is frequently ravaged by storms and inundations, and it is thereby exposed to extraordinary expenses. Upon such occasions the people assemble, and every one is said to declare with the greatest frankness what he is worth, in order to be taxed accordingly. At Zurich, the law orders, that in cases of necessity, every one should be taxed in proportion to his revenue; the amount of which he is obliged to declare upon oath. They have no suspicion, it is said, that any of their fellow citizens will deceive them. At Basil, the principal revenue of the state arises from a small custom upon goods exported. All the citizens make oath, that they will pay every three months all the taxes imposed by law. All merchants, and even all inn-keepers, are trusted with keeping themselves the account of the goods which they sell, either within or without the territory. At the end of every three months, they send this account to the treasurer, with the amount of the tax computed at the bottom of it. It is not suspected that the revenue suffers by this confidence. {Memoires concernant les Droits, tom. i p. 163, 167,171.}

To oblige every citizen to declare publicly upon oath, the amount of his fortune, must not, it seems, in those Swiss cantons, be reckoned a hardship. At Hamburg it would be reckoned the greatest. Merchants engaged in the hazardous projects of trade, all tremble at the thoughts of being obliged, at all times, to expose the real state of their circumstances. The ruin of their credit, and the miscarriage of their projects, they foresee, would too often be the consequence. A sober and parsimonious people, who are strangers to all such projects, do not feel that they have occasion for any such concealment.

In Holland, soon after the exaltation of the late prince of Orange to the stadtholdership, a tax of two per cent. or the fiftieth penny, as it was called, was imposed upon the whole substance of every citizen. Every citizen asseseed himself, and paid his tax, in the same manner as at Hamburg, and it was in general supposed to have been paid with great fidelity. The people had at that time the greatest affection for their new government, which they had just established by a general insurrection. The tax was to be paid but once, in order to relieve the state in a particular exigency. It was, indeed, too heavy to be permanent. In a country where the market rate of interest seldom exceeds three per cent., a tax of two per cent. amounts to thirteen shillings and four pence in the pound, upon the highest neat revenue which is commonly drawn from stock. It is a tax which very few people could pay, without encroaching more or less upon their capitals. In a particular exigency, the people may, from great public zeal, make a great effort, and give up even a part of their capital, in order to relieve the state. But it is impossible that they should continue to do so for any considerable time; and if they did, the tax would soon ruin them so completely, as to render them altogether incapable of supporting the state.

The tax upon stock, imposed by the land tax bill in England, though it is proportioned to the capital, is not intended to diminish or, take away any part of that capital. It is meant only to be a tax upon the interest of money, proportioned to that upon the rent of land; so that when the latter is at four shillings in the pound, the former may be at four shillings in the pound too. The tax at Hamburg, and the still more moderate taxes of Underwald and Zurich, are meant, in the same manner, to be taxes, not upon the capital, but upon the interest or neat revenue of stock. That of Holland was meant to be a tax upon the capital.

Taxes upon the Profit of particular Employments.

In some countries, extraordinary taxes are imposed upon the profits of stock; sometimes when employed in particular branches of trade, and sometimes when employed in agriculture.

Of the former kind, are in England, the tax upon hawkers and pedlars, that upon hackney-coaches and chairs, and that which the keepers of ale-houses pay for a licence to retail ale and spiritous liquors. During the late war, another tax of the same kind was proposed upon shops. The war having been undertaken, it was said, in defence of the trade of the country, the merchants, who were to profit by it, ought to contribute towards the support of it.

A tax, however, upon the profits of stock employed in any particular branch of trade, can never fall finally upon the dealers (who must in all ordinary cases have their reasonable profit, and, where the competition is free, can seldom have more than that profit), but always upon the consumers, who must be obliged to pay in the price of the goods the tax which the dealer advances; and generally with some overcharge.

A tax of this kind, when it is proportioned to the trade of the dealer, is finally paid by the consumer, and occasions no oppression to the dealer. When it is not so proportioned, but is the same upon all dealers, though in this case, too, it is finally paid by the consumer, yet it favours the great, and occasions some oppression to the small dealer. The tax of five shillings a-week upon every hackney coach, and that of ten shillings a-year upon every hackney chair, so far as it is advanced by the different keepers of such coaches and chairs, is exactly enough proportioned to the extent of their respective dealings. It neither favours the great, nor oppresses the smaller dealer. The tax of twenty shillings a-year for a licence to sell ale; of forty shillings for a licence to sell spiritous liquors; and of forty shillings more for a licence to sell wine, being the same upon all retailers, must necessarily give some advantage to the great, and occasion some oppression to the small dealers. The former must find it more easy to get back the tax in the price of their goods than the latter. The moderation of the tax, however, renders this inequality of less importance; and it may to many people appear not improper to give some discouragement to the multiplication of little ale-houses. The tax upon shops, it was intended, should be the same upon all shops. It could not well have been otherwise. It would have been impossible to proportion, with tolerable exactness, the tax upon a shop to the extent of the trade carried on in it, without such an inquisition as would have been altogether insupportable in a free country. If the tax had been considerable, it would have oppressed the small, and forced almost the whole retail trade into the hands of the great dealers. The competition of the former being taken away, the latter would have enjoyed a monopoly of the trade; and, like all other monopolists, would soon have combined to raise their profits much beyond what was necessary for the payment of the tax. The final payment, instead of falling upon the shop-keeper, would have fallen upon the consumer, with a considerable overcharge to the profit of the shop-keeper. For these reasons, the project of a tax upon shops was laid aside, and in the room of it was substituted the subsidy, 1759.

What in France is called the personal taille, is perhaps, the most important tax upon the profits of stock employed in agriculture, that is levied in any part of Europe.

In the disorderly state of Europe, during the prevalence of the feudal government, the sovereign was obliged to content himself with taxing those who were too weak to refuse to pay taxes. The great lords, though willing to assist him upon particular emergencies, refused to subject themselves to any constant tax, and he was not strong enough to force them. The occupiers of land all over Europe were, the greater part of them, originally bond-men. Through the greater part of Europe, they were gradually emancipated. Some of them acquired the property of landed estates, which they held by some base or ignoble tenure, sometimes under the king, and sometimes under some other great lord, like the ancient copy-holders of England. Others, without acquiring the property, obtained leases for terms of years, of the lands which they occupied under their lord, and thus became less dependent upon him. The great lords seem to have beheld the degree of prosperity and independency, which this inferior order of men had thus come to enjoy, with a malignant and contemptuous indignation, and willingly consented that the sovereign should tax them. In some countries, this tax was confined to the lands which were held in property by an ignoble tenure; and, in this case, the taille was said to be real. The land tax established by the late king of Sardinia, and the taille in the provinces of Languedoc, Provence, Dauphine, and Britany; in the generality of Montauban, and in the elections of Agen and Condom, as well as in some other districts of France; are taxes upon lands held in property by an ignoble tenure. In other countries, the tax was laid upon the supposed profits of all those who held, in farm or lease, lands belonging to other people, whatever might be the tenure by which the proprietor held them; and in this case, the taille was said to be personal. In the greater part of those provinces of France, which are called the countries of elections, the taille is of this kind. The real taille, as it is imposed only upon a part of the lands of the country, is necessarily an unequal, but it is not always an arbitrary tax, though it is so upon some occasions. The personal taille, as it is intended to be proportioned to the profits of a certain class of people, which can only be guessed at, is necessarily both arbitrary and unequal.

In France, the personal taille at present (1775) annually imposed upon the twenty generalities, called the countries of elections, amounts to 40,107,239 livres, 16 sous. {Memoires concernant les Droits, etc tom. ii, p.17.} the proportion in which this sum is assessed upon those different provinces, varies from year to year, according to the reports which are made to the king's council concerning the goodness or badness of the crops, as well as other circumstances, which may either increase or diminish their respective abilities to pay. Each generality is divided into a certain number of elections; and the proportion in which the sum imposed upon the whole generality is divided among those different elections, varies likewise from year to year, according to the reports made to the council concerning their respective abilities. It seems impossible, that the council, with the best intentions, can ever proportion, with tolerable exactness, either of these two assessments to the real abilities of the province or district upon which they are respectively laid. Ignorance and misinformation must always, more or less, mislead the most upright council. The proportion which each parish ought to support of what is assessed upon the whole election, and that which each individual ought to support of what is assessed upon his particular parish, are both in the same manner varied from year to year, according as circumstances are supposed to require. These circumstances are judged of, in the one case, by the officers of the election, in the other, by those of the parish; and both the one and the other are, more or less, under the direction and influence of the intendant. Not only ignorance and misinformation, but friendship, party animosity, and private resentment, are said frequently to mislead such assessors. No man subject to such a tax, it is evident, can ever be certain, before he is assessed, of what he is to pay. He cannot even be certain after he is assessed. If any person has been taxed who ought to have been exempted, or if any person has been taxed beyond his proportion, though both must pay in the mean time, yet if they complain, and make good their complaints, the whole parish is reimposed next year, in order to reimburse them. If any of the contributors become bankrupt or insolvent, the collector is obliged to advance his tax; and the whole parish is reimposed next year, in order to reimburse the collector. If the collector himself should become bankrupt, the parish which elects him must answer for his conduct to the receiver-general of the election. But, as it might be troublesome for the receiver to prosecute the whole parish, he takes at his choice five or six of the richest contributors, and obliges them to make good what had been lost by the insolvency of the collector. The parish is afterwards reimposed, in order to reimburse those five or six. Such reimpositions are always over and above the taille of the particular year in which they are laid on.

When a tax is imposed upon the profits of stock in a particular branch of trade, the traders are all careful to bring no more goods to market than what they can sell at a price sufficient to reimburse them from advancing the tax. Some of them withdraw a part of their stocks from the trade, and the market is more sparingly supplied than before. The price of the goods rises, and the final payment of the tax falls upon the consumer. But when a tax is imposed upon the profits of stock employed in agriculture, it is not the interest of the farmers to withdraw any part of their stock from that employment. Each farmer occupies a certain quantity of land, for which he pays rent. For the proper cultivation of this land, a certain quantity of stock is necessary; and by withdrawing any part of this necessary quantity, the farmer is not likely to be more able to pay either the rent or the tax. In order to pay the tax, it can never be his interest to diminish the quantity of his produce, nor consequently to supply the market more sparingly than before. The tax, therefore, will never enable him to raise the price of his produce, so as to reimburse himself, by throwing the final payment upon the consumer. The farmer, however, must have his reasonable profit as well as every other dealer, otherwise he must give up the trade. After the imposition of a tax of this kind, he can get this reasonable profit only by paying less rent to the landlord. The more he is obliged to pay in the way of tax, the less he can afford to pay in the way of rent. A tax of this kind, imposed during the currency of a lease, may, no doubt, distress or ruin the farmer. Upon the renewal of the lease, it must always fall upon the landlord.

In the countries where the personal taille takes place, the farmer is commonly assessed in proportion to the stock which he appears to employ in cultivation. He is, upon this account, frequently afraid to have a good team of horses or oxen, but endeavours to cultivate with the meanest and most wretched instruments of husbandry that he can. Such is his distrust in the justice of his assessors, that he counterfeits poverty, and wishes to appear scarce able to pay anything, for fear of being obliged to pay too much. By this miserable policy, he does not, perhaps, always consult his own interest in the most effectual manner; and he probably loses more by the diminution of his produce, than he saves by that of his tax. Though, in consequence of this wretched cultivation, the market is, no doubt, somewhat worse supplied; yet the small rise of price which this may occasion, as it is not likely even to indemnify the farmer for the diminution of his produce, it is still less likely to enable him to pay more rent to the landlord. The public, the farmer, the landlord, all suffer more or less by this degraded cultivation. That the personal taille tends, in many different ways, to discourage cultivation, and consequently to dry up the principal source of the wealth of every great country, I have already had occasion to observe in the third book of this Inquiry.

What are called poll-taxes in the southern provinces of North America, and the West India islands, annual taxes of so much a-head upon every negro, are properly taxes upon the profits of a certain species of stock employed in agriculture. As the planters, are the greater part of them, both farmers and landlords, the final payment of the tax falls upon them in their quality of landlords, without any retribution.

Taxes of so much a head upon the bondmen employed in cultivation, seem anciently to have been common all over Europe. There subsists at present a tax of this kind in the empire of Russia. It is probably upon this account that poll-taxes of all kinds have often been represented as badges of slavery. Every tax, however, is, to the person who pays it, a badge, not of slavery, but of liberty. It denotes that he is subject to government, indeed; but that, as he has some property, he cannot himself be the property of a master. A poll tax upon slaves is altogether different from a poll-tax upon freemen. The latter is paid by the persons upon whom it is imposed; the former, by a different set of persons. The latter is either altogether arbitrary, or altogether unequal, and, in most cases, is both the one and the other; the former, though in some respects unequal, different slaves being of different values, is in no respect arbitrary. Every master, who knows the number of his own slaves, knows exactly what he has to pay. Those different taxes, however, being called by the same name, have been considered as of the same nature.

The taxes which in Holland are imposed upon men and maid servants, are taxes, not upon stock, but upon expense; and so far resemble the taxes upon consumable commodities. The tax of a guinea a-head for every man-servant, which has lately been imposed in Great Britain, is of the same kind. It falls heaviest upon the middling rank. A man of two hundred a-year may keep a single man-servant. A man of ten thousand a-year will not keep fifty. It does not affect the poor.

Taxes upon the profits of stock, in particular employments, can never affect the interest of money. Nobody will lend his money for less interest to those who exercise the taxed, than to those who exercise the untaxed employments. Taxes upon the revenue arising from stock in all employments, where the government attempts to levy them with any degree of exactness, will, in many cases, fall upon the interest of money. The vingtieme, or twentieth penny, in France, is a tax of the same kind with what is called the land tax in England, and is assessed, in the same manner, upon the revenue arising upon land, houses, and stock. So far as it affects stock, it is assessed, though not with great rigour, yet with much more exactness than that part of the land tax in England which is imposed upon the same fund. It, in many cases, falls altogether upon the interest of money. Money is frequently sunk in France, upon what are called contracts for the constitution of a rent; that is, perpetual annuities, redeemable at any time by the debtor, upon payment of the sum originally advanced, but of which this redemption is not exigible by the creditor except in particular cases. The vingtieme seems not to have raised the rate of those annuities, though it is exactly levied upon them all.

APPENDIX TO ARTICLES I. AND II.—Taxes upon the Capital Value of Lands, Houses, and Stock

While property remains in the possession of the same person, whatever permanent taxes may have been imposed upon it, they have never been intended to diminish or take away any part of its capital value, but only some part of the revenue arising from it. But when property changes hands, when it is transmitted either from the dead to the living, or from the living to the living, such taxes have frequently been imposed upon it as necessarily take away some part of its capital value.

The transference of all sorts of property from the dead to the living, and that of immoveable property of land and houses from the living to the living, are transactions which are in their nature either public and notorious, or such as cannot be long concealed. Such transactions, therefore, may be taxed directly. The transference of stock or moveable property, from the living to the living, by the lending of money, is frequently a secret transaction, and may always be made so. It cannot easily, therefore, be taxed directly. It has been taxed indirectly in two different ways; first, by requiring that the deed, containing the obligation to repay, should be written upon paper or parchment which had paid a certain stamp duty, otherwise not to be valid; secondly, by requiring, under the like penalty of invalidity, that it should be recorded either in a public or secret register, and by imposing certain duties upon such registration. Stamp duties, and duties of registration, have frequently been imposed likewise upon the deeds transferring property of all kinds from the dead to the living, and upon those transferring immoveable property from the living to the living; transactions which might easily have been taxed directly.

The vicesima hereditatum, or the twentieth penny of inheritances, imposed by Augustus upon the ancient Romans, was a tax upon the transference of property from the dead to the living. Dion Cassius, { Lib.

55. See also Burman. de Vectigalibus Pop. Rom. cap. xi. and Bouchaud de l'impot du vingtieme sur les successions.} the author who writes concerning it the least indistinctly, says, that it was imposed upon all successions, legacies and donations, in case of death, except upon those to the nearest relations, and to the poor.

Of the same kind is the Dutch tax upon successions. {See Memoires concernant les Droits, etc. tom i, p. 225.} Collateral successions are taxed according to the degree of relation, from five to thirty per cent. upon the whole value of the succession. Testamentary donations, or legacies to collaterals, are subject to the like duties. Those from husband to wife, or from wife to husband, to the fiftieth penny. The luctuosa hereditas, the mournful succession of ascendants to descendants, to the twentieth penny only. Direct successions, or those of descendants to ascendants, pay no tax. The death of a father, to such of his children as live in the same house with him, is seldom attended with any increase, and frequently with a considerable diminution of revenue; by the loss of his industry, of his office, or of some life-rent estate, of which he may have been in possession. That tax would be cruel and oppressive, which aggravated their loss, by taking from them any part of his succession. It may, however, sometimes be otherwise with those children, who, in the language of the Roman law, are said to be emancipated; in that of the Scotch law, to be foris-familiated; that is, who have received their portion, have got families of their own, and are supported by funds separate and independent of those of their father. Whatever part of his succession might come to such children, would be a real addition to their fortune, and might, therefore, perhaps, without more inconveniency than what attends all duties of this kind, be liable to some tax. The casualties of the feudal law were taxes upon the transference of land, both from the dead to the living, and from the living to the living. In ancient times, they constituted, in every part of Europe, one of the principal branches of the revenue of the crown.

The heir of every immediate vassal of the crown paid a certain duty, generally a year's rent, upon receiving the investiture of the estate. If the heir was a minor, the whole rents of the estate, during the continuance of the minority, devolved to the superior, without any other charge besides the maintenance of the minor, and the payment of the widow's dower, when there happened to be a dowager upon the land. When the minor came to be of age, another tax, called relief, was still due to the superior, which generally amounted likewise to a year's rent. A long minority, which, in the present times, so frequently disburdens a great estate of all its incumbrances, and restores the family to their ancient splendour, could in those times have no such effect. The waste, and not the disincumbrance of the estate, was the common effect of a long minority.

By a feudal law, the vassal could not alienate without the consent of his superior, who generally extorted a fine or composition on granting it. This fine, which was at first arbitrary, came, in many countries, to be regulated at a certain portion of the price of the land. In some countries, where the greater part of the other feudal customs have gone into disuse, this tax upon the alienation of land still continues to make a very considerable branch of the revenue of the sovereign. In the canton of Berne it is so high as a sixth part of the price of all noble fiefs, and a tenth part of that of all ignoble ones. {Memoires concernant les Droits, etc, tom.i p.154} In the canton of Lucern, the tax upon the sale of land is not universal, and takes place only in certain districts. But if any person sells his land in order to remove out of the territory, he pays ten per cent. upon the whole price of the sale. {id. p.157.} Taxes of the same kind, upon the sale either of all lands, or of lands held by certain tenures, take place in many other countries, and make a more or less considerable branch of the revenue of the sovereign.

Such transactions may be taxed indirectly, by means either of stamp duties, or of duties upon registration; and those duties either may, or may not, be proportioned to the value of the subject which is transferred.

In Great Britain, the stamp duties are higher or lower, not so much according to the value of the property transferred (an eighteen-penny or half-crown stamp being sufficient upon a bond for the largest sum of money), as according to the nature of the deed. The highest do not exceed six pounds upon every sheet of paper, or skin of parchment; and these high duties fall chiefly upon grants from the crown, and upon certain law proceedings, without any regard to the value of the subject. There are, in Great Britain, no duties on the registration of deeds or writings, except the fees of the officers who keep the register; and these are seldom more than a reasonable recompence for their labour. The crown derives no revenue from them.

In Holland {Memoires concernant les Droits, etc. tom. i. p 223, 224, 225.} there are both stamp duties and duties upon registration; which in some cases are, and in some are not, proportioned to the value of the property transferred. All testaments must be written upon stamped paper, of which the price is proportioned to the property disposed of; so that there are stamps which cost from three pence or three stivers a-sheet, to three hundred florins, equal to about twenty-seven pounds ten shillings of our money. If the stamp is of an inferior price to what the testator ought to have made use of, his succession is confiscated. This is over and above all their other taxes on succession. Except bills of exchange, and some other mercantile bills, all other deeds, bonds, and contracts, are subject to a stamp duty. This duty, however, does not rise in proportion to the value of the subject. All sales of land and of houses, and all mortgages upon either, must be registered, and, upon registration, pay a duty to the state of two and a-half per cent. upon the amount of the price or of the mortgage. This duty is extended to the sale of all ships and vessels of more than two tons burden, whether decked or undecked. These, it seems, are considered as a sort of houses upon the water. The sale of moveables, when it is ordered by a court of justice, is subject to the like duty of two and a-half per cent.

In France, there are both stamp duties and duties upon registration. The former are considered as a branch of the aids of excise, and, in the provinces where those duties take place, are levied by the excise officers. The latter are considered as a branch of the domain of the crown and are levied by a different set of officers.

Those modes of taxation by stamp duties and by duties upon registration, are of very modern invention. In the course of little more than a century, however, stamp duties have, in Europe, become almost universal, and duties upon registration extremely common. There is no art which one government sooner learns of another, than that of draining money from the pockets of the people.

Taxes upon the transference of property from the dead to the living, fall finally, as well as immediately, upon the persons to whom the property is transferred. Taxes upon the sale of land fall altogether upon the seller. The seller is almost always under the necessity of selling, and must, therefore, take such a price as he can get. The buyer is scarce ever under the necessity of buying, and will, therefore, only give such a price as he likes. He considers what the land will cost him, in tax and price together. The more he is obliged to pay in the way of tax, the less he will be disposed to give in the way of price. Such taxes, therefore, fall almost always upon a necessitous person, and must, therefore, be frequently very cruel and oppressive. Taxes upon the sale of new-built houses, where the building is sold without the ground, fall generally upon the buyer, because the builder must generally have his profit; otherwise he must give up the trade. If he advances the tax, therefore, the buyer must generally repay it to him. Taxes upon the sale of old houses, for the same reason as those upon the sale of land, fall generally upon the seller; whom, in most cases, either conveniency or necessity obliges to sell. The number of new-built houses that are annually brought to market, is more or less regulated by the demand. Unless the demand is such as to afford the builder his profit, after paying all expenses, he will build no more houses. The number of old houses which happen at any time to come to market, is regulated by accidents, of which the greater part have no relation to the demand. Two or three great bankruptcies in a mercantile town, will bring many houses to sale, which must be sold for what can be got for them. Taxes upon the sale of ground-rents fall altogether upon the seller, for the same reason as those upon the sale of lands. Stamp duties, and duties upon the registration of bonds and contracts for borrowed money, fall altogether upon the borrower, and, in fact, are always paid by him. Duties of the same kind upon law proceedings fall upon the suitors. They reduce to both the capital value of the subject in dispute. The more it costs to acquire any property, the less must be the neat value of it when acquired.

All taxes upon the transference of property of every kind, so far as they diminish the capital value of that property, tend to diminish the funds destined for the maintenance of productive labour. They are all more or less unthrifty taxes that increase the revenue of the sovereign, which seldom maintains any but unproductive labourers, at the expense of the capital of the people, which maintains none but productive.

Such taxes, even when they are proportioned to the value of the property transferred, are still unequal; the frequency of transference not being always equal in property of equal value. When they are not proportioned to this value, which is the case with the greater part of the stamp duties and duties of registration, they are still more so. They are in no respect arbitrary, but are, or may be, in all cases, perfectly clear and certain. Though they sometimes fall upon the person who is not very able to pay, the time of payment is, in most cases, sufficiently convenient for him. When the payment becomes due, he must, in most cases, have the more to pay. They are levied at very little expense, and in general subject the contributors to no other inconveniency, besides always the unavoidable one of paying the tax. In France, the stamp duties are not much complained of. Those of registration, which they call the Controle, are. They give occasion, it is pretended, to much extortion in the officers of the farmers-general who collect the tax, which is in a great measure arbitrary and uncertain. In the greater part of the libels which have been written against the present system of finances in France, the abuses of the controle make a principal article. Uncertainty, however, does not seem to be necessarily inherent in the nature of such taxes. If the popular complaints are well founded, the abuse must arise, not so much from the nature of the tax as from the want of precision and distinctness in the words of the edicts or laws which impose it.

The registration of mortgages, and in general of all rights upon immoveable property, as it gives great security both to creditors and purchasers, is extremely advantageous to the public. That of the greater part of deeds of other kinds, is frequently inconvenient and even dangerous to individuals, without any advantage to the public. All registers which, it is acknowledged, ought to be kept secret, ought certainly never to exist. The credit of individuals ought certainly never to depend upon so very slender a security, as the probity and religion of the inferior officers of revenue. But where the fees of registration have been made a source of revenue to the sovereign, register-offices have commonly been multiplied without end, both for the deeds which ought to be registered, and for those which ought not. In France there are several different sorts of secret registers. This abuse, though not perhaps a necessary, it must be acknowledged, is a very natural effect of such taxes.

Such stamp duties as those in England upon cards and dice, upon newspapers and periodical pamphlets, etc. are properly taxes upon consumption; the final payment falls upon the persons who use or consume such commodities. Such stamp duties as those upon licences to retail ale, wine, and spiritous liquors, though intended, perhaps, to fall upon the profits of the retailers, are likewise finally paid by the consumers of those liquors. Such taxes, though called by the same name, and levied by the same officers, and in the same manner with the stamp duties above mentioned upon the transference of property, are, however, of a quite different nature, and fall upon quite different funds.

ARTICLE III.—Taxes upon the Wages of Labour

The wages of the inferior classes of work men, I have endeavoured to show in the first book are everywhere necessarily regulated by two different circumstances; the demand for labour, and the ordinary or average price of provisions. The demand for labour, according as it happens to be either increasing stationary or declining; or to require an increasing, stationary, or declining population, regulates the subsistence of the labourer, and determines in what degree it shall be either liberal, moderate, or scanty. The ordinary average price of provisions determines the quantity of money which must be paid to the workman, in order to enable him, one year with another, to purchase this liberal, moderate, or scanty subsistence. While the demand for the labour and the price of provisions, therefore, remain the same, a direct tax upon the wages of labour can have no other effect, than to raise them somewhat higher than the tax. Let us suppose, for example, that, in a particular place, the demand for labour and the price of provisions were such as to render ten shillings a-week the ordinary wages of labour; and that a tax of one-fifth, or four shillings in the pound, was imposed upon wages. If the demand for labour and the price of provisions remained the same, it would still be necessary that the labourer should, in that place, earn such a subsistence as could be bought only for ten shillings a-week; so that, after paying the tax, he should have ten shillings a-week free wages. But, in order to leave him such free wages, after paying such a tax, the price of labour must, in that place, soon rise, not to twelve shillings a week only, but to twelve and sixpence; that is, in order to enable him to pay a tax of one-fifth, his wages must necessarily soon rise, not one-fifth part only, but one-fourth. Whatever was the proportion of the tax, the wages of labour must, in all cases rise, not only in that proportion, but in a higher proportion. If the tax for example, was one-tenth, the wages of labour must necessarily soon rise, not one-tenth part only, but one-eighth.

A direct tax upon the wages of labour, therefore, though the labourer might, perhaps, pay it out of his hand, could not properly be said to be even advanced by him; at least if the demand for labour and the average price of provisions remained the same after the tax as before it. In all such cases, not only the tax, but something more than the tax, would in reality be advanced by the person who immediately employed him. The final payment would, in different cases, fall upon different persons. The rise which such a tax might occasion in the wages of manufacturing labour would be advanced by the master manufacturer, who would both be entitled and obliged to charge it, with a profit, upon the price of his goods. The final payment of this rise of wages, therefore, together with the additional profit of the master manufacturer would fall upon the consumer. The rise which such a tax might occasion in the wages of country labour would be advanced by the farmer, who, in order to maintain the same number of labourers as before, would be obliged to employ a greater capital. In order to get back this greater capital, together with the ordinary profits of stock, it would be necessary that he should retain a larger portion, or, what comes to the same thing, the price of a larger portion, of the produce of the land, and, consequently, that he should pay less rent to the landlord. The final payment of this rise of wages, therefore, would, in this case, fall upon the landlord, together with the additional profit of the farmer who had advanced it. In all cases, a direct tax upon the wages of labour must, in the long-run, occasion both a greater reduction in the rent of land, and a greater rise in the price of manufactured goods than would have followed from the proper assessment of a sum equal to the produce of the tax, partly upon the rent of land, and partly upon consumable commodities.

If direct taxes upon the wages of labour have not always occasioned a proportionable rise in those wages, it is because they have generally occasioned a considerable fall in the demand of labour. The declension of industry, the decrease of employment for the poor, the diminution of the annual produce of the land and labour of the country, have generally been the effects of such taxes. In consequence of them, however, the price of labour must always be higher than it otherwise would have been in the actual state of the demand; and this enhancement of price, together with the profit of those who advance it, must always be finally paid by the landlords and consumers.

A tax upon the wages of country labour does not raise the price of the rude produce of land in proportion to the tax; for the same reason that a tax upon the farmer's profit does not raise that price in that proportion.

Absurd and destructive as such taxes are, however, they take place in many countries. In France, that part of the taille which is charged upon the industry of workmen and day-labourers in country villages, is properly a tax of this kind. Their wages are computed according to the common rate of the district in which they reside; and, that they may be as little liable as possible to any overcharge, their yearly gains are estimated at no more than two hundred working days in the year. {Memoires concernant les Droits, etc. tom. ii. p. 108.} The tax of each individual is varied from year to year, according to different circumstances, of which the collector or the commissary, whom intendant appoints to assist him, are the judges. In Bohemia, in consequence of the alteration in the system of finances which was begun in 1748, a very heavy tax is imposed upon the industry of artificers. They are divided into four classes. The highest class pay a hundred florins a year, which, at two-and-twenty pence half penny a-florin, amounts to £9:7:6. The second class are taxed at seventy; the third at fifty; and the fourth, comprehending artificers in villages, and the lowest class of those in towns, at twenty-five florins. {Memoires concernant les Droits, etc. tom. iii. p. 87.}

The recompence of ingenious artists, and of men of liberal professions, I have endeavoured to show in the first book, necessarily keeps a certain proportion to the emoluments of inferior trades. A tax upon this recompence, therefore, could have no other effect than to raise it somewhat higher than in proportion to the tax. If it did not rise in this manner, the ingenious arts and the liberal professions, being no longer upon a level with other trades, would be so much deserted, that they would soon return to that level.

The emoluments of offices are not, like those of trades and professions, regulated by the free competition of the market, and do not, therefore, always bear a just proportion to what the nature of the employment requires. They are, perhaps, in most countries, higher than it requires; the persons who have the administration of government being generally disposed to regard both themselves and their immediate dependents, rather more than enough. The emoluments of offices, therefore, can, in most cases, very well bear to be taxed. The persons, besides, who enjoy public offices, especially the more lucrative, are, in all countries, the objects of general envy; and a tax upon their emoluments, even though it should be somewhat higher than upon any other sort of revenue, is always a very popular tax. In England, for example, when, by the land-tax, every other sort of revenue was supposed to be assessed at four shillings in the pound, it was very popular to lay a real tax of five shillings and sixpence in the pound upon the salaries of offices which exceeded a hundred pounds a-year; the pensions of the younger branches of the royal family, the pay of the officers of the army and navy, and a few others less obnoxious to envy, excepted. There are in England no other direct taxes upon the wages of labour.

ARTICLE IV.—Taxes which it is intended should fall indifferently upon every different Species of Revenue

The taxes which it is intended should fall indifferently upon every different species of revenue, are capitation taxes, and taxes upon consumable commodities. Those must be paid indifferently, from whatever revenue the contributors may possess; from the rent of their land, from the profits of their stock, or from the wages of their labour.

Capitation Taxes.

Capitation taxes, if it is attempted to proportion them to the fortune or revenue of each contributor, become altogether arbitrary. The state of a man's fortune varies from day to day; and, without an inquisition, more intolerable than any tax, and renewed at least once every year, can only be guessed at. His assessment, therefore, must, in most cases, depend upon the good or bad humour of his assessors, and must, therefore, be altogether arbitrary and uncertain.

Capitation taxes, if they are proportioned, not to the supposed fortune, but to the rank of each contributor, become altogether unequal; the degrees of fortune being frequently unequal in the same degree of rank.

Such taxes, therefore, if it is attempted to render them equal, become altogether arbitrary and uncertain; and if it is attempted to render them certain and not arbitrary, become altogether unequal. Let the tax be light or heavy, uncertainty is always a great grievance. In a light tax, a considerable degree of inequality may be supported; in a heavy one, it is altogether intolerable.

In the different poll-taxes which took place in England during the reign of William III. the contributors were, the greater part of them, assessed according to the degree of their rank; as dukes, marquises, earls, viscounts, barons, esquires, gentlemen, the eldest and youngest sons of peers, etc. All shop-keepers and tradesmen worth more than three hundred pounds, that is, the better sort of them, were subject to the same assessment, how great soever might be the difference in their fortunes. Their rank was more considered than their fortune. Several of those who, in the first poll-tax, were rated according to their supposed fortune were afterwards rated according to their rank. Serjeants, attorneys, and proctors at law, who, in the first poll-tax, were assessed at three shillings in the pound of their supposed income, were afterwards assessed as gentlemen. In the assessment of a tax which was not very heavy, a considerable degree of inequality had been found less insupportable than any degree of uncertainty.

In the capitation which has been levied in France, without any interruption, since the beginning of the present century, the highest orders of people are rated according to their rank, by an invariable tariff; the lower orders of people, according to what is supposed to be their fortune, by an assessment which varies from year to year. The officers of the king's court, the judges, and other officers in the superior courts of justice, the officers of the troops, etc are assessed in the first manner. The inferior ranks of people in the provinces are assessed in the second. In France, the great easily submit to a considerable degree of inequality in a tax which, so far as it affects them, is not a very heavy one; but could not brook the arbitrary assessment of an intendant.

The inferior ranks of people must, in that country, suffer patiently the usage which their superiors think proper to give them.

In England, the different poll-taxes never produced the sum which had been expected from them, or which it was supposed they might have produced, had they been exactly levied. In France, the capitation always produces the sum expected from it. The mild government of England, when it assessed the different ranks of people to the poll-tax, contented itself with what that assessment happened to produce, and required no compensation for the loss which the state might sustain, either by those who could not pay, or by those who would not pay (for there were many such), and who, by the indulgent execution of the law, were not forced to pay. The more severe government of France assesses upon each generality a certain sum, which the intendant must find as he can. If any province complains of being assessed too high, it may, in the assessment of next year, obtain an abatement proportioned to the overcharge of the year before; but it must pay in the mean time. The intendant, in order to be sure of finding the sum assessed upon his generality, was empowered to assess it in a larger sum, that the failure or inability of some of the contributors might be compensated by the overcharge of the rest; and till 1765, the fixation of this surplus assessment was left altogether to his discretion. In that year, indeed, the council assumed this power to itself. In the capitation of the provinces, it is observed by the perfectly well informed author of the Memoirs upon the Impositions in France, the proportion which falls upon the nobility, and upon those whose privileges exempt them from the taille, is the least considerable. The largest falls upon those subject to the taille, who are assessed to the capitation at so much a-pound of what they pay to that other tax. Capitation taxes, so far as they are levied upon the lower ranks of people, are direct taxes upon the wages of labour, and are attended with all the inconveniencies of such taxes.

Capitation taxes are levied at little expense; and, where they are rigorously exacted, afford a very sure revenue to the state. It is upon this account that, in countries where the case, comfort, and security of the inferior ranks of people are little attended to, capitation taxes are very common. It is in general, however, but a small part of the public revenue, which, in a great empire, has ever been drawn from such taxes; and the greatest sum which they have ever afforded, might always have been found in some other way much more convenient to the people.

Taxes upon Consumable Commodities.

The impossibility of taxing the people, in proportion to their revenue, by any capitation, seems to have given occasion to the invention of taxes upon consumable commodities. The state not knowing how to tax, directly and proportionably, the revenue of its subjects, endeavours to tax it indirectly by taxing their expense, which, it is supposed, will, in most cases, be nearly in proportion to their revenue. Their expense is taxed, by taxing the consumable commodities upon which it is laid out.

Consumable commodities are either necessaries or luxuries.

By necessaries I understand, not only the commodities which are indispensibly necessary for the support of life, but whatever the custom of the country renders it indecent for creditable people, even of the lowest order, to be without. A linen shirt, for example, is, strictly speaking, not a necessary of life. The Greeks and Romans lived, I suppose, very comfortably, though they had no linen. But in the present times, through the greater part of Europe, a creditable day-labourer would be ashamed to appear in public without a linen shirt, the want of which would be supposed to denote that disgraceful degree of poverty, which, it is presumed, nobody can well fall into without extreme bad conduct. Custom, in the same manner, has rendered leather shoes a necessary of life in England. The poorest creditable person, of either sex, would be ashamed to appear in public without them. In Scotland, custom has rendered them a necessary of life to the lowest order of men; but not to the same order of women, who may, without any discredit, walk about barefooted. In France, they are necessaries neither to men nor to women;

the lowest rank of both sexes appearing there publicly, without any discredit, sometimes in wooden shoes, and sometimes barefooted. Under necessaries, therefore, I comprehend, not only those things which nature, but those things which the established rules of decency have rendered necessary to the lowest rank of people. All other things I call luxuries, without meaning, by this appellation, to throw the smallest degree of reproach upon the temperate use of them. Beer and ale, for example, in Great Britain, and wine, even in the wine countries, I call luxuries. A man of any rank may, without any reproach, abstain totally from tasting such liquors. Nature does not render them necessary for the support of life; and custom nowhere renders it indecent to live without them.

As the wages of labour are everywhere regulated, partly by the demand for it, and partly by the average price of the necessary articles of subsistence; whatever raises this average price must necessarily raise those wages; so that the labourer may still be able to purchase that quantity of those necessary articles which the state of the demand for labour, whether increasing, stationary, or declining, requires that he should have. {See book i.chap. 8} A tax upon those articles necessarily raises their price somewhat higher than the amount of the tax, because the dealer, who advances the tax, must generally get it back, with a profit. Such a tax must, therefore, occasion a rise in the wages of labour, proportionable to this rise of price.

It is thus that a tax upon the necessaries of life operates exactly in the same manner as a direct tax upon the wages of labour. The labourer, though he may pay it out of his hand, cannot, for any considerable time at least, be properly said even to advance it. It must always, in the long-run, be advanced to him by his immediate employer, in the advanced state of wages. His employer, if he is a manufacturer, will charge upon the price of his goods the rise of wages, together with a profit, so that the final payment of the tax, together with this overcharge, will fall upon the consumer. If his employer is a farmer, the final payment, together with a like overcharge, will fall upon the rent of the landlord.

It is otherwise with taxes upon what I call luxuries, even upon those of the poor. The rise in the price of the taxed commodities, will not necessarily occasion any rise in the wages of labour. A tax upon tobacco, for example, though a luxury of the poor, as well as of the rich, will not raise wages. Though it is taxed in England at three times, and in France at fifteen times its original price, those high duties seem to have no effect upon the wages of labour. The same thing maybe said of the taxes upon tea and sugar, which, in England and Holland, have become luxuries of the lowest ranks of people; and of those upon chocolate, which, in Spain, is said to have become so.

The different taxes which, in Great Britain, have, in the course of the present century, been imposed upon spiritous liquors, are not supposed to have had any effect upon the wages of labour. The rise in the price of porter, occasioned by an additional tax of three shillings upon the barrel of strong beer, has not raised the wages of common labour in London. These were about eighteen pence or twenty pence a-day before the tax, and they are not more now.

The high price of such commodities does not necessarily diminish the ability of the inferior ranks of people to bring up families. Upon the sober and industrious poor, taxes upon such commodities act as sumptuary laws, and dispose them either to moderate, or to refrain altogether from the use of superfluities which they can no longer easily afford. Their ability to bring up families, in consequence of this forced frugality, instead of being diminished, is frequently, perhaps, increased by the tax. It is the sober and industrious poor who generally bring up the most numerous families, and who principally supply the demand for useful labour. All the poor, indeed, are not sober and industrious; and the dissolute and disorderly might continue to indulge themselves in the use of such commodities, after this rise of price, in the same manner as before, without regarding the distress which this indulgence might bring upon their families. Such disorderly persons, however, seldom rear up numerous families, their children generally perishing from neglect, mismanagement, and the scantiness or unwholesomeness of their food. If by the strength of their constitution, they survive the hardships to which the bad conduct of their parents exposes them, yet the example of that bad conduct commonly corrupts their morals; so that, instead of being useful to society by their industry, they become public nuisances by their vices and disorders. Through the advanced price of the luxuries of the poor, therefore, might increase somewhat the distress of such disorderly families, and thereby diminish somewhat their ability to bring up children, it would not probably diminish much the useful population of the country.

Any rise in the average price of necessaries, unless it be compensated by a proportionable rise in the wages of labour, must necessarily diminish, more or less, the ability of the poor to bring up numerous families, and, consequently, to supply the demand for useful labour; whatever may be the state of that demand, whether increasing, stationary, or declining; or such as requires an increasing, stationary, or declining population.

Taxes upon luxuries have no tendency to raise the price of any other commodities, except that of the commodities taxed. Taxes upon necessaries, by raising the wages of labour, necessarily tend to raise the price of all manufactures, and consequently to diminish the extent of their sale and consumption. Taxes upon luxuries are finally paid by the consumers of the commodities taxed, without any retribution. They fall indifferently upon every species of revenue, the wages of labour, the profits of stock, and the rent of land. Taxes upon necessaries, so far as they affect the labouring poor, are finally paid, partly by landlords, in the diminished rent of their lands, and partly by rich consumers, whether landlords or others, in the advanced price of manufactured goods; and always with a considerable overcharge. The advanced price of such manufactures as are real necessaries of life, and are destined for the consumption of the poor, of coarse woollens, for example, must be compensated to the poor by a farther advancement of their wages. The middling and superior ranks of people, if they understood their own interest, ought always to oppose all taxes upon the necessaries of life, as well as all taxes upon the wages of labour. The final payment of both the one and the other falls altogether upon themselves, and always with a considerable overcharge. They fall heaviest upon the landlords, who always pay in a double capacity; in that of landlords, by the reduction, of their rent; and in that of rich consumers, by the increase of their expense. The observation of Sir Matthew Decker, that certain taxes are, in the price of certain goods, sometimes repeated and accumulated four or five times, is perfectly just with regard to taxes upon the necessaries of life. In the price of leather, for example, you must pay not only for the tax upon the leather of your own shoes, but for a part of that upon those of the shoemaker and the tanner. You must pay, too, for the tax upon the salt, upon the soap, and upon the candles which those workmen consume while employed in your service; and for the tax upon the leather, which the saltmaker, the soap-maker, and the candle-maker consume, while employed in their service.

In Great Britain, the principal taxes upon the necessaries of life, are those upon the four commodities just now mentioned, salt, leather, soap, and candles.

Salt is a very ancient and a very universal subject of taxation. It was taxed among the Romans, and it is so at present in, I believe, every part of Europe. The quantity annually consumed by any individual is so small, and may be purchased so gradually, that nobody, it seems to have been thought, could feel very sensibly even a pretty heavy tax upon it. It is in England taxed at three shillings and fourpence a bushel; about three times the original price of the commodity. In some other countries, the tax is still higher. Leather is a real necessary of life. The use of linen renders soap such. In countries where the winter nights are long, candles are a necessary instrument of trade. Leather and soap are in Great Britain taxed at three halfpence a-pound; candles at a penny; taxes which, upon the original price of leather, may amount to about eight or ten per cent.; upon that of soap, to about twenty or five-and-twenty per cent.; and upon that of candles to about fourteen or fifteen per cent.; taxes which, though lighter than that upon salt, are still very heavy. As all those four commodities are real necessaries of life, such heavy taxes upon them must increase somewhat the expense of the sober and industrious poor, and must consequently raise more or less the wages of their labour.

In a country where the winters are so cold as in Great Britain, fuel is, during that season, in the strictest sense of the word, a necessary of life, not only for the purpose of dressing victuals, but for the comfortable subsistence of many different sorts of workmen who work within doors; and coals are the cheapest of all fuel. The price of fuel has so important an influence upon that of labour, that all over Great Britain, manufactures have confined themselves principally to the coal counties; other parts of the country, on account of the high price of this necessary article, not being able to work so cheap. In some manufactures, besides, coal is a necessary instrument of trade; as in those of glass, iron, and all other metals. If a bounty could in any case be reasonable, it might perhaps be so upon the transportation of coals from those parts of the country in which they abound, to those in which they are wanted. But the legislature, instead of a bounty, has imposed a tax of three shillings and threepence a-ton upon coals carried coastways; which, upon most sorts of coal, is more than sixty per cent. of the original price at the coal pit. Coals carried, either by land or by inland navigation, pay no duty. Where they are naturally cheap, they are consumed duty free; where they are naturally dear, they are loaded with a heavy duty.

Such taxes, though they raise the price of subsistence, and consequently the wages of labour, yet they afford a considerable revenue to government, which it might not be easy to find in any other way. There may, therefore, be good reasons for continuing them. The bounty upon the exportation of corn, so far as it tends, in the actual state of tillage, to raise the price of that necessary article, produces all the like bad effects; and instead of affording any revenue, frequently occasions a very great expense to government. The high duties upon the importation of foreign corn, which, in years of moderate plenty, amount to a prohibition; and the absolute prohibition of the importation, either of live cattle, or of salt provisions, which takes place in the ordinary state of the law, and which, on account of the scarcity, is at present suspended for a limited time with regard to Ireland and the British plantations, have all had the bad effects of taxes upon the necessaries of life, and produce no revenue to government. Nothing seems necessary for the repeal of such regulations, but to convince the public of the futility of that system in consequence of which they have been established.

Taxes upon the necessaries of life are much higher in many other countries than in Great Britain. Duties upon flour and meal when ground at the mill, and upon bread when baked at the oven, take place in many countries. In Holland the money-price of the bread consumed in towns is supposed to be doubled by means of such taxes. In lieu of a part of them, the people who live in the country, pay every year so much a-head, according to the sort of bread they are supposed to consume. Those who consume wheaten bread pay three guilders fifteen stivers; about six shillings and ninepence halfpenny. Those, and some other taxes of the same kind, by raising the price of labour, are said to have ruined the greater part of the manufactures of Holland {Memoires concernant les Droits, etc. p. 210, 211.}. Similar taxes, though not quite so heavy, take place in the Milanese, in the states of Genoa, in the duchy of Modena, in the duchies of Parma, Placentia, and Guastalla, and the Ecclesiastical state. A French author {Le Reformateur} of some note, has proposed to reform the finances of his country, by substituting in the room of the greater part of other taxes, this most ruinous of all taxes. There is nothing so absurd, says Cicero, which has not sometimes been asserted by some philosophers.

Taxes upon butcher's meat are still more common than those upon bread. It may indeed be doubted, whether butcher's meat is any where a necessary of life. Grain and other vegetables, with the help of milk, cheese, and butter, or oil, where butter is not to be had, it is known from experience, can, without any butcher's meat, afford the most plentiful, the most wholesome, the most nourishing, and the most invigorating diet. Decency nowhere requires that any man should eat butcher's meat, as it in most places requires that he should wear a linen shirt or a pair of leather shoes.

Consumable commodities, whether necessaries or luxuries, may be taxed in two different ways. The consumer may either pay an annual sum on account of his using or consuming goods of a certain kind; or the goods may be taxed while they remain in the hands of the dealer, and before they are delivered to the consumer. The consumable goods which last a considerable time before they are consumed altogether, are most properly taxed in the one way; those of which the consumption is either immediate or more speedy, in the other. The coach-tax and plate tax are examples of the former method of imposing; the greater part of the other duties of excise and customs, of the latter.

A coach may, with good management, last ten or twelve years. It might be taxed, once for all, before it comes out of the hands of the coach-maker. But it is certainly more convenient for the buyer to pay four pounds a-year for the privilege of keeping a coach, than to pay all at once forty or forty-eight pounds additional price to the coach-maker; or a sum equivalent to what the tax is likely to cost him during the time he uses the same coach. A service of plate in the same manner, may last more than a century. It is certainly-easier for the consumer to pay five shillings a-year for every hundred ounces of plate, near one per cent. of the value, than to redeem this long annuity at five-and-twenty or thirty years purchase, which would enhance the price at least five-and-twenty or thirty per cent. The different taxes which affect houses, are certainly more conveniently paid by moderate annual payments, than by a heavy tax of equal value upon the first building or sale of the house.

It was the well-known proposal of Sir Matthew Decker, that all commodities, even those of which the consumption is either immediate or speedy, should be taxed in this manner; the dealer advancing nothing, but the consumer paying a certain annual sum for the licence to consume certain goods. The object of his scheme was to promote all the different branches of foreign trade, particularly the carrying trade, by taking away all duties upon importation and exportation, and thereby enabling the merchant to employ his whole capital and credit in the purchase of goods and the freight of ships, no part of either being diverted towards the advancing of taxes, The project, however, of taxing, in this manner, goods of immediate or speedy consumption, seems liable to the four following very important objections. First, the tax would be more unequal, or not so well proportioned to the expense and consumption of the different contributors, as in the way in which it is commonly imposed. The taxes upon ale, wine, and spiritous liquors, which are advanced by the dealers, are finally paid by the different consumers, exactly in proportion to their respective consumption. But if the tax were to be paid by purchasing a licence to drink those liquors, the sober would, in proportion to his consumption, be taxed much more heavily than the drunken consumer. A family which exercised great hospitality, would be taxed much more lightly than one who entertained fewer guests. Secondly, this mode of taxation, by paying for an annual, half-yearly, or quarterly licence to consume certain goods, would diminish very much one of the principal conveniences of taxes upon goods of speedy consumption; the piece-meal payment. In the price of threepence halfpenny, which is at present paid for a pot of porter, the different taxes upon malt, hops, and beer, together with the extraordinary profit which the brewer charges for having advanced than, may perhaps amount to about three halfpence. If a workman can conveniently spare those three halfpence, he buys a pot of porter. If he cannot, he contents himself with a pint; and, as a penny saved is a penny got, he thus gains a farthing by his temperance. He pays the tax piece-meal, as he can afford to pay it, and when he can afford to pay it, and every act of payment is perfectly voluntary, and what he can avoid if he chuses to do so. Thirdly, such taxes would operate less as sumptuary laws. When the licence was once purchased, whether the purchaser drunk much or drunk little, his tax would be the same. Fourthly, if a workman were to pay all at once, by yearly, half-yearly, or quarterly payments, a tax equal to what he at present pays, with little or no inconveniency, upon all the different pots and pints of porter which he drinks in any such period of time, the sum might frequently distress him very much. This mode of taxation, therefore, it seems evident, could never, without the most grievous oppression, produce a revenue nearly equal to what is derived from the present mode without any oppression. In several countries, however, commodities of an immediate or very speedy consumption are taxed in this manner. In Holland, people pay so much a-head for a licence to drink tea. I have already mentioned a tax upon bread, which, so far as it is consumed in farm houses and country villages, is there levied in the same manner.

The duties of excise are imposed chiefly upon goods of home produce, destined for home consumption. They are imposed only upon a few sorts of goods of the most general use. There can never be any doubt, either concerning the goods which are subject to those duties, or concerning the particular duty which each species of goods is subject to. They fall almost altogether upon what I call luxuries, excepting always the four duties above mentioned, upon salt, soap, leather, candles, and perhaps that upon green glass.

The duties of customs are much more ancient than those of excise. They seem to have been called customs, as denoting customary payments, which had been in use for time immemorial. They appear to have been originally considered as taxes upon the profits of merchants. During the barbarous times of feudal anarchy, merchants, like all the other inhabitants of burghs, were considered as little better than emancipated bondmen, whose persons were despised, and whose gains were envied. The great nobility, who had consented that the king should tallage the profits of their own tenants, were not unwilling that he should tallage likewise those of an order of men whom it was much less their interest to protect. In those ignorant times, it was not understood, that the profits of merchants are a subject not taxable directly; or that the final payment of all such taxes must fall, with a considerable overcharge, upon the consumers.

The gains of alien merchants were looked upon more unfavourably than those of English merchants. It was natural, therefore, that those of the former should be taxed more heavily than those of the latter. This distinction between the duties upon aliens and those upon English merchants, which was begun from ignorance, has been continued front the spirit of monopoly, or in order to give our own merchants an advantage, both in the home and in the foreign market.

With this distinction, the ancient duties of customs were imposed equally upon all sorts of goods, necessaries as well its luxuries, goods exported as well as goods imported. Why should the dealers in one sort of goods, it seems to have been thought, be more favoured than those in another? or why should the merchant exporter be more favoured than the merchant importer?

The ancient customs were divided into three branches. The first, and, perhaps, the most ancient of all those duties, was that upon wool and leather. It seems to have been chiefly or altogether an exportation duty. When the woollen manufacture came to be established in England, lest the king should lose any part of his customs upon wool by the exportation of woollen cloths, a like duty was imposed upon them. The other two branches were, first, a duty upon wine, which being imposed at so much a-ton, was called a tonnage; and, secondly, a duty upon all other goods, which being imposed at so much a-pound of their supposed value, was called a poundage. In the forty-seventh year of Edward III., a duty of sixpence in the pound was imposed upon all goods exported and imported, except wools, wool-felts, leather, and wines which were subject to particular duties. In the fourteenth of Richard II., this duty was raised to one shilling in the pound; but, three years afterwards, it was again reduced to sixpence. It was raised to eightpence in the second year of Henry IV.; and, in the fourth of the same prince, to one shilling. From this time to the ninth year of William III., this duty continued at one shilling in the pound. The duties of tonnage and poundage were generally granted to the king by one and the same act of parliament, and were called the subsidy of tonnage and poundage. The subsidy of poundage having continued for so long a time at one shilling in the pound, or at five per cent., a subsidy came, in the language of the customs, to denote a general duty of this kind of five per cent. This subsidy, which is now called the old subsidy, still continues to be levied, according to the book of rates established by the twelfth of Charles II. The method of ascertaining, by a book of rates, the value of goods subject to this duty, is said to be older than the time of James I. The new subsidy, imposed by the ninth and tenth of William III., was an additional five per cent. upon the greater part of goods. The one-third and the two-third subsidy made up between them another five per cent. of which they were proportionable parts. The subsidy of 1747 made a fourth five per cent. upon the greater part of goods; and that of 1759, a fifth upon some particular sorts of goods. Besides those five subsidies, a great variety of other duties have occasionally been imposed upon particular sorts of goods, in order sometimes to relieve the exigencies of the state, and sometimes to regulate the trade of the country, according to the principles of the mercantile system.

That system has come gradually more and more into fashion. The old subsidy was imposed indifferently upon exportation, as well as importation. The four subsequent subsidies, as well as the other duties which have since been occasionally imposed upon particular sorts of goods, have, with a few exceptions, been laid altogether upon importation. The greater part of the ancient duties which had been imposed upon the exportation of the goods of home produce and manufacture, have either been lightened or taken away altogether. In most cases, they have been taken away. Bounties have even been given upon the exportation of some of them. Drawbacks, too, sometimes of the whole, and, in most cases, of a part of the duties which are paid upon the importation of foreign goods, have been granted upon their exportation. Only half the duties imposed by the old subsidy upon importation, are drawn back upon exportation; but the whole of those imposed by the latter subsidies and other imposts are, upon the greater parts of the goods, drawn back in the same manner. This growing favour of exportation, and discouragement of importation, have suffered only a few exceptions, which chiefly concern the materials of some manufactures. These our merchants and manufacturers are willing should come as cheap as possible to themselves, and as dear as possible to their rivals and competitors in other countries. Foreign materials are, upon this account, sometimes allowed to be imported duty-free; spanish wool, for example, flax, and raw linen yarn. The exportation of the materials of home produce, and of those which are the particular produce of our colonies, has sometimes been prohibited, and sometimes subjected to higher duties. The exportation of English wool has been prohibited. That of beaver skins, of beaver wool, and of gum-senega, has been subjected to higher duties; Great Britain, by the conquests of Canada and Senegal, having got almost the monopoly of those commodities.

That the mercantile system has not been very favourable to the revenue of the great body of the people, to the annual produce of the land and labour of the country, I have endeavoured to show in the fourth book of this Inquiry. It seems not to have been more favourable to the revenue of the sovereign; so far, at least, as that revenue depends upon the duties of customs.

In consequence of that system, the importation of several sorts of goods has been prohibited altogether. This prohibition has, in some cases, entirely prevented, and in others has very much diminished, the importation of those commodities, by reducing the importers to the necessity of smuggling. It has entirely prevented the importation of foreign wollens; and it has very much diminished that of foreign silks and velvets, In both cases, it has entirely annihilated the revenue of customs which might have been levied upon such importation.

The high duties which have been imposed upon the importation of many different sorts of foreign goods in order to discourage their consumption in Great Britain, have, in many cases, served only to encourage smuggling, and, in all cases, have reduced the revenues of the customs below what more moderate duties would have afforded. The saying of Dr. Swift, that in the arithmetic of the customs, two and two, instead of making four, make sometimes only one, holds perfectly true with regard to such heavy duties, which never could have been imposed, had not the mercantile system taught us, in many cases, to employ taxation as an instrument, not of revenue, but of monopoly.

The bounties which are sometimes given upon the exportation of home produce and manufactures, and the drawbacks which are paid upon the re-exportation of the greater part of foreign goods, have given occasion to many frauds, and to a species of smuggling, more destructive of the public revenue than any other. In order to obtain the bounty or drawback, the goods, it is well known, are sometimes shipped, and sent to sea, but soon afterwards clandestinely re-landed in some other part of the country. The defalcation of the revenue of customs occasioned by bounties and drawbacks, of which a great part are obtained fraudulently, is very great. The gross produce of the customs, in the year which ended on the 5th of January 1755, amounted to £5,068,000. The bounties which were paid out of this revenue, though in that year there was no bounty upon corn, amounted to £167,806. The drawbacks which were paid upon debentures and certificates, to £2,156,800. Bounties and drawbacks together amounted to £2,324,600. In consequence of these deductions, the revenue of the customs amounted only to £2,743,400; from which deducting £287,900 for the expense of management, in salaries and other incidents, the neat revenue of the customs for that year comes out to be £2,455,500. The expense of management, amounts, in this manner, to between five and six per cent. upon the gross revenue of the customs; and to something more than ten per cent. upon what remains of that revenue, after deducting what is paid away in bounties and drawbacks.

Heavy duties being imposed upon almost all goods imported, our merchant importers smuggle as much, and make entry of as little as they can. Our merchant exporters, on the contrary, make entry of more than they export; sometimes out of vanity, and to pass for great dealers in goods which pay no duty gain a bounty back. Our exports, in consequence of these different frauds, appear upon the custom-house books greatly to overbalance our imports, to the unspeakable comfort of those politicians, who measure the national prosperity by what they call the balance of trade.

All goods imported, unless particularly exempted, and such exemptions are not very numerous, are liable to some duties of customs. If any goods are imported, not mentioned in the book of rates, they are taxed at 4s:9¾d. for every twenty shillings value, according to the oath of the importer, that is, nearly at five subsidies, or five poundage duties. The book of rates is extremely comprehensive, and enumerates a great variety of articles, many of them little used, and, therefore, not well known. It is, upon this account, frequently uncertain under what article a particular sort of goods ought to be classed, and, consequently what duty they ought to pay. Mistakes with regard to this sometimes ruin the custom-house officer, and frequently occasion much trouble, expense, and vexation to the importer. In point of perspicuity, precision, and distinctness, therefore, the duties of customs are much inferior to those of excise.

In order that the greater part of the members of any society should contribute to the public revenue, in proportion to their respective expense, it does not seem necessary that every single article of that expense should be taxed. The revenue which is levied by the duties of excise is supposed to fall as equally upon the contributors as that which is levied by the duties of customs; and the duties of excise are imposed upon a few articles only of the most general used and consumption. It has been the opinion of many people, that, by proper management, the duties of customs might likewise, without any loss to the public revenue, and with great advantage to foreign trade, be confined to a few articles only.

The foreign articles, of the most general use and consumption in Great Britain, seem at present to consist chiefly in foreign wines and brandies; in some of the productions of America and the West Indies, sugar, rum, tobacco, cocoa-nuts, etc. and in some of those of the East Indies, tea, coffee, china-ware, spiceries of all kinds, several sorts of piece-goods, etc. These different articles afford, the greater part of the perhaps, at present, revenue which is drawn from the duties of customs. The taxes which at present subsist upon foreign manufactures, if you except those upon the few contained in the foregoing enumeration, have, the greater part of them, been imposed for the purpose, not of revenue, but of monopoly, or to give our own merchants an advantage in the home market. By removing all prohibitions, and by subjecting all foreign manufactures to such moderate taxes, as it was found from experience, afforded upon each article the greatest revenue to the public, our own workmen might still have a considerable advantage in the home market; and many articles, some of which at present afford no revenue to government, and others a very inconsiderable one, might afford a very great one.

High taxes, sometimes by diminishing the consumption of the taxed commodities, and sometimes by encouraging smuggling frequently afford a smaller revenue to government than what might be drawn from more moderate taxes.

When the diminution of revenue is the effect of the diminution of consumption, there can be but one remedy, and that is the lowering of the tax. When the diminution of revenue is the effect of the encouragement given to smuggling, it may, perhaps, be remedied in two ways; either by diminishing the temptation to smuggle, or by increasing the difficulty of smuggling. The temptation to smuggle can be diminished only by the lowering of the tax; and the difficulty of smuggling can be increased only by establishing that system of administration which is most proper for preventing it.

The excise laws, it appears, I believe, from experience, obstruct and embarrass the operations of the smuggler much more effectually than those of the customs. By introducing into the customs a system of administration as similar to that of the excise as the nature of the different duties will admit, the difficulty of smuggling might be very much increased. This alteration, it has been supposed by many people, might very easily be brought about.

The importer of commodities liable to any duties of customs, it has been said, might, at his option, be allowed either to carry them to his own private warehouse; or to lodge them in a warehouse, provided either at his own expense or at that of the public, but under the key of the custom-house officer, and never to be opened but in his presence. If the merchant carried them to his own private warehouse, the duties to be immediately paid, and never afterwards to be drawn back; and that warehouse to be at all times subject to the visit and examination of the custom-house officer, in order to ascertain how far the quantity contained in it corresponded with that for which the duty had been paid. If he carried them to the public warehouse, no duty to be paid till they were taken out for home consumption. If taken out for exportation, to be duty-free; proper security being always given that they should be so exported. The dealers in those particular commodities, either by wholesale or retail, to be at all times subject to the visit and examination of the custom-house officer; and to be obliged to justify, by proper certificates, the payment of the duty upon the whole quantity contained in their shops or warehouses. What are called the excise duties upon rum imported, are at present levied in this manner; and the same system of administration might, perhaps, be extended to all duties upon goods imported; provided always that those duties were, like the duties of excise, confined to a few sorts of goods of the most general use and consumption. If they were extended to almost all sorts of goods, as at present, public warehouses of sufficient extent could not easily be provided; and goods of a very delicate nature, or of which the preservation required much care and attention, could not safely be trusted by the merchant in any warehouse but his own.

If, by such a system of administration, smuggling to any considerable extent could be prevented, even under pretty high duties; and if every duty was occasionally either heightened or lowered according as it was most likely, either the one way or the other, to afford the greatest revenue to the state; taxation being always employed as an instrument of revenue, and never of monopoly; it seems not improbable that a revenue, at least equal to the present neat revenue of the customs, might be drawn from duties upon the importation of only a few sorts of goods of the most general use and consumption; and that the duties of customs might thus be brought to the same degree of simplicity, certainty, and precision, as those of excise. What the revenue at present loses by drawbacks upon the re-exportation of foreign goods, which are afterwards re-landed and consumed at home, would, under this system, be saved altogether. If to this saving, which would alone be very considerable, were added the abolition of all bounties upon the exportation of home produce; in all cases in which those bounties were not in reality drawbacks of some duties of excise which had before been advanced; it cannot well be doubted, but that the neat revenue of customs might, after an alteration of this kind, be fully equal to what it had ever been before.

If, by such a change of system, the public revenue suffered no loss, the trade and manufactures of the country would certainly gain a very considerable advantage. The trade in the commodities not taxed, by far the greatest number would be perfectly free, and might be carried on to and from all parts of the world with every possible advantage. Among those commodities would be comprehended all the necessaries of life, and all the materials of manufacture. So far as the free importation of the necessaries of life reduced their average money price in the home market, it would reduce the money price of labour, but without reducing in any respect its real recompence. The value of money is in proportion to the quantity of the necessaries of life which it will purchase. That of the necessaries of life is altogether independent of the quantity of money which can be had for them. The reduction in the money price of labour would necessarily be attended with a proportionable one in that of all home manufactures, which would thereby gain some advantage in all foreign markets. The price of some manufactures would be reduced, in a still greater proportion, by the free importation of the raw materials. If raw silk could be imported from China and Indostan, duty-free, the silk manufacturers in England could greatly undersell those of both France and Italy. There would be no occasion to prohibit the importation of foreign silks and velvets. The cheapness of their goods would secure to our own workmen, not only the possession of a home, but a very great command of the foreign market. Even the trade in the commodities taxed, would be carried on with much more advantage than at present. If those commodities were delivered out of the public warehouse for foreign exportation, being in this case exempted from all taxes, the trade in them would be perfectly free. The carrying trade, in all sorts of goods, would, under this system, enjoy every possible advantage. If these commodities were delivered out for home consumption, the importer not being obliged to advance the tax till he had an opportunity of selling his goods, either to some dealer, or to some consumer, he could always afford to sell them cheaper than if he had been obliged to advance it at the moment of importation. Under the same taxes, the foreign trade of consumption, even in the taxed commodities, might in this manner be carried on with much more advantage than it is at present.

It was the object of the famous excise scheme of Sir Robert Walpole, to establish, with regard to wine and tobacco, a system not very unlike that which is here proposed. But though the bill which was then brought into Parliament, comprehended those two commodities only, it was generally supposed to be meant as an introduction to a more extensive scheme of the same kind. Faction, combined with the interest of smuggling merchants, raised so violent, though so unjust a clamour, against that bill, that the minister thought proper to drop it; and, from a dread of exciting a clamour of the same kind, none of his successors have dared to resume the project.

The duties upon foreign luxuries, imported for home consumption, though they sometimes fall upon the poor, fall principally upon people of middling or more than middling fortune. Such are, for example, the duties upon foreign wines, upon coffee, chocolate, tea, sugar, etc.

The duties upon the cheaper luxuries of home produce, destined for home consumption, fall pretty equally upon people of all ranks, in proportion to their respective expense. The poor pay the duties upon malt, hops, beer, and ale, upon their own consumption; the rich, upon both their own consumption and that of their servants.

The whole consumption of the inferior ranks of people, or of those below the middling rank, it must be observed, is, in every country, much greater, not only in quantity, but in value, than that of the middling, and of those above the middling rank. The whole expense of the inferior is much greater titan that of the superior ranks. In the first place, almost the whole capital of every country is annually distributed among the inferior ranks of people, as the wages of productive labour. Secondly, a great part of the revenue, arising from both the rent of land and the profits of stock, is annually distributed among the same rank, in the wages and maintenance of menial servants, and other unproductive labourers. Thirdly, some part of the profits of stock belongs to the same rank, as a revenue arising from the employment of their small capitals. The amount of the profits annually made by small shopkeepers, tradesmen, and retailers of all kinds, is everywhere very considerable, and makes a very considerable portion of the annual produce. Fourthly and lastly, some part even of the rent of land belongs to the same rank; a considerable part to those who are somewhat below the middling rank, and a small part even to the lowest rank; common labourers sometimes possessing in property an acre or two of land. Though the expense of those inferior ranks of people, therefore, taking them individually, is very small, yet the whole mass of it, taking them collectively, amounts always to by much the largest portion of the whole expense of the society; what remains of the annual produce of the land and labour of the country, for the consumption of the superior ranks, being always much less, not only in quantity, but in value. The taxes upon expense, therefore, which fall chiefly upon that of the superior ranks of people, upon the smaller portion of the annual produce, are likely to be much less productive than either those which fall indifferently upon the expense of all ranks, or even those which fall chiefly upon that of the inferior ranks, than either those which fall indifferently upon the whole annual produce, or those which fall chiefly upon the larger portion of it. The excise upon the materials and manufacture of home-made fermented and spirituous liquors, is, accordingly, of all the different taxes upon expense, by far the most productive; and this branch of the excise falls very much, perhaps principally, upon the expense of the common people. In the year which ended on the 5th of July 1775, the gross produce of this branch of the excise amounted to £3,341,837:9:9.

It must always be remembered, however, that it is the luxuries, and not the necessary expense of the inferior ranks of people, that ought ever to be taxed. The final payment of any tax upon their necessary expense, would fall altogether upon the superior ranks of people; upon the smaller portion of the annual produce, and not upon the greater. Such a tax must, in all cases, either raise the wages of labour, or lessen the demand for it. It could not raise the wages of labour, without throwing the final payment of the tax upon the superior ranks of people. It could not lessen the demand for labour, without lessening the annual produce of the land and labour of the country, the fund upon which all taxes must be finally paid. Whatever might be the state to which a tax of this kind reduced the demand for labour, it must always raise wages higher than they otherwise would be in that state; and the final payment of this enhancement of wages must, in all cases, fall upon the superior ranks of people.

Fermented liquors brewed, and spiritous liquors distilled, not for sale, but for private use, are not in Great Britain liable to any duties of excise. This exemption, of which the object is to save private families from the odious visit and examination of the tax-gatherer, occasions the burden of those duties to fall frequently much lighter upon the rich than upon the poor. It is not, indeed, very common to distil for private use, though it is done sometimes. But in the country, many middling and almost all rich and great families, brew their own beer. Their strong beer, therefore, costs them eight shillings a-barrel less than it costs the common brewer, who must have his profit upon the tax, as well as upon all the other expense which he advances. Such families, therefore, must drink their beer at least nine or ten shillings a-barrel cheaper than any liquor of the same quality can be drank by the common people, to whom it is everywhere more convenient to buy their beer, by little and little, from the brewery or the ale-house. Malt, in the same manner, that is made for the use of a private family, is not liable to the visit or examination of the tax-gatherer but, in this case the family must compound at seven shillings and sixpence a-head for the tax. Seven shillings and sixpence are equal to the excise upon ten bushels of malt; a quantity fully equal to what all the different members of any sober family, men, women, and children, are, at an average, likely to consume. But in rich and great families, where country hospitality is much practised, the malt liquors consumed by the members of the family make but a small part of the consumption of the house. Either on account of this composition, however, or for other reasons, it is not near so common to malt as to brew for private use. It is difficult to imagine any equitable reason, why those who either brew or distil for private use should not be subject to a composition of the same kind.

A greater revenue than what is at present drawn from all the heavy taxes upon malt, beer, and ale, might be raised, it has frequently been said, by a much lighter tax upon malt; the opportunities of defrauding the revenue being much greater in a brewery than in a malt-house; and those who brew for private use being exempted from all duties or composition for duties, which is not the case with those who malt for private use.

In the porter brewery of London, a quarter of malt is commonly brewed into more than two barrels and a-half, sometimes into three barrels of porter. The different taxes upon malt amount to six shillings a-quarter; those upon strong ale and beer to eight shillings a-barrel. In the porter brewery, therefore, the different taxes upon malt, beer, and ale, amount to between twenty-six and thirty shillings upon the produce of a quarter of malt. In the country brewery for common country sale, a quarter of malt is seldom brewed into less than two barrels of strong, and one barrel of small beer; frequently into two barrels and a-half of strong beer. The different taxes upon small beer amount to one shilling and fourpence a-barrel. In the country brewery, therefore, the different taxes upon malt, beer, and ale, seldom amount to less than twenty-three shillings and fourpence, frequently to twenty-six shillings, upon the produce of a quarter of malt. Taking the whole kingdom at an average, therefore, the whole amount of the duties upon malt, beer, and ale, cannot be estimated at less than twenty-four or twenty-five shillings upon the produce of a quarter of malt. But by taking off all the different duties upon beer and ale, and by trebling the malt tax, or by raising it from six to eighteen shillings upon the quarter of malt, a greater revenue, it is said, might be raised by this single tax, than what is at present drawn from all those heavier taxes.

In 1772, the old malt tax produced	£722,023: 11: 11
The additional	£356,776: 7: 9¾
In 1775, the old tax produced	£561,627: 3: 7½
The additional	£278,650: 15: 3¾
In 1774, the old tax produced	£624,614: 17: 5¾
The additional	£310,745: 2: 8½
In 1775, the old tax produced	£657,357: 0: 8¼
The additional	£323,785: 12: 6¼
	£5,855,580: 12: 0¾
Average of these four years	£958,895: 3: 0
In 1772, the country excise produced	£1,243,120: 5: 3
The London brewery	408,260: 7: 2¾
In 1773, the country excise	£1,245,808: 3: 3
The London brewery	405,406: 17: 10½
In 1774, the country excise	£1,246,373: 14: 5½
The London brewery	320,601: 18: 0¼
In 1775, the country excise	£1,214,583: 6: 1¼
The London brewery	463,670: 7: 0¼
	4) £6,547,832: 19: 2¼
Average of these four years	£1,636,958: 4: 9½
To which adding the average malt tax	958,895: 3: 0¼
The whole amount of those different taxes comes out to be	£2,595,835: 7: 10
But, by trebling the malt tax, or by raising it from six to eighteen shillings upon the quarter of malt, that single tax would produce	£2,876,685: 9: 0
A sum which exceeds the foregoing by	280,832: 1: 3

Under the old malt tax, indeed, is comprehended a tax of four shillings upon the hogshead of cyder, and another of ten shillings upon the barrel of mum. In 1774, the tax upon cyder produced only £3,083:6:8. It probably fell somewhat short of its usual amount; all the different taxes upon cyder, having, that year, produced less than ordinary. The tax upon mum, though much heavier, is still less productive, on account of the smaller consumption of that liquor. But to balance whatever may be the ordinary amount of those two taxes, there is comprehended under what is called the country excise, first, the old excise of six shillings and eightpence upon the hogshead of cyder; secondly, a like tax of six shillings and eightpence upon the hogshead of verjuice; thirdly, another of eight shillings and ninepence upon the hogshead of vinegar; and, lastly, a fourth tax of elevenpence upon the gallon of mead or metheglin. The produce of those different taxes will probably much more than counterbalance that of the duties imposed, by what is called the annual malt tax, upon cyder and mum.

Malt is consumed, not only in the brewery of beer and ale, but in the manufacture of low wines and spirits. If the malt tax were to be raised to eighteen shillings upon the quarter, it might be necessary to make some abatement in the different excises which are imposed upon those particular sorts of low wines and spirits, of which malt makes any part of the materials. In what are called malt spirits, it makes commonly but a third part of the materials; the other two-thirds being either raw barley, or one-third barley and one-third wheat. In the distillery of malt spirits, both the opportunity and the temptation to smuggle are much greater than either in a brewery or in a malt-house; the opportunity, on account of the smaller bulk and greater value of the commodity, and the temptation, on account of the superior height of the duties, which amounted to 3s. 10 2/3d. upon the gallon of spirits. {Though the duties directly imposed upon proof spirits amount only to 2s. 6d per gallon, these, added to the duties upon the low wines, from which they are distilled, amount to 3s 10 2/3d. Both low wines and proof spirits are, to prevent frauds, now rated according to what they gauge in the wash.}

By increasing the duties upon malt, and reducing those upon the distillery, both the opportunities and the temptation to smuggle would be diminished, which might occasion a still further augmentation of revenue.

It has for some time past been the policy of Great Britain to discourage the consumption of spiritous liquors, on account of their supposed tendency to ruin the health and to corrupt the morals of the common people. According to this policy, the abatement of the taxes upon the distillery ought not to be so great as to reduce, in any respect, the price of those liquors. Spiritous liquors might remain as dear as ever; while, at the same time, the wholesome and invigorating liquors of beer and ale might be considerably reduced in their price. The people might thus be in part relieved from one of the burdens of which they at present complain the most; while, at the same time, the revenue might be considerably augmented.

The objections of Dr. Davenant to this alteration in the present system of excise duties, seem to be without foundation. Those objections are, that the tax, instead of dividing itself, as at present, pretty equally upon the profit of the maltster, upon that of the brewer and upon that of the retailer, would so far as it affected profit, fall altogether upon that of the maltster; that the maltster could not so easily get back the amount of the tax in the advanced price of his malt, as the brewer and retailer in the advanced price of their liquor; and that so heavy a tax upon malt might reduce the rent and profit of barley land.

No tax can ever reduce, for any considerable time, the rate of profit in any particular trade, which must always keep its level with other trades in the neighbourhood. The present duties upon malt, beer, and ale, do not affect the profits of the dealers in those commodities, who all get back the tax with an additional profit, in the enhanced price of their goods. A tax, indeed, may render the goods upon which it is imposed so dear, as to diminish the consumption of them. But the consumption of malt is in malt liquors; and a tax of eighteen shillings upon the quarter of malt could not well render those liquors dearer than the different taxes, amounting to twenty-four or twenty-five shillings, do at present. Those liquors, on the contrary, would probably become cheaper, and the consumption of them would be more likely to increase than to diminish.

It is not very easy to understand why it should be more difficult for the maltster to get back eighteen shillings in the advanced price of his malt, than it is at present for the brewer to get back twenty-four or twenty-five, sometimes thirty shillings, in that of his liquor. The maltster, indeed, instead of a tax of six shillings, would be obliged to advance one of eighteen shilling upon every quarter of malt. But the brewer is at present obliged to advance a tax of twenty-four or twenty-five, sometimes thirty shillings, upon every quarter of malt which he brews. It could not be more inconvenient for the maltster to advance a lighter tax, than it is at present for the brewer to advance a heavier one. The maltster does not always keep in his granaries a stock of malt, which it will require a longer time to dispose of than the stock of beer and ale which the brewer frequently keeps in his cellars. The former, therefore, may frequently get the returns of his money as soon as the latter. But whatever inconveniency might arise to the maltster from being obliged to advance a heavier tax, it could easily be remedied, by granting him a few months longer credit than is at present commonly given to the brewer.

Nothing could reduce the rent and profit of barley land, which did not reduce the demand for barley. But a change of system, which reduced the duties upon a quarter of malt brewed into beer and ale, from twentyfour and twenty-five shillings to eighteen shillings, would be more likely to increase than diminish that demand. The rent and profit of barley land, besides, must always be nearly equal to those of other equally fertile and equally well cultivated land. If they were less, some part of the barley land would soon be turned to some other purpose; and if they were greater, more land would soon be turned to the raising of barley. When the ordinary price of any particular produce of land is at what may be called a monopoly price, a tax upon it necessarily reduces the rent and profit of the land which grows it. A tax upon the produce of those precious vineyards, of which the wine falls so much short of the effectual demand, that its price is always above the natural proportion to that of the produce of other equally fertile and equally well cultivated land, would necessarily reduce the rent and profit of those vineyards. The price of the wines being already the highest that could be got for the quantity commonly sent to market, it could not be raised higher without diminishing that quantity; and the quantity could not be diminished without still greater loss, because the lands could not be turned to any other equally valuable produce. The whole weight of the tax, therefore, would fall upon the rent and profit; properly upon the rent of the vineyard. When it has been proposed to lay any new tax upon sugar, our sugar planters have frequently complained that the whole weight of such taxes fell not upon the consumer, but upon the producer; they never having been able to raise the price of their sugar after the tax higher than it was before. The price had, it seems, before the tax, been a monopoly price; and the arguments adduced to show that sugar was an improper subject of taxation, demonstrated perhaps that it was a proper one; the gains of monopolists, whenever they can be come at, being certainly of all subjects the most proper. But the ordinary price of barley has never been a monopoly price; and the rent and profit of barley land have never been above their natural proportion to those of other equally fertile and equally well cultivated land. The different taxes which have been imposed upon malt, beer, and ale, have never lowered the price of barley; have never reduced the rent and profit of barley land. The price of malt to the brewer has constantly risen in proportion to the taxes imposed upon it; and those taxes, together with the different duties upon beer and ale, have constantly either raised the price, or, what comes to the same thing, reduced the quality of those commodities to the consumer. The final payment of those taxes has fallen constantly upon the consumer, and not upon the producer.

The only people likely to suffer by the change of system here proposed, are those who brew for their own private use. But the exemption, which this superior rank of people at present enjoy, from very heavy taxes which are paid by the poor labourer and artificer, is surely most unjust and unequal, and ought to be taken away, even though this change was never to take place. It has probably been the interest of this superior order of people, however, which has hitherto prevented a change of system that could not well fail both to increase the revenue and to relieve the people.

Besides such duties as those of custom and excise above mentioned, there are several others which affect the price of goods more unequally and more indirectly. Of this kind are the duties, which, in French, are called peages, which in old Saxon times were called the duties of passage, and which seem to have been originally established for the same purpose as our turnpike tolls, or the tolls upon our canals and navigable rivers, for the maintenance of the road or of the navigation. Those duties, when applied to such purposes, are most properly imposed according to the bulk or weight of the goods. As they were originally local and provincial duties, applicable to local and provincial purposes, the administration of them was, in most cases, entrusted to the particular town, parish, or lordship, in which they were levied; such communities being, in some way or other, supposed to be accountable for the application. The sovereign, who is altogether unaccountable, has in many countries assumed to himself the administration of those duties; and though he has in most cases enhanced very much the duty, he has in many entirely neglected the application. If the turnpike tolls of Great Britain should ever become one of the resources of government, we may learn, by the example of many other nations, what would probably be the consequence. Such tolls, no doubt, are finally paid by the consumer; but the consumer is not taxed in proportion to his expense, when he pays, not according to the value, but according to the bulk or weight of what he consumes. When such duties are imposed, not according to the bulk or weight, but according to the supposed value of the goods, they become properly a sort of inland customs or excise, which obstruct very much the most important of all branches of commerce, the interior commerce of the country.

In some small states, duties similar to those passage duties are imposed upon goods carried across the territory, either by land or by water, from one foreign country to another. These are in some countries called transit-duties. Some of the little Italian states which are situated upon the Po, and the rivers which run into it, derive some revenue from duties of this kind, which are paid altogether by foreigners, and which, perhaps, are the only duties that one state can impose upon the subjects of another, without obstruction in any respect, the industry or commerce of its own. The most important transit-duty in the world, is that levied by the king of Denmark upon all merchant ships which pass through the Sound.

Such taxes upon luxuries, as the greater part of the duties of customs and excise, though they all fall indifferently upon every different species of revenue, and are paid finally, or without any retribution, by whoever consumes the commodities upon which they are imposed; yet they do not always fall equally or proportionally upon the revenue of every individual. As every man's humour regulates the degree of his consumption, every man contributes rather according to his humour, than proportion to his revenue: the profuse contribute more, the parsimonious less, than their proper proportion. During the minority of a man of great fortune, he contributes commonly very little, by his consumption, towards the support of that state from whose protection he derives a great revenue. Those who live in another country, contribute nothing by their consumption towards the support of the government of that country, in which is situated the source of their revenue. If in this latter country there should be no land tax, nor any considerable duty upon the transference either of moveable or immoveable property, as is the case in Ireland, such absentees may derive a great revenue from the protection of a government, to the support of which they do not contribute a single shilling. This inequality is likely to be greatest in a country of which the government is, in some respects, subordinate and dependant upon that of some other. The people who possess the most extensive property in the dependant, will, in this case, generally chuse to live in the governing country. Ireland is precisely in this situation; and we cannot therefore wonder, that the proposal of a tax upon absentees should be so very popular in that country. It might, perhaps, be a little difficult to ascertain either what sort, or what degree of absence, would subject a man to be taxed as an absentee, or at what precise time the tax should either begin or end. If you except, however, this very peculiar situation, any inequality in the contribution of individuals which can arise from such taxes, is much more than compensated by the very circumstance which occasions that inequality; the circumstance that every man's contribution is altogether voluntary; it being altogether in his power, either to consume, or not to consume, the commodity taxed. Where such taxes, therefore, are properly assessed, and upon proper commodities, they are paid with less grumbling than any other. When they are advanced by the merchant or manufacturer, the consumer, who finally pays them, soon comes to confound them with the price of the commodities, and almost forgets that he pays any tax. Such taxes are, or may be, perfectly certain; or may be assessed, so as to leave no doubt concerning either what ought to be paid, or when it ought to be paid; concerning either the quantity or the time of payment. What ever uncertainty there may sometimes be, either in the duties of customs in Great Britain, or in other duties of the same kind in other countries, it cannot arise from the nature of those duties, but from the inaccurate or unskilful manner in which the law that imposes them is expressed.

Taxes upon luxuries generally are, and always may be, paid piecemeal, or in proportion as the contributors have occasion to purchase the goods upon which they are imposed. In the time and mode of payment, they are, or may be, of all taxes the most convenient. Upon the whole, such taxes, therefore, are perhaps as agreeable to the three first of the four general maxims concerning taxation, as any other. They offend in every respect against the fourth.

Such taxes, in proportion to what they bring into the public treasury of the state, always take out, or keep out, of the pockets of the people, more than almost any other taxes. They seem to do this in all the four different ways in which it is possible to do it.

First, the levying of such taxes, even when imposed in the most judicious manner, requires a great number of custom-house and excise officers, whose salaries and perquisites are a real tax upon the people, which brings nothing into the treasury of the state. This expense, however, it must be acknowledged, is more moderate in Great Britain than in most other countries. In the year which ended on the 5th of July, 1775, the gross produce of the different duties, under the management of the commissioners of excise in England, amounted to £5,507,308:18:8¼, which was levied at an expense of little more than five and a-half per cent. From this gross produce, however, there must be deducted what was paid away in bounties and drawbacks upon the exportation of exciseable goods, which will reduce the neat produce below five millions. {The neat produce of that year, after deducting all expenses and allowances, amounted to £4,975,652:19:6.} The levying of the salt duty, and excise duty, but under a different management, is much more expensive. The neat revenue of the customs does not amount to two millions and a-half, which is levied at an expense of more than ten per cent., in the salaries of officers and other incidents. But the perquisites of custom-house officers are everywhere much greater than their salaries; at some ports more than double or triple those salaries. If the salaries of officers, and other incidents, therefore, amount to more than ten per cent. upon the neat revenue of the customs, the whole expense of levying that revenue may amount, in salaries and perquisites together, to more than twenty or thirty per cent. The officers of excise receive few or no perquisites; and the administration of that branch of the revenue being of more recent establishment, is in general less corrupted than that of the customs, into which length of time has introduced and authorised many abuses. By charging upon malt the whole revenue which is at present levied by the different duties upon malt and malt liquors, a saving, it is supposed, of more than £50,000, might be made in the annual expense of the excise. By confining the duties of customs to a few sorts of goods, and by levying those duties according to the excise laws, a much greater saving might probably be made in the annual expense of the customs.

Secondly, such taxes necessarily occasion some obstruction or discouragement to certain branches of industry. As they always raise the price of the commodity taxed, they so far discourage its consumption, and consequently its production. If it is a commodity of home growth or manufacture, less labour comes to be employed in raising and producing it. If it is a foreign commodity of which the tax increases in this manner the price, the commodities of the same kind which are made at home may thereby, indeed, gain some advantage in the home market, and a greater quantity of domestic industry may thereby be turned toward preparing them. But though this rise of price in a foreign commodity, may encourage domestic industry in one particular branch, it necessarily discourages that industry in almost every other. The dearer the Birmingham manufacturer buys his foreign wine, the cheaper he necessarily sells that part of his hardware with which, or, what comes to the same thing, with the price of which, he buys it. That part of his hardware, therefore, becomes of less value to him, and he has less encouragement to work at it. The dearer the consumers in one country pay for the surplus produce of another, the cheaper they necessarily sell that part of their own surplus produce with which, or, what comes to the same thing, with the price of which, they buy it. That part of their own surplus produce becomes of less value to them, and they have less encouragement to increase its quantity. All taxes upon consumable commodities, therefore, tend to reduce the quantity of productive labour below what it otherwise would be, either in preparing the commodities taxed, if they are home commodities, or in preparing those with which they are purchased, if they are foreign commodities. Such taxes, too, always alter, more or less, the natural direction of national industry, and turn it into a channel always different from, and generally less advantageous, than that in which it would have run of its own accord.

Thirdly, the hope of evading such taxes by smuggling, gives frequent occasion to forfeitures and other penalties, which entirely ruin the smuggler; a person who, though no doubt highly blameable for violating the laws of his country, is frequently incapable of violating those of natural justice, and would have been, in every respect, an excellent citizen, had not the laws of his country made that a crime which nature never meant to be so. In those corrupted governments, where there is at least a general suspicion of much unnecessary expense, and great misapplication of the public revenue, the laws which guard it are little respected. Not many people are scrupulous about smuggling, when, without perjury, they can find an easy and safe opportunity of doing so. To pretend to have any scruple about buying smuggled goods, though a manifest encouragement to the violation of the revenue laws, and to the perjury which almost always attends it, would, in most countries, be regarded as one of those pedantic pieces of hypocrisy which, instead of gaining credit with anybody, serve only to expose the person who affects to practise them to the suspicion of being a greater knave than most of his neighbours. By this indulgence of the public, the smuggler is often encouraged to continue a trade, which he is thus taught to consider as in some measure innocent; and when the severity of the revenue laws is ready to fall upon him, he is frequently disposed to defend with violence, what he has been accustomed to regard as his just property. From being at first, perhaps, rather imprudent than criminal, he at last too often becomes one of the hardiest and most determined violators of the laws of society. By the ruin of the smuggler, his capital, which had before been employed in maintaining productive labour, is absorbed either in the revenue of the state, or in that of the revenue officer; and is employed in maintaining unproductive, to the diminution of the general capital of the society, and of the useful industry which it might otherwise have maintained.

Fourthly, such taxes, by subjecting at least the dealers in the taxed commodities, to the frequent visits and odious examination of the tax-gatherers, expose them sometimes, no doubt, to some degree of oppression, and always to much trouble and vexation; and though vexation, as has already been said, is not strictly speaking expense, it is certainly equivalent to the expense at which every man would be willing to redeem himself from it. The laws of excise, though more effectual for the purpose for which they were instituted, are, in this respect, more vexatious than those of the customs. When a merchant has imported goods subject to certain duties of customs; when he has paid those duties, and lodged the goods in his warehouse; he is not, in most cases, liable to any further trouble or vexation from the custom-house officer. It is otherwise with goods subject to duties of excise. The dealers have no respite from the continual visits and examination of the excise officers. The duties of excise are, upon this account, more unpopular than those of the customs; and so are the officers who levy them. Those officers, it is pretended, though in general, perhaps, they do their duty fully as well as those of the customs; yet, as that duty obliges them to be frequently very troublesome to some of their neighbours, commonly contract a certain hardness of character, which the others frequently have not. This observation, however, may very probably be the mere suggestion of fraudulent dealers, whose smuggling is either prevented or detected by their diligence.

The inconveniencies, however, which are, perhaps, in some degree inseparable from taxes upon consumable communities, fall as light upon the people of Great Britain as upon those of any other country of which the government is nearly as expensive. Our state is not perfect, and might be mended; but it is as good, or better, than that of most of our neighbours.

In consequence of the notion, that duties upon consumable goods were taxes upon the profits of merchants, those duties have, in some countries, been repeated upon every successive sale of the goods. If the profits of the merchant-importer or merchant-manufacturer were taxed, equality seemed to require that those of all the middle buyers, who intervened between either of them and the consumer, should likewise be taxed. The famous alcavala of Spain seems to have been established upon this principle. It was at first a tax of ten per cent. afterwards of fourteen per cent. and it is at present only six per cent. upon the sale of every sort of property whether moveable or immoveable; and it is repeated every time the property is sold. {Memoires concernant les Droits, etc. tom. i, p. 15} The levying of this tax requires a multitude of revenue officers, sufficient to guard the transportation of goods, not only from one province to another, but from one shop to another. It subjects, not only the dealers in some sorts of goods, but those in all sorts, every farmer, every manufacturer, every merchant and shopkeeper, to the continual visit and examination of the tax-gatherers. Through the greater part of the country in which a tax of this kind is established, nothing can be produced for distant sale. The produce of every part of the country must be proportioned to the consumption of the neighbourhood. It is to the alcavala, accordingly, that Ustaritz imputes the ruin of the manufactures of Spain. He might have imputed to it, likewise, the declension of agriculture, it being imposed not only upon manufactures, but upon the rude produce of the land.

In the kingdom of Naples, there is a similar tax of three per cent. upon the value of all contracts, and consequently upon that of all contracts of sale. It is both lighter than the Spanish tax, and the greater part of towns and parishes are allowed to pay a composition in lieu of it. They levy this composition in what manner they please, generally in a way that gives no interruption to the interior commerce of the place. The Neapolitan tax, therefore, is not near so ruinous as the Spanish one.

The uniform system of taxation, which, with a few exception of no great consequence, takes place in all the different parts of the united kingdom of Great Britain, leaves the interior commerce of the country, the inland and coasting trade, almost entirely free. The inland trade is almost perfectly free; and the greater part of goods may be carried from one end of the kingdom to the other, without requiring any permit or let-pass, without being subject to question, visit or examination, from the revenue officers. There are a few exceptions, but they are such as can give no interruption to any important branch of inland commerce of the country. Goods carried coastwise, indeed, require certificates or coast-cockets. If you except coals, however, the rest are almost all duty-free. This freedom of interior commerce, the effect of the uniformity of the system of taxation, is perhaps one of the principal causes of the prosperity of Great Britain; every great country being necessarily the best and most extensive market for the greater part of the productions of its own industry. If the same freedom in consequence of the same uniformity, could be extended to Ireland and the plantations, both the grandeur of the state, and the prosperity of every part of the empire, would probably be still greater than at present.

In France, the different revenue laws which take place in the different provinces, require a multitude of revenue officers to surround, not only the frontiers of the kingdom, but those of almost each particular province, in order either to prevent the importation of certain goods, or to subject it to the payment of certain duties, to the no small interruption of the interior commerce of the country. Some provinces are allowed to compound for the gabelle, or salt tax; others are exempted from it altogether. Some provinces are exempted from the exclusive sale of tobacco, which the farmers-general enjoy through the greater part of the kingdom. The aides, which correspond to the excise in England, are very different in different provinces. Some provinces are exempted from them, and pay a composition or equivalent. In those in which they take place, and are in farm, there are many local duties which do not extend beyond a particular town or district. The traites, which correspond to our customs, divide the kingdom into three great parts; first, the provinces subject to the tariff of 1664, which are called the provinces of the five great farms, and under which are comprehended Picardy, Normandy, and the greater part of the interior provinces of the kingdom; secondly, the provinces subject to the tariff of 1667, which are called the provinces reckoned foreign, and under which are comprehended the greater part of the frontier provinces; and, thirdly, those provinces which are said to be treated as foreign, or which, because they are allowed a free commerce with foreign countries, are, in their commerce with the other provinces of France, subjected to the same duties as other foreign countries. These are Alsace, the three bishoprics of Mentz, Toul, and Verdun, and the three cities of Dunkirk, Bayonne, and Marseilles. Both in the provinces of the five great farms (called so on account of an ancient division of the duties of customs into five great branches, each of which was originally the subject of a particular farm, though they are now all united into one), and in those which are said to be reckoned foreign, there are many local duties which do not extend beyond a particular town or district. There are some such even in the provinces which are said to be treated as foreign, particularly in the city of Marseilles. It is unnecessary to observe how much both the restraints upon the interior commerce of the country, and the number of the revenue officers, must be multiplied, in order to guard the frontiers of those different provinces and districts which are subject to such different systems of taxation.

Over and above the general restraints arising from this complicated system of revenue laws, the commerce of wine (after corn, perhaps, the most important production of France) is, in the greater part of the provinces, subject to particular restraints arising from the favour which has been shown to the vineyards of particular provinces and districts above those of others. The provinces most famous for their wines, it will be found, I believe, are those in which the trade in that article is subject to the fewest restraints of this kind. The extensive market which such provinces enjoy, encourages good management both in the cultivation of their vineyards, and in the subsequent preparation of their wines.

Such various and complicated revenue laws are not peculiar to France. The little duchy of Milan is divided into six provinces, in each of which there is a different system of taxation, with regard to several different sorts of consumable goods. The still smaller territories of the duke of Parma are divided into three or four, each of which has, in the same manner, a system of its own. Under such absurd management, nothing but the great fertility of the soil, and happiness of the climate, could preserve such countries from soon relapsing into the lowest state of poverty and barbarism.

Taxes upon consumable commodities may either be levied by an administration, of which the officers are appointed by govermnent, and are immediately accountable to government, of which the revenue must, in this case, vary from year to year, according to the occasional variations in the produce of the tax; or they may be let in farm for a rent certain, the farmer being allowed to appoint his own officers, who, though obliged to levy the tax in the manner directed by the law, are under his immediate inspection, and are immediately accountable to him. The best and most frugal way of levying a tax can never be by farm. Over and above what is necessary for paying the stipulated rent, the salaries of the officers, and the whole expense of administration, the farmer must always draw from the produce of the tax a certain profit, proportioned at least to the advance which he makes, to the risk which he runs, to the trouble which he is at, and to the knowledge and skill which it requires to manage so very complicated a concern. Government, by establishing an administration under their own immediate inspection, of the same kind with that which the farmer establishes, might at least save this profit, which is almost always exorbitant. To farm any considerable branch of the public revenue requires either a great capital, or a great credit; circumstances which would alone restrain the competition for such an undertaking to a very small number of people. Of the few who have this capital or credit, a still smaller number have the necessary knowledge or experience; another circumstance which restrains the competition still further. The very few who are in condition to become competitors, find it more for their interest to combine together; to become copartners, instead of competitors; and, when the farm is set up to auction, to offer no rent but what is much below the real value. In countries where the public revenues are in farm, the farmers are generally the most opulent people. Their wealth would alone excite the public indignation; and the vanity which almost always accompanies such upstart fortunes, the foolish ostentation with which they commonly display that wealth, excite that indignation still more.

The farmers of the public revenue never find the laws too severe, which punish any attempt to evade the payment of a tax. They have no bowels for the contributors, who are not their subjects, and whose universal bankruptcy, if it should happen the day after the farm is expired, would not much affect their interest. In the greatest exigencies of the state, when the anxiety of the sovereign for the exact payment of his revenue is necessarily the greatest, they seldom fail to complain, that without laws more rigorous than those which actually took place, it will be impossible for them to pay even the usual rent. In those moments of public distress, their commands cannot be disputed. The revenue laws, therefore, become gradually more and more severe. The most sanguinary are always to be found in countries where the greater part of the public revenue is in farm; the mildest, in countries where it is levied under the immediate inspection of the sovereign. Even a bad sovereign feels more compassion for his people than can ever be expected from the farmers of his revenue. He knows that the permanent grandeur of his family depends upon the prosperity of his people, and he will never knowingly ruin that prosperity for the sake of any momentary interest of his own. It is otherwise with the farmers of his revenue, whose grandeur may frequently be the effect of the ruin, and not of the prosperity, of his people.

A tax is sometimes not only farmed for a certain rent, but the farmer has, besides, the monopoly of the commodity taxed. In France, the duties upon tobacco and salt are levied in this manner. In such cases, the farmer, instead of one, levies two exorbitant profits upon the people; the profit of the farmer, and the still more exorbitant one of the monopolist. Tobacco being a luxury, every man is allowed to buy or not to buy as he chuses; but salt being a necessary, every man is obliged to buy of the farmer a certain quantity of it; because, if he did not buy this quantity of the farmer, he would, it is presumed, buy it of some smuggler. The taxes upon both commodities are exorbitant. The temptation to smuggle, consequently, is to many people irresistible; while, at the same time, the rigour of the law, and the vigilance of the farmer's officers, render the yielding to the temptation almost certainly ruinous. The smuggling of salt and tobacco sends every year several hundred people to the galleys, besides a very considerable number whom it sends to the gibbet. Those taxes, levied in this manner, yield a very considerable revenue to government. In 1767, the farm of tobacco was let for twenty-two millions five hundred and forty-one thousand two hundred and seventy-eight livres a-year; that of salt for thirty-six millions four hundred and ninety-two thousand four hundred and four livres. The farm, in both cases, was to commence in 1768, and to last for six years. Those who consider the blood of the people as nothing, in comparison with the revenue of the prince, may, perhaps, approve of this method of levying taxes. Similar taxes and monopolies of salt and tobacco have been established in many other countries, particularly in the Austrian and Prussian dominions, and in the greater part of the states of Italy.

In France, the greater part of the actual revenue of the crown is derived from eight different sources; the taille, the capitation, the two vingtiemes, the gabelles, the aides, the traites, the domaine, and the farm of tobacco. The five last are, in the greater part of the provinces, under farm. The three first are everywhere levied by an administration, under the immediate inspection and direction of government; and it is universally acknowledged, that in proportion to what they take out of the pockets of the people, they bring more into the treasury of the prince than the other five, of which the administration is much more wasteful and expensive.

The finances of France seem, in their present state, to admit of three very obvious reformations. First, by abolishing the taille and the capitation, and by increasing the number of the vingtiemes, so as to produce an additional revenue equal to the amount of those other taxes, the revenue of the crown might be preserved; the expense of collection might be much diminished; the vexation of the inferior ranks of people, which the taille and capitation occasion, might be entirely prevented; and the superior ranks might not be more burdened than the greater part of them are at present. The vingtieme, I have already observed, is a tax very nearly of the same kind with what is called the land tax of England. The burden of the taille, it is acknowledged, falls finally upon the proprietors of land; and as the greater part of the capitation is assessed upon those who are subject to the taille, at so much a-pound of that other tax, the final payment of the greater part of it must likewise fall upon the same order of people. Though the number of the vingtiemes, therefore, was increased, so as to produce an additional revenue equal to the amount of both those taxes, the superior ranks of people might not be more burdened than they are at present; many individuals, no doubt, would, on account of the great inequalities with which the taille is commonly assessed upon the estates and tenants of different individuals. The interest and opposition of such favoured subjects, are the obstacles most likely to prevent this, or any other reformation of the same kind. Secondly, by rendering the gabelle, the aides, the traites, the taxes upon tobacco, all the different customs and excises, uniform in all the different parts of the kingdom, those taxes might be levied at much less expense, and the interior commerce of the kingdom might be rendered as free as that of England. Thirdly, and lastly, by subjecting all those taxes to an administration under the immediate inspection and direction or government, the exorbitant profits of the farmers-general might be added to the revenue of the state. The opposition arising from the private interest of individuals, is likely to be as effectual for preventing the two last as the first-mentioned scheme of reformation.

The French system of taxation seems, in every respect, inferior to the British. In Great Britain, ten millions sterling are annually levied upon less than eight millions of people, without its being possible to say that any particular order is oppressed. From the Collections of the Abbé Expilly, and the observations of the author of the Essay upon the Legislation and Commerce of Corn, it appears probable that France, including the provinces of Lorraine and Bar, contains about twenty-three or twenty-four millions of people; three times the number, perhaps, contained in Great Britain. The soil and climate of France are better than those of Great Britain. The country has been much longer in a state of improvement and cultivation, and is, upon that account, better stocked with all those things which it requires a long time to raise up and accumulate; such as great towns, and convenient and well-built houses, both in town and country. With these advantages, it might be expected, that in France a revenue of thirty millions might be levied for the support of the state, with as little inconvenience as a revenue of ten millions is in Great Britain. In 1765 and 1766, the whole revenue paid into the treasury of France, according to the best, though, I acknowledge, very imperfect accounts which I could get of it, usually run between 308 and 325 millions of livres; that is, it did not amount to fifteen millions sterling; not the half of what might have been expected, had the people contributed in the same proportion to their numbers as the people of Great Britain. The people of France, however, it is generally acknowledged, are much more oppressed by taxes than the people of Great Britain. France, however, is certainly the great empire in Europe, which, after that of Great Britain, enjoys the mildest and most indulgent government.

In Holland, the heavy taxes upon the necessaries of life have ruined, it is said, their principal manufacturers, and are likely to discourage, gradually, even their fisheries and their trade in ship-building. The taxes upon the necessaries of life are inconsiderable in Great Britain, and no manufacture has hitherto been ruined by them. The British taxes which bear hardest on manufactures, are some duties upon the importation of raw materials, particularly upon that of raw silk. The revenue of the States-General and of the different cities, however, is said to amount to more than five millions two hundred and fifty thousand pounds sterling; and as the inhabitants of the United Provinces cannot well be supposed to amount to more than a third part of those of Great Britain, they must, in proportion to their number, be much more heavily taxed.

After all the proper subjects of taxation have been exhausted, if the exigencies of the state still continue to require new taxes, they must be imposed upon improper ones. The taxes upon the necessaries of life, therefore, may be no impeachment of the wisdom of that republic, which, in order to acquire and to maintain its independency, has, in spite of its meat frugality, been involved in such expensive wars as have obliged it to contract great debts. The singular countries of Holland and Zealand, besides, require a considerable expense even to preserve their existence, or to prevent their being swallowed up by the sea, which must have contributed to increase considerably the load of taxes in those two provinces. The republican form of government seems to be the principal support of the present grandeur of Holland. The owners of great capitals, the great mercantile families, have generally either some direct share, or some indirect influence, in the administration of that government. For the sake of the respect and authority which they derive from this situation, they are willing to live in a country where their capital, if they employ it themselves, will bring them less profit, and if they lend it to another, less interest; and where the very moderate revenue which they can draw from it will purchase less of the necessaries and conveniencies of life than in any other part of Europe. The residence of such wealthy people necessarily keeps alive, in spite of all disadvantages, a certain degree of industry in the country. Any public calamity which should destroy the republican form of government, which should throw the whole administration into the hands of nobles and of soldiers, which should annihilate altogether the importance of those wealthy merchants, would soon render it disagreeable to them to live in a country where they were no longer likely to be much respected. They would remove both their residence and their capital to some other country, and the industry and commerce of Holland would soon follow the capitals which supported them.

CHAPTER III

OF PUBLIC DEBTS

In that rude state of society which precedes the extension of commerce and the improvement of manufactures; when those expensive luxuries, which commerce and manufactures can alone introduce, are altogether unknown; the person who possesses a large revenue, I have endeavoured to show in the third book of this Inquiry, can spend or enjoy that revenue in no other way than by maintaining nearly as many people as it can maintain. A large revenue may at all times be said to consist in the command of a large quantity of the necessaries of life. In that rude state of things, it is commonly paid in a large quantity of those necessaries, in the materials of plain food and coarse clothing, in corn and cattle, in wool and raw hides. When neither commerce nor manufactures furnish any thing for which the owner can exchange the greater part of those materials which are over and above his own consumption, he can do nothing with the surplus, but feed and clothe nearly as many people as it will feed and clothe. A hospitality in which there is no luxury, and a liberality in which there is no ostentation, occasion, in this situation of things, the principal expenses of the rich and the great. But these I have likewise endeavoured to show, in the same book, are expenses by which people are not very apt to ruin themselves. There is not, perhaps, any selfish pleasure so frivolous, of which the pursuit has not sometimes ruined even sensible men. A passion for cock-fighting has ruined many. But the instances, I believe, are not very numerous, of people who have been ruined by a hospitality or liberality of this kind; though the hospitality of luxury, and the liberality of ostentation have ruined many. Among our feudal ancestors, the long time during which estates used to continue in the same family, sufficiently demonstrates the general disposition of people to live within their income. Though the rustic hospitality, constantly exercised by the great landholders, may not, to us in the present times, seem consistent with that order which we are apt to consider as inseparably connected with good economy; yet we must certainly allow them to have been at least so far frugal, as not commonly to have spent their whole income. A part of their wool and raw hides, they had generally an opportunity of selling for money. Some part of this money, perhaps, they spent in purchasing the few objects of vanity and luxury, with which the circumstances of the times could furnish them; but some part of it they seem commonly to have hoarded. They could not well, indeed, do any thing else but hoard whatever money they saved. To trade, was disgraceful to a gentleman; and to lend money at interest, which at that time was considered as usury, and prohibited bylaw, would have been still more so. In those times of violence and disorder, besides, it was convenient to have a hoard of money at hand, that in case they should be driven from their own home, they might have something of known value to carry with them to some place of safety. The same violence which made it convenient to hoard, made it equally convenient to conceal the hoard. The frequency of treasure-trove, or of treasure found, of which no owner was known, sufficiently demonstrates the frequency, in those times, both of hoarding and of concealing the hoard. Treasure-trove was then considered as an important branch of the revenue of the sovereign. All the treasure-trove of the kingdom would scarce, perhaps, in the present times, make an important branch of the revenue of a private gentleman of a good estate.

    The same disposition, to save and to hoard, prevailed in the sovereign, as well as in the subjects. Among nations, to whom commerce and manufacture are little known, the sovereign, it has already been observed in the Fourth book, is in a situation which naturally disposes him to the parsimony requisite for accumulation. In that situation, the expense, even of a sovereign, cannot be directed by that vanity which delights in the gaudy finery of a court. The ignorance of the times affords but few of the trinkets in which that finery consists. Standing armies are not then necessary; so that the expense, even of a sovereign, like that of any other great lord can be employed in scarce any thing but bounty to his tenants, and hospitality to his retainers. But bounty and hospitality very seldom lead to extravagance; though vanity almost always does. All the ancient sovereigns of Europe, accordingly, it has already been observed, had treasures. Every Tartar chief, in the present times, is said to have one.

    In a commercial country, abounding with every sort of expensive luxury, the sovereign, in the same manner as almost all the great proprietors in his dominions, naturally spends a great part of his revenue in purchasing those luxuries. His own and the neighbouring countries supply him abundantly with all the costly trinkets which compose the splendid, but insignificant, pageantry of a court. For the sake of an inferior pageantry of the same kind, his nobles dismiss their retainers, make their tenants independent, and become gradually themselves as insignificant as the greater part of the wealthy burghers in his dominions. The same frivolous passions, which influence their conduct, influence his. How can it be supposed that he should be the only rich man in his dominions who is insensible to pleasures of this kind? If he does not, what he is very likely to do, spend upon those pleasures so great a part of his revenue as to debilitate very much the defensive power of the state, it cannot well be expected that he should not spend upon them all that part of it which is over and above what is necessary for supporting that defensive power. His ordinary expense becomes equal to his ordinary revenue, and it is well if it does not frequently exceed it. The amassing of treasure can no longer be expected; and when extraordinary exigencies require extraordinary expenses, he must necessarily call upon his subjects for an extraordinary aid. The present and the late king of Prussia are the only great princes of Europe, who, since the death of Henry IV. of France, in 1610, are supposed to have amassed any considerable treasure. The parsimony which leads to accumulation has become almost as rare in republican as in monarchical governments. The Italian republics, the United Provinces of the Netherlands, are all in debt. The canton of Berne is the single republic in Europe which has amassed any considerable treasure. The other Swiss republics have not. The taste for some sort of pageantry, for splendid buildings, at least, and other public ornaments, frequently prevails as much in the apparently sober senate-house of a little republic, as in the dissipated court of the greatest king.

The want of parsimony, in time of peace, imposes the necessity of contracting debt in time of war. When war comes, there is no money in the treasury, but what is necessary for carrying on the ordinary expense of the peace establishment. In war, an establishment of three or four times that expense becomes necessary for the defence of the state; and consequently, a revenue three or four times greater than the peace revenue. Supposing that the sovereign should have, what he scarce ever has, the immediate means of augmenting his revenue in proportion to the augmentation of his expense; yet still the produce of the taxes, from which this increase of revenue must be drawn, will not begin to come into the treasury, till perhaps ten or twelve months after they are imposed. But the moment in which war begins, or rather the moment in which it appears likely to begin, the army must be augmented, the fleet must be fitted out, the garrisoned towns must be put into a posture of defence; that army, that fleet, those garrisoned towns, must be furnished with arms, ammunition, and provisions. An immediate and great expense must be incurred in that moment of immediate danger, which will not wait for the gradual and slow returns of the new taxes. In this exigency, government can have no other resource but in borrowing.

The same commercial state of society which, by the operation of moral causes, brings government in this manner into the necessity of borrowing, produces in the subjects both an ability and an inclination to lend. If it commonly brings along with it the necessity of borrowing, it likewise brings with it the facility of doing so.

A country abounding with merchants and manufacturers, necessarily abounds with a set of people through whose hands, not only their own capitals, but the capitals of all those who either lend them money, or trust them with goods, pass as frequently, or more frequently, than the revenue of a private man, who, without trade or business, lives upon his income, passes through his hands. The revenue of such a man can regularly pass through his hands only once in a year. But the whole amount of the capital and credit of a merchant, who deals in a trade of which the returns are very quick, may sometimes pass through his hands two, three, or four times in a year. A country abounding with merchants and manufacturers, therefore, necessarily abounds with a set of people, who have it at all times in their power to advance, if they chuse to do so, a very large sum of money to government. Hence the ability in the subjects of a commercial state to lend.

Commerce and manufactures can seldom flourish long in any state which does not enjoy a regular administration of justice; in which the people do not feel themselves secure in the possession of their property; in which the faith of contracts is not supported by law; and in which the authority of the state is not supposed to be regularly employed in enforcing the payment of debts from all those who are able to pay. Commerce and manufactures, in short, can seldom flourish in any state, in which there is not a certain degree of confidence in the justice of government. The same confidence which disposes great merchants and manufacturers upon ordinary occasions, to trust their property to the protection of a particular government, disposes them, upon extraordinary occasions, to trust that government with the use of their property. By lending money to government, they do not even for a moment diminish their ability to carry on their trade and manufactures; on the contrary, they commonly augment it. The necessities of the state render government, upon most occasions willing to borrow upon terms extremely advantageous to the lender. The security which it grants to the original creditor, is made transferable to any other creditor; and from the universal confidence in the justice of the state, generally sells in the market for more than was originally paid for it. The merchant or monied man makes money by lending money to government, and instead of diminishing, increases his trading capital. He generally considers it as a favour, therefore, when the administration admits him to a share in the first subscription for a new loan. Hence the inclination or willingness in the subjects of a commercial state to lend.

The government of such a state is very apt to repose itself upon this ability and willingness of its subjects to lend it their money on extraordinary occasions. It foresees the facility of borrowing, and therefore dispenses itself from the duty of saving.

In a rude state of society, there are no great mercantile or manufacturing capitals. The individuals, who hoard whatever money they can save, and who conceal their hoard, do so from a distrust of the justice of government; from a fear, that if it was known that they had a hoard, and where that hoard was to be found, they would quickly be plundered. In such a state of things, few people would be able, and nobody would be willing to lend their money to government on extraordinary exigencies. The sovereign feels that he must provide for such exigencies by saving, because he foresees the absolute impossibility of borrowing. This foresight increases still further his natural disposition to save.

The progress of the enormous debts which at present oppress, and will in the long-run probably ruin, all the great nations of Europe, has been pretty uniform. Nations, like private men, have generally begun to borrow upon what may be called personal credit, without assigning or mortgaging any particular fund for the payment of the debt; and when this resource has failed them, they have gone on to borrow upon assignments or mortgages of particular funds.

What is called the unfunded debt of Great Britain, is contracted in the former of those two ways. It consists partly in a debt which bears, or is supposed to bear, no interest, and which resembles the debts that a private man contracts upon account; and partly in a debt which bears interest, and which resembles what a private man contracts upon his bill or promissory-note. The debts which are due, either for extraordinary services, or for services either not provided for, or not paid at the time when they are performed; part of the extraordinaries of the army, navy, and ordnance, the arrears of subsidies to foreign princes, those of seamen's wages, etc. usually constitute a debt of the first kind. Navy and exchequer bills, which are issued sometimes in payment of a part of such debts, and sometimes for other purposes, constitute a debt of the second kind; exchequer bills bearing interest from the day on which they are issued, and navy bills six months after they are issued. The bank of England, either by voluntarily discounting those bills at their current value, or by agreeing with government for certain considerations to circulate exchequer bills, that is, to receive them at par, paying the interest which happens to be due upon them, keeps up their value, and facilitates their circulation, and thereby frequently enables government to contract a very large debt of this kind. In France, where there is no bank, the state bills (billets d'etat {See Examen des Reflections Politiques sur les Finances.}) have sometimes sold at sixty and seventy per cent. discount. During the great recoinage in king William's time, when the bank of England thought proper to put a stop to its usual transactions, exchequer bills and tallies are said to have sold from twenty-five to sixty per cent. discount; owing partly, no doubt, to the supposed instability of the new government established by the Revolution, but partly, too, to the want of the support of the bank of England.

When this resource is exhausted, and it becomes necessary, in order to raise money, to assign or mortgage some particular branch of the public revenue for the payment of the debt, government has, upon different occasions, done this in two different ways. Sometimes it has made this assignment or mortgage for a short period of time only, a year, or a few years, for example; and sometimes for perpetuity. In the one case, the fund was supposed sufficient to pay, within the limited time, both principal and interest of the money borrowed. In the other, it was supposed sufficient to pay the interest only, or a perpetual annuity equivalent to the interest, government being at liberty to redeem, at any time, this annuity, upon paying back the principal sum borrowed. When money was raised in the one way, it was said to be raised by anticipation; when in the other, by perpetual funding, or, more shortly, by funding.

In Great Britain, the annual land and malt taxes are regularly anticipated every year, by virtue of a borrowing clause constantly inserted into the acts which impose them. The bank of England generally advances at an interest, which, since the Revolution, has varied from eight to three per cent., the sums of which those taxes are granted, and receives payment as their produce gradually comes in. If there is a deficiency, which there always is, it is provided for in the supplies of the ensuing year. The only considerable branch of the public revenue which yet remains unmortgaged, is thus regularly spent before it comes in. Like an improvident spendthrift, whose pressing occasions will not allow him to wait for the regular payment of his revenue, the state is in the constant practice of borrowing of its own factors and agents, and of paying interest for the use of its own money.

In the reign of king William, and during a great part of that of queen Anne, before we had become so familiar as we are now with the practice of perpetual funding, the greater part of the new taxes were imposed but for a short period of time (for four, five, six, or seven years only), and a great part of the grants of every year consisted in loans upon anticipations of the produce of those taxes. The produce being frequently insufficient for paying, within the limited term, the principal and interest of the money borrowed, deficiencies arose; to make good which, it became necessary to prolong the term.

In 1697, by the 8th of William III., c. 20, the deficiencies of several taxes were charged upon what was then called the first general mortgage or fund, consisting of a prolongation to the first of August 1706, of several different taxes, which would have expired within a shorter term, and of which the produce was accumulated into one general fund. The deficiencies charged upon this prolonged term amounted to £5,160,459: 14: 9½.

In 1701, those duties, with some others, were still further prolonged, for the like purposes, till the first of August 1710, and were called the second general mortgage or fund. The deficiencies charged upon it amounted to £2,055,999: 7: 11½.

In 1707, those duties were still further prolonged, as a fund for new loans, to the first of August 1712, and were called the third general mortgage or fund. The sum borrowed upon it was £983,254:11:9¼.

In 1708, those duties were all (except the old subsidy of tonnage and poundage, of which one moiety only was made a part of this fund, and a duty upon the importation of Scotch linen, which had been taken off by the articles of union) still further continued, as a fund for new loans, to the first of August 1714, and were called the fourth general mortgage or fund. The sum borrowed upon it was £925,176:9:2¼.

In 1709, those duties were all (except the old subsidy of tonnage and poundage, which was now left out of this fund altogether) still further continued, for the same purpose, to the first of August 1716, and were called the fifth general mortgage or fund. The sum borrowed upon it was £922,029:6s.

In 1710, those duties were again prolonged to the first of August 1720, and were called the sixth general mortgage or fund. The sum borrowed upon it was £1,296,552:9:11¾.

In 1711, the same duties (which at this time were thus subject to four different anticipations), together with several others, were continued for ever, and made a fund for paying the interest of the capital of the South-sea company, which had that year advanced to government, for paying debts, and making good deficiencies, the sum of £9,177,967:15:4d, the greatest loan which at that time had ever been made.

Before this period, the principal, so far as I have been able to observe, the only taxes, which, in order to pay the interest of a debt, had been imposed for perpetuity, were those for paying the interest of the money which had been advanced to government by the bank and East-India company, and of what it was expected would be advanced, but which was never advanced, by a projected land bank. The bank fund at this time amounted to £3,375,027:17:10½, for which was paid an annuity or interest of £206,501:15:5d. The East-India fund amounted to £3,200,000, for which was paid an annuity or interest of £160,000; the bank fund being at six per cent., the East-India fund at five per cent. interest.

In 1715, by the first of George I., c. 12, the different taxes which had been mortgaged for paying the bank annuity, together with several others, which, by this act, were likewise rendered perpetual, were accumulated into one common fund, called the aggregate fund, which was charged not only with the payment of the bank annuity, but with several other annuities and burdens of different kinds. This fund was afterwards augmented by the third of George I., c.8., and by the fifth of George I., c. 3, and the different duties which were then added to it were likewise rendered perpetual.

In 1717, by the third of George I., c. 7, several other taxes were rendered perpetual, and accumulated into another common fund, called the general fund, for the payment of certain annuities, amounting in the whole to £724,849:6:10½.

In consequence of those different acts, the greater part of the taxes, which before had been anticipated only for a short term of years were rendered perpetual, as a fund for paying, not the capital, but the interest only, of the money which had been borrowed upon them by different successive anticipations.

Had money never been raised but by anticipation, the course of a few years would have liberated the public revenue, without any other attention of government besides that of not overloading the fund, by charging it with more debt than it could pay within the limited term, and not of anticipating a second time before the expiration of the first anticipation. But the greater part of European governments have been incapable of those attentions. They have frequently overloaded the fund, even upon the first anticipation; and when this happened not to be the case, they have generally taken care to overload it, by anticipating a second and a third time, before the expiration of the first anticipation. The fund becoming in this manner altogether insufficient for paying both principal and interest of the money borrowed upon it, it became necessary to charge it with the interest only, or a perpetual annuity equal to the interest; and such improvident anticipations necessarily gave birth to the more ruinous practice of perpetual funding. But though this practice necessarily puts off the liberation of the public revenue from a fixed period, to one so indefinite that it is not very likely ever to arrive; yet, as a greater sum can, in all cases, be raised by this new practice than by the old one of anticipation, the former, when men have once become familiar with it, has, in the great exigencies of the state, been universally preferred to the latter. To relieve the present exigency, is always the object which principally interests those immediately concerned in the administration of public affairs. The future liberation of the public revenue they leave to the care of posterity.

During the reign of queen Anne, the market rate of interest had fallen from six to five per cent.; and, in the twelfth year of her reign, five per cent. was declared to be the highest rate which could lawfully be taken for money borrowed upon private security. Soon after the greater part of the temporary taxes of Great Britain had been rendered perpetual, and distributed into the aggregate, South-sea, and general funds, the creditors of the public, like those of private persons, were induced to accept of five per cent. for the interest of their money, which occasioned a saving of one per cent. upon the capital of the greater part or the debts which had been thus funded for perpetuity, or of one-sixth of the greater part of the annuities which were paid out of the three great funds above mentioned. This saving left a considerable surplus in the produce of the different taxes which had been accumulated into those funds, over and above what was necessary for paying the annuities which were now charged upon them, and laid the foundation of what has since been called the sinking fund. In 1717, it amounted to £523,454:7:7½. In 1727, the interest of the greater part of the public debts was still further reduced to four per cent.; and, in 1753 and 1757, to three and a-half, and three per cent., which reductions still further augmented the sinking fund.

A sinking fund, though instituted for the payment of old, facilitates very much the contracting of new debts. It is a subsidiary fund, always at hand, to be mortgaged in aid of any other doubtful fund, upon which money is proposed to be raised in any exigency of the state. Whether the sinking fund of Great Britain has been more frequently applied to the one or to other of those two purposes, will sufficiently appear by and by.

Besides those two methods of borrowing, by anticipations and by a perpetual funding, there are two other methods, which hold a sort of middle place between them; these are, that of borrowing upon annuities for terms of years, and that of borrowing upon annuities for lives.

During the reigns of king William and queen Anne, large sums were frequently borrowed upon annuities for terms of years, which were sometimes longer and sometimes shorter. In 1695, an act was passed for borrowing one million upon an annuity of fourteen per cent., or £140,000 a-year, for sixteen years. In 1691, an act was passed for borrowing a million upon annuities for lives, upon terms which, in the present times, would appear very advantageous; but the subscription was not filled up. In the following year, the deficiency was made good, by borrowing upon annuities for lives, at fourteen per cent. or a little more than seven years purchase. In 1695, the persons who had purchased those annuities were allowed to exchange them for others of ninety-six years, upon paying into the exchequer sixty-three pounds in the hundred; that is, the difference between fourteen per cent. for life, and fourteen per cent. for ninety-six years, was sold for sixty-three pounds, or for four and a-half years purchase. Such was the supposed instability of government, that even these terms procured few purchasers. In the reign of queen Anne, money was, upon different occasions, borrowed both upon annuities for lives, and upon annuities for terms of thirty-two, of eighty-nine, of ninety-eight, and of ninety-nine years. In 1719, the proprietors of the annuities for thirty-two years were induced to accept, in lieu of them, South-sea stock to the amount of eleven and a-half years purchase of the annuities, together with an additional quantity of stock, equal to the arrears which happened then to be due upon them. In 1720, the greater part of the other annuities for terms of years, both long and short, were subscribed into the same fund. The long annuities, at that time, amounted to £666,821: 8:3½ a-year. On the 5th of January 1775, the remainder of them, or what was not subscribed at that time, amounted only to £136,453:12:8d.

During the two wars which began in 1739 and in 1755, little money was borrowed, either upon annuities for terms of years, or upon those for lives. An annuity for ninety-eight or ninety-nine years, however, is worth nearly as much as a perpetuity, and should therefore, one might think, be a fund for borrowing nearly as much. But those who, in order to make family settlements, and to provide for remote futurity, buy into the public stocks, would not care to purchase into one of which the value was continually diminishing; and such people make a very considerable proportion, both of the proprietors and purchasers of stock. An annuity for a long term of years, therefore, though its intrinsic value may be very nearly the same with that of a perpetual annuity, will not find nearly the same number of purchasers. The subscribers to a new loan, who mean generally to sell their subscription as soon as possible, prefer greatly a perpetual annuity, redeemable by parliament, to an irredeemable annuity, for a long term of years, of only equal amount. The value of the former may be supposed always the same, or very nearly the same; and it makes, therefore, a more convenient transferable stock than the latter.

During the two last-mentioned wars, annuities, either for terms of years or for lives, were seldom granted, but as premiums to the subscribers of a new loan, over and above the redeemable annuity or interest, upon the credit of which the loan was supposed to be made. They were granted, not as the proper fund upon which the money was borrowed, but as an additional encouragement to the lender.

Annuities for lives have occasionally been granted in two different ways; either upon separate lives, or upon lots of lives, which, in French, are called tontines, from the name of their inventor. When annuities are granted upon separate lives, the death of every individual annuitant disburdens the public revenue, so far as it was affected by his annuity. When annuities are granted upon tontines, the liberation of the public revenue does not commence till the death of all the annuitants comprehended in one lot, which may sometimes consist of twenty or thirty persons, of whom the survivors succeed to the annuities of all those who die before them; the last survivor succeeding to the annuities of the whole lot. Upon the same revenue, more money can always be raised by tontines than by annuities for separate lives. An annuity, with a right of survivorship, is really worth more than an equal annuity for a separate life; and, from the confidence which every man naturally has in his own good fortune, the principle upon which is founded the success of all lotteries, such an annuity generally sells for something more than it is worth. In countries where it is usual for government to raise money by granting annuities, tontines are, upon this account, generally preferred to annuities for separate lives. The expedient which will raise most money, is almost always preferred to that which is likely to bring about, in the speediest manner, the liberation of the public revenue.

In France, a much greater proportion of the public debts consists in annuities for lives than in England. According to a memoir presented by the parliament of Bourdeaux to the king, in 1764, the whole public debt of France is estimated at twenty-four hundred millions of livres; of which the capital, for which annuities for lives had been granted, is supposed to amount to three hundred millions, the eighth part of the whole public debt. The annuities themselves are computed to amount to thirty millions a-year, the fourth part of one hundred and twenty millions, the supposed interest of that whole debt. These estimations, I know very well, are not exact; but having been presented by so very respectable a body as approximations to the truth, they may, I apprehend, be considered as such. It is not the different degrees of anxiety in the two governments of France and England for the liberation of the public revenue, which occasions this difference in their respective modes of borrowing; it arises altogether from the different views and interests of the lenders.

In England, the seat of government being in the greatest mercantile city in the world, the merchants are generally the people who advance money to government. By advancing it, they do not mean to diminish, but, on the contrary, to increase their mercantile capitals; and unless they expected to sell, with some profit, their share in the subscription for a new loan, they never would subscribe. But if, by advancing their money, they were to purchase, instead of perpetual annuities, annuities for lives only, whether their own or those of other people, they would not always be so likely to sell them with a profit. Annuities upon their own lives they would always sell with loss; because no man will give for an annuity upon the life of another, whose age and state of health are nearly the same with his own, the same price which he would give for one upon his own. An annuity upon the life of a third person, indeed, is, no doubt, of equal value to the buyer and the seller; but its real value begins to diminish from the moment it is granted, and continues to do so, more and more, as long as it subsists. It can never, therefore, make so convenient a transferable stock as a perpetual annuity, of which the real value may be supposed always the same, or very nearly the same.

In France, the seat of government not being in a great mercantile city, merchants do not make so great a proportion of the people who advance money to government. The people concerned in the finances, the farmers-general, the receivers of the taxes which are not in farm, the court-bankers, etc. make the greater part of those who advance their money in all public exigencies. Such people are commonly men of mean birth, but of great wealth, and frequently of great pride. They are too proud to marry their equals, and women of quality disdain to marry them. They frequently resolve, therefore, to live bachelors; and having neither any families of their own, nor much regard for those of their relations, whom they are not always very fond of acknowledging, they desire only to live in splendour during their own time, and are not unwilling that their fortune should end with themselves. The number of rich people, besides, who are either averse to marry, or whose condition of life renders it either improper or inconvenient for them to do so, is much greater in France than in England. To such people, who have little or no care for posterity, nothing can be more convenient than to exchange their capital for a revenue, which is to last just as long, and no longer, than they wish it to do.

The ordinary expense of the greater part of modern governments, in time of peace, being equal, or nearly equal, to their ordinary revenue, when war comes, they are both unwilling and unable to increase their revenue in proportion to the increase of their expense. They are unwilling, for fear of offending the people, who, by so great and so sudden an increase of taxes, would soon be disgusted with the war; and they are unable, from not well knowing what taxes would be sufficient to produce the revenue wanted. The facility of borrowing delivers them from the embarrassment which this fear and inability would otherwise occasion. By means of borrowing, they are enabled, with a very moderate increase of taxes, to raise, from year to year, money sufficient for carrying on the war; and by the practice of perpetual funding, they are enabled, with the smallest possible increase of taxes, to raise annually the largest possible sum of money. In great empires, the people who live in the capital, and in the provinces remote from the scene of action, feel, many of them, scarce any inconveniency from the war, but enjoy, at their ease, the amusement of reading in the newspapers the exploits of their own fleets and armies. To them this amusement compensates the small difference between the taxes which they pay on account of the war, and those which they had been accustomed to pay in time of peace. They are commonly dissatisfied with the return of peace, which puts an end to their amusement, and to a thousand visionary hopes of conquest and national glory, from a longer continuance of the war.

The return of peace, indeed, seldom relieves them from the greater part of the taxes imposed during the war. These are mortgaged for the interest of the debt contracted, in order to carry it on. If, over and above paying the interest of this debt, and defraying the ordinary expense of government, the old revenue, together with the new taxes, produce some surplus revenue, it may, perhaps, be converted into a sinking fund for paying off the debt. But, in the first place, this sinking fund, even supposing it should be applied to no other purpose, is generally altogether inadequate for paying, in the course of any period during which it can reasonably be expected that peace should continue, the whole debt contracted during the war; and, in the second place, this fund is almost always applied to other purposes.

The new taxes were imposed for the sole purpose of paying the interest of the money borrowed upon them. If they produce more, it is generally something which was neither intended nor expected, and is, therefore, seldom very considerable. Sinking funds have generally arisen, not so much from any surplus of the taxes which was over and above what was necessary for paying the interest or annuity originally charged upon them, as from a subsequent reduction of that interest; that of Holland in 1655, and that of the ecclesiastical state in 1685, were both formed in this manner. Hence the usual insufficiency of such funds.

During the most profound peace, various events occur, which require an extraordinary expense; and government finds it always more convenient to defray this expense by misapplying the sinking fund, than by imposing a new tax. Every new tax is immediately felt more or less by the people. It occasions always some murmur, and meets with some opposition. The more taxes may have been multiplied, the higher they may have been raised upon every different subject of taxation; the more loudly the people complain of every new tax, the more difficult it becomes, too, either to find out new subjects of taxation, or to raise much higher the taxes already imposed upon the old. A momentary suspension of the payment of debt is not immediately felt by the people, and occasions neither murmur nor complaint. To borrow of the sinking fund is always an obvious and easy expedient for getting out of the present difficulty. The more the public debts may have been accumulated, the more necessary it may have become to study to reduce them; the more dangerous, the more ruinous it may be to misapply any part of the sinking fund; the less likely is the public debt to be reduced to any considerable degree, the more likely, the more certainly, is the sinking fund to be misapplied towards defraying all the extraordinary expenses which occur in time of peace. When a nation is already overburdened with taxes, nothing but the necessities of a new war, nothing but either the animosity of national vengeance, or the anxiety for national security, can induce the people to submit, with tolerable patience, to a new tax. Hence the usual misapplication of the sinking fund.

In Great Britain, from the time that we had first recourse to the ruinous expedient of perpetual funding, the reduction of the public debt, in time of peace, has never borne any proportion to its accumulation in time of war. It was in the war which began in 1668, and was concluded by the treaty of Ryswick, in 1697, that the foundation of the present enormous debt of Great Britain was first laid.

On the 31st of December 1697, the public debts of Great Britain, funded and unfunded, amounted to £21,515,742:13:8½. A great part of those debts had been contracted upon short anticipations, and some part upon annuities for lives; so that, before the 31st of December 1701, in less than four years, there had partly been paid off; and partly reverted to the public, the sum of £5,121,041:12:0¾d; a greater reduction of the public debt than has ever since been brought about in so short a period of time. The remaining debt, therefore, amounted only to £16,394,701:1:7¼d.

In the war which began in 1702, and which was concluded by the treaty of Utrecht, the public debts were still more accumulated. On the 31st of December 1714, they amounted to £53,681,076:5:6½. The subscription into the South-sea fund, of the short and long annuities, increased the capital of the public debt; so that, on the 31st of December 1722, it amounted to £55,282,978:1:3 5/6. The reduction of the debt began in 1723, and went on so slowly, that, on the 31st of December 1739, during seventeen years-of profound peace, the whole sum paid off was no more than £8,328,554:17:11 3/12, the capital of the public debt, at that time, amounting to £46,954,623:3:4 7/12.

The Spanish war, which began in 1739, and the French war which soon followed it, occasioned a further increase of the debt, which, on the 31st of December 1748, after the war had been concluded by the treaty of Aix-la-Chapelle, amounted to £78,293,313:1:10¾. The most profound peace, of 17 years continuance, had taken no more than £8,328,354, 17:11¼ from it. A war, of less than nine years continuance, added £31,338,689:18: 6 1/6 to it. {See James Postlethwaite's History of the Public Revenue.}

During the administration of Mr. Pelham, the interest of the public debt was reduced, or at least measures were taken for reducing it, from four to three per cent.; the sinking fund was increased, and some part of the public debt was paid off. In 1755, before the breaking out of the late war, the funded debt of Great Britain amounted to £72,289,675. On the 5th of January 1763, at the conclusion of the peace, the funded debt amounted debt to £122,603,336:8:2¼. The unfunded debt has been stated at £13,927,589:2:2. But the expense occasioned by the war did not end with the conclusion of the peace; so that, though on the 5th of January 1764, the funded debt was increased (partly by a new loan, and partly by funding a part of the unfunded debt) to £129,586,789:10:1¾, there still remained (according to the very well informed author of Considerations on the Trade and Finances of Great Britain) an unfunded debt, which was brought to account in that and the following year, of £9,975,017: 12:2 15/44d. In 1764, therefore, the public debt of Great Britain, funded and unfunded together, amounted, according to this author, to £139,561,807:2:4. The annuities for lives, too, which had been granted as premiums to the subscribers to the new loans in 1757, estimated at fourteen years purchase, were valued at £472,500; and the annuities for long terms of years, granted as premiums likewise, in 1761 and 1762, estimated at twenty-seven and a-half years purchase, were valued at

£6,826,875. During a peace of about seven years continuance, the prudent and truly patriotic administration of Mr. Pelham was not able to pay off an old debt of six millions. During a war of nearly the same continuance, a new debt of more than seventy-five millions was contracted.

On the 5th of January 1775, the funded debt of Great Britain amounted to £124,996,086, 1:6¼d. The unfunded, exclusive of a large civil-list debt, to £4,150,236:3:11 7/8. Both together, to £129,146,322:5:6. According to this account, the whole debt paid off, during eleven years of profound peace, amounted only to £10,415,476:16:9 7/8. Even this small reduction of debt, however, has not been all made from the savings out of the ordinary revenue of the state. Several extraneous sums, altogether independent of that ordinary revenue, have contributed towards it. Amongst these we may reckon an additional shilling in the pound land tax, for three years; the two millions received from the East-India company, as indemnification for their territorial acquisitions; and the one hundred and ten thousand pounds received from the bank for the renewal of their charter. To these must be added several other sums, which, as they arose out of the late war, ought perhaps to be considered as deductions from the expenses of it. The principal are,

The produce of French prizes	£690,449: 18: 9
Composition for French prisoners	670,000: 0: 0
What has been received from the sale of the ceded islands	95,500: 0: 0
Total,	£1,455,949: 18: 9

If we add to this sum the balance of the earl of Chatham's and Mr. Calcraft's accounts, and other army savings of the same kind, together with what has been received from the bank, the East-India company, and the additional shilling in the pound land tax, the whole must be a good deal more than five millions. The debt, therefore, which, since the peace, has been paid out of the savings from the ordinary revenue of the state, has not, one year with another, amounted to half a million a-year. The sinking fund has, no doubt, been considerably augmented since the peace, by the debt which had been paid off, by the reduction of the redeemable four per cents to three per cents, and by the annuities for lives which have fallen in; and, if peace were to continue, a million, perhaps, might now be annually spared out of it towards the discharge of the debt. Another million, accordingly, was paid in the course of last year; but at the same time, a large civil-list debt was left unpaid, and we are now involved in a new war, which, in its progress, may prove as expensive as any of our former wars. {It has proved more expensive than any one of our former wars, and has involved us in an additional debt of more than one hundred millions. During a profound peace of eleven years, little more than ten millions of debt was paid; during a war of seven years, more than one hundred millions was contracted.} The new debt which will probably be contracted before the end of the next campaign, may, perhaps, be nearly equal to all the old debt which has been paid off from the savings out of the ordinary revenue of the state. It would be altogether chimerical, therefore, to expect that the public debt should ever be completely discharged, by any savings which are likely to be made from that ordinary revenue as it stands at present.

The public funds of the different indebted nations of Europe, particularly those of England, have, by one author, been represented as the accumulation of a great capital, superadded to the other capital of the country, by means of which its trade is extended, its manufactures are multiplied, and its lands cultivated and improved, much beyond what they could have been by means of that other capital only. He does not consider that the capital which the first creditors of the public advanced to government, was, from the moment in which he advanced it, a certain portion of the annual produce, turned away from serving in the function of a capital, to serve in that of a revenue; from maintaining productive labourers, to maintain unproductive ones, and to be spent and wasted, generally in the course of the year, without even the hope of any future reproduction. In return for the capital which they advanced, they obtained, indeed, an annuity of the public funds, in most cases, of more than equal value. This annuity, no doubt, replaced to them their capital, and enabled them to carry on their trade and business to the same, or, perhaps, to a greater extent than before; that is, they were enabled, either to borrow of other people a new capital, upon the credit of this annuity or, by selling it, to get from other people a new capital of their own, equal, or superior, to that which they had advanced to government. This new capital, however, which they in this manner either bought or borrowed of other people, must have existed in the country before, and must have been employed, as all capitals are, in maintaining productive labour. When it came into the hands of those who had advanced their money to government, though it was, in some respects, a new capital to them, it was not so to the country, but was only a capital withdrawn from certain employments, in order to be turned towards others. Though it replaced to them what they had advanced to government, it did not replace it to the country. Had they not advanced this capital to government, there would have been in the country two capitals, two portions of the annual produce, instead of one, employed in maintaining productive labour.

When, for defraying the expense of government, a revenue is raised within the year, from the produce of free or unmortgaged taxes, a certain portion of the revenue of private people is only turned away from maintaining one species of unproductive labour, towards maintaining another. Some part of what they pay in those taxes, might, no doubt, have been accumulated into capital, and consequently employed in maintaining productive labour; but the greater part would probably have been spent, and consequently employed in maintaining unproductive labour. The public expense, however, when defrayed in this manner, no doubt hinders, more or less, the further accumulation of new capital; but it does not necessarily occasion the destruction of any actually-existing capital.

When the public expense is defrayed by funding, it is defrayed by the annual destruction of some capital which had before existed in the country; by the perversion of some portion of the annual produce which had before been destined for the maintenance of productive labour, towards that of unproductive labour. As in this case, however, the taxes are lighter than they would have been, had a revenue sufficient for defraying the same expense been raised within the year; the private revenue of individuals is necessarily less burdened, and consequently their ability to save and accumulate some part of that revenue into capital, is a good deal less impaired. If the method of funding destroys more old capital, it, at the same time, hinders less the accumulation or acquisition of new capital, than that of defraying the public expense by a revenue raised within the year. Under the system of funding, the frugality and industry of private people can more easily repair the breaches which the waste and extravagance of government may occasionally make in the general capital of the society.

It is only during the continuance of war, however, that the system of funding has this advantage over the other system. Were the expense of war to be defrayed always by a revenue raised within the year, the taxes from which that extraordinary revenue was drawn would last no longer than the war. The ability of private people to accumulate, though less during the war, would have been greater during the peace, than under the system of funding. War would not necessarily have occasioned the destruction of any old capitals, and peace would have occasioned the accumulation of many more new. Wars would, in general, be more speedily concluded, and less wantonly undertaken. The people feeling, during continuance of war, the complete burden of it, would soon grow weary of it; and government, in order to humour them, would not be under the necessity of carrying it on longer than it was necessary to do so. The foresight of the heavy and unavoidable burdens of war would hinder the people from wantonly calling for it when there was no real or solid interest to fight for. The seasons during which the ability of private people to accumulate was somewhat impaired, would occur more rarely, and be of shorter continuance. Those, on the contrary, during which that ability was in the highest vigour would be of much longer duration than they can well be under the system of funding.

When funding, besides, has made a certain progress, the multiplication of taxes which it brings along with it, sometimes impairs as much the ability of private people to accumulate, even in time of peace, as the other system would in time of war. The peace revenue of Great Britain amounts at present to more than ten millions a-year. If free and unmortgaged, it might be sufficient, with proper management, and without contracting a shilling of new debt, to carry on the most vigorous war. The private revenue of the inhabitants of Great Britain is at present as much incumbered in time of peace, their ability to accumulate is as much impaired, as it would have been in the time of the most expensive war, had the pernicious system of funding never been adopted.

In the payment of the interest of the public debt, it has been said, it is the right hand which pays the left. The money does not go out of the country. It is only a part of the revenue of one set of the inhabitants which is transferred to another; and the nation is not a farthing the poorer. This apology is founded altogether in the sophistry of the mercantile system; and, after the long examination which I have already bestowed upon that system, it may, perhaps, be unnecessary to say anything further about it. It supposes, besides, that the whole public debt is owing to the inhabitants of the country, which happens not to be true; the Dutch, as well as several other foreign nations, having a very considerable share in our public funds. But though the whole debt were owing to the inhabitants of the country, it would not, upon that account, be less pernicious.

Land and capital stock are the two original sources of all revenue, both private and public. Capital stock pays the wages of productive labour, whether employed in agriculture, manufactures, or commerce. The management of those two original sources of revenue belongs to two different sets of people; the proprietors of land, and the owners or employers of capital stock.

The proprietor of land is interested, for the sake of his own revenue, to keep his estate in as good condition as he can, by building and repairing his tenants houses, by making and maintaining the necessary drains and inclosures, and all those other expensive improvements which it properly belongs to the landlord to make and maintain. But, by different land taxes, the revenue of the landlord may be so much diminished, and, by different duties upon the necessaries and conveniencies of life, that diminished revenue may be rendered of so little real value, that he may find himself altogether unable to make or maintain those expensive improvements. When the landlord, however, ceases to do his part, it is altogether impossible that the tenant should continue to do his. As the distress of the landlord increases, the agriculture of the country must necessarily decline.

When, by different taxes upon the necessaries and conveniencies of life, the owners and employers of capital stock find, that whatever revenue they derive from it, will not, in a particular country, purchase the same quantity of those necessaries and conveniencies which an equal revenue would in almost any other, they will be disposed to remove to some other. And when, in order to raise those taxes, all or the greater part of merchants and manufacturers, that is, all or the greater part of the employers of great capitals, come to be continually exposed to the mortifying and vexatious visits of the tax-gatherers, this disposition to remove will soon be changed into an actual removing. The industry of the country will necessarily fall with the removal of the capital which supported it, and the ruin of trade and manufactures will follow the declension of agriculture.

To transfer from the owners of those two great sources of revenue, land, and capital stock, from the persons immediately interested in the good condition of every particular portion of land, and in the good management of every particular portion of capital stock, to another set of persons (the creditors of the public, who have no such particular interest), the greater part of the revenue arising from either, must, in the long-run, occasion both the neglect of land, and the waste or removal of capital stock. A creditor of the public has, no doubt, a general interest in the prosperity of the agriculture, manufactures, and commerce of the country; and consequently in the good condition of its land, and in the good management of its capital stock. Should there be any general failure or declension in any of these things, the produce of the different taxes might no longer be sufficient to pay him the annuity or interest which is due to him. But a creditor of the public, considered merely as such, has no interest in the good condition of any particular portion of land, or in the good management of any particular portion of capital stock. As a creditor of the public, he has no knowledge of any such particular portion. He has no inspection of it. He can have no care about it. Its ruin may in some cases be unknown to him, and cannot directly affect him.

The practice of funding has gradually enfeebled every state which has adopted it. The Italian republics seem to have begun it. Genoa and Venice, the only two remaining which can pretend to an independent existence, have both been enfeebled by it. Spain seems to have learned the practice from the Italian republics, and (its taxes being probably less judicious than theirs) it has, in proportion to its natural strength, been-still more enfeebled. The debts of Spain are of very old standing. It was deeply in debt before the end of the sixteenth century, about a hundred years before England owed a shilling. France, notwithstanding all its natural resources, languishes under an oppressive load of the same kind. The republic of the United Provinces is as much enfeebled by its debts as either Genoa or Venice. Is it likely that, in Great Britain alone, a practice, which has brought either weakness or dissolution into every other country, should prove altogether innocent?

The system of taxation established in those different countries, it may be said, is inferior to that of England. I believe it is so. But it ought to be remembered, that when the wisest government has exhausted all the proper subjects of taxation, it must, in cases of urgent necessity, have recourse to improper ones. The wise republic of Holland has, upon some occasions, been obliged to have recourse to taxes as inconvenient as the greater part of those of Spain. Another war, begun before any considerable liberation of the public revenue had been brought about, and growing in its progress as expensive as the last war, may, from irresistible necessity, render the British system of taxation as oppressive as that of Holland, or even as that of Spain. To the honour of our present system of taxation, indeed, it has hitherto given so little embarrassment to industry, that, during the course even of the most expensive wars, the frugality and good conduct of individuals seem to have been able, by saving and accumulation, to repair all the breaches which the waste and extravagance of government had made in the general capital of the society. At the conclusion of the late war, the most expensive that Great Britain ever waged, her agriculture was as flourishing, her manufacturers as numerous and as fully employed, and her commerce as extensive, as they had ever been before. The capital, therefore, which supported all those different branches of industry, must have been equal to what it had ever been before. Since the peace, agriculture has been still further improved; the rents of houses have risen in every town and village of the country, a proof of the increasing wealth and revenue of the people; and the annual amount of the greater part of the old taxes, of the principal branches of the excise and customs, in particular, has been continually increasing, an equally clear proof of an increasing consumption, and consequently of an increasing produce, which could alone support that consumption. Great Britain seems to support with ease, a burden which, half a century ago, nobody believed her capable of supporting. Let us not, however, upon this account, rashly conclude that she is capable of supporting any burden; nor even be too confident that she could support, without great distress, a burden a little greater than what has already been laid upon her.

When national debts have once been accumulated to a certain degree, there is scarce, I believe, a single instance of their having been fairly and completely paid. The liberation of the public revenue, if it has ever been brought about at all, has always been brought about by a bankruptcy; sometimes by an avowed one, though frequently by a pretended payment.

The raising of the denomination of the coin has been the most usual expedient by which a real public bankruptcy has been disguised under the appearance of a pretended payment. If a sixpence, for example, should, either by act of parliament or royal proclamation, be raised to the denomination of a shilling, and twenty sixpences to that of a pound sterling; the person who, under the old denomination, had borrowed twenty shillings, or near four ounces of silver, would, under the new, pay with twenty sixpences, or with something less than two ounces. A national debt of about a hundred and twenty-eight millions, near the capital of the funded and unfunded debt of Great Britain, might, in this manner, be paid with about sixty-four millions of our present money. It would, indeed, be a pretended payment only, and the creditors of the public would really be defrauded of ten shillings in the pound of what was due to them. The calamity, too, would extend much further than to the creditors of the public, and those of every private person would suffer a proportionable loss; and this without any advantage, but in most cases with a great additional loss, to the creditors of the public. If the creditors of the public, indeed, were generally much in debt to other people, they might in some measure compensate their loss by paying their creditors in the same coin in which the public had paid them. But in most countries, the creditors of the public are, the greater part of them, wealthy people, who stand more in the relation of creditors than in that of debtors, towards the rest of their fellow citizens. A pretended payment of this kind, therefore, instead of alleviating, aggravates, in most cases, the loss of the creditors of the public; and, without any advantage to the public, extends the calamity to a great number of other innocent people. It occasions a general and most pernicious subversion of the fortunes of private people; enriching, in most cases, the idle and profuse debtor, at the expense of the industrious and frugal creditor; and transporting a great part of the national capital from the hands which were likely to increase and improve it, to those who are likely to dissipate and destroy it. When it becomes necessary for a state to declare itself bankrupt, in the same manner as when it becomes necessary for an individual to do so, a fair, open, and avowed bankruptcy, is always the measure which is both least dishonourable to the debtor, and least hurtful to the creditor. The honour of a state is surely very poorly provided for, when, in order to cover the disgrace of a real bankruptcy, it has recourse to a juggling trick of this kind, so easily seen through, and at the same time so extremely pernicious.

Almost all states, however, ancient as well as modern, when reduced to this necessity, have, upon some occasions, played this very juggling trick. The Romans, at the end of the first Punic war, reduced the As, the coin or denomination by which they computed the value of all their other coins, from containing twelve ounces of copper, to contain only two ounces; that is, they raised two ounces of copper to a denomination which had always before expressed the value of twelve ounces. The republic was, in this manner, enabled to pay the great debts which it had contracted with the sixth part of what it really owed. So sudden and so great a bankruptcy, we should in the present times be apt to imagine, must have occasioned a very violent popular clamour. It does not appear to have occasioned any. The law which enacted it was, like all other laws relating to the coin, introduced and carried through the assembly of the people by a tribune, and was probably a very popular law. In Rome, as in all other ancient republics, the poor people were constantly in debt to the rich and the great, who, in order to secure their votes at the annual elections, used to lend them money at exorbitant interest, which, being never paid, soon accumulated into a sum too great either for the debtor to pay, or for any body else to pay for him. The debtor, for fear of a very severe execution, was obliged, without any further gratuity, to vote for the candidate whom the creditor recommended. In spite of all the laws against bribery and corruption, the bounty of the candidates, together with the occasional distributions of coin which were ordered by the senate, were the principal funds from which, during the latter times of the Roman republic, the poorer citizens derived their subsistence. To deliver themselves from this subjection to their creditors, the poorer citizens were continually calling out, either for an entire abolition of debts, or for what they called new tables; that is, for a law which should entitle them to a complete acquittance, upon paying only a certain proportion of their accumulated debts. The law which reduced the coin of all denominations to a sixth part of its former value, as it enabled them to pay their debts with a sixth part of what they really owed, was equivalent to the most advantageous new tables. In order to satisfy the people, the rich and the great were, upon several different occasions, obliged to consent to laws, both for abolishing debts, and for introducing new tables; and they probably were induced to consent to this law, partly for the same reason, and partly that, by liberating the public revenue, they might restore vigour to that government, of which they themselves had the principal direction. An operation of this kind would at once reduce a debt of £128,000,000 to £21,333,333:6:8. In the course of the second Punic war, the As was still further reduced, first, from two ounces of copper to one ounce, and afterwards from one ounce to half an ounce; that is, to the twenty-fourth part of its original value. By combining the three Roman operations into one, a debt of a hundred and twenty-eight millions of our present money, might in this manner be reduced all at once to a debt of £5,333,333:6:8. Even the enormous debt of Great Britain might in this manner soon be paid.

By means of such expedients, the coin of, I believe, all nations, has been gradually reduced more and more below its original value, and the same nominal sum has been gradually brought to contain a smaller and a smaller quantity of silver.

Nations have sometimes, for the same purpose, adulterated the standard of their coin; that is, have mixed a greater quantity of alloy in it. If in the pound weight of our silver coin, for example, instead of eighteen pennyweight, according to the present standard, there were mixed eight ounces of alloy; a pound sterling, or twenty shillings of such coin, would be worth little more than six shillings and eightpence of our present money. The quantity of silver contained in six shillings and eightpence of our present money, would thus be raised very nearly to the denomination of a pound sterling. The adulteration of the standard has exactly the same effect with what the French call an augmentation, or a direct raising of the denomination of the coin.

An augmentation, or a direct raising of the denomination of the coin, always is, and from its nature must be, an open and avowed operation. By means of it, pieces of a smaller weight and bulk are called by the same name, which had before been given to pieces of a greater weight and bulk. The adulteration of the standard, on the contrary, has generally been a concealed operation. By means of it, pieces are issued from the mint, of the same denomination, and, as nearly as could be contrived, of the same weight, bulk, and appearance, with pieces which had been current before of much greater value. When king John of France, {See Du Cange Glossary, voce Moneta; the Benedictine Edition.} in order to pay his debts, adulterated his coin, all the officers of his mint were sworn to secrecy. Both operations are unjust. But a simple augmentation is an injustice of open violence; whereas an adulteration is an injustice of treacherous fraud. This latter operation, therefore, as soon as it has been discovered, and it could never be concealed very long, has always excited much greater indignation than the former. The coin, after any considerable augmentation, has very seldom been brought back to its former weight; but after the greatest adulterations, it has almost always been brought back to its former fineness. It has scarce ever happened, that the fury and indignation of the people could otherwise be appeased.

In the end of the reign of Henry VIII., and in the beginning of that of Edward VI., the English coin was not only raised in its denomination, but adulterated in its standard. The like frauds were practised in Scotland during the minority of James VI. They have occasionally been practised in most other countries.

That the public revenue of Great Britain can never be completely liberated, or even that any considerable progress can ever be made towards that liberation, while the surplus of that revenue, or what is over and above defraying the annual expense of the peace establishment, is so very small, it seems altogether in vain to expect. That liberation, it is evident, can never be brought about, without either some very considerable augmentation of the public revenue, or some equally considerable reduction of the public expense.

A more equal land tax, a more equal tax upon the rent of houses, and such alterations in the present system of customs and excise as those which have been mentioned in the foregoing chapter, might, perhaps, without increasing the burden of the greater part of the people, but only distributing the weight of it more equally upon the whole, produce a considerable augmentation of revenue. The most sanguine projector, however, could scarce flatter himself, that any augmentation of this kind would be such as could give any reasonable hopes, either of liberating the public revenue altogether, or even of making such progress towards that liberation in time of peace, as either to prevent or to compensate the further accumulation of the public debt in the next war.

By extending the British system of taxation to all the different provinces of the empire, inhabited by people either of British or European extraction, a much greater augmentation of revenue might be expected. This, however, could scarce, perhaps, be done, consistently with the principles of the British constitution, without admitting into the British parliament, or, if you will, into the states-general of the British empire, a fair and equal representation of all those different provinces; that of each province bearing the same proportion to the produce of its taxes, as the representation of Great Britain might bear to the produce of the taxes levied upon Great Britain. The private interest of many powerful individuals, the confirmed prejudices of great bodies of people, seem, indeed, at present, to oppose to so great a change, such obstacles as it may be very difficult, perhaps altogether impossible, to surmount. Without, however, pretending to determine whether such a union be practicable or impracticable, it may not, perhaps, be improper, in a speculative work of this kind, to consider how far the British system of taxation might be applicable to all the different provinces of the empire; what revenue might be expected from it, if so applied; and in what manner a general union of this kind might be likely to affect the happiness and prosperity of the different provinces comprehended within it. Such a speculation, can, at worst, be regarded but as a new Utopia, less amusing, certainly, but no more useless and chimerical than the old one.

The land-tax, the stamp duties, and the different duties of customs and excise, constitute the four principal branches of the British taxes.

Ireland is certainly as able, and our American and West India plantations more able, to pay a land tax, than Great Britain. Where the landlord is subject neither to tythe nor poor's rate, he must certainly be more able to pay such a tax, than where he is subject to both those other burdens. The tythe, where there is no modus, and where it is levied in kind, diminishes more what would otherwise be the rent of the landlord, than a land tax which really amounted to five shillings in the pound. Such a tythe will be found, in most cases, to amount to more than a fourth part of the real rent of the land, or of what remains after replacing completely the capital of the farmer, together with his reasonable profit. If all moduses and all impropriations were taken away, the complete church tythe of Great Britain and Ireland could not well be estimated at less than six or seven millions. If there was no tythe either in Great Britain or Ireland, the landlords could afford to pay six or seven millions additional land tax, without being more burdened than a very great part of them are at present. America pays no tythe, and could, therefore, very well afford to pay a land tax. The lands in America and the West Indies, indeed, are, in general, not tenanted nor leased out to farmers. They could not, therefore, be assessed according to any rent roll. But neither were the lands of Great Britain, in the 4th of William and Mary, assessed according to any rent roll, but according to a very loose and inaccurate estimation. The lands in America might be assessed either in the same manner, or according to an equitable valuation, in consequence of an accurate survey, like that which was lately made in the Milanese, and in the dominions of Austria, Prussia, and Sardinia.

Stamp duties, it is evident, might be levied without any variation, in all countries where the forms of law process, and the deeds by which property, both real and personal, is transferred, are the same, or nearly the same.

The extension of the custom-house laws of Great Britain to Ireland and the plantations, provided it was accompanied, as in justice it ought to be, with an extension of the freedom of trade, would be in the highest degree advantageous to both. All the invidious restraints which at present oppress the trade of Ireland, the distinction between the enumerated and non-enumerated commodities of America, would be entirely at an end. The countries north of Cape Finisterre would be as open to every part of the produce of America, as those south of that cape are to some parts of that produce at present. The trade between all the different parts of the British empire would, in consequence of this uniformity in the custom-house laws, be as free as the coasting trade of Great Britain is at present. The British empire would thus afford, within itself, an immense internal market for every part of the produce of all its different provinces. So great an extension of market would soon compensate, both to Ireland and the plantations, all that they could suffer from the increase of the duties of customs.

The excise is the only part of the British system of taxation, which would require to be varied in any respect, according as it was applied to the different provinces of the empire. It might be applied to Ireland without any variation; the produce and consumption of that kingdom being exactly of the same nature with those of Great Britain. In its application to America and the West Indies, of which the produce and consumption are so very different from those of Great Britain, some modification might be necessary, in the same manner as in its application to the cyder and beer counties of England.

A fermented liquor, for example, which is called beer, but which, as it is made of molasses, bears very little resemblance to our beer, makes a considerable part of the common drink of the people in America. This liquor, as it can be kept only for a few days, cannot, like our beer, be prepared and stored up for sale in great breweries; but every private family must brew it for their own use, in the same manner as they cook their victuals. But to subject every private family to the odious visits and examination of the tax-gatherers, in the same manner as we subject the keepers of ale-houses and the brewers for public sale, would be altogether inconsistent with liberty. If, for the sake of equality, it was thought necessary to lay a tax upon this liquor, it might be taxed by taxing the material of which it is made, either at the place of manufacture, or, if the circumstances of the trade rendered such an excise improper, by laying a duty upon its importation into the colony in which it was to be consumed. Besides the duty of one penny a-gallon imposed by the British parliament upon the importation of molasses into America, there is a provincial tax of this kind upon their importation into Massachusetts Bay, in ships belonging to any other colony, of eight-pence the hogshead; and another upon their importation from the northern colonies into South Carolina, of five-pence the gallon. Or, if neither of these methods was found convenient, each family might compound for its consumption of this liquor, either according to the number of persons of which it consisted, in the same manner as private families compound for the malt tax in England; or according to the different ages and sexes of those persons, in the same manner as several different taxes are levied in Holland; or, nearly as Sir Matthew Decker proposes, that all taxes upon consumable commodities should be levied in England. This mode of taxation, it has already been observed, when applied to objects of a speedy consumption, is not a very convenient one. It might be adopted, however, in cases where no better could be done.

Sugar, rum, and tobacco, are commodities which are nowhere necessaries of life, which are become objects of almost universal consumption, and which are, therefore, extremely proper subjects of taxation. If a union with the colonies were to take place, those commodities might be taxed, either before they go out of the hands of the manufacturer or grower; or, if this mode of taxation did not suit the circumstances of those persons, they might be deposited in public warehouses, both at the place of manufacture, and at all the different ports of the empire, to which they might afterwards be transported, to remain there, under the joint custody of the owner and the revenue officer, till such time as they should be delivered out, either to the consumer, to the merchant-retailer for home consumption, or to the merchant-exporter; the tax not to be advanced till such delivery. When delivered out for exportation, to go duty-free, upon proper security being given, that they should really be exported out of the empire. These are, perhaps, the principal commodities, with regard to which the union with the colonies might require some considerable change in the present system of British taxation.

What might be the amount of the revenue which this system of taxation, extended to all the different provinces of the empire, might produce, it must, no doubt, be altogether impossible to ascertain with tolerable exactness. By means of this system, there is annually levied in Great

Britain, upon less than eight millions of people, more than ten millions of revenue. Ireland contains more than two millions of people, and, according to the accounts laid before the congress, the twelve associated provinces of America contain more than three. Those accounts, however, may have been exaggerated, in order, perhaps, either to encourage their own people, or to intimidate those of this country; and we shall suppose, therefore, that our North American and West Indian colonies, taken together, contain no more than three millions; or that the whole British empire, in Europe and America, contains no more than thirteen millions of inhabitants. If, upon less than eight millions of inhabitants, this system of taxation raises a revenue of more than ten millions sterling; it ought, upon thirteen millions of inhabitants, to raise a revenue of more than sixteen millions two hundred and fifty thousand pounds sterling. From this revenue, supposing that this system could produce it, must be deducted the revenue usually raised in Ireland and the plantations, for defraying the expense of the respective civil governments. The expense of the civil and military establishment of Ireland, together with the interest of the public debt, amounts, at a medium of the two years which ended March 1775, to something less than seven hundred and fifty thousand pounds a year. By a very exact account of the revenue of the principal colonies of America and the West Indies, it amounted, before the commencement of the present disturbances, to a hundred and forty-one thousand eight hundred pounds. In this account, however, the revenue of Maryland, of North Carolina, and of all our late acquisitions, both upon the continent, and in the islands, is omitted; which may, perhaps, make a difference of thirty or forty thousand pounds. For the sake of even numbers, therefore, let us suppose that the revenue necessary for supporting the civil government of Ireland and the plantations may amount to a million. There would remain, consequently, a revenue of fifteen millions two hundred and fifty thousand pounds, to be applied towards defraying the general expense of the empire, and towards paying the public debt. But if, from the present revenue of Great Britain, a million could, in peaceable times, be spared towards the payment of that debt, six millions two hundred and fifty thousand pounds could very well be spared from this improved revenue. This great sinking fund, too, might be augmented every year by the interest of the debt which had been discharged the year before; and might, in this manner, increase so very rapidly, as to be sufficient in a few years to discharge the whole debt, and thus to restore completely the at-present debilitated and languishing vigour of the empire. In the meantime, the people might be relieved from some of the most burdensome taxes; from those which are imposed either upon the necessaries of life, or upon the materials of manufacture. The labouring poor would thus be enabled to live better, to work cheaper, and to send their goods cheaper to market. The cheapness of their goods would increase the demand for them, and consequently for the labour of those who produced them. This increase in the demand for labour would both increase the numbers, and improve the circumstances of the labouring poor. Their consumption would increase, and, together with it, the revenue arising from all those articles of their consumption upon which the taxes might be allowed to remain.

The revenue arising from this system of taxation, however, might not immediately increase in proportion to the number of people who were subjected to it. Great indulgence would for some time be due to those provinces of the empire which were thus subjected to burdens to which they had not before been accustomed; and even when the same taxes came to be levied everywhere as exactly as possible, they would not everywhere produce a revenue proportioned to the numbers of the people. In a poor country, the consumption of the principal commodities subject to the duties of customs and excise, is very small; and in a thinly inhabited country, the opportunities of smuggling are very great. The consumption of malt liquors among the inferior ranks of people in Scotland is very small; and the excise upon malt, beer, and ale, produces less there than in England, in proportion to the numbers of the people and the rate of the duties, which upon malt is different, on account of a supposed difference of quality. In these particular branches of the excise, there is not, I apprehend, much more smuggling in the one country than in the other. The duties upon the distillery, and the greater part of the duties of customs, in proportion to the numbers of people in the respective countries, produce less in Scotland than in England, not only on account of the smaller consumption of the taxed commodities, but of the much greater facility of smuggling. In Ireland, the inferior ranks of people are still poorer than in Scotland, and many parts of the country are almost as thinly inhabited. In Ireland, therefore, the consumption of the taxed commodities might, in proportion to the number of the people, be still less than in Scotland, and the facility of smuggling nearly the same. In America and the West Indies, the white people, even of the lowest rank, are in much better circumstances than those of the same rank in

England; and their consumption of all the luxuries in which they usually indulge themselves, is probably much greater. The blacks, indeed, who make the greater part of the inhabitants, both of the southern colonies upon the continent and of the West India islands, as they are in a state of slavery, are, no doubt, in a worse condition than the poorest people either in Scotland or Ireland. We must not, however, upon that account, imagine that they are worse fed, or that their consumption of articles which might be subjected to moderate duties, is less than that even of the lower ranks of people in England. In order that they may work well, it is the interest of their master that they should be fed well, and kept in good heart, in the same manner as it is his interest that his working cattle should be so. The blacks, accordingly, have almost everywhere their allowance of rum, and of molasses or spruce-beer, in the same manner as the white servants; and this allowance would not probably be withdrawn, though those articles should be subjected to moderate duties. The consumption of the taxed commodities, therefore, in proportion to the number of inhabitants, would probably be as great in America and the West Indies as in any part of the British empire. The opportunities of smuggling, indeed, would be much greater; America, in proportion to the extent of the country, being much more thinly inhabited than either Scotland or Ireland. If the revenue, however, which is at present raised by the different duties upon malt and malt liquors, were to be levied by a single duty upon malt, the opportunity of smuggling in the most important branch of the excise would be almost entirely taken away; and if the duties of customs, instead of being imposed upon almost all the different articles of importation, were confined to a few of the most general use and consumption, and if the levying of those duties were subjected to the excise laws, the opportunity of smuggling, though not so entirely taken away, would be very much diminished. In consequence of those two apparently very simple and easy alterations, the duties of customs and excise might probably produce a revenue as great, in proportion to the consumption of the most thinly inhabited province, as they do at present, in proportion to that of the most populous.

The Americans, it has been said, indeed, have no gold or silver money, the interior commerce of the country being carried on by a paper currency; and the gold and silver, which occasionally come among them, being all sent to Great Britain, in return for the commodities which they receive from us. But without gold and silver, it is added, there is no possibility of paying taxes. We already get all the gold and silver which they have. How is it possible to draw from them what they have not?

The present scarcity of gold and silver money in America, is not the effect of the poverty of that country, or of the inability of the people there to purchase those metals. In a country where the wages of labour are so much higher, and the price of provisions so much lower than in England, the greater part of the people must surely have wherewithal to purchase a greater quantity, if it were either necessary or convenient for them to do so. The scarcity of those metals, therefore, must be the effect of choice, and not of necessity.

It is for transacting either domestic or foreign business, that gold or silver money is either necessary or convenient.

The domestic business of every country, it has been shewn in the second book of this Inquiry, may, at least in peaceable times, be transacted by means of a paper currency, with nearly the same degree of conveniency as by gold and silver money. It is convenient for the Americans, who could always employ with profit, in the improvement of their lands, a greater stock than they can easily get, to save as much as possible the expense of so costly an instrument of commerce as gold and silver; and rather to employ that part of their surplus produce which would be necessary for purchasing those metals, in purchasing the instruments of trade, the materials of clothing, several parts of household furniture, and the iron work necessary for building and extending their settlements and plantations; in purchasing not dead stock, but active and productive stock. The colony governments find it for their interest to supply the people with such a quantity of paper money as is fully sufficient, and generally more than sufficient, for transacting their domestic business. Some of those governments, that of Pennsylvania, particularly, derive a revenue from lending this paper money to their subjects, at an interest of so much per cent. Others, like that of Massachusetts Bay, advance, upon extraordinary emergencies, a paper money of this kind for defraying the public expense; and afterwards, when it suits the conveniency of the colony, redeem it at the depreciated value to which it gradually falls. In 1747, {See Hutchinson's History of Massachusetts Bay vol. ii. page 436 et seq.} that colony paid in this manner the greater part of its public debts, with the tenth part of the money for which its bills had been granted. It suits the conveniency of the planters, to save the expense of employing gold and silver money in their domestic transactions; and it suits the conveniency of the colony governments, to supply them with a medium, which, though attended with some very considerable disadvantages, enables them to save that expense. The redundancy of paper money necessarily banishes gold and silver from the domestic transactions of the colonies, for the same reason that it has banished those metals from the greater part of the domestic transactions in Scotland; and in both countries, it is not the poverty, but the enterprizing and projecting spirit of the people, their desire of employing all the stock which they can get, as active and productive stock, which has occasioned this redundancy of paper money.

In the exterior commerce which the different colonies carry on with Great Britain, gold and silver are more or less employed, exactly in proportion as they are more or less necessary. Where those metals are not necessary, they seldom appear. Where they are necessary, they are generally found.

In the commerce between Great Britain and the tobacco colonies, the British goods are generally advanced to the colonists at a pretty long credit, and are afterwards paid for in tobacco, rated at a certain price. It is more convenient for the colonists to pay in tobacco than in gold and silver. It would be more convenient for any merchant to pay for the goods which his correspondents had sold to him, in some other sort of goods which he might happen to deal in, than in money. Such a merchant would have no occasion to keep any part of his stock by him unemployed, and in ready money, for answering occasional demands. He could have, at all times, a larger quantity of goods in his shop or warehouse, and he could deal to a greater extent. But it seldom happens to be convenient for all the correspondents of a merchant to receive payment for the goods which they sell to him, in goods of some other kind which he happens to deal in. The British merchants who trade to Virginia and Maryland, happen to be a particular set of correspondents, to whom it is more convenient to receive payment for the goods which they sell to those colonies in tobacco, than in gold and silver. They expect to make a profit by the sale of the tobacco; they could make none by that of the gold and silver. Gold and silver, therefore, very seldom appear in the commerce between Great Britain and the tobacco colonies. Maryland and Virginia have as little occasion for those metals in their foreign, as in their domestic commerce. They are said, accordingly, to have less gold and silver money than any other colonies in America.

They are reckoned, however, as thriving, and consequently as rich, as any of their neighbours.

In the northern colonies, Pennsylvania, New York, New Jersey, the four governments of New England, etc. the value of their own produce which they export to Great Britain is not equal to that of the manufactures which they import for their own use, and for that of some of the other colonies, to which they are the carriers. A balance, therefore, must be paid to the mother-country in gold and silver and this balance they generally find.

In the sugar colonies, the value of the produce annually exported to Great Britain is much greater than that of all the goods imported from thence. If the sugar and rum annually sent to the mother-country were paid for in those colonies, Great Britain would be obliged to send out, every year, a very large balance in money; and the trade to the West Indies would, by a certain species of politicians, be considered as extremely disadvantageous. But it so happens, that many of the principal proprietors of the sugar plantations reside in Great Britain. Their rents are remitted to them in sugar and rum, the produce of their estates. The sugar and rum which the West India merchants purchase in those colonies upon their own account, are not equal in value to the goods which they annually sell there. A balance, therefore, must necessarily be paid to them in gold and silver, and this balance, too, is generally found.

The difficulty and irregularity of payment from the different colonies to Great Britain, have not been at all in proportion to the greatness or smallness of the balances which were respectively due from them. Payments have, in general, been more regular from the northern than from the tobacco colonies, though the former have generally paid a pretty large balance in money, while the latter have either paid no balance, or a much smaller one. The difficulty of getting payment from our different sugar colonies has been greater or less in proportion, not so much to the extent of the balances respectively due from them, as to the quantity of uncultivated land which they contained; that is, to the greater or smaller temptation which the planters have been under of over-trading, or of undertaking the settlement and plantation of greater quantities of waste land than suited the extent of their capitals. The returns from the great island of Jamaica, where there is still much uncultivated land, have, upon this account, been, in general, more irregular and uncertain than those from the smaller islands of Barbadoes, Antigua, and St. Christopher's, which have, for these many years, been completely cultivated, and have, upon that account, afforded less field for the speculations of the planter. The new acquisitions of Grenada, Tobago, St. Vincent's, and Dominica, have opened a new field for speculations of this kind; and the returns front those islands have of late been as irregular and uncertain as those from the great island of Jamaica.

It is not, therefore, the poverty of the colonies which occasions, in the greater part of them, the present scarcity of gold and silver money. Their great demand for active and productive stock makes it convenient for them to have as little dead stock as possible, and disposes them, upon that account, to content themselves with a cheaper, though less commodious instrument of commerce, than gold and silver. They are thereby enabled to convert the value of that gold and silver into the instruments of trade, into the materials of clothing, into household furniture, and into the iron work necessary for building and extending their settlements and plantations. In those branches of business which cannot be transacted without gold and silver money, it appears, that they can always find the necessary quantity of those metals; and if they frequently do not find it, their failure is generally the effect, not of their necessary poverty, but of their unnecessary and excessive enterprise. It is not because they are poor that their payments are irregular and uncertain, but because they are too eager to become excessively rich. Though all that part of the produce of the colony taxes, which was over and above what was necessary for defraying the expense of their own civil and military establishments, were to be remitted to Great Britain in gold and silver, the colonies have abundantly wherewithal to purchase the requisite quantity of those metals. They would in this case be obliged, indeed, to exchange a part of their surplus produce, with which they now purchase active and productive stock, for dead stock. In transacting their domestic business, they would be obliged to employ a costly, instead of a cheap instrument of commerce; and the expense of purchasing this costly instrument might damp somewhat the vivacity and ardour of their excessive enterprise in the improvement of land. It might not, however, be necessary to remit any part of the American revenue in gold and silver. It might be remitted in bills drawn upon, and accepted by, particular merchants or companies in Great Britain, to whom a part of the surplus produce of America had been consigned, who would pay into the treasury the American revenue in money, after having themselves received the value of it in goods; and the whole business might frequently be transacted without exporting a single ounce of gold or silver from America.

It is not contrary to justice, that both Ireland and America should contribute towards the discharge of the public debt of Great Britain. That debt has been contracted in support of the government established by the Revolution; a government to which the protestants of Ireland owe, not only the whole authority which they at present enjoy in their own country, but every security which they possess for their liberty, their property, and their religion; a government to which several of the colonies of America owe their present charters, and consequently their present constitution; and to which all the colonies of America owe the liberty, security, and property, which they have ever since enjoyed. That public debt has been contracted in the defence, not of Great Britain alone, but of all the different provinces of the empire. The immense debt contracted in the late war in particular, and a great part of that contracted in the war before, were both properly contracted in defence of America.

By a union with Great Britain, Ireland would gain, besides the freedom of trade, other advantages much more important, and which would much more than compensate any increase of taxes that might accompany that union. By the union with England, the middling and inferior ranks of people in Scotland gained a complete deliverance from the power of an aristocracy, which had always before oppressed them. By a union with Great Britain, the greater part of people of all ranks in Ireland would gain an equally complete deliverance from a much more oppressive aristocracy; an aristocracy not founded, like that of Scotland, in the natural and respectable distinctions of birth and fortune, but in the most odious of all distinctions, those of religious and political prejudices; distinctions which, more than any other, animate both the insolence of the oppressors, and the hatred and indignation of the oppressed, and which commonly render the inhabitants of the same country more hostile to one another than those of different countries ever are. Without a union with Great Britain, the inhabitants of Ireland are not likely, for many ages, to consider themselves as one people.

No oppressive aristocracy has ever prevailed in the colonies. Even they, however, would, in point of happiness and tranquillity, gain considerably by a union with Great Britain. It would, at least, deliver them from those rancourous and virulent factions which are inseparable from small democracies, and which have so frequently divided the affections of their people, and disturbed the tranquillity of their governments, in their form so nearly democratical. In the case of a total separation from Great Britain, which, unless prevented by a union of this kind, seems very likely to take place, those factions would be ten times more virulent than ever. Before the commencement of the present disturbances, the coercive power of the mother-country had always been able to restrain those factions from breaking out into any thing worse than gross brutality and insult. If that coercive power were entirely taken away, they would probably soon break out into open violence and bloodshed. In all great countries which are united under one uniform government, the spirit of party commonly prevails less in the remote provinces than in the centre of the empire. The distance of those provinces from the capital, from the principal seat of the great scramble of faction and ambition, makes them enter less into the views of any of the contending parties, and renders them more indifferent and impartial spectators of the conduct of all. The spirit of party prevails less in Scotland than in England. In the case of a union, it would probably prevail less in Ireland than in Scotland; and the colonies would probably soon enjoy a degree of concord and unanimity, at present unknown in any part of the British empire. Both Ireland and the colonies, indeed, would be subjected to heavier taxes than any which they at present pay. In consequence, however, of a diligent and faithful application of the public revenue towards the discharge of the national debt, the greater part of those taxes might not be of long continuance, and the public revenue of Great Britain might soon be reduced to what was necessary for maintaining a moderate peace-establishment.

    The territorial acquisitions of the East India Company, the undoubted right of the Crown, that is, of the state and people of Great Britain, might be rendered another source of revenue, more abundant, perhaps, than all those already mentioned. Those countries are represented as more fertile, more extensive, and, in proportion to their extent, much richer and more populous than Great Britain. In order to draw a great revenue from them, it would not probably be necessary to introduce any new system of taxation into countries which are already sufficiently, and more than sufficiently, taxed. It might, perhaps, be more proper to lighten than to aggravate the burden of those unfortunate countries, and to endeavour to draw a revenue from them, not by imposing new taxes, but by preventing the embezzlement and misapplication of the greater part of those which they already pay.

If it should be found impracticable for Great Britain to draw any considerable augmentation of revenue from any of the resources above mentioned, the only resource which can remain to her, is a diminution of her expense. In the mode of collecting and in that of expending the public revenue, though in both there may be still room for improvement, Great Britain seems to be at least as economical as any of her neighbours. The military establishment which she maintains for her own defence in time of peace, is more moderate than that of any European state, which can pretend to rival her either in wealth or in power. None of these articles, therefore, seem to admit of any considerable reduction of expense. The expense of the peace-establishment of the colonies was, before the commencement of the present disturbances, very considerable, and is an expense which may, and, if no revenue can be drawn from them, ought certainly to be saved altogether. This constant expense in time of peace, though very great, is insignificant in comparison with what the defence of the colonies has cost us in time of war. The last war, which was undertaken altogether on account of the colonies, cost Great Britain, it has already been observed, upwards of ninety millions. The Spanish war of 1739 was principally undertaken on their account; in which, and in the French war that was the consequence of it, Great Britain, spent upwards of forty millions; a great part of which ought justly to be charged to the colonies. In those two wars, the colonies cost Great Britain much more than double the sum which the national debt amounted to before the commencement of the first of them. Had it not been for those wars, that debt might, and probably would by this time, have been completely paid; and had it not been for the colonies, the former of those wars might not, and the latter certainly would not, have been undertaken. It was because the colonies were supposed to be provinces of the British Empire, that this expense was laid out upon them. But countries which contribute neither revenue nor military force towards the support of the empire, cannot be considered as provinces. They may, perhaps, be considered as appendages, as a sort of splendid and shewy equipage of the empire. But if the empire can no longer support the expense of keeping up this equipage, it ought certainly to lay it down; and if it cannot raise its revenue in proportion to its expense, it ought at least to accommodate its expense to its revenue. If the colonies, notwithstanding their refusal to submit to British taxes, are still to be considered as provinces of the British empire, their defence, in some future war, may cost Great Britain as great an expense as it ever has done in any former war. The rulers of Great Britain have, for more than a century past, amused the people with the imagination that they possessed a great empire on the west side of the Atlantic. This empire, however, has hitherto existed in imagination only. It has hitherto been, not an empire, but the project of an empire; not a gold mine, but the project of a gold mine; a project which has cost, which continues to cost, and which, if pursued in the same way as it has been hitherto, is likely to cost, immense expense, without being likely to bring any profit; for the effects of the monopoly of the colony trade, it has been shewn, are to the great body of the people, mere loss instead of profit. It is surely now time that our rulers should either realize this golden dream, in which they have been indulging themselves, perhaps, as well as the people; or that they should awake from it themselves, and endeavour to awaken the people. If the project cannot be completed, it ought to be given up. If any of the provinces of the British empire cannot be made to contribute towards the support of the whole empire, it is surely time that Great Britain should free herself from the expense of defending those provinces in time of war, and of supporting any part of their civil or military establishment in time of peace; and endeavour to accommodate her future views and designs to the real mediocrity of her circumstances.

Printed by Amazon Italia Logistica S.r.l.
Torrazza Piemonte (TO), Italy